Jihadists and Weapons of Mass Destruction

Jihadists and Weapons of Mass Destruction

Edited by
Gary Ackerman and Jeremy Tamsett

CRC Press
Taylor & Francis Group
Boca Raton London New York

CRC Press is an imprint of the
Taylor & Francis Group, an **informa** business

CRC Press
Taylor & Francis Group
6000 Broken Sound Parkway NW, Suite 300
Boca Raton, FL 33487-2742

Printed in the United States of America on acid-free paper
10 9 8 7 6 5 4 3 2 1

International Standard Book Number-13: 978-1-4200-6964-8 (Hardcover)

Library of Congress Cataloging-in-Publication Data

Jihadists and weapons of mass destruction / editor, Gary Ackerman, Jeremy Tamsett.
p. cm.
Includes bibliographical references and index.
ISBN 978-1-4200-6964-8 (alk. paper)
1. Weapons of mass destruction. 2. Jihad. 3. Qaida (Organization) 4. Security, International. 5. Terrorism. I. Ackerman, Gary, 1973- II. Tamsett, Jeremy. III. Title.

U793.J54 2008
363.325'3--dc22 2008048739

Visit the Taylor & Francis Web site at
http://www.taylorandfrancis.com

and the CRC Press Web site at
http://www.crcpress.com

Contents

Contributors

Gary A. Ackerman (Editor)
Research Director
National Consortium for the Study of Terrorism and Responses to Terrorism (START)
University of Maryland
College Park, Maryland

Victor H. Asal
Assistant Professor of Political Science
Rockefeller College
University at Albany–SUNY
Albany, New York

Jeffrey M. Bale
Director
Monterey Terrorism Research and Education Program (MonTREP)
Associate Professor
Graduate School of International Policy Studies
Monterey Institute of International Studies
Monterey, California

Marcus Binder
Independent Consultant
MKB Consulting
Ithaca, New York

Charles Blair
Director
Center for Terrorism and Intelligence Studies (CETIS)
San Jose, California

Edith Bursac
Program Coordinator/Research Associate
International Organizations and Nonproliferation Program
James Martin Center for Nonproliferation Studies
Monterey Institute of International Studies
Monterey, California

Mark Dechesne
Senior Researcher
Center for Terrorism and Counterterrorism
University of Leiden–Campus The Hague
The Hague, The Netherlands

Charles D. Ferguson
Fellow, Science and Technology
Council on Foreign Relations
Washington, DC

Brian Finlay
Senior Associate
The Henry L. Stimson Center
Washington, DC

James Forest
Director of Terrorism Studies
Combating Terrorism Center
Associate Professor
United States Military Academy
West Point, New York

Cheryl Loeb
Research Associate
Center for Technology and National Security Policy
National Defense University
Washington, DC

Erin McNerney
Visiting Scholar
National Consortium for the Study of Terrorism and Responses to Terrorism (START)
University of Maryland
College Park, Maryland

Michael Moodie
Independent Consultant, Proliferation Issues
Washington, DC

Randall S. Murch
Associate Director
Research Program Development
Associate Director
Center for Technology, Security, and Policy
Virginia Tech University
Blacksburg, Virginia

R. Karl Rethemeyer
Assistant Professor
Rockefeller College
University at Albany–SUNY
Albany, New York

Matthew Rhodes
Research Assistant
National Consortium for the Study of Terrorism and Responses to Terrorism (START)
University of Maryland
College Park, Maryland

Brad Roberts
Research Staff Member
Institute for Defense Analyses
Alexandria, Virginia

Patrick S. Roberts
Visiting Fellow
Harvard University
Cambridge, Massachusetts
Assistant Professor
Center for Public Administration and Policy
School of Public and International Affairs
Virginia Tech University
Blacksburg, Virginia

Sammy Salama
Fellow
Combating Terrorism Center
United States Military Academy
West Point, New York

Jeremy Tamsett (Editor)
Research Analyst
Henley-Putnam University
San Jose, California
Research Analyst
Center for Terrorism and Intelligence Studies
San Jose, California

Acknowledgments

We realized early on in the process of preparing this volume that despite dealing with two topics at the forefront of official and public discourse, to properly explore the intersection of jihadism and weapons of mass destruction would require more than the participation of any single scholar or academic discipline. Such a multi-faceted phenomenon demanded a multidisciplinary and collaborative effort if we wanted to achieve more than to merely scratch the surface of our subject. We are, therefore, indebted above all to the contributors to this book, each of whom gave wholeheartedly of their time and expertise to this endeavor. In particular, we are thankful that each and every author graciously acquiesced to our vision for this volume and enthusiastically adopted our stylistic and conceptual design. Their accommodation forged the links that allowed us to bind chapters that often dealt with very unique subject matter into a consistent and hopefully cohesive chain. We also extend heartfelt thanks to the many eminent scholars and practitioners who provided valuable feedback on individual chapters, especially Jarret Brachman, Jonathan Tucker, Keith Keener, Assaf Moghadam, and Kesten Green. The final result is all the better for their input. We would like to single out Jeffrey Bale, who not only contributed greatly to the book with his chapter on jihadist strategy and ideology, but also spent a significant amount of time reviewing several chapters and submitting pointed comments and corrections to subtle errors. Our respective home institutions were exceedingly patient with us during the book's production and we thank our colleagues at the National Consortium for the Study of Terrorism and Responses to Terrorism (START), especially Gary Lafree and Kathleen Smarick, in addition to Peter Neumann at the Department of War Studies, King's College, London; we are grateful as well to Nirmalya Bhowmick at the Center for Terrorism and Intelligence Studies (CETIS) and Greg Von Gehr, Jim Killin, Michael Corcoran, and the rest of the outstanding administration of Henley-Putnam University. We were supported by an excellent editorial and production team at Taylor and Francis, headed up by Mark Listewnik and Susan Horwitz. Matthew Rhodes was instrumental in creating the charts in Chapter 14 and in coordinating the Delphi study. Last, but certainly not least, we want to thank our wives, Nancy and Angela, who had to bear the burden of our agreeing to produce a book outside of our normal working hours.

Introduction

Gary Ackerman and Jeremy Tamsett

> Ali pulled the pick-up over onto the dirt strip that bordered the road. The small rise where he parked the truck overlooked much of the city and he could see the thousands of lights twinkling below him like multi-colored stars. He would have considered them beautiful were it not for the fact that he knew what those lights were busy shining on this very moment. Gambling. Fornication. Businesses whose profits would go to the Zionist alliance to be used to oppress and kill the Faithful. Clean-shaven and dressed in a simple T-shirt and jeans, Ali looked to the outside world like any other modern young man interested in parties and girls and sports. But Ali was different. He was making sure that his life would mean something. The day he had made his bayat and swore to follow the Shaykh on the path of jihad, he had been told that he was special, that he had a great destiny—to be the loftiest of all *shuhadah*. What he was preparing to do would bring honor to his family and hope to the entire Ummah. It was the only way to once and for all make the infidels cease their intrusions and bring them to their knees. And he would be rewarded in heaven by sitting at the right hand of the Prophet, peace be upon him. Ali got out and walked around to the truck bed, where he began to unfasten one of the bungee cords that held the tarpaulin covering "al-Naqoori." Everything had been placed in readiness before his journey—all that remained was for him to disable the safety mechanism and check that the green light was flashing, which meant that the components were still properly aligned. He took a deep breath. The months of hard training could not stop his hand from shaking a little. He recited the verses as he had been instructed: "Then when one blast is sounded on the Trumpet, And the earth is moved, and its mountains, and they are crushed to powder at one stroke, On that Day shall the Great Event come to pass."[1] He immediately felt better, more relaxed, and even a little joyful as he completed his preparations. The next few seconds would change everything, would right all the wrongs. Ali placed his hand on the switch and looked around one last time at the sleeping suburb and the vista below. He closed his eyes and loudly proclaimed the *shahada*. Then he pressed the switch...A microsecond later the high explosive in the device detonated, releasing gases that propelled a plug of 30 percent highly enriched uranium at a speed of 5,000 meters per second down a short tube. When the plug reached the end of tube, it slammed into a similar hemisphere of uranium, causing the combined mass to become supercritical and releasing the most devastating energy known to mankind. Before the destructive blast wave had crested the hill, Ali had been proven right—the world would never be the same again.

The above passage is fictional, to be sure, with more than a little license taken in several of its assumptions. Far from seeking to arouse alarm, since there has been more than enough of that already, this hypothetical scenario is presented with a single purpose—namely, to highlight the change in popular thinking that has occurred with respect to the likelihood of terrorists successfully employing weapons of mass destruction. Just two decades ago, the description of Ali and his bomb would have been dismissed as mere fantasy by the vast majority of both policymakers and the general public the world over. Today, such a frightening scenario sounds an eerie ring of plausibility for many within and outside of government. Much of the change in threat perception can be linked to the rise of a global jihadist movement bent on converting, subordinating, or punishing all those it regards as unbelievers. This has been accompanied by profuse hype about the insidious motives and apocalyptic capabilities of these newly prominent actors. The task remains, however, to explore how much of the assessment of this threat is based on sober analysis and how much has been influenced by unfounded fears and political exigencies; hence the need for a thorough evaluation of the likelihood of jihadists using the ultimate weapons.

This volume focuses on the nexus between two of the most prominent themes in current articulations of threats to international security, a nexus formed where malevolent actors meet malignant means. The first component bound up in this pernicious union is the global jihadist movement, which consists of a loose ideational network of violent actors whose actions are usually terroristic in nature. Jihadists, at least in the minds of many Western governments and academics, are presently the most dangerous nonstate actors worldwide, and are expected to remain so for some time to come. For example, a 2007 National Intelligence Estimate (NIE), the highest level product published by the U.S. intelligence community, states that "The main threat [to the U.S. homeland] comes from Islamic terrorist groups and cells, especially al-Qa'ida, driven by their undiminished intent to attack the Homeland and a continued effort by these terrorist groups to adapt and improve their capabilities,"[2] while the British MI5 security service asserts on its public Web site that, "The most significant terrorist threat comes from Al Qaida [sic] and associated networks."[3]

There are several reasons why the current crop of violent Islamic extremists might be painted with such a frighteningly negative brush. The most obvious is their recent track record. Jihadists have demonstrated both a willingness and ability to launch sophisticated attacks that have caused numbers of civilian casualties almost unparalleled in the annals of acts of nonstate violence. They have also proven themselves to be quintessential asymmetric opponents, using relatively meager physical and financial resources to circumvent the vaunted defensive capabilities of the developed world and strike at the heart of the countries of the West (and elsewhere). Not only have jihadists employed wily and adaptive behavior on the offensive, but the movement has also shown a surprising robustness in the face of sustained international counterterrorist efforts. This is reflected in the ability of the al-Qa'ida central command to regroup and ensconce itself in ungoverned spaces in Pakistan's northwest provinces after their Taliban hosts were routed in Afghanistan.[4]

The movement's resilience is perhaps even more apparent in the "disaggregation" of the larger movement into small, ephemeral groups of plotters, often linked by not much more than a common worldview and a virtual, Internet-based connection to the wider community of likeminded jihadists. The aspect of jihadism (that is to say, the pursuit of violent jihad) that is perhaps most alarming to many is its rapid growth. By capitalizing on widespread dissatisfaction of the status quo within Muslim communities throughout the world—especially among youth—and utilizing a sophisticated and seemingly successful global propaganda campaign[5] through a variety of media, their message of violent opposition to both the West and extant Muslim regimes is spreading.[6] It is thus little surprise that the 9/11 Commission decried that "The catastrophic threat at this moment in history is...the threat posed by *Islamist* terrorism—especially the al Qaeda [sic] network, its affiliates, and its ideology"[7] (emphasis in original).

The second theme present in the threat nexus is that of so-called weapons of mass destruction (WMD). While the precise nature of these weapons will be discussed below, the dual-core conceptualization of WMD entails their potentially catastrophic effects and their consummate utility as asymmetric weapons that, for all intents and purposes, act as "force multipliers." These features of WMD make them at least nominally attractive to those actors that lack the ability to challenge their enemies on the conventional military battlefield. WMD and their proliferation to new state or nonstate actors have thus been identified as cardinal dangers to global security in the post–Cold War world. For instance, in a February 5, 2008 statement to the U.S. Senate Select Committee on Intelligence, Mike McConnell, U.S. Director of National Intelligence, conceded that, "The time when only a few states had access to the most dangerous technologies has been over for many years."[8]

The possibility of WMD falling into the hands of terrorists or other violent nonstate actors (as well as their capacity to produce WMD) has ostensibly elicited particular concern among policymakers, and is often presented, at least in the United States and the United Kingdom, as one of the major security threats (if not the single gravest threat) to national or international security.[9] Concern for this eventuality was encapsulated in U.S. President George W. Bush's 2002 National Security Strategy[10] and has been reinforced several times since, most notably in the 2006 U.S. National Strategy for Combating Terrorism, which contends that "Our greatest and gravest concern…is WMD in the hands of terrorists. Preventing their acquisition and the dire consequences of their use is a key priority of this strategy."[11]

Based on the prominence of both of the above topics within national security discourse in several countries, even in the absence of any tangible evidence of jihadist involvement with WMD, it would be natural that the potential nexus between jihadists and WMD would be a topic of more than passing relevance. Add to this the wealth of information, available even in open sources, of jihadist interest in and attempts to acquire WMD and their constituent materials and it is little wonder that the prospect of jihadist-inspired WMD terrorism has gained considerable traction in both intelligence and law enforcement circles. The 2007 National Intelligence Estimate goes so far as to assert that, "al-Qa'ida [sic] will continue to try to acquire and employ chemical, biological, radiological, or nuclear material in attacks and would not hesitate to use them if it develops what it deems is sufficient capability."[12] Such sentiments are not confined to officialdom—in a survey conducted on behalf of this volume and presented herein, the overwhelming majority of expert participants viewed Sunni jihadists as the most pressing short- to medium-term threat vis-à-vis WMD.[13] All this attention provides at least *prima facie* justification for examining the unique characteristics of the jihadist–WMD nexus more closely.

Unfortunately, while the official assertions are bold and the news reports alarming, there is rarely substantial (read: sufficient) depth to many of their arguments, at least not in the way they are presented in the public sphere. For instance, we need to incorporate more subtlety and discrimination in our analyses than presuming that because our enemies hate us, they will blindly pursue WMD and would use them as soon as they succeeded in acquiring them. For a detailed approach to such issues, we usually rely on scholars, as represented in both institutions of higher learning and what are popularly referred to as "think tanks" or policy institutes. It is to previous work on the current topic that has emerged from this quarter that we now turn.

STORY SO FAR: PAST AND PRESENT RESEARCH ON JIHADISTS AND WMD

The March 1995 sarin nerve agent attack on the Tokyo subway by the Japanese "doomsday" cult Aum Shinrikyo served as a catalyst for the rapid growth not only of sensationalist media reports on "WMD terrorism" and new government policies to combat the use of WMD by nonstate actors,[14] but also of a host of academic and policy-oriented studies and commentaries on what previously had been a largely under-researched topic.[15] This corpus, which we will refer to for convenience as the "WMD terrorism literature,"[16] contained few explicit references to jihadists in the context of WMD between 1995 and 2001. Nevertheless, the burgeoning activities of Islamic extremists and the implications of what was then sometimes referred to as the "New Terrorism" were implicit in much of the discussion at the time, which yielded several useful insights, particularly with respect to the links between religious ideologies and the use of unconventional weapons.

One of the pivotal contributions in this regard is the understanding that since the worldview of a terrorist group or individual demarcates allies and enemies and forms the basis for deciding between legitimate and illegitimate targets and tactics,[17] an actor's ideology is likely to be a prominent factor in any decision to resort to the use of WMD. Another important conclusion, widely accepted by terrorism experts in this original tranche of publications, is that groups motivated by religion, which are focused on cosmic as opposed to this-worldly concerns, are far more willing to engage in attacks involving mass casualties and, hence, would be more prone to use WMD.[18] As Jeffrey M. Bale (author of the first chapter in this volume) has observed, "to the extent that violent extremist groups are absolutely convinced that they are doing God's bidding, virtually any action that they decide to undertake can be justified, no matter how heinous, since the 'divine' ends are thought to justify the means."[19] According to this line of reasoning, the resurgence in religiously inspired terrorism in recent decades implies that there is now a greater possibility of terrorists seeking to use weapons of mass destruction.

Although some scholars have questioned the logic of this relationship altogether,[20] it is more likely that the connection between religion and WMD exists, but is more complex and nuanced than initially presented. First, not all religious terrorists are equally likely to pursue mass destruction—many religiously motivated terrorist organizations have political components, represent constituencies that are well-defined geographically (and thus are subject to retribution), or depend for financial or logistical support on state parties or diaspora communities whose views may not be quite as radical as their own. Second, it is the theological and cultural content of the particular strand of religious belief that is of greatest significance,[21] rather than the mere fact that a group has a religious predilection. It has been asserted that the ideologies that are the most conducive to the pursuit of catastrophic violence are those that simultaneously reflect an apocalyptic millenarian character, in which an irremediably corrupt world must be purged to make way for a utopian future, and those that emphasize the capacity for purification from sins through sacrificial acts of violence.[22] It is interesting to note straightaway that at least some strains of jihadists, with their desire for a universal Caliphate (and occasionally also the advent of the Mahdi[23]) together with the glorification of martyrdom through suicide attacks, fit quite neatly into these categories.[24] Third, Jessica Stern has also suggested that religious terrorists might embrace WMD as a means of "emulat[ing] God."[25] Thus, while possessing an ideology with a religious characteristic is by no means determinative,[26] it is likely to be a contributing factor to any desire to engage in WMD terrorism. In any event, it must be borne in mind that in this volume we are not making any assertions about correlations between religion and WMD in general, but we are instead focusing in particular on one set of actors representing the modern manifestation of jihadism. Nonetheless, the early WMD terrorism literature is certainly suggestive of what might be expected from jihadists with respect to WMD.

In the wake of the spectacular jihadist attacks on the United States on September 11, 2001, the WMD terrorism literature began to focus more directly on the particular brand of extremism behind these attacks, together with its organizational adherents. While we continue to see many works on the more general aspects of WMD terrorism,[27] it has now become rare indeed that a report or book does not make at least a passing reference to al-Qa'ida or the broader community of jihadists. There have also been several monographs dealing with one or the other particular weapon type (CBRN—chemical, biological, radiological, and nuclear) that allude to jihadists to varying extents.[28] Significantly, for the first time, several articles and book chapters have been published that specifically address the topic of jihadists and WMD.[29]

These latter publications, in particular, have sought to introduce a greater degree of nuance and refinement into the analyses. First, commentators have emphasized the importance to jihadists of theological legitimacy for their actions. We must therefore remain cognizant of ideological developments like the lengthy 2003 *fatwa* by a radical Saudi cleric legitimizing the use of WMD against the West.[30] Second, several authors have also highlighted the distinction between the WMD potential of different components of the jihadist movement.[31] For example, while al-Qa'ida central might seek to inflict mass casualties brought about by sophisticated WMD, smaller groupings of self-radicalized jihadists are argued to be more likely to resort to smaller scale CBRN attacks that have mainly psychological and economic effects.[32] Even jihadist groups within the same context might approach the question of WMD differently, such as when interviews with members of Izz a-Din al-Qassam (the military wing of Hamas) revealed enthusiastic support for the use of WMD, while Palestinian Islamic Jihad members expressed concern over their use.[33] Third, this new literature has engaged areas of analysis that have only recently come to the fore, such as the role played by virtual communities of jihadists on the Internet in the dissemination of instructional and ideological information on WMD. Last, recent scholarly publications seem to appreciate far better the inherent dynamism and nonlinearity[34] of the relationship between jihadists and WMD. For example, although al-Qa'ida initially seemed to view WMD in primarily defensive terms as a means of deterrence, it is now recognized that a shift has occurred wherein WMD is currently perceived by many jihadists as a legitimate first strike weapon that can be used for offensive purposes.[35] Even skeptics who have pointed to the relative dearth of discussion of CBRN weapons in jihadist writings (when compared to the volume of other tactical subjects), admit that the threat space is extremely fluid, and that the emergence of better-educated jihadists from Western nations, as well as new strategic approaches such as those espoused in the treatises of Abu Musab al-Suri, may be tipping the jihadists' equation in favor of WMD use.[36]

For all its welcome contributions, however, this incipient literature exploring the nexus between jihadists and WMD is piecemeal, with no single source taking a comprehensive look at the topic from multiple vantage points. Moreover, the approach to analyzing the subject has remained largely within the purview of traditional scholars of terrorism, who mostly represent the academic disciplines of history, qualitative political science, and international relations. We believe that a topic of such obvious complexity, one that demands an understanding of a diverse set of issues ranging from Islamic theology to the technical requirements for creating a nuclear weapon, would benefit from the theories and methods of several other academic disciplines. This is made all the more vital when one considers the difficulties surrounding the data that are available to researchers, which includes a lot of uncorroborated reports and thus requires careful analysis from a variety of contexts. To paraphrase Brad Roberts, one of the contributors to this volume: "Experts interested in jihadism have devoted only a tiny fraction of their time and effort to thinking about weapons of mass destruction. Similarly, experts on weapons of mass destruction have devoted little time and effort to thinking about jihadism."[37]

We have conceived of the current effort as a more holistic treatment of the nexus between jihadists and WMD and, therefore, gathered a multi-disciplinary group of contributors, who number among them not only historians and qualitative political scientists, but also a psychologist, a quantitative political scientist, a public policy scholar, a physicist, and a biologist. We have attempted to take a structured approach to exploring the threat of jihadists acquiring WMD from a multitude of perspectives, while simultaneously applying a range of methodologies to analyzing the problem.

TROUBLING TERMINOLOGY: DEFINITIONS AND DISTINCTIONS BETWEEN CONCEPTS

Thus far we have referred to the key concepts of this volume in a general sense, but since none of the terms involved are devoid of either complexity or controversy, we will now proceed to specifically define how each of the major terms in the book will be used. While we concede that the existing terminology might be deficient in several respects, we feel that the substitution of terms that have obtained purchase in popular descriptions by completely new (albeit technically more accurate) constructions may serve only to muddy the definitional waters further and make the discussion somewhat removed from the current discourse. Therefore, we have retained such references as "weapons of mass destruction," with the proviso that they are to be understood (at least in the context of this volume) solely as we define them below.

The Jihadists

In this volume, we are focusing in particular on the motives and behavior of jihadists, which we define to be Islamist actors who employ violence in order to further their goals.[38]

In order for this definition to be of practical use to many readers, we will need to briefly explore the concept of Islamism. However, since this book is not centered on Islamism per se and there are many excellent texts devoted to this and related subjects,[39] we will limit our discussion to those aspects of Islamism necessary to provide definitional clarity.

Islamism

At the outset, we should clear up some common misinterpretations of the term *Islamism*.[40] First, and most basically, Islamism (and its Islamist adherents) must be clearly distinguished from the broader term *Islam*, which is a neutral reference to the religion that originated in the Arabian Peninsula with the teachings of the prophet Muhammad (ca. 570–632) and has become one of the three major monotheistic faiths (Christianity and Judaism being the other two). We henceforth take pains in this volume to draw a solid line between general followers of the Islamic faith (Muslims) and the strain of violent extremists currently espousing a set of radical interpretations of Islam (jihadists). Islamism should also not be equated with the locution of *Muslim fundamentalism*, which more generally describes various attempts throughout Islamic history to return to what its proponents perceive as the unadulterated foundations of the faith. Like other forms of religious fundamentalism, Muslim fundamentalism usually involves literal interpretations and strict constructions of Islam's sacred texts, primarily the *Qur'an* and the *hadith* (the collected sayings and actions of Muhammad). Because not all Muslim fundamentalist movements seek to actively change the existing social and political order, Islamism is best viewed as merely a subset of Muslim fundamentalism. Neither is Islamism the same thing as *political Islam*. The latter is a more expansive term covering a whole range of movements seeking to place Islam at the core of their political agendas, and includes such diverse movements as pan-Islam (*al-wahda al-islamiyya*), Ottomanism (*Osmancilik*), Islamic "Socialism," and moderate reformist Islam. Islamism is, therefore, only one strain of "political Islam." Figure 1 attempts to illustrate how Islamism and, as we shall see, jihadists are situated within the broader Islamic milieu.

But what do Islamists believe that makes them distinct from other Islamic movements? Their basic ideological outlook entails the belief that Muslims have been corrupted by secular ideologies from the West—including capitalism, communism, atheism, modernism, and materialism—which has in turn enabled the *infidels* (nonbelievers) in Western nations to dominate and exploit the Muslim world. Islamists believe that the solution to this problem consists of returning to a puritanical interpretation and application of Qur'anic precepts, Islamic tradition (*ahadith*), and Islamic law (*shari'a*), creating a truly Islamic state modeled on these principles, and thereby expunging Western social and cultural influences from Islam. This is accompanied by hostility toward those Muslims who are perceived as less pious or committed, with particular ire directed toward current rulers of Muslim lands who are often denounced as apostates and portrayed as traitors and puppets of the Western imperialist powers. Islamists always draw a marked distinction between the *dar-al-Islam* (the Abode of Islam) and the *dar-al-harb* (the Abode of War, a reference to the non-Islamic world), treating the latter and all it contains with contempt.[42] Indeed, many Islamists express the belief that Islam is locked in an eternal struggle with the evil forces of *jahiliyya* ("ignorance" or "barbarism"), which is presently represented by the West and most egregiously by the United States. Islamism, with its objective of

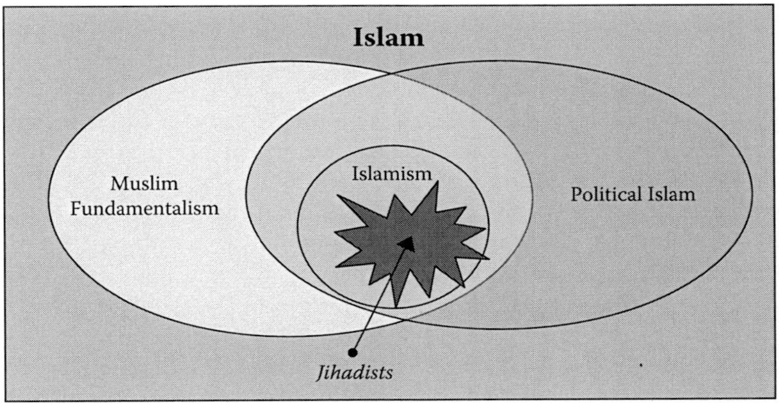

FIGURE 1 Orienting Islamism within Islam.

overthrowing the existing political order in Muslim lands and elsewhere, is an inherently radical ideology and one that contains both revivalist and revolutionary elements.

Despite sharing certain elements with previous Islamic reform movements, Islamism (in its present incarnation) is a relatively recent political phenomenon. While heavily influenced by earlier movements such as Wahhabism, Salafism, and even some Sufi movements (all of which called for a return to the earliest Islamic practices and a cleansing of the Muslim world[42]), Islamism also reflects several characteristics of the mass revolutionary movements that dominated Europe in the nineteenth and twentieth centuries. So, while Islamists refer to some relatively early Islamic scholars, such as Ibn Taymiyya (1263–1328), for inspiration, much of their worldview is based on the writings and teachings of Islamic thinkers of more recent vintage, to a large degree the Egyptians Hasan al-Banna (1906–1949) and Sayyid Qutb (1906–1966), and the Pakistani Mawlana Mawdudi (1903–1979). Islamism is also not restricted solely to the Sunni branch of Islam, but has Shi'ite variants, such as that espoused by Ayatollah Ruhollah Khomeini in Iran.

While sharing most of the same ultimate goals for radical societal change, not all variants of Islamism are necessarily inherently violent. Some Islamist groups have adopted a strategy of gradual "Islamization from below," which is reflected in an "accommodationist" approach to the existing political order, and usually consists of proselytizing to the Muslim masses and providing social services to encourage a return to what the Islamists believe to be the true path of Islam. This approach is to be contrasted with that of the *jihadists*, who are those Islamists who believe that waging armed struggle against unbelievers (*jihad bi-al-sayf*, i.e., "jihad of the sword") is the only path to victory over the forces of "unbelief." Many of the current groups of jihadists, especially al-Qa'ida, further characterizes the current *jihad* against the West as "defensive" rather than "offensive," which under Islamic law arguably allows its members a greater latitude in terms of recruitment and tactics.

It must also be noted that even the jihadist movement itself is not monolithic—while subscribing to the same general tenets, and thus constituting a "community" in a fairly loose sense of the word, there are several groupings that differ in terms of cultural background, tactical and strategic priorities, and mechanisms of control and organization. In organizational terms, the movement consists, at one end of the scale, of fairly hierarchical, centralized, transnational establishments led by dedicated ideologues such as the so-called "al-Qa'ida central" thought to currently reside somewhere along the Afghan–Pakistani border and, at the other end of the scale, of small cells of disparate, self-radicalized extremists with no formal training or direct connections to outside logistical assistance. The most important division within the jihadist movement, however, is based on the strategic focus of the actors, with national or regionally focused groups (such as HAMAS and Hizb`allah) directing the bulk of their energies to defeating the "near enemy" (the apostate or "occupying" regimes in their parts of the Muslim world), while the more transnational-focused groups, exemplified by the al-Qa'ida movement, believing that it is first necessary to "cut the head off of the snake" and defeat the "far enemy" (led by the United States) before it will be possible to instill shari'a in the Muslim world. As these two types of orientations have become increasingly networked in recent years, however, the distinction has in practice become increasingly blurred in several areas of the world.

One final aspect of the use of the term *jihadist* needs to be addressed. Some commentators have argued that since most Muslims regard *jihad* (whether internal or external) as a religious duty, and since the jihadists themselves often enthusiastically embrace the label, the use of the term *jihadist* serves to lend some degree of legitimacy to these actors and their violent behaviors. Alternative, more derogatory appellations, such as *Qutbists* referring to the aforementioned Islamist Sayyed Qutb have been posted (thus associating the jihadists with a mortal source rather than a divine one). However, jihadism as we have described it is a delineative label for a particular set of actors that does not necessarily imply legitimacy and, consequently, we feel it is more accessible to a general reading audience than the more erudite alternatives.

Weapons of Mass Destruction

Unlike jihadism, the use of the phraseology *weapons of mass destruction* in popular discourse is not so much confusing as it is controversial and, at times, even counterproductive. Each element of the term is subject to some degree of dispute, but the primary controversy surrounds the identification of which weapons are included (and, by extension, which are excluded) from the definition.[43] Although the roots of the expression have been traced back as far as descriptions of the aerial bombardment of Guernica during the Spanish Civil War, it was only after the U.S. use of nuclear weapons during World War II that the usage of the term became widespread. Thus, from the outset, nuclear weapons—in other words, weapons that employ an atomic fission or fusion reaction for their explosive power—were unequivocally regarded as WMD because of the singular scale of destruction they cause. During the Cold War era, the WMD label was applied, both by the United States Department of Defense and the United Nations, to nuclear, biological, and chemical weapons, with radiological weapons added intermittently.[44]

After the Cold War, however, the treatment of the term became far murkier, at least in the United States, when its domestic criminal code (enacted by Congress) expanded the use of WMD to cover a much wider range of weapons, including conventional explosives, incendiary charges, missiles, and mines (18 U.S.C. §2332a). For example, Zacarias Moussaoui, one of the conspirators involved with the September 11, 2001 attacks, was indicted and tried for attempting to use an airplane as a weapon of mass destruction.[45] The U.S. military has done little to clarify matters; instead it has arguably added to the confusion by adopting a similarly broad, yet in some ways also an overly restrictive approach to WMD, which it currently defines as

> Weapons that are capable of a high order of destruction and/or of being used in such a manner as to destroy large numbers of people. Weapons of mass destruction can be high-yield explosives or nuclear, biological, chemical, or radiological weapons, but exclude the means of transporting or propelling the weapon where such means is a separable and divisible part of the weapon. [46]

In addition to the inclusion of high explosives, the above definition excludes, for instance, missiles that contain nuclear warheads or artillery tubes that launch chemical shells. This usage is unfortunate in that it obscures a fundamental aspect of WMD—namely, that chemical, biological, radiological, or nuclear (CBRN) agents must not only be capable of inflicting harm, but must also be deliverable to their intended target before they can qualify as practical weapons, let alone WMD.[47] Indeed, except for nuclear weapons, the efficacy and, hence, utility of WMD depends almost entirely on delivery.[48] The scale of the effects of many of these weapons thus depends very much on how they are used.[49]

The most comprehensive analysis of the term *WMD* has been undertaken by W. Seth Carus,[50] who prefers limiting WMD to nuclear, chemical, and biological weapons, but is—somewhat begrudgingly—willing to include radiological weapons, in line with international treaty usage. At the same time, he emphatically rejects the inclusion of large-scale conventional weapons despite their ability to wreak massive destruction. Carus, however, reaches his conclusion partially based on what would be most serviceable for the U.S. Department of Defense, which is not one of the decision criteria that concern us here, so we need a further reason if we seek to exclude conventional weapons from our definition.

The factor that differentiates CBRN from conventional weapons does not lie in the asymmetric nature of CBRN weapons. After all, as the September 11 attacks amply demonstrated, conventional means can also be used in an asymmetric fashion to cause massive damage and loss of life. Rather, the most obvious argument in favor of placing CBRN weapons into a category of their own is that, at least in the case of nuclear, chemical, and biological weapons, there is the potential (in principle) to cause a greater scale of casualties (on the order of tens of thousands to millions) than any conceivable conventional explosive weapon.

Since in practice this potential is almost never realized and the scale of damage from terrorists using conventional weapons has historically dwarfed the effects achieved through chemical, biological, and radiological weapons, why should CBRN be elevated above conventional weapons on the basis of theoretical potential alone? The answer lies in a less tangible direction. In addition to their tremendous mass casualty potential, CBRN weapons possess an arguably even more important distinguishing characteristic—the inordinate psychological and social impact of these weapons. In other words, CBRN weapons are inherently more frightening than guns and bombs. There are many reasons for this phenomenon, including the invasiveness of many agents, particularly biological organisms, and a natural human fear of contamination. Perhaps the most important anxiety-provoking factor is the intangible nature of most of these agents (take, for example, radiation, which cannot be seen, smelled, or felt) that can lead to both gnawing doubt over whether or not one has been exposed and a sense of powerlessness against an unseen hazard. For instance, the 1995 Tokyo subway attack involving the chemical agent sarin killed 12 people, but over 4,400 of the 5,510 ostensible casualties who reported to medical facilities showed no symptoms of nerve agent exposure and were classified as "worried well."[51] That same year, the bombing of the federal building in Oklahoma City killed 168 people and injured more than 500. Yet there were no "worried well" in the latter case, which is one indication of the greater psychological impact of WMD compared to conventional weapons.

The notion of "mass" in weapons of mass destruction also presents some difficulties. Exactly how much destruction or how many casualties must a weapon cause before it qualifies as WMD? The answer to this question is largely subjective, making attempts at specific quantification seem arbitrary. While some CBRN weapons (such as nuclear weapons or aerosolized *Bacillus anthracis* spores) are likely to cause thousands of casualties and, therefore, undoubtedly qualify as WMD, smaller scale terrorist attacks using other CBR materials (for example, an assassination using ricin or sarin) do not. When the news media or public officials conflate these two very different types of attacks and use the more dramatic moniker of "WMD" to describe *any* CBRN incident, public anxiety regarding CBRN might actually increase. Paradoxically, this could make even small-scale CBRN attacks increasingly attractive to terrorists, which consequently compounds the problem. When used inappropriately, then, the term WMD can be counterproductive in our efforts to prevent the use of CBRN weapons. One method that has been used to provide a reference point for the scale required to constitute a genuine WMD is an attack where the effects exceed the capabilities of local responders. This solution is problematic since the same weapon could then be regarded as a WMD if used in one locale with meager response resources, but would not qualify as such in a second locale with abundant emergency services. The best solution is perhaps to refrain from precisely enumerating the measurement of "mass" and instead to specify that, in the context of terrorism, in order for a weapon to qualify, its effects, whether physical or otherwise, should be at least on the order of those experienced in the largest conventional terrorist attacks, such as the attacks of September 11, 2001.

The last component of the formulation WMD, namely, the term *destruction*, presents problems of its own. *Destruction* traditionally connotes annihilation and physical ruin, and its use as an umbrella term for CBRN weapons can obscure important differences between the various agents and the effects they cause. For example, a release of *Bacillus anthracis* in downtown New York City, unlike a nuclear weapon, would not leave a large crater where skyscrapers once stood. Moreover, while CBRN weapons do have some characteristics in common—particularly the singular levels of anxiety they invariably will provoke in target populations—there are significant differences between chemical, biological, radiological, and nuclear weapons in terms of the capabilities required for terrorists to acquire and deploy them. Therefore, if one is not careful, the use of the homogenous label of WMD can lead to generalized and erroneous statements about a very diverse set of weapons. For instance, while the terrorist detonation of a nuclear weapon is generally regarded by many commentators as a "low-probability, high-consequence" event, it would be a mistake to ascribe a similar characterization to a rudimentary attack using toxic chemicals.

Another problem with the "destruction" component is that it is often not the physical destruction or even the casualties caused by these weapons that exerts the bulk of their effects on target societies, but rather the far-reaching *disruption* they cause. Both the physical and psychosocial consequences of using CBRN can jeopardize the functioning of critical infrastructures and services. Just two examples suffice: A chemical weapons attack using a persistent agent would immediately contaminate an area and hinder the functioning of essential services, while the use of a contagious biological agent may provoke mass evacuations and necessitate socially and economically disruptive quarantines.

One way to avoid the complications surrounding the term *weapons of mass destruction* is to refrain from using it altogether and to substitute a more well-defined descriptor. Several alternatives have been proposed, among the most promising of which are "weapons of mass effect" and "weapons of mass disruption" (the latter term has the added advantage of retaining the same acronym). This is not, however, as satisfactory a resolution as it might at first seem. First, while these substitutes may address some of the deficiencies discussed above by more accurately describing the consequences of these weapons, they do nothing to address such core concerns as which weapons are included or the scale of "mass," making them only partial solutions at best. Moreover, just as chemical and biological weapons might not cause destruction per se, stating that nuclear weapons cause disruption is more than a little euphemistic and merely flips the initial problem on its head. Second, the term *weapons of mass destruction* is used ubiquitously[52] and, despite being derided in several quarters,[53] it is still used by scholars and practitioners as well as in national and international legal instruments and, thus, cannot be easily jettisoned. We will, therefore, retain the term *weapons of mass destruction* in this volume, with the important stipulation that we will be careful and explicit in how we define and use the term.

In light of the above discussion, we have chosen in this volume to restrict the term *weapons of mass destruction* and its acronym WMD to *chemical, biological, radiological, and nuclear weapons that, if used, would inflict catastrophic casualties, widespread social disruption, or devastating economic consequences greater than those brought about by the largest conventional attacks carried out thus far.* This usage can include both CBRN[54] agents that are specifically designed for use in a military context (e.g., nuclear warheads or VX nerve agent) and materials developed for nonmilitary purposes that can be misused in ways that cause significant harm (e.g., pesticides, or radioactive isotopes used for industry or research). Each author in this work was supplied with the above definition and was also requested to make a clear distinction in their analysis between smaller scale CBRN attacks and genuine WMD attacks as we have defined them, with the focus of the book lying squarely on WMD.

Terrorism and WMD Terrorism

We focus in this volume on jihadists as a distinct set of nonstate actors and thus are not directly concerned with whether it is proper to label a specific group of jihadists as terrorists or not. Nonetheless, we cannot completely avoid the use of the term "terrorism" throughout the various chapters and, therefore, we engage in a brief discussion here, with the proviso that we are seeking only a usable definition for the purposes of the current text and do not aspire to stake any claims in the broader definitional fray.

The first thing to realize about terrorism is that there is no broad consensus (either among governments or academics) on what a terrorist is, leading to a host of divergent definitions.[55] Since an objective definition of terrorism has proven elusive, the subject has become prone to subjective manipulation by political actors, leading to the aphorism that "one person's terrorist is another's freedom fighter." What almost everyone can agree on, however, is that the word "terrorist" carries a negative connotation and that it continues to be politically expedient to label any opponent as a terrorist, a predilection that can sometimes lead to almost farcical results.[56]

Several observers who do acknowledge the definitional morass surrounding terrorism sometimes—out of exasperation or laxity—seek to avoid the issue entirely by appealing to an alleged intuitive "terrorism radar," that is, "we'll know terrorism when we see it." The only problem with this approach is that in the case of terrorism, by the time we see it, it is generally too late to do anything about it.[57] In other words, the importance of the loss of meaning of the concept of a terrorist group transcends mere academic nitpicking—the official definition of terrorism often forms the basis of the political, legal, or military response to it.

We offer a definition that attempts to differentiate between terrorism and other forms of violence (such as guerilla warfare), while capturing what many believe are the distinguishing elements of terrorism, namely, an intention on the part of the perpetrator to have a broader psychological impact and the noncombatant status of the victims. We therefore define *terrorism* to be

> The intentional use or threatened use of violence, directed against noncombatant victims selected for their symbolic or representative value, as a means of instilling anxiety in, transmitting one or more messages to, and thereby manipulating the attitudes and behavior of a wider target audience or audiences.[58]

An actor can be termed a terrorist, then, if the majority of his or her violent activities can be classed as terrorism. In this volume, we further restrict the usage of the term to nonstate actors, at the same time acknowledging that terrorism committed by states is often the most egregious type. It follows that the term "WMD terrorism" refers to acts of terrorism involving weapons of mass destruction, as we have defined them previously.

While offering the above definition of terrorism in order to provide clarity to the discussion, we take heed of the words of J. Bowyer Bell, who stated that, "no matter what tools of analysis a scholar carries into the terrorist thicket, rarely is the venture begun or ended disinterestedly"[59] and acknowledge that our definition may not be suitable for all. Therefore, we have allowed the various authors in this volume to depart from the above definition if they wish, so long as they do so explicitly.

FRAMING QUESTIONS

Beyond the basic goal of more comprehensively exploring a topic of substantial significance to international security, we have endeavored to provide more structure to our inquiry by orienting the discussion around a set of four central questions. While the authors in this volume were not explicitly required to address these questions in any formulaic way, they are implicit in the work as a whole. By listing the questions that frame the discourse at the outset, we will hopefully aid the reader in understanding each chapter in the context of the larger topic of the potential use by jihadists of weapons of mass destruction.

How Serious Is the Threat of Jihadists Using WMD, Really?

While the threat, or at least the potential threat, of jihadists obtaining and using WMD might seem obvious to some, there are several skeptics who argue that the threat is far lower than it is popularly believed to be and further that it has been exaggerated, either unwittingly or by design, by politicians, journalists, and the so-called homeland security industry[60] (which is posited as a somewhat updated incarnation of Eisenhower's military–industrial complex). Rather than ignoring such views, we must pay them careful consideration, lest we open this enterprise up to accusations of hyping the threat in order to justify our own or our authors' academic existence or to secure a place at the trough of government funding. Therefore, the most basic question we will pose in this volume is whether there exists a genuine threat in the first place. The fundamental elements in assessing such a threat consist of establishing whether the potential perpetrator(s) possess both the motivation to cause a particular type of harm and the capability to successfully do so.[61] In the case of assessing motivation, we will consider whether there is a sufficiently strong ideological, strategic, or tactical basis for jihadists to use WMD, which culminates in the question, "Are they really trying?" To get at the extent of jihadist capabilities with respect to WMD we will endeavor to answer the question: "How close are they to succeeding?" By subsequently combining current levels of jihadist motivation and capability, we will seek to establish a minimum level of objective threat that may at least dampen (though doubtfully silence) any accusations of threat exaggeration.

Which Aspects of the WMD Terrorism Problem Are Specific, and Consequentially So, to Jihadists?

Much ink has been spilled on the topic of WMD terrorism and perhaps even more on recent explorations of radical Islamic movements. Part of the rationale behind the current volume is that there are at least some salient features occurring at the nexus of jihadism and WMD that merit deeper exploration and which could add to the current discourse on both subjects. The chapters in this volume are therefore structured to identify elements in the behavioral progression from ideology to strategy and thence to operations and tactics that are particular to jihadists and would, therefore, translate into unique manifestations of WMD pursuit or use in the jihadist context. This could include such considerations as which weapon type (of CBRN) would be most likely to be pursued by jihadists, how this would be justified to the jihadists' perceived constituency, as well as the probable scale and sophistication of any jihadist WMD attacks.

Which Measures Are Likely to Be Effective in Countering or Preventing WMD Attacks by Jihadists and Which Are Not? How Do These Relate to Current Counterterrorism Tools and Practices?

Moving beyond characterization of the threat itself, this volume also investigates which methods are needed to address the unique threat elements identified in answering the previous question. The methods that will be considered range from preventative measures such as early interdiction of plots and hardening of targets, to prompt detection of a CBRN attack and consequence management efforts for mitigating post-attack effects. Presuming that the threat has been verified and that it possesses distinct features, the primary question in this regard becomes: Will general CBRN countermeasures be adequate to deal with the particular manifestation of the threat likely to emanate from the jihadist quarter, or will extant approaches need to be tweaked, or perhaps even reformulated wholesale? Once the requirements for effective means to combat the jihadist WMD threat have been established, a preliminary evaluation of the extent to which counterterrorist practitioners at all levels are incorporating these requirements into their standard operating procedures can be undertaken.

What Does the Future Hold for the Prospects of WMD Use by Jihadists?

Terrorism and technology are inherently dynamic phenomena. Jihadist terrorism and the technologies underlying WMD have proven themselves to be doubly so. A static picture of the WMD jihadist threat is therefore likely to be of extremely limited utility as both the actors involved and the availability of the weapons they seek constantly evolve. Each author was therefore instructed to give some thought to future developments as these pertained to their individual facets of the overall issue. Furthermore, the last part of the book is devoted to an explicit consideration of how the threat might develop in the coming decades.

CHAPTER STRUCTURE

It is the nature, and indeed one of the strengths, of any edited volume that a diversity of approaches and opinions is presented. At the same time, one of the objectives of this volume is to ensure that the topic is examined as thoroughly as possible and in greater depth than has previously been the case. In designing the structure of the book, our task as editors was thus to attempt to strike a balance between encouraging multiple perspectives and breadths of interpretation, while at the same time creating a cogent text with minimal redundancies. Thanks to a set of very attentive and enthusiastic contributing authors, the resulting text exceeded our expectations in this regard. Nevertheless, the reader should not be surprised if the conclusions of some of the authors differ, or if some elements of the analysis receive more attention than others, since this reflects the latitude given to each author to pursue his or her own analysis as he or she feels fit.

Section I of the book examines the jihadists themselves and their orientation toward WMD. It is focused primarily on the motivational element, but also includes references to generic jihadist capabilities. Jeffrey M. Bale begins the section by discussing how jihadist ideology translates into strategy in the context of the archetypical transnational jihadist organization—al-Qaʿida—and how ideological and strategic exigencies relate specifically to the employment of WMD. Bale's chapter is followed by Mark Dechesne's psychologically inspired approach to understanding the jihadist relationship to weapons selection and WMD, built around a model of the jihadist "lifespace." Moving from a focus on the broader jihadist worldview, James Forest and Sammy Salama investigate how this might translate into the use of WMD at the tactical level, with a particular focus on jihadist target selection were they to employ WMD. Sammy Salama and Edith Bursac round out the first section with the chapter on the methods by which WMD knowledge is disseminated by jihadists using the World Wide Web and the extent to which this might augment jihadist capabilities to successfully deploy WMD.

Section II takes a closer look at the weapons themselves. Since the availability and the degree of difficulty involved in acquiring and using each of the four CBRN weapon types differ in several important respects, a separate chapter is devoted to each type of WMD. Each chapter follows a similar structure, beginning with a brief introduction to the weapon type and how it causes harm and then tracing the obstacles jihadists would face in obtaining or using the weapon. This is followed by a description of previous jihadist activities involving the type of weapon under consideration, accompanied by an analysis of the progress jihadists have made toward employing the weapon on the scale of a WMD attack. Markus Binder and Michael Moodie explore the jihadist use of chemical weapons, including the looming threat of toxic industrial chemicals. This is followed by Cheryl Loeb's survey of jihadist involvement with biological and toxin weapons. Charles P. Blair provides a detailed description of the potential for jihadists to detonate a nuclear explosive in a fission or fusion reaction. Charles D. Ferguson discusses the prospect of massive disruption brought about by jihadists dispersing radiological materials.

Having painted a detailed picture of the threat of jihadists using WMD, the discussion in Section III turns to various aspects of countering or defending against the threat. Randall S. Murch and Jeremy Tamsett explore the role of intelligence and law enforcement in anticipating and interdicting WMD terrorist attacks by jihadists, while Brad Roberts discusses the complexities surrounding attempts to deter jihadists from going down the WMD path. An important element in the prevention of WMD terrorism is denying would-be perpetrators access to the requisite raw materials with which WMD are constructed; thereupon, Brian Finlay and Jeremy Tamsett provide an overview of nonproliferation policies as well as an analysis of the efficacy of so-called "supply-side" efforts to limit the availability of WMD materials to jihadists. When the layers of prevention and protection fail, consequence mitigation comes to the fore and Patrick S. Roberts describes the strategic aspects of robust responses to WMD attacks.

Section IV of the book is forward looking in that it considers the extent to which we can anticipate future developments concerning jihadists and WMD. Victor H. Asal and R. Karl Rethemeyer conduct a groundbreaking quantitative empirical analysis of historical jihadist behavior in an attempt to identify a set of characteristics of jihadist groups that might serve as future indicators of an intent and capability to use, or at least pursue, CBRN weapons. This is followed by Gary Ackerman's chapter, in which he discusses the difficulties of anticipating behavioral trends and conducts a forecasting exercise to examine the future likelihood of jihadists using WMD over an extended time period.

The conclusion provides a summary of the book's major findings and recommendations and attempts to develop a response to the framing questions posed in this introduction. The first appendix includes a list of open-source reports of plots or other activities involving al-Qaʻida and CBRN matériel. The second reference appendix is a substantial compilation of statements and discussions of WMD attributed to jihadists and drawn from the open sources.

Two more preliminary notes are warranted. First, although the focus of this book is on the jihadist movement more generally, which includes both Sunni and Shiʻi variants of Islamism, many of the authors chose to focus primarily on Sunni groups, no doubt reflecting the greater amount of activity by these groups with respect to WMD, and the fact that Shiʻi involvement with WMD seems to center around the activities of a state actor, Iran, and its radical leader, Mahmud Ahmadinejad, as opposed to the nonstate groups that are the focus of this book. Nonetheless, it should be recognized that Shiʻi-based jihadist groups also have the potential to pursue WMD, as can be seen in some of the references in the text to Shiʻi groups such as Hizb`allah. Second, certain authors chose to conduct their analysis by highlighting the dynamics of a particular jihadist organization, the al-Qaʻida network. This is also hardly surprising when one considers that al-Qaʻida is currently both the primary jihadist antagonist and has been involved in one way or another with the majority of jihadist activities involving WMD.

Having thus laid out the structure and context of the book, we can now proceed to the analysis of the nexus between jihadists and WMD. It is here where the reader will be exposed to a number of different perspectives regarding the threat and hopefully propelled to a greater understanding of what is one of the key security issues of the first part of the twenty-first century.

NOTES

1. *Qur'an* (69:13–15), following Hafiz Abdullah Yusuf Ali's translation.
2. National Intelligence Estimate, "The Terrorist Threat to the U.S. Homeland," Office of the Director of National Intelligence, July 2007, available at http://www.dni.gov/press_releases/press_releases.htm.
3. "The Threats," MI5 Security Service Web site, available at http://www.mi5.gov.uk/output/Page16.html.

4. Statement of Gen. Michael Hayden, Director U.S. Central Intelligence Agency, "A Conversation with Michael Hayden," Council on Foreign Relations, September 7, 2007, available at http://www.cfr.org/publication/14162/conversation_with_michael_hayden_rush_transcript_federal_news_service.html.
5. "EU Terrorism Situation and Trend Report," *Europol*, March 2007, 3, available at http://www.europol.europa.eu/publications/EU_Terrorism_Situation_and_Trend_Report_TE-SAT/TESAT2007.pdf.
6. J. Michael McConnell, Director of National Intelligence, Annual Threat Assessment of the Director of National Intelligence for the Senate Select Committee on Intelligence, February 5, 2008.
7. "What to Do? A Global Strategy," 9/11 Commission Report, Chapter 12, 362, available at http://www.9-11commission.gov/report/911Report_Ch12.pdf.
8. Op. cit.
9. Somewhat paradoxically, there is some evidence to suggest that al-Qa'ida might only have become substantially interested in CBRN weapons as a result of American officials and experts continually highlighting the dangers of terrorists using these weapons in the wake of the 1995 Tokyo subway attacks; see: Toby Archer, ""WMD" Terrorism—How Scared Should We Be?" UPI Briefing Paper 2, Finnish Institute of International Affairs, May 31, 2005, 4.
10. President Bush contends that "Weapons of mass destruction (WMD)—nuclear, biological, and chemical—in the possession of hostile states and terrorists represent one of the greatest security challenges facing the United States. We must pursue a comprehensive strategy to counter this threat in all of its dimensions." See George W. Bush, National Security Strategy of the United States of America, White House, September 17, 2002, 5. This is not only an American concern. In a 2006 speech, Dame Eliza Manningham-Buller, then-Director General of Britain's MI5, declared: "Today we see the use of home-made improvised explosive devices; tomorrow's threat may include the use of chemicals, bacteriological agents, radioactive materials and even nuclear technology." Eliza Manningham-Buller, "The International Terrorist Threat to the UK," Queen Mary's College London, November 9, 2006.
11. National Strategy for Combating Terrorism, White House, September 2006, 12. Another recent example appeared in a 2008 report by the U.S. State Department: "The nexus of weapons of mass destruction (WMD) and terrorism poses one of the gravest potential risks to the national security of the United States and its global partners. A successful major WMD terrorist attack could result in mass casualty events and produce far-reaching economic and political consequences that would affect all members of the international community." See "The Global Challenge of WMD Terrorism," *Country Reports on Terrorism* (2007), Chapter 4, U.S. State Department, April 30, 2008.
12. National Intelligence Estimate, 2007. Compare with McConnell, op. cit.: "Al-Qa'ida and other terrorist groups are attempting to acquire chemical, biological, radiological, and nuclear weapons and materials (CBRN). We assess al-Qa'ida will continue to try to acquire and employ these weapons and materials; some chemical and radiological materials and crude weapons designs are easily accessible, in our judgment."
13. See the results of the Delphi study by Gary Ackerman in Chapter 14 in this volume.
14. For example, in the United States, the Defense Against Weapons of Mass Destruction Act of 1996 and Nunn-Lugar-Domenici amendment to the National Defense Authorization Act for FY97 provided for the training of first responders to deal

with WMD terrorist incidents; see: "Nunn-Lugar-Domenici Domestic Preparedness and WMD Civil Support Teams," Center for Nonproliferation Studies (2001), available at http://cns.miis.edu/research/cbw/120city.htm.

15. Among the better-researched book-length studies written between 1995 and 2001 are Brad Roberts, ed., *Terrorism with Chemical and Biological Weapons: Calibrating Risks and Responses* (Alexandria, VA: Chemical and Biological Arms Control Institute, 1997); Richard A. Falkenrath, Robert D. Newman, and Bradley A. Thayer, *America's Achilles' Heal: Nuclear, Biological, and Chemical Terrorism and Covert Attack* (Cambridge, MA: MIT Press, 1998); Jessica Stern, *The Ultimate Terrorists* (Cambridge, MA: Harvard University Press, 1999); Brad Roberts, ed., *Hype or Reality?: The "New Terrorism" and Mass Casualty Attacks* (Alexandria, VA: Chemical and Biological Arms Control Institute, 2000); Jonathan B. Tucker, ed., *Toxic Terror: Assessing Terrorist Use of Chemical and Biological Weapons* (Cambridge, MA: MIT Press, 2000); and Nadine Gurr and Benjamin Cole, *The New Face of Terrorism: Threats from Weapons of Mass Destruction* (New York: I. B. Tauris, 2002). Some of the more influential article commentaries from the same time period include: Ron Purver, "Chemical and Biological Terrorism: New Threat to Public Safety," *Conflict Studies* 295 (December 1996–January 1997); Bruce Hoffman, "Terrorism and WMD: Some Preliminary Hypotheses," *Nonproliferation Review* 4:3 (Spring–Summer 1997); Jonathan B. Tucker and Amy Sands, "An Unlikely Threat," *Bulletin of the Atomic Scientists* 55:4 (July–August 1999); Jean Pascal Zanders, "Assessing the Risk of Chemical and Biological Weapons Proliferation to Terrorists," *Nonproliferation Review* 6:4 (Fall 1999); Ehud Sprinzak, "The Great Superterrorism Scare," *Foreign Policy* (Fall 1998); John V. Parachini, "Comparing Motives and Outcomes of Mass Casualty Terrorism involving Conventional and Unconventional Weapons," *Studies in Conflict and Terrorism* 24:5 (September 2001); and Daniel S. Gressang IV, "Audience and Message: Assessing Terrorist WMD Potential," *Terrorism and Political Violence* 13:3 (Autumn 2001).
16. We understand that this term carries with it several definitional concerns, especially since not all the CBRN activities of terrorists are likely to qualify as WMD, and not all nonstate users of WMD will necessarily be terrorists. Nonetheless, this term has entered popular parlance and we use it in place of the technically more accurate yet simultaneously more cumbersome phrase "the literature on the use of CBRN weapons by nonstate actors." A more detailed discussion of both these terms will be presented later in this chapter.
17. Albert Bandura has discussed various ways in which terrorist groups legitimize their violent behavior, several of which can flow from a group's ideological outlook, including moral justification, displacement of responsibility, ignoring the actual suffering of victims, and dehumanizing victims (Albert Bandura, "Mechanisms of Disengagement," in Walter Reich, *Origins of Terrorism:* Psychologies, Ideologies, Theologies, States of Mind [Washington, DC: Woodrow Wilson Center Press, 1988]).
18. See, for example, Hoffman, *Inside Terrorism*, New York: Columbia University Press, 1998, 94; idem, "Terrorism and WMD: Some Preliminary Hypotheses," op cit., 45–50; idem, *"Holy Terror": The Implications of Terrorism Motivated by a Religious Imperative* (Santa Monica, CA: RAND Corporation, 1993); Gavin Cameron, "WMD Terrorism in the United States," *Nonproliferation Review* 7(1): 156–170 (Spring 2000); James K. Campbell, "On Not Understanding the Problem," in *Hype or Reality?: The "New Terrorism" and Mass Casualty Attacks*, ed. Brad Roberts (Alexandria, VA: Chemical and Biological Arms Control Institute, 2000), 30–33; Gurr and Cole, *New*

Face of Terrorism, 22–32, 126–148; Tucker, "Lessons from the Case Studies," in *Toxic Terror*, 261–262; and Marlo, "WMD Terrorism and US Intelligence Collection," *Terrorism and Political Violence* 11:3 (1999).

19. Jeffrey M. Bale, Islamism, in *Encyclopedia of Bioterrorism Defense*, Richard F. Pilch and Raymond Zilinskas, eds. (New York: Wiley, 2005), 296–298.Compare Hoffman, "*Holy Terror,*" op. cit., 12.
20. These authors have questioned the connection between a desire on the part of religious terrorists to cause mass casualties and the potential use of WMD, as well as the extent to which religious actors are oblivious to political concerns. They have also pointed to the large number of CBRN plots on the part of ethno-nationalist terrorists. See, for example, David C. Rapoport, "Terrorism and Weapons of the Apocalypse," *Nonproliferation Review* 6:3 (1999), 49–67; Parachini, op. cit., 399; and Adam Dolnik, "All God's Poisons: Re-evaluating the Threat of Religious Terrorism with Respect to Non-conventional Weapons," in *Terrorism and Counterterrorism: Understanding the New Security Environment*, eds. R. D. Howard and R. L. Guilford Sawyer (New York: McGraw-Hill, 2004). While these concerns must be taken into consideration, to consequently deny the connection completely is, in our opinion, letting the pendulum swing too far in the other direction.
21. For a full discussion, see Daniel Gressang, op cit. 88.
22. Jeffrey M. Bale and Gary Ackerman, "Profiling the WMD Terrorist Threat," in *WMD Terrorism: Science and Policy Choices*, Stephen M. Maurer and Christine Hartmann-Siantar eds. (Cambridge, MA: MIT Press, 2009), 29–30.
23. The precise nature of the Mahdi differs according to interpretation, but generally, in Islamic eschatology, the Mahdi (literally: "guided one") is the savior who, often together with Jesus, will bring to perfect fruition the Islamic ideal of a just and peaceful global community of believers in anticipation of the Muslim Final Day of Judgment (*yaum al-Qiyamah*, literally "Day of Resurrection").
24. See Adam Dolnik, "Die and Let Die: Exploring the Links between Suicide Terrorism and Terrorist Use of Chemical, Biological, Radiological, and Nuclear Weapons," *Studies in Conflict and Terrorism*, 26 (2003), 17–35.
25. Jessica Stern, *The Ultimate Terrorists* (Cambridge, MA: Harvard University Press, 1999), 70.
26. This has been validated empirically: see Victor H. Asal, Gary A. Ackerman, and R. Karl Rethemeyer, *Connections Can Be Toxic: Terrorist Organizational Factors and the Pursuit and Use of CBRN Terrorism*, Unpublished manuscript (2008).
27. A recent book-length publication on WMD terrorism is Randall Howard and James, J. F. Forest, *Weapons of Mass Destruction and Terrorism* (New York: McGraw-Hill, 2008). An excellent survey of recent publications and research on terrorism involving WMD is Nancy Hayden, "Terrifying Landscapes," Advanced Systems and Concepts Office, Defense Threat Reduction Agency, June 2007.
28. For example, Charles D. Ferguson, William Potter, Amy Sands, Leonard Spector, and Fred Wehling, *The Four Faces of Nuclear Terrorism* (Monterey, CA: Center for Nonproliferation Studies, 2004); Graham Allison, *Nuclear Terrorism: The Ultimate Preventable Catastrophe* (New York: Henry Holt, 2004); Michael Levi, *On Nuclear Terrorism* (Cambridge, MA: Harvard University Press, 2007); Jonathan Tucker, *War of Nerves: Chemical Warfare from World War I to al-Qaeda* (New York: Pantheon, 2006); Eric Croddy, *Chemical and Biological Warfare: A Comprehensive Survey*

for the Concerned Citizen (New York: Springer-Verlag, 2002); and Barry Kellman, *Bioviolence: Preventing Biological Terror and Crime* (Cambridge: Cambridge University Press, 2007).

29. These include Gary Ackerman and Laura Snyder, "Would They if They Could? WMD Terrorism in the Middle East," *Bulletin of the Atomic Scientists* (May/June 2002); Jonathan Spyer, "The Al-Qa'ida Network and Weapons of Mass Destruction," *Middle East Review of International Affairs*, 8:3 (2004); Reuven Paz, "Global Jihad and WMD: Between Martyrdom and Mass Destruction," in *Current Trends in Islamist Ideology*, Vol. 2, ed. Hillel Fradkin et al. (Washington, DC: Hudson Institute, 2005); Jerry Mark Long, "Strategic Culture, Al-Qaida, and Weapons of Mass Destruction," Advanced Systems Concepts Office, Defense Threat Reduction Agency, 2007; Robert Wesley "Al-Qaeda's WMD Strategy After the U.S. Intervention in Afghanistan," *Jamestown Terrorism Monitor* 3:20 (October 21, 2005); Adam Dolnik, "13 Years since Tokyo: Re-Visiting the 'Superterrorism' Debate," *Perspectives on Terrorism* 2:2 (2008); and Andrea Plebani, "Attractiveness of WMD for Radical Islamist Movements: Ideological Constraints, Black-Spots, and Failed-Weak States," *Strategic Insights* 4:5 (2007).
30. Nasir bin Hamd al-Fahd, *A Treatise on the Legal Status of Using Weapons of Mass Destruction Against Infidels*, Rabi` I 1424 (May 2003).
31. Jeffrey Mark Long,.4, op. cit.
32. Bruce Hoffman, "CBRN Terorrism Post-9/11" in Forest and Howard, op. cit., 275. As we discuss below, it should be noted that, as we define the concept, in certain circumstances even those CBRN attacks that inflict minimal casualties might qualify as WMD if they result in genuinely extensive social disruption and devastating economic consequences.
33. Jerrold Post, Ehud Sprinzak, and Laurita Denny, "The terrorists in their own words: Interviews with 35 incarcerated Middle Eastern terrorists" *Terrorism and Political Violence*, 15:1 (2003) 180–181.
34. See Hayden, 13.
35. Robert Wesley, "Al-Qaeda's WMD Strategy Prior to the U.S. Intervention in Afghanistan," *Jamestown Terrorism Monitor* 3:19 (October 7, 2005); Robert Wesley, "Al-Qaeda's WMD Strategy After the U.S. Intervention in Afghanistan," *Jamestown Terrorism Monitor* 3:20 (October 21, 2005).
36. Paz, op. cit.
37. Originally quoted as "...experts interested in the terrorism subject had devoted only a tiny fraction of their time and effort to thinking about weapons of mass destruction. Similarly, experts on weapons of mass destruction had devoted little time and effort to thinking about terrorism." Brad Roberts, "Motivations for Terrorists to use Weapons of MassDestruction," Confronting Terrorism, a Workshop Held at the Los Alamos National Laboratory, March 25–29, 2002, *Proceędings*, edited by Rajan Gupta and Mario R. Perez. Passage quoted in Hayden, op. cit., 5.
38. We are restricting our definition to the description of a specific set of violent actors and intentionally avoiding engaging the contemporary meaning of the word *jihad*. The connotations of the term *jihad* (derived from the Arabic root connoting the action of "striving," "struggling," or "exerting oneself") have been a topic of some controversy, since the term has historically had more than one application. Our focus here is on those actors who regard themselves as being involved in an active armed

struggle against their external enemies. For more detail on the debate surrounding the essential meaning of *jihad* in Islam, see footnote 51 in the chapter by Jeffrey M. Bale in this volume.

39. For a general introduction to the broader subject of radical Islamic movements, compare Mary Habeck, *Knowing the Enemy* (New Haven, CT: Yale University Press, 2006); Rudolph Peters, *Jihad in Classical and Modern Islam* (Princeton, NJ: Markus Wiener Publishers, 2005); Olivier Roy, *Globalized Islam* (New York: Columbia University Press, 2006); Fawaz A. Gerges, *The Far Enemy,* (Cambridge: Cambridge University Press, 2005); Bassam Tibi, *The Challenge of Fundamentalism: Political Islam and the New World Disorder* (Berkeley: University of California Press, 2002); Jeffrey M. Bale, op cit., 296–298. For more on this see Emmanuel Sivan, *Radical Islam: Medieval Theology and Modern Politics* (New Haven, CT: Yale University Press, 1990).
40. The authors are indebted to Jeffrey M. Bale for his insights on the nature of contemporary Islamism. For a greater level of detail on Islamist doctrine(s) than that presented here, see Jeffrey M. Bale, "Islamism," op. cit.
41. The ultimate goal is to bring the entire world within the fold of the *dar-al-Islam*, after which a new and peaceful global *umma* (Islamic community) can be established, in which everyone will accede to the will of Allah.
42. Faisal Devji, *Landscapes of Jihad: Militancy, Morality, Modernity* (Ithaca, NY: Cornell University Press, 2005).
43. We thank Jarret Brachman for pointing out that the jihadists themselves have applied the WMD moniker to a variety of weapons, including characterizing disease, famine, poverty, political turmoil, social unrest, environmental pollution, popular culture, capitalism and more as WMD that are intentionally being deployed against Muslim populations by Western governments. This characterization might serve a useful propaganda purpose or even influence the jihadists' own willingness to use unconventional weapons against the West and will be taken up by contributing authors in this context. However, we are less concerned at this juncture with the jihadist conception of WMD because we are seeking in this volume to explore the likelihood and consequences of a particular type and level of harm as faced by the potential victims of jihadist attacks, irrespective of how the jihadists themselves might label the weapons used.
44. A brief background of each of these weapons types is provided in the four chapters in Section II of this volume.
45. Even U.S. law enforcement discourse has used the term inconsistently. For example, former FBI Director Louis Freeh has used the term *WMD* to include large amounts of conventional explosive on some occasions: Louis Freeh, "Statement on President's Fiscal Year 2000 Budget Before the Senate Committee on Appropriations," available at http://www.fbi.gov/congress/congress99/freehct2.htm, and not others; Freeh, "Testimony Before the United States Senate, Committees on Appropriations, Armed Services, and Select Committee on Intelligence," May 10, 2001, available at http://www.fbi.gov/congress/congress01/freeh051001.htm.
46. Joint Publication 1-02, *Department of Defense Dictionary of Military and Associated Terms*, U.S. Department of Defense, available at http://www.dtic.mil/doctrine/jel/new_pubs/jp1_02.pdf.
47. For more detail see Jeffrey M. Bale and Gary Ackerman, "Profiling the WMD Terrorist Threat," op. cit.

48. Chemical weapons, for instance, can dissipate quickly if they are improperly aerosolized or if the weather is unfavorable.
49. For example, one can easily imagine that the same amount of agent could kill twenty people in an enclosed area or cause serious but nonmortal injuries to thousands if released outdoors.
50. W. Seth Carus, "Defining 'Weapons of Mass Destruction,'" Center for the Study of Weapons of Mass Destruction Occasional Paper 4, National Defense University Press, Washington, DC, February 2006.
51. See A. E. Smithson and L. A. Levy, "Ataxia: The Chemical and Biological Terrorism Threat and the U.S. Response," Henry L. Stimson Center, Report No. 35 (October 2000).
52. This is to the extent that the American Dialect Society selected "weapons of mass destruction" and its abbreviation "WMD" as its word (or phrase) of the year in 2002; see http://www.americandialect.org/index.php/amerdial/2002_words_of_the_y/.
53. In 2003, the term received the more dubious honor of appearing on Lake Superior State University's List of Banished Words rejected for misuse, overuse, and general uselessness; see http://www.lssu.edu/banished/archive/2003.php.
54. We recognize that in the future, new technologies might arise that could be incorporated into weapons that would cause casualty, social, and psychological effects similar to those caused by CBRN. A plausible candidate would be nanotechnology, although it has thankfully not yet matured to this stage of posing a viable threat. If, however, such novel weapon types do arise at some point, we are open to including them within our definition of WMD.
55. See, for example, the extensive discussion of the variety of definitions of terrorism in Alex P. Schmid and Albert J. Jongman, *Political Terrorism: A New Guide to Actors, Authors, Concepts, Data Bases, Theories and Literature* (Amsterdam: North-Holland, 1988), especially 1– 38; and Bruce Hoffman, *Inside Terrorism*, 1–42.
56. Some governments use the word terrorism to describe their enemies without paying any attention to the way the word is used elsewhere. So, while the United States and many other countries view Iran as a major sponsor of terrorism, the Iranian government chooses to use this word as propaganda to criticize Israeli policies, as can be seen in the words of Iran's President Khatami: "In the midst of the global terrorism crisis, the world faces an intensive and severe genre of terrorism in the Middle East. Occupation of the Palestinian territories, Syrian Golan and Lebanese Shaba'a, expulsion of the Palestinian people from their homeland, judaization of Palestine and in particular al-Quds al-Sharif [Jerusalem], planning and building of illegal settlements, killing and terrorizing of defenseless Palestinian civilians in their homes and cities, destruction of historical sites, civil institutions and residential areas, are examples of this phenomenon" (from "Text of the Address by Mohammad Khatami, President of the Islamic Republic of Iran, before The 56th Session of The United Nations General Assembly," United Nations, New York, November 10, 2001, available at http://www.un.org/webcast/ga/56/statements/011110iranE.htm).
57. All the above definitional problems are exacerbated by the fact that terrorism is itself a dynamic phenomenon that is affected by geopolitical, structural, and other developments as well as the strong influences of public perception; any suitable definition must be able to reflect this dynamism and will furthermore be subject to some revision, while at the same time maintaining core concepts as constants.
58. This is a slightly modified version of the definition used by Jeffrey M. Bale. While we thank Dr. Bale for his input, we bear full responsibility for the definition offered.

59. J. Bowyer Bell, "Trends on Terror: The Analysis of Political Violence," *World Politics* 29:3 (April 1977), 487.
60. The two most prominent disquisitions in this regard are those of John Mueller and Ian Lustick, both professors of political science who have argued that the true threat of Islamic terrorists has been overblown and that the so-called Global War on Terror (GWOT) has been in some respects manufactured by fear-mongering politicians and other vested interests. In particular, both authors question the likelihood of terrorists being able to successfully use WMD on a large scale. See John Mueller, *Overblown: How Politicians and the Terrorism Industry Inflate National Security Threats, and Why We Believe Them* (New York: Simon & Schuster, 2006); and Ian S. Lustick, *Trapped in the War on Terror* (Philadelphia: University of Pennsylvania Press, 2006).
61. For applications of this methodology, see Gary Ackerman and Kevin Moran, *Bioterrorism and Threat Assessment*, *Weapons of Mass Destruction Commission* (The "Blix" Commission), Stockholm (2005); and Gary Ackerman, "Beyond Arson? A Threat Assessment of the Earth Liberation Front," *Terrorism and Political Violence* 15:4 (Winter 2004).

SECTION I

The Jihadists

CHAPTER 1

Jihadist Ideology and Strategy and the Possible Employment of WMD[1]

Jeffrey M. Bale

CONTENTS

INTRODUCTION

Those who work without knowledge will damage more than they can fix and those who walk quickly on the wrong path will only distance themselves from their goal.

ancient Arab proverb[2]

The aim of carrying out resistance missions and individual jihad terrorism [*jihad al-irhabi al-fardi*] is to inflict the largest human and material casualties possible on American interests and its allied countries.

Abu Mus'ab al-Suri[3]

If the objective and subjective conditions materialize, and there are soldiers, weapons, and money—even if this means using biological, chemical, and bacterial [sic] weapons—we will conquer the world, so that "There is no God but Allah, and Muhammad is His Prophet" will be triumphant over the domes of Moscow, Washington, and Paris.

Grand Ayatollah Ahmad Husayni al-Baghdadi[4]

One of the peculiarities of the literature on "WMD terrorism" is the disparity between the large amount of attention paid to terrorist capabilities and the relatively small amount of attention paid to terrorist motivations.[5] As Bruce Hoffman has rightly noted, "the need for a better understanding of the motivations, thought processes, mindsets and historical consciousness of terrorists...is essential if the [terrorism] field is to grow in new and beneficial directions, retain its relevance, and provide insightful and thoughtful analysis..."[6] Indeed, as Jerrold Post long ago emphasized, "absent a clear understanding of the adversary's intentions, the strategies and tactics developed [to counter them] are based primarily on knowledge of terrorists [sic] technological capabilities and give insufficient weight to psychological motivations."[7] This same observation is likewise true with respect to the *ideological motivations* and *operational objectives* of different types and groups of terrorists.

Properly assessing the general ideological and strategic objectives of jihadist groups—Islamist groups that are focused on waging *jihad bi al-sayf* ("jihad with the sword") or armed struggle against "unbelievers" (including "apostate" Muslims)—much less predicting the precise means they intend to employ in the future to achieve those objectives, is a formidable task.[8] At first glance, this might appear to be a counterintuitive if not a nonsensical claim. After all, al-Qa'ida and the various terrorist organizations and factions with which it has been affiliated have been attacking the United States and its Muslim and European allies for well over a decade, and these attacks should in and of themselves reveal distinctive patterns of action and provide careful observers with a reasonably clear idea of what their operational objectives are. Moreover, Usama bin Ladin, his lieutenants, and his supporters have often publicly announced their supposed political and strategic objectives in an effort to influence the perception and behavior of their enemies and followers. Yet these sources alone cannot, if not properly interpreted, provide observers with a clear picture of al-Qa'ida's strategic thinking, including with respect to chemical, biological, radiological, and nuclear (CBRN) agents and weapons. First of all, the pattern of al-Qa'ida attacks, to the extent that such a pattern exists and is discernable, has not only evolved over time but must be viewed from the enemy's own point of view. Second, al-Qa'ida's proclaimed rationales for carrying out its terrorist assaults, both those that it has launched in the past and those that it threatens to make in the future, can rarely if ever be taken at face value.

These intrinsic problems have been further compounded because intelligence and military analysts in the United States and Europe who are charged with comprehending and interdicting jihadist terrorism have all too often employed entirely secular, materialistic types of reasoning and exclusively Western military frames of reference, above all—whether consciously or not—certain ideas derived from well-known nineteenth-century military theorists such as the Prussian officer Carl von Clausewitz (1780–1831),[9] in an effort to explain what it is that al-Qa'ida is currently up to.[10] Unfortunately, this is a classic case of analytical "mirror-imaging," since to the extent that transnational jihadists operate on the basis of some sort of military logic and rationality, which remains debatable, it is often a logic and rationality rooted in a profoundly religious worldview that is intrinsically nonrational and arguably both utopian and delusional in terms of its intermediate and ultimate aims. Indeed, one might carry this argument further and suggest that al-Qa'ida is prone to engaging in a peculiar form of "magical thinking,"[11] in this case one that is derived from essentially theological precepts associated with Islam. Hence the group's strategic reasoning, such as it is, is generally based on radically different principles than those that are characteristic of sovereign nation-states or conventional Western military forces.

ORGANIZATIONAL FACTORS

Before actually turning to the question of al-Qa'ida's strategic concepts and objectives, it is necessary to highlight how the group's complex organizational structure may affect the implementation of those objectives. Al-Qa'ida proper is a relatively small organization, numerically speaking, which is divided into two basic levels. First, there are a few dozen members of the Majlis al-Shura (Consultative Council), which is internally subdivided into several committees, one of which is concerned explicitly with military affairs.[12] This council effectively constitutes the strategic directorate or officer corps of the group. Second, al-Qa'ida consists of somewhere between several hundred and several thousand rank-and-file members who take their marching orders directly from leading figures in the Majlis al-Shura.[13] That is essentially all there is to al-Qa'ida as an actual organization. If Bin Ladin or his principal lieutenants wish to organize an attack themselves, they will either employ existing members of al-Qa'ida's rank-and-file or recruit suitable volunteers who have already received—or are currently receiving—training from those rank-and-file members in the group's camps. Strictly speaking, if one was limiting one's analysis to al-Qa'ida as an organization, it would only be necessary to consider the actions carried out by its rank-and-file members or those seemingly promising individuals who its leaders had recruited specifically to carry out particular operations, wherever in the world they may be operating.

Unfortunately, there is much more to the Islamist terrorist threat than that which is represented by the leaders and rank-and-file members of the al-Qa'ida organization. The issue under consideration here is complicated enormously by two developments. First, al-Qa'ida has established affiliations with a host of other Islamist terrorist organizations or factions thereof, both within and outside of the Middle East. These affiliated groups and factions have more or less officially embraced al-Qa'ida's transnational jihadist agenda, including its emphasis on attacking the "far enemy," that is, the United States. At the same time, they have not entirely abandoned their former local, national, or regional concerns and objectives, much less their armed struggles against the "near enemy" in their respective areas. There is no doubt, for example, that proclaimed supporters of a global jihad such as Jemaah Islamiyah (JI: Islamic Association) in Indonesia, the Jama'at al-Salafiyya li-al-Da'wa wa al-Qital/Groupe Salafiste pour la Prédication et le Combat (GSPC: Salafist Group for Preaching and Fighting) in Algeria, the Juma'a Abu Sayyaf (Bearer of Swords Group) in the Philippines, and the Jama'at al-Islamiyya al-Muqatila al-Maghribiyya/Groupe Islamique Combattant Marocain (GICM: Moroccan Islamic Combat Group) are still interested, perhaps even more so, in eventually overthrowing the "infidel" regimes in their own areas or countries. This should not come as a surprise, since despite his advocacy of a worldwide jihad Bin Ladin himself has retained a particular interest in destabilizing the Saudi regime in his own homeland, the "Land of the Two Holy Places," and Ayman al-Zawahiri still remains embroiled in Egyptian Islamist infighting despite having left Egypt and opted to merge his own "internationalist" faction of the Tanzim al-Jihad al-Islami (Islamic Jihad Organization) into the al-Qa'ida organization to form Qa'idat al-Jihad (the Base [or Foundation] of the Jihad).[14]

Moreover, as many analysts have argued, in recent years al-Qa'ida has transmogrified from an actual, relatively delimited organization into a diffuse ideological current that nowadays serves to inspire hundreds of thousands if not millions of people across the Muslim world.[15] Although only a small segment of this radicalized population may end up having recourse to terrorism, the result is an ever-growing increase in the threat posed by alleged "self-starter" groups inspired by Bin Ladin's ideology—which some have referred to as "Bin Ladinism"—but that seem at first glance to have few if any tangible organizational, operational, or logistical connections to al-Qa'ida itself.[16] For example, some have argued that the March 11, 2004 Madrid bombings and the July 7, 2005 London bombings were carried out mainly by small cells composed of disaffected Muslim citizens or permanent residents who, inspired to respond by the exhortations of al-Qa'ida and other jihadist spokesmen, endeavored to carry out devastating acts of violence against "infidel" Westerners at home.[17] Although Bin Ladin has always claimed, sometimes disingenuously in an effort to conceal the actual operational involvement of al-Qa'ida, that his primary role was to function as an instigator rather than an actual organizer of jihadist actions, as time goes on this may be more and more the case.[18] What this means, effectively speaking, is that would-be "amateur" jihadists with no observable prior associations with al-Qa'ida or any other established Islamist terrorist groups may suddenly take it upon themselves to translate exhortations made by ideologues such as Bin Ladin and al-Zawahiri into action—whether or not they understand or correctly interpret the strategic aims of those figures. In short, actions taken by individuals who claim to be inspired by Bin Ladin but who may not even be correctly divining his real aims can only complicate the analysis of the objectives of al-Qa'ida proper. That is why, for the purposes of this study, the focus has been on al-Qa'ida itself and its more or less "official" organizational branches.

GENERAL IDEOLOGICAL FACTORS: ARE AL-QA'IDA'S OBJECTIVES TRULY "RATIONAL" OR "STRATEGIC"?

There can be no doubt that specific military or paramilitary actions and operations carried out within the context of what is generally referred to as unconventional, asymmetric, or "fourth-generation" warfare, like those carried out in the course of conventional wars, are generally intended to accomplish some objective. Such actions are rarely, if ever, utterly random, purely pathological, entirely whimsical, or so idiosyncratic in their etiology as to be incomprehensible to others. Nor are they generally undertaken with no purpose at all in mind, initiated simply "for their own sake," or carried out just because of a perceived need to do something, anything. Unless a particular political or military leader has suddenly descended into outright madness, i.e., mental illness in the clinical sense of that term, it must be assumed that his actions are directed toward some purpose. This is all the more true of terrorism per se, which by definition involves the carrying out of acts of violence that are specifically intended to influence the perceptions and behavior of wider target audiences. Terrorism is thus indisputably a technique or tactic that various parties adopt for purposive reasons.[19]

To put it another way, although terrorists and other nonstate actors rarely, if ever, engage in the sort of formal "cost–benefit" analyses that many social scientists futilely seek to model, and their "rationality" may not be comprehensible to outsiders, they normally carry out their acts of violence in order to achieve more or less calculated operational objectives.[20] To the extent that this is true, whether terrorist choose to attack targets with CBRN materials and weapons will largely depend—assuming that (1) they have the technical capabilities to do so, and that (2) using such agents is not utterly antithetical to their ideological agendas and/or psychological makeup—on whether the operational advantages that their use might be perceived to confer is seen as outweighing the operational disadvantages that their uses might incur.[21] From this perspective, a group's decision to employ CBRN, like its other decisions concerning targeting weapons and tactics, will often be based on some degree of rational strategic calculation or choice.

This does not mean, however, that terrorists are entirely or even essentially "rational" actors. Indeed, it would be incorrect to assume, as many observers have, that extremist groups behave and operate primarily, if not exclusively, in accordance with "rational choice" models, that the important actions they undertake are decided upon only after a careful calculation of "costs and benefits," and consequently that those whose responsibility it is to counter their nefarious schemes will be able to ascertain their most likely potential targets simply by determining the tangible value of the targets themselves and the objective difficulties any attacker would encounter if they chose to attack those targets.[22] Since in the real world it appears self-evident that individuals and organizations rarely, if ever, make decisions based entirely on rational processes and objective calculations, the adoption of such an abstract, hyper-rational theoretical approach is not only quite unrealistic, but is more likely than not to yield results that are seriously misleading.

Artificially rational decision-making models are even more flawed when applied uncritically or mechanically to predict the behavior of extremist groups, which almost by definition are far more prone to carry out actions for arguably less rational—or at least less discernibly rational—"expressive" reasons than, say, staid business firms, entrenched policy-making bureaucracies, or conventional military units (although these latter entities do not invariably behave rationally either). Indeed, extremist groups tend to carry out acts of violence both (1) for reasons that one can characterize as broadly rational, in particular to produce certain tangible impacts (e.g., cause casualties or physical damage) and/or to provoke certain desired psychological responses in wider audiences (i.e., terrorism proper), and (2) to satisfy more arcane ideological, subjective, impulsive, or partially conscious and hence ostensibly less rational needs.[23] These latter "internal" motives, which are herein being characterized as "expressive," include such things as doctrinal obsessions (e.g., compulsions to attack designated enemies or smite "evildoers," longings to precipitate a prophesied Armageddon, injunctions promoting individual or collective martyrdom, technological fetishism), group pathologies (e.g., excessive insularity, charismatic and/or authoritarian leadership, extreme forms of peer pressure, suppression of internal dissent, "groupthink"), collective emotional impulses (e.g., a burning desire to get revenge, a passion for gaining glory or grabbing the spotlight, a perceived need to demonstrate prowess or outdo rival groups, a desire to evoke past triumphs or tragedies), or—in the case of "lone wolves"—an incalculably diverse range of potential personal idiosyncrasies.[24] It is in fact the varying importance, fluidity, and precise configuration of such "expressive" factors that serve to distinguish particular extremist groups from one another, including those operating within the same ideological milieu, and these very distinctions can be crucially important in terms of influencing a group's selection of targets and/or its chosen methods for attacking those targets.

That is why the never-ending flood of terrorist threat assessments that are based primarily on rational choice models or on standard "Clausewitzian" strategic or geopolitical frames of reference, which almost invariably downplay or even ignore altogether the important "expressive" motivational factors that derive from a particular group's ideologies, internal organizational dynamics, and general emotional orientation (which is in turn strongly influenced by regnant cultural values within their respective societies), are so often misguided or erroneous. As long as this type of analytical "mirror-imaging" of the enemy persists, both inside and outside of the intelligence community, serious flaws in the ongoing assessment of future terrorist threats, whether they involve CBRN weapons or not, are likely to occur.

Again, this is not to say that extremist groups are entirely irrational or that they do not usually make various types of strategic calculations, especially on the operational level, where they are often brutally effective, but simply that their reasoning processes and decision-making concerning target selection, weapons selection, and attack modalities are also influenced by a host of other, less predictable and less recognizably rational if not predominantly semi-rational or nonrational factors, including their frequently obtuse ideological proclivities and their often unrealistic ultimate goals. This is especially true in the cases of secular or religious extremists who seek to achieve utopian and arguably delusional aims, that is, those that promote what Lee Harris has referred to as "fantasy ideologies," whether these envision the forging of preternaturally harmonious, cooperative, strife-free communities on the international level (communists) or the national level (fascists); the creation of racially "pure" havens (white and black supremacists); the extirpation of human "despoilers" of the environment (fringe eco-radicals); the precipitation or hastening of catastrophic "end times" prophecies (apocalyptic millenarians); or the restoration of the Caliphate, the unification of the Muslim *umma*, and ultimately the Islamization of the entire world (the most radical elements within the global jihadist milieu).[25]

Nor does the fact that terrorism is by definition purposive mean that the short-term, intermediate, or long-term goals that the perpetrators of particular acts of violence are trying to accomplish are necessarily realistic, nor that the specific actions they carry out will necessarily produce the actual effects that they were designed to achieve. Indeed, in the real world it is very often the case that (1) the ultimate objectives pursued by terrorist groups and states are unrealizable, utopian, and indeed chimerical, and/or that (2) their specific acts of violence regularly produce effects on wider audiences—both potential supporters and designated enemies—which are contrary if not antithetical to those they were aiming for. To the extent that particular parties, whether states or extremist groups, promote phantasmagoric, unachievable goals and regularly miscalculate the impact of and reactions to their acts of violence, they can be characterized as essentially nonrational or, at best, as only being rational within the framework of or in accordance with the tenets of a "fantasy ideology." It seems obvious that if a violence-prone group begins by embracing absurd notions or fundamentally flawed premises, then even if it acts perfectly logically on the basis of those premises, the results will inevitably be disastrous. Such a group cannot ultimately achieve its desired objectives, no matter how much mayhem it causes, but until it implodes or is effectively neutralized or destroyed it may well be capable of doing a tremendous amount of material and psychological damage to those it has designated as enemies.

With this background, the extent to which al-Qa'ida's objectives may be considered realistic and therefore realizable can perhaps begin to be addressed. As it happens, influential terrorism analysts cannot even agree on this most basic of questions. Some view al-Qa'ida through the prism of a traditional Western military perspective, as an essentially rational strategic actor, whereas others argue that the group and its leaders are essentially irrational. Still others seek to forge a middle ground by arguing that although al-Qa'ida may be said to operate more or less rationally as opposed to completely irrationally, it does so primarily within the restrictive confines of a basically nonrational theological framework. In short, whatever rationality it may display is seriously constrained or "bounded."

The "rationalist" interpretation has been championed by analysts such as George Friedman, founder of the private Strategic Forecasting (Stratfor) firm, which generally promulgates a "realist" geopolitical and strategic perspective, and Michael Scheuer, the former head of Alec Station, the "Bin Ladin Unit" within the U.S. Central Intelligence Agency (CIA). Although Friedman acknowledges that al-Qa'ida ultimately aims to reestablish the Caliphate and restore it to its former position of greatness, an objective that is almost certainly unrealizable, he nevertheless gives the overall impression that Bin Ladin's organization is an extraordinarily calculating if not a thoroughly rational strategic actor.[26] Indeed, he explicitly contrasts the often dramatic but less effective approaches adopted by terrorist groups that were active during the 1970s and 1980s, groups that he considers to have been overly hierarchical and dangerously dependent upon the support of various foreign intelligence services, with the strategic seriousness of al-Qa'ida. As he puts it, instead of devoting their energies primarily to "making symbolic gestures," as earlier terrorists purportedly did, al-Qa'ida "saw itself as trying to put into motion certain political processes that would result in achieving its political goals."[27] This is a rather peculiar statement insofar as it implies, falsely, that earlier generations of terrorists were not trying to set certain processes in motion in order to achieve specific political goals, however utopian those goals might have been. In reality, even the most "symbolic" and arguably "expressive" of the terrorist actions in previous decades, such as the demonstrative "propaganda of the deed" assassinations perpetrated by nineteenth- and early twentieth-century anarchists, were intended to achieve certain hoped-for political results. Friedman is certainly correct to argue that al-Qa'ida is much more dangerous than most of the terrorist organizations in the past, but if one were to accept his general portrayal of al-Qa'ida at face value, one could easily be led to conclude that Bin Ladin has not only carefully planned out every phase of some ostensible strategic "master plan" in advance, but that his terrorist group has so far been singularly successful in carrying out the phases of that master plan and, consequently, in achieving its supposed strategic objectives. These claims are, to say the least, contestable.

Scheuer also rightly recognizes and indeed goes out of his way to emphasize that Bin Ladin and al-Qa'ida are motivated primarily by religious imperatives.[28] Yet although he begins with this perfectly sound premise, he inexplicably draws a number of seriously flawed and misleading conclusions. For one thing, he argues that Bin Ladin does not preach or practice an "aberrant form" of Islam, and indeed that the al-Qa'ida leader is "in the Islamic mainstream."[29] This statement is in certain respects overdrawn inasmuch as it erroneously conflates Islam with Islamism, an inherently radical political ideology with openly imperialistic aims. While it is certainly true that many of Bin Ladin's militant interpretations of traditional Islamic concepts and generic anti-"infidel" attitudes are based on texts from the most authoritative Islamic sources (including key Qur'anic passages and the relevant sections in various collections of *ahadith* that are considered to be reliable [*sahih*, literally "sound"]), and that some are widely accepted by Muslims, this does not mean that the latter fully share his puritanical interpretation of the Islamic faith or his extremely radical ideology, much less that they generally support his utopian transnational jihadist agenda or his brutal terrorist methods. For another, despite highlighting Bin Ladin's fundamentally religious motivations, which should have led him to expect the al-Qa'ida leader to periodically display faith-based and arguably nonrational patterns of behavior, Scheuer, like Friedman, nonetheless proceeds to ascribe far too much rationality and pragmatism to Bin Ladin and his fellow jihadists, especially in his second book. Therein he vehemently denies, despite the existence of masses of evidence to the contrary, that they have an intrinsic and theologically based hatred toward the secular United States, an apocalyptic worldview, or fundamentally unrealistic ultimate objectives.[30] Quite the contrary, in fact: "Bin Laden and most Islamists, therefore, can be said to be motivated by their love of Allah and their hatred of a few, specific U.S. policies and actions they believe are damaging—and threatening to destroy—the things they love. Theirs is a war against a specific target and for specific, limited purposes."[31] From this, it follows that if the United

States and its key allies were willing to alter their foolish, counterproductive, oppressive, and exploitive policies toward the Muslim world, Bin Ladin would then cease attacking the West.[32] However, as will be argued below, what Scheuer does not seem to grasp is that the global jihadists' "love of Allah" is infused with extremely irrational notions that make their objectives anything but limited or fully rational. This immediately becomes apparent as soon as one carefully examines Bin Ladin's own pronouncements, provided that the reader is familiar enough with Islam and Islamic history to understand his historical references and code words.[33]

In marked contrast to this "rationalist" perspective, which might be more aptly characterized as "hyper-rationalist," both Lee Harris and Ralph Peters adopt the "nonrationalist" perspective in that they emphasize what they regard as the inherently irrational objectives and characteristics of global jihadists such as Bin Ladin. Harris begins by explicitly challenging the appropriateness of using Clausewitzian analytical frameworks to explain the 9/11 attacks, and by extension to understanding al-Qa'ida's entire agenda. Instead, he argues that al-Qa'ida operates in accordance with a "fantasy ideology," a phenomenon he considers operative whenever "political and ideological symbols and tropes [are] used not for political purposes, but entirely for the benefit of furthering a specific personal or collective fantasy."[34] Many individuals behave at least in part in accordance with their own personal fantasy ideology, but in most such cases—serial killers and other delusional maniacs excluded—they tend to be obnoxious but relatively harmless. However, such fantasy ideologies can become very dangerous indeed when they are embraced collectively by members of a certain group. This can occur when there is a "preexisting collective need" for such a fantasy that stems "from a conflict between a set of collective aspirations and desires, on one hand, and the stern dictates of brutal reality, on the other—a conflict in which the lack of realism is gradually transformed into a penchant for fantasy."[35] Moreover, according to Harris, the groups that are especially prone to adopt fantasy ideologies are those that "history has passed by or rejected—groups that feel that they are under attack from forces which, while more powerful perhaps than they are, are nonetheless inferior in terms of true virtue." This is why the "theme of reviving ancient glory is an important key to understanding fantasy ideologies..." Just as "uncivilized" Ethiopia served as the prop for Mussolini's fantasy of restoring the Roman Empire, so too does the United States, cast in the image of an inherently corrupt and imperialistic Crusader power out to destroy Islam, serve as the prop for Bin Ladin's jihadist fantasy of purifying and unifying the *umma*, restoring the Caliphate, and regaining Muslim supremacy vis-à-vis the world of "unbelief."[36] From this standpoint, the attacks on 9/11 were not really designed to achieve a concrete strategic objective, but instead constituted a spectacular and symbolic act of theater designed to confirm al-Qa'ida's fantasy that a few Muslim martyrs could defeat the "Great Satan" and, in the process, inspire and rouse the Muslim masses in support of that fantasy. Since al-Qa'ida supposedly "has no strategic purpose in anything [it] does" and is allegedly incapable of making a "realistic assessment," Harris argues that there is nothing that the United States can do, policy-wise, to "change the attitudes of our enemies—short, perhaps, of a massive nationwide conversion to fundamentalist Islam."[37] However, while the transnational jihadists do in fact adhere to a "fantasy ideology," this does not mean that they eschew strategic calculations. Moreover, Harris commits the very same error that Scheuer makes in that he fails to draw a clear distinction between jihadist ideological vanguard organizations such as al-Qa'ida and the Muslim masses. Although no changes in U.S. foreign policies are likely to induce those vanguard groups to cease attacking us, the adoption of more sensible policies could very well help to reduce their growing base of popular support.

As for Peters, he makes an even harsher judgment about al-Qa'ida's supposed rationality. He begins by drawing a relatively hard and fast distinction between what he terms "practical terrorists" and "apocalyptic terrorists." He argues that the actions of the practical terrorist are "calculated to change political circumstances, while for the apocalyptic terrorist, destruction is an end in itself, despite his extravagant statements about strategic objectives."[38] Practical terrorists "may behave savagely, but they have tangible goals and a logical approach to achieving them," and although ideology can "dominate their thinking...it does not break loose entirely from mundane reality."[39] In contrast, apocalyptic terrorists like Bin Ladin are "mentally divorced from our world and its values...view the greater world as their enemy...[and] are merciless [because] they view themselves as tools of a divine and uncompromising retribution."[40] Indeed, he goes so far as to claim, with considerable plausibility, that retribution against "unbelievers, heretics, and even their own brethren whose belief is less pure, is the real strategic goal of apocalyptic terrorists, even when they do not fully realize it themselves or cannot articulate it." Hence "we cannot know apocalyptic terrorists by their pronouncements as well as by their deeds, since much of what they say is meant to make their intentions seem more innocent or justified than they are."[41] For this reason Peters concludes, as Harris did concerning his fantasist, that "[n]o change in the world order will ever content the apocalyptic terrorist, since his actual discontents are internal to himself and no alteration in the external environment could sate his appetite for retribution against those he needs to believe are evil and guilty of causing his personal sufferings and disappointments."[42] It follows that such people cannot be controlled, like practical terrorists, but instead need to be killed. There are, however, two fundamental problems with Peters' analysis. First, his two categories of terrorists should be seen as representing Weberian "ideal types" rather than living human beings, who—apart from clinical lunatics—are never either entirely rational or entirely irrational in their behavior. Since in any given case it is difficult if not impossible for observers to artificially separate their "rational" from their "expressive" motives and actions, one simply cannot accept Peters' overly sharp distinction between practical and apocalyptic terrorists. Second, even extremists who are in fact impelled by their adherence to Manichean ideological or theological doctrines (and perhaps also by personal demons) to smite "evildoers" are at times capable of rational calculation and understanding basic cause-and-effect relationships. Indeed, the historical record is replete with examples of violence-prone extremist groups whose members simultaneously espoused delusional worldviews and exhibited a ruthless efficiency on the operational level.

Given such acute disagreements among analysts concerning the strategic rationality of al-Qa'ida, it should come as no surprise to learn that they cannot even agree on the most important fundamental questions. Take, for example, the seemingly straightforward matter of whether al-Qa'ida carried out the 9/11 attacks with the specific intention, among others, of provoking a massive and hopefully ham-fisted and therefore counterproductive American military invasion of Muslim territories. According to the "rationalists," this was precisely Bin Ladin's intention, and certain al-Qa'ida theorists even retrospectively claimed that this was indeed part of his original plan.[43] Yet many other high-ranking al-Qa'ida insiders have revealed that Bin Ladin had ignored the concerns expressed by his confidants and seriously miscalculated by believing that the Americans would not carry out aggressive actions against the group's Afghan base and its Taliban hosts. Indeed, there was a good deal of retrospective bitterness and post-facto criticism of Bin Ladin for naively believing his own propaganda about American cowardice and weakness.[44] Furthermore, it is also clear that Bin Ladin was himself surprised by the collapse of the Twin Towers, which he did not anticipate despite his relative optimism about the probable success of the "planes operation."[45] This serves to illustrate just how difficult it is to divine the real intentions of the jihadist adversary, especially in lieu of reliable inside information.

In any case, in between these overly dichotomous postulations of either full strategic rationality or essential nonrationality lie various middle positions. One version of such a stance, "pragmatic messianism," has been proffered by Christopher Blanchard, who comes to the following eminently sensible conclusion:

> Bin Ladin has outlined specific political demands that support the image of Al Qaeda as a pliable, pragmatic political actor. Nevertheless, Al Qaeda's operational record seems to indicate that its leaders' commitment to specific national causes and strategic objectives are *rhetorical tools designed to elicit support* for their broader ideological agenda of confrontation with the West and puritanical reform in the Islamic world.[46]

Another is the notion of "pragmatic fanaticism" offered by Arabist Michael Doran who, despite making some problematic assertions, ends up concluding that al-Qa'ida's "long-term goals are set by its fervent devotion to a radical religious ideology, but in its short-term behavior, it is a rational political actor operating according to the dictates of realpolitik."[47] Although one may question just how rational and wedded to *realpolitik* the organization is even in the short term, Doran's view nonetheless has certain similarities to that promoted herein, which seeks to differentiate between two distinct levels of al-Qa'ida activity—a "strategic" level that concerns the realism or lack thereof of Bin Ladin's ultimate goals, and an "operational" level that concerns the group's actual mechanics of planning and executing attacks. This is arguably a more nuanced approach that seems to better reflect the mindset and behavior of al-Qa'ida and other transnational jihadist groups. From this point of view, al-Qa'ida can be said to behave rationally on the "strategic" level, at least in part, but that to the extent that this is the case it does so largely within certain historically and culturally conditioned theological and thus arguably nonrational parameters. In contrast, on the "operational" level, al-Qa'ida often displays considerable sophistication, which allows it to plan and carry out devastatingly effective and often spectacular terrorist attacks that allow the group to achieve its narrowly "tactical" aims, if not to further its unachievable strategic goals. Let us begin by considering the strategic objectives of al-Qa'ida.

The key point that needs to be emphasized is that, far from accepting modern Western conceptions of international law, which presuppose "the existence of a family of nations composed of a community of states enjoying full sovereign rights and equality of status"—the leaders of al-Qa'ida instead adhere to what they consider—quite rightly—to be authentically Islamic conceptions.[48] These conceptions, which were first laid down in the era of the "virtuous forefathers" of the faith (*al-salaf al-salih*)—Muhammad, his companions, and his "rightly-guided" caliphal successors—in order to govern the relations between the growing Islamic community and non-Muslims, do not involve the recognition of other sovereign states, since "the ultimate goal of Islam was the subordination of the whole world to one [universal] system of law and religion."[49] This "classical" notion has in fact been augmented rather than abandoned by today's jihadists, who regard modern nation-states as artificial creations that the "enemies of Islam" intentionally designed to prevent the restoration of a unified Muslim *umma*.

The first and most important of these traditional Islamic conceptions was clearly articulated in the *Qur'an* itself: One of the primary responsibilities incumbent upon all Muslims is to spread the divine word of Allah, which was thought to have been revealed directly by the archangel Gabriel to the Prophet Muhammad, throughout the entire world, since it was ostensibly meant for all of humanity, not restricted to Arabs alone.[50] Therefore, whenever the Muslims encountered "unbelievers," they were admonished to offer them three options: convert to Islam, pay a poll tax (*jizya*) and accept a subordinate status (as *dhimmi*) in a Muslim-dominated society, or prepare to fight.[51] Second, the methods Muslims traditionally used to spread and universalize Islam involved a combination of proselytization (*da'wa*) and "jihad of the sword for the sake of Allah" (*jihad bi al-sayf fi sabil Allah*), i.e., armed struggle for the faith.[52] During periods of relative weakness, Muslims tended to rely primarily on *da'wa*, but when they were militarily strong, they often waged *jihad bi al-sayf* in a frankly imperialistic effort to expand the boundaries of the Islamic world by conquest (*fath*, literally "opening") at the expense of non-Muslims.[53] Third, on the basis of the examples reportedly set by the Prophet himself or his close companions and successors,[54] medieval jurists soon formulated a geopolitical conception that was based upon a clear-cut division of the world into two antithetical parts: the *dar al-Islam* (Abode of Islam), "territories in which the law of Islam prevails," and the *dar al-harb* (Abode of War), "territories under perpetual threat of missionary war."[55] The latter included all of the territories that were not ruled by the *khalif* (Caliph) or an imam in accordance with Islamic law (the *shari'a*). In theory, if the rulers who governed portions of the *dar al-harb* refused to allow Muslims to freely practice their religion within their realms, the leaders of the *umma* were obliged to wage war against those rulers, defeat them, and incorporate their lands into the *dar al-Islam*. This was, if taken at face value, a doctrine that postulated a state of more or less permanent war against unbelievers, albeit one that could be periodically interrupted, until such time as they agreed to convert to Islam.

In practice, of course, the decision to initiate military action against segments of the *dar al-harb* was affected by a host of practical considerations, above all the existing correlation of forces between particular Muslim and non-Muslim rulers. Therefore, if non-Muslim rulers were simply too powerful to fight and defeat, or if they freely allowed Muslims to practice their religion, it was not considered necessary to fight them, at least not immediately. In fact, two new categories were developed by jurists to accommodate political and military realities and thereby allow Muslims to avoid having to wage war continually or at once: the concept of the *dar al-sulh* (Abode of Truce), "territories not conquered by Muslim troops but by buying peace by the giving of tribute, the payment of which guarantees a truce or armistice (*hudna*, *sulh*)," and that of the *dar al-'ahd* (Abode of the Covenant), territories existing under the temporary proprietorship of non-Muslims that fall neither within the boundaries of the *dar al-Islam* nor of the *dar al-harb*.[56] Although rejected as legitimate by many influential jurists, these temporary and intermediate categories allowed Muslim rulers to maintain peaceful relations with non-Muslim rulers as long as the latter were not actively engaged in the repression of their co-religionists. However, despite these concessions to reality, in the pre-modern era Muslims were convinced that such arrangements were strictly temporary and that at some point these transitional territories would be incorporated, along with the remaining portions of the *dar al-harb*, into the *dar al-Islam*. Indeed, for them "the duty of *djihad* exists as long as the universal domination of Islam has not been attained," from which it follows that "[p] eace with non-Muslim nations is...a provisional state of affairs only...[and] there can be no question of genuine peace treaties" with such states.[57]

Such uncompromising, expansionist, and imperialistic notions were problematic enough during the extraordinary period of Arab conquest and rapid Islamization that lasted from the seventh to the tenth centuries, but maintaining them today, when the

Muslim world is politically, economically, and militarily weak, can only be characterized as delusional and potentially suicidal. That is why most Muslim states, and indeed the vast majority of Muslims, have not only reluctantly abandoned their former universalist and expansionist pretensions but also accommodated themselves to the ever-growing power imbalances between the *dar al-kufr* (Abode of Unbelief) and the *dar al-Islam*, as well as to international norms and institutions that are nowadays accepted throughout most of the rest of the world. Some Muslims may still secretly hope that, with the help of Allah, the status quo ante of Muslim glory and supremacy can one day be restored, but in the meantime they are generally willing to face reality.

Not so with Bin Ladin and the transnational jihadists, for whom such eminently practical considerations do not count for much. Indeed, despite their often intimate familiarity with the functioning of complex modern Western societies, as well as their willingness to adopt modern technology and their penchant for periodically employing modern-sounding "anti-imperialist" rhetoric of the sort normally associated the secular revolutionary left and right, the jihadists are essentially living in a seventh-century mental universe. As Walid Phares has rightly noted:

> The jihadist logic is historicist and theological at the same time. In the mind of its authors, leaders, and militants, the initial *rissala* (mission) bestowed on the Prophet, and carried on by the caliphs for more than thirteen centuries, is also theirs.... The jihadists believe that what was initiated in Muslim history ages ago is still moving forward today, just as it was in the beginning. They also believe that Allah is still commanding them to perform these *wajibat*, or duties, without interruption. And they are firmly convinced that the enemies of their ancestors as perceived in those times are still the enemies of today, in a war that has not ended for the last millennium and a half.... Put simply, in the mind of the jihadists...they are in line to fulfill a mission launched centuries ago.[58]

He adds that "[w]hen Osama bin Laden traveled to Afghanistan eight centuries later, he was executing the orders of [militant thirteenth-century century scholar] Bin Taymiya: fighting the infidels, reestablishing the pure Islamic state, and laying the groundwork for the return of the Caliphate."[59] Furthermore, having deluded themselves into thinking that their victory over the "atheistic" Soviet superpower in Afghanistan was due solely to their own divinely sanctioned efforts and to the intervention of Allah, as opposed to the operational assistance provided by the Pakistani secret service and the external financial and logistical support they received from the Gulf States and the United States, the "Afghan Arabs" became convinced that with Allah's help they could also defeat the world's only remaining superpower, the United States, which they viewed as unremittingly hostile to Islam but inherently corrupt, weak, and decadent. Although Phares acknowledges that it may be hard for Western analysts to accept the fact that "the modern jihadists of al Qaeda and its sister organizations embody thirteenth-century jihad in the framework of twenty-first century global politics," he nonetheless justly concludes that "this reality explains most of the irrational behavior of modern-day jihadists, including suicide bombers, and the litany of extreme, violent acts and statements for which they have been responsible—which to reasonable people seem to belong to another age."[60]

Indeed, it is precisely their failure to recognize this fundamental reality that explains why the "rationalist" interpreters of al-Qa'ida have mistakenly projected their own modern Western military and strategic analytical frameworks onto the enemy and thereby seriously misconstrued jihadist objectives. Such a perspective is perhaps most clearly expressed by Scheuer, when he insists that Bin Ladin's struggle has "specific, limited purposes" and is narrowly calculated to deter the Unted States from pursuing certain policies. Similarly, he scoffs at the view that al-Qa'ida has utopian imperialistic goals by arguing that "[a]t this point in history we need worry little about the threat of an offensive and expansionist jihad meant to conquer new lands for Islam and convert new peoples to the faith" since "[s]uch a jihad is the collective—not individual—responsibility of Muslims, and must be called by a Caliph..."[61] He also claims that the Islamists are "not so offended by our democratic...system of politics, guarantees of personal rights and civil liberties, and separation of church and state that [they are] willing to wage war against overwhelming odds in order to stop Americans from voting, speaking freely, and praying, or not, as they wish."[62] These statements are both analytically problematic and in large part factually incorrect.

First, Scheuer accepts Bin Ladin's assertions that al-Qa'ida is waging a "defensive jihad" against the enemies of Islam at face value, which makes no sense at all.[63] The fact that Bin Ladin and other jihadists are convinced that Muslims are everywhere under attack, when in fact Muslims themselves are so often the party doing the attacking, and that they view American actions as intrinsically anti-Islamic, ignoring the fact that during the 1990s the United States militarily defended Muslims in Kuwait, Bosnia, and Kosovo; criticized brutal Russian policies and actions in Chechnya; and sought to provide humanitarian relief and a measure of security in Somalia, is a sign that they have collective, ideologically derived paranoid delusions and are prone to adopt nonsensical conspiracy theories, not that they have accurately and realistically interpreted world events.[64] In this context it should be remembered that political and religious extremists of all varieties almost invariably portray themselves as victims of persecution, oppression, and aggression in order to rationalize and justify their own initiation of violence and aggression against real and imagined enemies. For example, Hitler and Stalin—the two biggest mass murderers of the twentieth century—both portrayed themselves and their nations, also not without some justification, as targets and victims of Western imperialism. Even the worst, most bellicose tyrants and fanatics often manage to delude themselves that they are the real victims, and Bin Ladin seems to be no exception. However, there are also two eminently practical reasons why he might wish to emphasize the ostensibly "defensive" nature of al-Qa'ida's struggle against the West. On the one hand, it allows him to exploit the widespread Muslim sense of victimization and thereby mobilize a larger base of public support in the Islamic world, as well as to pose as a resistance fighter against "U.S. imperialism" in order to gain more international sympathy. On the other hand, insofar as he is able to convince Muslims that his jihad really is "defensive" rather than "offensive," he has better jurisprudential grounds to argue that it is every individual Muslim's duty to wage this jihad and that doing so does not require the authorization of a Caliph or another accepted Muslim political authority, as is the case with "offensive jihad."[65]

Hence, whether he has a "persecution complex" and has therefore actually managed to convince himself that he and his murderous followers are the real victims, or is cynically seeking to elicit the sympathy that is all too often uncritically granted to self-proclaimed victims, or a combination of both, it would be naïve to accept Bin Ladin's statements at face value. This is all the more true given that he has explicitly repudiated his own propagandistic public claims to be waging a "defensive jihad" in the course of internal debates with other Muslims, especially those whom he regards as having abandoned fundamental Muslim principles out of cynicism or cowardice. An excellent illustration of his real underlying agenda, which is in fact to wage "offensive jihad" until the entire "infidel" world is subjected to Islam, can be seen clearly in a letter entitled "Moderate Islam is a Prostration to the West," which he sent in 2002 in response to the reply by

153 prominent Saudi scholars ("How We Can Coexist") to an open letter ("What We're Fighting For") that had earlier been sent to Saudi Arabia by 60 American intellectuals in the wake of 9/11. In his harsh response to the arguments of the Saudi "court 'ulama," Bin Ladin insists that attempts to promote a dialogue between civilizations is "an infidel notion imported from the West verbatim"[66] and continues as follows:

> As for this atmosphere of shared understandings, what evidence is there for Muslims to strive for this? What did the Prophet, the Companions after him, and the righteous forebears [*al-salaf al-salih*] do? Did they wage *jihad* against the infidels, attacking them all over the earth, in order to place them under the suzerainty of Islam in great humility and submission? Or did they send messages to discover "shared understandings" between themselves and the infidels in order that they may reach an understanding whereby universal peace, security, and natural relations would spread—in such a satanic manner as this?[67]

He then goes on to bitterly chastise those scholars for ignoring the Muslim religious duty to wage "offensive jihad":

> We never thought that such words [promoting dialogue and understanding] would ever appear from those who consider themselves adherents of this religion. Such expressions, and more like them, would lead the reader to believe that those who wrote them are Western intellectuals, not Muslims! Those previous expressions are true *only* by tearing down the wall of enmity from the infidels [an allusion to the traditional Islamic doctrine of "loyalty and enmity" (*al wala' wa al-bara'*), which mandates that Muslims must always support one another against, and not befriend, "infidels"] and by rejecting *jihad*—especially Offensive *Jihad*. The problem, however, is that Offensive *Jihad* is an established and basic tenet of this religion. It is a religious duty rejected only by the most deluded. So how can they call off this religious obligation ["offensive *jihad*"], while imploring the West to understandings and talks "under the umbrella of justice, morality, and rights"? The essence of all this comes from right inside the halls of the United Nations, instead of the Divine Foundations that are built upon hating the infidels, repudiating them with tongue and teeth until they embrace Islam or pay the *jizya* with willing submission and humility.[68]

Nor was he finished. After citing the bellicose Qur'anic passage that advocates and justifies frightening or terrorizing the enemy (8:60), the *sura* and *aya* that are among those most favored by today's jihadists, he claims that "whoever refuses the principle of terror[ism] against the enemy also refuses the commandment of Allah, the Exalter, the Most High, and His *sharia*."[69] So much for the misleading notion that al-Qa'ida is waging a purely "defensive jihad."

Second, Scheuer is on decidedly shaky ground when he argues that Bin Ladin is "a practical warrior, not an apocalyptic terrorist in search of Armageddon."[70] As several scholars have documented, there is no doubt at all that apocalyptic, messianic, and millenarian themes are common within today's Sunni jihadist circles, including those close to al-Qa'ida, just as they have always been intrinsic to the Shi'i tradition and have been systematically stoked since the late 1970s by certain Khomeini-linked and -inspired Islamist milieus.[71] For an example of such themes on al-Qa'ida-linked Web sites, note the March 9, 2003 article by Usama 'Azzam, who made the following statement on the eve of the American invasion of Iraq:

> Is there anyone who still doubts that we are approaching the end of the world? Does anyone think the hour is far? We are on the eve of the total dismantling that will be followed by our clear victory.... After this war, which has no precedence in human history and in the fight between the community of believers and the Devil and his followers, does anyone doubt that these are the days of the Mahdi?[72]

'Azzam then adds the following revealing remark: "I have no doubt that the leaders of the *mujahidin* of al-Qa'ida and the Taliban are the owners of the black banners who will assist the Mahdi."[73] In support of these apocalyptic notions, 'Azzam cited the now-famous work by Abu Qatada al-Filastini, the imprisoned "spiritual leader" of al-Qa'ida in Europe, *Ma'alim al-ta'ifa al-mansura (Signs of the Victorious Side).* Nor was 'Azzam alone in predicting imminent "end-of-the-world" scenarios that would pave the way for the prophesied return of the Mahdi, notions which at that moment apparently caught the imagination of many young anti-Western Saudis. See, for example, the postings on the Muntada al-Jinn wa al-'Afarit Internet forum, a section of which deals primarily with dreams and visions. In the words of the Saudi supervisor of this particular section:

> These [apocalyptic] visions and their like, many of which were sent to me, propagate the destruction of this evil country [the United States] and the punishments, disasters, and dismantling that will occur there. This is the way Allah deals with oppressors.... The punishment of this super oppressor is very close. We ask Allah to heal the hearts of the believers of its influence, and grant the Muslims all of its finance and equipment as booty.[74]

Indeed, such notions had become so widespread, along with the idea that Bin Ladin himself was the Mahdi, that al-Qa'ida's leaders felt compelled to openly criticize them, in part because they were afraid that overly optimistic expectations of Islam's looming final triumph might induce jihadist supporters not to take action and in part, perhaps, because Bin Ladin has never claimed to be the Mahdi and does not seem to believe that he is.[75] Thus, in February 2003, on the Web site of the Markaz al-Dirasat wa al-Buhuth al-Islamiyya (Center for Islamic Studies and Research), a Saudi-based entity closely linked to al-Qa'ida, an anonymous author leveled an attack on such apocalyptic ideas, firstly by claiming that the *ahadith* concerning "the black banners that will appear in the East" are very weak (*da'if*), and secondly by advising would-be supporters to "support the jihad against Allah's enemies rather than harm the jihad and the mujahidin with nonsensical ideas."[76] Perhaps even more tellingly, one of the most supposedly "rational," "pragmatic," and "secularized" of the jihadist military analysts linked to al-Qa'ida, Abu Mus'ab al-Suri, devotes the entire final chapter of his 1600-page strategic treatise, *Da'wa al-muqawwama al-islamiyya al-'alamiyya* (*The Call for Global Islamic Resistance*), to apocalyptic Islamic prophecies concerning the return of the Mahdi and the cataclysmic "end of days."[77] Hence, although this is an inordinately complex matter that can only be touched upon here, suffice to say that Scheuer is as wrong to deny that there are any apocalyptic tendencies observable in the al-Qa'ida milieu as Peters is to argue that Bin Ladin and his cohorts are entirely apocalyptic.

Third, there is plenty of evidence indicating that the global jihadists are pursuing an expansionist imperialistic agenda, though the cleverer ones like Bin Ladin seek to divert attention from or otherwise disguise their aggressive and expansionist underlying designs by continually harping on their more reasonable and legitimate grievances in an effort to both rally support from the Muslim masses and foment divisions within "infidel" ranks in order to prevent the formation of a common anti-jihadist front.[78] However, even in his own public propaganda statements, Bin Ladin regularly juxtaposes seemingly rational and morally justifiable objectives with bizarre theological imperatives that can only be said to "make sense" within an Islamic cultural and historical context that has long since been superseded. Indeed, even the most restrained and *proximate* demands of al-Qa'ida and other global jihadist groups—the complete withdrawal of foreign military forces from "Muslim lands," the abandonment of all Western support for "apostate" Muslim regimes and Israel, the elimination of all "corrupting" Western cultural influences from the *dar al-Islam*, and the end of Western "exploitation" of Muslim resources, above all the paying of artificially low prices for oil—are in large part non-negotiable and therefore virtually impossible to achieve, whatever their moral merits or demerits might be.

Worse still, when one considers jihadist *long-term* objectives, one has truly entered the realm of total unreality. These long-term goals can be divided into three categories: minimal, intermediate, and maximal. The *minimal* objective of the jihadists is to "liberate" all Muslim-majority territories that are currently "occupied" by hostile "infidel" military forces, including Palestine, Iraq, Chechnya, Kashmir, southern Thailand, the southern Philippines, and "Eastern Turkestan," which effectively brings them into direct conflict with Israel, the United States, Russia, India, the Thai and Philippine governments, and China.[79] The *intermediate* long-term objective of the global jihadists is to recover all of the territory that was once under Muslim control but then subsequently lost to "infidel" powers, including Spain, Sicily and parts of southern Italy, a substantial portion of the Balkans, huge swaths of territory in Turkic Central Asia, all of northern India, and large segments of northwestern China, which adds Spain, Italy, Croatia, Serbia, Bulgaria, and Greece to their list of enemies.[80] Their *maximal* long-term goal, of course, is the very same one promoted by both the "rightly-guided" Caliphs and several later Umayyad, 'Abbasid, and Ottoman rulers—to spread the word of Allah to the "unbelievers" (*kuffar*), by force if necessary, and ultimately to Islamize every corner of the globe at the expense of both the *ahl al-kitab* and the "polytheists," which in practice would nowadays amount to completely overturning and transforming the existing world order. As Phares sums it up, al-Qa'ida aims to humiliate and ultimately destroy America, the military and economic bastion of the *dar al-harb*, in order to lay the groundwork for Islam's final triumph over the West and other non-Muslims.[81] It was this very decision to shift the target of jihadist terrorism away from the "near enemy" (*al-'adu al-qarib*), that is, "apostate" Muslim regimes, and instead strike directly at the "far enemy" (*al-'adu al-ba'id*), the United States, that constituted Bin Ladin's chief strategic innovation, one that has already had incalculable geopolitical implications.[82]

Alas, similarly aggressive, expansionist goals were enunciated by virtually all of the Islamist ideologues who served to inspire today's jihadist groups. For example, in Sayyid Abu al-A'la Mawdudi's famous speech from 1939, later published as *Al-Jihad fi sabil Allah* (*Jihad for the Sake of Allah*), one can find the following exhortations:

> Islam is a revolutionary ideology which seeks to alter the social order of the entire world and rebuild it in conformity with its own tenets and ideals. "Muslim" is the title of that International Revolutionary Party organized by Islam to carry into effect its revolutionary programme....Islam wishes to do away with all states and governments which are opposed to the ideology and programme of Islam....Islam requires the earth—not just a portion, but the entire planet—...because the whole of mankind should benefit from Islam, and its ideology and welfare programme....Islam is not merely a religious creed... but a comprehensive system which seeks to annihilate all tyrannical and evil systems in the world and enforce its own programme for reform which it deems best for the well-being of mankind....The objective of Islamic jihad is to eliminate the rule of an

> un-Islamic system and establish in its stead an Islamic system of rule. Islam does not intend to confine this revolution to a single state or a few countries; the aim of Islam is to bring about universal revolution.[83]

Compare the remarks of Hasan al-Banna, the founder of the Jam'iyyat al-Ikhwan al-Muslimin (Society of the Muslim Brothers, or Muslim Brotherhood), who stated that "[i]t is in the nature of Islam to dominate, not to be dominated, to impose its law on all nations and to extend its power to the entire planet."[84] See further the following illustrative remarks by fellow Muslim Brother Sayyid Qutub, the most influential of all Sunni jihadist theorists, who contemptuously rejected the concept of "defensive *jihad*" and repeatedly chastised those who sought to limit jihad in this way as "defeatists"[85]:

> Islam is a general declaration of the liberation of man on earth from subjugation to other creatures, including his own desires, through the acknowledgement of Allah's lordship over the universe and all creation...this declaration signifies a total revolution against assigning sovereignty to human beings, whatever forms, systems and situations such sovereignty may take [i.e., against all non-Islamic political systems].[86]

From this it follows that *jihad bi al-sayf* must be waged to "establish Allah's authority and to remove tyranny. It liberates mankind from submission to any authority other than Allah.... It wants the system laid down by Allah to replace the [other] systems established by his creatures."[87] Moreover, as far as Qutub and his contemporary jihadist disciples are concerned, this armed struggle against worldwide unbelief or *jahiliyya* (non-Islamic ignorance and barbarism) "is not a temporary phase but an eternal state—an eternal state, as truth and falsehood cannot co-exist on this earth."[88]

Lest anyone doubt that defeating and destroying "infidel" powers and spreading Islam throughout the world is the global jihadists' ultimate objective, one should—in addition to Bin Ladin's letter to the Saudi scholars cited above—consider the inflammatory, unequivocal remarks of the aforementioned Abu Qatada:

> Muslims' target is the West. We will split Rome open. The destruction must be carried out by sword. Those who will destroy Rome are already preparing the swords. Rome will not be conquered with the word but with the force of arms.[89]

Equally explicit are two August 2002 articles penned by Sayf al-Din al-Ansari, which appeared in the al-Qa'ida-linked journal *Majallat al-Ansar* (*The Magazine of the Supporters*) and openly advocated the extermination of infidels by means of jihad. In one such article, he wrote the following:

> Just as the law of extermination was applied to the infidel forces among the nations in previous days and no one could escape it, so it will be applied to the infidel forces in our day and no one will escape it. Namely, similar to the fate of the Thamud and 'Ad peoples, so the American state, the Jewish state, and all other infidel countries will surely be destroyed.[90]

In the second article, he claims that Allah has the power to exterminate the infidels directly, without using intermediaries, but that instead He has laid down that "the infidels' extermination is part of Islamic law, which is operative until the Day of Judgment" and that its "principal element will be fulfilled only at the hands of the believers, meaning through jihad, which is also to be operative until the Day of Judgment.[91] This is meant as a direct criticism of those Islamist scholars and organizations which argue that gradual, less violent approaches involving missionary work, education, and the provision of social services are nowadays the preferred methods for expanding the faith and ensuring the ultimate victory of Islam.

Nor are such sentiments confined to jihadists with an avowedly global agenda who are focusing on targeting the "far enemy." One can also find them expressed in unguarded moments by leaders of jihadist groups with a more local or national focus who are currently targeting only the "near enemy," such as the Harakat al-Muqawwama al-Islamiyya (HAMAS: Islamic Resistance Movement) in Palestine. For example, in an April 11, 2008, Friday sermon broadcast on HAMAS' al-Aqsa television channel, Yunis al-Astal, a cleric and HAMAS Minister of Parliament, made the following remarks to his congregation:

> Allah has chosen you for Himself and for His religion, so that you will serve as the engine pulling this nation [*umma*] to the phase of succession, security, and consolidation of power, and even to conquests through *da'wa* and military conquests of the capitals of the entire world.... Very soon, Allah willing, Rome will be conquered, just like Constantinople was, as was prophesized by our Prophet Muhammad.... Today, Rome is the capital of the Catholics, or the Crusader capital, which had declared its hostility to Islam, and has planted the brothers of pigs and apes [i.e., the Jews] in Palestine in order to prevent the reawakening of Islam. This capital of theirs will be an advanced post for the Islamic conquests, which will spread through Europe in its entirety, and then will turn to the two Americas, and even Eastern Europe.... I believe that our children, or our grandchildren, will inherit our *jihad* and our sacrifices, and Allah willing, [that] the commanders of the conquest [of the world] will come from among them.[92]

So much for the naive notion, expressed by many academicians, that Islamist and jihadist groups with a seemingly "nationalist" focus have no wider global ambitions.[93]

Furthermore, it should be pointed out that even ostensibly nonviolent Islamist groups, such as the Muslim Brotherhood and Hizb al-Tahrir al-Islami (HT: Islamic Liberation Party), likewise intend to spread the faith and eventually raise the banner of Islam over the "infidel" world by means of a combination of *da'wa*, infiltration and penetration operations, demographic "reconquest," and/or outright armed struggle (jihad).[94] See, for example, the illustrative remarks of the Muslim Brotherhood's supposedly "moderate" spiritual guide, Yusuf al-Qaradhawi:

> Islam will return once more to Europe as a conqueror and as a victorious power after it was expelled twice from the continent...I assume that next time the conquest will not be achieved by the sword but by preaching [*da'wa*] and spreading the ideology [of Islam]...The conquest of Rome and the expansion of Islam will reach all the areas where the sun shines and the moon appears [i.e., the entire world]....That will be the result of a planted seed and the beginning of the righteous Caliphate's return....[The Islamic Caliphate] deserves to lead the umma to the plains of victory.[95]

Compare further the even more militaristic June 2003 remarks of Anjem Choudary, one of the leaders of the radical London-based group al-Muhajirun (The Émigrés or Exiles), an offshoot of Hizb al-Tahrir:

> One day the black flag of Islam will be flying over [Number 10] Downing Street. Lands will not be liberated by individuals, but by an army. Eventually there'll have to be a Muslim army. It's just a matter of time before it happens.[96]

How anyone can characterize such extreme views as "limited" in their focus or "defensive" in their aims is beyond comprehension.

Indeed, Scheuer fails even to acknowledge, much less give sufficient weight to, al-Qa'ida's less-than-rational "expressive" motives for carrying out attacks, above all (1) its religiously grounded obsession with slaughtering and ultimately cleansing the world of "apostates," "hypocrites," and "infidels," and (2) its burning desire to exact revenge against "Crusaders" and perfidious Jews for a host of proclaimed "crimes," real or imagined, that these "servants of Satan" are supposed to have committed against innocent Muslims. Such atavistic or retributional impulses are well-expressed by numerous al-Qa'ida–linked spokesmen. For example, in his book Ayman al-Zawahiri perfectly captures both sentiments. He advocates that the *mujahidin* inflict massive casualties on the enemy whenever possible, since this is supposedly the only language that the West understands, and also clearly reveals his thirst for revenge when he opines that the jihadist movement

> promises destruction and ruin for the new Crusades against the lands of Islam. It is ready for revenge against the heads of the world's gathering of infidels, the United States, Russia, and Israel. It is anxious to seek retribution for the blood of the martyrs, the grief of the mothers, the deprivation of the orphans, the suffering of the detainees, and the sores of the tortured people throughout the land of Islam.[97]

Nor are al-Zawahiri's sentiments at all unique in jihadist circles. In a December 1998 interview with al-Jazira, Bin Ladin himself openly appealed to Allah to help his fellow jihadists "wreak revenge on the Jews and Crusaders" for their alleged crimes against Muslims.[98] Note also the telling remarks of Shaykh Husayn b. Mahmud (the pseudonym for an al-Qa'ida leader whose writings often appear on jihadist fora):

> Allah commanded the believers to be firm, forceful, ruthless and radical in killing the enemies who fight against [Islam], and to show them no mercy or compassion...[Since] this applies to offensive jihad...what about [the case in which] the infidels attack the Muslim states, shed blood, violate women's honor and offend [Islam]? In that case, there is no doubt that they must be struck and killed with even greater ruthlessness, as a lesson to others and in order to fill them with awe for the *umma*, so that no one will wish to attack Muslims anywhere, ever again.... Our righteous forefathers [*al-salaf al-salih*] implemented [these] principles, and the results were amazing: they gained victory after victory and Allah's triumph was realized, because they defended his faith and obeyed his command to kill, disperse and smite the enemies of the faith....[99]

To prevent his readers from misconstruing his open support for extreme violence, Mahmud ended his text by lauding the ruthlessness and brutality of Sayf al-Islam Khattab, the notorious Arab commander who fought and died in Chechnya, and Abu Mus'ab al-Zarqawi, the even more fanatical *'amir* of al-Qa'ida fi Bilad al-Rafidayn (al-Qa'ida in the Land of the Two Rivers, i.e., Mesopotamia).[100]

Similarly illustrative statements calling for the indiscriminate mass murder of infidels, although ostensibly justified on the basis of reciprocity, can easily be multiplied. Thus Sayf al-Din al-Ansari, in his section of a book entitled *Ghazwa 11 Sibtimbir* (*The September 11 Raid*), claimed that the deaths of nearly 3,000 Americans in the attacks on New York and Washington, DC, was justified both in accordance with the principle of retaliation and because Islamic doctrine approves the destruction of enemy fortresses, even in circumstances where it may be impossible to distinguish between soldiers and civilians.[101] Compare also "The Truth about the New Crusade: A Ruling on the Killing of Women and Children of the Non-Believers," the draft of an ideological justification for the 9/11 attacks by Ramzi b. al-Shayb, one of the actual hijackers:

> Concerning the operations of the blessed Tuesday [9/11]...they are legally legitimate, because they are committed against a country at war with us, and the people in that country are combatants. Someone might say that it is the innocent, the elderly, the women, and the children who are victims, so how can these operations be legitimate according to *sharia*? And we say that the sanctity of women, children, and the elderly is not absolute. There are special cases....Muslims may respond in kind if infidels have targeted women and children and elderly Muslims, [or if] they are being invaded, [or if] the non-combatants are helping with the fight, whether in action, word, or any other type of assistance, [or if they] need to attack with heavy weapons, which do not differentiate between combatants and non-combatants...Now that we know that the operations were permissible from the Islamic point of view, we must answer or respond to those who prohibit the operations from the point of view of benefits or harms.... Because of Saddam and the Baath Party, America punished a whole population. Thus its bombs and its embargo killed millions of Iraqi Muslims. And because of Osama bin Laden, America surrounded Afghans and bombed them, causing the death of tens of thousands of Muslims ... God said to assault whoever assaults you, in a like manner.... In killing Americans who are ordinarily off limits, Muslims should not exceed four million non-combatants, or render more than ten million of them homeless. We should avoid this, to make sure the penalty [that we are inflicting] is no more than reciprocal. God knows what is best.[102]

No less radical are the views expressed in a series of public letters by al-Qa'ida spokesman Sulayman Abu Ghayth, a Kuwaiti *shaykh*, who argues that the number of American casualties resulting from the 9/11 attacks was not nearly high enough to balance the historical ledger. As he sees it, the *mujahidin* have a right to kill at least four million Americans (including one million children), displace eight million, and maim hundreds of thousands more, since this is approximately how many Muslim deaths, displacements, and injuries he calculates have been directly or indirectly attributable to anti-Islamic U.S. policies and actions.[103] Finally, Saudi scholar Nasir ibn Hamid al-Fahd, in a May 2003 *fatwa*, approved the use of weapons of mass destruction (WMDs) against the United States, since a combination of military necessity and the law of retaliation supposedly gave Muslims the right to kill as many as ten million Americans.[104]

Even if one discounts the bloodthirsty rhetoric that is the norm on innumerable jihadist Web sites, one might think that such blatant "official" justifications and open calls for mass murder, revenge, and retribution might temper Scheuer's overemphasis on al-Qa'ida's rationality, but this is not the case. In that sense the attitudes of the "rationalists" are reminiscent of those observers in the 1930s who insisted, despite massive evidence to the contrary, that Hitler had pragmatic goals that could actually be satisfied rather than an irrational hatred of real and imagined enemies, a passionate desire to exact revenge against them, and an outright will to exterminate them. It was precisely their failure to take Nazi ideological fanaticism seriously that led to so many misplaced efforts to appease the German chancellor. The same, alas, is true today inasmuch as many observers and analysts persistently downplay or ignore the intrinsic ideological fanaticism of al-Qa'ida and other jihadist groups.

Unfortunately, the "nonrationalist" interpreters have themselves only gotten things partially right. After all, it is a fairly short step between arguing that the jihadists' basic worldview is not only archaic and anachronistic but hallucinatory, which is essentially true, and concluding—wrongly—that this means that they are incapable of displaying any strategic or operational rationality. This unwarranted leap is perhaps best epitomized by French scholar Olivier Roy, who like Harris claims that al-Qa'ida "has no strategic vision" at all, and that "most of its targets have no military or strategic value."[103] To say the least, this is an overstatement, even if one is willing to admit that Bin Ladin's organization has carried out particular actions in part for ideologically induced "expressive" reasons, such as a compulsion to smite "infidels" or obtain retribution, rather than for purely rational "strategic" reasons.[106]

Bin Ladin's ultimate aims, as noted above, are to unite the Muslim *umma*, restore the power and glory of the Caliphate, and secure the triumph of the *dar al-Islam* over the *dar al-kufr.* He recognizes, however, that this objective cannot be achieved until a truly Islamic state is established in the heart of the Muslim world and until the power of the United States is undermined and destroyed, two objectives that are viewed as closely interrelated.[107] What, then, is al-Qa'ida's basic strategy for accomplishing its ultimate objectives? Since at least the mid-1990s, its principal aim has been to precipitate a titanic "conflict of civilizations" between the Islamic world and the West, and in the process create a global Islamic insurgent movement that even the unmatched power and vast resources of America would be unable to cope with or quell.[108] In order to accomplish this preliminary aim, al-Qa'ida carried out a series of provocative attacks marked by increasing lethality, culminating on 9/11, that were intended to goad the United States into launching a massive attack on the Islamic world, which would only serve to confirm Bin Ladin's long-standing claims that the "Great Satan" and its allies were waging a war against Islam.[109] An incautious, brutal response by the U.S. military would in turn hopefully have the effect of arousing the increasingly angry Muslim masses from their slumber and compelling them at long last to answer al-Qa'ida's call to wage a "defensive jihad" against the invading "infidels," who could now be more plausibly seen as trying to militarily subjugate the *dar al-Islam* and directly exploit its resources.

The beauty of this scheme, apart from its breathtaking simplicity, was that it provided the transnational jihadists with a virtual "win-win" situation. If the United States lashed out indiscriminately, on the one hand, or did not react forcefully at all, on the other, it would inadvertently hand a huge propaganda victory to al-Qa'ida. Only a measured, precisely targeted, and quietly lethal response might have foiled Bin Ladin's plan, since such a relatively restrained but highly efficacious middle course would have served to demonstrate American power and resolve without causing unnecessary civilian casualties, in the process further radicalizing the Muslim "street" and providing al-Qa'ida with new recruits.[110] For several years the United States actually failed this test, in that it did not respond decisively or effectively to jihadist attacks, thereby repeatedly allowing al-Qa'ida to display its operational prowess and also serving as an inspiration to both jihadists and other anti-Western Muslims by mistakenly giving them the impression that America really was a weak, decadent "paper tiger" that had no stomach for fighting or taking casualties, just as Bin Ladin had been saying ever since the 1993 Somali debacle. After 9/11, however, by cracking down on anti-Muslim vigilante violence inside the United States and precisely targeting al-Qa'ida and the Taliban regime in Afghanistan, America for a time deprived Bin Ladin of such an easy anticipated victory.[111] It was only later, when the U.S. military failed to seal off the retreat of the *mujahidin* at Tora Bora, thereby not dealing al-Qa'ida a knockout blow,[112] and when the Bush administration embarked on its ill-conceived invasion and occupation of Iraq, that Bin Ladin was handed a golden opportunity to rally his scattered, disillusioned fighters, recruit new generations of *mujahidin*, and more effectively tap and exploit Muslim popular anger.[113]

It has been argued above that al-Qa'ida has extremely utopian aims, rooted in "classical" Islamic juridical and political conceptions about the relations between the Islamic world and the non-Islamic world, that could only be achieved in the present era if some unanticipated combination of natural and human cataclysms brought about the collapse of the existing world order. However, this does not mean that Bin Ladin and his principal lieutenants are incapable of formulating particular strategic concepts in an effort to achieve those fundamentally unrealistic goals. In his recent assessment of global jihadist objectives, Thomas Hegghammer argues that there are "five principal categories of actors that shape contemporary global jihadist ideology" and, more narrowly, endeavor to define global jihadist strategy. The first is "represented by the leadership of the 'old al-Qa'ida,'" that is, Bin Ladin and Ayman al-Zawahiri, who communicate primarily through sound and visual recordings diffused on Arab television stations. According to Hegghammer,

> The statements by Bin Ladin and al-Zawahiri are often quite general in content, and their main purpose seems to be to convince and motivate believers to take up arms against the enemy. Their approximately 40 statements since the Autumn of 2001 have focused on the political reasons to fight the Crusaders. They rarely provide specific strategic or tactical advice, and hence their declarations are always subject to interpretation by other writers.[114]

This does not mean that they do not discuss specific strategic matters at all,[115] but that the primary responsibility for defining and clarifying global jihadist strategy falls to the other four categories, namely, pro-jihadist religious scholars (the *'ulama al-jihad*), actual military and strategic thinkers linked to al-Qa'ida, members of other active militant organizations (including branches of al-Qa'ida), and what Hegghammer refers to as "grassroots radicals, i.e., the thousands of anonymous participants on radical Islamist discussion forums on the Internet."[116]

In this context, there is no need to devote any attention to the exhortative and juridical materials produced by the jihadist *'ulama*, most of whom have in any case since been arrested by the Saudi or European authorities, nor to focus on the voluminous materials produced by Islamist terrorist groups with their own agendas or by jihadist sympathizers who post all sorts of messages on jihadist forums and blogsites. Rather, what is perhaps most significant is that since 9/11, and especially since the autumn of 2002, the number of texts produced by the third group above, which can be broadly characterized as "strategic studies" texts, has increased considerably. In particular, the online magazine *Majallat al-Ansar* and the Web site of the Markaz al-Dirasat wa al-Buhuth al-Islamiyya have provided forums for materials of this type. Unlike other jihadist materials, these strategic analyses tend to be more "secular in style, academic in their approach, and objective in their assessments."[117] One indication of this is that the authors of some of these works have evidently examined and analyzed Western military writings, as the example of Sayf al-Ansar's article on "Fourth Generation Warfare" indicates.[118] Hence it cannot be denied that certain al-Qa'ida military leaders, such as Abu Ubayd al-Qurashi, the now deceased Saudi 'Abd al-'Aziz al-Muqrin, and the recently captured Abu Mus'ab al-Suri, do possess a relatively clear strategic vision, one that is informed by years of operational experience.

However, the extent to which al-Qa'ida engages in coherent strategic thinking should not be exaggerated. Three examples should suffice to demonstrate the limitations in al-Qa'ida's strategic thinking.[119] First, there is a 113-page strategic treatise written by Abu Bakr Naji, *Idarat al-tawahhush* (*The Management of Savagery*), which was produced by the aforementioned Markaz and posted in March 2005 on the al-Ikhlas online forum by someone using the moniker "Irhabi3," that is, "Terrorist 3." The jihadist strategic plan outlined by Naji is extremely schematic, so much so that one wonders how seriously to take it. He begins by hypothesizing a three-phase strategy. In the first phase, the "vexation and exhaustion" phase, the jihadists will bleed "infidel" forces and rally Muslim youth by means of exemplary targeting (such as the 2002 Bali bombing); in the second, the "management of savagery" phase, they will establish zones under their own control, where they can establish authentically Islamic institutions and impose the *shari'a*; and in the third, the empowerment phase, they will extend the above phases and link up various jihadist zones of control until a greater Islamic state has been re-established.[120] Among the targeting objectives Naji lists are tourist resorts, "Crusader" banks, and oil installations (in order to force the enemy to expend resources to raise security for refineries, pipelines, and shipping), and he especially advocates striking hard, since a superior enemy can only be defeated by means of economic and military attrition.

Second, in another text posted on the Internet, "Al-Qa'ida's Strategy to the Year 2020," Muhammad Ibrahim Makkawi—a pseudonym used by Sayf al-Adl—outlined a similar five-phase strategy.[121] In the first phase, the goal was to induce the "ponderous American elephant" to invade Muslim lands. In the second phase, this invasion would in turn anger and galvanize the resistance of the *umma*, while in the process providing more jihadist recruits. In the third, the conflict with the Crusaders would be expanded throughout the region, thereby trapping and bleeding U.S. forces within a "*jihad* triangle of horror" running through Afghanistan, currently neutral Iran, and southern Iraq, and then into southern Turkey, southern Lebanon, and Syria. In the fourth phase, the movement would be expanded globally, with the result that independent jihadist cells would spring up autonomously, including in the West. In the fifth and final phase, the United States will become so overextended militarily that its economy will collapse, paving the way for the final victory of the *mujahidin* over the *dar al-kufr*.

Third, in a 2005 book by journalist Fu'ad Husayn, which is entitled *Al-Zarqawi, al-jil al-thani li-al-Qa'ida* (*Al-Zarqawi: Al-Qa'ida's Second Generation*), the author purports to describe a strategy for victory that has been carefully outlined by al-Qa'ida's own leaders.[122] This particular scheme has seven rather than three phases, and is thus even more elaborate—and arguably more of an exercise in wishful thinking—than Naji's. The first is the "awakening" stage from 2000 to 2003, during which the *umma* will be awakened from its state of hibernation by the jihadist precipitation of an American invasion of the Muslim world. The second is the "eye-opening" stage from 2003 to 2006, during which the United States will open the eyes of the believers by occupying Muslim lands and thence be engaged directly by the *mujahidin* on Muslim soil. The third is the "standing upright" stage, from 2007 to 2010, during which the jihadist vanguard and the *umma* will develop the capacity to take effective offensive action, especially in the al-Sham region (Syria, Lebanon, and Jordan). The fourth is the "recuperation of power" stage, from 2010 to 2013, during which apostate Muslim regimes will be overthrown by means of direct combat, thereby accelerating the deterioration of U.S. power and influence in the region. The fifth is the "declaration" and establishment of an Islamic state stage, from 2013 to 2016, during which the Caliphate will be restored even as American and European power declines in relation to that of China, India, and the Islamic world. The sixth is the "all-out confrontation" stage, from 2017 to 2020, during which there will be total war between the *dar al-islam* and the *dar al-kufr* and the creation of a new balance of power. The seventh and last is the "final victory" stage, after 2020, during which the unbelievers will suffer complete defeat at the hands of the Islamic *umma*. Interestingly, from the second stage on, the *mujahidin* plan to "burn" Arab oil in order to deprive the West of vital revenues and to wage a campaign of electronic jihad, that is, cyber-sabotage, against the U.S. economy. More bizarrely, in the fourth stage they plan to gradually reinstitute the gold standard in order to devalue Western currency, an idea first proposed by Hizb al-Tahrir. What particularly strikes the outside observer is not only the overly schematic and absurdly optimistic "strategy" outlined here, but also the apparent reliance on a vaguely numerological system to determine the length of the successive stages.[123] In short, beyond the most rudimentary and seemingly unrealistic projections and prognostications, one finds precious little coherent strategic thinking in these two works.[124]

Nevertheless, al-Qa'ida has repeatedly shown itself to be devastatingly effective on the operational and "tactical" levels, irrespective of whether its leaders always display a coherent and realistic "strategic" vision. As is now well known, the principal modus operandi employed by al-Qa'ida, especially in the major attacks officially authorized by Bin Ladin and his Majlis al-Shura, is characterized by thorough, time-consuming, and at times meticulous planning; the careful surveillance of prospective targets; and the gradual insertion of operatives into the target zone, followed by the sudden execution of near simultaneous attacks by well-prepared "martyrs" (*shuhada*), that is, suicide terrorists. These traits were clearly displayed in, among other actions, the destructive 1998 attacks on the two U.S. embassies in Africa, the attack on the *U.S.S. Cole*, and the "planes operation" on 9/11, and they have since been adopted by other jihadist organizations that are affiliated with or directly inspired by al-Qa'ida, for example, by Jemaah Islamiyah in its horrific 2002 and 2005 attacks on areas frequented by tourists in Bali. On the operational level, al-Qa'ida generally displays a serious, realistic, and fundamentally rational approach. This is illustrated by a series of articles authored by Sayf al-Adl, who was appointed head of al-Qa'ida's military committee after the death of Muhammad Atif, that appeared during 2004 in *Mu'askar al-Battar*, an important but now defunct al-Qa'ida military and operations journal.[125] In one such article, al-Adl urged the *mujahidin* to develop a "creative" and "flexible" attack plan marked by the following characteristics:

1. A plan should be reasonable. In other words, alternatives should be examined properly and weighed carefully so that the best of them can be chosen.
2. There should be a major—specific—target and other secondary targets for the operation.
3. The plan should be realistic.
4. It should be coherent, tight, and accurate. There should be no gaps in it. Rather, each part of the plan should complement the other part. It should appear to the enemy as a connected sequence of events.
5. It should be simple. In other words, every member [of the operational cell] should easily understand it and be able to implement it without difficulty.[126]

Such an approach is unfortunately typical of the sound, realistic (para)military thinking that permeates al-Qa'ida's operational and tactical planning. Therefore, no matter how bizarre and absurd the maximal objectives of the global jihadists may in fact be, it would be a terrible mistake to underestimate their undeniably effective operational methods and capabilities. Hence, if the aforementioned notions of "pragmatic fanaticism" or "pragmatic messianism" are in fact applicable to al-Qa'ida, they would seem to be particularly relevant in this sense.

JIHADIST IDEOLOGY AND THE POTENTIAL EMPLOYMENT OF CBRN WEAPONS

Just as there continue to be disputes among specialists about the overall objectives and strategy of jihadist groups with a global agenda, especially al-Qa'ida, so too are there ongoing disagreements about whether such groups are likely to employ "weapons of mass destruction" should they manage to acquire or produce them. Although there is no doubt whatsoever that Usama bin Ladin and other leading al-Qa'ida figures have repeatedly expressed an interest in obtaining CBRN materials, agents, and weapons, nor that the organization has already sought to provide Islamic theological and moral justifications for employing them, has periodically made efforts to acquire them,[127] has actually attempted to produce certain of them in makeshift laboratories in Afghanistan,[128] and has openly advocated using them against the United States and its "infidel" allies, experts and pundits continue to argue about the likelihood of such an eventuality.[129] Most of these debates have hitherto concentrated on whether al-Qa'ida and affiliated groups actually have or are likely to be able to develop the technical capabilities required to deploy such weapons, but the focus here will instead be on their intentions.

One fact that is undeniable is that spokesmen for al-Qa'ida and associated groups have repeatedly advocated the acquisition, if not always the first or immediate use, of CBRN weapons. The arguments for doing so have generally been based on Qur'anic verses and supporting *ahadith* that explicitly authorize the killing and terrorizing of infidels, coupled with—although barely tempered by—certain Islamic "just war" doctrines concerning the appropriate conduct of warfare *fi sabil Allah*. These latter arguments are primarily based on two key notions.[130] The first is the concept of reciprocity with respect to the enemy—"an eye for an eye"—both in terms of the actual means and the scale of the actions that can and should be employed. In short, if the enemy is said to be behaving barbarously and without restraint or using terrible weapons, then Muslims have the right to use the same brutal methods even if such methods are normally prohibited (*haram*). The second is based on simple practicality and expediency, in that it would normally be impossible to carry out attacks on enemy territory at all without inadvertently killing women, children, the aged, and the infirm, classes of people that it is normally forbidden to kill deliberately. The same is true for Muslims who happen to reside in areas of the *dar al-harb*, who according to classical doctrines are enjoined to leave those areas and return to territories of the *dar al-Islam* so that they will not be "corrupted" by infidels and so that no harm will inadvertently come to them in the course of Muslim raids.[131] These themes often appear in statements and texts prepared by jihadists who are trying to provide "Islamically correct" theological and legal justifications for their surprise attacks and depredations against both non-Muslim and Muslim civilians.[132] Worse still, their arguments often fall on sympathetic ears given that atrocity stories and conspiracy theories concerning the "enemies of Islam" are so widely disseminated and so often uncritically accepted throughout the Muslim world. Even so, it should be noted that some Islamist intellectuals have severely criticized al-Qa'ida's reliance on these arguments to justify its proposed employment of "weapons of mass destruction," especially nuclear weapons, which indicates that there remain strong differences of opinion even within jihadist circles concerning these weighty matters.[133]

In addition to basing their rationales for attacking "infidels" on Qur'anic injunctions and the *sunna* of the Prophet Muhammad, al-Qa'ida leaders have also increasingly sought to behave in other "Islamically correct" ways with respect to their designated enemies. For example, stung by the attacks of certain respected Muslim religious scholars who criticized them for carrying out the 9/11 attacks without first calling their enemies to embrace Islam—as is in theory mandated by the *Qur'an* and other medieval Islamic theological and juridical sources—Usama bin Ladin and other al-Qa'ida spokesmen have since repeatedly invited their prospective "infidel" targets to convert to Islam and follow Allah's true path, thereby satisfying accepted precedents and, at least in theory, giving their "satanic" foes an opportunity to avoid being attacked. Therefore, in his October 2002 letter to the Americans, after enumerating a long litany of alleged U.S. political and moral "crimes" to explain why he was fighting the "great Satan," the al-Qa'ida leader explained what he wanted from the Americans: "The first thing we are calling you to is Islam...the seal of all the previous religions...the religion of *jihad* in the way of Allah so that Allah's word and religion reign supreme."[134] Furthermore, al-Qa'ida's "official" American spokesman, 'Azzam al-Amriki (né Adam Gadahn), has likewise repeatedly demanded that Americans convert to Islam in order to avoid further jihadist attacks. In a September 2006 videotape, Gadahn invited "all Americans and unbelievers to Islam, whatever their role and status in Bush and Blair's world order," and then warned them that they had better "[d]ecide today, because today could be [their] last day."[135] More recently, in January 2008, Gadahn again urged Americans to "abandon their corrupt ungodly religion for the simple, moderate, and reasonable religion of Islam."[136] These offers, whether they are simply ignored or are publicly rejected (as Bin Ladin surely knows they will be), serve to open the way, legally and theologically, for jihadist attacks on Americans at any time and any place, including in their own homeland.

In any event, Usama bin Ladin himself has made several pronouncements indicating that he enthusiastically supports the Muslim acquisition of CBRN weapons. For example, in a January 11, 1999 interview with *Time* magazine, he made the following statement in response to a question about whether he was trying to acquire chemical and nuclear weapons (as the Americans were then claiming):

> Acquiring [such] weapons for the defense of Muslims is a religious duty. If I have indeed acquired these weapons, then I thank Allah for enabling me to do so. And if I seek to acquire these weapons, I am carrying out a [religious] duty. It would be a sin for Muslims not to try to possess the weapons that would prevent the infidels from inflicting harm on Muslims. *But how we would use these weapons if we possessed them is up to us.*[137]

Elsewhere in the interview he said that America, which was allegedly "acting on behalf of Israel and the Jews, paving the way for the Jews to divide the Muslim world once again, enslave it, and loot the rest of its wealth," "should expect reactions from the Muslim world that are proportionate to the injustice they inflict."[138] Once again, one can observe al-Qa'ida's shrewd public emphases on the "defense" of the *umma* and the legitimacy of "proportional" responses to supposed enemy aggression.

In June 2002, as noted above, Kuwaiti al-Qa'ida spokesman Sulayman Abu Ghayth published a three-part article on the group's al-Nida' (The Call) Web site entitled "In the Shade of Lances."[139] In the first part, he argues that the world should not have been surprised by the 9/11 attacks, which was "something natural" given that America has tyrannized and oppressed Muslims and other peoples for so long. In the second part, he claims that America "disseminates abomination and licentiousness among the people via the cheap media and vile curricula" and "is the reason for all oppression, injustice, licentiousness, or suppression that is the lot of the Muslims." Moreover, it is "immersed in the blood of Muslims" due to its support for Israeli "abominations" and its invasions of

Afghanistan and Iraq. Hence, according to his own calculations of the number of Muslim casualties attributable to American actions, and on the basis of the divinely sanctioned law of reciprocal punishment, he concludes (in the third part of the article) that Muslims

> have the right to kill 4 million Americans—2 million of them children—and to exile twice as many and wound and cripple hundreds of thousands. Furthermore, it is our right to fight them with chemical and biological weapons, so as to afflict them with the fatal maladies that have afflicted the Muslims because of [the Americans'] chemical and biological weapons.... America knows only the language of force...[and] is kept at bay by blood alone.[140]

Lest anyone think that Abu Ghayth was simply promoting the "legitimate" defense of the *umma* against U.S. "aggression" herein, note that in part two he openly advocates the standard imperialistic jihadist notion that "the entire earth must be subjected to the religion of Islam—not to the East, not to the West—to no ideology and no path except for the path of Allah."[141]

Still another crucially important document is the *fatwa* authorizing Muslim use of WMDs that was issued in May 2003 by Saudi *shaykh* Nasir ibn Hamid al-Fahd and posted on his Web site.[142] The arguments al-Fahd uses in this *fatwa* are the standard Islamic "just war" arguments referred to above, especially those favored by jihadists because they appear to sanction actions that they fervently wish or actually intend to undertake, that is, attack infidels, "apostates," and "hypocrites"—that it is permissible for Muslims to retaliate in kind against their enemies, both with respect to means and scale; that it is permissible for Muslims to kill women, children, and the infirm if they do so inadvertently or cannot avoid doing so in the course of military operations against the enemy; and that it is permissible to kill Muslims accidentally in the same context. Moreover, he argues that Muslims are authorized to employ CBRN if it is "necessary": "If the infidels can be repelled from the Muslims only by using such weapons, their use is permissible, even if you kill them without exception and destroy their tillage and stock." He also claims that, according to Islamic scholars, "there is no obligation when there is inability; *there is no prohibited thing when there is necessity*."[143] Elsewhere he goes much further than "*shari'a* reasoning" normally allows by arguing that it is permissible to use CBRN weapons "if those engaged in jihad decide that there is benefit in using them," which effectively eliminates the need to adhere to any *jus in bello* legal restraints, Islamic or otherwise. Finally, he makes two arguments with respect to WMD, one that is commonly made by Islamists and one that is somewhat more original. The common one is that Muslims are not bound by international agreements, including those banning WMD, simply because such agreements were established by infidels and therefore have "no standing in Islamic law." The one that is less common is that the term "weapons of mass destruction" has been unfairly restricted by those same infidels to refer solely to CBRN weapons. As al-Fahd cynically observes, if one belligerent "should strike another with tons of 'conventional' bombs, killing tens of thousands, this use of weapons would be allowed internationally," which indicates that the enemies of Islam, including those who previously used chemical or nuclear weapons, "want to protect themselves and monopolize such weapons on the pretext of 'banning them internationally.'"

Finally, in his post-7/7 bombing message to the British and Europeans, Abu Mus'ab al-Suri likewise resorts to arguments concerning the necessity and justness of responding in kind to the West with respect to "destructive" weapons:

> You have acquired all kinds of destructive conventional and strategic weapons, such as nuclear, chemical and biological, legal weapons as well as weapons that are internationally banned, and you have used all this in your wars against us and against others without any deterrent or any law. Hence, we are serious about acquiring all possible weapons and means and will deal with you the same way, in accordance with our true religion.[144]

Little needs to be added by way of clarification, since the text is quite explicit.

One can see from the above statements and jurisprudential arguments that al-Qa'ida has repeatedly claimed to possess, justified the employment of, or threatened to use CBRN materials and weapons. However, even if one was to assume that the group does in fact already have such weapons in its possession, these bellicose remarks do not really answer the question of when and under what circumstances al-Qa'ida might actually have recourse to deploying them. The two main questions are whether Usama bin Ladin and his cohorts plan to use them (1) defensively, that is, to deter or repel prospective conventional or CBRN attacks by the "enemies of Islam," or (2) offensively, that is, to carry out either a tactical or strategic "first strike" against the "far enemy" in their own homelands. These questions are in turn related to the operational issue of whether, capabilities permitting, al-Qa'ida would be more likely to use CB agents to carry out small-scale attacks on "infidel" forces occupying Muslim lands or in their overseas bases, or spectacular, large-scale attacks with BRN weapons against the homelands of the United States or its European allies. Perhaps not surprisingly, the available indicators of al-Qa'ida's short-, medium-, and long-term intentions remain somewhat ambiguous, which has in turn caused outside observers to come to rather different conclusions.

For this very reason, it is necessary to discuss al-Qa'ida's possible purposes for using CBRN weapons at greater length. There are some indications that the organization had hoped to obtain or develop these weapons, at least in part, for "defensive" purposes, specifically in order to deter the United States and its allies from taking certain extreme military measures against jihadist networks. For example, in a November 2001 interview with Pakistani journalist Hamid Mir, Usama bin Ladin made the following claim:

> I wish to declare that if America used chemical or nuclear weapons against us, then we may retort with chemical and nuclear weapons. We have the weapons as [a] deterrent.[145]

In a subsequent conversation with journalist and terrorism analyst Peter Bergen, Mir paraphrased Bin Ladin's earlier answer as follows: "We have nuclear deterrence and this is for our defense."[146]

One might easily be tempted to dismiss these claims to have obtained or developed WMD merely for "defensive" or deterrence purposes as blatantly deceptive propaganda, much like the global jihadists' public claims to be waging "defensive jihad" and be pursuing limited objectives. However, certain inside sources have lent some additional support, however partial, to Usama bin Ladin's public "deterrence" claims. First, Abu Mus'ab al-Suri made the following arguments in a booklet published on November 5, 1999 by the al-Ghuraba' Center for Islamic Studies in Kabul:

> The difference in armament and number between Muslims and their enemies, between the oppressed and the strong, has never been larger.... Military logic shows us that it is almost absurd to launch a classical confrontational war to restore the balance of power...[Hence] the renascent Islamic forces in...Central Asia...must attempt to acquire weapons of mass destruction (nuclear, biological, bacteriological) in exactly the same way as the aggressive, oppressive world represented by the Jews and the West possesses these weapons. One has

> to threaten with them [these weapons] and deter the enemy exactly like they [the enemy] have been doing....The Central Asian region has developed factories, and they have raw material for these weapons, which has made a base and a hope for Muslims to acquire these weapons....This is a strategic goal which is within reach, but only Allah knows.[147]

Similar sentiments were expressed by Abu Mus'ab in his huge military treatise, where he warns that unless the American public is able to deter its own "Zionist" government from continuing its "aggression on all mankind," the nations under attack have the right to respond "with all means and reciprocally, including the use of weapons of mass destruction, and [by] breaking the enemy's back via genocides and the killing of civilians."[148] As is common in jihadist tracts, advocacy of the procurement of dangerous WMD is here justified as an appropriate response to, and a necessary means to counterbalance or even deter, the methods and arsenal of the "infidel" enemy.

Second, a disillusioned al-Qa'ida insider named Abu al-Walid al-Masri, in his book manuscript entitled *Tarikh al-Afghan al-'Arab* (*The History of the Afghan Arabs*), subsequently provided important details about secret discussions that had occurred between "hawks" and "doves" within the group's leadership circles concerning CBRN weapons. The account of Abu al-Walid in this connection is important enough to be quoted at length:

> The dreams of the hardline wing in al-Qa'ida, which sometimes appeared in the forms of demands, dealt with the need and importance of possessing weapons of mass destruction and storing some of them on American territory to be used in a fast and direct response to any American aggression against Afghanistan....The conclusion reached was that al-Qa'ida must possess weapons for defense, based on what can be obtained or supplied in the nuclear, biological, or chemical fields, so that in a crisis, if the other side used weapons of mass destruction, it will not escape a deadly punishment.... Another group believed that these types of weapons, if Bin Ladin could obtain them, would [only] be tactical by virtue of their primitiveness and weak destructive capability. However, they will continue to call them "weapons of mass destruction" to create fear. They are primitive weapons with tactical and not strategic capabilities. In other words, using them will give the mujahidin credibility, prestige, and psychological influence.... The people close to Bin Ladin believed that these destructive weapons would greatly enhance the combat capability and psychological influence of the al-Qa'ida fighters. The most important questions were: if such weapons could be obtained, will they be used against the enemy on Muslim territory or against the enemy on his own territory? Will the enemy forces be targeted by these weapons (if they were obtained), or will the civilians in their country also be targeted? There were different interpretations and views in this respect, and then more questions were asked. Which of these weapons will be more appropriate for the current situation of the mujahidin: the nuclear, chemical, or biological? Should the information regarding the ways of obtaining such weapons remain secret, or should it be disseminated among the mujahidin groups in all the areas?...Others raised questions about the possibility of mixing the weapon of suicide action (the only remaining deterrent weapon in the hands of Muslims) and those weapons [of mass destruction]. They noted that the security measures by the enemy have greatly reduced the effect of suicide operations, and the introduction of these weapons could greatly enhance the value of suicide operations and their effect on the enemy.... As to the WMD proposals, Bin Ladin did not approve them in the first place and that was obvious from his repeated theory that the United States could not bear two or three strikes from him. But he refused to voice publicly his rejection of the idea, probably because of his extreme politeness with those around him. Another reason was that his right-hand man in al-Qa'ida, Abu Hafs [al-Masri], led the hawks' wing and strongly supported the acquisition of new resources, especially WMD. But he did not make up his mind about the strategy of using these weapons, postponing

> this until they were actually acquired. Abu Hafs took charge of the WMD issue and acted with his known stubbornness and determination.[149]

This, however, does not fully resolve the matter of al-Qa'ida's reasons for pursuing a CBRN weapons' capability. For one thing, such discussions may well have been context-specific inasmuch as they took place in the periods prior to and after 9/11, when the group's leaders were particularly worried about just how terrible America's reaction to the "planes operation" might be. Hence at that time they were heatedly debating the possible development of new weapons or the adoption of other measures that might serve to deter or at least mitigate an overwhelming and decisive U.S. military response. For another, from the account itself it is clear that Usama bin Ladin and his henchmen had not yet come to definitive conclusions about how best to employ such weapons, and that despite being pressured by certain "hawks," the *shaykh* preferred to postpone making any final decisions about this until the weapons were actually available in his arsenal. At the same time, references to storing WMD in America *in advance of their use* could easily open the way to using them as a first strike weapon, and not necessarily in response to threatening U.S. military actions.

Indeed, there are numerous other indications that al-Qa'ida fully intends to, or at least hopes to, carry out "offensive" strikes if and when they do actually manage to obtain or develop CBRN weapons. For example, in an undated handwritten letter addressed to the Americans, al-Qa'ida "brother" Abu 'Abdullah al-Kuwayti, after claiming that the jihadists' war was with "the Jews" and not the American people, warned that if the latter continued to involve themselves in this struggle, "our combat groups, along with our military, nuclear, and biological equipment, will kill hundreds of thousands of people we don't wish to fight."[150] Despite the transparent attempt to persuade the American public to withdraw support from the Bush administration, this nonetheless constituted a threat to cause mass casualties by using a combination of conventional, biological, and nuclear weapons. Such a threat may, of course, not have been genuine, but simply part and parcel of a crude psychological warfare campaign directed against the United States. Even so, it again suggests that elements within al-Qa'ida seem to have no qualms whatsoever about killing huge numbers of Americans in their own homeland or about employing WMD to do so.

More ominously, on December 26, 2002, Abu Shihab al-Qandahari, a former Yemeni *mujahid* in the anti-Soviet war in Afghanistan who served as the moderator of the al-Qa'ida–linked Internet forum al-Mujahidun, published a short article with the provocative title, "Nuclear War is the Solution to the Destruction of the United States." The most illuminating sections of this article are reproduced below:

> Indeed, you did read that [the title] correctly. This is the only way to kill the maximum number of Americans. This is the nuclear terror[ism], which the Americans have never feared....The United States attacked Iraq using weapons that contaminated the lands and water with radiation for thousands of years. It also enhances its bombs with depleted uranium to cause even greater harm to the people and the environment....Eye for eye and tooth for tooth. If the Americans have bombs that no one else owns, al-Qa'ida is stronger. It owns "dirty bombs" and "bombs with lethal viruses," which could cover American cities with deadly diseases and turn this nation...into a crowd of contaminated and sick people. The coming days will prove that Qa'idat al-Jihad is capable, with Allah's help, of turning the United States into a lake of lethal radiation, which would seem like the last days of humanity. It would also prove that al-Qa'ida is very popular all over the Islamic world....Yes, we will destroy America and its allies because they have used their

> power for evil against the weak....Their end is closer now, at the hand of the awakening [Islamic] youth who, [sitting] astride their steeds, will [in the end] dismount either as victors or martyrs.[151]

Although the sentiments expressed by Abu Shihab concerning the desire to slaughter and terrorize Americans and destroy the United States are crystal clear, and apparently elicited a favorable response among his radical readers, in an analysis of the text Reuven Paz is right to caution that this incendiary article could represent nothing more than an empty threat, or deliberate disinformation concerning al-Qa'ida's supposed possession of CBRN materials, or propaganda aimed at encouraging Islamists and jihadist sympathizers.[152]

The same cautionary remarks also apply to several frightening statements made the following year in a series of emails to the London-based magazine *al-Majalla* by Abu Muhammad al-Ablaj, who described himself as the *'amir* (commander) overseeing the "mujahidin training center" for al-Qa'ida and the Taliban. In a May 2003 email, he made these barely veiled threats:

> As to the use of sarin gas and nuclear [weapons], we will talk about them then and the infidels will know what harms them. They spared no effort in their war on us in Afghanistan and left no weapon unused. They should not therefore rule out the possibility that we will present them with our capabilities.[153]

He also said in that same message that al-Qa'ida "would not rule out the use of sarin gas and the poisoning of the drinking water in American and Western cities."[154] On June 27, he followed this up by issuing the following warning:

> Crushing and devastating strikes against America will come at the suitable time. In other words, after wearing it out with injuries our strike must be a knockout....The wings of the U.S. eagle must be clipped. This stage will be followed by the stage of cutting off the veins. The last stage will be the stage of slaughtering according to the Islamic method, and it will be a major surprise for the entire nation.[155]

Later, in a September 21 article in *al-Majalla*, al-Ablaj replied thusly to a question from reporter Mahmud Khalil about al-Qa'ida's possession and possible use of "strategic biological, chemical, or nuclear weapons":

> Is there a sane person who discloses his [operational] secrets? Brother, the strategic weapons are not just [a matter of] remov[ing] the pin and strik[ing]. If such was the case, then [they] would have been available and [an attack] would have been carried out before the "blessed strike" [9/11]. The matter needs time. Such a massive strategic weapon is bound to have reactions commensurate with its size. It must therefore be used at a time that makes the Crusader enemy beg on his knee that he does not want more strikes and that he will withdraw into himself and occupy himself with his misfortune with the tails of shame, failure, and disgrace between his legs and licking his wounds after the utter defeat.[156]

Elsewhere in that email exchange, al-Ablaj claimed that "action and planning are afoot" and that the United States is "on its way to the abyss, disappearance, and breakdown."[157] Still more bellicose comments were made by al-Ablaj in late December 2003, when he warned that a new al-Qa'ida strike against the United States was imminent:

> Let them prepare now for more sorrows and let them prepare the coffins and the largest number of hospitals and graves. The coming days are full of surprises and major events

> that will make them an historic example. We will teach them painful lessons that they will never forget.[158]

He then outlined a number of possible attack scenarios that would be "distinguished by lethal strikes in depth," including the "poisoning of a drinking water plant that supplies an entire U.S. city and using the lethal sarin gas against U.S. human crowds" (as Aum Shinrikyo had done in Japan).[159]

As in the case of the remarks of Abu Shihab al-Qandahari, those of al-Ablaj may well be nothing more than examples of false jihadist bravado or components of intentional disinformation and psychological warfare campaigns designed to mislead or frighten Western audiences, especially since al-Ablaj made various other assertions that were either undeniably false or arguably fantastic.[160] Hence these and other jihadist claims implying that al-Qa'ida already possesses and/or is simply waiting for the right moment to employ CBRN weapons cannot be taken at face value, all the more so since such weapons have been neither displayed nor used during the intervening period.

However that may be, the objective of attacking the U.S. homeland with WMD was explicitly articulated by Abu Mus'ab al-Suri in an open letter to the U.S. administration published in December 2004, in which he implicitly criticized Usama bin Ladin for not employing WMD on 9/11 and went on to make other provocative remarks:

> If I had been consulted in the case of [the 9/11] operation I would have advised them to select aircraft from other countries and to have put weapons of mass destruction aboard them. Attacking America with weapons of mass destruction was—and still is—a difficult and complicated matter, but it is still a possibility in the end, if Allah permits us. More importantly, it is becoming a necessity....if those engaged in *jihad* establish that the evil of the infidels can be repelled only by attacking them with weapons of mass destruction, they may be used *even if they annihilate all the infidels.*[161]

He then went on to claim that "defeating America and ending its ambitions of global hegemony is a matter of life and death for Muslims," but said this could only be achieved in one of three ways. The first was if Allah would "send a calamity down upon it and destroy it by natural disasters, comets, earthquakes, volcanoes, or a drowning flood," as some scholars have prophesied, but in the meantime he cautioned Muslims not to neglect their duty to continue the fight. The second was in the wake of Muslim resistance and guerrilla campaigns, but this would "require a long period of time and great sacrifices..." The third was through the use of WMD:

> Finally, the last option: to destroy America through strategic and decisive operations involving weapons of mass destruction—nuclear, chemical, or biological. The mujahidin may be able to obtain these weapons by cooperating with whomever already possesses them, by buying them, or by building and using primitive radioactive weapons known as "dirty bombs"...it is not a far cry from justice to adopt the slogan, "Dirty Bombs for a Dirty Nation." This is practically equal treatment. Let the American people—those who voted for killing, destruction, the looting of other nations' wealth, megalomania, and the desire to control others—be contaminated with radiation! We apologize for the radioactive fallout.

Here, in short, Abu Mus'ab is looking forward to the destruction of America, if necessary by means of the use of CBRN weapons.

Even more revealing, in a 1999 videotaped lecture series entitled "Jihad is the Solution"—that is, long before the post-9/11 American invasions of Afghanistan and Iraq—Abu Mus'ab had already clearly indicated his desire to carry out a strategic strike on American soil designed to cause mass casualties and widespread psychological trauma. Here are some telling excerpts from one of his lectures:

> Guerrilla warfare in [infidel] countries should be based upon the infliction of large human losses. This is very important! To cause large human losses! Secondly, in their countries, we have to start thinking about the use of weapons of mass destruction in terrorism. You understand? In their countries, we have to use weapons of mass destruction in terrorism. You add one kilogram of uranium to some explosives and you go and pollute some 50 countries altogether....Why? Because between us and these people there has to be a strategic balance...If you take away weapons of mass destruction, there is no parity.... These human losses [in their countries] must be caused by weapons of mass destruction....Weapons of mass destruction are nuclear. They are quick and easy and can be obtained from most mafias in the world. This is a strategic weapon. Nuclear weapons have become mafia merchandise. They are sold...in Uzbekistan and Pakistan. It is a beautiful and fantastic thing that the uranium sources in the world are located in the region in which we are now moving. Understand? The reservoirs of uranium in the world are in Central Asia.[162]

Although Norwegian Arabist Brynjar Lia rightly notes that several of Abu Mus'ab's assertions here reveal a lack of technical expertise and effectively gloss over the great difficulties of obtaining, storing, and deploying such materials and weapons, there can be no doubt that the jihadist theoretician would like to be able to carry out acts of terrorism in Western countries using them.[163]

It is in this context that one must consider a couple of the lesser known actions undertaken or proposed by al-Qa'ida that seem designed to facilitate the eventual acquisition or deployment of CBRN weapons. First, in an internal document describing the organizational committees within al-Qa'ida, there is a reference to both a "Nuclear Weapons Section" (*qism al-aslaha al-nawa'iyya [sic]*) and a "Special Operations Section" (*qism al-'amal al-khass*) within the group's Military Committee (*al-lajnat al-'askariyya*). Under the description of the Special Operations Section, it indicates that the section's supervisor must "possess the appropriate amount of scientific knowledge which qualifies him for performing his job," that is, not "less than [that of] a university graduate," and, ideally, also be a "military academy graduate."[164] This brief document may assume a more ominous significance given that in his military treatise, Abu Mus'ab al-Suri specifically advocates the creation of "strategic operations brigades" (*saraya al-'amaliyyat al-istratijiyya*) that "must possess knowledge of operational capabilities and be in possession of, and able to utilize, weapons of mass destruction in time of need for either reciprocal treatment or for the *strategic termination of the conflict with America*."[165] The latter phrase is clearly an oblique reference to an offensive nuclear or biological attack on American soil. This should not come as any surprise considering Abu Mus'ab's frequent emphases on the need to cause mass casualties.

Although it is very clear that al-Qa'ida and certain affiliated groups have a great interest in acquiring or producing CBRN weapons, from the conflicting statements provided above it is still not entirely clear exactly how they might eventually decide to employ such weapons should they ever manage to obtain or produce them. At present there are ambiguous indications that they might be used for deterrence, in a tactical manner on selected battlegrounds (in the case of chemical agents, as some 2007 attacks in Iraq suggest), or in a strategic strike on Western territories, and it may well be that final operational decisions concerning their deployment will not actually be made by key jihadist leaders until they actually have these weapons at their disposal.

In this context it needs to be emphasized yet again that it is often simply assumed, especially by uninformed or casual observers and the general public, that the only purpose terrorists might have for employing so-called "weapons of mass destruction" would be to cause mass casualties and massive physical damage. This assumption is generally false.[166] First of all, as experts have periodically noted, the only type of weapon included within the category of "weapons of mass destruction" that is actually capable of causing massive physical destruction is a nuclear weapon. None of the other types of WMD, that is, chemical, biological, or radiological (CBR) materials and weapons, are capable of causing such extensive physical damage. Indeed, of these three types of substances, only properly weaponized and disseminated biological agents could potentially generate a truly catastrophic number of casualties, meaning a number ranging from the tens of thousands to the millions. In marked contrast, chemical weapons proper, even if deployed in ideal conditions, would be capable of killing at most several thousand people, and the number of people who might be killed or wounded in an attack with a radiological dispersal device or "dirty bomb" would be dependent primarily upon just how powerful the conventional explosives with which the radiological materials were mixed turned out to be (although, depending on the type of radiological materials used, many others could instead be killed by direct exposure to radiation).

Second, CBRN materials and weapons can be—and indeed historically have been—used for a wide variety of purposes.[167] The most obvious of these purposes, as noted above, would be to try and inflict mass casualties on declared enemies. However, the most important single factor that would arguably motivate terrorists—in the strictest sense of that term[168]—to employ CBRN weapons would be the desire to exert a tremendous psychological influence on one or more target audiences, perhaps including both their enemies, who would be stunned if not cowed, and their supporters, who would be impressed if not inspired. Given the ubiquity of mass casualty Islamist bombings using a variety of improvised explosive devices (IEDs), it seems likely that only attacks using similar types of "conventional" materials that resulted in many hundreds or thousands of deaths would nowadays have the same psychological *frisson* as successful acts of CBR terrorism, whatever their scale. In that sense CBRN weapons are almost ideally suited for terrorism proper, since their employment is almost guaranteed to exert a disproportionate impact upon the emotional states of the wider audiences that terrorists are by definition trying to influence or traumatize with their acts of violence.[169] Finally, in addition to these two primary motivations, there are also a number of other reasons why jihadists might opt to employ CBR materials—to assassinate individual "Crusaders," "polytheists," or "apostates" with toxic materials; to contaminate key facilities or vital areas of Western cities; or even because they are generally well-suited for covert delivery.[170]

Finally, one noteworthy point in this context is that the number of references to WMD is surprisingly limited in available jihadist primary sources. This relative paucity can be interpreted in one of two ways. If one is inclined toward skepticism regarding jihadist claims, one might concur with Paz's suggestion that this may well be an indication that the development and use of CBRN materials are not operational priorities for al-Qa'ida and affiliated groups, an interpretation that tends to reinforce the more generalized arguments of those specialists who believe that terrorists are unlikely to employ WMD because they tend to be conservative with respect to both weapons selection and operational techniques. After all, why should veteran terrorist groups bother experimenting with new and dangerous weapons that are difficult to handle and might not actually be effective when they can more easily continue to rely on weapons and techniques that are tried and true, such as IEDs? However, those with a more pessimistic or alarmist disposition might instead interpret the relative absence of discussion about "weapons of mass destruction" in jihadist sources as an indicator that key groups within this milieu are jealously guarding vital information concerning their presumably top secret CBRN efforts in order not to provide their enemies with any indications of what they plan to do, as certain above-cited comments of al-Ablaj suggest. Although this question will undoubtedly be answered, one way or another, with the passage of time, at present it remains difficult to determine exactly where the truth lies between these contending positions.

Lest anyone find the historical patterns of actual CBR terrorism, the relative lack of references to WMD in jihadist sources, or al-Qa'ida's reported internal disputes about how to employ these materials to be overly reassuring, it should by now be clear that key figures or factions within the jihadist milieu seem motivated and indeed determined to employ "weapons of mass destruction"—at some point—in a strategic strike against the homeland of the United States or, if that is not possible, one of its close European allies. Their fanatical hatred of "infidels," their propensity for carrying out spectacular mass casualty attacks, and their oft-stated desire to eradicate "evil" and annihilate the "enemies of Islam" make them especially prone to try to carry out catastrophic attacks of this sort, irrespective of their propagandistic blather about "defensive jihad" and their periodic references to "deterrence." For that reason, it is probably only their apparent inability to acquire or produce effective CBRN weapons that has thus far inhibited them from attempting such a strike. In any case, the world cannot afford to blithely assume that such weapons will never end up in jihadist hands, much less that those *mujahidin* who prefer to target the "far enemy" would have serious moral scruples about employing them.

CONCLUSION

In sum, it is precisely the above-noted combination of (1) delusional, utopian, and non-negotiable goals, which ultimately derive from a theologically based and fanatical "fantasy ideology," and (2) a ruthless operational efficiency capable of causing tremendous damage, that makes al-Qa'ida and its affiliates such dangerous and formidable adversaries. If these groups actually had rational, limited, negotiable aims, as Scheuer insists, it would be vastly preferable.[171] In that case, compromises could be made by both sides, and it might well be possible to come to some sort of acceptable agreement or settlement that would serve to limit the ongoing campaign of jihadist violence that is nowadays being incited and partially organized and executed by Bin Ladin. No serious observer can honestly believe, however, that even if the United States and its allies suddenly acceded to all of Bin Ladin's proximate and relatively limited but still expansive demands, that the *mujahidin* affiliated with al-Qa'ida and the other Islamist terrorist groups would then be willing to lay down their arms, say "thank you," and initiate peaceful and mutually beneficial relations with the *dar al-kufr*.[172] Such a naïve illusion, which completely ignores their underlying religious intolerance and fanaticism, can scarcely be reconciled with the ongoing flood of utterly uncompromising statements that Bin Ladin and other jihadist spokesmen have made over the years, above all in Arabic-language materials that most Westerners cannot read. Yet even in his December 1998 interview for al-Jazira, Bin Ladin made the following revealing statement: "Every Muslim, from the moment they realize the distinction in their hearts, hates Americans, hates Jews, and hates Christians. That is part of our belief and our religion." Or elsewhere in that same interview, when he refers to non-Muslims as mankind's "devils and demons" and boasts that "we are continuing on this path [of *jihad*] until we meet God Almighty."[173] Nor is his meaning any less clear in another interview for al-Jazira, this one dating from October 21, 2001, when he says that the "disbelieving fornicators" may choose whether or not to fight Muslims, but the latter have no choice but to fight everyone in the "ranks of the Jews."[174] Similar hardline views have also repeatedly been expressed by Shi'i Islamists, as when the then leader of al-Amal al-Islami (Islamic Amal), the Iranian-backed Shi'i militia in Lebanon, Husayn Musavi, made the following bellicose statement on November 14, 1985: "We are not fighting so that the enemy recognizes us and offers us something. We are fighting to wipe out the enemy."[175] Needless to say, when the only alternatives that presently remain open to Western "infidels" are capitulating and converting to a strict, puritanical version of Islam, on the one hand, or fighting to defend the values, interests, and territories of Western civilization, on the other, there is absolutely no choice but to fight, and to fight ruthlessly and effectively. This, in turn, requires that Western democracies understand the true nature of their enemy, properly interpret his intentions and objectives, and take appropriate countermeasures. Up until now, governments in the West have generally failed on all three counts.

In the final analysis, there is one seemingly insurmountable difficulty that faces any state or society that is confronted by hostile, violence-prone religious extremists: their stubborn maintenance of faith that their agendas and actions are "divinely sanctioned," even in the face of looming defeat and disaster. This is because when things are going their way, they attribute all of their good fortune to the support and will of God, but when things cease going their way, they rarely draw the equally logical but opposing conclusion—that God, in his supposedly infinite wisdom, has decided to withdraw that favor because they have sinned or are otherwise no longer worthy of it. On the contrary, they almost invariably conclude that God is increasing their suffering and misfortune precisely in order to test their faith, and then respond by renewing and redoubling their efforts to achieve their goals. In short, to the extent that they are absolutely convinced that God is on their side and that the enemy is inherently evil and ungodly, they are unusually hard to deter or permanently undermine the morale of. Such an attitude is particularly problematic if such extremists are determined, however long it may take them, to acquire, produce, and deploy CBRN weapons, as some global jihadists seem to be.

NOTES

1. In recent years the author has profited from informal interactions concerning (1) the "rationality" of political and religious extremists and/or (2) Islamism with a number of specialists, including Gary Ackerman, Sammy Salama, Adam Dolnik (three former colleagues at the Monterey Institute of International Studies), Kevin Coogan, Martha Crenshaw, Walter Laqueur, Bassam Tibi, Lorenzo Vidino, Phil Williams, and Alex P. Schmid, although none of them should be blamed for any errors or presumed to share the interpretations herein. I would also like to thank Douglas Borer at the Naval Postgraduate School for allowing me to offer lectures on these topics in his classes.
2. Proverb quoted by the disgruntled al-Qa'ida insider Abu al-Walid al-Masri, in the context of a blistering critique of Usama bin Ladin's strategic blunders in a book serialized by *al-Sharq al-Awsat* and thence cited by Fawaz A. Gerges, *The Far Enemy:*

Why Jihad Went Global (New York: Cambridge University, 2005), 195. Here it applies to the general failure of Western analysts and policymakers to understand the ideologies and objectives of global jihadist networks and, as a result of that failure, their unfortunate pursuit of mistaken and counterproductive policies in the "war against terrorism."

3. Abu Mus'ab al-Suri, *Da'wa al-muqawwama al-islamiyya al-'alamiyya* [*The Call for Global Islamic Resistance*], 1381.
4. These remarks were made on al-Jazira by a Shi'i cleric in Iraq, but one who was an advocate of Sunni–Shi'i collaboration in resisting the Americans and was therefore exempted from attack back in 2004 (along with Muqtada al-Sadr and Jawad al-Khalisi, other Shi'i figures with similarly radical views) by the sectarian, rabidly anti-Shi'i Sunni leader of al-Qa'ida fi Bilad al-Rafidayn (Al-Qa'ida in Mesopotamia), Abu Mus'ab al-Zarqawi. Excerpts from the Grand Ayatollah's remarks have been translated as "Iraqi Ayatollah Ahmad al-Baghdadi Talks of America's Annihilation and the Muslim Conquest of the World; Declares Support for Nuclear Bombs for Muslim and Arab Countries," MEMRI #1166, May 18, 2006, available at http://www.memri.org/bin/articles.cgi?Page=archives&Area=sd&ID=SP116606. Note, however, that henceforth this chapter will be focused primarily on Sunni jihadist groups with a global agenda, especially al-Qa'ida "central."
5. Among the noteworthy exceptions are Jeffrey M. Bale and Gary Ackerman, "How Serious is the 'WMD Terrorism' Threat?: Terrorist Motivations and Capabilities for Using Chemical, Biological, Radiological, and Nuclear (CBRN) Weapons," report prepared by the WMD Terrorism Research Program, Center for Nonproliferation Studies, 2005, Part II on motivations; the two volumes edited by Brad Roberts, *Terrorism with Chemical and Biological Weapons: Calibrating Risks and Responses* (Alexandria, VA: Chemical and Biological Arms Control Institute, 1997), and especially *Hype or Reality?: The "New Terrorism" and Mass Casualty Attacks* (Alexandria, VA: Chemical and Biological Arms Control Institute, 2000); Nadine Gurr and Benjamin Cole, *The New Face of Terrorism: Threats from Weapons of Mass Destruction* (London: I. B. Tauris, 2002), chapters 4–7; and Gavin Cameron, *Nuclear Terrorism: A Threat Assessment for the 21st Century* (New York: Palgrave Macmillan, 1999), chapters 2–4.
6. Bruce Hoffman, "Foreword," in Andrew Silke, ed., *Research on Terrorism: Trends, Achievements and Failures* (Portland, OR and London: Frank Cass, 2004),. xviii.
7. Jerrold M. Post, "Prospects for Nuclear Terrorism: Psychological Motivations and Constraints," in Paul Leventhal and Yonah Alexander, eds., *Preventing Nuclear Terrorism* (Lexington, MA: D. C. Heath, 1987), 91. Although this remark is nearly 20 years old and was made solely in reference to nuclear terrorism, the overall situation has unfortunately not changed all that much since then. For every article that discusses terrorist motivations for using WMD, there are dozens of "threat" and "vulnerability" assessments that focus almost exclusively on narrowly technical matters, including the technological capabilities that terrorists would need in order to launch a successful "WMD" attack.
8. Indeed, even using the term "strategy" is somewhat problematic when discussing relatively small, sectarian extremist groups that rarely if ever field conventional military forces or employ conventional military methods. The word, which derives from the ancient Greek term *strategia* (meaning "generalship"), has both a general meaning and one that is specifically related to the conduct of military operations. In the general sense, it can be defined as "a plan of action or policy designed to achieve a

major or overall aim," whereas in a narrowly military context it signifies "the art of planning and directing overall military operations and movements" in a war or campaign. See *The Oxford American English Dictionary* (New York: G. P. Putnam, 2002), 1361. In the latter context, it is usually distinguished from the term "tactics," which refers to "the art of disposing armed forces in order of battle and of organizing operations, especially during contact with the enemy,"that is, the actual disposition and maneuvering of forces on the battlefield. See ibid., 1407. There are, of course, further distinctions that can be drawn between "grand strategy" (which refers to the most general decisions made concerning the deployment of armed forces to achieve national policies), "strategy," "grand tactics" (which concerns the maneuvering of forces in a particular region prior to engaging in battle), and "tactics," but these need not concern us here. For our purposes, the terms "strategy" and "strategic" will be used loosely to refer to both al-Qa'ida's broader political objectives and the quasi-military operational methods they have opted to employ to achieve those objectives.

9. For more on von Clausewitz's ideas about war and its relation to politics, see especially Carl von Clausewitz, *On War*, translated by Michael Howard and Peter Paret (Princeton, NJ: Princeton University PRess, 1989). For scholarly analyses of his ideas and their influence on modern strategic thought, see Peter Paret, *Understanding War: Essays on Clausewitz and the History of Military Power* (Princeton, NJ: Princeton University Press, 1993), especially Part Two; and idem and Gordon A. Craig, eds., *Makers of Modern Strategy from Machiavelli to the Nuclear Age* (Princeton, NJ: Princeton University Press, 1986), especially Chapter 7. Clausewitz's most famous maxim is that "War is the continuation of politics by other means." This alone should imply that his ideas have little or no relation to those held by Usama bin Ladin.
10. Even al-Qa'ida military analysts have pointed out the shortcomings of Clausewitzian approaches. Note, for example, the comments of Abu Ubayd al-Qurashi, which in this case concern the impact of al-Qa'ida's organizational structure on U.S. military analyses and actions: "America today is facing a huge problem with Clausewitz's theories. The latter are premised on the existence of a centralized hostile power with a unified command. Assuredly, the mujahidin, with the al-Qa'ida organization in their vanguard, believe in decentralized organizations. Thus the enemy cannot ascertain the [mujahidin's] center of gravity, let alone aim a mortal blow at it." See Abu Ubayd al-Qurashi, "A Lesson in War," *Al-Ansar*, December 19, 2002.
11. *Magical thinking* is a term that seems to have been used first by nineteenth-century cultural anthropologists who sought to explain how members of traditional societies viewed the world, in particular the manner in which they explained natural phenomena in a prescientific context. Perhaps the most notable characteristic of magical thinking has to do with misperceiving or misunderstanding causation processes by, for example, confusing correlation with causation. Several classic examples of magical thinking were provided by E. E. Evans-Pritchard, *Witchcraft, Magic, and Oracles among the Azande* (Oxford: Clarendon, 1967), Chapter 2, in which the Azande explained diverse events by attributing them to witchcraft rather than natural causes.
12. This is somewhat misleading, however, insofar as it suggests that the other committees of the Majlis al-Shura are concerned primarily with "nonmilitary" affairs. In fact, what the military committee is concerned with are operational matters, whereas the financial committee and training committees are both concerned with logistical matters and the so-called *fatwa* committee is concerned with evaluating the religious appropriateness of the tangible actions to be undertaken by the group.

13. The precise number of rank-and-file members has fluctuated considerably over time and probably reached its lowest ebb after the U.S. military and its Afghan allies toppled the Taliban regime and drove the surviving al-Qa'ida fighters across the Afghan frontier into the Pashtun tribal zones of Pakistan.
14. Bin Ladin's obsession with the apostasy of the Saudi regime and its ongoing persecution of radicals is frequently reflected in his public statements. Likewise, to this day al-Zawahiri is engaged in polemics with former jihadist comrades in Egypt over tactics and their decision to renounce violent struggle. See, for example, his bitter polemics with Muntasir al-Zayyat, which can in part be followed by comparing Montasser al-Zayyat, *The Road to Al-Qaeda: The Story of Bin Laden's Right-Hand Man* (London: Pluto, 2004), especially chapters 4–8, and al-Zawahiri, *Fursan tahta rayat al-nabi' [Knights under the Prophet's Banner]*, serialized in *Al-Sharq al-Awsat* in December 2001, parts 8-9. Compare also Gerges, *Far Enemy*, especially chapters 3 and 4.
15. See, for example, Jason Burke, *Al Qaeda: Casting a Shadow of Terror* (London: I. B. Tauris, 2003), 7–22; Erik Schechter, "Generic Jihad," *Jerusalem Post*, December 5, 2003; and Jerry Mark Long, "Strategic Culture, al-Qaida, and Weapons of Mass Destruction," SAIC report prepared for the Defense Threat Reduction Agency, November 20, 2006, 3–4.
16. This interpretation has been promoted by Marc Sageman in two influential books, *Understanding Terror Networks* (Philadelphia: University of Pennsylvania, 2004) and, with even more force, in idem, *Leaderless Jihad: Terror Networks in the Twenty-First Century* (Philadelphia: University of Pennsylvania Press, 2008).
17. However, these cells did have some reported links, at least indirectly, to members of certain terrorist networks linked to al-Qa'ida (respectively, the Groupe Islamique Combattant Marocain [GICM: Moroccan Islamic Combat Group] and Lashkar-i Tayyiba [Army of the Pure] in Pakistan). For the Madrid bombings as the product of a purely local cell, see Daniel Benjamin and Steven Simon, *The Next Attack: The Failure of the War on Terror and a Strategy for Getting it Right* (New York: Henry Holt, 2005), 3–16; and, more recently, Scott Atran and Marc Sageman, "The Great Train Bombing," preliminary draft report, October 10, 2007, 5–12 and passim, available at www.healthsystem.virginia.edu/internet/ciag/london/Madrid-Bombing-10Oct07.pdf. For the view that the Madrid cell was in various ways connected to broader jihadist networks, including those linked to al-Qa'ida, see Lorenzo Vidino, *Al Qaeda in Europe: The New Battleground of International Jihad* (Amherst, NY: Prometheus, 2005), 295–340. The most detailed account of the Madrid bombings is provided in Administración de Justicia, Juzgado Central de Instrucción No. 6, Audencia Nacional, Madrid, *Sumario No. 20/2004*, April 10, 2006. See further Casimiro García-Abadillo, *11-M: La venganza* (Madrid: Esfera de los Libros, 2004); José Maria Irujo, *El agujero: España invadida por la yihad* (Madrid: Santillana, 2005); Juan Poyatos and Rachid Boutarbouch, *Viaje al origen del 11-M: Un análisis criminológico para saber por que?* (Mallorca: Centro Balear de Estudios para la Cooperación, 2005); and, for the political effects, Miguel Platón, *11-M: Como la Yihad puso de rodillas en España* (Madrid: Esfera de los Libros, 2005). For the ideological background of jihadist animosity toward Spain, see Gustavo de Arístegui, *La Yihad en España: La obsesión por reconquistar Al-Andalus* (Madrid: Esfera de los Libros, 2005). For the 7/7 bombings, see the recent report by the British authorities, United Kingdom, House of Commons, Intelligence and Security Committee, *Report of the Official Account of the Bombings in London on 7 July 2005, 11 May 2006* (London: Stationery Office, 2006). See

further Sean O'Neill and Daniel McGrory, *The Suicide Factory: Abu Hamza and the Finsbury Park Mosque* (London: Harper, 2006), esp. 269–76; Crispin Black, *7/7, the London Bombs: What went Wrong?* (London: Gibson Square, 2005); and Nafeez Mossadeq Ahmed, *The London Bombings: An Independent Inquiry* (Woodstock, NY: Overlook, 2006), which, despite the author's political biases, provides much useful material. New information has recently surfaced which indicates that the London bombers—like their Spanish counterparts—did not appear to have been an entirely autonomous group of disaffected locals, as was originally claimed. On the contrary, two members of the cell had reportedly traveled to South Asia and established direct contact with Pakistani jihadists linked to Bin Ladin.

18. For examples of Bin Ladin's public and indeed proud claims to function as an instigator of jihadist terrorism, see Bruce Lawrence, ed., *Messages to the World: The Statements of Osama Bin Laden* (London and New York: Verso, 2005), 69 (where he says it is his duty is to motivate the *umma* to wage *jihad* against the United States, Israel, and their allies) and 107–108 (where he admits that he incited "martyrs" to carry out the 9/11 attacks in "self-defense," as well as inciting other attacks on Americans and Jews, which is a religious duty, and says that if this makes him a terrorist, so be it).
19. Compare Daniel S. Gressang IV, "Audience and Message: Assessing Terrorist WMD Potential," *Terrorism and Political Violence* 13:3 (Autumn 2001), 91: "Terrorist actions are purposive acts, designed to produce, directly or indirectly, expected outcomes.... Each act serves a purpose, whether the audience understands that purpose or not."
20. See especially Martha Crenshaw, "The Logic of Terrorism: Terrorist Behavior as a Product of Strategic Choice," in ed. Walter Reich, *Origins of Terrorism: Psychologies, Ideologies, Theologies, States of Mind* (Washington, DC: Woodrow Wilson International Center for Scholars, 1998), 7–24; Gordon H. McCormick, "Terrorist Decision Making," *Annual Reviews in Political Science* 6 (2003), 481.
21. Compare, for example, Gurr and Cole, *New Face of Terrorism*, 91. See also ibid., 80. Note, however, that these arguments were made in connection with terrorists' use of CBRN weapons, not in the context of general terrorist targeting.
22. This is the approach that is typically adopted, for example, by the insurance industry. In that context it makes some degree of sense, since the industry is primarily concerned with assessing the objective value of potential targets, as well as determining the probabilities that certain targets or types of targets will be hit, in order to establish economically viable rates. When counterterrorism analysts rely entirely on the same more or less "objective" criteria, however, they are bound to make errors.
23. From the days of Karl Heinzen in the mid-nineteenth century, certain radicals and observers have drawn a distinction between terrorism as a utilitarian and thus a relatively rational act and terrorism as an expressive act, above all an act of personal redemption. See McCormick, "Terrorist Decision Making," 477–478. Although these two categories are not necessarily discrete, much less mutually exclusive, some scholars rightly emphasize the individual and collective (i.e., group-oriented) psychological functions that terrorism serves rather than only its narrowly instrumental functions. See, for example, Jerrold M. Post, "Terrorist Psycho-Logic: Terrorist Behavior as a Produce of Psychological Forces," in ed. Walter Reich, *Origins of Terrorism*, 25–40.
24. For one such "expressive" motive, personal glorification, see Albert Borowitz, *Terrorism for Self-Glorification: The Herostratos Syndrome* (Kent, OH: Kent State University, 2005). For another, a burning desire to get revenge, see the psychological

analysis of Ramond H. Hamden, "Unresolved Trauma and the Thirst for Revenge: The Retributional Terrorist," in *The Making of a Terrorist: Recruitment, Tarning, and Root Causes*, ed. James. J. F. Forest, 1: Recruitment: 165–175 (Westport, CT: Prager, 2006)

25. For the "fantasy ideologies" characteristic of extremists, see Lee Harris, "Al Qaeda's Fantasy Ideology: War without Clausewitz," *Policy Review* 114 (August–September 2002), 19–36; and idem, *Civilization and its Enemies: The Next Stage of History* (New York: Free Press, 2004), 1–20. His ideas will be discussed further below.
26. George Friedman, *America's Secret War: Inside the Hidden Worldwide Struggle between the United States and its Enemies* (New York: Doubleday, 2004), 28, 33–38.
27. Ibid., 58.
28. Michael Scheuer, *Through Our Enemies' Eyes: Osama Bin Laden, Radical Islam, and the Future of America* (Washington, DC: Brassey's, 2006), xxiii–xxiv, 3–5, and especially 19: "What must be understood is that what bin Laden has said and done has everything to do with religion.... When U.S. and other Western leaders describe bin Laden as a terrorist problem, not a religious one, they mislead their publics"; and idem, *Imperial Hubris: Why the West is Losing the War on Terrorism* (Washington, DC: Potomac, 2004), xviii and passim, but especially xi: "The war bin Laden is waging has everything to do with the tenets of the Islamic faith." Note that this author shares Scheuer's view that "ideas are the main drivers of human history" and that, as per historian Perry Miller, they are "coherent and powerful imperatives to human behavior." See ibid, xvii. This is even more true for the leaders and members of extremist groups, whose raison d'être, identities, and purposes all derive primarily from their adherence to particular political and religious ideologies.
29. Ibid., 1–2.
30. Ibid., xviii, 8, 16–18.
31. Ibid., 17. Compare the politically distorted view of Michael Mann as it appeared in a blurb on the back cover of Lawrence, ed., *Messages to the World*: "Despite his religious rhetoric and the bloody means, Bin Laden is a rational man. There is a simple reason why he attacked the United States: American imperialism." The fact that Bin Ladin views the conflict between the believers and "infidels" to be a theological imperative that is "eternal" seems to have utterly escaped the attention of such people.
32. This is the clear implication of his analysis in ibid., 11–15, 17. Compare the argument of Mohammad-Mahmoud Ould Mohamedou, *Understanding Al Qaeda: The Transformation of War* (London: Pluto, 2007), 63–73. This particular work, which (according to a favorable blurb on the rear cover) "provides a much-needed secular understanding of Al Qaeda" [!!!], is very misleading.
33. See, however, the cautionary note by Thomas Hegghammer, "Global Jihadism after the Iraq War," *Middle East Journal* 60:1 (Winter 2006), 15: "the study of ideology is not an exact science and...our current concepts do not adequately capture the complexity of the phenomenon of Islamist militancy."
34. Harris, "Al Qaeda's Fantasy Ideology," 23.
35. Ibid., 25, for this and the two quotes immediately below.

36. For al-Qa'ida's desire to unite the *umma*, restore the historic power of the "righteous" Caliphate, and wage jihad against "Crusaders" and other unbelievers, compare the remarks of Bin Ladin in his October 21, 2001 interview for al-Jazira, cited in Lawrence, ed., *Messages to the World*, 121; and those of al-Zawahiri in *Fursan*, part 11.
37. Harris, "Al Qaeda's Fantasy Ideology," 33, 32.
38. Ralph Peters, "When Devils Walk the Earth: The Mentality and Roots of Terrorism, and How to Respond," in idem, *Beyond Terror: Strategy in a Changing World* (Mechanicsburg, PA: Stackpole, 2002), 22.
39. Ibid., 23.
40. Ibid., 27, 28, 29.
41. Ibid., 29.
42. Ibid., 30. Peters further argues, persuasively, that since the "health of any religious community can be gauged by the degree to which it rejects these bloody apostles of terror...the Islamic world's acceptance of apocalyptic terrorists as heroes is perhaps the most profound indicator of its spiritual crisis and decay."
43. For the rationalist view, see Friedman, *America's Secret War*, 34–6. Al-Qa'ida's own retrospective claims have been reported by journalist Fu'ad Husayn in his recent biography of Abu Mus'ab al-Zarqawi, *Al-Zarqawi, al-jil al-thani li-al-Qa'ida [Al-Zarqawi: Al-Qa'ida's Second Generation]* (Beirut: Al-Khayal, 2005), as serialized in *Al-Quds al-'Arabi* in May 2005, part 14; and by Bassam al-Baddarin, "Al-Qa'ida Drew Up Working Strategy Lasting until 2020: Plans for Broad 'Jihadist Front' Covering Afghanistan, Iraq, Iran, and Lebanon," *Al-Quds al-'Arabi*, March 11, 2005, citing an Internet text written by Muhammad Ibrahim Makkawi, "Al Qa'ida's Strategy to the Year 2020." Compare Abdel Bari Atwan, editor-in-chief of that same newspaper, in *The Secret History of al-Qa'ida* (London: Saqi, 2006), 221–222.
44. Compare Gerges, *Far Enemy*, 191–199; Bari Atwan, *Secret History of al-Qa'ida*, 180; and the recent book by Abu al-Walid al-Masri, a top Afghan Arab operative, *Tarikh al-Afghan al-'Arab* [*The History of the Afghan Arabs*], which was serialized in *Al-Sharq al-Awsat* in December 2004, part 2. Abu al-Walid is highly critical of Bin Ladin's judgment. Similar critiques were leveled against Bin Ladin and other global jihadists by Islamists who have repudiated violence and by jihadists who prefer to focus their efforts on overthrowing the apostate regimes in their own countries. See Gerges, *Far Enemy*, 200–214, 218–228, 234–340.
45. As his videotaped comments at a private November 9, 2001 dinner in Jalalabad, together with his lieutenants and a Saudi militant and guest named Khalid al-Harbi, clearly indicate. See Ben Fenton, "Damned by his Gloating Smile," *The Telegraph*, December 14, 2001. Bin Ladin's most revealing remarks on that occasion are also cited by Fawaz A. Gerges, *Journey of the Jihadist: Inside Muslim Militancy* (Orlando, FL: Harcourt, 2007), 206–209.
46. See Christopher Blanchard, "Al Qaeda: Statements and Evolving Ideology," *CRS [Congressional Research Service] Report*, November 16, 2004, 5 (italics added). Compare also his further conclusions: "Experience suggests that Al Qaeda's leaders believe that regular attempts to characterize Al Qaeda's actions as defensive and religiously sanctioned will increase tolerance of and support for their broader ideological program. *The identification of limited political objectives and the implication that their fulfillment will resolve broader grievances may help to mask the group's underlying ideological agenda.*" See ibid., 6 (italics again added).

47. Michael Doran, "The Pragmatic Fanaticism of al Qaeda: An Anatomy of Extremism in Middle Eastern Politics," *Political Science Quarterly* 117:2 (2002), esp. 177–182. Among those problematic assertions are (1) that "[f]anaticism...played no role in al Qaeda's miscalculation" in launching the 9/11 attacks (based on a disputable analogy between its decision and the miscalculations of the Arab powers in 1967 and Iraq in 1990); (2) that given their religious differences Usama bin Ladin's documented cooperation with Hizballah and the Iranian regime in the mid-1990s was ascribable solely to "pragmatism" (ignoring the facts that a) the *shaykh* has long consciously sought to dampen doctrinal disputes between Sunni jihadists; and b) not all of the factions within that milieu were equally sectarian or hostile towards the Shi'i); and (3) that al-Qa'ida, being an allegedly "rational actor," is "susceptible to the same kinds of analyses that...would apply to any other state or political movement in the Middle East" (as if there were no differences between the behavior of religious zealots, secular nationalists, and nation-states!!!). See ibid., 177–178.
48. For the general Muslim rejection of Western and other non-Islamic international laws, norms, and institutions, see Majid Khadduri, *War and Peace in the Law of Islam* (Baltimore: Johns Hopkins University Press, 1955), 44–46. Furthermore, in theory, Muslims also reject standard Western conceptions of international relations, including notions such as the balance of power and *realpolitik*. That this is also the jihadist and al-Qa'ida view is apparent. See Mary Habeck, *Knowing the Enemy: Jihadist Ideology and the War on Terror* (New Haven: Yale University Press, 2006), 74–75. This is confirmed by the comments of Bin Ladin, who stated that "no sane Muslim should take his grievances to the United Nations" or any other international bodies, which are "infidel, man-made organizations." See his December 1998 interview for al-Jazira, cited in Lawrence, ed., *Messages to the World*, 67–68. Compare also the remarks of al-Zawahiri, who argues that the battle between unbelief and Islam is universal, and specifically identifies the U.N., multinational corporations, international communications and exchange systems, international news agencies and satellite channels, and international relief agencies, "which are being used as a cover for espionage, proselytizing, coup planning, and the transfer of weapons," as being in the enemy camp. See al-Zawahiria, *Fursan*, part 11. Ironically, it is Islamic relief agencies that are often engaged in the sordid activities that he ascribes to their Western counterparts.
49. Khadduri, *War and Peace*, 45.
50. See, for example, *Qur'an* 9.33.
51. Compare *Qur'an* 9.5, 9.124, 47.4. The second option was originally confined to believers in the Abrahamic faiths or "people of the book" (*ahl al-kitab*), that is, Christians and Jews, but was subsequently extended to Zoroastrians and, at various times and places, even polytheists (such as Hindus).
52. In recent years there has been a lot of nonsense written on the subject of jihad, both by Muslims who have intentionally sought to conceal its nature and by naive academic apologists for both Islam and Islamism. The term *jihad* is derived from the verbal root *jahada*, which means to "strive," "struggle," or "exert oneself," especially in the path of Allah. While it is true that the *Qur'an* makes a distinction between the "greater jihad," that is, struggling against the evil within oneself, and the "lesser jihad," that is, waging armed struggle against unbelievers, and that medieval jurists recognized several distinct categories of jihad (e.g., jihad of the heart, of the tongue, of the hands, and of the sword), the fact remains that in both the *ahadith* and the early Muslim historical chronicles—apart from texts dealing exclusively with personal

piety and Sufism—the term normally refers to armed struggle against unbelievers. See E[mile] Tyan, "Djihad," in Bernard Lewis et al., *Encyclopedia of Islam: New Edition* [hereafter *EI2*] (Leiden: E. J. Brill, 1983 [1965]), 2: 538: "In law, according to general doctrine and in historical tradition, the *djihad* consists of military action with the object of the expansion of Islam and, if need be, of its defence...The notion stems from the fundamental principle of the universality of Islam: this religion, along with the temporal power which it implies, ought to embrace the whole universe, if necessary by force." For excellent analyses of the evolution of the meaning of *jihad*, see Michael Bonner, *Jihad in Islamic History: Doctrines and Practice* (Princeton, NJ: Princeton University, 2006); David Cook, *Understanding Jihad* (Berkeley and Los Angeles: University of California Press, 2005); Reuven Firestone, *Jihad: The Origin of Holy War in Islam* (New York and Oxford: Oxford University Press, 1999); and Rudolph Peters, *Jihad in Classical and Modern Islam* (Princeton, NJ: Marcus Weiner, 1996). In any event, despite the existence of multiple meanings, it is undeniable that radical Islamists invariably use the term *jihad* to refer to an armed struggle against unbelievers, and also that they have repeatedly sought to transform jihad (*bi-al-sayf*) from being a sixth "unofficial" pillar (*rukn*) of the Islamic faith into one of its official de jure pillars.

53. For the imperialistic nature of the early Islamic conquests, as well as of current global jihadist objectives, see Efraim Karsh, *Islamic Imperialism: A History* (New Haven, CT: Yale University, 2006), esp. 1–8, 207–234. Although Karch is a controversial figure, it is hard to deny that the term "imperialist" is applicable in this context.
54. The cases that are most often cited as examples of this practice are Muhammad's invitation to the Persians and Jews to adopt Islam under pain of invasion. See, for example, Muhammad ibn Isma'il al-Bukhari, *Kitab al-Jihad*, 147, 148, 149, and 151. However, the prototypical case is the invitation by a Muslim commander to the people of Yamama.
55. See, respectively, A[rmand] Abel, "Dar al-Islam," *EI2*, vol. 2, 127; and idem, "Dar al-Harb," *EI2*, vol. 2, 126. This bipartite division of the world seems to have first emerged during the 'Abbasid period, specifically in the later eighth century. See Roy Parviz Mottahedeh and Ridwan al-Sayyid, "The Idea of Jihad before the Crusades," in Angeliki E. Laiou and Roy Parviz Mottahedeh, eds., *The Crusades from the Perspective of Byzantium and the Muslim World* (Washington, DC: Dumbarton Oaks Research Library and Collection, 2001), 28.
56. See, respectively, D. B. McDonald and A[rmand] Abel, "Dar al-Sulh," *EI2*, vol 2, 131; and Halil Inalcik, "Dar al-'Ahd," *EI2*, vol. 2, 116.
57. Tyan, "Djihad," 539. Compare Rudolph Peters, "Jihad," in Mircea Eliade, ed., *The Encyclopedia of Religion* (New York: Macmillan, 1987), vol. 8. This traditional view is clearly accepted by Bin Ladin, who in an October 21, 2001 interview for al-Jazira argued that the clash of civilizations between the *dar al-Islam* and the *dar al-kufr* (Abode of Unbelief) is a reality proven in the *Qur'an* and *ahadith* of Muhammad, in contrast to the "fairytale" of "world peace" promoted by the West. Cited in Lawrence, ed., *Messages to the World*, 124–125.
58. Phares, *Future Jihad*, 50, 49.
59. Ibid., 56.
60. Ibid.
61. Scheuer, *Imperial Hubris*, 6–7.

62. Ibid., 8. In reality, there can be no doubt whatsoever that the jihadists are intrinsically and intransigently opposed to virtually every defining characteristic of modern Western civilization, including secularism (above all), pluralism, democracy, individual freedom (especially freedom of choice), materialism, and hedonism (which they regard as "immorality" and "decadence"). For an excellent overview, see Habeck, *Knowing the Enemy*, chapter 4. Anything that they perceive as undermining Allah's rule or sovereignty (*hakimiyya*), including man-made political systems of all types, is anathema to them.
63. He also fails to point out that Bin Ladin and his cohorts have consistently sought to manipulate the circumstances and terms under which jihad can legitimately be waged. See Gerges, *Far Enemy*, 3–4. Note also that for the jihadists, as for most medieval jurists, forcibly recovering territories that were once under Muslim control but were subsequently lost to Islam is considered "defensive jihad." Hence, if the jihadists sought to expel the Spaniards from Spain, the Serbs and Croats from the Balkans, the Russians from Turkic Central Asia, the Chinese from Uighur territory, the Christians from the southern Philippines, and the Indians from Kashmir and other Muslim-majority parts in northern India, from their point of view this would be considered "defensive" rather than "offensive" jihad.
64. For the penchant of the Islamists, and indeed Muslims in general, to believe in a host of absurd conspiracy theories, in the pejorative sense of that term, see Daniel Pipes, *The Hidden Hand: Middle East Fears of Conspiracy* (New York: St. Martin's, 1996). For more on the nature of conspiracy theories, see Jeffrey M. Bale, "Political Paranoia v. Political Realism: On Distinguishing between Bogus Conspiracy Theories and Genuine Conspiratorial Politics," *Patterns of Prejudice* 41(1): 45–60, 2007. However, the remarks above are not meant to imply that U.S. policies toward the Muslim world have not often been foolish and counterproductive, or that Muslims do not have many legitimate complaints and grievances about those policies.
65. Compare Long, "Strategic Culture, al-Qaida, and Weapons of Mass Destruction," 15–16. Still another benefit, according to al-Zawahiri, is that in the context of defensive jihad, "there are no rules or conditions" in the effort to "repulse the invading enemy who corrupts faith and the world...he must be expelled by all possible means." In short, there are no limitations on the methods that might be employed by the *mujahidin*. See his "Jihad, Martyrdom, and the Killing of Innocents," translated in Raymond Ibrahim, ed., *The Al Qaeda Reader* (New York: Broadway, 2007), 170.
66. See Usama b. Ladin, "Moderate Islam is a Prostration to the West," which has now been translated in ibid., 28.
67. Ibid., 31.
68. Ibid., 32.
69. Ibid., 54. A much more elaborate argument in support of terrorism can be found in the military treatise of Abu Mus'ab al-Suri, *Da'wa al-muqawwama*, 1374–1378. Therein Abu Mus'ab bitterly attacks Muslim scholars who criticize the jihadist employment of terrorism, argues that terrorizing the enemy is specifically sanctioned in the *Qur'an* and that assassinating enemy leaders is supported by the example of the Prophet, and draws a distinction between what he calls "blameworthy terrorism" (*irhab madhmum*), the "terrorism of falsehood [*irhab al-batil*]...which inflicts harm [on] and fear among the innocent without true cause," and "praiseworthy [or blessed] terrorism" (*irhab mahmud*), which is "carried out by the righteous that have been unjustly treated...[and] removes injustice from the oppressed...by terrorizing

and repelling the oppressor." See ibid., 1374–1375. Elsewhere, he proudly states "[y]es, we are terrorists towards God's enemies" (1376), and later devotes a small section to the "strategy of deterrence through terrorism" (1391–1393).

70. Scheuer, *Imperial Hubris*, xviii.
71. See, for example, David Cook, *Contemporary Muslim Apocalyptic Literature* (Syracuse, NY: Syracuse University, 2005), especially Chapters 6–9, which reveals that such literature is filled with apocalyptic notions stemming from the Christian, Jewish, and—perhaps most surprisingly—secular Western as well as the Islamic traditions; Timothy R. Furnish, *Holiest Wars: Islamic Mahdis, their Jihads, and Osama bin Laden* (Westport, CT: Praeger, 2005), especially Chapters 4 and 6 and Jean-Pierre Filiu, *L'Apocalypse dans l'Islam* (Paris: Fayand, 2008), esp. 105–206, 291–289. Compare also a forthcoming study by Yvonne Haddad. For earlier Muslim apocalyptic conceptions, see the outstanding study by David Cook, *Studies in Muslim Apocalyptic* (Princeton, NJ: Darwin, 2002). The term *mahdi* (literally "the [rightly] guided one") applies above all to the prophesied redeemer of Islam who is destined to emerge and transform the world into a perfect Islamic society before the Day of Resurrection (*yawm al-qiyama*), at which point he will fight alongside the returned Jesus (who has forsaken Christianity and embraced the authentic revelation, i.e., Islam) against the Dajjal (the Deceiver, i.e., Antichrist or false messiah). The word does not appear first in the *Qur'an* itself, but rather in early collections of *ahadith* that are considered reliable. See W[ilfred] Madelung, "Al-Mahdi," *EI2*, vol. 5, 1230–1238; and Furnish, *Holiest Wars*, 10–17.
72. Usama 'Azzam, "Are the Taliban and al-Qa'ida those who will Raise the Black Banners?," *al-Da'wa* Web site, March 9, 2003. Cited by Reuven Paz, "Global Jihad and the Sense of Crisis: Al-Qa'idah's Other Front," undated [but 2003] report, Intelligence and Terrorism Information Center at the Center for Special Studies, 1, available at http://www.intelligence.org.il/g_j/rp_d_11_03.html.
73. Ibid.
74. Muntada al-Jinn wa al-'Afarit Web site, available at http://www.jazanvoice.net/vb/forumdisplay.php?s=09676bd441afa83467c79a96220906c1&forumid=32. The name of the Web site means The Jinn [Spirits] and the Demons. Cited in ibid., 2.
75. One work that openly discusses whether Bin Ladin might in fact be the Mahdi is by Ihyab al-Badawi and Hasan al-Zawami, *Usama bin Ladin: Al-Mahdi al-muntazar am al-masikh al-Dajjal? Harb al-fana' wa barunat al-CIA [Usama bin Ladin: The Awaited Mahdi or the Dajjal? The War of Extermination and the Barons of the CIA]* (Cairo: Madbuli al-Saghir, 2002). Moreover, Furnish argues that Bin Ladin is not only perceived by many Sunnis to be the Mahdi, but that he may even view himself in this way. See Furnish, *Holiest Wars*, 156–160; and idem, "Bin Ladin: The Man Who Would Be Mahdi," *Middle East Quarterly* 9:2 (Spring 2002), esp. 56–59.
76. "Allah has not assigned our umma to know the person of the Mahdi prior to his Appearance," Markaz al-Dirasat wa al-Buhuth al-Islamiyya Web site, February 2003, previously available at http://www.conrado.net/_vit_inf/print.php?id=989&ty=pr&img=no. Cited in ibid., 2–3.
77. Al-Suri, *Da'wa al-muqawwama*, 1517–1599. Just prior to that chapter, he has a section concerning "omens" that forecast the eventual triumph of Islam, including the West's abandonment of God and all of the spiritual ills that have allegedly resulted therefrom: intellectual alienation, mental illness, rampant sexuality, alcohol and drug

use, high suicide and crime rates, "rebellion in phenomena like the Beatles and the hippies," and "sexually deviant individuals [homosexuals]." See ibid., 1502–1516 [quoted passages from 1507].

78. The more rational grievances expressed by Bin Ladin have been usefully categorized and summarized by Scheuer in *Imperial Hubris*, 11–14.
79. This was essentially the objective of 'Abdallah 'Azzam, who sought to form a jihadist "rapid deployment force" that could come to the aid of Muslims being subjected to "infidel" military control. See Gerges, *Far Enemy*, 135–138. Compare also the key texts of 'Azzam himself, such as *Ilhaq bi al-qafila [Join the Caravan]* (London: 'Azzam, 2001); and idem, *Al-difa' 'an ard al-muslimin, aham furud al-'ayn [The Defense of Muslim Lands: The Most Important of the Individual Duties]* (Jedda: Al-Mujtama', 1987). Both can also be found online, with partial English translations, on the Islamist Watch Web site: http://www.islamistwatch.org.
80. For one illustrative example, note the Islamist obsession to recover control over al-Andalus, that is, Spain. See Arístegui, *Yihad en España*, especially 119–155. Compare Bin Ladin's remarks in his December 1994 letter to Saudi religious scholar 'Abd al-'Aziz ibn Baz, head of the pro-regime "palace 'ulama," which he closes by asking Allah to help the *umma* re-establish *tawhid* (belief in the unity of God) in "stolen" Islamic lands such as Palestine and Spain. Cited in Lawrence, ed., *Messages to the World*, 14.
81. Phares, *Future Jihad*, 134–135, 161–169. Compare al-Zawahiri, *Fursan*, part 11; and Bari Atwan, *Secret History of al-Qa'ida*, 222, who, on the basis of Muhammad Makkawi's strategic treatise, notes that al-Qa'ida intends to bring down the United States, just as it previously brought down the Soviet Union, after which an "ultimate, definitive military clash between a mighty Islamic army and the 'nonbelievers,' often mentioned by bin Laden, will result in the victory and *global dominance of the Caliphate*. This is, at any rate, al-Qa'ida's dream." Italics added.
82. For analyses of this crucial reorientation of jihadist objectives, based primarily upon internal jihadist sources, compare Gerges, *Far Enemy*, especially 143–150; and al-Zayyat, *Road to Al Qaeda*, 68–70.
83. Sayyid Abul Al'a Maudoodi, *Jihad in Islam* (Lahore: Islamic Publications, 2001 [1939]), 8, 9, 19, 24.
84. Cited in Amir Taheri, *Holy Terror: Inside the World of Islamic Terrorism* (Bethesda, MD: Adler & Adler, 1987), unnumbered page directly before introduction.
85. See, for example, Sayyid Qutb, *In the Shade of the Qur'an*, translated and edited by Adil Salahi (Leicester: Islamic Foundation, 2003), vol. viii, 266. Compare the similarly intransigent views of Egyptian jihadist 'Abd al-Salam al-Faraj, author of *al-Farida al-Gha'iba*, cited in the translation of Johannes J. G. Jansen, *The Neglected Duty: The Creed of Sadat's Assassins* (New York: Macmillan, 1986), 193.
86. Qutb, *Shade of the Qur'an*, vol. vii, 133–134.
87. Ibid., vol. viii, 306.
88. Sayyid Qutb, *Milestones* (Beirut and Damascus: International Islamic Federation of Student Organizations, 1978), 139. Compare al-Suri, *Da'wa al-muqawwama*, 201–202, though he claims it is the enemies of Islam that cannot abide the coexistence of Islam, rather than vice versa.
89. Abu Qatada, as cited in Philip Webster and Richard Ford, "Extremist Clerics Face Prosecution for Backing Terror," *[London] Times*, 14 July 2005. In this passage the term *Rome*, although based upon an alleged prediction of Muhammad concerning the Muslim seizure of the city of Rome, refers not simply to the capital of Italy

and the locale of the Papal States, but to Christendom as a whole, that is, the West. Similar sentiments concerning the coming "opening" (*fath*), that is., conquest, of the West appear frequently on jihadist Web sites.

90. Sayf al-Din al-Ansari, "Wa yimhaq al-kafirin [And Exterminate the Infidels]," *Majallat al-Ansar* 16, August 10, 2002, 4–8, cited by Jonathan D. Halevi, "Al-Qaeda's Intellectual Legacy: New Radical Islamic Thinking Justifying the Genocide of Infidels," *Jerusalem [Center for Public Affairs] Viewpoints* 508, December 1, 2003, electronic 10–11. The 'Ad and the Thamud were pagan Arab tribes that were totally destroyed by God because they both rejected the efforts of ancient Arabian prophets, respectively Hud (Hebrew 'Eber) and Salih (Hebrew Shelah), to call them to abandon polytheism and embrace the one true God. Allusions to these stories can be found in the *Qur'an* 7:65–67, 11:58–59, and 26: 124–125, 142–143. Note also that the term *al-ansar* (the supporters) has a very precise and historically important meaning for Muslims, in that it was the name given to Muhammad's earliest supporters in the town of Medina, in contradistinction to the earliest Meccan Muslims who emigrated with the Prophet from Mecca to Medina in 622, who were known as *al-muhajirun* (the émigrés).
91. Sayf al-Din al-Ansari, "Yi'adhibuhum Allah bi-'aydikum," *Majallat al-Ansar* 16, August 24, 2002, 4–9, cited in Halevi, "Al-Qaeda's Intellectual Legacy," 11.
92. Cited in "Hamas MP/Cleric's Friday Sermon: We Will Conquer Rome, the Two Americas, and Eastern Europe," MEMRI, April, 14, 2008, available at http://www.memri.org/bin/articles/cqi?Page=countries&Area=Palestinian&ID=SP189508.
93. Given HAMAS' origins s a militarized component of the Palestinian branch of the Muslim Brotherhood as well as its bitter long-standing opposition to the secularism of the PLO (a genuine ethno-nationalist group), it is astonishing that many scholars continue to characterize HAMAS as a "nationalist" group rather than as a religiously-motivated Islamist group. Although there is no doubt that HAMAS has pronounced nationalist elements in its ideology, which is hardly surprising due to the context within which it is operating, its agenda has always been and still remains primarily religious—to establish a strict, puritanical Islamic state in Palestine and thence expel the Israeli "occupiers" from the al-Aqsa mosque and surrounding regions, at which point certain less circumspect HAMAS leaders (such as al-Astal) evidently hope to continue waging "offensive" *jihad* until the rest of the world is subjected to Islam.
94. For a secret Muslim Brotherhood plan to gain influence and eventual supremacy in the West via stealth and subversion, see Sylvain Besson, *La conquête de l'Occident: Le projet secret des islamistes* (Paris: Seuil, 2005), especially Chapters 1–2, 5–7. The actual document, entitled "The Project," appears in French translation on 193–205. For the universalist and frankly imperialistic objectives of HT, it is sufficient to visit its Web site, which among other items contains PDF files of numerous pamphlets put out by the group. See http://www.hizb-ut-tahrir.org.
95. Cited by Halevi, "Al-Qaeda's Intellectual Legacy," electronic 4.
96. Cited by Oni Golan, "One Day the Black Flag of Islam will be Flying over Downing Street," *Jerusalem Post*, July 2, 2003. Another al-Muhajirun member, Abu Yusuf, made the following alarming statement in 2004: "I would like to see the Mujahidin coming into London and killing thousands, whether with nuclear weapons or germ warfare. And if they need a safehouse, they can stay in mine." Cited in David Cohen, "Terror on the Dole," *Evening Standard*, April 20, 2004. This is the very same group that organized demonstrations in Britain in early 2006, ostensibly to protest the Danish cartoons satirizing Muhammad, at which marchers carried signs with messages such

as "Islam Will Dominate the World," "Exterminate Those Who Slander Islam," "Be Prepared for the Real Holocaust," "Freedom Go to Hell," "Europe is the Cancer, Islam is the Answer," and "Europe You Will Pay, Your 9/11 Is on Its Way!"

97. Al-Zawahiri, *Fursan*, part 11. Note also that he is a vociferous advocate of the Islamic doctrine of "loyalty and enmity" (*al-wala' wa al-bara'*), which enjoins eternal enmity toward, as well as dissociation from, unbelievers. See his treatise, "Loyalty and Enmity: An Inherited Doctrine and a Lost Reality," in Ibrahim, ed., *Al Qaeda Reader*, 66–115. This injunction derives from several rather explicit Qur'anic passages, including 3:28 and 5:51.
98. Cited in Lawrence, ed., *Messages to the World*, 69.
99. Shaykh Husayn b. Mahmud, "Let Them Find Ruthlessness in You," Sada al-Jihad online magazine, April–May 2007. For English excerpts, see "Senior Al-Qaeda Sheik: 'May Allah Send Someone Who will Kill them Even More Savagely...Tear their Hearts Out...Cut Their Heads Off, Tear Them Limb from Limb, and Shed Their Blood in Rivers,'" in MEMRI No. 1635, June 27, 2007, available at http://www.memri.org/bin/articles.cgi?Page=archives&Area=sd&ID=SP163507. Note, however, that Bin Mahmud points out that one of the benefits of ruthlessly killing the enemies of Islam is to deter others from attacking Muslims.
100. Ibid.
101. Sayf al-Din al-Ansari, "Ghazawat New York wa Washington," in Ghazwa 11 Sibtimbir: Kitab al-ansar li-muwajahat al-harb al-salibiyya, September 2002, 10–11. In pre-Islamic Arabia, the noun of unity *ghazwa* (pl. *ghazawat*) referred to an "expedition, usually of limited scope, conducted with the aim of gaining plunder." However, after the triumph of Islam, it was used specifically to refer to Muhammad's expeditions against "infidels." See T. M. Johnstone, "Ghazw," *EI2*, 2: 1055.
102. Cited in Alan Cullison, "Inside Al Qaeda's Hard Drive," *Atlantic Monthly* 294:2 (September 2004), 68.
103. Sulayman Abu Ghayth, "In the Shade of Lances: Why We Fight America," which first appeared on jihadist Web sites in June 2002. Portions of this text have since been translated into English and published in *The Al-Qaeda Documents*, vol. 3, 107–110 ed. Ben N. Venzke, (Alexandria, VA: Tempest/IntelCenter, 2003).
104. The actual text was formerly available at http://www.al-fhd.com/rsayl/doc/rsayl.damar.doc. It has been usefully cited and analyzed by Reuven Paz, "Yes to WMD: The First Islamist Fatwah on the Use of Weapons of Mass Destruction," *PRISM Special Dispatches* 1:1 (May 2003), 4–7. See the more extensive discussion below, in the section on possible WMD use.
105. Olivier Roy, *Globalized Islam: The Search for a New Ummah* (New York: Columbia University Press, 2004), 294. Compare also 55–56.
106. Here it may be worth briefly discussing the remarks of Norwegian Arabist Brynjar Lia concerning al-Qa'ida's rationality. At first sight, he seems to fall clearly within the "rationalist" camp: "In the aftermath of 9/11, it was commonplace to assert that al-Qaida pursued no underlying strategic plan. The accepted argument was that the obsessive fanaticism of jihadi terrorists, their religious dogmas, their pursuit of martyrdom, and visceral hatred for the West made them blind, and their behavior was not rooted in any kind of rational strategy. While this school of thought still has numerous protagonists, a growing number of studies have already begun to debunk the myth of a non-existent al-Qaida strategy." See his *Architect of Global Jihad: The Life of Al-Qaida Strategist Abu Mus'ab al-Suri* (New York: Columbia University Press, 2008), 4. Even so, Lia also emphasizes that Abu Mus'ab al-Suri, the subject

of his outstanding book, is atypical inasmuch as he was "a dissident, a critic, and an intellectual in an ideological current in which one would expect to find obedience rather than dissent, conformity rather than self-criticism, doctrinaire ideologues rather than introspective individuals," and a person who "discarded traditional jihadi rhetoric about God's promised victory in favor of brutal honesty, putting hard-nosed realism before religious wish-fulfillment and pragmatic long-term strategies before utopianism." See ibid., 3–4. Despite this, as will become clearer below, one can find many religiously based arguments and even some apocalyptic formulations in Abu Mus'ab's relatively pragmatic and "rational" writings.

107. See the extended discussion of al-Zawahiri, *Fursan*, part 11.

108. For example, Bin Ladin has explicitly stated that his goal was to "move, incite and mobilize the umma" until such time as it reached a "revolutionary ignition point." See, respectively, "Usama Bin Ladin's Message to Iraq," Al-Jazira, February 11, 2003; and "Bin Ladin Interviewed on Jihad Against U.S.," *Al-Quds al-'Arabi*, November 27, 1996. Both of these quotes are conveniently cited in Blanchard, "Al Qaeda: Statements and Evolving Ideology," 6. Compare the remarks of Bari Atwan, *Secret History of al-Qa'ida*, 225: "Al-Qa'ida wishes to foment a 'clash of civilizations,' with Christian fundamentalism opposed to Islamic fundamentalism, resulting in an eventual all-out war between the 'believers' and the *kafir*."

109. See al-Zawahiri, *Fursan*, part 11. On this point, many analysts who otherwise disagree seem to concur. See, for example, the remarks of Sarah E. Zabel, "The Military Strategy of the Global Jihad," U.S. Army, Strategic Studies Institute, Report, October 2007, 6–7: "Strikes against U.S. interests are planned *with the intention* that they incur a military response. Thus, in addition to the destruction of the direct object of the attack, the jihadis also benefit from drawing U.S. forces into hostile territory, an expensive effort that makes them vulnerable to attrition. At the same time, the barefaced U.S. invasion…incites Muslim wrath against the invaders" (italics in original). Compare the illuminating remarks of al-Qa'ida security chief Sayf al-Adl on the purposes of the 9/11 attacks, cited in ibid., 7. One should, however, keep in mind that claims like al-Adl's were post-facto explanations designed to make the jihadists seem especially prescient.

110. This was explicitly recognized by Usama bin Ladin himself. See his October 3, 2001 letter to Mullah 'Umar, where he wrote: "Keep in mind that America is currently facing two contradictory problems: (a) If it refrains from responding to *jihad* operations, its prestige will collapse, thus forcing it to withdraw its troops abroad and restrict itself to U.S. internal affairs. This will transform it from a major power to a third-rate power, similar to Russia; (b) On the other hand, a campaign against Afghanistan will impose great long-term economic burdens, leading to further economic collapse, which will force America, God willing, to resort to the former Soviet Union's only option: withdrawal from Afghanistan, disintegration, and contraction." Cited in Cullison, "Inside Al-Qaeda's Hard Drive," 70.

111. Phares, *Future Jihad*, 166–168.

112. For the factors involved in the U.S. failure to trap Bin Ladin's fighters at Tora Bora, a military blunder of tremendous import, see Philip Smucker, *Al Qaeda's Great Escape: The Military and the Media on Terror's Trail* (Washington, DC: Brassey's, 2004).

113. On the disastrous impact of the invasion of Iraq on support for global jihadism, see, e.g., Benjamin and Simon, *Next Attack*, xiv, 31–50; and Gerges, *Far Enemy*, 251–276. There is no doubt that jihadist leaders see the U.S. invasion of Iraq as a

golden opportunity to "bleed" the Crusaders and eventually erect an Islamic state in the historic heart of the *dar al-islam*. See Hegghammer, "Global Jihadism after the Iraq War," 17–24.

114. Hegghammer, "Global Jihadism," 15.
115. See, for example, al-Zawahiri's comments on the potential geostrategic impact should the Caucasus fall into the hands of local and global jihadists: "The liberation of the Caucasus would constitute a hotbed of jihad (or fundamentalism as the United States describes it) and that region would become the shelter of thousands of Muslim mujahidin from various parts of the Islamic world, particularly Arab parts. This poses a direct threat to the United States represented by the growing support for the jihadist movement everywhere in the Islamic world. If the Chechens and other Caucasian mujahidin reach the shores of the oil-rich Caspian Sea, the only thing that will separate them from Afghanistan will be the neutral state of Turkmenistan. This will form a mujahid Islamic belt to the south of Russia that will be connected in the east to Pakistan, which is brimming with mujahidin movements in Kashmir. The belt will be linked to the south with Iran and Turkey that are sympathetic to the Muslims of Central Asia. This will break the cordon that is struck around the Muslim Caucasus and allow it to communicate with the Islamic world in general, but particularly with the mujahidin movement." See al-Zawahiri's *Fursan*, part 7.
116. Hegghammer, "Global Jihadism after the Iraq War," 16–17. For the *fatawa* of the radical *'ulama*, see the book by Shmuel Bar, *Warrant for Terror: The Fatwas of Radical Islam and the Duty to Jihad* (Stanford, CA: Hoover Institution, 2006).
117. Ibid., 28.
118. Sayf al-Ansar, "Hurub al-jil al-rabi," *Majallat al-Ansar* 2, January 28, 2002). Compare also Abu Ubayd al-Qurashi, "Amrika wa mabadi' al-harb: Bayna al-nazariyya ila al-tatbiq [America and the Principles of War: From Theory to Practice]," *Majallat al-Ansar* 24, January 2, 2003.
119. Three unresolved questions concerning the texts cited below are (1) whether they amount to different versions of the same basic strategy, which may well be the case; (2) whether they constitute hyper-rationalist post-facto analyses of what has already occurred that are designed retrospectively to display al-Qa'ida's supposed "prescience," together with future optimistic prognostications; and (3) the extent to which they can be said to reflect al-Qa'ida's "official" strategy. The fact that they all surfaced around the same time period suggests that there was an effort by the group to make its strategic intentions known.
120. See Abu Bakr Naji, *Idarat al-tawahhush*, 11–22, for the general scheme, and 23–62, for specifics on how to manage the first two phases. Compare the brief analyses by Stephen Ulph, "New Online Book Lays Out al-Qaeda's Military Strategy," *Terrorism Focus* [Jamestown Foundation] 2:6 (March 17, 2005), 4–6; Bruce Tefft, "Al-Qa'ida Book on Managing Savagery," *Isralert*, March 8, 2005; and Jarrett M. Brachman and William F. McCants, "Stealing Al-Qa'ida's Playbook," *CTC [West Point Counterterrorism Center] Report*, February 2006, 6–10. This scheme echoes traditional guerrilla warfare strategies, which likewise involve weakening the enemy and rallying the masses, gradually establishing "liberated zones," and then expanding those zones at the enemy's expense until such time as the latter is fatally weakened. In short, this is little more than an Islamic version of the classic "oil spot" strategy. After the establishment of an Islamic state in the third stage, of course, Naji says that Muslims "will begin liberating the earth and humanity from the hegemony of unbelief and tyranny through the power of Allah." See ibid., 61.

121. See the analysis in Bari Atwan, *Secret History of al-Qa'ida*, 221–222. Compare al-Baddarin, "Al-Qa'ida Drew Up Working Strategy," *Al-Quds al-'Arabi*, March 11, 2005.
122. See Husayn, *Al-Zarqawi*, parts 14 and 15. This analysis may well represent a synthesis of the two texts cited directly above, as opposed to being based on other, unspecified jihadist sources. Unfortunately, the author was unable to obtain a copy of the actual book, given its relative scarcity in Western libraries.
123. Note, however, that the less histrionic jihadist proponents recognize that the hoped-for divinely ordained triumph of the *umma* over the West, above all America, may take decades if not centuries. See, for example, Qutub, *Milestones*, 7–9; Abu Mus'ab al-Suri, interview, *Al-Sharq al-Awsat*, January 23, 2005.
124. Ironically, because of the Bush administration's terrible mistakes in Iraq, the initial phases of these projected schemes seem to be developing according to jihadist projections.
125. Some of his analyses have been conveniently quoted verbatim in Michael Scheuer, "Assessing London and Sharm al-Sheikh: The Role of Internet Intelligence and Urban Warfare Planning," *Terrorism Focus* 2:15 (August 15, 2005), 6–8. A total of 22 issues of *Mu'askar al-Battar* were produced.
126. Sayf al-Adl, "Planning Special Operations," *Mu'askar al-Battar*, September 13, 2004.
127. For media reports on al-Qa'ida's alleged WMD activities, including the group's efforts to obtain CBRN weapons or materials, see Kimberly McCloud et al., "Chart: Al-Qa'ida's WMD Activities," Center for Nonproliferation Studies Web site, available at http://cns.miis.edu/pubs/other/sjm_cht.htm. Note that this chart only covers the period up to mid-2004, and that many of the claims reported in various media outlets were never actually substantiated.
128. Compare some of the entries in ibid.; Nic Robertson, "Disturbing Scenes of Death Show Capability with Chemical Gas," CNN, August 19, 2002; Alan Cullison and Andrew Higgens, "A Computer in Kabul Yields a Chilling Array of al Qaida Memos," *Wall Street Journal*, December 31, 2001; and Cullison, "Inside Al Qaeda's Hard Drive," 61–62. Note also the recent story by Josh Meyer, "Al Qaeda Said to Focus on WMDs," *Los Angeles Times*, February 3, 2008, which suggests that in the Pakistan frontier zone the group, under the auspices of its notorious CW expert, Midhat Mursi al-Sayyid 'Umar (or Abu Khabab al-Masri), "has regenerated at least some of the robust research and development effort that it lost when the U.S. military bombed its Afghanistan headquarters and training camps in late 2001...[and] is once again trying to develop or obtain chemical, biological, radiological or even nuclear weapons to use in attacks on the United States and other enemies." For more on Abu Khabab, see Evan Kohlmann, "Abu Khabab al-Masri: A Master of Terror," Counterterrorism Blog, January 18, 2006, available at http://counterterrorismblog.org/2006/01/abu_khabab_almasri_a_master_of.php. This individual was killed in South Wasiristan by a CIA drone on July 28, 2008. See "Al Queda confirms death of leading commander Al-MAsri," Associated Press, August 5, 2008.
129. Compare the alarmist views of Paul L. Williams in a series of books, including *Osama's Revenge: The Next 9/11—What the Media and the Government Haven't Told You* (Amherst, NY: Prometheus, 2004); *The Al Qaeda Connection: International Terrorism, Organized Crime, and the Coming Apocalypse* (Amherst, NY: Prometheus, 2005); and *The Day of Islam: The Annihilation of America and the Western World* (Amherst, NY: Prometheus, 2007), and the perhaps overly sanguine if not dismissive

views of Robin M. Frost, *Nuclear Terrorism after 9/11* (Abingdon and New York: Routledge/International Institute for Strategic Studies, 2005); and William R. Clark, Bracing for Armageddon? *The Science and Politics of Bioterrism in America* (New York: Oxford University Press, 2008), esp. Chapter 10. For a sober assessment see Brian Michael Jenkins, *Will Terrorists Go Nuclear?* (Amherst, NY: Prometheus Books, 2008.)

130. For an excellent short discussion of these matters, see Quintan Wiktorowicz and John Kaltner, "Killing in the Name of Islam: Al-Qaeda's Justification for September 11," *Middle East Policy* 10:2 (Summer 2003), esp. 85–90. Therein the authors further parse jihadist arguments concerning appropriate Muslim "rules of engagement and civilian targeting" by listing them under seven "conditions."

131. For more on these matters, see John Kelsay, *Islam and War: A Study in Comparative Ethics* (Louisville, KY: Westminster/John Knox, 1993), 59–-67; and idem, *Arguing the Just War in Islam* (Cambridge, MA, and London: Harvard University, 2007), esp. 104–110. Kelsay emphasizes that classical Muslim treatises on war "exhibit a strong inclination toward a position one might characterize as 'military realism,'" since once a war was determined to be "just," that is, initiated to expand or defend the *dar al-Islam*, their authors were "willing to grant wide latitude to commanders in the determination of appropriate means" even though such latitude was not "total." See ibid, 106, in his analysis of Muhammad ibn al-Hasan al-Shaybani's famous treatise, the *Kitab al-siyar*. For modern debates between jihadists and their critics over the appropriate aims and means for waging *jihad* to "resist" the enemy, see ibid., 129–151.

132. For explicit justifications for inadvertently killing other Muslims in the course of waging jihad and carrying out "martyrdom" operations, see al-Zawahiri, "Jihad, Martyrdom, and the Killing of Innocents," in Ibrahim, ed., *Al Qaeda Reader*, 161–173; and Abu Mus'ab al-Zarqawi, "The Return of Bin al-'Alqami's Grandchildren," speech posted by al-Qa'ida fi Bilad al-Rafidayn on jihadist message boards on May 18, 2005, originally available (among other sites) on the al-Hisba forum at http://www.alhesbah.com/v/showthread.php?t=23027. For an English translation of key excerpts from the latter, see "Abu Mus'ab al-Zarqawi: Collateral Killing of Muslims is Legitimate," MEMRI No. 917, June 7, 2005, available at http://www.memri.org/bin/articles.cgi?Page=archives&Area=sd&ID=SP91705. Note, however, that the Shi'i are not even considered to be genuine Muslims by the most sectarian Sunni radicals, who therefore have no qualms about intentionally killing them. See "Leader of Al-Qaeda in Iraq Al-Zarqawi Declares 'Total War' on Shi'ites, States that the Sunni Women of Tel'Afar Had 'Their Wombs Filled with the Sperm of the Crusaders,'" speech translated in MEMRI No. 987, September 16, 2005, available at http://www.memri.org/bin/articles.cgi?Page=archives&Area=sd&ID=SP98705, wherein al-Zarqawi refers to the Shi'i as *rafidiyin* (literally "rejectors [of the Truth]"), a term often applied by Sunni extremists to the Shi'i. Such provocative arguments nonetheless generated considerable debate and even outright opposition from other, less sectarian Sunni Islamist circles. For the justifiability of *intentionally targeting* as well as inadvertently killing categories of "infidels" that Muslims are ostensibly forbidden to attack, see [al-Qa'ida], "A Statement from Qa'idat al-Jihad Regarding the Mandates of the Heroes and the Legality of the Operations in New York and Washington," which was originally posted on the Markaz al-Dirasat wa al-Buhuth al-Islamiyya Web site on April 24, 2002—a text that unfortunately does not appear in the existing collections of English-language translations of al-Qa'ida statements—see the discussion in Wiktorowicz and Kaltner, "Killing in the Name of Islam," 76–92.

133. For an example of Islamist opposition to the possible use of nuclear weapons against the United States, see Abu Zabadi, "Religious Grounds for [Launching] a Nuclear Attack," al-Firdaws Web site, April 12, 2007, some excerpts from which (and hostile responses to) can be found in "Is it Legitimate to Use Nuclear Weapons against the West? A Debate on an Islamist Forum," MEMRI #1538, available at http://www.memri.org/bin/articles.cgi?Page=archives&Area=sd&ID=SP153807.
134. See Ibrahim, ed., *Al Qaeda Reader*, 201–202.
135. "American Al-Qaeda: U.S. Should Convert to Islam," CNN, September 3, 2006, available at http://www.cnn.com/2006/WORLD/asiapcf/09/02/zawahiri.tape/index.html. Excerpts from this address, "An Invitation to Islam," along with the actual tape, which was produced by al-Qa'ida's media company, al-Sahab, can be accessed at Laura Mansfield's Web site, lauramansfield.com, at http://www.lauramansfield.com/j/zawahiri090106.asp.
136. Adam Gadahn, "An Invitation for Reflection and Repentence," translated by Laura Mansfield and posted in Jeffrey Imm, "Al-Qaeda's Gadahn—Transcript of the January 6 Message," *Counterterrorism Blog*, January 7, 2008, available at http://counterterrorismblog.org/2008/01/gadahn_010608_transcript.php.
137. Italics added. See Rahimullah Yusufzai, "Osama bin Ladin Lashes Out Against the West," *Time* magazine, January 11, 1999, available at http://www.time.com/time/asia/asia/magazine/1999/990111/osama1.html. Note that the last sentence cited in the above paragraph does not appear on the *Time* site itself, but rather in an October 7, 2001 version of the interview posted on ABC News, available at http://www.islamistwatch.org/blogger/localstories/05-06-03/ABCInterview.html.
138. Ibid.
139. This article has been translated as "Why We Fight America: Al-Qa'ida Spokesman Explains September 11 and Declares Intentions to Kill 4 Million Americans with Weapons of Mass Destruction," MEMRI Special Dispatch Series 388, June 12, 2002, available at http://www.memri.org/gin/printerfriendly/pf.cgi. All of the quotes in this paragraph have been drawn from that source.
140. Ibid.
141. Ibid.
142. Nasir ibn Hamid al-Fahd, "Risala fi hukm istikhdam 'aslihat al-damar al-shamil didh al-kuffar [A Treatise on the Legal Status of Using Weapons of Mass Destruction against Infidels]," May 21, 2003, originally available at http://www.al-fhd.com/rsayl/doc/rsayl.damar.doc. All the quotes in this paragraph are from this document.
143. Ibid. (italics added).
144. Abu Mus'ab al-Suri, "Message to the British and the Europeans—Its People and Governments—Regarding the London Explosions, July 2005," posted on various jihadist Web sites in August 2005, cited by Lia, *Architect of Global Jihad*, 307. Oddly, another version of this "final" Abu Mus'ab text does not include the passage referring to NBC weapons. See "Abu Musab al-Suri's Final 'Message to the British and Europeans,'" Global Terror Alert Web site, August 2005, available at http://www.globalterroralert.com/pdf/1205/abumusabeurope.pdf.
145. See Hamid Mir, "Osama Claims He Has Nukes: If US Uses N-Arms It Will Get Same Response," *Dawn* [Karachi], November 10, 2001, available at http://www.dawn.com/2001/11/10/top1.htm. In this context, the term "retort" is obviously employed in the archaic sense of "repay."

146. Cited in Peter L. Bergen, ed., *The Usama bin Laden I Know: An Oral History of al Qaeda's Leader* (New York: Free Press, 2006), 348. Mir also made a couple of other interesting remarks. First, he emphasized that the al-Qa'ida leader spoke only about chemical and nuclear weapons, and that he explicitly denied that the group had any link to the post-9/11 *Bacillus anthracis* letter mailings in the United States. Second, when Mir expressed skepticism that al-Qa'ida actually had nuclear weapons, al-Zawahiri replied that it was not difficult to purchase them: "If you have thirty million dollars, you can have these kind of [nuclear] suitcase bombs from the black market of Central Asia."
147. Abu Mus'ab al-Suri, *The Muslims in Central Asia and the Coming Battle of Islam*, cited and translated by Lia, *Architect of Global Jihad*, 307. Note further that there has been much speculation about Abu Mus'ab's involvement, along with Abu Khabab al-Masri, in training jihadists in the use of poisons and chemicals at the Darunta camp. Compare ibid., 299–304; and Paul Cruickshank and Mohamad Hage Ali, "Jihadist of Mass Destruction," *Washington Post*, June 11, 2006. Here it is also worth pointing out that Abu Mus'ab's reference to former Soviet-controlled areas of Central Asia and the Caucasus as a likely future source for nuclear and biological materials is echoed in a letter prepared by Hasan al-Tajiki, the "fifth letter" in a file addressed to al-Qa'ida's African Corps and entitled "Hawla al-jihad fi al-qawqaz" ["Concerning Jihad in the Caucasus"], wherein the author argues that Chechen mafia gangs "could let the Muslims of the Caucasus defy 'strategic impossibility' and set an historical precedent by becoming the first movement to engage in guerrilla warfare armed with nuclear weapons," since in theory nothing could "prevent the Chechen mafia from arming its people with nuclear weapons." Elsewhere he claims that once nuclear weapons become a "people's weapon" rather than one that is solely in the hands of the superpowers, "history will take a new course…" See Harmony document AFGP-2002-600053, 38, 33, available at http://ctc.usma.edu/aq.pdf/AFGP-2002-600053-Orig-Meta.pdf.
148. Al-Suri, *Da'wa al-muqawwama*, 1121.
149. Cited by Bergen, ed., *Usama bin Laden I Know*, 342–343. These quotes were combined by Bergen after being drawn from the following two sources: "Al-Sharq al-Awsat Review of a Draft Copy of…'The Story of the Afghan Arabs'…, Part 1," *Al-Sharq al-Awsat*, December 8, 2004, 11; and "Al Qa'ida's Hawks Sought Weapons of Mass Destruction through Fighter Khattab in Chechnya, Part 2," *Al-Sharq al-Awsat*, December 9, 2004, 15.
150. See Harmony document AFGP-2002-001120, 1–2, available from the Combating Terrorism Center at West Point at http://ctc.usma.edu/aq/pdf/AFGP-2002-001120-Orig.pdf. In that same letter, he claims that al-Qa'ida has already given some combat groups present in America and Europe the "green light to move." See ibid., 1.
151. The original Arabic text is no longer available online, but it has been translated both by Reuven Paz on the Israeli International Insitute for Counterterrorism in Herzliya's Web site as "The First Nuclear Threat against the United States," available at http://212.150.54.123/spotlight/comment/cfm?id=861, and in the book by Williams, *Day of Islam*, 13–14.
152. Paz, introduction to "The First Nuclear Threat against the United States."
153. For an analysis of this communiqué from al-Ablaj, see Ben Venzke, "al-Qaeda/al-Ablaj Threat Assessment, volume 1.0," IntelCenter report, May 30, 2003, 7, available at http://www.intelcenter.com/ATA-PUB-v1-0.pdf.
154. Ibid., 6–7.

155. Mahmud Khalil, "Report on An interview by Email with Abu Muhammad al-Ablaj, al-Qa'ida Training Official," *al-Majalla*, June 27, 2003, 10–11, translation available at http://alphabetcity.blogspot.com/2003/06/al-ablajs-latest-rant-mahmud-khalil-of.html.
156. Mahmud Khalil, "Al-Qa'ida's Abu Muhammad al-Ablaj on Bin Ladin, Weapons, U.S. Targets," *al-Majalla*, September 21, 2003, translation available at http://www.why-war.com/news/2003/09/21/alqaidas.html.
157. Ibid.
158. Mahmud Khalil, "Al-Qa'ida's al-Ablaj Warns 'Zero Hour' for Strike Inside U.S. Has Been Set," *al-Majalla*, December 28, 2003, translation available at http://www.why-war.com/news/2003/12/28/alqaidas.html.
159. Ibid. Such an attack on America never actually occurred within the period specified as "zero hour."
160. For example, al-Ablaj falsely claimed responsibility for the sudden failure of the electrical grid in parts of the United States and discussed an alleged al-Qa'ida plan to cause a catastrophe by setting off bombs on earthquake fault lines or in volcanic zones within the United States. See, respectively, Mahmud, "al-Ablaj on Bin Ladin," and idem, "al-Ablaj Warns 'Zero Hour.'"
161. "Communique from the Office of Abu Mus'ab al-Suri," December 22, 2004, 6. Italics added. For translated excerpts, compare Lia, *Architect of Global Jihad*, 306; and "Abu Mus'ab al-Suri and his Plan for the Destruction of America: "Dirty Bombs for a Dirty Nation," July 11, 2005, Global Terror Alert Web site, available at http://www.globalterroralert.com/pdf/0705/abumusabalsuri.pdf. All of the quotes in this paragraph below are from the latter source.
162. Transcript of Abu Mus'ab al-Suri, "Jihad is the Solution" videotape, cited by Lia, *Architect of Global Jihad*, 310–312. Of course, as per usual he justifies the adoption of such destructive weapons and extreme measures by claiming that the infidels are the aggressors who originally established the laws of "barbarous warfare."
163. For Lia's cautionary remarks, see ibid., 312. He also points out, quite rightly, that Abu Mus'ab's comments may have been designed to play on Western fears, and that the development of CBRN capabilities would require the kind of organizational centralization and hierarchy that is antithetical to his own emphasis on jihadist "leaderless resistance." See ibid, 313.
164. See untitled document, Harmony document #AFGP-2002-000078, 9, 11, available at http://ctc.usma.edu/aq/pdf/AFGP-2002-000078-Orig.pdf.
165. Al-Suri, *Da'wa al-muqawwama*, 1400 (italics added). In the HTML Arabic version of the text, this description appears on page 1398.
166. The points emphasized in the next two paragraphs summarize the more extended arguments made in Bale and Ackerman, "How Serious is the 'WMD Terrorism' Threat?," 14–20.
167. This can be determined from even the most cursory perusal of the cases in the Monterey WMD Terrorism Database, which is currently the most comprehensive open-source catalog of prior CBRN terrorist threats, hoaxes, and attacks. Therein one can find a plethora of schemes for using CBR agents, most of which involve poisoning or contaminating specific individuals and locales rather than generating mass casualties. For a nonsubscription version of this database, see http://cns.miis.edu/db/wmdt_demo/index.htm.

168. The definition of terrorism that I have been using for the past 25 years is as follows: "the use or threatened use of violence, directed against victims selected for their symbolic or representative value, as a means of instilling anxiety in, transmitting one or more messages to, and thereby manipulating the perceptions and behavior of wider target audience(s)." In short, terrorism is nothing more than a violent technique of psychological manipulation, and like all other techniques or tactics, it can be—and historically has been—employed by all sorts of protagonists and for a vast array of causes (e.g., by states, on behalf of states, and in opposition to states, by leftists, rightists, and centrists, by the religious and the irreligious, etc.). One qualification that needs to be made, however, is that the term *terrorism* should only be applied to asymmetric conflicts lest it be confused or conflated with efforts to influence wider audiences in the context of conventional military operations. Note also, in the interests of terminological precision, that the term *terror* refers to a psychological state marked by fear and anxiety, and must therefore be distinguished from terrorism. There is no such thing as a "terror network," only a "terrorist network."
169. Compare the remarks of Jonathan B. Tucker and Amy Sands, "An Unlikely Threat," *Bulletin of the Atomic Scientists* 55:4 (July–August 1999), 49, wherein some of the reasons for this disproportionate psychological impact are highlighted: "[CBW weapons] are generally invisible, odorless, tasteless, silent, and insidious," and as a result they tend to "evoke deep human anxieties and instill a qualitatively different type of terror" than, say, sudden explosions. The same is true of radiological contamination. In contrast, nuclear devices are so massively destructive that they would have a huge psychological impact for that reason alone.
170. Indeed, far from being used primarily to inflict large numbers of casualties in catastrophic attacks, CBR materials have thus far generally been deployed in "tactical or discrete attacks" to achieve limited and far more practical effects. See Jonathan B. Tucker, "Lessons from the Case Studies," in idem, ed., *Toxic Terror: Assessing Terrorist Use of Chemical and Biological Weapons* (Cambridge, MA: M.I.T., 2000), 267.
171. Compare Harris, "Al Qaeda's Fantasy Ideology," 33. Even Bari Atwan, whose portrayal of Bin Ladin and his group is relatively sympathetic, is forced to admit that "the prospect of opening negotiations with al-Qa'ida seems remote indeed...[although] this notion should not be completely ruled out...The problem, of course, is that al-Qa'ida's demands are global...." See *Secret History of al-Qa'ida*, 234.
172. Bin Ladin occasionally gives the impression that he is reasonable and would stop attacking "unbelievers" if only they would cease and desist. In his October 21, 2001 interview for al-Jazira, for example, he said "if our violators stop violating us, there is a way out." Cited in Lawrence, ed., *Messages to the World*, 126. However, his rare conciliatory statements seem to be designed primarily to sow confusion or dissension within "infidel" ranks.
173. Cited in ibid., 81, 92.
174. Cited in ibid., 128.
175. Cited in Taheri, *Holy Terror*, 16. Therein one can find numerous other quotations from Iranian clerics reflecting equally intolerant and extreme attitudes.

CHAPTER 2

Obedience to Divinity? The Psychology of Jihadist WMD Terrorism

Mark Dechesne

CONTENTS

> The ruling to kill the Americans and their allies—civilians and military—is an individual duty for every Muslim who can do it in any country in which it is possible to do it, in order to liberate the al-Aqsa Mosque and the holy mosque [Mecca] from their grip, and in order for their armies to move out of all the lands of Islam, defeated and unable to threaten any Muslim.
>
> **Usama bin Ladin, 1998**

INTRODUCTION

Quite a few terrorism scholars have read in these and other statements of Usama bin Ladin the emergence of a new form of terrorism that is assumed to deviate from traditional terrorism in a number of ways.[1] A moniker originally coined in a *Newsweek* article that appeared just after Ramzi Youssef led the first attack on the World Trade Center in 1993,[2] the "new terrorists" are described as being (1) focused on killing as a goal rather than as a means to achieve or advance a specific political agenda; (2) inspired by very general, often transcendental or millenarian ideologies; (3) in pursuit of a global agenda rather than a local agenda; and (4) characterized by an interest in and access to technologically advanced weaponry.

Given these characteristics, it should not come as a surprise that the concept of new terrorism is, at least superficially, intimately intertwined with the use of weapons of mass destruction (WMD). Weapons of mass destruction, as implied by their very name, are highly instrumental in maximizing death and destruction. Their potential to fundamentally alter reality and to materialize theodicean representations make WMD of particular interest to pursue and use among those adhering to all-encompassing, transcendent worldviews. Moreover, a WMD attack will never go by unnoticed and will almost certainly have global impact. In this respect, too, the new terrorists may feel particularly drawn to acquire WMD. Finally, although still considered a scenario of low likelihood, the prospect of a terrorist organization that is able to successfully manufacture or acquire WMD is not completely unrealistic.

Although the label "New Terrorism" has been of importance in highlighting the increased global threat stemming from religiously inspired terrorism, the concept can be considered controversial at best within the academic community. The explanatory power of the construct for the understanding of the mindset of a WMD terrorist may actually be very limited. For example, Martha Crenshaw[3] has questioned the label, in part because upon closer scrutiny, "old" terrorists may not be that different in their intentions and ideals from "new" terrorists. It is not so much the psychology of new terrorists that is different from old terrorists but, rather, their capability to use more modern weaponry that sets them apart.

Beyond the validity of the distinction, a further liability concerns its application potential. The construct of a new terrorism is too amorphous to deal with the diversity and complexity that characterizes globalized WMD terrorism. For example, a terrorist organization may want to acquire WMD to coerce a community into action, without actually intending to use the weapon. Moreover, although WMD may bring about great destructiveness, the concept of new terrorism fails to specify the exact nature of the link between transcendental ideology and WMD. If new terrorists are primarily interested in death and destruction, and conventional weapons are much easier to acquire than WMD, and thereby have far greater utility in reaching strategic goals, why would new terrorists not stick to and specialize in conventional weaponry?

Hence, in order to describe the psychology of WMD terrorism, while taking into account the complexities of WMD terrorism and adding predictive validity, it is imperative to go beyond the simple distinction of old vs. new terrorism, and incorporate the complex interplay of tactical, strategic, ideological, and psychological dynamics that drives terrorists to the pursuit and use of WMD. This chapter aims to do so. It proposes a model that specifies the tactical, strategic, ideological, and psychological indicators of the appeal of WMD terrorism and their interaction. The model will be applied to describe the threat of WMD terrorism stemming from jihad-inspired terrorists.

"LIFESPACE" OF A WMD TERRORIST

The focal point of this analysis is the lifespace[4] of the terrorist. Operating within a specific configuration of physical, political, military, and psychological circumstances, the terrorist is assumed to implicitly or explicitly consider and weigh the options available to most effectively advance the cause.[5] Within this general conceptualization, we consider the tactical, strategic, ideological, and psychological factors that contribute to the acquisition and/or use of WMD.[6] Essentially, it is proposed that the motivation to engage in WMD terrorism is the result of the confluence of (1) an actual or perceived necessity for tactical extremeness; (2) strategic considerations concerning the minimization and maximization of personal and oppositional interests; (3) an ideology that stresses themes of control and dominance, of anger and revenge, and of essence and identity; and (4) a mindset that limits the consideration of options to only the clearest and least ambiguous. A substantial portion of this chapter seeks to justify these propositions.

A WMD terrorist is considered a representative of an organization that uses WMD as an instrument to advance a political or religious cause. It should be apparent that what we term "WMD psychology" does not specifically concern the footsoldiers in a terrorist organization who might actually deploy WMD. The relevant mindset may in fact often be an emergent property of an organization rather than of an individual, with the individual constituents representing only a part of the whole. In all cases, we assume that the use of WMD is considered by an individual or an organization to be a general tactical behavior by which to take a stance in a conflict.

The lifespace perspective holds that the analysis of individual overt and covert behavior requires consideration of the interplay between current pressing concerns, elements of the material and social environment, and individual psychological properties. Behavior emerges out of a perceived tension between individual intentions and environmental circumstances. The tension triggers an analysis of the situation and of goals and a search for available means to deal with the tension. This analysis and search may involve consideration of the causes and effects of the tension, of means to change the situation, of interest in changing the situation, of background beliefs, of access to these beliefs, and of individual motivation. Jointly, these elements enable the individual to determine a new course of action to deal with the situation.[7]

Transposing these general notions to the particular lifespace of the WMD terrorist, we conceive of the struggle of the terrorist organization to be the result of a perceived tension between collective ideals and environmental circumstances. WMD are considered the most effective means to deal with this tension. From the perspective of the terrorist, determining the effectiveness of WMD involves tactical, strategic, ideological, and personal considerations (concepts that have received additional scrutiny elsewhere in this volume). Following this reasoning, in order to understand the psychology of WMD terrorism, it is important to scrutinize the tactical, strategic, ideological, and psychological "modules" that lead the terrorist to conclude that WMD are the most effective way of reducing the tension and thus of giving shape to the struggle.

Tactical Extremeness: Bringing about Dramatic Change

The destructiveness of WMD and their potential to disrupt a society and to psychologically disturb its citizens are unmatched. Extremeness may thus be considered their key tactical feature. The extremeness of WMD stems in part from its effect on the target. A genuine WMD, like a nuclear explosion or virulent biological attack, potentially maximizes the number of casualties. The aftermath of a WMD attack may even be more encompassing than its immediate effects, both physically and psychologically.[8] The psychological impact of merely the threat of a WMD attack has been recognized by the U.S. National Academy of Sciences to be far greater than that of conventional attacks, even in instances where both are considered equally lethal.[9]

WMD are also extreme in the sense of negotiability.[10] Given the destructive, disruptive, and disturbing potential of WMD, an actual attack with a WMD can only lead to three possible futures: further escalation of conflict, immediate surrender, or collapse of the targeted enemy. Thus, WMD use is particularly instrumental in the context of a zero-sum conflict, the most extreme and irrevocable type of conflict. Moreover, to the extent that the use of WMD terrorism fosters irrevocable escalation, it is also likely to minimize the duration of conflict. Therefore, the use of WMD may force a quick decision in a conflict. In this respect, too, WMD use as a tactic may be considered extreme.

Strategic Use of WMD

Above and beyond its tactical extremeness, WMD terrorism may be used to affect various strategies to reach military and ideological goals. Six strategic uses of WMD terrorism and three corresponding ideological themes are of particular relevance. We consider these strategies and corresponding themes and describe various considerations pertinent to understanding and countering the threat of WMD attacks. The six strategies are deterrence, coercion, destruction, scorched earth, transformation, and mimesis. The three ideological themes are control, revenge, and truth. For each strategy, we consider whether there are alternative means to WMD available to achieve the strategy, whether the strategy implies the actual use of the weapons or merely their acquisition, and whether the focus of the strategy is maximization of gains or minimization of losses for the self and for the opponent.

1. *Deterrence* has figured as the hallmark concept of nuclear strategy for many years.[11] It refers to the capability of WMD to frighten an opponent into refraining from offensive action. This strategy essentially helps to minimize potential losses, as it serves to prevent others from attacking, rather than to damage an opponent or to maximize gains. Importantly, effective deterrence does not require the actual use of WMD; their mere acquisition is sufficient. Moreover, conventional weaponry may very well fulfill a similar strategic aim of deterrence as WMD. There is not something inherently "nuclear" about deterrence strategy, although WMD may be more effective in deterring than conventional weaponry.
2. *Coercion* refers to the maximization of one's own gain through the threat of using WMD. In many respects, coercion can be considered a key element in the strategy of terrorist organizations. By coercing an opponent, the actor using the

strategy maximizes its own gain. Similarly to deterrence, coercion relies heavily on the threat of WMD, rather than on their actual use. Also, similarly to deterrence, quite a number of alternative means are available, and indeed more easily accessible than WMD, to achieve the same end.

3. *Destruction* implies the actual use of WMD rather than their mere acquisition. The primary strategic aim of destruction is the maximization of the opponent's loss. To achieve this aim, other, more conventional weaponry is available, although, as implied by their name, weapons of mass destruction may very well be the most effective means to this end.
4. *Scorched earth* serves to minimize the opponent's gain. It is a strategy of last resort whereby a party in conflict eradicates its own ground to prevent the opponent from capturing it. Given their destructive, disrupting, and disturbing potential, WMD may be particularly effective toward this end. Nonetheless, similarly to destruction, other weapons may be equally effective and perhaps more readily accessible.
5. *Transformation* is a fifth strategy. Here, WMD are used to bring about structural changes to reality. They are considered a means to realize a millenarian agenda.[12] The transformation notion pertains to reality as a whole and thus includes both the self and the opponent. Clearly, transformation is about the use of WMD rather than about their acquisition. Although transformation may be realized by alternative means, WMD are likely to be far more effective.[13]
6. *Mimesis* constitutes an attempt to manifest a deeper "true" reality that is often depicted in religious scriptures. While the strategy of transformation entails the creation of something new, the strategy of mimesis seeks to create something modeled on a preconceived idea. Apocalyptic violence[14] is guided by the goal of mimesis. It pertains to both the self and the opponent. Furthermore, because of the specifics of a true reality, these are likely to constrain the choice of weaponry. Oftentimes, to match the dramatic images depicted in the scriptures,[15] specific weapons, including WMD, are the only means available in the context of mimesis.

Ideological Themes: Control, Revenge, and Truth

The six strategic uses correspond to various elements present in an ideology that legitimize and instigate WMD violence. An ideology is considered here an organized set of ideas, ideals, and values of relevance in describing the current and desired states of a collective and in describing the ways in which discrepancies between the current and desired states are thought to be most efficiently reduced. Three themes in an ideology may be of particular pertinence in this context: control, revenge, and truth.

The *theme of control* refers to the sense of autonomy of a people as held by the people or a political organization claiming to represent them. The theme of control can be depicted on a dimension ranging from a sense of being completely oppressed to a sense of being completely autonomous. In ideological discourse, feelings of oppression or concern with control and autonomy may be manifested in references to dominance, resistance, or power. Critically, the theme of control corresponds to a great extent with the strategies of deterrence and coercion and to a much lesser extent with the other four strategies. Deterrence and coercion are both considered to be strategies to (re)gain control over a situation. Thus by highlighting oppression and dominance in a current situation, the ideology that capitalizes on the issue of control legitimizes the use of deterrence and coercion as strategies.

The *theme of revenge* refers to a sense of wrongdoing committed against a particular group of people by an external party, in conjunction with a strategy for retribution. The theme of revenge, in many ways, has its counterpart in the theme of gratitude. In ideological discourse, the theme of revenge may be encompassed by references to inequality, injustice, and grievance. Similarly to the theme of control, the theme of revenge corresponds to specific strategies. The theme of revenge provides the legitimization for destruction or for scorched earth strategies.

The *theme of truth* refers to a strong epistemic interest and a strong claim by a particular party to hold the absolute truth. The ideological discourse that encompasses the theme of truth will contain reference to issues such as the true nature of reality, to essence, and to identity. Particular conceptions of truth may motivate or legitimate a forceful transformation of the current reality. Furthermore, epistemic motivation may give rise to or legitimize the use of violence to represent the true nature of reality and hence facilitates the strategy of mimesis and transformation.

The interplay of ideological and strategic elements determining the appeal of WMD is summarized in Table 2.1.

In the table, the six strategies are represented on the left side and the corresponding ideological themes on the right side of the table. The table also reiterates other relevant issues, including whether there are alternative means than WMD available to enforce the strategy, whether the strategy implies the actual use of the weapons or merely their acquisition, and whether the focus of the strategy is maximization of gains or minimization of losses for the self and for the opponent.

Decision-Making Process

The foregoing analysis of the interplay between strategic and ideological factors describes the general framework of factors that *may be* involved in the appeal of WMD. In order to understand the specific factors that actually are involved in a situation, it is also of relevance to consider the decision-making process that leads the leadership of a terrorist organization to conclude that WMD use is desirable.

In this decision-making process, the tactical, strategic, and ideological considerations discussed above play a critically important role. They serve as the resources to fuel judgment. However, before tactical extremeness, strategic objectives, and ideological themes converge to enhance the appeal of WMD terrorism, these elements need to fit with the leader's perception and motivations. In this context, the capability and motivation of the terrorist to consider tactical, strategic, and ideological elements that favor WMD terrorism, as well as to consider the elements that discourage their acquisition and use, are of particular pertinence. Following the *unimodel of social judgment*,[16] the capability of the decision-maker depends on the salience of relevant information and the cognitive capacity to process the information. Furthermore, the motivation depends on specific personality characteristics and personal motivation.

Salience of relevant information refers to the extent to which tactical, strategic, and ideological information is accessible to the decision-maker. Information may gain in salience as a result of access to particular reports, media, intelligence, and advisors. A critically important factor in this context is the direct social environment. Like-minded

TABLE 2.1 Summary of Stategy x Ideology elements

Strategy	Alternative Means?	Acquisition/Use		Focus				Theme
		Acquire	Use	Minimize Loss to Self	Maximize Loss to Self	Maximize to Enemy	Minimize Gain to Enemy	
Deterrence	Yes	x		x				Control
Coercion	Yes	x			x			Control
Destruction	Yes	x	x			x		Anger
Scorched earth	Yes	x	x				x	Anger
Transformation	Yes	x	x	x	x	x	x	Epistemic
Mimesis	No	x	x	x	x	x	x	Epistemic

others may contribute to the salience of particular information, whereas the presence of pluralism and ambivalence may diminish the persuasive impact of that information.

Information processing capacity is another factor related to the decision-maker's capability, rather than motivation, to process particular information. At times, such as in "the fog of war," the amount, complexity, and ambiguity of information may exceed the human capability to process it. Similarly, an urgency to act in response to developments may constrain a decision-maker from considering all relevant information. In such cases, research shows that decision-makers often rely on the simplest, most deeply rooted beliefs, or in the absence of prior beliefs, on the first thing that will be brought to their attention.

Personality constitutes another factor that impacts the decision-making process. A number of factors are potentially relevant in this context. For example, research has identified stable individual differences in the need for control.[17] Also, research has shown that individuals differ in the extent to which they engage in violent retribution.[18] Moreover, research suggests that individuals vary in the extent to which they look for and embrace absolutism and closed-mindedness.[19] Finally, research has shown stable individual differences in the extent to which one prefers to avoid losses versus the extent to which one is motivated to achieve gains.[20]

For all these individual difference variables, the relevance for decision-making based on tactical, strategic, and ideological reasons should be apparent. Individuals high in the desire for control should, for example, feel particularly attracted to strategies of deterrence and coercion. Also, people chronically high in prevention focus (i.e., a focus on preventing losses rather than achieving gains) may feel particularly inclined to adopt a scorched earth strategy. The desire for absolutism may not only bring about an inclination to adapt transformational or mimetic strategies, but may also entail a preference for extreme tactics.

Apart from personality, particular personal experience may also constitute *motivational forces* that drive decision-makers into favoring specific options. Accordingly, a personal experience of humiliation and oppression may increase the appeal of strategies that serve to gain or regain control. Similarly, experienced or perceived injustice in one's personal life may enhance the perception of legitimacy of the use of violence as a retributive device. Also, personal fascinations with higher, absolute truth may motivate one to perceive viability in the use of WMD to transform reality or seek out "core" truths. Motivation may also play a key role in the preference for extreme tactics. Typically, a strong desire to achieve certainty and avoid ambiguity is associated with a strong conviction of the zero-sum nature of the conflict, and a desire to minimize the duration of the conflict.

SUMMARY

To summarize, the present analysis proposes that the appeal of WMD is a function of the joint factors of (1) the urge for tactical extremeness, (2) various strategic options, (3) ideological themes, and (4) components of the decision-making process. The starting point of the analysis is the perceived struggle of the terrorist organization, resulting from a perceived tension between collective ideals and sociopolitical realities. WMD are considered by the terrorist organization the most effective means to deal with this tension. Following this reasoning, in order to understand the psychology of WMD terrorism, it is important to scrutinize the tactical, strategic, ideological, and psychological "modules" that lead the terrorist to conclude that WMD are the most effective way of giving shape to the struggle.

Accordingly, the selection of WMD may be the result of a preference for extreme tactics, a consideration of various strategies, specific ideological themes, and characteristics of a particular decision-making process. A perceived zero-sum nature of the conflict, an urge for maximum destructiveness, and an urge to minimize the duration of the conflict all contribute to the appeal of extreme tactics. Strategic considerations may include whether to maximize one's own gains, minimize one's own losses, minimize the opponent's gain, maximize the opponent's loss, or completely alter reality. Deterrence, coercion, destruction, scorched earth, transformation, and mimesis all represent strategies that could potentially help to realize these strategic aims. These strategic aims, in turn, correspond to and are facilitated and legitimized by ideologies that emphasize control and oppression, revenge and anger, and/or truth and identity. The extent to which the tactical, strategic, and ideological factors contribute to the appeal of WMD depends in part on the decision-makers within the organization. To the extent that the decision-maker has access to information that is conducive to encouraging tactical extremeness, has access to information promoting the specific strategic options and ideological considerations associated with WMD that are discussed above, is able to process such information, and has the personality and is motivated to do so, the appeal of WMD terrorism is likely to be enhanced.

The equation that summarizes the model is depicted in Figure 2.1. We proceed by applying this model to the case of jihadist terrorism.

Case of Jihadist Terrorism

The origins, history, and current state of jihadist terrorism have been well documented in this book and elsewhere.[21] The current model may provide insight into the interplay of the psychological, tactical, strategic, and ideological elements that determine the risk of jihadist-inspired WMD terrorism. As will be explicated, the analysis yields the conclusion that although jihadist ideology may fuel the appeal of WMD terrorism, it is essential

WMD Terrorism Appeal
=
Tactical Extremeness
{maximal destructiveness, minimal duration, zero sum}
×
Strategic Priorities
{deterrence, coercion, destruction, scorched earth, transformation, mimesis}
×
Ideological Motivation
{control, anger, epistemic}
×
Decision Making
{salience of information, processing capability, affective states, motivations, personality factors}

FIGURE 2.1 Summary of model.

to differentiate between the types of WMD terrorism in order to describe the variety of positions regarding the appeal and strategic use of WMD among jihadist ideologues.

It is commonly known that *jihad* literally translates as "struggle." In this respect, the question of the appeal of WMD to jihadists quite literally coincides with the model's assertion that the appeal of WMD should be understood against the backdrop of specific struggles stemming from a perceived discrepancy between ideal and actual circumstances. In the case of the global jihad, the perceived discrepancies between actual and current states may be plotted on multiple dimensions. The International Crisis Group,[22] for example, demarcates three contexts of jihadist political struggle: internal, irredentist, and global. The *internal struggle* pertains to dissatisfaction experienced under the current regimes in the Muslim world. These regimes are considered to betray governance on the basis of "pure" Shari'a law and are considered to engage in a cowardly emulation of non-Islamic Western values. *Irredentist struggle* pertains to the ideal to free the *dar al-Islam* (i.e., the land formerly under Islamic governance) from non-Muslim rule and oppression. The *global struggle* pertains to the perceived global conflict of the Arabic world with the United States and its allies. A critical, overarching element within the jihadist movement is the emphasis on unity of thought and an aversion toward plurality.[23] Indeed, in this respect, jihadist ideology inflames an extremeness of tactics since, in principle, a final compromise is ruled out by the fundamentalist religious legitimization of the jihadist stance.

With regard to ideological themes conducive to WMD appeal, control, revenge, and truth are omnipresent in explications of jihadist ideology. The theme of control, as expressed in discussions of issues such as domination, oppression, power, and resistance, can be found in many of the foremost jihadist texts and interviews, in particular in reference to the irredentist and global struggles. Moreover, the theme of revenge as expressed through feelings of anger and reference to injustice may also be found in the writing of virtually all jihadist ideologues. Finally, with emphasis on *takfir* practice (i.e., the practice of distinguishing between true believers and infidels, and emphasis on purity of beliefs in Salafi ideology), the issue of truth is similarly commonly addressed, especially in the context of internal and global struggles. Indeed, it would go far beyond the scope of this chapter to aim for comprehensiveness regarding the ways in which the jihadists have expressed the ideological themes of control, revenge, and truth. Instead, therefore, the focus will be on several landmark writings.

The themes of control, revenge, and truth are clearly present in Bin Ladin's 1996 declaration of war against America. The declaration marks the starting point of a continuing campaign of violence. In it, (re)establishing control appears to be a central motive. In the opening sentences, for example, Bin Ladin notes

> The latest and the greatest of these aggressions, incurred by the Muslims since the death of the Prophet, is the occupation of the land of the two Holy Places—the foundation of the house of Islam, the place of the revelation, the source of the message and the place of the noble Ka'ba, the Qiblah of all Muslims—by the armies of the American Crusaders and their allies. (We bemoan this and can only say: "No power and power acquiring except through Allah.")

The theme of revenge can also be found, although it is less pronounced. For example, Bin Ladin notes that

> It was a pleasure for the "heart" of every Muslim and a remedy to the "chests" of believing nations to see you [i.e., the United States] defeated.

There are also a number of references to the theme of truth:

> In the shadow of these discussions and arguments truthfulness is covered by the falsehood, and personal feuds and partisanship created among the people increasing the division and the weakness of the Ummah; priorities of the Islamic work are lost while the blasphemy and polytheism continue its grip and control over the Ummah. We should be alert to these atrocious plans carried out by the Ministry of Interior. The right answer is to follow what have been decided by the people of knowledge, as was said by Bin Taymiyyah (Allah's mercy upon him): "people of Islam should join forces and support each other to get rid of the main "Kufr" who is controlling the countries of the Islamic world, even to bear the lesser damage to get rid of the major one, that is the great Kufr." (Kufr = disbelief[24])

Although all three ideological themes are present, emphasis is given to the theme of control. It is, for example, noted that "the ill effect of ignoring these differences [i.e., minor differences among Muslims], at a given period of time, is much less than the ill effect of the occupation of the Muslims' land by the main Kufr."

Given the emphasis on the theme of control, the model implies that the main strategic consideration is deterrence. This assertion is substantiated by Bin Ladin's exclamations. The threat of terrorism is primarily considered a deterrent:

> Few days ago the news agencies had reported that the Defence Secretary of the Crusading Americans had said that "the explosion at Riyadh and Al-Khobar had taught him one lesson: that is not to withdraw when attacked by coward terrorists."
>
> We say to the Defence Secretary that his talk can induce a grieving mother to laughter! And shows the fears that had enshrined you all. Where was this false courage of yours when the explosion in Beirut took place on 1983 AD (1403 A.H). You were turned into scattered pits [sic] and pieces at that time; 241 mainly marines solders [sic] were killed. And where was this courage of yours when two explosions made you to [sic] leave Aden in lees [sic] than twenty four hours!
>
> But your most disgraceful case was in Somalia; where—after vigorous propaganda about the power of the USA and its post cold war leadership of the new world order—you moved tens of thousands of international force, including twenty eight thousands American solders [sic] into Somalia. However, when tens of your solders [sic] were killed in minor battles and one American Pilot was dragged in the streets of Mogadishu you left the area carrying disappointment, humiliation, defeat and your dead with you.

There are also references to destruction, although primarily as a way to deal with occupation, rather than as a goal in itself:

> Terrorising you, while you are carrying arms on our land, is a legitimate and morally demanded duty. It is a legitimate right well known to all humans and other creatures. Your example and our example is like a snake which entered into a house of a man and got killed by him.

Interestingly, though, no reference to the use of WMD can be found, while martyrdom operations are explicitly and frequently celebrated in the text. Given Usama bin Ladin's emphasis on the ideological themes of control, and the strategies of deterrence, this should not come as a surprise. Martyrdom operations may be just as effective in gaining control as WMD terrorism.[25]

More generally, the lack of attention to WMD terrorism may in fact represent a trend within al-Qa'ida's ideological exclamations.[26] Indeed, although ample evidence exists that al-Qa'ida has sought ways to either buy or construct and use WMD, several of the (very few) scholarly treaties on jihadists' appeal of WMD[27,28] have noted that the use of WMD represents a rarely discussed and, in fact, controversial topic within the ranks of al-Qa'ida leadership.

Jihadist WMD Doctrine

The dynamics of the WMD debate within the al-Qa'ida leadership can be explained in terms of psychological, tactical, strategic, and ideological factors.

Scholars have traced Usama bin Ladin's interest in acquiring and using WMD to his stay in Sudan in 1994.[29] Of interest, Salama and Hansell[30] have suggested that the initial interest in WMD was primarily sparked by psychological factors. After being expelled from Saudi Arabia, and having survived two assassination attempts, Usama bin Ladin's interest in extreme measures and his urge for retaliation were significantly increased.

The first public references to the potential use of WMD for jihadist purposes come in 1998. The increased interest in WMD coincided with an increased need for tactically extreme means reflecting the more global ambitions that resulted from that year's fusion of al-Qa'ida with al-Zawahiri's branch of Egyptian Islamic Jihad, the embassy bombings in Kenya and Tanzania, and the U.S. retaliatory missile strike against an al-Qa'ida training camp. At least two interviews with Usama bin Ladin appear in the Western press explicitly dealing with WMD. In both interviews, WMD are considered strategic deterrents.

In a *Time* magazine interview published in December 1998,[31] Bin Ladin famously replies to the question asking whether he is trying to acquire chemical and nuclear weapons:

> Acquiring weapons for the defense of Muslims is a religious duty. If I have indeed acquired these weapons, then I thank God for enabling me to do so. And if I seek to acquire these weapons, I am carrying out a duty. It would be a sin for Muslims not to try to possess the weapons that would prevent the infidels from inflicting harm on Muslims.

Although clearly militant, the tone of the interview is rather moderate. Indeed, it should be noted that, although suggested by the interview question, Bin Ladin does not speak explicitly about chemical and nuclear weapons, but rather speaks of acquiring weapons in general. Importantly, the use of weaponry (including WMD) is only discussed as a means for defense.

In a face-to-face interview with ABC's *Frontline* journalist John Miller,[32] Bin Ladin further explicates the defensive nature of jihadist WMD acquisition and use. It is legitimized as a retaliatory instrument in a defensive power struggle:

> Those who threw atomic bombs and used the weapons of mass destruction against Nagasaki and Hiroshima were the Americans. Can the bombs differentiate between military and women and infants and children? America has no religion that can deter her from exterminating whole peoples. Your position against Muslims in Palestine is despicable and disgraceful. America has no shame.... We believe that the worst thieves in the world today and the worst terrorists are the Americans. Nothing could stop you except perhaps retaliation in kind.

Daly, Parachini, and Rosenau report[33] an additional interview of March 1998 testifying to a more offensive (as opposed to defensive) use of WMD, befitting more the strategic aim of destruction:

> The United States is the biggest terrorist and rogue and it is the duty of every Muslim to struggle for its annihilation.

In 2001, Bin Ladin's tone regarding the use of WMD implies tactical moderation. There is no call for all-out destruction, there are no clear indicators of a need for a decisive blow in the conflict, nor any calls for the elimination of all forms of negotiation. In an interview with Pakistani journalist Hamid Mir in 2001,[34] Bin Ladin still emphasizes the defensive use of WMD. Deterrence remains the main strategic aim, at least in terms of pronouncements from the jihadists themselves:

> Hamid Mir: Some Western media claim that you are trying to acquire chemical and nuclear weapons. How much truth is there in such reports?
>
> Usama bin Ladin: I heard the speech of American President Bush yesterday [Oct 7, 2001]. He was scaring the European countries that Osama wanted to attack with weapons of mass destruction. I wish to declare that if America used chemical or nuclear weapons against us, then we may retort with chemical and nuclear weapons. We have the weapons as deterrent.

In fact, the retaliatory and defensive aims of jihad are emphasized:

> HM: Can it be said that you are against the American government, not the American people?
> OSB: Yes! We are carrying on the mission of our Prophet, Muhammad (peace be upon him). The mission is to spread the word of God, not to indulge massacring people. We ourselves are the target of killings, destruction and atrocities. We are only defending ourselves. This is defensive Jihad. We want to defend our people and our land. That is why I say that if we don't get security, the Americans, too would not get security.

At that time, U.S. military activities in Afghanistan were substantially threatening the very existence of al-Qa'ida. Such a threat had practical and ideological consequences with regard to the contemporaneous appeal of WMD. First, the U.S. activities had reduced the control of al-Qa'ida's executive command. As a consequence, small pockets of jihadists, isolated from the central leadership, began to formulate their own version of the struggle, which often lead to more nonspecific and much more radical intentions. Illustrative in this context is a text by an Islamist Internet forum moderator called Abu Shihab Al-Kandahari. At the end of the 2002 he wrote a treaty entitled "The Nuclear War Is the Solution for the Destruction of the United States,"[35] in which he described a much more offensive strategy for jihadist WMD use that is based on revenge and aims for destruction:

> Yes, you did read the title correctly. It is the only way to kill the maximum number of Americans.
>
> Yes, the United States and its allies would be destroyed, as a result of the misuse of their power against the weak. Their end is closer now, by the arms of the uprising youngsters, who while riding their horses, never step down but victorious or martyrs. In both cases this is their victory.

A second result of the U.S. successes in Afghanistan was a search for ideologically warranted countermeasures. A "Treatise on the Legal Status of Using Weapons of Mass Destruction Against Infidels" by Nasir Bin Hamd al-Fahd of May 2003[36] is exemplary, because it mandates the use of WMD by jihadists. Al-Fahd gives three reasons for the legitimacy of WMD use. The first is defensive:

> Thus, the situation in this regard is that if those engaged in jihad establish that the evil of the infidels can be repelled only by attacking them at night with weapons of mass destruction, they may be used even if they annihilate all the infidels.

The second and third reasons, however, are for more offensive in nature, and aim specifically for destruction rather than control. In discussing the second reason for the legitimacy of WMD use, he notes:

> Al-'Ayni said in 'Umdat al-Qari, 14:270: Bin 'Umar's hadith proves that Muslims may employ any stratagems that will sap their polytheist enemy strength, weaken their cunning, and facilitate victory over them....
>
> The hadith is clear in its indicating that setting fire to enemy territory is permissible if the fighting requires it.

The third argument justifies indiscriminate killing based on an analogy between catapults and WMD:

> Scholars have agreed that it is permissible to bombard the enemy with a catapult and similar things. As everyone knows, a catapult stone does not distinguish between women, children, and others; it destroys anything that it hits, buildings or otherwise.
>
> This proves that the principle of destroying the infidels' land and killing them if the jihad requires it and those in authority over the jihad decide it so legitimate; for the Muslims bombarded these countries with catapults until they were conquered.

In 2004, the radicalization of strategy and ideology following the effective diminution of the control of al-Qa'ida's central command is reflected in a call among jihadists to reorganize. Former al-Qa'ida training camp leader Abu Mus'ub al-Suri is influential in this context. While emphasizing the need for a strong organization, al-Suri embraces the enhanced strategic and ideological radicalism that has accompanied decentralized jihad. His motivation has always been revenge. In 2000, he already wrote: [37]

> Let us unite against Allah's enemies and give these enemies the succinct response to their crime and to their killing of those who bid justice among people—"go back to them, and be sure we shall come to them with such hosts as they will never be able to meet.

By the end of 2004, the juxtaposition of radicalism and organization gives rise to two treaties on the "Islamist global resistance" that favors the use of WMD. In one, al-Suri argues in an open letter to the U.S. State department:[38]

> Hitting the US with WMD was and is still very complicated. Yet, it is possible after all, with Allah's help, and more important than being possible—it is vital.
>
> The ultimate choice is the destruction of the United States by operations of strategic symmetry through weapons of mass destruction.

General Trends

The trajectory of WMD appeal from 1994 to 2005 as expressed in public exclamations by jihadist leaders illustrates the importance of taking the tactical, strategic, ideological, and psychological factors into consideration. Regarding the psychological factors, it is particularly noteworthy that WMD discourse within the al-Qa'ida leadership has emerged primarily after events that pose a threat to the core of al-Qa'ida's leadership or the organization. Usama bin Ladin's initial interest in acquiring and using WMD emerged after two failed assassination attempts in 1994. Furthermore, the increase in WMD discourse in 1998 followed after the U.S. missile strike on one of al-Qa'ida's training camps in Afghanistan. The increased public debate on WMD potential use by al-Qa'ida in 2002 followed the U.S. military endeavors in Afghanistan, which had effectively eradicated the al-Qa'ida organization. Generally, then, personal threat may pose a particularly powerful contributor to the appeal of WMD use.[39]

The attacks on al-Qa'ida may also have contributed to an increased urgency for a firm response, thereby enhancing the preference for tactical extremeness. This appeal of tactical extremeness may have further been enhanced by the globalization of the jihadist cause. Globalization, for example, as a result of the merger of Bin Ladin's al-Qa'ida with al-Zawahiri's Egyptian Islamic Jihad, enhances the appeal of WMD because these weapons are sufficiently extreme to have a global impact.

On a strategic level, the increased globalization and decentralization may have changed the primary organizational goals of al-Qa'ida and thereby changed the appeal of WMD. Whereas al-Qa'ida's immediate strategic aim was to deter the United States and the West from interfering in the Islamic world, more recent strategic exclamations, for example, by al-Suri, have highlighted the centrality of inflicting harm on the United States and the West. Destruction rather than deterrence has become the primary aim of jihadists. Globalization and decentralization of the organization may have played a role in this development. Originally, al-Qa'ida appeared to have pursued a primarily regional agenda, in which the issue of control and the strategy of deterrence may have found greater resonance than in a more global context, where possession of a specific land may be considered of less concern than the harm inflicted on the global community of Muslims.

The shift in priority from deterrence to destruction has its analogue on an ideological level. Whereas the theme of control, as reflected in discussions of autonomy and power, predominate early jihadist discourse, subsequent, more recent discourse appears to be dominated by the theme of revenge for the perceived injustices inflicted on the Islamic global community. This shift in ideological theme and strategic aim has important ramifications for assessments of the WMD terrorism threat, because control motivation and deterrence strategies capitalize on the acquisition of WMD, but revenge motivation and destruction strategies are associated with their actual use.

WMD terrorism may be an effective means by which to reach these goals of deterrence and destruction. Nonetheless, the strategic goals can also be achieved using alternative means. For example, martyrdom operations with conventional explosives may also be effective to deter and destroy, with a far easier and feasible production process and far lower costs. Given the strategic objectives and the greater accessibility of these alternative means, the ranking of WMD among weapons choices for most jihadists should not be considered extremely high. The relatively lower appeal of WMD is also reflected in the relatively rare discussion on the topic within the community of jihadist ideologues.

However, to state that there is no appeal of WMD among jihadists is to deny the facts. A long list of well-documented events suggests otherwise.[40] Bin Ladin and other representatives of al-Qa'ida have actively sought to acquire WMD, have conducted experiments to develop them, and have claimed to possess them.[41] Why, then, this activity if WMD are seemingly not the weapon of first choice, at least currently? The interest in WMD by jihadists may stem in part from the immense power associated with possessing these weapons. While they may be difficult to acquire, actually acquiring them would imply a very significant increase in the chances of achieving strategic objectives. Perhaps an analogy to the lottery can be made. Despite the extremely slim chances of actually winning, the thought of winning may in itself be rewarding. However, despite such fantasies, very few people would actually rely on the lottery to cover the expenses of daily living. Similarly, given their low feasibility for causing mass casualties—at least currently—it would be unwise for any organization that relies on violence to focus exclusively on the possession of WMD to achieve its core ambitions.

The appeal of WMD is based on more than unrealistic optimism, however. In fact, even in the absence of a prospect of actual deployment, a statement that al-Qa'ida possesses WMD, or indications that it is experimenting with WMD, is in itself sufficient to spread fear across the Western world. Thus, even without acquiring or using WMD, the mere attempt to acquire WMD has the potential to directly or indirectly influence policy. Note, however, that these uses are essentially to be discussed in the context of jihadist use of psychological warfare rather than in the context of the jihadist acquisition of WMD. Also, these tactics are not effective in isolation. Only when the possibility of WMD is raised in the midst of highly lethal, non-WMD–based attacks, is it sufficiently credible to cause serious panic, and thereby to disrupt society. The main point for the current analysis is, however, that even an attempt or a statement about an attempt to acquire WMD has the potential to cause disruption, and this may be another factor that explains why WMD show up sporadically in jihadist ideological discourse.

Future Trajectories

As maintained throughout this chapter, the appeal of WMD to jihadists may be relatively low among its central leadership as a result of the availability of more feasible and perhaps equally effective alternative weapons, most notably suicide bombers. This analysis should not be taken to suggest that the risk of a WMD attack by jihadists is minimal, however, particularly when thinking about the risks beyond the near future. Indeed, the presently advanced model may not only be used to describe the past and current states of affairs regarding WMD use among jihadists, but it may also be used to delineate the dimensions of relevance for describing future developments that may signal increases in WMD appeal. In this regard, various developments suggest that the attractiveness of WMD is on the rise.

Two trends within the jihadist movement may be especially noteworthy: the increased globalization of the jihadist movement, and the decentralization of the al-Qa'ida organization. The primary implication of the globalization of the jihadist movement has been a shift in priority of the jihadists' original political goal of removing Western influences out of the Arabian Peninsula into a more abstract metaphorical concept of jihad that helps Muslims to construe and maintain identity in a global society.

With this more abstract conception of jihad, the appeal of a cosmic struggle between global forces, as opposed to a specific political struggle, increases. The emphasis on identity and cosmic struggle between true believers and infidels, in turn, gives jihad an increasingly cultic status, while the central leadership of al-Qa'ida has lost its authority to canalize these developments. Among the new jihadist cultists, strategic aims become more focused on representing and defending identity and truth. Also, given the abstractness of this aim, the tactics become increasingly extreme, partially because of a decreasing relevance of negotiation or coexistence. The extremeness of tactics may also be enhanced as a result of the individual that feels drawn to this newest incarnation of the jihad. Given its abstract, messianic message and lack of formal organization, this form of jihad is especially likely to attract marginalized and unstable individuals, of which Richard Reid may serve as prototype (for more details about Reid and so-called "dirty bombs," see Chapter 7 of this volume).

Thus, all the parameters identified in the model play a role in increasing the attractiveness of using WMD. Specifically, the predominant ideological theme shifts from control and destruction to truth and identity. With it, there is an increased strategic aim of transforming society and representing true identity. These issues of truth and identity make negotiation less likely and encourage the use of extreme tactics. People in need of identity may be particularly receptive to this specific interplay of ideological, strategic, and tactical factors. The ideological, strategic, psychological, and tactical factors are particularly tangible among the disenchanted Islamic diaspora youth in Western (European) countries. Although they lack the capability to develop nuclear weapons and employ these weapons to destroy major cities, small-scale chemical, biological, or radiological attacks are within their reach. Indeed, the current analysis is highly consistent with Bruce Hoffman's suggestion that the use of small-scale chemical, biological, and radiological devices may constitute major short-term threats in the fight against terrorism. Whether jihadists will be able to graduate to true WMD is a question addressed in several other chapters of this volume (see the chapters on each CBRN weapon type in Section II, "The Agents of Harm").

CONCLUSION AND IMPLICATIONS

The present chapter has adopted a lifespace perspective to come to a better understanding of the appeal of WMD terrorism among jihadists. The guiding idea behind the lifespace perspective is that, among its users, WMD terrorism is considered to have the greatest appeal in the midst of alternatives to take action in a struggle resulting from discrepancies between ideals and current circumstances. Four levels of factors are of relevance in understanding when WMD terrorism has the highest appeal: (1) tactical extremeness; (2) strategic objectives; (3) ideological themes; and (4) psychological factors.

A perceived zero-sum nature of the conflict, an urge for maximum destructiveness, and a desire to minimize the duration of the conflict (i.e., to bring it to a swift and successful conclusion) all contribute to the appeal of extreme tactics. Strategic considerations may include whether to maximize one's own gains, minimize one's own losses, minimize the opponent's gain, or maximize the opponent's loss, or completely alter reality. Deterrence, coercion, destruction, scorched earth, transformation, and mimesis all represent strategies that could potentially help to realize such aims. These strategic aims, in turn, correspond with and are facilitated and legitimized by ideologies that emphasize control and perceived oppression by an outside party, revenge and anger, and/or truth and identity. The ideological theme of control facilitates deterrence and coercion strategies. The theme of revenge facilitates destruction and scorched earth. The themes of truth and identity may bring about strategies of transformation and mimesis. Additionally, the extent to which the tactical, strategic, and ideological factors contribute to the appeal of WMD depends in part on the leadership of the organization. To the extent that leadership has access to information conducive to tactical extremeness, strategic options, and ideological consideration, to the extent the leadership is able to process such information, and has the requisite personality type and is motivated to do so, the appeal of WMD terrorism is likely to be enhanced.

We believe the current framework has implications for the analysis of WMD terrorism in general and the understanding of jihadist WMD terrorism in particular.

Analyzing WMD Terrorism

WMD terrorism is considered to be among the greatest threats of our time. Nonetheless, its analysis has yet to yield a unified framework in which to understand and predict the appeal of WMD terrorism. Such frameworks are essential for objective knowledge formation, and increase the accountability of intelligence gathering efforts.

Thus far, WMD terrorism has been primarily understood as a new development, a "new terrorism," that is contrasted with a perceived former dominant terrorism paradigm. The new terrorism is considered to be (1) focused on killing as a goal rather than as a means to achieve or advance a specific political agenda, (2) inspired by very general—often transcendental or millenarian—ideologies, (3) manifested in the pursuit of a global agenda rather than a local agenda, and (4) characterized by an interest in and access to technologically advanced weaponry. The use of this new terrorism model has been criticized, however, for insufficiently attending to the complexity of factors involved in the motivation to seek WMD. To incorporate the complexity of tactical, strategic, ideological, and psychological considerations involved, the present chapter advanced a new, tentative framework in which particular historical events can be interpreted, and future scenarios be drawn. The framework encompasses various features that are of pertinence for the detection of WMD.

Analysis of Ideology Is Useful in Detecting WMD Appeal

By identifying ideological themes and corresponding strategic aims, the present model may help to detect organizations that are particularly at risk of developing and using WMD. The analysis of the ideological content of terrorist organizations to detect intent to acquire and use WMD may in fact function much as a Geiger counter does to help to detect the physical presence of radioactive material. The high presence of the ideological themes of control, revenge, and truth should be treated as a heightened risk, and the organization exclaiming these themes should therefore be subjected to closer scrutiny. As we have suggested throughout, the themes of control and perceived oppression, the theme of revenge, and the theme of truth and identity may bring about an interest in the strategic use of WMD. Checking for the presence of these themes may thus help to estimate the appeal of WMD terrorism. The present framework suggests that the themes of control and revenge may give rise to strategic aims that can also be achieved with other means than WMD, whereas this is less the case for themes of truth and identity. The theme of identity and truth should therefore be particularly subjected to closer scrutiny.

The Analysis of Ideological Themes for Detecting WMD Should Be Conducted in Conjunction with an Analysis of Tactical, Strategic, and Psychological Factors

The presence of the themes of control, revenge, and truth do not necessarily imply that WMD will be selected. A person may, for example, be obsessed by themes of truth and identity control, but may be unable or unwilling to translate this into specific strategic aims. Also, removal of oppression and restoration of autonomy can often be achieved through means less extreme than WMD. The theme of control may, for example, be associated with increased WMD appeal only in the case of a perceived necessity for tactical extremeness. Hence, once the particular "risky" ideological themes have been identified, it is essential to put the themes in perspective by including tactical, strategic, and psychological factors in the risk assessment.

A Variety of Factors May Be Involved in Changes in the Motivation to Use WMD

The assessment of future threats of WMD attacks may be as relevant as the assessment of current threat levels. The current model suggests that in order to understand and predict changes in the intent to acquire WMD, a variety of factors need to be taken into account. Critical factors that have been identified in describing changes in WMD appeal among jihadists include shifts from regional to global focus, changes in ideological focus in response to events, and changes in organizational structure. All these factors affect the dynamic interplay of tactics, strategy, ideology, and psychology. Greater globalization increases the emphasis on the themes of identity and truth and thereby creates a greater perceived need for tactical extremeness and transformational strategy. The U.S. efforts in Afghanistan have considerably enhanced the ideological theme of revenge and thereby caused a shift from the strategic aim of deterrence to the strategic aim of destruction. These efforts also brought about a change in organization that made the central command of Bin Ladin less influential and gave rise to those whose interest may have been less overtly political and more intrinsically violent. All these developments have increased the appeal of WMD, although, simultaneously, these developments may also have significantly reduced the actual capability to engage in WMD terrorism.

Understanding Jihadist Motives to Use WMD

The appeal of WMD for jihadist terrorists was highlighted in the current chapter. Despite frequent mention of such appeal in popular media and policy circles, there are various indicators that the issue of WMD is subject to controversy within the circles of jihadist ideologues. The presently advanced framework and concepts may help to understand this controversy.

Jihadist ideology centers around three struggles: an internal struggle concerning the establishment of pure Islamic governance, a terrestrial irredentist struggle concerning the reestablishment of the Caliphate, and a global struggle concerning the distinction between true believers and infidels and apostates. Initially, jihadist struggle as personified in the early years of Usama bin Ladin's al-Qa'ida focused primarily on the second, irredentist struggle. Given this particular struggle, the ideological theme of control and the overcoming of domination were particularly salient. Deterrence was the primary strategy. Because other means than WMD are potentially effective to this end, and much easier to acquire and use, the appeal of WMD was thus present, but rather low.

After the U.S. efforts in Afghanistan decentralized al-Qa'ida, and the 9/11 attacks and other missions throughout the world led to a globalized Islamist movement, the ideological themes of revenge and identity became more prominent in jihadist thinking. With this emphasis on revenge comes the strategic urge for destruction of "the enemy." Although not unique in serving this purpose, WMD could help to fulfill this strategic aim. The globalization of the jihadist struggle has also led to an increased emphasis on Islamic identity. In combination with the ideological theme of revenge, the global struggle for Islamic identity has the potential to create a new jihadist cultic worldview in which its endorsers seek out WMD because they represent the only means to significantly transform reality.

NOTES

1. See R. Howard, "The New Terrorism and Weapons of Mass Destruction," in *Weapons of Mass Destruction and Terrorism*, eds. R. Howard and J. Forest (New York: McGraw-Hill, 2008), 6–22.
2. "The New Terrorism," *Newsweek* (1993), available at http://www.newsweek.com/id/113743.
3. For example, see M. Crenshaw, "'New' versus 'Old' Terrorism," *Palestine-Israel Journal of Politics*, Economics and Culture, Special Issue on "Violence and its Alternatives," 10 (2003), 48--53.
4. K. Lewin, *Principles of Topological Psychology* (New York: McGraw-Hill Publications in Psychology, 1936).
5. See Arie W. Kruglanski and S. Fishman, "Terrorism Between 'Syndrome' and 'Tool'," *Current Directions in Psychological Science,* 15 (2006), 44–48.
6. J. Post, "The Psychology of WMD Terrorism," *International Studies Review*, 7 (2005), 148–151.
7. See, for example, R. C. Schank and R. P. Abelson, *Scripts, Plans, Goals and Understanding: An Inquiry into Human Knowledge Structures* (Chapters 1–3) (Hillsdale, NJ: Lawrence Erlbaum Associates, 1977). See also J. R. Anderson and C. Lebiere, *The Atomic Components of Thought* (Hillsdale, NJ: Lawrence Erlbaum Associates, 1998).
8. B. P. Bem, "After the Missiles: Sociopsychological Effects of Nuclear War," *American Psychologist,* 40 (1985), 927–937.
9. National Research Council, *Long Term Worldwide Effects of Multiple Nuclear-Weapons Detonations* (Washington, DC: National Academy of Sciences, 1975).
10. For example, K. Lieber and D. Press, *The Rise of U.S. Nuclear Primacy* (Foreign Affairs, 2006), 42–55.
11. T. Schelling, *Arms and Influence* (New Haven, CT: Yale University Press, 1996).
12. For example, W. Pierce, ("Andrew Macdonald"), *The Turner Diaries* (the National Alliance Washington, DC, 1978).
13. See also M. Sageman, *Leaderless Jihad: Terror Networks in the Twenty-first Century* (Philadelphia: University of Pennsylvania Press, 2007) for an up-to-date treatment of the topic.
14. See, for example, R. Lifton, *Destroying the World to Save It: Aum Shinrikyo, Apocalyptic Violence, and the New Global Terrorism* (New York: Owl Books, 2000). See also M. Juergensmeyer, *Terror in the Mind of God: The Global Rise of Religious Violence* (Berkeley: University of California Press, 2000).
15. N. Cohn, *The Pursuit of the Millennium. Revolutionary Millenarians and Mystical Anarchists of the Middle Ages* London, 1984).
16. A. Kruglanski and E. Thompson, "Persuasion by a Single Route: A View from the Unimodel," *Psychological Inquiry*, 10 (1999), 83–109. See also A. Kruglanski, M. Dechesne, and E. Orehek, "Explorations in Lay Epistemics: The Why, How and Who of Knowledge Formation," unpublished manuscript, University of Maryland, College Park, 2008.
17. J. Burger, "Desire for Control and Achievement-Related Behaviors," *Journal of Personality and Social Psychology*, 48 (1985), 1520–1533.

18. C .Spielberger and S. Sydeman, "State-Trait Anxiety Inventory and State-Trait Anger Expression Inventory," in *The Use of Psychological Testing for Treatment Planning and Outcome Assessment*, ed. **M.** Maruish (Hillsdale, NJ: Lawrence Erlbaum Associates, 1994), 292–321.
19. A. Kruglanski, *The Psychology of Closed Mindedness* (New York: Psychology Press, 2004).
20. E. T. Higgins, "Beyond Pleasure and Pain," *American Psychologist*, 52 (1997), 1280–1300.
21. R. Gunaratna, *Inside Al Qaeda: Global Network of Terror* (New York: Columbia University Press, 2002). J. Stern, *Terror in the Name of God: Why Religious Militants Kill* (New York: HarperCollins Publishers, 2003). M. Sageman, *Understanding Terror Networks* (Philadelphia: University of Pensylvania Press, 2004).
22. International Crisis Group, *Understanding Islamism* (2005), available at http://www.crisisgroup.org/home/index.cfm?id=3300&l=1.
23. W. McCants and J. Brachman, *The Militant Ideology Atlas* (Highland Falls, NY: West Point Military Academy, 2006), available at http://ctc.usma.edu/atlas/atlas.asp.
24. See, for example, http://www.islamicgarden.com/kaffirkufr.html; http://www.pwhce.org/takfiri.html.
25. Robert Pape, "The Strategic Logic of Suicide Terrorism," *American Political Science Review*, 97 (2003), 343–361.
26. P. Bergen, *The Osama bin Ladin I Know: An Oral History of Al Qaeda's Leader* (New York: Simon and Schuster, 2006).
27. R. Paz, "Global Jihad and WMD: Between Martyrdom and Mass Destruction," *Current Trends in Islamist Ideology*, 2 (2005), 74–87.
28. J. M. Long, *Strategic Culture, Al-Qaida, and Weapons of Mass Destruction* (McClean, VA: SIAC, 2006).
29. R. Gunaratna, *Inside Al Qaeda: Global Network of Terror*.
30. S. Salama and L. Hansell, "Does Intent Equal Capability? Al-Qaeda and Weapons of Mass Destruction," *The Nonproliferation Review*, 12 (2005), 615–653.
31. http://www.time.com/time/printout/0,8816,174550,00.html.
32. See http://www.pbs.org/wgbh/pages/frontline/shows/binLadin/who/interview.html.
33. S. Daly, J. Parachini, and W. Rosenau, *Aum Shinrikyo, Al Qaeda, and the Kinshasa Reactor Implications of Three Case Studies for Combating Nuclear Terrorism* (Washington, DC: RAND Corp., 2005).
34. http://www.robert-fisk.com/usama_interview_hamid_mir_ausaf.htm.
35. Source: http://www.ict.org.il/apage/13140.php.
36. http://www.carnegieendowment.org/static/npp/fatwa.pdf.
37. http://ctc.usma.edu/aq/pdf/AFGP-2002-600966-trans1.pdf.
38. Quotations taken from Paz, "Global, Jihad, and WMD," 82.
39. T. Pyszczynski, S. Solomon, and J. Greenberg, *In the Wake of September 11: The Psychology of Terror* (Washington, DC: American Psychological Association, 2003).
40. See http://cns.miis.edu/pubs/other/sjm_cht.htm.
41. See Salama and Hansell, "Does Intent Equal Capability,"note 30.

CHAPTER 3

Jihadist Tactics and Targeting

James J. F. Forest and Sammy Salama

CONTENTS

INTRODUCTION

On February 5, 2008, U.S. Director of National Intelligence J. Michael McConnell declared that "al-Qa'ida and other terrorist groups are attempting to acquire chemical, biological, radiological, and nuclear weapons and materials (CBRN)," and that "al-Qa'ida will continue to try to acquire and employ these weapons and materials."[1] Just a few days earlier, news reports emerged that Abu Khabab al-Masri—a chemical engineer and high-ranking Egyptian member of al-Qa'ida who had reportedly been killed in a 2006 U.S. airstrike—was now thought to be alive and well and in charge of resurrecting al-Qa'ida's program to develop or obtain weapons of mass destruction.[2] Described by several intelligence officials as a top explosives experts, Khabab is suspected of having had a role in a plot to attack New York in 2003 with a device called *al-mubtakkar* (or the "invention") to disperse hydrogen cyanide gas in subway cars, potentially killing dozens of people—a strike that, according to former CIA Director George Tenet's 2007 autobiography, Ayman al-Zawahiri canceled, saying, "We have something better in mind."[3]

According to one senior U.S. intelligence official, Khabab (whose real name is Midhat Mursi al-Sayid Umar) is now believed to have set up rudimentary labs with at least a handful of aides and is training Western recruits for chemical attacks in Europe and perhaps the United States, just as he did when he ran the "Khabab Camp" at al-Qa'ida's sprawling Darunta training complex in Afghanistan's Tora Bora region before the attacks of September 11, 2001. Clearly, the very notion that al-Qa'ida's fledgling weapons of mass destruction (WMD) program is moving forward again raised alarm bells throughout intelligence and security communities worldwide, largely due to the assumption that the acquisition by al-Qa'ida of a weapon of mass destruction would lead directly to its use. Steven Flynn, for example, has suggested that it is a question of "when, not if" terrorists will attack the United States with WMD.[4] However, as a number of scholars have observed, we must question this assumption if we are to gain a true understanding of the nature of the WMD terrorism threat.[5]

Building on the other chapters in this volume that address jihadist strategy, this chapter will examine their attack decision-making, as well as the tactical and operational advantages—and disadvantages—of using CBRN weapons to achieve their strategic and political objectives. The discussion begins by explaining how a terrorist group's tactics and targeting are directly related to their ideology, operational capabilities, and strategic constraints, and why in most cases analyzing these elements together explains why we have seen very few examples of WMD terrorism throughout history. Next, the chapter examines the target selection calculus of al-Qa'ida and seeks to address the question of how jihadists might use WMD if they were to acquire them. We then refine this analysis by focusing on the differing levels of interest in (and potential uses for) CBRN weapons by various elements of al-Qa'ida. Clearly, as other chapters in this volume demonstrate, it is dangerously misleading to assume that all jihadists think and act uniformly about strategy, tactics, and the role of CBRN weapons. Finally, we conclude with some thoughts on what our analysis suggests for further research and strategies to combat terrorism and WMD proliferation.

TACTICAL ADVANTAGES AND DISADVANTAGES OF CBRN WEAPONS

The general consensus among most scholars of international security is that CBRN weapons are sought by terrorists because of various assumed strategic and tactical benefits they offer. For example, as described by Jeffrey M. Bale in Chapter 1 of this volume, the possession of these weapons raises the profile and bargaining power of the group, and forces a government to take them very seriously. The tactical benefits of CBRN weapons vary widely, of course, as much as the weapons themselves. For example, a stolen nuclear warhead in the hands of a terrorist group brings a much different set of potential benefits than a small quantity of weaponized chemicals like ricin or chlorine gas. A group like al-Qa'ida is unlikely to be interested in a virulent, contagious biological pathogen that causes the slow painful death of indiscriminate millions worldwide, because avoiding counterproductive violence is necessary if they are to be considered a legitimate vanguard of the jihadist movement. Small-scale chemical weapons attacks might be possible (given the relatively easy access to key ingredients). But a nuclear device appears to be the most effective type of WMD to help eliminate U.S. and Western obstacles that stand in the way of jihadists achieving their objectives.

However, from an operational perspective, it is important to note that the actual use of CBRN weapons by terrorists has yet to produce any real tactical or long-term strategic benefits for those responsible. Given that emulation and copycat behavior is commonplace throughout the terrorist world,[6] it is very instructive that of the rare historical cases of WMD terrorism, none have been repeated or emulated by other terrorist groups. For example, in 1984, a cult led by the Bhagwan Shri Rajneesh in Oregon used a biological agent to contaminate several restaurant salad bars in a plot to influence a local election. Soon after, steady streams of patients were reporting to local physicians and hospitals with symptoms ranging from nausea and diarrhea to headache and fever. In total, 751 fell ill, but there were no fatalities. Two members of the group were prosecuted, and there is no evidence that the cult has since committed a similar act of violence. Furthermore, it is important to note that no other group has tried to emulate this tactic, despite its relative technical simplicity.

In June 1990, the Liberation Tigers of Tamil Eelam (LTTE) became the first insurgent, guerrilla, or terrorist organization to stage a chemical weapons attack when it used chlorine gas in its assault on a Sri Lankan Armed Forces camp at East Kiran. As Bruce Hoffman notes, this attack was relatively crude: Several large drums of the chemical were transported from a nearby paper mill and positioned around the camp's perimeter, and when the wind currents were judged right, the attackers released the gas, which wafted into the camp.[7] More than sixty military personnel were injured, and the LTTE captured the facility. However, though this was part of the first round in a renewed military offensive, the LTTE did not use a similar weapon in subsequent attacks, in part due to revulsion among their core supporters and constituencies.[8]

Chlorine is a fairly common chemical, particularly in industrialized societies where it is used for a broad range of applications from municipal sewage treatment plants to plastics and other industries. Recently, insurgents in Iraq tried to use chlorine gas in a small number of their attacks against U.S. and coalition forces, but the practice was short-lived, probably because of the same disadvantageous results that the LTTE encountered and because overall the casualties from those attacks were not significantly greater than what we have seen from conventional roadside and suicide bombings. Thus, with limited tactical benefit or return on investment, combined with increased risk to a group's own operatives and supporters, using this form of WMD may not be as attractive to jihadists as some observers have assumed.

In another example, Aum Shinrikyo—a Japanese religious cult—launched an attack in March 1995 on the Tokyo subway using sarin gas, killing nearly a dozen people, injuring approximately 1,000 others, and sending 5,000 to hospitals for checkups. Their objective in this attack was to disrupt an anticipated effort by law enforcement authorities to arrest members of the group (which is why they attacked subway lines leading to many government ministries). This attack was similar to their use of sarin the previous year in Matsumoto against judicial officials who were involved in a judicial proceeding against them.[9] Here again, the tactic has not been replicated by jihadists or other groups, despite the recipes and instructions for manufacturing sarin that are widely available on the Internet. As a weapon, sarin will garner a group or individual some level of media attention, but it has a limited capability for generating the kind of strategic effect that would help them achieve their overall objectives (for a more detailed description and analysis of Aum Shinrikyo, see Chapter 5 on chemical weapons).

More recently, when Bob Stevens, a tabloid photo editor in Boca Raton, Florida, died of anthrax in the months following the 9/11 attacks, he became the first U.S. casualty in a new era of bioterrorism threats. In the days and weeks to follow, four others succumbed to anthrax after handling tainted mail—two postal workers in Washington, DC; a New York City hospital stockroom employee; and an elderly Connecticut woman. At least seventeen others fell ill but survived the still-unsolved post-9/11 bioterrorism attack.[10] Here again, a tactical and operating model has been offered for jihadists seeking to deploy Bacillus anthracis against their enemies, and yet to date none of them have. One could argue that the security measures put in place after October 2001 have much to do with it. However, worldwide there remain a plethora of vulnerabilities and opportunities for jihadists to acquire and use Bacillus anthracis. Thus, perhaps the more likely reason we have not seen follow-on anthrax attacks anywhere else, by jihadists or others, is that as a weapon this agent yields very limited (if any) strategic benefit and a low return on investment. It is not contagious; requires careful handling and sophistication to transform the spores into a weaponized, deliverable form; and has other disadvantages that, when compared with other items on the menu of weapons options at the jihadists disposal, render it less attractive.

In each of these cases, the WMD terrorist attack failed to achieve any recognizable objectives other than to sicken or kill a relatively small number of people and garner media attention. This review of the historical record thus raises questions about what real tactical or strategic benefits can be derived from the use of these weapons—especially compared with the more popular and comparatively easier-to-deploy conventional explosives. Indeed, according to the 2008 Threat Assessment of the Director of National Intelligence, "the use of a conventional explosive [will] be the most probable al-Qa'ida attack scenario because the group is proficient with conventional small arms and improvised explosive devices and is innovative in creating capabilities and overcoming security obstacles."[11]

Jihadists are not stupid; they will not invest substantial money, personnel, and other resources toward the acquisition and use of weapons whose strategic benefit is questionable, particularly when there are significant disadvantages associated with these weapons. For example, from the perspective of tactical deployment, CBRN materials pose many risks to operatives throughout the planning and preparation stages of an attack. A lack of familiarity and comfort with toxins, pathogens, or radiological materials could expose would-be perpetrators to greater operational risks than they may be willing to accept (assuming that they are aware of such risks and do not take precautions to mitigate or protect against them). In any case, many of the elements and materials necessary for these weapons are expensive and regulated through various domestic licensing systems and export control regimes, making it difficult to acquire them without attracting the attention of local authorities. Further, these central elements are notoriously difficult to weaponize and deploy effectively, and the highly specialized knowledge required for a successful WMD attack is rare among terrorists. Overall, there are a lot more things that can go wrong with CBRN weapons than with conventional explosives. With all these considerations, the return on investment in CBRN is seen as lower than that associated with conventional, homemade explosives like those used in Bali, Madrid, London, and so many other jihadist attacks in recent years.

Finally, terrorist groups must consider the ideological and strategic ramifications of using WMD. By definition, terrorist groups are willing to use some level of violence in the pursuit of their objectives, ranging from a desire for religious governance (e.g., Islamist militants seeking to establish a caliphate, where Shari`a law reigns supreme) to Maoist-style communism (e.g., insurgencies in Peru and Nepal). However, terrorists also generally seek to avoid counterproductive violence, so from a strategic standpoint weapons of mass destruction may not be all that useful.

Indeed, there are relatively few political ideologies that articulate a need for the end of the world, or at least the end of all mankind, and thus relatively few groups are seeking weapons and targets that would achieve this scale of carnage. Examples of those that might include extreme environmentalist cults like the Church of Euthanasia and the Voluntary Human Extinction Movement (both of whom call for the elimination of the human race in order to save the planet) and apocalyptic (doomsday or final judgment) cults. In fact, there is a threshold of catastrophic terrorism (based on the amount of death and destruction caused), a threshold that relatively few groups have crossed. Among the groups that have crossed the threshold of catastrophic terrorism (or at least intend to if given the capability and opportunity), most appear unconstrained by earthly considerations, and instead see themselves as fulfilling the mandate of a higher power—in essence, the threat they pose is limited solely by the weapons they can acquire. A common thread among these groups is the need for mass destruction and death (indeed, the elimination of all humans, in some cases) in order to bring about a better world envisioned and articulated through some form of catastrophic ideology. Most commonly, this future utopian world is envisioned through the lens of some type of religious interpretation. Among these, the most prominent in recent years has been Aum Shinrikyo, whose leader, Shoko Asahara, came to believe that a catastrophic world war was imminent, and that only his followers would survive.

Jihadists recognize the risk of being portrayed in the same category as these fringe apocalyptic groups. Indeed, al-Qa'ida and many of its affiliated groups are quite concerned with monitoring and controlling their public image. These considerations impact the WMD calculations of jihadists—clearly, they are not seeking the end of the world, but, rather, they want their Salafi-Islamist vision of the future to dominate world affairs. Despite what some ill-informed observers in the media suggest, jihadists will not invest resources in a weapon that is unlikely to yield positive results and may even negatively affect their image and support among key constituencies.

Overall, despite globalization and numerous technological advances over the past decade, it is noteworthy that we have not seen more (and more successful) attacks using weapons of mass destruction. Indeed, based on predictions of the past decade, we should be awash in terrorist attacks using improvised chemical, biological, radiological, or nuclear weapons by now. But we are not, and for several good reasons, including the limited availability of CBRN materials, the relatively rare ideological justification for their use, the limited tactical and strategic benefits they offer, and the many operational disadvantages that are associated with a WMD attack. Understanding the advantages and disadvantages of CBRN weapons is necessary in order to appreciate the difficulties that jihadists face in rationalizing their acquisition and use. Indeed, as the next section of this chapter illustrates, there are relatively narrow parameters within which jihadists consider WMD attacks useful.

JIHADIST MOTIVATIONS AND RATIONALE FOR THE USE OF WMD

A terrorist group's tactics, weapons choices, and targeting are directly related to their ideology, operational capabilities, and strategic constraints. Generally speaking, the jihadists' vision of the future requires them to overthrow what they consider to be "postate" regimes in the Middle East and replace them with governments that rule by Shari`a law, but only until the Islamic Caliphate can be reestablished to rule over the entire Muslim world. Attacks against Western targets (such as those that have been carried out against New York City and the Pentagon, London, and Madrid) are necessary because it is through alliances with powerful, industrialized Western nations that these apostate regimes are sustained. It is here that we see the jihadists' overarching rationale for the use of CBRN weapons—they are perceived as offering the power necessary for the jihadists to achieve their political objectives.

Saudi Cleric, Shaykh Nasir ibn Hamd al-Fahd, attempted to religiously legitimize the use of WMD by stating that laws and treaties established by infidels against the use of nuclear, biological, and chemical weapons have no standing in Islamic law; that pronouncements of historical Islamic jurists legitimate the use of CBRN weapons and provide exceptions to the prohibition against killing women and children; and that the cumulative damage American bombs have caused to Muslim lands over many years justifies the kind of retaliation that can only be produced by a weapon of mass destruction. Whether the target is foreign or domestic, their interest in a WMD attack is predicated on the notion that America and the West have it coming; a WMD attack is necessary to "even the score." Similar rationalizations have been offered by other ideologues within the al-Qa'ida movement, such as when Abu Musab al-Suri said in 2002, "Let the American people—those who voted for killing, destruction, the looting of other nations' wealth, megalomania and the desire to control others—be contaminated with radiation."[12] More recently, in September 2006, Abu Hamza al-Muhajir—a leader of al-Qa'ida in Iraq—encouraged his fellow terrorists to consider testing these weapons in Iraq: "The field of jihad (holy war) can satisfy your scientific ambitions, and the large American bases (in Iraq) are good places to test your unconventional weapons, whether biological or dirty, as they call them."[13]

For members of al-Qa'ida, the acquisition and use of WMD is necessary to annihilate the enemies of Islam. They rationalize the need for these weapons as part of a power/capability/force multiplier calculation within the context of the larger socio-political vision being pursued. According to statements made on various jihadist web forums, supporters of the global salafi-jihadist movement want and expect a "spectacular" event even bigger than 9/11. Bin Ladin, al-Zawahiri, and their immediate leadership cadres no doubt recognize that al-Qa'ida is in competition with other "voices" in the Muslim world, and a catastrophic terrorist attack will allow them to claim center stage. They also understand that intentional state sponsorship of a WMD attack is unlikely, but believe that if such weapons are made available, then Allah must intend for them to be used in the service of jihad. The question, then, is how they envision using these weapons in the event that they someday, somehow, possess them.

THE ROLE OF WMD WITHIN AL-QA'IDA'S TARGET SELECTION CALCULUS

In recent years, jihadists have chosen targets largely related to public transportation (subways, commuter trains, airports, ferries, and airlines), commerce (hotels, office buildings, cafes, nightclubs, etc.), and civil authority (government offices, police stations, etc.). What does this tell us about their potential for conducting a WMD attack? As mentioned earlier, it is dangerously misleading to assume all jihadists think and act uniformly about strategy, tactics, and the role of CBRN weapons. Certainly there are patterns and commonalities from which general themes can be inferred. But most of what we know about jihadists' strategic objectives—and the tactical and operational means by which they seek to achieve these objectives—is drawn from documents disseminated by key ideologues and thinkers within the al-Qa'ida movement. Thus, a careful assessment of al-Qa'ida's own operational manuals and literature provides a valuable case study for how jihadists choose their targets.

To begin with, the primary strategic objective of the network has direct relevance for the question of targeting: to "bleed" (exhaust) the United States economically and militarily both by directly causing inordinate economic losses and forcing the United States to spend excessive amounts of money to protect its vast infrastructure. According to al-Qa'ida's main literature and manuals, the United States derives its considerable military power and political influence from its superior economy. It is believed, therefore, that disrupting the American economy will in turn defeat the United States as an opponent and end its military hegemony and presence overseas. Therefore, impeding Western economies is, as one al-Qa'ida member aptly stated, "the most dangerous and effective arena of Jihad, because we live in a materialistic world."[14] Consequently, al-Qa'ida cells are encouraged to attack targets with high economic value that will result in serious economic losses in the United States.

The following excerpts from *Sawt al-Jihad* (*The Voice of Jihad*), al-Qa'ida's official publication in Saudi Arabia, underscore the network's primary strategic objective of weakening the United States economically by forcing it to expend enormous sums of money on protecting its vast infrastructure, as well as by attacking its economic assets directly:

> What else is there to say about September 11?
>
> Since September 11th America has been spending billions of dollars to protect its infrastructure and interests around the world.... The attacker determines the timing of the strike. He will carry a concentrated strike one time at a weak point and then sit in ambush again. So the enemy will look for a gap and close it, this is not necessarily where he was hit but all other similar targets. So striking the American embassies in Kenya and Tanzania means protecting every American embassy in the world. Striking the [USS] *Cole* at sea means protecting all American assets in the seas. Diversifying targets means protecting all American things in every land that may have terrorists!!
>
> If the enemy used his economy to rule the world and hire collaborators, then we need to strike this economy with harsh attacks to bring it down on the heads of its owners. If the enemy has built its economy on the basis of open markets and free trade by getting the monies of investors, then we have to prove to these investors that the enemy's land is not safe for them, that his economy is not capable of guarding their monies, so they would abandon him to suffer alone the fall of his economy.
>
> This is about Jihad against the crusader enemy, so what about the September 11th operation? Hijacking planes is a well known tactic, which was used by various fighters and freedom fighters, so what's new about this operation? People used to hijack planes and consider them a target, but those who are willing to put in the extra effort turned these planes into a method only, a projectile shot in the heart of the enemy.... The enemy used to protect his external interests and spend exorbitant sums for this protection, so he was surprised when he was struck inside his borders. The enemy used to protect a thousand interests outside his country, now he has to protect a million interests inside his country that need continuing protection!! The attack on the Trade Center forced America since that day to spend billions to protect the huge economic infrastructure that runs the American economy. Using planes in this attack has forced America to spend billions to protect the planes and airports in all possible ways. This protection is not limited to the hundreds of American airports but also to every airport in the world. Anyone related to the aviation field is spending excessive amounts to guard air travel; the matter has reached protecting the skies.... This is how America was transformed after one strike, protecting all that can be struck, as they guard all that can be used to strike with!! This is related to armed protection. As for surveillance, now America monitors everything, it even needed to change its laws and to give up on what it used to pride itself of civil rights and personal freedoms. It has violated all previous taboos searching for terrorists.[15]

In October 2005, Abu Mus`ab al-Najdi, a Saudi al-Qa'ida affiliate, published a short manuscript that emphasized the network's strategic objective of attacking economic targets. In a seven-page document entitled "Al-Qa'ida's Battle is Economic not Military," he outlines in great detail the rationale behind attacking soft targets of high economic value by noting the following:

> The Islamic nation [umma] has entered through al-Qa'ida's war with America a new period that is different from all the other periods experienced by Muslims against their

enemies. This period is based on the economic war due to the peculiar nature of the adversary in this ferocious battle. Usually, wars that are based on military strength and victory belong to those who are militarily superior on the battlefield. But our war with America is fundamentally different for the first priority is defeating her economically. For that, anything that negatively affects their economy is considered for us a step in the right direction in the path to victory. Military defeats do not greatly affect how we measure total victory, but these defeats indirectly impinge on the economy, which can be demonstrated with breaching the confidence of capitalists and investors in this nation's ability to safeguard its various trade and dealings.

In light of this matter, the difficulty and ease of the task becomes apparent. In addition, it becomes apparent why additional al-Qa'ida strikes inside the United States have been delayed. When thinking about military strikes, it is not difficult to carry out an attack that would kill a good number of American civilians, but in my opinion this is a waste of resources without much benefit. However, when directing these resources against economic targets, it is more effective and can get us many steps closer toward victory. An attack that kills a large number of Americans cannot achieve a tenth of this effectiveness. This reveals the importance of the blessed September 11th attack, which is not that it killed a large number of infidels, but what is more important is the economic effect that this strike achieved.... I will not be exaggerating if I said that striking the Pentagon was purely symbolic and had no noticeable effect on the course of the battle. It is symbolic for it shows the Americans that their foremost military facility can be destroyed by a handful of individuals, which is a blow to their morale and a point of pride for the Islamic peoples who have been drowning in defeat for many years.

An operation targeting a field of infrastructure in a new country that does not have a history of countering these operations is considered as bleeding (exhausting) to the greater enemy America and the targeted nation itself. It is so because these nations will be required to protect all similar potential targets which results in economic exhaustion (bleeding).... For example, if a hotel that caters to Western tourists in Indonesia is targeted, the enemy will be required to protect all hotels that cater to Western tourists in all countries, which may become a target of similar attacks. You can say the same thing about living residences, economic establishments, embassies, and others.[16]

An assessment of al-Qa'ida's targeting rationale reveals that the network's most likely targets will be facilities of high economic value in the United States and Europe. Although the network's literature does not specify which precise sectors it intends to target, such facilities would most likely include financial districts and buildings, airports and planes, train and bus stations, ports and ships, subways, shopping malls, hotels, resorts, tourist attractions, sports arenas, entertainment centers, and embassies. For many of these types of targets, the interconnected, network-centric infrastructures within which they are situated would lead to a ripple effect of any WMD terrorist attack. That is, an attack on a critical component of a country's transportation infrastructure would impact upon such things as power distribution, food and water supply chains, waste management, the domestic retail sector, and so forth. As noted earlier, tactical decisions include "return on investment" considerations, and thus if jihadists were to acquire a weapon of mass destruction, it would likely be deployed in such a manner that our interconnected infrastructure vulnerabilities would amplify its effect. This would especially be the case if jihadists were in possession of only one or a few CBRN weapons and would want to maximize the potential benefits derived from using them.

In addition to "bleeding" the United States economically, attacking American targets in Muslim countries is also aimed at discouraging alliances between the United States and regional "apostate" governments. As described above, according to al-Qa'ida's own training manuals and literature, its primary targets are Western facilities of high economic value, in addition to Western corporations and Western individuals conducting business in Muslim countries, and targets related to the oil and tourism industries either locally or in the West.

The rationale for attacking economic targets is also articulated in al-Qa'ida's urban guerrilla training manual, entitled "Military Sciences—Targets Inside the Cities." In this manual, which is aimed at instructing jihadist formations on the tactics for conducting operations inside cities in the Muslim world, author Abi Hajin Abd al-Aziz al-Muqrin (a former al-Qa'ida commander in Saudi Arabia) specifically tells his students to concentrate their attacks on economic targets. He states

> The objective of attacking these targets: breaching the security and climate of stability that is necessary for economic growth, such as the bombing of oil pipelines in Iraq which has made it less appealing for foreign corporations. At the very least it prevents a secure climate that is needed for robbing the assets of Muslims.

Additional objectives described in this manual include

> Removal of foreign capitalists from domestic markets; also negative economic consequences on their native lands as occurred very quickly following the blessed strikes in Madrid which affected the entire European economy. Among these are double strikes that affect the economy of the Crusader or Jewish or apostates regimes.

Among the examples of strikes suggested by al-Muqrin are

- striking Jewish Crusader investments in Muslim lands.
- striking international corporations.
- striking international economists and business experts.
- striking imports from crusader nations through military means (as occurred in the bombing and burning of certain American restaurants), or through political means like boycotts.
- striking raw materials stolen from Muslim lands, such as the strike on the French oil carrier or the strikes on Iraqi oil pipelines. These kinds of economic strikes are determined by the high leadership who wait for the appropriate time and place.
- assassination of Jews who work in business and disciplining those who cooperate with them economically following a proper warning. Only those who are proven to be collaborating apostates should be assassinated.[17]

In addition to attacking targets of high economic value, al-Qa'ida also aims at deterring Westerners from carrying out business in the Muslim world. According to statements by the network, Western commerce has led to corrupt and "apostate" regimes in Muslim countries (especially Saudi Arabia, Egypt, Jordan, and Morocco—the home countries of many al-Qa'ida members). As demonstrated in the past several years, al-Qa'ida has routinely attacked Western targets (including hotels and resorts) in Muslim countries such as Iraq, Saudi Arabia, Jordan, Egypt, and Indonesia. While killing people indiscriminately may not always be in the jihadists' best interest (as was demonstrated, for example, by the infamous letter from Ayman al-Zawahiri to Abu Musab al-Zarqawi imploring him to tone down the violence in Iraq), several of al-Qa'ida's more prominent ideologues (e.g., Suleiman Abu Ghayth) have argued that targeting certain populations of people is not only strategically sanctioned but ideologically justified. In his manual, Abi Hajin al-Muqrin also specifies to the readers in sinister detail the categories of "human targets" that al-Qa'ida wishes to attack. He states:

> We should target and kill Jews and Christians. We say to all who fight god and his prophet, we bring you slaughter. In our current reality we should not be deterred by borders or geography, all Muslim dwellings and lands are ours. We should turn the lands of the infidels into a hell as they have turned our lands into a hell. For that, all operational cells should not pay attention to geographic borders as described by the enemies, but aim to transform infidel lands into battlefronts, as they have turned Muslim lands into fields of experimentation for their weapons and inventions. We need to transform their lands into hell and destruction, and the sons of the Muslim nations are capable of this, god permitting.

Clearly, CBRN weapons would be an important and effective means to achieving the goals outlined in this particular passage. Al-Muqrin's manual continues:

> The priority in these operations should be given to Jews and Christians with official connection to Muslim lands. It is advisable to start with targeting unprotected easy targets. Priority is given to the dependants of infidel nations that are directly involved in supporting local apostates. For example, in Saudi Arabia first target Americans, then the English. In Iraq, the Americans. In Afghanistan, the Americans. In Algeria, the French. In Indonesia, the Australians...etc.

Al-Muqrin also categorizes human targets by importance:

1. Jews: They are divided into various degrees by importance. First American and Israeli Jews, then British Jews, then French...etc.
2. Christians: They are categorized by order of importance as follows:

- Americans
- British
- Spanish
- Australians
- Canadians
- Italians

These groups are further divided into:

- businessmen. For business has global importance in this age.
- diplomats, politicians, intellectuals, analysts, and political emissaries.
- scientists and experts.
- military commanders and soldiers.
- tourists, visiting entertainers, and all which have received a warning from the Mujahideen to abstain from or evacuate Muslim lands.[18]

CBRN weapons would play an important role in enhancing al-Qa'ida's target selection calculus because, despite their relatively modest killing capability (with the exception of nuclear weapons), their deployment against civilian and transportation facilities is likely to cause significant economic damage. For example, the al-Qa'ida manual for the manufacture of the previously mentioned *al-Mubtakkar,* entitled *Al-mubtakkar al-farid: Li irsaal al-safah al-athiri ila al-kafir al-`anid (The Unique Invention: To Deliver the*

Gaseous Killer to the Stubborn Infidel), which instructs jihadists on how to manufacture a hydrogen cyanide dispersal device, outlines the following specific locations and facilities where *al-Mubtakkar* can be used:[19]

- brothels
- theaters
- markets and shopping malls
- jewish temples
- dancing halls
- trains (not stations due to camera surveillance)
- schools
- hospitals
- bars and restaurants
- banks and loan facilities
- cinemas
- gyms
- casinos
- churches on Muslim lands
- government offices (security and intelligence)

As this target list demonstrates, al-Qa'ida is not only concerned with causing mass civilian casualties, but additionally causing considerable economic damage, achieving a symbolic effect and gaining media coverage by attacking these soft targets. One can easily imagine how significant an attack using *al-Mubtakkar* on trains, subways, or shopping malls would be. Even if the attack only resulted in a handful of deaths, it would surely result in the extended closure of these facilities, a massive search of the facilities, and an expensive period of reconstruction. Such an attack would surely have a significant economic impact on the community targeted and the nation as a whole, for it would necessitate that all similar facilities throughout the country are adequately protected and prepared to deal with such an event. And constant media coverage and political fear-mongering would negatively impact consumer confidence, a key economic indicator.

Another CBRN manual further enforces this point. The document, entitled "Instances of Radiation Pollution from 1945–1987," and published on a well-known al-Qa'ida Web site, highlights the group's aim of causing severe economic losses to the United States and its allies. In an effort to cause serious economic damage, the document encourages jihadists to attack the West by employing Cesium-137 in radiological dispersal devices (RDDs). It specifically underscores the economic repercussions of RDD attacks by stating the following:

> The important thing is to disperse radioactive material in a large commercial area so the government is forced to shut down this area, which will cause this country massive economic disruption due to the following reasons:
>
> - the high costs of decontamination of radioactive areas
> - the high economic losses in this large commercial area due to closure
> - subsequent unemployment and loss of jobs
> - stoppage of general life in that area
> - large compounded problems are to follow due to these losses.

> Suggested cities: Las Vegas (the city of fornication and gambling that does not sleep)—New York—London—Sydney—Tokyo—Moscow—Other large tourist cities—and commercial capitals of all infidel nations.[20]

In sum, numerous statements, manuals, and other al-Qa'ida documents reveal a fairly consistent pattern of target selection and strategic rationales for those targets. However, to truly understand the WMD threat posed by al-Qa'ida, it is necessary to examine the differences among the members and followers of this movement, along with their different strategic and operational constraints and objectives.

REFINING OUR ANALYSIS OF AL-QA'IDA'S TARGETING

Most observers have described al-Qa'ida in the generic sense of being a unified, monolithic entity. However, nothing could be further from the truth. In reality, as terrorism expert Bruce Hoffman recently explained, al-Qa'ida should be viewed as a globally networked movement with at least four dimensions, each of which has its own distinct set of operational preferences, organizational capabilities and constraints, and attack decision-making parameters.[21]

The first, called "al-Qa'ida central," is comprised of leftover leaders of the pre-9/11 organization, ostensibly led by Usama bin Ladin, Ayman al-Zawahiri, and a small cadre of others who are believed to be hiding in the mountainous border region of Afghanistan and Pakistan. This dimension of al-Qa'ida may be actively engaged in commissioning some attacks, directing surveillance and collating reconnaissance, planning operations, and approving their execution. But their most important role in a WMD attack will probably be in providing ideological inspiration and perhaps financial support and some knowledge of strategic or tactical value to others within the movement who have greater operational capabilities and fewer constraints.

At the same time, however, we should be mindful of recent intelligence reports that indicate that al-Qa'ida central is reconstituting itself in the tribal areas of Pakistan and could in time regain the operational capabilities it once enjoyed during the late 1990s. As the July 2007 National Intelligence Estimate observes, this group "is and will remain the most serious terrorist threat to the Homeland, as its central leadership continues to plan high-impact plots, while pushing others in extremist Sunni communities to mimic its efforts and to supplement its capabilities. We assess the group has protected or regenerated key elements of its Homeland attack capability, including: a safehaven in the Pakistan Federally Administered Tribal Areas (FATA), operational lieutenants, and its top leadership."[22] Perhaps over the long-term horizon, barring any extensive military deployment (by Pakistan or the United States) in Waziristan, al-Qa'ida central will re-emerge as the foremost threat behind a potential WMD terrorist attack.

The second dimension of al-Qa'ida is comprised of formally established insurgent or terrorist groups like those mentioned above, which have received training, arms, money, "spiritual guidance," and other assistance from al-Qa'ida central. These groups are located in dozens of countries across Asia, the Middle East, and North Africa. These so-called "al-Qa'ida affiliate groups"—like Jemaah Islamiyah (in Indonesia), the Islamic Army of Aden (in Yemen), Harkat al-Mujahideen (in Kashmir), and the Moroccan Islamic Combatant Group—have been responsible for hundreds of terrorist attacks since before 9/11. Because of these groups' ideological (and sometimes logistical) relationship with al-Qa'ida central, we have often attributed these attacks to Usama bin Ladin and his close colleagues, regardless of the absence of any direct command or control linkages. This is precisely what Bin Ladin envisioned for al-Qa'ida: armed groups inspired to act on behalf of the global movement.

However, the geographically specific nature of virtually all these groups—that is, with nationally or regionally oriented memberships, political agendas, and available targets—poses some constraints on the viability of CBRN weapons. Most of these affiliate groups focus their targeting primarily on the "near enemy" (local apostate or non-Mulsim regimes) as opposed to the "far enemy" (the United States and the West), and thus a WMD attack would in essence wreak havoc "in their own backyard" and diminish the likelihood of helping the group achieve their political aspirations. For example, if the Moroccan Islamic Combatant Group were to carry out a WMD attack in Morocco, they would surely lose whatever local support and operational flexibility they have within the region. Furthermore, attacks that negatively impact the economic well-being of a group's local support base would make it harder for the group to sustain operations, possibly weakening their ability to conduct future attacks. The same could be said for the jihadists in Bangladesh, Indonesia, Malaysia, the Philippines, Yemen, Libya, Tunisia, and so forth. Thus, while these groups may currently be considered more operationally capable than al-Qa'ida central of conducting a WMD attack, they are only slightly more likely to do so because of strategic constraints, and would have to carefully weigh the kinds of blowback ramifications that do not concern Bin Ladin, al-Zawahiri, and the other members of the stateless al-Qa'ida central.

The third dimension of the movement is comprised of dispersed, ad hoc groupings of al-Qa'ida adherents that may have (or previously had) some direct connection with al-Qa'ida, but are no longer members of any formal group. There are two subcategories within this dimension: individuals who have had some prior terrorism experience, and may have been involved in some previous jihadist campaigns in Algeria, the Balkans, or Chechnya—or perhaps more recently in Iraq—and may have trained in some al-Qa'ida facility, perhaps in Afghanistan, Yemen, or Sudan before 9/11. Examples include Ahmad Ressam (the so-called "Millennium Plot" bomber, whose target was Los Angeles International Airport), Kamal Bourgass (who was indicted in the United Kingdom for conspiracy to use ricin in a terrorist attack), and Dhiren Barot (who was arrested in the United Kingdom after authorities discovered a plot to use radioactive "dirty bombs" in a series of attacks against U.S. financial targets and London hotels and train stations). All of these individuals had at some point in time trained in jihadist camps in Pakistan, Kashmir, Malaysia, or the Philippines. This category also includes trained but unaffiliated individuals like the suicide bombers who attacked the London underground on July 7, 2005, two of whom are believed to have received explosives training by an al-Qa'ida operational commander in Pakistan.

This dimension of al-Qa'ida is perhaps the most dangerous when considering the threat of WMD terrorism. These individuals may have just enough tactical training to be competent, along with significant personal motivation, and yet lack the geographically based constraints of the formal al-Qa'ida affiliate groups. They may have the ability to conduct covert operations, or the requisite level of self-discipline and commitment to earn an advanced degree in biology, chemistry, or physics. They may be loosely connected with criminal underground networks—as was the case with the 2004 Madrid bombers—who provide them with access to knowledge, explosives, and other weapons that are useful for conducting basic terrorist attacks, and perhaps even more exotic CBRN materials. And their lack of membership in any formal group could make it more difficult for authorities to gather intelligence about any planned attack.

Further, individuals within this realm of al-Qa'ida may wish to distinguish themselves by acquiring a more sophisticated tactical capability. There is a certain level of competition within the global jihadist movement among groups and members, sometimes fueled by a need to attract greater support and resources from the global community of sympathizers, which may lead them down a path toward CBRN weapons. Competition often breeds innovation, creativity, and other attributes of human nature that can be harnessed for good or, in this case, for potentially catastrophic terrorism. And at the same time, these ad hoc groupings of al-Qa'ida adherents may be relatively unconcerned about managing perceptions or community blowback, and may not feel constrained by the strategic considerations that influence the tactical and targeting decisions of other elements of al-Qa'ida. Overall, the levels of knowledge and motivation found among groups and individuals in this category suggest a greater WMD attack potential than in the others.

The fourth dimension of al-Qa'ida includes radicalized individuals who have absolutely no direct connection with al-Qa'ida or any other identifiable terrorist group, but nonetheless are prepared to carry out attacks in solidarity with or support of al-Qa'ida's jihadist agenda. Their relationship with al-Qa'ida is more inspirational than actual. They are typically motivated by a shared sense of enmity and grievance felt toward the United States and the West, as well as the apostate regimes they support, and more generally complain about the oppression of Muslims in Palestine, Kashmir, Chechnya, and elsewhere.

Most individuals within this dimension of al-Qa'ida have been rank amateurs, lacking any real disciplined training and unable to successfully pull off a dramatic terrorist attack. The likelihood of a WMD terrorist attack from this quarter is thus relatively low, but because of inadequate operational capabilities rather than divergent ideological or strategic considerations. However, one cannot rule out the possibility of a highly skilled individual becoming inspired by the justifications for WMD violence put forth by al-Qa'ida's ideologues. After all, a primary objective of Usama bin Ladin has always been to encourage and facilitate a worldwide Islamic revolution—to launch a socio-political action movement of global proportion, and to inspire, motivate, and animate radicalized Muslims to join the movement's fight. "Join the Jihad." "Think globally, act locally." These are the core messages of al-Qa'ida's massive strategic communications effort. One can only hope that their messages do not find resonance with an angry, disenfranchised nuclear lab technician or a biochemist with access to some of the world's most lethal pathogens.

Equally important, al-Qa'ida–inspired individuals or cells may desire to prove themselves to al-Qa'ida central or simply wish to acquire greater glory (or notoriety) within the global jihadist movement by aspiring to develop a WMD capability themselves or by accumulating and proliferating WMD knowledge for others. This is illustrated in the case of the "Nuclear Preparation Encyclopedia," an extensive manual consisting of multiple chapters compiled by a jihadist activist operating under the *nom de guerre* Layth al-Islam (Lion of Islam), who states that "I have been studying nuclear physics for two years on various scientific and Jihadist Web sites."[23] He adds that his posting is "a present to the Emir [Commander] of the Mujahideen Sheikh Usama Bin Ladin, God bless him, for the Jihad in the path of God," and that it aims to empower the jihadist community with knowledge of nuclear weapons.[24] Following its posting on the *al-Firdaws* jihadist Web site in October 2005, this manual was viewed by more than 57,000 viewers and received considerable attention in jihadist circles.[25]

CONCLUSION

All four variations of al-Qa'ida, as discussed in this chapter, are likely to employ similar tactical and targeting behaviors. For example, suicide bombings will surely remain prominent within their attack arsenal, and their targeting preferences will seek to have a strategic, economic, and symbolic effect. Operational constraints—including the difficulty in acquiring certain toxins, pathogens, and radiological materials, and the high levels of risks that these items pose to operatives during the planning and preparation stages of an attack—may be a key deterrent for most (but clearly not all) jihadists. Some devices like the aforementioned *al-Mubtakkar* can be readily assembled by jihadist operatives, provided they can procure the precursor chemicals. They may also find it useful to identify and use "pre-positioned weapons." Through the attacks of September 11, 2001, al-Qa'ida central modeled a strategy of using "pre-positioned weapons"—no weapons were smuggled into the country, no exotic chemicals or pathogens were needed, and no disgruntled scientists or black market profiteers were involved in that attack. Rather, the success of 9/11 (from their perspective) was the product of commitment, training, funds, flight information, and box cutters. Thus, when considering the WMD terrorism threat, we should certainly be concerned about the vulnerabilities associated with nuclear power plants, chemical storage facilities, biotechnology labs, dams, water protection infrastructure (a la Hurricane Katrina), and railway tanker cars carrying toxic chemicals through or near populated areas, or near economically critical targets, particularly those related to energy security.

In the future, al-Qa'ida central may emerge as the most likely threat for carrying out acts of WMD terrorism, especially if Abu Khabab is indeed able to resurrect al-Qa'ida's program to obtain or develop weapons of mass destruction. However, this analysis suggests that currently the most likely threat of WMD terrorism may stem from ad hoc groupings of al-Qa'ida adherents who may have (or previously had) some direct connection with al-Qa'ida but are not now members of any formal group. They will likely face greater financial and operational constraints than al-Qa'ida central or affiliate groups, but are also less likely to be constrained by the ideological or strategic concerns about causing counterproductive violence. Assuming that they follow the targeting guidance issued by leaders of al-Qa'ida central, they are likely to attack energy, transportation, or other infrastructure targets in the West, but they may also attack these kinds of targets in the Muslim world, arguing that these are the sources of power for an "apostate" local regime. Furthermore, because of globalization and the increasing interdependence among all nations, attacking energy-related targets in the Middle East and Asia would have a strategic ripple effect in the West. And, unlike the regional affiliates or other elements of al-Qa'ida, these ad hoc groups of motivated jihadists are less likely to be constrained by strategic or ideological "counterproductive violence" considerations, and thus may deploy WMD on Muslim lands regardless of whether or not it would provoke dire condemnation from the Muslim masses.

Our analysis supports the suggestion that future al-Qa'ida attacks are more likely to involve conventional high explosives—whether or not via suicide bombings—than CBRN weapons. Targeting guidance emphasizes economic impact over mass casualties, and jihadists have already become familiar (and had some success) with conventional high explosives, so overall there are relatively few vectors of ideological or strategic justification for taking on the additional risks that would come with WMD. Further, as noted earlier in this chapter, it is likely that only a small minority of CBRN weapons would be useful to jihadists. Overall, within the jihadist world fueled by al-Qa'ida's ideology, there are relatively few groups or individuals with the requisite combination of both tactical competence and strategic freedom to actually benefit from investing the time, money, manpower, and effort into planning and carrying out a WMD attack.

And yet, all of the available intelligence indicates that members of al-Qa'ida—all dimensions, al-Qa'ida central and its supporters and inspired cells—are keenly interested in acquiring CBRN weapons. Al-Qa'ida central seeks to develop or acquire these weapons through the resurrected work of Abu Khabab, and the movement as a whole encourage this through the proliferation of WMD manuals on the Internet. The economic damage these weapons could inflict would surely aid them in their quest to degrade the strength and political will of the United States and reduce our willingness to maintain a presence in the Middle East or to support the "infidel, corrupt regimes" in the region that are the true intermediate-term targets of al-Qa'ida's wrath. While conventional explosives and suicide bombings will remain predominant in the jihadist milieu, it is only a matter of time before their motivations and opportunities converge to produce a WMD attack.

NOTES

1. J. Michael McConnell, "Annual Threat Assessment of the Director of National Intelligence for the Senate Select Committee on Intelligence," February 5, 2008, 7
2. Josh Meyer, "Al Qa'ida Said to Focus on WMDs," *Los Angeles Times,* February 3, 2008.
3. Ibid.
4. This is a catch phrase used—some may say abused—by several government officials, security experts, academics, and comedians to discuss the likelihood of the use of WMD against the United States. Stephen Flynn, in his book *America the Vulnerable* (New York: HarperCollins, 2004), spoke of containers as "the poor man's missile" and implied that the question is "when, not if" such containers will be used to deliver WMD into the United States.
5. For example, see Sammy Salama and Lydia Hansell, "Does Intent Equal Capability? Al Qa'ida and Weapons of Mass Destruction," *Nonproliferation Review* 12, no. 3 (November 2003), 615–653.
6. For a thorough analysis of this, see *Teaching Terror: Strategic and Tactical Learning in the Terrorist World,* eds. James J. F. Forest (Lanham, MD: Rowman & Littlefield, 2008).
7. Bruce Hoffman, "CBRN Terrorism Post-9/11" in *Weapons of Mass Destruction and Terrorism*, eds. Russell Howard and James J.F. Forest (New York: McGraw-Hill, 2007).
8. John V. Parachini, "Comparing Motives and Outcomes of Mass Casualty Terrorism Involving Conventional and Unconventional Weapons," *Studies in Conflict and Terrorism*, vol. 24, no. 5, (September 2001), 389–406.
9. This Matsumoto attack did not kill the three judges, but it did inflict deaths and casualties on neighbors and succeeded in delaying the trial that the Aum thought it might lose. For a list of Aum attacks with biological agents, see David E. Kaplan, "Aum Shinrikyo (1995)," in *Toxic Terror: Assessing Terrorist Use of Chemical and Biological Weapons*, ed. Jonathan B. Tucker (Cambridge, MA: MIT Press, 2000), 221.

10. Peter Franceschina, "Anthrax Attacks Remain Unsolved," *Baltimore Sun*, October 15, 2006, 1. See Russell Howard, "Preface" in *Weapons of Mass Destruction and Terrorism*, edited by Russell Howard and James Forest (New York: McGraw-Hill, 2008). However, in July 2008, Bruce Iving—a suspect in the case—committed suicide before the FBI could proceed with its indictment and is considered by some as the perpertrator of this attack.
11. J. Michael McConnell, "Annual Threat Assessment of the Director of National Intelligence for the Senate Select Committee on Intelligence," February 5, 2008, 7
12. Al-Suri is a Syrian who spent the 1990s working with al-Qa'ida leaders to train fighters in the use of poisons and chemicals at two camps near Jalalabad and Kabul. Statement made on October 21, 2002.
13. Statement made September 28, 2006. MEMRI Special Dispatch Series—No. 1309.
14. Nur al-Din al-Kurdi, "The Arenas of Jihad," *Dharwat al-Sunam* (*Peak of the Camel's Hump*), an online magazine, 2006, 3: 27–28.
15. Akhu Man Ta`a Allah, "What Else is There to Say About September 11," *Sawt al-Jihad (Voice of Jihad Magazine)*, 2004, vol. 26, 35–42.
16. Abu Mus`ab al-Najadi, "Al-Qa'ida's Battle Is Economic Not Military," October 3, 2005.
17. Abi Hajin Abd al-Aziz al-Muqrin, "Military Sciences—Targets in the Cities," *Mu`askar al-Battar (al-Battar Camp) Magazine*, 7: 23–27.
18. Ibid.
19. "Al-Mubtakkar al-Farid: Li Irsaal al-Safah al-Athiri Ila al-Kafir al-`Anid—The Unique Invention: To Deliver the Gaseous Killer to the Stubborn Infidel," *al-Firdaws*, October 2005.
20. Abu al-Usud al-Faqir, "Instances of Radiation Pollution from 1945–1987," *al-Faruq*.
21. Testimony before Congress, *Combating Terrorism Center's Web site*, February 14, 2007, available at http://ctc.usma.edu/Hoffman_ Testimony021407.pdf.
22. National Intelligence Council, "National Intelligence Estimate: The Terrorist Threat to the US Homeland," July 2007. Office of the Director of National Intelligence, Washington, DC: NIC.
23. "Al-Qa'ida Jihadi Website Publishes 'Nuclear Preparation Encyclopedia,'" *WMDInsights*, December 2005/January 2006.
24. Ibid.
25. Uzi Mahnaimi and Tom Walker, "Al-Qa'ida woos recruits with nuclear bomb Web site," *The Sunday Times*, November 6, 2005.

CHAPTER 4

Jihadist Capabilities and the Diffusion of Knowledge

Sammy Salama and Edith Bursac

CONTENTS

INTRODUCTION

It has been often stated that the prospect of weapons of mass destruction (WMD) terrorism is the foremost danger to American national security. Since the September 11 attacks on the United States, this has become a more realistic danger because of al-Qa'ida's increasing global network and demonstrated desire to kill thousands of innocent civilians, as described by Jeffrey M. Bale in Chapter 1 of this volume. Evidence suggests that the network has made multiple attempts to acquire and weaponize chemical, biological, radioactive, and nuclear (CBRN) agents and to disseminate technical information to its supporters. Reportedly, al-Qa'ida cells or affiliates have attempted to acquire biological agents, various chemical agents, radiological material, and uranium since the mid-1990s. The individual chapters in Section II ("Agents of Harm") of this book discuss each weapon type in greater detail. There are also allegations that the network has planned to use biological and chemical agents in terrorist attacks, in addition to its plans for attacking nuclear facilities.[1]

The first important question to ask is whether al-Qa'ida's current capability to engage in WMD matches their actual sinister intent.[2] To answer this question one needs to examine the evolution of al-Qa'ida's technical familiarity with WMD and, most particularly, the merit of actual CBRN production instructions as depicted and disseminated in the group's own training manuals and literature. Monitoring and analysis of primary al-Qa'ida literature provide the most revealing window into the concrete motivations, goals, and capabilities of this network. This chapter will discuss al-Qa'ida's interest in WMD and its attitude toward these agents, explore how al-Qa'ida uses the Internet to facilitate and proliferate training, and, most importantly, it will analyze the network's likely capabilities with respect to WMD by evaluating the merit of CBRN production instructions as portrayed in al-Qa'ida's training manuals and Web sites.

AL-QA'IDA'S INTEREST AND ATTITUDE TOWARD WMD

Usama bin Ladin's initial interest in the acquisition of CBRN agents began during his stay in Sudan in 1994. With the support of the Sudanese military and elements of the ruling National Islamic Front (NIF), Bin Ladin began research into chemical weapons in a laboratory in Khartoum.[3] Bin Ladin also allegedly hired an Egyptian scientist to purchase one kilogram of uranium from South Africa.[4] WMD acquisition has since been a consistent theme in Usama bin Ladin's public statements. In December 1999, he declared that "Acquiring weapons for the defense of Muslims is a religious duty. If I indeed have acquired these weapons I am carrying out a duty. It would be a sin for Muslims not to try and possess weapons that would prevent the infidels from inflicting harm on Muslims."[5]

Following the official union of Usama bin Ladin's al-Qa'ida with Ayman al-Zawahiri's faction of the Egyptian Islamic Jihad in Afghanistan on February 23, 1998, a new and more dangerous transnational network called "The World Islamic Front for Jihad Against the Jews and Crusaders" emerged.[6] Subsequently, this new incarnation of al-Qa'ida's ruling body, the *Majlis al-Shura*, debated the possibility of acquiring WMD capability. At the time, the leadership was concerned about the prospects of American deployment in Afghanistan. The al-Qa'ida hierarchy was particularly interested in achieving WMD capability as a deterrent in order to prevent the United States from invading Afghanistan and to counterbalance existing American and Israeli WMD arsenals. As a result of these internal discussions, the al-Qa'ida leadership decided to pursue a very ambitious WMD strategy. Al-Qa'ida's ultimate goal was to acquire nuclear weapons as a defensive option in order to retaliate against possible American aggression in Afghanistan and other Muslim territories. Furthermore, al-Qa'ida leaders decided that the acquisition of nuclear, chemical, and biological weapons would be a priority for their organization.[7]

Throughout the early 1990s, al-Qa'ida's WMD policy has evolved from defensive to offensive. Following the 9/11 attacks and America's subsequent invasion of Afghanistan, the network has been planning to use WMD as a first strike weapon against the United States and its allies. In light of the U.S.-led occupation of Afghanistan and Iraq, al-Qa'ida leaders view WMD attacks against the United States and the resulting mass casualties as a legitimate retribution for current and past killings of Muslims. In November 2002, Bin Ladin emphasized this sentiment by stating that: "This is an unfair division. The time has

FIGURE 4.1 Cover page of CBW manual *A Course in Popular Poisons and Deadly Gases* by Abu Hadhifa al-Shami.

come for us to be equal... Just as you kill, you are killed. Just as you bombard, you are bombarded. Rejoice at the harm coming to you."[8]

Another important milestone that enhanced al-Qa'ida's posture toward and quest for WMD capability occurred in May 2003, when the leadership obtained religious justification from a young but respected Saudi Islamic scholar, Shaykh Nasir bin Hamid al-Fahd, to permit WMD use against the United States. In his twenty-five–page document entitled, "A Treatise on the Legal Status of Using Weapons of Mass Destruction against Infidels," the Sunni Muslim scholar empowered al-Qa'ida with a *fatwa* (religious decree) and thus provided the network with the religious justification needed to carry out such an attack in the future.[9] In this *fatwa*, Shaykh Nasir al-Fahd stated, "This matter is so obvious to Muslims that it needs no demonstration.... Anyone who considers America's aggression against Muslims and their lands during the past decades...will conclude that striking her is permissible merely on the rule of treating as one has been treated. No other arguments need be mentioned. Some brothers have totaled the number of Muslims killed directly or indirectly by their weapons and come up with a figure of nearly 10 million."[10] He also argued in his treatise that, in a state of jihad, the mass killings of American civilians is permissible, "Thus the situation in this regard is that if those engaged in jihad establish that the evil of the infidels can be repelled only by attacking them at night with weapons of mass destruction, they may be used even if they annihilate all the infidels."[11] Shaykh al-Fahd concluded by arguing that while the killing of other Muslims is usually forbidden by God, in the path of jihad it should be permitted. He stated, "as long as jihad has been commanded...and it can be carried out only in this way [i.e., with Muslims being killed in attacks by Muslims], it is permitted."[12]

In more recent al-Qa'ida statements it is abundantly clear that if and when the network acquires WMD capability, it would not hesitate to use such weapons against suitable targets. As the late Abu Musab al-Zarqawi—the leader of al-Qa'ida in Iraq—claimed, "if we had such a bomb—and we ask God that we have such a bomb soon—we would not hesitate for a moment to strike Israeli towns, such as Eilat, Tel Aviv and others."[13] Al-Zarqawi's sentiments were reiterated by another important jihadist thinker and one of the most prolific al-Qa'ida strategists, Mustafa Sit Maryam Nasar—better known as Abu Musab al-Suri—who published the famous manuscript, "The International Islamic Resistance Call."[14] In this 1,600-page treatise for global jihadists and in his "Letter of Reply to the U.S. State Department," al-Suri claims that weapons of mass destruction should be used against the United States. In addition, he criticizes Usama bin Ladin for not employing WMD in the 9/11 attacks by asserting that, "If I were consulted in the case of that operation I would advise the use of planes in flights from outside the US that would carry WMD. Hitting the US with WMD was and is still very complicated. Yet, it is possible after all, with Allah's help, and more important than being possible—it is vital."[15]

HOW JIHADIS DISSEMINATE TRAINING—OVERVIEW OF JIHADIST WEB SITES

It is difficult to imagine that the rapid spread of radical jihad, coupled with the immense growth of jihadist organizations worldwide, would have been possible without the facilitation of the Internet. Following the American invasion of Afghanistan in 2001, when al-Qa'ida was denied a cohesive geographic safe haven where it could attract and train members en masse, it resorted to the Internet to attract, recruit, and train jihadists worldwide. The al-Qa'ida network, its affiliates, and other jihadists have actively exploited the Internet in order to further their global propaganda campaign, attract new recruits to their cause, and empower the jihadist community with instructions on how to plan and carry out terrorist attacks against important targets worldwide.[16]

Since 9/11, a range of jihadist Web sites have surfaced on the Internet. Although exact numbers do not exist, experts estimate that over the past few years the number of jihadist Web sites has increased exponentially, from about 20 in the year 2000 to roughly 4,000 by 2005.[17] Others argue that the increase has been more dramatic and claim that the number of terrorist Web sites has grown from 12 to more than 4,800 from 2000 to 2006.[18] The study of such Web sites provides analysts with insight into the strategic thinking, capabilities, and intentions of the jihadist community.

The importance of these Web sites cannot be overemphasized, because the al-Qa'ida network relies heavily on the Internet to advance its mission. For example, Web sites provide al-Qa'ida with an effective tool to publicize its message and circulate a considerable amount of information. This in turn enables al-Qa'ida affiliates, supporters, and independent jihadist cells all over the world to learn from experienced al-Qa'ida operatives, such as senior operational chiefs and leading strategists. In addition to the daily postings by al-Qa'ida members, these outlets contain practically all extant material related to al-Qa'ida. The majority of these Web sites cover a large swath of material, including books by al-Qa'ida figures, statements by leaders, historical texts, writings of famous ideologues (e.g., Bin Taymiyya, Sayyid Qutb, and Abdullah Azzam), discussions on apostate and secular Muslim regimes, religious doctrines, and anti-Western discourse. A relatively small subset of these Web sites contains links to dozens of military magazines and operational training manuals, and an even smaller subset deals specifically with WMD. By, for instance, posting detailed operational instructions on how to attack potential targets, such Web sites can provide a virtual training camp for new recruits, and are designed to enable additional cells in various locations to successfully carry out terrorist acts.

OPERATIONAL WEB SITES

Operational Web sites make up a fraction of all jihadist Web sites, yet they are most menacing because they equip cell members and sympathizers with considerable numbers of operational manuals on facets of terrorism written by actual terror trainers. In addition to al-Qa'ida, several of its regional affiliates and countless independent jihadists have constructed their own Web sites. It is also apparent that many supporters of al-Qa'ida's global propaganda campaign are investing a great deal of effort to spread their message by utilizing multiple uniform resource locators (URL) and password-protected Web sites. Furthermore, it appears that contributors to jihadist Web sites are posting nearly identical information on various alternative Web sites whenever an operational jihadist Web site is taken down. The end result is that the counterterrorism community faces a great challenge in removing or blocking the dangerous information contained in these Web sites.

Efforts to remove jihadist Web sites are similar to American attempts to neutralize Soviet nuclear missiles in the 1980s, when the Reagan administration started the Star Wars program—ostensibly to destroy Soviet ballistic missiles in space in the event of a nuclear missile exchange. The Soviets responded by indicating that they would produce and launch a massive number of ballistic missiles simultaneously with the aim of overwhelming the planned American missile defense system. The jihadist community is following a similar pattern. Well aware that some of their Web sites will be removed or hacked by Western intelligence agencies, jihadist Web site administrators launch dozens of Web sites containing operational information continuously and in parallel fashion, thereby overwhelming the counterterrorism community. As a result, manuals initially posted in one place are quickly disseminated to other Web sites where they can be downloaded by al-Qa'ida sympathizers worldwide.

It is likely that the number of jihadists viewing operationally oriented Web sites falls somewhere between 40,000 and 60,000.[19] As these Web sites gain in popularity and are circulated to other outlets, the number of viewers is likely to continue to grow. It is important to note, however, that a sizeable number of persons surfing these Web sites are comprised of terrorism analysts, intelligence professionals, media reporters, academics, and researchers, and, thus, the number attributed to the online jihadist community is likely to be inflated.

Structure of an Average Operational Jihadist Web Site

Although there are numerous variations, most operational jihadist Web sites contain the following pages:

- General information
- *Da'wa*—the "Call to god" (i.e., religious proselytization, and indoctrination)
- Islamic poetry and writing
- News about jihadist cells (activities, advise and announcements)
- News and latest developments (current events)

- Communiqués from and news about Iraq, the current primary jihadist arena
- Other jihadist communiqués
- Video and audio postings (short videos or operations and/or lectures by important jihadist figures)
- Preparations for jihad (military preparation, which usually includes terrorist manuals and training books)
- Jihadist sisters (how women can help and participate in the jihad)
- Electronic jihad (hacking and other computer sabotage skills)
- Programs to download
- Mechanisms for recording suggestions and complaints
- Graphics and design elements

Depending on the standing of the Web site in the jihadist community and the significance of the topics discussed, each of these web pages may contain hundreds, if not thousands, of postings. Although a minority of jihadist Web sites display operational information, during the past years the number of these operational Web sites has increased as much as 1,500%, displaying inflammatory information and training materials that can be used by the jihadist community in order to enhance their skills in combat.[20]

NATURE OF INSTRUCTIONS PROVIDED ON THE INTERNET

As it relates to conventional skills and tactics, the danger of instruction in operational training manuals circulated on these Web sites should not be underestimated and, in many cases, constitutes first-class terrorist training. While the average Western observer may not have a clear understanding of the significance of these Web sites and mistakenly assume that the information contained therein is of poor quality, many of these manuals have been prepared by seasoned al-Qa'ida veterans and high-level operational planners. In fact, some of the operational manuals are written by leading al-Qa'ida trainers and operatives, including Saif al-Adel, the current head of al-Qa'ida's military committee; Yousef bin Saleh al-`Ayeeri (who is also known as Sheikh al-Battar), former trainer in Afghanistan and former head of al-Qa'ida in Saudi Arabia; and his heir, Abi Hajer Abd al-Aziz al-Muqrin. The size of these operational manuals varies from the massive 1,081-page "Encyclopedia of Jihad," to Saif al-Adel's short two-page manual detailing the ideal "Safe-House." Yet the majority of operational manuals provide jihadists and would-be jihadists with precious insight and detailed levels of instruction, thus equipping them with deadly skills.

The following three manuals illustrate the nefariousness of instructions provided on these Web sites:

1. *Al-`Amn Wal–Istikhbarat* (*Security and Intelligence*; often referred to as the "Encyclopedia of Jihad")—This massive 1,081-page manual is the most comprehensive and detailed training manual ever produced by al-Qa'ida. It has been found in homes of suspected terrorists in numerous countries. This well-written and extensive text empowers cell members with detailed terrorist tradecraft through step-by-step instructions dealing with each of the following subjects: basic security guidelines, reconnaissance, information gathering, arrests, interrogation methods, clandestine covers, communication equipment and communication security, wiretaps and equipment, jihadist cell formations, cell security,

intelligence and counterintelligence, spying and recruiting, training and operating spies, secret searches, surveillance, disguises and hiding, assassination, kidnapping and hostage taking, remote detonators, explosive letters, psychological warfare, propaganda, utility of rumors, VIP protection and escort, security details, search methods, protecting VIPs in transition in cars or boats, vehicle security, planning and studying transportation roads, manufacturing poisons, basic demolition principles, manufacturing various explosives, fuses, detonators, using handguns, marksmanship, manufacturing silencers, assassination with rockets, lock picking, how to act during home searches, sniper training and marksmanship, using motorcycles for assassination operations, using cars for assassination operations, how to attack an armored vehicle, secret communications, and using machine guns. This is perhaps the most alarming of all al-Qa'ida manuals, for it contains a considerable amount of dangerous information for cell members.[21]

2. *Harb al-`Isabat* (*Guerrilla Warfare*)—In this 35-page manual published in 2004, former al-Qa'ida commander in Saudi Arabia Yousef bin Saleh al-`Ayeeri (Sheikh al-Battar) explains four types of guerrilla warfare campaigns fought in the mountains, jungles, cities, and deserts. Concerning guerrilla warfare in the cities, he states that "if fought correctly it can paralyze the enemy...but it is also among the most difficult types of warfare." Al-`Ayeeri teaches his students that guerrilla warfare is divided into three phases, namely, engagement, balance, and victory. He states that in the initial phase of attrition, which tends to be the longest, jihadists are to utilize underground cellular formations to exhaust the enemy. In the second phase, jihadist formations will adopt a semi-organized structure; and in the final phase, when the enemy is on the ropes, the jihadists will engage in a full-blown overt confrontation to reach a decisive victory. In the final pages, the author details the cell formations that are used by al-Qa'ida in urban warfare, including the number of members and squads that the leaders of cells should aspire to, and the required skills needed to conduct their activities and manage their actions.[22]
3. The *Abdullah Dhu al-Bajadeen Encyclopedia for the Manufacture of Explosives in Pictures Parts I–III*—The *Abdullah Dhu al-Bajadeen Encyclopedia* is the most detailed and complete jihadist manual dealing with explosives. In this 187-page, 3-part encyclopedia, the author provides cell members with complete and easy-to-follow instructions, together with dozens of images to familiarize readers with the science of demolition, as well as the manufacture of numerous different types of explosives, fuses, detonators, and precursor materials. In Part I, the author provides instruction on the preparation of sulfuric acid, potassium nitrate, acetone peroxide, ammonium nitrate, basic fuses, a simple timing device, nitroglycerin, electronic fuses, methyl ethyl ketone peroxide, and many other explosive designs. Part II of the encyclopedia illustrates the production of nitroglycerin, acetone peroxide, liquid nitroglycol, ammonium nitrate, potassium nitrate, capacitors, mercuric fulminate, RDX, and nitrocellulose. Part III explores nitronaphthalene, smoke and pipe bombs, aluminum powder, armor piercing shaped explosives, anti-ship bombs, and hydrogen peroxide.[23]

Al-Qa'ida's virtual training academy thus eliminates the need to establish training camps or to transfer training materials across borders. Michael Scheuer, former head of the so-called CIA Bin Ladin Unit, articulated this progress by stating that, "It used to be they had to go to Sudan, they had to go to Yemen, they had to go to Afghanistan to train."[24] Currently, the Internet provides an al-Qa'ida operative with the necessary information and materials, and, as a result, he "no longer has to carry anything that's incriminated. He doesn't need his schematics, he doesn't need his blueprints, he doesn't need his formulations."[25] The material "can be sent ahead by encrypted Internet, and it gets lost in the billions of messages that are out there."[26]

Perhaps one of the best examples of the high quality of instruction found on jihadi Web sites can be illustrated by the premier al-Qa'ida operational magazine *Mu`askar al-Battar* (*Camp al-Battar* [the name of the sword of the prophet]), which was published in 2004 and 2005. At present, 22 issues of this publication have been posted on countless jihadist Web sites. Each issue of *Mu`askar al-Battar* magazine contains approximately 30–40 pages of text. Of particular concern within these pages are lessons by the aforementioned Saif al-Adel, Yousef al-`Ayiri, and Abd al-Aziz al-Muqrin. Specifically, among the lessons taught by Saif al-Adel to the jihadi community through this magazine include:

- Religious justification and precedents for covert jihadist operations
- Ways to erect and enhance the security of the jihadist cell
- Principles of security
- Counterintelligence
- Communication security (how to secure communications)
- Security and intelligence (how to secure transportation, money transfers, weapons training)
- Counter activity and propaganda
- Covert operations
- Secret meetings
- Secret searches (how to enter forbidden locations and acquire information without leaving a trace and how to protect your safe house from secret searches)
- Safe houses
- Planning special operations
- Examples of security plans

Al-Batter magazine gives would-be terrorists the opportunity of learning from the same master terrorist practitioner who personally trained the 1998 embassy bombers and the 9/11 hijackers.

The most notable of all operational jihadist Web sites, and by far the most informative and comprehensive source on jihadist terrorism, is *Mawsu`at al-I`dad* (*The Nuclear Preparation Encyclopedia*).[27] This Web site contains links to dozens of portals describing numerous tactical skills utilized and developed by seasoned jihadists. It also includes several thousand listed pages on various terrorist topics and provides specific instructions and illustrations on light weapons, guerrilla tactics, silencers, marksmanship, self-defense, physical education, survival and sabotage techniques, martial arts, espionage, rocket manufacture, explosives manufacture, suicide belt production, CBW agents, bombs and landmines, timed explosives, first aid and warnings, basic information about nuclear weapons and electronics, radar, and airplane-hindering techniques.[28] In addition, there are links to several Western Web sites in English providing information on similar topics.

Although the exact number of people viewing operational CBRN manuals and postings is difficult to determine, one can safely assume that the number of viewers who have accessed such manuals ranges in the tens of thousands worldwide. For example, *The*

Nuclear Preparation Encyclopedia attracted over 57,000 visitors after it was first posted on the *al-Firdaws* Web site in October of 2005.[29] Now that the general characteristics of online operational jihadi resources have been described, those dealing specifically with materials that could be used in WMD are discussed below.

CHEMICAL AND BIOLOGICAL WEAPONS (CBW)

Since the September 11 terrorist attacks on the United States, the possibility that groups associated with the al-Qa'ida network may attempt an attack on the United States using chemical weapons remains very likely. There is sufficient evidence that al-Qa'ida remains committed to producing or acquiring chemical weapons (see Chapter 5 of this volume for a more detailed discussion of this and the points that follow). Especially troubling is the prevalence of information found on jihadist Web sites and other sources for the production of chemical and biological weapons. Up to now, hydrogen cyanide, ricin, and toxic industrial chemicals (TICs), such as sulfuric acid, cyanide salts, and pesticides, seem to be the chemical agents of choice for would-be terrorists. Several al-Qa'ida–related publications, including "cookbooks" coveted the world over by amateur terrorists, explain various methods for acquiring hydrogen cyanide and ricin.[30] Indeed, the methods by which to extract ricin from castor plant beans illustrated in a jihadist manual entitled *Military Studies in the Jihad against the Tyrants* is a direct translation from *The Poisoner's Handbook*.[31] Because of the proliferation of jihadist Web sites, discussion forums, and blogs, the number of training materials containing information about chemical devices and the production of chemical agents has been on the rise. In addition to scanned copies of "cookbooks" written in English, some of these Web sites even include homemade videos.[32] For example, a popular jihadist Web site recently posted a video that demonstrates a procedure for obtaining ricin, which is a passage from a famous amateur video, *The Poor Man's James Bond Greets the Russians*.[33]

In 2005, an *al-Tawhid wal Jihad* (al-Qa'ida in Iraq) Web site posted an eight-page document containing a detailed history of biological weapons and indirectly encouraged the use of these weapons against the United States. The group emphasized that biological weapons are an effective and affordable weapon that could bring jihadists to parity with the United States. Following a brief chronology about the uses of biological weapons throughout history, the author states:

> Biological weapons are considered the least complicated and the easiest to manufacture from [sic] all weapons of mass destruction. All the information concerning the production of these weapons is readily available in academic books, scholarly publications and even on the internet.... In addition to the ease of production, these weapons are also considered to be the most affordable. With $50,000 a group of amateurs can possess a biological weapon sufficient to threaten a superpower. It is for this reason that biological weapons are called the poor man's atomic weapon.[34]

Some of the most worrisome sections of material dealing with WMD are the instructional pages that provide detailed directions on how to manufacture numerous important CBW agents. In most cases, these instructions are very specific and easy to follow. In other cases, the instructions are very vague and lack important technical information. The most notable instructions include information for the preparation of the following chemical and biological agents: cyanide, hydrogen sulfide gas, mustard agent, ricin, *Yersinia pestis,* and botulinum toxin, in addition to several low-end, non-WMD poisons.

AL-MUBTAKKAR DEVICE

In February 2006, a report published by *WMD Insights* revealed that a manual for the production of the *al-Mubtakkar,* a crude hydrogen cyanide dispersal mechanism (Figure 4.2), had been available on two jihadist Web sites, *al-Firdaws* and *al-Farouq*, between October 2005 and early 2006.[35] Following the shutting down of both sites, the manual has since been disseminated to other Web sites and was most recently observed on the *al-Nusra* site in April 2006. As a result, it is highly likely that instructions for the *al-Mubtakkar* assembly are no longer limited only to al-Qa'ida but are available to other terrorist groups worldwide.[36]

This device is designed to work as a crude binary munition containing a cyanide salt (potassium cyanide) that is separated by a barrier from an acid (hydrochloric acid).[37] Once the barrier separating the two containers is broken by a detonator, it produces hydrogen cyanide, a so-called "blood agent" that poisons cells by preventing them from utilizing oxygen.[38] According to Ron Suskind's book, *The One Percent Doctrine,* an al-Qa'ida affiliate based in Saudi Arabia planned an attack on the New York City subway in 2003 with the *al-Mubtakkar* device.[39] Surprisingly, according to reports, al-Zawahiri decided to cancel the operation forty-five days before the planned attack.[40] It is unclear if the online version of *al-Mubtakkar* is identical to the one al-Qa'ida planned to use in New York, but they seem from descriptions to be very similar.

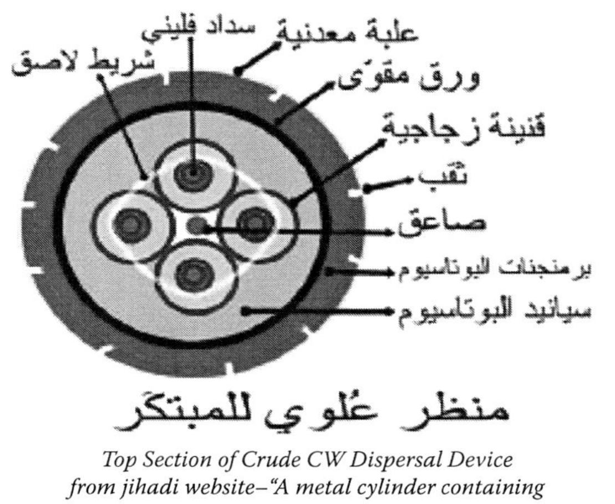

Top Section of Crude CW Dispersal Device from jihadi website–"A metal cylinder containing 4 Coca Cola bottles (each filled with 250 mg of hydrochloric acid), cork (in each bottle), held together by scotch tape, surrounded by potassium cyanide, potassium permanganate, cardboard, and activated by a detonator in the middle." Translated from original caption in Arabic

FIGURE 4.2 Top section of *al-Mubtakkar* hydrogen cyanide dispersal device. (Source: WMDInsights.com.)

The online manual for the production of *al-Mubtakkar* is an eight-page text entitled *Al-Mubtakkar al-Farid: Li Irsaal al-Safah al-Athiri Ila al-Kafir al-`Anid* [*The Unique Invention: To Deliver the Gaseous Killer to the Stubborn Infidel*]. It provides al-Qa'ida members and supporters with specific instructions for the production and dispersal of hydrogen cyanide by combining specific quantities of hydrochloric acid with potassium cyanide in a rudimentary device, consisting of four glass bottles in a metal container. To further enhance the readers' understanding, the manual provides thirty-four images that carefully illustrate the materials and components used in the device and also instruct cell members on precise step-by-step assembly and precautionary guidance to enhance the potency of *al-Mubtakkar.* In total, the manual consists of six short chapters that discuss the advantages of this device, suggested targets, words of caution, a list of the specific necessary ingredients and quantities, and the assembly of the *Mubtakkar* device and the detonator. In its discussion of potential targets, the manual specifically advocates that this weapon be used against "soft targets" and states that "the most effective way to disperse this gas is in closed quarters by using the central air conditioning and ventilation systems within a building or by using multiple devices if available." It also adds, "When placing these devices inside buildings it should specifically be placed by the entrances and the emergency exits."[41]

RADIOLOGICAL AND NUCLEAR WEAPONS

Despite strong evidence that al-Qa'ida has made various attempts in procuring radiological and nuclear material, there are no indications that the network has been successful in this endeavor. Similar to the network's claims about acquiring chemical and biological agents, most allegations concerning the movement's procurement of radiological and nuclear material focus on Afghanistan and the former Soviet Union (FSU). Al-Qa'ida's interest in pursuing nuclear weapons is emphasized by declarations of al-Qa'ida operatives and statements posted on jihadist Web sites.

Perhaps the most alarming al-Qa'ida-related nuclear text is a manual entitled *Nuclear Preparation Encyclopedia* that was posted in October 2005 on the *al-Firdaws* jihadist Web site. In this vast 287-page document, consisting of 14 chapters, the author, a jihadist activist named Layth al-Islam (Lion of Islam), asserts "I have been studying nuclear physics for two years on various scientific and jihadist Web sites." He states that his manual is aimed at "empowering the jihadi community with knowledge about nuclear weapons."[42]

The posting of his encyclopedia demonstrates an increase in the quality of instructions on nuclear technology available on jihadist Web sites. While the manual does not provide the would-be terrorist with detailed instructions for the construction of a nuclear weapon, the document contains historical surveys of nuclear technology, including explanations of nuclear experiments in Arabic, and overviews of famous nuclear scientists. Most disturbing, however, is information about critical mass and information concerning the amounts of fissile material needed for the manufacture of nuclear weapons. Additionally, the manual provides several sketches in English and Arabic of gun-type and implosion-type nuclear warheads, which appear to be borrowed from open-source information available on the Internet. While the manual does not provide jihadists with a step-by-step blueprint for the manufacture of nuclear weapons, it does outline steps for the extraction of radium and the assembly of a radium-based radiological dispersion device (RDD) or "dirty bomb."[43]

ASSESSMENT OF QUALITY OF CBRN PRODUCTION INSTRUCTIONS

Active monitoring and analysis of primary al-Qa'ida literature and manuals can reveal the underlying motivations, goals, and capabilities of the al-Qa'ida network. It also enables analysts to assess the validity of actual CBRN production instructions. Various books, manuals, and web pages produced by al-Qa'ida and its supporters contain important information on the history and utility of various poisons, chemical agents, biological agents, and nuclear weapons; however, an ongoing examination of al-Qa'ida's operational manuals indicates that the quality of instructions for CBRN production is largely subpar (see Table 4.1).

Although al-Qa'ida literature includes instructions on CBRN agents, only a small percentage of such information consists of actual formulations and recipes necessary for the production and manufacture of CBRN agents. With regard to instructions on biological weapons, most of them are considered amateurish and are only adequate for producing small amounts of crude agents that are not suitable for carrying out attacks resulting in mass casualties.[44] Furthermore, the al-Qa'ida network would need significant technical assistance in order to weaponize biological agents for use in a terrorist attack. For example, although anthrax bacteria are lethal in aerosol form, it is extremely difficult to weaponize *Bacillus anthracis* spores. In addition to spore size, maintaining the virulence of the bacteria are essential factors for successful deployment. As for plague, the instructions for the extraction of *Yersinia pestis* are amateurish and fail to mention that plague is a very fragile agent and therefore difficult to weaponize and disperse.[45] It is clear that the author of the instructions borrowed mainly text and sketches from a 1977 book written by Michael J. Pelzcar, Roger D. Reig, and E.C.S. Chan, entitled *Microbiology*.[46]

The five different formulations for the toxin ricin illustrated in al-Qa'ida–related publications are only sufficient for producing small amounts of crude agent.[47] With regard to mustard agent, the information provided in these manuals is incomplete and lacks specific instructions for the actual production of the agent.[48] In the case of cyanide, the instructions fail to mention that the precursor chemicals are difficult to procure.[49] In the case of botulinum toxin, the process described would be very difficult to master and would most likely not result in the successful production of the agent.[50] The synthesis process for nerve agents requires a certain amount of expertise and is far more difficult than the instructions illustrated in "cookbooks" and al-Qa'ida–related manuals.[51] More so, as the Aum Shinrikyo's nerve agent attacks showed effective dispersion of nerve agents is not an easy task.[52]

Of all the CBW concoctions described in jihadist manuals or proliferated on jihadist Web sites, *al-Mubtakkar* is perhaps the most nefarious and dangerous. Potentially it can be very deadly if used under optimal atmospheric conditions in a confined area such as a subway system, where the closed spaces of subway cars would dramatically enhance the effectiveness of this hydrogen cyanide dispersal device. Equally troubling, it is relatively easy to assemble and deploy if terrorists are able to acquire precursor chemicals of suitable potency. Yet at the same time, although in theory hydrogen cyanide is a very lethal CW agent, in reality it is doubtful that deploying such a crude device would truly produce mass casualties. The CW attack on the Tokyo subway in March 1995 is a relevant point of reference. In that attack, Aum Shinrikyo members disseminated the deadlier sarin nerve agent by puncturing small bags containing the agent with sharpened umbrellas tips. Yet, although Aum members attacked five subway cars during the morning rush hour, this attack resulted in only 12 deaths, while 1,000 persons were injured.[53] The actual mass killing potential of *al-Mubtakkar* would depend on numerous variables specific to the scale and efficiency of the particular attack and remains largely uncertain.

Currently, al-Qa'ida and its affiliates are not likely to possess the technical skills required to manufacture chemical warfare agents and to disperse them in an efficient manner. In fact, many al-Qa'ida members commonly presented as chemical weapons "experts" are actually terrorists that received limited training in crude procedures in training camps in Afghanistan.[54] For instance, Shukhrat Masirokhunov, a former leading operative of the Islamic Movement of Uzbekistan (IMU; an al-Qa'ida affiliate) who fought American forces in Afghanistan and was captured in Peshawar by the Pakistani authorities, told of his CBW training in Afghanistan. He states, "In 2000, I took a 20-day training course in making chemical agents and explosives. A poison can be made literally from any material—cigarettes, honey, and even bread. We worked at a special laboratory near Jalalabad. Our instructor was Abu Habbob Misriy, a former chemistry teacher from Egypt. There were about 200 men taking that course, including 14 or 15 from the North Caucasus who returned to Russia a year later."[55]

While would-be terrorists would have to overcome several difficulties in order to obtain a true WMD capability with CBW agents, evidence suggests that these substances even in crude form are suitable as a terrorist weapon. The employment of chemical or biological agents has the potential of causing fear and panic among the population, despite the limited physical effect of the agent. Therefore, if a terrorist attack is indeed intended to terrorize, then the CBW agents outlined in these manuals would do the job adequately. Nevertheless, while these weapons may succeed in terrorizing a population and causing economic damage, it is very unlikely that these agents would be capable of causing mass fatalities.

As for the various postings on Islamist Web sites dealing with nuclear and radiological weapons, at least one posting appears to be a translation of a document posted on several American Web sites.[56] Another posting surveys international instances of radiological contamination from 1945 to 1987 and explores the possible usage of Cesium-137 in an RDD. This posting does not offer detailed instructions for the assembly of the RDD, nor does it detail the amount of cesium-137 or explosives that would be needed for such an attempt. It does, however, accurately outline the expected economic damage such an attack might produce and lists possible Western cities as targets.[57] A third posting that claimed to provide instructions for the enrichment of uranium and the manufacture of a nuclear weapon bordered on the absurd. The instructions were borrowed from an English-language publication that was subpar and lacking any real scientific expertise.[58]

Even al-Qa'ida's most reliable nuclear manual, the *Nuclear Preparation Encyclopedia*, is riddled with numerous technical errors. Although the author instructs his audience on how to extract the radioactive material radium and illustrates methods for assembling a gun-type bomb, he erroneously claims that this device can yield a nuclear explosion; this is incorrect because radium is not a fissionable material. In fact, the instructions depicted in the manual would lead to an RDD, provided the would-be terrorist possessed sufficient amounts of radium as described in the crude methods and techniques.[59]

An evaluation of al-Qa'ida's literature and manuals as posted reveals many flaws in WMD production instructions. As the summary assessment in Table 4.1 illustrates, al-Qa'ida has yet to display publicly the types of WMD knowledge needed in order to achieve mass destruction. As mentioned earlier, al-Qa'ida literature contains basic technical flaws and fails to address the manufacture of munitions, weaponization, and effective delivery systems. A potent agent alone does not equal a weapon of mass destruction; rather, the transformation of an agent into a bona fide WMD requires multiple stages of

TABLE 4.1 Summary Assessment of Production Instructions for CBRN Agents as Displayed in al-Qa'ida and Other Jihadist Manuals

Agent	Are these instructions valid?	Expected quality of agent/device produced	Do these instructions outline the manufacture of munitions?	Do these instructions outline credible delivery systems?	What is the mass casualty potential of this agent if produced following these instructions?
Cyanide – CW (multiple recipes)	Yes; but ingredients are difficult to procure	Very crude	No	No	Very low; more suitable for poisoning or assassination
Hydrogen Sulfide Gas – CW (2 recipes)	Yes	Crude	No	No	Low; this agent will only work if deployed in a confined area; awful odor will force people to evacuate the area
Mustard Gas – CW	No	These instructions are not sufficient for production	No	No	None
Botulinum Toxin – BW	Yes; but the process is very difficult to master	Crude; may not work	No	No	Very low; more suitable for poisoning or assassination
Ricin – BW (5 different recipes)	Yes; but the process is amateurish	A small amount of crude agent	No	No	Very low; more suitable for poisoning or assassination
Plague – BW (*Yersinia pestis*)	Yes; but the process is very difficult to master	Crude; will likely not work	No	Vague unspecific instructions are provided	Very low

Cesium-137 (radiological dispersal devise 'RDD')	Yes; but ingredients are difficult to procure	Very crude; RDD instructions are not precise	No	Vague unspecific instructions are provided	Very low; depends on amount of and type of explosives used
Highly Enriched Uranium	No; instructions are laughable	These instructions are not sufficient for production	No	No	None
Radium based gun-type nuclear explosive device	No; radium is not a fissionable material	These instructions are not suitable for production of a nuclear explosive device	No	No; method described is not a credible nuclear warhead delivery system	Very low; this device would amount to a RDD; accordingly, casualty potential depends on amount of and type of explosives used

Note: Recipe is the set of instructions used to manufacture a CBW agent, also referred to as a formulation.

weaponization. For example, the difficulty in successfully carrying out a terrorist attack utilizing biological agents is highlighted by Pilch and Zilinskas in the *Encyclopedia of Bioterrorism Defense*:

> Acquiring an effective biological weapon and carrying out a successful biological attack requires the criminal to take four vital steps: (1) secure a culture of a suitable pathogen or a quantity of toxin; (2) develop an appropriate formulation; that is, a combination of the pathogen or toxin and the substrate in which it is suspended or dissolved; (3) obtain an appropriate container to safely store and transport the formulations; and (4) apply an efficient mechanism to disperse the pathogen or toxin over or onto the target population. In addition, if the biological warfare (BW) agent is to be delivered by aerosol, a fifth factor is essential, namely, favorable meteorological conditions for the act of dispersion.[60]

In addition, al-Qa'ida manuals also fail to include specific information on the impact of atmospheric conditions (i.e., temperatures, sunlight, rain, altitude, wind speed, wind direction, and turbulence) on the deployment of CBW agents. These atmospheric conditions directly affect the performance and potency of CBW agents and are thus vital considerations.[61]

An analysis of al-Qa'ida's WMD manuals reveals that the instructions displayed are incomplete and not suitable for the production of actual weapons of mass destruction. Many experts agree that al-Qa'ida has not yet demonstrated the means to effectively manufacture, weaponize, and deploy WMD. Nevertheless, it is also important to note that, according to Western sources and al-Qa'ida's own statements and publications, the network and its affiliates are actively pursuing such a capability. While one should not preclude the possibility that some al-Qa'ida–related outfit is clandestinely opting to develop deadlier WMD agents and delivery systems, currently there are no credible reports to demonstrate that the network has acquired such a capability. At this juncture, despite their tremendous hostility and desire for mass casualties, in all likelihood al-Qa'ida has yet to develop a true WMD capability. Achieving such an important landmark requires rigorous scientific mastery and technical accomplishment, which cannot be replaced by religious zeal, anti-Western animosity, or downright coldblooded acrimony. Yet, while these CBRN agents and devices discussed are not capable of mass casualties, they remain suitable for mass disruption.

OTHER PROMINENT SUNNI JIHADIST ORGANIZATIONS

Unlike al-Qa'ida and its cohorts, who are clearly pursuing a WMD capability to further their global goals and increase their potential for inflicting massive casualties, other prominent Sunni jihadist organizations with regional orientations such as Hamas and the Palestinian Islamic Jihad (PIJ) have shown no real interest in the matter. There is no credible information in the open-source literature that demonstrates that these two prominent jihadist groups have seriously attempted to acquire or to weaponize CBRN agents. There are a variety of possible explanations for their lack of enthusiasm, including a multitude of political, technical, and economic constrains. Unlike al-Qa'ida and its affiliates, who show no hesitation for killing thousands of Westerners and Muslims, Hamas and the PIJ have thus far pursued a more measured approach of controlled tit-for-tat violence against Israel. They routinely target buses, restaurants, clubs, and markets but have not yet embarked on mega terrorist attacks that exceed tens of casualties. Doing so will be a considerable escalation in the violence and will certainly be met with a stern Israeli response.

In addition, their hesitation may be partly explained by their desire to maintain legitimate political standing in the Arab world and among the Palestinian populace. While viewed as terror organizations in the West and in Israel; in the Arab world and in the eyes of constitutes in the Palestinian territories these organizations are viewed as legitimate resistance movements that target Israelis in response for their occupation of Palestinian lands and to avenge Palestinian casualties. Hamas in particular is viewed by most Arabs as a legitimate political party that for decades has furnished considerable social welfare programs to the population of Gaza. Hamas also participated in and won the Palestinian parliamentary elections in early 2006 and formed a Palestinian government headed by Prime Minister Isma`il Haniyya. The subsequent international embargo and the internal power struggle with Fatah ultimately brought about the demise of the Hamas-led government. Carrying out a mass casualty attack by employing conventional weapons or WMD will adversely diminish their legitimacy and standing within the Palestinian populace and the region as a whole. More so, it will almost certainly end all political and financial aid that Hamas and the PIJ receive from Arab governments as such actions will be viewed as disproportionate and unjustifiable violence that threaten to delve the region toward further instability.

In addition, there is no indication that Hamas and the PIJ have the indigenous technical capability or scientific expertise to pursue the manufacture of WMD even if they wished it. Also, such endeavors are likely very costly and somewhat unattainable considering the dire economic circumstances currently in Gaza. Furthermore, as the Gaza strip is among the most overpopulated regions in the world, this hinders the prospects of developing and experimenting with CBRN agents that carry the risk of accidents and contamination that could harm Palestinian civilians. If these organizations were to cause Palestinian civilian deaths through contamination or poisoning by CBRN agents, their standing within the Palestinian community will be irreversibly damaged. This also brings into question the indiscriminate nature of CBRN agents, for deploying them on Israeli targets is likely to also harm Palestinians because of the close proximity of Israeli and Palestinian populations in the holy land.

But perhaps most important, unlike al-Qa'ida, which is elusive and cannot be pinned down to a single geographic location, Hamas and the PIJ have a "return address." Most of the leadership apparatus of Hamas and the PIJ and their families reside in Gaza, while Khalid Meshal, Abu Musa Marzuq, and Ramadan Abdullah Shalah reportedly reside in Damascus. This is a very important distinction, for if these groups were to perpetrate a true mass casualty attack on an Israeli city that results in hundreds or thousands of Israeli casualties, there is little doubt that Israel will respond harshly by targeting the leadership and operational cadres of Hamas and the PIJ in the Gaza strip and subsequently cause unprecedented levels of destruction in the Palestinian areas. Israel is also likely to target Damascus if it is implicated in such an attack. In contrast, al-Qa'ida is not deterred from undertaking WMD operations for it does not have a "return address," nor does it have a constituency that it represents or caters to. Currently, the upper leadership of al-Qa'ida is hiding in unknown locations or possibly out of the reach of American and Pakistani security services in the largely protected tribal areas of Pakistan. In short, numerous serious political, logistical, and strategic impediments hinder the pursuit and deployment of WMD by Palestinian jihadis.

SHI'I JIHADISTS AND WEAPONS OF MASS DESTRUCTION

In contrast to global Sunni jihadists, who have made WMD acquisition a major focus of their jihad, for the most part Shi'i jihadists have largely not shown a sincere and robust interest in CBRN agents. While there are numerous reports that allege and examine concrete efforts by Sunni jihadists like al-Qa'ida and its supporters to pursue WMD capability, there are no credible open-source reports that indicate the same is true of Shi'i jihadists. In this regard, it is important to clarify that this may be partly the result of Shi'i jihadists' control of operational materials, unlike al-Qa'ida and its supporters, who are extensively circulating operational manuals online. In contrast, regional jihadist terror organizations in the Levant use their Web sites mainly for informational and propaganda purposes and not for operational training, and as such it is difficult to come across any credible primary sources that provide insight into their capabilities.

The open-source literature does not indicate that Hizballah, the vanguard of Shi'i jihadists, has thus far shown any real interest in the development of WMD. This is likely for numerous reasons: First, Hizballah has significant state sponsorship from its main benefactor, the Islamic Republic of Iran, which has provided Hizballah since its inception in 1982 with extensive military training, armaments, and millions of dollars in financial aid. In fact, Hizballah has acquired a formidable rocket arsenal from Iran, and if it was to desire CBRN agents, it would likely opt to acquire them from their main sponsor rather than endeavor to produce them indigenously. Second, Hizballah is an official party in the Lebanese political system, and it is considered as such a legitimate resistance organization by most governments in the Middle East, with whom it maintains normalized diplomatic relations and affiliation. Opting for WMD capability will likely hinder Hizballah's relations with other political parties in Lebanon and other Arab governments because of the perceived nefariousness of such weapons systems.

Third, Hizballah controls a cohesive geographic location and enjoys a strong standing among its primary constituents, the Shi'i Lebanese population, because of its perceived resistance to Israel and, equally important, its long history of providing considerable social welfare to the Shi'i population. WMD experimentation can be a threat to Hizballah's standing within the Shi'i population if contamination or pollution were to occur as a result of an accident or due to an Israeli aerial bombing of a Hizballah facility. In contrast, al-Qa'ida has no loyal constituency and is not loyal to a specific geographic location. Fourth, it can be argued that WMD acquisition does not provide Hizballah with any actual tangible benefits. Since the 1980s Hizballah has been successful in its battles with Israel primarily because of its superior guerilla tactics and, more recently, by its deployment of rocket attacks. It has blunted Israeli advances, forced Israel to withdraw from Lebanese territories, penetrated Israeli air space with thousands of rocket attacks, and practically shut down northern Israel for more than a month. No other Arab army has been able to replicate these achievements, as such; Hizballah is perceived as the victorious party in its conflicts with Israel and has little to gain from utilizing CBRN agents.

Finally, and perhaps most important, one needs to keep in mind the considerable devastation that Israel visited on the Lebanese civilian infrastructure following the kidnapping of its soldiers by Hizballah in July 2006, which practically brought the fragile democracy to its knees following decades of development and growth; one can imagine how Israel would respond to a true mass casualty attack on its soil if it is perpetrated by Hizballah. During the July–August 2006 war, Hizballah Secretary-General Hassan Nasrallah told *al-Jazeera* that he would not have authorized the kidnapping of Israeli

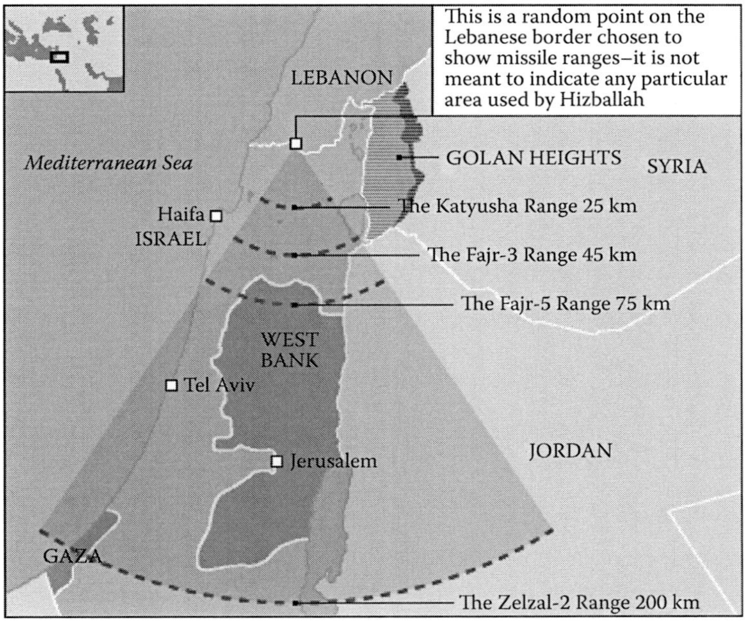

FIGURE 4.3 Range of Hizballah rockets used in July–August 2006 war. (Source: http://news.bbc.co.uk.)

soldiers had he anticipated the sternness of the Israeli response. The anticipated severity of the Israeli response to a WMD attack on its soil practically diminishes the chances of such an occurrence. Hizballah is likely to continue to engage Israel in a war of attrition but not escalate the conflict by carrying out a mass casualty attack on Israeli soil.

Yet, the specter of a WMD-capable Hizballah should not be dismissed altogether. In its latest thirty-four–day war with Israel in July–August 2006, Hizballah utilized a formidable arsenal of rockets and missile systems (see Table 4.2). The war erupted on July 12 after Hizballah operatives infiltrated the northern Israeli border, killed a group of Israeli soldiers, and kidnapped two additional soldiers. Israel retaliated with extensive bombardment of Hizballah strongholds in southern Lebanon and in Beirut, and by extensively targeting the Lebanese civil infrastructure, including the Beirut airport, bridges, roads, fuel depots, and a full navel blockade of Lebanese shores. Early in the conflict, Hizballah launched a daily barrage of Katyusha rockets, *Fajr-3* and *Fajr-5* long-range bombardment rockets, into northern Israel. Also on July 14, 2006, Hizballah used a Chinese-made Iranian modified C-802 anti-ship cruise missile to attack the *Spear*, an Israeli Saar-5 class missile ship off the shore of Tyre.[62] The attack killed a number of Israeli sailors and severely damaged the *Spear*, which was towed back to an Israeli port. During the conflict Hizballah did not utilize any of its *Zelzal-2* long-range bombardment rockets with a reported range of 200 kilometers that are capable of reaching Tel-Aviv, although it was reported that Israel was successful in neutralizing numerous *Zelzal-2* rockets before they could be launched.[63]

These rockets and missiles systems were supplied to Hizballah by Iran, which imported and modified some of these systems since the 1980s. This daily barrage of rockets was sustained by Hizballah until the end of the conflict and mainly targeted Israel's third largest

TABLE 4.2 Missile and Rocket Systems Used by Hizballah during the July/August 2006 War with Israel

Name	Length (m)	Diameter (cm)	Weight (kg)	Range (km)	Payload (kg)	Comments
C-802 [2]	6.392m	36cm	715kg	120km	165kg	"Land attack anti-ship cruise missile," initially imported by Iran from the People's Republic of China. The missile attacks at 5-7 meters above sea-level and has radar jamming capability that makes it difficult to shoot down.
Fajr-3 [3]	5.2m	24cm	408kg	43km	45kg	The Iranian *Fajr*-3 was developed in reaction to the Iran/Iraq war and is a modified DPRK 240mm M-1985 multiple rocket launcher, production reportedly began in 1990. It is a "long-range bombardment rocket system."
Fajr-5 [4]	6.46m	33.3cm	860kg	75km	90kg	The Iranian *Fajr*-5 is based on China's 302mm WS-1 MRL (with modifications). It is a "long-range bombardment rocket system," fired from a rail launcher.
Katyusha [5]	1.8m	13cm	42kg	12-22km	22kg	Originally a Soviet WWII-era rocket–there are reports that Hizballah has the ability to fire Katyusha rockets from static and mobile launchers. More recent reports have spoken of "long-range" Katyusha. Israel and the United States are developing the Tactical High Energy Laser to destroy the Katyusha being fired from Lebanon.
Zelzal-2 [6]	8.46m	61cm	3,545kg	200km	600kg	The Iranian *Zelzal*-2 is a "long-range bombardment rocket" similar to an unguided Scud. It was developed to retaliate against Iraq during the Iran/Iraq war.

1 This table was created by Alexis Zeiger and Sammy Salama in 2006 at the James Martin Center for non-proliferation Studies

2 Raytheon, "C-801 (SY-2/HY-5) / C-802," *Missile Systems of the World*, AMI International, 1999, 228; "C-802 / YJ-2 / Ying Ji-802 / CSS-C-8 / SACCADE / C-8xx / YJ-22," Federation of American Scientists, 17 February 2000; "C-802 / YJ-2 / Ying Ji-802 / CSS-C-8 / SACCADE C-8xx / YJ-22 / YJ-82," GlobalSecurity.org, 17 July 2006; Bryan Bender, "Hezbollah Arsenal May Be Substantial," *Boston Globe*, 18 July 2006.

3 "Israel: New Hezbollah Rockets Can Reach Tel Aviv and Be'er Sheva," Ha'aretz, 14 July 2006; "Iran: Missile Capabilities: Long-Range Artillery Rocket Programs," Nuclear Threat Initiative, February 2006; Raytheon, "Fadjr Series," *Missile Systems of the World*, AMI International, 1999, 425; "Hizballah Rockets," GlobalSecurity.org, 17 July 2006.

4 "Israel: New Hezbollah Rockets Can Reach Tel Aviv and Be'er Sheva," Ha'aretz, 14 July 2006; "Iran: Missile Capabilities: Long-Range Artillery Rocket Programs," Nuclear Threat Initiative, February 2006; Raytheon, "Fadjr Series," *Missile Systems of the World*, AMI International, 1999, 425; "Hizballah Rockets," GlobalSecurity.org, 17 July 2006.

5 "Israel: New Hezbollah Rockets Can Reach Tel Aviv and Be'er Sheva," *Ha'aretz*, 14 July 2006; "Weapons and Warfare," Federation of American Scientists, 2006; "Katyusha Rocket," GlobalSecurity.org, 17 July 2006; Ross Dunn, "Correspondent Report," Voice of America / Federation of American Scientists, 4 May 2000; "Hizballah Rockets," GlobalSecurity.org, 17 July 2006; Bryan Bender, "Hezbollah Arsenal May Be Substantial," *Boston Globe*, 18 July 2006.

6 "Zelzal-2 / Mushak-200," GlobalSecurity.org, 28 April 2005; "Israel: New Hezbollah Rockets Can Reach Tel Aviv and Be'er Sheva," Ha'aretz, 14 July 2006; "Iran: Missile Capabilities: Long-Range Artillery Rocket Programs," Nuclear Threat Initiative, February 2006; Raytheon, "Zelzal-2," *Missile Systems of the World*, AMI International, 1999, 427.

city, Haifa, in addition to Acre, Nahariya, and northern Israel as a whole. Despite extensive efforts by the Israeli Air Force to find and neutralize rocket launchers, "Hizbollah succeeded in firing approximately 3,970 rockets during the hostilities—an average of 120 rockets a day."[64] While the extensive rocket barrage did not result in mass casualties within Israel, it did cause tens of casualties and considerable economic damage by practically shutting down Haifa and northern Israel for more than a month and forcing thousands of Israeli residents to flee south.

MIRSAD-1 UNMANNED AERIAL VEHICLE (UAV)

Alarm over Hizballah's budding missile capability was raised even prior to the 2006 war, specifically in November 2004 and in April 2005, when Hizballah flew an unmanned aerial vehicle (UAV) called the *Mirsad-1* over Israeli airspace.[65] It is widely believed that the *Mirsad-1* is an Iranian-made UAV given to Hizballah in 2004. The London-based Arabic periodical *Al-Sharq al-Awsat* reported that in August 2004 Hizballah received eight Iranian-made *Mohajer* UAV drones. According to a senior Iranian official cited in the article, "the *Mohajer-4* drone, which Hizballah named *Al-Mirsad-1*, carries three cameras, digital radar, and an electronic transmission system. It can fly at an altitude of 6,000 feet and at a maximum speed of 120 kilometers per hour."[66] More so, the article alleges that Iran has trained about thirty Hizballah fighters to pilot these UAVs in the Pasdaran air base in Esfahan.

In a speech on November 12, 2004, Hizballah Secretary-General Hassan Nasrallah proudly claimed that the *Mirsad-1* drone was indigenously made and boasted about the range and the payload of this UAV; he stated "*Mirsad-1* cannot only reach Nahariya, but anywhere you want to the deepest part of occupied Palestine, there is no problem here ... with a quantity of explosives ranging from 40 to 50 kilos and sent to its target. It is programmed and goes to the target you want. Take your choice! Do you want a power plant, water plant, military base, or whatever? Therefore, we now do not only have the ability to face penetration with penetration, and not also to reconnoiter only, but also the possibility of replying to any air attack with action from the air, if we wished that."[67] In August 2006, the Israeli Air Force downed three *Mirsad-1* drones flying over the Mediterranean and over Lebanese and Israeli territory.[68]

RELEVANCE TO CBRN

The July–August 2006 war was testament to the Shi'i jihadist group's formidable military prowess, making Hizballah the only jihadist organization that has to date displayed a mastery of rocket and missile technology, in addition to its superior ground formations and guerrilla tactics. Although there are no credible reports that Hizballah is currently pursuing WMD, this demonstrated rocket capability and the use of sophisticated UAVs does at least raise the potential of these becoming delivery systems for CBRN agents. Keeping in mind that artillery shells and aerial bombs were the main methods used by the Iraqis during the Iran–Iraq war in the 1980s to deploy mustard gas and other CW agents against advancing Iranian forces and the Kurdish population. In theory, if Hizballah were to pursue and acquire CBRN agents, it certainly has the delivery systems to project them deep into Israeli territory, reaching up to Tel-Aviv. Specifically, the *Mirsad-1* is potentially the most suitable for delivering WMD, largely because of the precise and accurate nature of UAVs and cruise missiles as opposed to other delivery systems. As stated by missile expert Dennis M. Gormley, "The cruise missile's steady horizontal flight pattern permits release of the agent along a line of contamination, and enables the cruise missile to release and spray agent at right angles to the wind direction and upwind of the target area, greatly increasing dissemination efficiency.... Extensive modeling shows that cruise missile delivery of biological agents enlarges the effective lethal area of an attack by at least a factor of ten over ballistic missile delivery."[69]

This is quite significant for the discussion of jihadists and weapons of mass destruction, for Shi'i Hizballah is the sole jihadi organization known to possess actual delivery systems potentially capable of deploying WMD. In contrast, al-Qa'ida and its supporters have shown great interest in the manufacture of WMD, yet there is no indication that they posses any sophisticated means for delivering such agents. In fact, all the previously discussed Sunni jihadi WMD concoctions relied on primitive delivery methods, including injection, contamination of food, spraying crude agents into air conditioning openings, mixing CBW agents with hand lotion and applying it to desired objects, or using explosives to disperse radiological materials. In the case of the *al-Mubtakkar*, the most nefarious al-Qa'ida WMD invention to date, cell members are instructed to leave the CW dispersal device in confined crowded locations or to utilize the central air conditioning and ventilation systems to disperse the agent.[70] In short, an analysis of Sunni and Shi'i jihadi WMD capabilities infers the ironic conclusion that while Sunni Salafi-jihadists aspire and labor to acquire weapons of mass destruction they do not posses suitable delivery systems, yet Shi'i jihadists possess advanced and capable delivery systems although they have not shown serious interest in acquiring WMD agents.

CONCLUSION

One of the most pressing security threats facing the United States today is the possible use of WMD by the al-Qa'ida network and other religious extremist movements. While Usama bin Ladin has been interested in acquiring a formidable WMD capability since the early 1990s, the al-Qa'ida network has yet to do so. An analysis of al-Qa'ida's WMD training manuals reveals that the instructions displayed are more suitable for the production of modest amounts of crude agent that can be used in assassinations and poisoning, but are not suitable for the production of the types of WMD capable of mass killing. Many experts agree that al-Qa'ida has not yet demonstrated the means to effectively manufacture, weaponize, and deploy weapons of mass destruction. On the other hand, while these CBRN agents and devices discussed are not capable of mass casualties, they remain suitable for causing mass disruption.

Nevertheless, it is also important to note that, according to Western sources and al-Qa'ida's own statements and publications, the network and its affiliates are actively pursuing such a capability. Despite their relative modest killing potential, al-Qa'ida's CBRN capabilities fall in line with the group's target selection calculus and should not be casually brushed off or ignored as they are still capable of causing the West considerable economic damage. However, the fact that al-Qa'ida and its affiliates may be far from perpetrating a mass casualty CBRN attack does not warrant reduced vigilance against them. To the contrary, al-Qa'ida cells and formations should be aggressively pursued to curtail their activities and to disrupt their quest for a true WMD capability. At the same time, it is important to keep the threat in perspective and not attribute to these terrorists any capabilities that they still do not posses. Doing so serves no purpose but increasing fear and escalating public alarm. At this juncture, the risk from al-Qa'ida's use of conventional terror tactics exceeds the risk from their attempts to acquire and deploy CBRN agents. While the killing potential of CBRN agents is high in theory, given al-Qa'ida's modest technical prowess and delivery means, it pales in comparison to the proven threat of conventional weapons, as seen in the deadly attacks carried out in recent years by al-Qa'ida in the United States, Europe, Asia, Africa, and the Middle East. Overall, al-Qa'ida's current technical knowledge and WMD capability are likely most suitable for assassinations and poisoning rather than large-scale attacks aimed at mass casualties. In the near term, al-Qa'ida and its affiliates are likely to continue to use conventional weapons and atypical weapons in creative ways.

At the same time, some discussion of the limits of publicly available information is warranted. While the examination of the operational jihadi manuals described above that were proliferated on various jihadi Web sites or found in homes of jihadi militants provides valuable insight into the general levels of WMD knowledge in the broader jihadi milieu, it is not meant to be presented as the totality of jihadi WMD knowledge. Just because the instructions and recipes provided in al-Qa'ida WMD manuals are largely subpar, this is not meant to infer that there can't be other dedicated elements of al-Qa'ida or other jihadist groups, or actual trained scientists with jihadi sympathies, working in secret with far greater capabilities and access to materials. Yet, current reports do not indicate that more advanced capabilities have been acquired by jihadi networks.

Equally important, the fact that al-Qa'ida and its affiliates have yet to employ actual WMD in their attacks is by itself an important indicator of their current capability. Unlike past enemies of the United States, who opted to acquire WMD arsenals to achieve deterrence and strategic parity with the West, al-Qa'ida and its cohorts are not so inclined. Their statements and literature indicate that they view weapons of mass destructions as a first strike weapon to target the American homeland and American allies around the world. As such, the fact that they have yet to carry out a WMD attack may be construed as that they simply do not possess the capability to produce these weapons at this time.

Nevertheless, despite their hostile rhetoric, there may be some reservations among al-Qa'ida's leaders concerning the use of WMD. That in 2003 al-Qa'ida's second-in-command, Ayman al-Zawahiri, decided to call off the aforementioned plot employing *al-Mubtakkar* is an important occurrence and warrants examination. While the reasons for this reversal are not known, one can speculate that numerous considerations may have influenced al-Zawahiri's decision. It may be that the jihadi cell responsible for this undertaking was not able to procure the necessary precursor materials to manufacture a sufficient number of *al-Mubtakkar* devices to attack multiple subway cars. It is also plausible that al-Zawahiri and other al-Qa'ida leaders understood the limits of this hydrogen cyanide dispersal device and reasoned that it would likely not produce a true mass casualty attack that is capable of inflicting fatalities comparable to 9/11 and as such would be seen as a disappointment by their jihadi supporters. However, other considerations are also likely. It may be that al-Qa'ida believed that an *al-Mubtakkar* device would be deadly but decided to hold off on carrying out this plot to pursue a larger and more devastating undertaking that has yet to be revealed.

Finally, it is also plausible that in 2003 the leadership of al-Qa'ida was simply not positioned to carry out a second mass casualty attack on the American homeland. Keep in mind that following the American invasion of Afghanistan in late 2001, Usama bin Ladin and other al-Qa'ida leaders narrowly escaped in Tora Bora and subsequently found refuge in Pakistan's tribal areas. Since then, the United States has hesitated to carry out military operations in Waziristan in order not to undermine the authority of the Pakistani government, which is an important American ally. It is plausible that in 2003, during the time of the alleged *al-Mubtakkar* plot, al-Qa'ida's leadership, which had just settled into their new safe haven, concluded that carrying a second mass casualty attack against the American homeland would strengthen American resolve and force the United States to throw caution to the wind and pursue extensive military actions against suspected al-Qa'ida and Taliban positions in Waziristan. Such operations would have likely killed or captured the fugitive upper leadership of al-Qa'ida. A final consideration may be that following the American invasion of Iraq in March 2003, Zawahiri and other al-Qa'ida leaders simply preferred to carry out a sustained guerrilla war against the large American presence in Iraq.

Regardless, in the future, the threat of WMD usage by jihadists is likely to continue as WMD manuals such as *al-Mubtakkar* continue to be proliferated by jihadi outlets. More so, one should not discount the possibility that in the future jihadi operatives will acquire access to CBRN agents or even ready-made weapons if favorable political circumstances arise that facilitate such transfers or theft. Most notably, an Islamist takeover of Pakistan by parties sympathetic to the Taliban or al-Qa'ida would increase the risk of WMD proliferation to jihadists exponentially, as would a pre-emptive attack on Iran's nuclear facilities that would deteriorate the security of Iranian nuclear and other WMD related facilities or may simply motivate members of the Iranian security services to proliferate CBRN agents to jihadi terrorist organizations as payback.

NOTES

1. Dave Saltonstall, "Pakistan Reportedly Warned U.S. Targets," *New York Daily News*, August 23, 1998; Laura Mansnerus, "Testimony at Bombing Trial Outlines Recipe for Mayhem," *New York Times*, July 6, 2001, B2; C. L. Staten, "Dirty Bomb Plot Thwarted Says Attorney General," *Emergency Net News*, June 10, 2002; Elaine Sciolino, "Terror Verdict Due Today for a Frenchman on Trial in Morocco," *New York Times*, Sept. 18, 2003; Jordan TV Channel 1, "Confessions of Group Planning Jordan Chemical Attack," BBC Monitoring, April 26, 2004.
2. Due to the proliferation of primary manuals, we have unique insight into al-Qa'ida and their methods and capabilities that we do not have on other jihadi organizations. In contrast, other jihadi organizations do not disseminate operational materials on their Web sites; for that reason, we do not have the same level of knowledge of their capabilities. In sum, we decided not to mix two types of analyses: one derived from primary al-Qa'ida manuals vs. an analysis of other jihadi capabilities based on statements in the open-source literature. Therefore, the bulk of this chapter is focused on al-Qa'ida.
3. U.S. District Court, Southern District of New York, *United States of America vs. Usama bin Laden: Testimony of Jamal Ahmad al-Fadl*, February 6–13, 2001, 292, 366, 524–526.
4. Rohan Gunaratna, *Inside Al Qa'ida Global Network of Terror* (New York: Columbia University Press, 2002), 49.
5. Jason Burke, *Al-Qa'ida Casting a Shadow of Terror* (London: I. B. Tauris, 2003), 187.
6. "Jihad Against the Jews and Crusaders—World Islamic Front Statement," *Federation of American Scientists*, February 23, 1998, http://www.fas.org/irp/world/para/docs/980223-fatwa.htm.

7. In 2004, the Arabic newspaper *Asharq Alawsat* obtained a manuscript authored by Abu Walid al-Masri, a member of Usama Bin Ladin's inner circle. In this manuscript, "The Story of the Afghan Arabs: From the Entry to Afghanistan to the Final Exodus with [the?] Taliban," Abu Walid reveals many of the internal dynamics that led to al-Qa'ida's decision to pursue WMD capability. Through his membership in al-Qa'ida's Majlis al-Shura, al-Masri participated in the meetings in which the leadership debated the benefits of pursuing WMD capability and the impact such a move would have on the global jihadi movement and the actions of the United States in the Middle East. "Book: The Story of the Arab Afghans," *Asharq Alawsat*, December 8, 2004.
8. Anonymous, *Imperial Hubris: Why the West is Losing the War on Terror* (Dulles: Brassey's, 2004), 153.
9. Ibid., 154–155.
10. Nasir Bin Hamid al-Fahd, "A Treatise on The Legal Status of Using Weapons of Mass Destruction Against Infidels," May 2003, 5, 8.
11. Ibid., 10.
12. Ibid., 22.
13. "Al-Qa'ida Denies Jordan WMD Plot," *BBC*, April 30, 2004.
14. Peter Bergen, "Reading al-Qaeda," *Washington Post,* September 11, 2005.
15. Reuven Paz, "Global Jihad and WMD: Between Martyrdom and Mass Destruction," in Hillel Fradkin, Husain Haqqani, and Eric Brown, eds., *Current Trends in Islamist Ideology* (Washington, DC: Hudson Institute, 2005), 82.
16. MEMRI Special Report No. 374, "The Enemy Within: Where are the Islamist/jihadist Websites Hosted, and What Can Be Done About It?" July 17, 2007.
17. "Suicide Bombers Turning to Web sites," *Agence France Presse*, September 29, 2005. More current numbers are not available.
18. "Terrorism on the Internet," *Voice of America,* April 11, 2006.
19. While it is not possible to provide the precise number of jihadi online viewers, occasionally, a high-profile posting on an operational jihadi Web site will attract a disproportionately large number of viewers and will generate much interest within online jihadi circles. For example, the "Nuclear Preparation Encyclopedia," which was posted on *al-Firdaws* jihadi Web site in October 2005, attracted more than 57,000 viewers. Please see Uzi Mahnaimi and Tom Walker, "Al-Qaeda Woos Recruits with Nuclear Bomb Website," *The Sunday Times*, November 6, 2005.
20. Based on author's own observations between 2004 and 2007.
21. Maktab al-Khidamat, "Security and Intelligence."
22. Yousef Bin Saleh al-`Ayeeri, "Guerilla Warfare," 2004.
23. Abdullah Dhu al-Bajadeen, "The Abdullah Dhu al-Bajadeen Encyclopedia for the Manufacture of Explosives in Pictures, Parts I–III."
24. Steve Coll and Susan B. Glasser, "Terrorists Turn to the Web as Base of Operations," *Washington Post,* August 7, 2005.
25. Ibid.
26. Ibid.
27. "Table of Contents," *Mausu'a al 'Aidad, The Nuclear Preparation Encyclopedia.*
28. Ibid.
29. Uzi Mahnaimi and Tom Walker, "al-Qa'ida Woos Recruits with Nuclear Bomb Web site," *Sunday Times,* November 6, 2005. Presumably the number of visitors pertains to visits in October 2005.

30. René Pita, "Assessing al-Qa'ida's Chemical Threat," *International Journal of Intelligence and Counterintelligence,* 20:3, 2007, 491.
31. Jeffrey M. Bale et al., "Ricin Found in London: An *al-Qa'ida* Connection?" *Center for Nonproliferation Studies*, January 23, 2003.
32. René Pita, "Assessing al-Qa'ida's Chemical Threat," 491–492.
33. Ibid.
34. "Biological Weapons," *al Tawhid Wal Jihad.*
35. Sammy Salama, "Special Report: Manual for Producing Chemical Weapon To Be Used in New York Subway Plot Available On Al-Qaeda Websites Since Late 2005," *WMD Insights*, July/August 2006 issue.
36. Ibid.
37. René Pita, "Assessing al-Qa'ida's Chemical Threat," 491–492.
38. Ron Suskind, "The Untold Story of al-Qaeda's Plot to Attack the Subways," *TIME,* June 19, 2006.
39. Ron Suskind, *The One Percent Doctrine: Deep Inside America's Pursuit of Its Enemies Since 9/11* (New York: Simon & Schuster, 2006), 217–218.
40. Ibid.
41. "Al-Mubtakkar al-Farid: Li Irsaal al-Safah al-Athiri Ila al-Kafir al-`Anid—The Unique Invention: To Deliver the Atheric Killer to the Stubborn Infidel," *al-Firdaws,* October 2005 [translated by author].
42. Layth al-Islam, "Nuclear Preparation Encyclopedia," *al-Firdaws*, October 6, 2005.
43. Ibid.
44. Dr. Raymond Zilinskas, Director of the Chemical and Biological Weapons Nonproliferation Program at the Center for Nonproliferation Studies, Interview by author, Monterey, California, August 4, 2005.
45. "The Biological Weapon," *Mawsu`a al I`adad—The Preparation Encyclopedia.*
46 Michael Pelczar, Roger Reid, and E.C.S. Chan, *Microbiology* (New York: McGraw-Hill, 1977), 97, 108–110, 114, 129–130, 136–140, 145, 217, 224, 644–645, 659.
47. "Declaration of Jihad Against the Tyrants—Lesson Sixteen," *The Smoking Gun*; Abu Hadhifa al-Shami, "A Course in Popular Poisons and Deadly Gases," Islamic Media Center, *Mausu'a al 'Aidad—The Preparation Encyclopedia*; Abdel-Aziz, "The Mujahideen Poison Handbook," February 7, 1996; Ansar al-Qa'ida, "Encyclopedia of Poisons," *Mausu'a al 'Aidad—The Preparation Encyclopedia*; "Maktab al-Khidamat, "Security and Intelligence."
48. Ansar a-Qai`da, "Encyclopedia of Poisons," *Mawsu`a al I`adad—The Preparation Encyclopedia*; "All That Relates to the Chemical Weapon (Mustard Gas) a Lot of Important and Rare Information for the First Time," *al-Ma`asada al jihadiya—The jihadi Lion's Den.*
49. Abu Hadhifa al-Shami, "A Course in Popular Poisons and Deadly Gases," Islamic Media Center, *Mawsu`a al I`adad—The Preparation Encyclopedia*; Abdel-Aziz, "The Mujahideen Poison Handbook," February 7, 1996; Ansar al-Qa'ida, "Encyclopedia of Poisons," *Mawsu`a al I`adad—The Preparation Encyclopedia.*
50. Abu Hadhifa al-Shami, "A Course in Popular Poisons and Deadly Gases," Islamic Media Center, *Mawsu`a al I`adad—The Preparation Encyclopedia*; Abdel-Aziz, "The Mujahideen Poison Handbook," February 7, 1996; Ansar al-Qa'ida, "Encyclopedia of Poisons," *Mawsu`a al I`adad—The Preparation Encyclopedia.*
51. Pita, "*Assessing al-Qa'ida's Chemical Threat,*" 493.
52. Jonathan B. Tucker, *War of Nerves: Chemical Warfare from World War I to Al-Qaeda*, (New York: Pantheon Books, 2006), 331–332.

53. Sammy Salama, "Special Report: Manual for Producing Chemical Weapon To Be Used in New York Subway Plot Available On Al-Qaeda Websites Since Late 2005," *WMD Insights*, July/August 2006 issue.
54. Pita, "*Assessing al-Qa'ida's Chemical Threat*," 493.
55. Bakhtiyar Akhmedkhanov, "International Terrorist Reveals Secrets," *Moscow News*, 2005.
56. "The Nuclear Bomb," *al-Khayma* (the Tent); "Documentation and Diagrams of the Atomic Bomb," *Outlaw Labs* (no publication or posting date provided).
57. Abu al-Usood al-Faqir, "Instances of Radiation Pollution from 1945-1987," *al-Farouq*.
58. "How to Build Your Own H-Bomb at Home," *al-Ma`asada al jihadiya—The Jihadi Lion's Den*, March 2005.
59. Layth al-Islam, "Nuclear Preparation Encyclopedia," *al-Firdaws* Web site, October 6, 2005.
60. Richard Pilch and Raymond Zilinskas eds., *Encyclopedia of Bioterrorism Defense* (Hoboken, NJ: Wiley-Liss, 2005), 76.
61. Eric Croddy, *Chemical and Biological Warfare: A Comprehensive Survey for the Concerned Citizen* (New York: Copernicus, 2002), 14.
62. For a detailed discussion of Hizballah's missiles and of Iranian support please see Jennifer Kline, "Special Report: Challenges of Iranian Missile Proliferation—Part II, Assistance to Hezbollah," *WMD Insights*, October 2006.
63. Ibid.
64. Noam Ophir, "Look Not to the Skies: The IAF vs. Surface-to-Surface Rocket Launchers," Jaffee Center for Strategic Studies, 9:3, November 2006.
65. Lisa Myers, "Hezbollah Drone Threatens Israel," *NBC Nightly News*, April 12, 2005.
66. "Lebanese Hezbollah Receives Eight Iranian-made Drones," *Al-Sharq al-Awsat*, November 10, 2004, in OSC document GMP20041110000085.
67. "Speech by Hezbollah's Nasrallah on Jerusalem Day, Mirsad-1," *Al-Manar TV*, November 12, 2004, in OSC document GMP20041112000278.
68. J. Kline, "Special Report: Challenges of Iranian Missile Proliferation—Part II, Assistance to Hezbollah." *WMD Insights*, October 2006.
69. Dennis M. Gormley, "North Korean Cruise Missile Tests—and Iraqi Cruise Missile Attacks—Raise Troubling Questions for Missile Defenses," *Center for Nonproliferation*, April 8, 2003.
70. For example, see Sammy Salama and Lydia Hansell, "Does Intent Equal Capability? Al Qa'ida and Weapons of Mass Destruction," *Nonproliferation Review* 12:3, (November 2003) 637–638; S. Salama, "Special Report: Manual for Producing Chemical Weapon To Be Used in New York Subway Plot Available On Al-Qaeda Websites Since Late 2005."

SECTION II

The Agents of Harm

CHAPTER 5

Jihadists and Chemical Weapons

Markus Binder and Michael Moodie

CONTENTS

INTRODUCTION

Chemical weapons are one of the oldest of those capabilities frequently described as "weapons of mass destruction," also commonly referred to simply as WMD. Strictly speaking, neither chemical nor biological weapons are capable of inflicting mass destruction, and for this reason, a more useful term is chemical biological radiological and nuclear (CBRN) that acknowledges their unconventional nature without overstating the extent to which they have similar destructive capabilities. The history of the use of various chemicals as agents of harm is as extensive as it is eclectic. For example, toxic fumes were used as a weapon in India as far back as 2000 BC. In 400 BC, Sparta reportedly used wood saturated with pitch and sulfur under besieged city walls to choke defenders. In 1591, Germans burned stink bombs containing a mixture of shredded hooves and horns with a fetid gum resin to disrupt enemy forces.[1] But it was the chemical scientific revolution of the late nineteenth century that gave chemicals the potential to become a major weapon of war. The crippling potential inherent in chemical weapons was revealed in 1915 near the Belgian town of Ypres when the Germans unleashed clouds of chlorine gas against Allied lines, breaking the defense and inflicting serious casualties. This successful attack led to an ever-increasing use of chemical weapons on the battlefields of World War I by all participants; by the final stages of the war, up to one-third of all artillery shells were chemical rounds. The chemical genie was unleashed, and chemical weapons have since been considered a scourge upon mankind. Regrettably, even as the final years of the twentieth century saw reductions in the threat from state-run chemical weapons programs, there were increasing signs that chemical weapons might become a significant weapon in the hands of terrorists, especially jihadists.

Based on their characteristics, physical properties, and effects, chemical weapons differ significantly from their nuclear and biological counterparts. The effects of chemical weapons are normally seen over a smaller area, and they have been traditionally viewed as more effective at the tactical or operational level rather than at the strategic level. In contrast to biological weapons, which are generally slow-acting, the effects of exposure to chemical weapons can become apparent within minutes or at most hours of initial contact. The strategic value of chemical weapons derives primarily from their psychological impact. Forcing a frightened population, or even military units, to don gas masks or protective gear can produce both physical and psychological effects of significant magnitude.

It is perhaps both of these impacts that make chemical weapons potentially attractive to jihadist terrorists. Just as they were the first CBRN weapons to arise in the modern age, chemical weapons were also the first WMD used by terrorists in recent history, when the Japanese religious cult, Aum Shinrikyo, released the chemical warfare (CW) agent sarin in the Tokyo subway in 1995. Revelations regarding Usama bin Ladin's expressed interest in using unconventional weapons quickly followed; and both of these factors contributed to the increased concern over the potential for CBRN terrorism in the United States throughout the later 1990s. Then in late 2001, the antrax letter attacks, coming so soon after the unconventional (though non-CBRN) September 11th attacks, drove concerns over the potential terrorist use of CBRN weapons to the top of the U.S. national security agenda.

Although jihadists have demonstrated their interest in the full range of CBRN weapons, chemicals are the most likely weapons to be used in the near term. While nuclear weapons have the potential to be many orders of magnitude more devastating than chemical weapons, they are also significantly less likely to be used in the medium term or even long term. In short, a terrorist attack involving nuclear weapons constitutes the quintessential low-probability, high-consequence scenario. Biological weapons are somewhat less high-consequence vis-à-vis nuclear weapons while the probability of their use is slightly higher. Chemical weapons, on the other hand, are unique insofar as they combine significant potential consequences with a generally accepted high probability of use. The basic technologies underlying chemical weapons are essentially ubiquitous in the modern world, and many analysts have concluded that the required materials and processes are well within the capabilities of determined jihadist groups. This contrasts with nuclear weapons, for which the necessary materials are very hard to obtain, and biological weapons, where the technologies and methods have proven very difficult to master (see Chapters 8 and 6 in this volume, respectively, for detailed information about the nexus of the threat posed by jihadists and these specific weapon types).

This chapter will consider jihadist interest and potential exploitation of chemical weapons. It will proceed in four sections: The first section briefly describes the nature of chemical weapons. The second offers a short discussion of various acquisition strategies available to jihadist terror groups. The third provides a short history of chemical weapons use by jihadists, including several case studies that highlight acquisition and use modes. The fourth section considers trends that could affect the acquisition and use of chemical weapons by jihadist terrorists in the future.

CHEMICAL WEAPONS: TECHNICAL DIMENSIONS

CW agents may exist as solids, gases, or liquids. When filled in munitions—whether of a military nature such as gravity bombs, artillery shells, mortar rounds, and missile payloads, or in as simple a form as the plastic bags used by Aum Shinrikyo in the Tokyo subway cars—most chemical agents are in liquid form. Following their release, the agent is dispersed as a liquid, vapor, or aerosol. Each chemical agent uniquely combines a key set of characteristics, including

- *Lethality*: whether or not, and in what circumstances, the agent will cause fatalities;
- *Mode of action*: the route by which the agent will affect living organisms;
- *Speed of action*: the time between exposure and effect;
- *Toxicity*: the measure of a quantity of a substance required to achieve the desired effect;
- *Persistence*: the length of time an agent remains a hazard once released into the environment.

There are two types of chemical agent that jihadists may choose from. The first of these are agents traditionally developed for military use, while the second are an extensive range of toxic industrial chemicals (TICs) that are widely used for commercial purposes but remain highly dangerous to human health. This distinction is complicated by the fact that, since their initial use, several of the traditional military agents, most notably chlorine and phosgene, have become very widely used industrial chemicals. Although they have lost most of their military value, these chemicals retain a harmful potential that could make them appealing to jihadists.

Western categorization systems separate military CW agents into several different categories, largely depending on how they work in the body. These categories include the following:

- ***Blister agents***, or vesicants, are oily liquids that inflict chemical burns on the skin or any other part of the body with which they come into contact, including the lungs if they are inhaled. Blister agents, such as mustard gas, were used extensively in the last two years of the World War I. More recently, they were used to some effect in the war between Iraq and Iran in the 1980s.
- ***Blood agents*** refer to chemical agents that use cyanide as an important ingredient and achieve their effects by traveling through the blood stream to sites where the agent can interfere with oxygen utilization at the cellular level. Hydrogen cyanide, which is also a widely used industrial chemical, and cyanogen chloride are the most important agents in this group.
- ***Choking agents*** attack the airways and cause swelling and edema in the lung tissues. These were perhaps the most widely used agents during World War I, and include such chemicals as chlorine and phosgene, both of which are in

widespread commercial use today. Protection against these agents is relatively simple, and they have consequently lost most of their military value. However, the majority of TICs likely to be used as weapons by jihadists are toxic inhalation hazards (TIHs), which fall within this category.

- ***Incapacitating agents*** are intended not to be lethal but to disable the target personnel for hours if not days after exposure. Such agents tend to act on the central nervous system and can render the victim unconscious. Such agents can also disrupt key mental functions like memory, problem solving, attention, and comprehension. The anticholinergic agent 3-quinuclidinyl benzilate (BZ) and the more better-known drug LSD are examples of incapacitating agents.
- ***Nerve agents*** are perhaps the most widely feared category of chemical weapon because of the speed and severity of their impact. Discovered as a by-product of 1930's research into organophosphorous insecticides, these agents inhibit the function of vital enzymes in the human body that inactivates acetylcholine, which mediates the transmission of certain types of nerve impulses. Nerve agents include tabun (GA), sarin (GB), soman (GD), and other G-series agents, as well as V-agents (VE, VM, and VX) discovered by British scientists in the late 1940s. The Iraqis are believed to have used nerve agents in their war with Iran, and the Aum Shinrikyo cult used sarin in its attacks in Matsumoto (1994) and Tokyo (1995). Following the 1995 Tokyo attack, Japanese authorities discovered that the cult had also explored other nerve agents, including soman, tabun, and VX (in addition to its unsuccessful efforts to use the biological weapons anthrax and botulinum toxin).

Once a group has selected the agent that it would like to use, it must take appropriate measures to acquire the chemical and produce a weapon for subsequent use.

JIHADIST CHEMICAL WEAPON ACQUISITION STRATEGIES

Earlier chapters have made clear jihadists' interest in obtaining and using chemical weapons (in addition to other types of WMD). The jihadist community has two basic approaches available to them to obtain chemical weapons, each of which has unique attractions and drawbacks. The first approach is to acquire chemical weapons by theft, "gift" (such as from a state sponsor), or purchase. The second is to produce the chemical agent and its delivery mechanism using precursors and other materials that are themselves purchased, stolen, or otherwise obtained. A choice of whether to select one or both of these two basic approaches must be made irrespective of whether the group plans to employ military CW agents or the aforementioned toxic industrial chemicals.

Theft of Military CW Agents

The largest potential sources of ready-made CW agents are the stockpiles of the Russian Federation and the United States. The Russian stockpile is currently comprised of approximately 30,000 metric tons of CW agents stored at seven locations.[2] A substantial proportion of the Russian stockpile is stored in several million relatively portable munitions rather than large bulk containers.[3] Concerns regarding the security of the Russian stockpile continue to exist, but are less intense than in the early 1990s.[4]

The U.S. chemical weapons stockpile (approximately 15,000 metric tons) is located at six facilities spread across the lower forty-eight states.[5] All six facilities are part of the U.S. CW stockpile destruction program. The facilities in question store an assortment of filled unitary chemical munitions and bulk agent containers. Unlike Russian munitions, many U.S. artillery shells are already fitted with fuzes and burster charges, making it relatively easy to convert these munitions into potent, ready-to-use weapons. U.S. facilities also hold large numbers of bulk agent containers containing approximately 700 kilograms of sarin or VX.[6] However, the handling of these bulky items and their large quantities of lethal agent would be extremely difficult, thus reducing their attractiveness to terrorists.[7]

Both Russia and the United States are currently engaged in an ongoing process of CW destruction that is gradually reducing the quantity of agent available for potential seizure. Unfortunately, this process is slow and far behind schedule, substantially extending both the life of stockpiles and the period of associated risk. Moscow contends that the Russian stockpile will not be completely eliminated until 2012 (at the earliest), although some observers believe that the process could take considerably longer. According to U.S. estimates, its stockpiles may not be completely eliminated until 2023.[8] Although the process could be completed as early as 2017, if additional funding is made available for Blue Grass, Kentucky and Pueblo, Colorado.

Nevertheless, Russian and U.S. authorities are aware of the dangers posed by terrorists obtaining chemical weapons and have an interest in ensuring adequate security at all CW stockpile facilities. They have devoted considerable effort and money to enhancing security at those sites. As a general observation with respect to security, it seems that attempting to seize or divert weapons or CW agents from these facilities would be a high-risk action for jihadists, which is unlikely to ultimately result in acquisition and very likely to expose the planned operation. It is more difficult to make a determination regarding the ease of terrorist acquisition of CW agents or weapons from stockpiles in other countries such as India, North or South Korea, Libya, or Syria. Available information suggests that the Indian and South Korean stockpiles, both of which are expected to be completely eliminated by 2010 (at the latest), are stored under guard at single military facilities. The North Korean stockpile is very difficult to account for, but it seems unlikely that jihadists would be able to mount a successful operation to seize CW agents in that country. In the Syrian case, CW agents appear to be under tight central government control and are presumably not vulnerable to theft or seizure.

Purchase or Transfer of Military CW Agents

A number of governments, including Iran and Syria, have been accused of providing weapons, training, and/or funding to jihadist movements. In the past, concerns have been expressed that these countries might supply military CW agents, and presumably the necessary training, to ensure their effective use by jihadist organizations. Cooperation along these lines would greatly increase the likelihood that a jihadist group might successfully mount a devastating chemical terrorist attack. Although Syria is believed to have relatively sophisticated CW capabilities, it is important to note that, to date, no publicly available evidence exists of any transfer of CW or CW training to terrorist organizations by a sovereign government. Any action of this type—that led to a successful attack or even an exposed plot—would carry with it an extremely high risk that the provider of assistance would be exposed and punished. While it is unlikely that analysis of the CW agent used would identify the supplier, the operational details of terrorist attacks including information on training and support networks, are frequently exposed by post-facto investigations. This consideration makes it unlikely that any regime would endanger itself by directly providing CW to terrorists.

There is, however, the possibility that disaffected or corrupt elements within a national military or scientific structure might elect to make CW agents or weapons available to jihadists in contravention of state policy. In the 1990s, al-Qa'ida operatives apparently attempted to purchase nuclear materials from officials in a number of the Soviet Union's successor states. An unconfirmed allegation also claims that Aum Shinrikyo obtained blueprints for its sarin production facility from a corrupt Russian official in the early 1990s.[9] In addition to officials seeking private gain, it is also a challenge to ensure that states continue to make sufficient resources available to prevent production or storage facilities from allowing leakage of materials to criminals and other substate actors.

Nevertheless, as a general rule, it remains unlikely that governments would tolerate unauthorized attempts to transfer chemical weapons or relevant technical knowledge to jihadist terrorist groups. In the event of an attack, the danger that the transfer could be traced back to its source would place the state at risk of economic and political sanctions or even military attack. As such, state governments have strong incentives to ensure that officials with access to CW munitions or information do not engage in unauthorized transfers. On balance, this type of transfer seems unlikely to occur unless state authority is already severely compromised.

Production

A more likely alternative for those seeking access to military CW agents is to produce them indigenously along with the necessary delivery systems. This contingency has received extensive attention from many analysts who often differ on the ease of producing CW agents. Some contend that the production of military agents, especially nerve agents, is an extremely difficult enterprise. Others adopt the position that the production of relatively small quantities of agent, on the order of a few tens of kilograms, can be achieved without too much difficulty by moderately skilled personnel using widely available equipment. Still others contend that it is not so much the production of the agent that is the major barrier, but the mating of agent and delivery device in such a way that ensures that the agent will be disseminted effectively and act in the way it is intended.

The basic requirements for manufacturing chemical weapons from scratch include precursor chemicals and an assortment of dual-use chemical equipment, potentially including corrosuin resistant piping and reaction vessels. All else being equal, the more basic the initial precursor chemicals the terrorists obtain, the more reaction steps will be required to produce the desired chemical agent and the longer and more complex the production process becomes. Certain processes for more complex chemical agents (such as certain of the G-series nerve agents) are extremely dangerous and require specialized equipment that can withstand corrosion, high temperatures, and high pressures.[10] Nonetheless, several alternative synthesis methods exist for producing most CW agents, and it is likely that terrorists would try wherever possible to avoid those that use high-temperature and high-pressure reactions in order to obviate the need for special equipment and reduce the possibility of injury or discovery resulting from an accidental release.[11] Finally, the group producing the agents would need to take special precautions to avoid prematurely exposing themselves to the agents. Depending on the level of risk the group is willing to accept, these precautions could range from basic spill and inhalation protections such as impervious gloves and gas masks to obtaining nerve agent antidotes such as atropine. Although the latter step might increase the possibility of detection, it could be useful for ensuring that those involved in the production of the CW agent survive long enough to complete their task.

Acquiring the required equipment may or may not be difficult, depending on the location of the jihadist manufacturing effort. In heavily industrialized societies such as Europe, obtaining the necessary equipment for small-scale batch production of CW agents should not be an insurmountable obstacle. The dual-use nature of many precursor chemicals and equipment puts the synthesis of limited quantities of CW agents within the reach of almost all terrorist organizations with the requisite expertise. Even recognized precursor chemicals controlled by the Chemical Weapons Convention (CWC) may be available to terrorists. This international nonproliferation treaty focuses on state-level programs and international trafficking rather than small-scale purchases of precursor chemicals that remain within national borders. However, for jihadists engaged in attempted production of CW agents outside of the major industrialized economies, chemical nonproliferation measures have the potential to make their efforts to secure precursors much more complex (see Chapter 11 of this volume for more detailed information concerning global efforts to prevent the proliferation of chemical weapons and other WMD).

The Australia Group is an informal collaboration among forty countries to coordinate their export controls relating to materials and equipment relevant to chemical (and biological) weapons. The existence of such controls would make it more difficult to secure at least some chemical precursors and specialized equipment, and jihadists may have to resort to creating "front companies" or other subterfuges to circumvent them. But given that the chemical industry and chemical production facilities are expanding significantly to developing countries such as China, India, and Indonesia that are not members of the Australia Group and have less well-developed national export controls, this potential acquisition route could take on new dimensions.

Obtaining exotic precursor chemicals may be difficult, but those that cannot be purchased may be available through targeted thefts, depending on the level of chemical activity in the local economy. Once again, such attempting to steal CW agent precursors and related technology would increase the risk that the group might be detected. An alternative would be to produce precursors from their more basic chemical ingredients.[12] However, an effort of this sort would dramatically increase the complexity of the operation, extending its duration and cost.

Once a decision is made to produce CW agents, a further decision must be made regarding the particular type of agent to manufacture. It is unlikely that jihadists would attempt to manufacture choking and blood agents such as chlorine, phosgene, or hydrogen cyanide. Although the manufacture of these chemicals is relatively simple, the production of useful quantities would require a substantial infrastructure. Furthermore, both of these agents are bulk industrial chemicals and could be obtained more easily by theft or purchase—there is no apparent advantage to manufacturing these independently. Nevertheless, there are indications that al-Qa'ida operatives did seek to produce cyanide and phosgene in Afghanistan in the late 1990s. The rationale behind adopting this approach remains unclear. It is possible that the motivation for this production effort was more closely tied to al-Qa'ida's internal dynamics than to a decision by the leadership to pursue this particular agent. Evidence that these efforts were at least partially successful included testimony by Ahmed Ressam, a man trained by al-Qa'ida and convicted of plotting to bomb Los Angeles International Airport, about tests using cyanide to kill dogs.

Following the U.S. invasion of Afghanistan, Ressam's testimony was confirmed when, in August 2002, CNN came into possession of a number of al-Qa'ida videotapes, including one showing experiments in which dogs were killed using an unidentified gas.

Vesicants are simpler to produce than nerve agents, both in terms of the chemical precursors required and the processes and materials needed for manufacture, but it is unlikely, though not impossible, that these will be selected. These agents are generally slow in their effects, may require large quantities to have a widespread affect, and lack lethality, reducing their attractiveness to jihadists, who have frequently indicated their interest in generating mass casualties. The main attraction of vesicants would be the ease with which they can contaminate a large area and the potential they have to produce significant economic disruptions while efforts are undertaken to decontaminate all potentially exposed facilities and persons.

In contrast, nerve agents are lethal even in very small doses, have a rapid effect, and even trace quantities can produce distressing physical symptoms, such as dimming and blurring of vision. On the other hand, these attractive qualities are counterbalanced by the difficulties associated with nerve agent production, which requires a series of complex reactions between precursers and intermediates that are difficult to obtain and frequently corrosive or toxic. The services of a suitable chemical engineer would be a necessary requirement for success.[13] Once jihadists have obtained suitable personnel and precursors, the actual production of kilogram quantities of moderately pure CW agents could, theoretically at least, be accomplished in a matter of days.[14]

To date, there have been very few examples of terrorist groups attempting to produce their own CW agents. Some evidence exists of low-level activity by al-Qa'ida in Afghanistan in the late 1990s, and there are a number of unsubstantiated claims of production by other groups. There have been numerous alleged or actual plots to produce agents, few of which have actually involved the acquisition of chemical precursors or expert personnel. Finally, since 2003 there have been several attempts at production of military CW agents by jihadist groups in Iraq (discussed below). However, the only documented instance of successful CW agent production by a terrorist group, jihadist or otherwise, is the case of Aum Shinrikyo in Japan, which is discussed in some detail below.

Aum Shinrikyo

Although the Aum Shinrikyo cult was not a jihadist group, it shared similar ideological characteristics such as an extreme Manichean outlook, a strong sense superiority, and a desire to actively reshape the world rather than waiting for their deity to do it for them (for more information on jihadists strategy and ideology, see Chapter 1 of this volume). In any case, Aum Shinrikyo provides an instructive example highlighting aspects of terrorist group capabilities for the production of military-grade chemical weapons. Aum was a large, well-resourced group based in a highly developed industrial society. The group actively recruited educated individuals who possessed a multitude of useful technical skills in the fields of biology and chemistry. Drawing on the skills of its members, the group was able to successfully produce small quantities of nerve agents including sarin, soman, tabun, and VX. Over a period of six months, beginning in November 1993, the group produced some 30 kilograms of sarin, which was subsequently used in attacks against both individuals and large groups of people. The group also constructed a large facility that was intended to produce as much as two tons of sarin per day as part of a plan to amass a stockpile of 70 tons of agent. Although this large production facility was not able to produce any sarin before the group's activities were ended by Japanese authorities, Aum's ability to design, construct, and begin to operate the facility was unprecedented. However, it is not clear that a jihadist group would be able to duplicate Aum's success by constructing and operating a similar facility. A much more significant element of the Aum case is the group's ability to make several tens of kilograms of sarin using laboratory methods over approximately six months. In doing so, the group highlighted the point that the production of so-called classic CW agents does not require the latest cutting-edge science and technology, although access to skilled personnel remains critical. In fact, they exploited science that is over seventy years old and quite well understood by a large number of people worldwide. The agent was produced at a facility located in a Tokyo suburb that, while impressive for a nonstate actor, involved relatively crude production techniques and technologies.

In addition to producing useful quantities of the agent, Aum was also able to develop and deploy a somewhat effective vehicle-mounted delivery system, which was used in the 1994 Matsumoto attack. Nevertheless, not all of Aum's attempts to produce workable delivery systems were as successful or as sophisticated as that used in the Matsumoto attack. Most famously, the Tokyo subway attack was conducted using plastic bags filled with liquid sarin that were punctured by umbrella tips and left to evaporate. This crude delivery technique, combined with the relatively poor quality of the sarin in terms of its purity, were major factors in limiting the number of casualties in that attack to only twelve victims.

The Aum Shinrikyo case reinforces the view that terrorists will apply different standards to their acquisition of an unconventional weapons capability, including chemical weapons. It is not necessary for their system to meet the same demanding expectations of long-term agent stability, high reliability, performance, and effectiveness usually applied to the products of a military program. The Aum Shinrikyo case also suggests that terrorists will be willing to cut corners or skip steps that would likely receive considerable time and attention (as well as resources) in a national program. For the terrorist, the standard is often that the weapon be "just good enough" for the particular operation planned.

The Aum case is particularly interesting for what it says about the ability of a well-funded organization with access to skilled personnel to produce and deliver military-style CW agents. In contrast to Aum's successes, the efforts of al-Qa'ida, and jihadist groups in general to demonstrate a similar production capability have been much less impressive. Al-Qa'ida has been suspected of seeking to produce chemical weapons ever since the group came to the attention of U.S. authorities. However, to date, neither al-Qa'ida nor the wider jihadist movement has demonstrated the ability to produce even small quantities of military agents. The most significant effort to date was that undertaken in Afghanistan in the late 1990s and early 2000s. Investigations following the U.S. invasion of that country highlighted al-Qa'ida's interest in these weapons, noting the existence of laboratories and documentation related to CW agent production. The bulk of these efforts were focused on the manufacturing of cyanide derivatives and industrial chemicals. There was little or no evidence to suggest that the group had demonstrated an ability to manufacture nerve agents.

Ultimately, although jihadist groups have some familiarity with the use of chemicals and chemical processes, these skills have been limited to that basic subset required to manufacture high explosives. In general terms, the efforts of jihadist groups to produce their own chemical weapons have thus far proven ineffective. A fundamental problem appears to be an inadequate understanding of the chemical processes involved and the difficulties in securing personnel with the appropriate skills.

At the same time, jihadists' past lack of success in developing and producing CW agents should not be allowed to foster complacency when considering future prospects. Previous failures have to some degree been a product of the population base from which jihadist groups have drawn recruits. In the core regions of jihadist activity and support, the levels of technical education and competence in the general population are relatively low compared to those in more industrially developed areas. This has the effect of reducing, albeit not eliminating, the likelihood that a jihadist group will be able to recruit someone with the requisite skillset needed to produce CW agents. The increasing ability of jihadist organizations to recruit new members amongst immigrant and native communities in Western societies may alter the calculus by providing access to a deeper pool of educated members with a wider range of skills. So, too, might the spread of underlying chemical processes and production capabilities throughout the developing world.

Acquisition of Toxic Industrial Chemicals

The acquisition and use of toxic industrial chemicals may represent the most effective method for jihadist groups to obtain a chemical weapon capability. Many highly toxic chemicals including anhydrous ammonia, chlorine, hydrogen fluoride, phosgene, and others are produced, stored, and transported in very large quantities in support of normal day-to-day industrial activities. Security for these chemicals is frequently minimal or nonexistent, and it is reasonable to suppose that a determined terrorist group would be able to gain access to significant quantities without too much difficulty. In contrast to the acquisition and use of military style agents, obtaining TICs only requires traditional terrorist skillsets. If jihadists were able to secure a truck loaded with a large quantity of chlorine or ammonia, all they would need to do would be to place these chemicals in an optimal location to achieve maximum effects. In many instances, the agents would not even need to be transported to be used effectively, as they could be unleashed on surrounding communities from industrial facilities. One of the best examples of the potential that TICs offer to jihadist groups is the 1984 incident in Bhopal, India, in which the release of 40 metric tons of methyl isocyanate (MIC) gas killed several thousand people and left many thousands of others severely injured. In the United States, the Department of Homeland Security considers the deliberate release of stored chlorine gas to have the potential to kill almost 20,000 people in a matter of hours.[15]

Most analysts who consider the issue of jihadist acquisition of chemical weapons are moving to the view that TICs represent the most likely future direction for these groups, as it avoids many of the complexities associated with the production or acquisition of traditional military agents. Although TICs are much less toxic than most CW agents on a weight-for-weight basis, the large amounts of a toxic industrial gas that might be released in a sabotage attack on a production or storage facility could still have catastrophic effects. TICs have the added advantage that the use of these chemicals as weapons would probably have a damaging effect on the economy of the affected country as it attempted to address the difficult issue of preventing future attacks of a similar nature. The next section will consider the available historical record highlighting jihadist attempts to develop and use chemical weapons.

HISTORICAL USE BY JIHADIST GROUPS

While the level of activity and accomplishment varied by group, location, and time period within elements of the jihadist community through the 1990s, the jihadist movement showed an increasing interest in the acquisition and use of chemical weapons. Many of the incidents recorded for the early to mid-1990s revolved around plans to use cyanide as a poison for assassination purposes, but no evidence indicates that any such attacks were successfully mounted. Other instances revolve around the use of cyanide to enhance the effects of bullets, bombs, or hand-held weapons such as knives. Again, none of these efforts—which allegedly included groups operating in Algeria, France, and Kashmir—appear to have produced significant results. Cyanide is a regular feature of these plots, most likely because of its relative abundance and the ease with which it can be secured.

Following the 1993 World Trade Center bombing, claims were made that the bomb maker, Ramzi Yousef, had intended to incorporate sodium cyanide into the bomb. Those claims were subsequently disputed.[16] Although he had threatened to use chemical weapons in correspondence on a number of occasions, there is no convincing evidence that the 1993 plot ever involved the use of a chemical agent. In the event that it had, it is difficult to see how the chemical agent could have avoided being consumed in the large initial explosion. If plans did exist to include this agent in the bomb, the case highlights the low level of understanding of the use of toxic chemicals within the jihadist community at the time, even on the part of a relatively accomplished and technically capable member.

An important element that helped increase sensitivity to the possibilities of jihadist use of chemical weapons within the global intelligence and security community was Aum Shinrikyo's Tokyo subway attack of April 1995. Even though this attack was not mounted by a jihadist group, it convinced many that other terrorists, including jihadists, could, and indeed eventually would, mount similar attacks. At the same time, it provided a counterexample to those who were arguing that the widespread availability of the underlying science and technology would inevitably foster a "catastrophic" event. Although the Aum Shinrikyo case can be seen to represent a unique confluence of factors, there were elements that worked together to render their attacks less effective than might have been the case if they had been mounted by a jihadist group. Despite investing large amounts of time and money in producing nerve agents, Aum was unable to make effective use of the limited quantities of the agents it managed to manufacture. The Tokyo subway attack resulted in 12 deaths and around 1,000 injuries, most of which were not serious. These results were much less than might have been anticipated for an attack of this sort directed against large numbers of people trapped in a confined space, especially when compared with the effects of the Madrid train bombings in 2003 and the 2005 London subway attack. The primary reasons for the poor results were the poor quality of the agent combined with the use of an inefficient dissemination method. A higher quality agent or, alternatively, a better dissemination method would almost certainly have resulted in more fatalities. An important consideration in this regard was the desire of the Aum perpetrators to survive the attack and escape the scene before the concentration of agent had reached a point at which it might seriously endanger their health. Jihadists are unlikely to operate under the same constraints, improving the chances of the agent being released in a fashion guaranteed to produce maximum immediate effect.

In early 2001, a jihadist ring with cells operating in London, Strasbourg, and Genoa was broken up. Initial reports claimed that the arrested cell members had been planning to release sarin nerve agent in subways and the European Parliament.[17] Although the group was reported to possess detailed instructions on the production and dissemination of the nerve agent, there were no indications that that they had secured suitable chemicals or produced any nerve agents. In 2002, a suspected plot by a group of jihadists to use cyanide in an attack on the U.S. embassy in Rome was uncovered by Italian authorities.[18] The arrested perpetrators possessed approximately 10 pounds of potassium ferrocyanide, a chemical that, although containing the label "cyanide" as part of its name, is not very toxic and is commonly used as an anti-caking agent and food additive. Although the intended use of the substance was unclear, speculation suggested that the perpetrators intended to poison the water supply of the U.S. embassy after a forced entry to service tunnels beneath the embassy. If this was their intent, it appears that their lack of technical expertise led them to choose a widely available but ineffective chemical agent for the attack.

Alleged plots unmasked in New York (2003) and Morocco (2005) highlighted jihadist interest in chemical weapons for wider effect.[19] The incidents also drew attention to the methods by which jihadists are making technical information available to groups and individuals. In both of these instances, jihadist cells appear to have been working toward completion of an improvised binary chemical weapon capable of generating hydrogen cyanide that could be carried in a backpack by a single person. This simple weapon, the so-called "mubtakker," is most interesting for what it suggests about the sophistication, or lack thereof, of potential jihadist chemical attacks. Although hydrogen cyanide is indeed a lethal substance, it is also subject to a number of serious limitations, including flammability, difficulties achieving lethal concentrations, and near complete ineffectiveness in nonlethal concentrations. The operation required no specialist skills. The most significant aspects of the planned attacks were the use of relatively easy to obtain chemicals and a preference for a single chemical reaction to take place at the point of delivery. A further significant element in these plots is their move away from a previous tendency to mix explosives with toxic chemicals. Ultimately, for unknown reasons, the plots were not carried out. However, the plans for the device have been widely circulated on the Internet, and the possibility remains that an attack using this device may be attempted in the future.

In late 2003, an Iraqi insurgent group that maintained ties to Abu Musab al- Zarqawi, the "*al-Abud* network," managed to secure the services of an Iraqi chemist with a view to manufacturing tabun nerve agent (GA) and nitrogen mustard (HN). The group's efforts appear to have failed in the face of inadequate skills and difficulties securing suitable precursors. An attempt by another Iraqi group to produce hydrogen cyanide for incorporation into improvised explosive devices (IEDs), discovered in late 2004, highlighted an ongoing problem facing jihadist efforts to effectively use chemicals as weapons—a fundamental lack of scientific or often even a practical understanding of the characteristics of the chemicals with which they are working. This is seen in the efforts to mix flammable agents such as hydrogen cyanide with relatively large quantities of explosives. Similar problems are seen in the plans of a London-based group to use osmium tetroxide as a chemical weapon, again using explosive dissemination, which would have transformed the substance into a nontoxic form.

A much murkier incident in 2004 is the alleged plot to release a large chemical cloud over the city of Amman, Jordan, in combination with a series of truck-bomb blasts. Public reports on this case have highlighted the confessions of several captured jihadists claiming that they planned a chemical attack, while Jordanian media aired images of large numbers of stacked containers filled with a variety of unnamed chemicals. The only chemical specifically identified was sulfuric acid, a chemical that is frequently discovered at jihadist bases. It is worth noting, however, that sulfuric, and nitric, acid are both ingredients in the manufacture of high explosives. This is probably the most likely explanation for the presence of these chemicals despite the "confessions" secured by Jordanian authorities.

In 2006, representatives of the *al-Aqsa* Martyrs Brigades, an armed wing of the Palestinian Fatah movement sometimes linked to Hizb'allah, claimed that the group had achieved success "in developing over 20 types of biological and chemical weapons after a three-year effort."[20] Although the *al-Aqsa* Martyrs Brigades is not itself a jihadist organization, the group has demonstrated a willingness to cooperate with those that are, such as Palestinian Islamic Jihad and Hamas. Many of the *al-Aqsa* Martyrs Brigades' operational techniques have been essentially indistinguishable from those of jihadist groups, and it is entirely possible that the group would be willing to share CW capabilities with other organizations. Even though the claims of CBW capability were clearly intended to have a deterrent effect on Israeli military operations, they were ultimately judged to be noncredible.[21] As such, these claims amounted to little more than posturing or an attempt to engage in "psychological warfare."[22]

By far the most significant development of the last ten years, in terms of jihadist use of chemical weapons, took place in Iraq in late 2006 and early 2007. Over the course of several months, al-Qa'ida in Iraq (an affiliate of the original al-Qa'ida organization) launched a series of attacks against civilians that featured the use of increasingly large quantities of chlorine gas. The objective in these attacks was to release a large cloud of chlorine gas that would cover an area and inflict larger numbers of casualties than might otherwise be achieved with the more typical car or truck bombs. Although these attacks were ultimately ineffective as chemical attacks, they evolved over time, thus demonstrating an improving understanding of the requirements for an effective attack.

The first attacks involved the use, as a supplement to traditional car bombs, of small 100-pound containers of chlorine gas stolen from water treatment facilities. These early attacks were not unlike the apocryphal attempt to add cyanide to the first World Trade Center bombing in 1993. The incorporation of chlorine cylinders into these attacks meant that they were able to eilcit more public attention than the increasingly routine explosive-only attacks, but there are no indications that the chlorine actually caused any injuries or deaths. Indeed, it is likely that the bulk of the chlorine was consumed in the initial explosion.

Subsequent attacks utilized one-ton containers of chlorine and were markedly more effective. In a series of attacks in early 2007, jihadists were able to release sufficient chlorine gas to inflict injuries and distress, though no deaths, on as many as 200 nearby individuals at a time. The chlorine attacks, which appear to have been the work of a relatively small element within the broader Iraq-based jihadist movement, ended unexpectedly in May 2007 for reasons that remain unclear. Although chlorine canisters have continued to be found on occasion as part of jihadist weapons caches, there has not been a continuing stream of chemical attacks. In public statements, U.S. officials have speculated that the turn to chlorine as a weapon represented a solution to a temporary shortage of explosives and that once the more usual explosive materials became available again the use of chlorine was abandoned. Additional factors may have been the arrests or deaths of key personnel behind the attacks. Unfortunately, there is simply not enough information available in the public domain to determine what led to the initiation, or the termination, of these attacks.

Although the Iraqi chlorine attacks generated significant numbers of casualties, most of these were relatively minor in nature. The primary reason for this was the use of insufficient quantities of agent, making it difficult or impossible to achieve lethal concentrations in an open-air environment. At no point did the Iraqi attacks employ more than a few tons of agent at a time. It is worth noting that the first series of German attacks using chlorine in 1915, which were launched under particularly favorable conditions against unprotected individuals, used anywhere from 15 to 150 tons of agent for each individual attack.[23]

The significance of these Iraqi chlorine attacks lies not in the numbers of casualties that they inflicted but in the transformation in approach to obtaining and using chemical weapons. These attacks represent the first time that jihadists have employed chemicals as a weapon with even a modicum of effectiveness. To mount their attacks the jihadists elected to forgo the lengthy and difficult process of manufacturing advanced CW agents, a process that may, in fact, be beyond their skill levels. Instead, the approach adopted was to secure prepackaged quantities of TICs and release them at a suitable time and place. To a significant degree, the limited impact of these attacks was a result of the severely disrupted and underdeveloped industrial infrastructure of Iraq. In more developed industrial societies, such as in Europe or North America, and increasingly in Asia as well, there are many more facilities storing or transporting much larger quantities of TICs in close proximity to large civilian population centers. Concerns that jihadist groups might turn to the use of TICs have been extant since at least the late 1990s, but until 2006 there were no instances of this occurring. To date, this style of attack has not been repeated outside Iraq, and the reasons for this absence should be thoroughly explored. Nevertheless, the necessary ingredients for a successful attack using commercial toxic industrial chemicals are present in almost every city in the world, and it may be only a matter of time until more such attacks occur.

This short overview of recent jihadist interest in and attempts to use chemical weapons highlights several points. In addition to the previously noted limitations in their technical understanding, a key element is the tendency on the part of jihadist groups to look at multiple agents and approaches when considering attacks. Many instances of chemical terrorism described in the popular media involve little more than an assortment of seized documents, some of which mention chemical weapons. Very few cases involve the acquisition of chemicals or indications that the plotters would be able to make effective use of chemical agents or precursors in the event that they were able to secure them. Nevertheless, it is clear that many jihadist groups and individuals are aware of the possibilities of chemical weapons despite their inability to deploy them effectively. In its most recent intelligence assessments of jihadist interest and capabilities in chemical weapons, the U.S. Defense Intelligence Agency (DIA) noted that "Al-Qa'ida continues its efforts to obtain chemical, biological, radiological and nuclear capabilities. In September 2006, al-Qa'ida in Iraq leader Abu Ayyub al-Masri publicly called upon scientists to help the terrorist group develop such weapons. These efforts will likely persist."[24] Although the jihadi's efforts have not yet produced any substantial results, this is not a guarantee that their attempts will continue to be unproductive. In addition to a continuation of jihadist efforts using the approaches outlined above, a number of developing trends in chemical technology and industry could improve the chances of success in the medium to long term.

CHANGING CW TERRORIST CHALLENGE

How the chemical terrorism challenge will evolve is a function of significant, ongoing, and often rapid change—first and foremost in the underlying science and technology, but also in the security landscape, social organization, strategic priorities, the form and function of conflict, and elsewhere. These changes are converging to create an environment marked by greater complexity and uncertainty, which, in turn, will heighten unpredictability. Managing risks in this environment will constitute the greatest challenge to policymakers in both counterterrorism and the CW arena in the future. But it will be an unfamiliar challenge. It will be less and less about what the terrorists have, and more and more about what they know and how they may try to misuse that knowledge. As the previous discussion highlights, in the past, their knowledge base and technical know-how have been limited; in light of current trends, that could change.

Challenge of Advancing Science and Technology

Science in today's world moves forward at an incredibly rapid pace. The result is that more and more scientific knowledge as well as the tools and technologies in which that knowledge is embeded are falling within the grasp of many more people. The world is witnessing a life sciences revolution; an explosion in knowledge about the processes of life at the molecular level. The speed of advance in certain branches of the life sciences is remarkable, moving faster even than Moore's Law that describes the incredible velocity of change in information technology.[25] In the face of such rapid change, it is difficult for national security, legal, regulatory, or ethical systems to keep up.

A notable aspect of this expanding knowledge, driven by the goals of the pharmaceutical, agricultural, and healthcare sectors, is the capability to package and deliver chemical agents. Increasing knowledge of these capabilities is especially important because, as a National Research Council (NRC) study points out, the materials, equipment, and technology for "disseminating and delivering the agent to their intended recipient(s) are equally, if not more important than the agents themselves...."[26] To date, this point has been insufficiently appreciated; most of the discussion of the life sciences-related threat has focused on biological and toxic agents. In the future, more attention should be paid to delivery devices.

This accelerating rate of change combines with the surprise inherent in scientific discovery to generate phenomena that are unexpected. The NRC study makes the point that scientific progress in the twentieth century was marked by successive serendipitous discoveries that had profound impacts, in some cases forcing complete revisions in how certain natural phenomena were understood. In the face of such a process, one can argue that the life sciences, including bio-chemistry, will continue to advance quickly, in a variety of directions, and that "new and previously unanticipated paradigm shifts are very likely to occur...."[27] Moreover, innovations need not come only from traditional research and development programs, but are likely to emerge from surprising quarters. Countries such as India and China are particularly well placed to achieve breakthroughs, but innovations with potential security implications could come from virtually any country or region of the world.[28] Moreover, such innovations are not likely to come from state-sponsored programs. Indeed, less and less of the process of technological innovation is supported by states, but rather by commercial and scientific imperatives. For that reason, the individuals who may be responsible for future use of unconventional weapons, including chemical weapons, need not be found in governmental programs, but may work for industrial or scientific ventures, and some of these individuals, especially in developing countries, may be sympathetic to the goals and aspirations of jihadists.

One key aspect of the scientific and technological trends that will have a major impact on the future proliferation environment is the convergence of various scientific fields. As analyst Alexander Kelle has noted, "many of the products flowing from the biotechnology revolution...are basically chemical compounds."[29] A *Nature* magazine survey of leading chemists found a clear consensus that many of chemistry's most urgent questions are ones that address aspects of living systems.[30] The increasingly blurred lines between biology and chemistry are especially apparent in new processes for drug discovery using combinatorial chemistry and high-throughput screening to generate significant numbers of potentially highly toxic chemical compounds. While these results may be rejected as the basis for developing a new drug, information about these toxic substances is maintained in corporate or other databases. Were jihadists able to access such information, they may be able to identify new and dangerous agents.

An important determinant of the success in this environment of converging technologies will be the ability to integrate, and what is true in the broader scientific and economic arenas of the life sciences is also true for the security sphere. Because the security sector now largely relies on the application of technologies from the commercial sector, the advantage here also rests with those—including terrorist groups—who can rapidly adapt, exploit, and integrate evolving technology. [31] Given the growing scientific and technological competence of many countries and individuals around the world, the United States should be under no illusion that it or its friends and allies are the only places where innovation in the security arena can occur or that such innovation will only be the product of government programs.

A second important implication of this development is that it creates a chance to pursue multiple routes to the same end point. It is vital for those responsible for managing CW risks to recognize that future efforts are likely to bear little resemblance to those of the past in terms of the pathways traveled to achieve success. No reason exists to believe that any future terrorist CW program will be similar to that, for example, of the Aum Shinrikyo.

Central Importance of Knowledge

These issues have come to the fore because current trends have shifted the center of gravity in the chemical weapons dynamic. Traditionally, the understanding of unconventional weapons—both chemical and biological—was based on two assumptions: (1) that sensitive materials and technologies were critical to the proliferation process and could be identified as inherently dangerous and (2) that suppliers of that material and technology could be controlled through a system of harmonized national export controls without unduly hampering legitimate commercial trade.[32] In today's globalized and networked world, neither of these assumptions is guaranteed. Rather than material and equipment, the fulcrum for CW has become that knowledge, and knowledge rests with individuals. The NRC study points out that today "matter" is transforming into "information."[33] Information becomes knowledge, and, as a result, technology transfers relating to chemistry are increasingly about knowledge, that is, "intangible" technology in the form of data, processes, and expertise. Moreover, knowledge is the currency of networks, the mode that has come to characterize more and more terrorist operations. This shift in the problem of the potential exploitation of CW to a knowledge-based risk is inherent in global scientific developments that result in more and more people in more and more places knowing more and more of the relevance to this challenge.

Impact of Globalization

The second trend with a major impact on the future of potential chemical weapons use by jihadists is globalization, which is characterized by interrelationships and transactions among actors at various levels that are distinguished by their worldwide scope, accelerating speed, growing magnitude, thickening density, and increasing complexity. Globalization has transformed patterns of industrial production at both the national and international levels. Together with new production processes, agile manufacturing, miniaturization, lower technology costs, and increased productivity of a global talent pool, these trends are restructuring business enterprises in fundamental ways, such as creating smaller enterprises, flatter organizational pyramids, and, particularly important in a terrorist context, more empowered employees.

It is in this context that scientific and technological trends have the potential to make it less difficult for jihadists to overcome some traditional barriers impeding the development of an effective CW program. The appearance of multi-purpose equipment, for example, the much-discussed microreactor and on-demand principles and practices create disturbing possibilities.[34] If such technology becomes widely used, it could transform, or at least alter significantly, the processes by which industry produces a wide range of chemicals. More importantly for this chapter, a microreactor's small size, flexibility, and precision could make it a particularly attractive technology for terrorists to explore.

This changing scientific and technological landscape has critical implications for security in general and the chemical terrorism challenge in particular:

- The number of regions of the world where people can be found with the requisite ability to exploit knowledge that can do harm has obviously grown significantly. That people might know how to apply this knowledge for malign purposes does not, of course, mean automatically that they will. Other factors as well are influential in moving down such a path. An increase in the number of people with the requisite knowledge, however, does imply an increase in the burden of potential risk that must be managed.
- These trends have created lower entry costs for terrorists if they want to pursue CW capabilities, and they allow for entering that pursuit at a higher point on the learning curve.
- The new structures of commercial and scientific enterprises will provide a wider range and more diverse array of legitimate dual-use covers for malign activities. They could also create multiple, parallel, possibly nontraditional pathways to the development of critical chemical weapons–related capabilities.
- The range of potential weapons options is expanding. Of particular concern in this regard is that developers—whether states or, to a lesser degree, nonstate actors—will be increasingly able "to identify biochemical pathways critical for physiological processes and engineer specific agents to exploit vulnerabilities..., [Such agents] will be able to target specific biological systems, such as the cardiovascular, immunological, neurological, and gastrointestinal systems...and produce a wide range of effects including death, incapacitation, or neurological

impairment."[35] A second aspect of this changing concept of a chemical weapon relates to delivery systems. The standard notion of "delivery" has evolved from the military context in which traditional munitions and missiles were the primary means. But here, too, options are expanding. As a result of efforts to find new mechanisms for drug delivery, for example, cutaneous absorption and improved aerosolization technologies are becoming available.

- The combination of what is interesting and what is doable—of curiosity and capability—could yield worrisome results. Nonstate actors might be willing to explore the CW potential of the life sciences, not because they are committed to developing a capability but because they have access to scientific or economic establishments, and they are interested in what possibilities these capabilities might offer.

BROAD SPECTRUM OF POTENTIAL USE OPTIONS

Most current thinking on potential chemical weapons use by terrorists emphasizes their desire to seek mass casualties. Such thinking, however, fails to encompass the full range of contingencies in which chemical weapons could be used. While such a contingency continues to receive the greatest attention from security planners and the media, it may not even be the most likely scenario for CW use. Much more probable are attacks that produce fewer casualties but still yield significant disruptive effects. The "Amerithrax" letters killed only five people. The Aum Shinrikyo attack in Tokyo resulted in only twelve fatalities. Nevertheless, both events demonstrated the enormous psychological and social impacts that even a limited attack with unconventional weapons could generate.

The "next use" of chemical weapons, especially if successful, could also have a profound impact on terrorists' perception of the utility of such capabilities, changing their calculations regarding the costs and benefits of pursuing chemical weapons. A more serious exploration of the potential utility and concepts of the use of chemical weapons could transform jihadist acquisition cost–benefit calculations. The technical and operational requirements for contingencies producing fewer victims are less stringent than those necessary for an attack producing catastrophic levels of casualties. It is important to understand the implications of these less demanding requirements so as to guard against underestimating the likelihood of such an event, which, even if it does not generate mass casualties, still could generate a catastrophic social or economic impact.

Since Aum Shinrikyo's 1995 sarin gas attack on the Tokyo subway, the question of whether terrorists could develop more effective chemical weapons has been the subject of intense debate. The Aum experience, however, is one of only a limited number of historical cases of terrorist attempts to exploit chemistry for malicious purposes. A key question is whether the case of the Aum Shinrikyo is, in fact, representative of the difficult challenges that nonstate actors face in trying to harness the life sciences and related technology, or whether the Aum was a unique situation, a one-of-a-kind combination of profound bad luck and organizational dysfunction that will not be repeated.[36]

Some experts contend that terrorists are both unwilling and unable to exploit the sciences. What these experts seem to forget, however, is a point made earlier, that is, that even if terrorists cannot exploit the most cutting-edge scientific and technological capabilities, it does not mean they can do nothing. Terrorists do not need the most advanced capabilities but could use what Paul Bracken calls "sidewise technology," older technology whose use is innovative with respect to processes, areas of application, or hitherto unforeseen combinations.[37] This point leads to the important realization that devastating harm need not come only from state-of-the-art chemical technology or techniques, but that modest levels of capability can, especially if used in unexpected ways, foster considerable damage. Moreover, terrorists do not demand the same operational performance from their technology that militaries require.[38] As previously argued, their science and technology has to be just "good enough."

CONCLUSION

At the present time it is clear that the undeniable, and threatening, desire of some jihadists to obtain and employ chemical weapons in a way that causes mass casualties greatly outstrips their collective ability to do so. Almost without exception, attempts to use chemicals as weapons have been unsuccessful. Documented efforts to incorporate toxic chemicals into more traditional jihadist weapons such as bombs have tended to be simplistic and almost invariably ineffective, generally demonstrating poor understanding of the characteristics and behavior of the chosen chemical. Weapons using chemicals alone have involved simple reactions undertaken at the point of delivery that may or may not produce an effective weapon. To date, no instances can be cited in which jihadist groups or individuals have demonstrated a capability to produce, let alone successfully employ, advanced CW agents such as nerve agents.

Having noted this, it is important to give due consideration to the potential for harmful interactions between changes in chemical technologies, global trends, and the structure of the jihadist movement. This is the case in two respects. First, one must consider that component of the jihadist movement that is focused on the "far enemy." The recruitment or inspiration of individuals from developed societies possessing relevant technical skills could rapidly transform the jihadist CW equation from one in which repeated demonstrations of incompetence cease to be the norm. Second, the combination of the trends in science and technology, with the impact of globalization that is resulting in a worldwide diffusion of that science and technology and its commercial exploitation is creating an environment far different than that which has characterized the recent past. The consequences of that combination, particularly the empowerment of individuals and the shift to a knowledge-based risk that can be facilitated by network operations, could play to the jihadist's advantage.

By far the most important recent development has been the exploration of the use of chlorine as a weapon by jihadists in Iraq. Although these attempts have demonstrated a poor understanding of the techniques required to make effective use of readily available TICs, they represent a change in approach that may, if followed up by jihadists operating outside of Iraq, presage a period in which the world begins to encounter increasingly deadly chemical terrorism producing mass casualties. The ineffectiveness of the chlorine attacks in Iraq was a failure of technique, not a failure of imagination. We cannot presume that such failures will continue to be the norm. In the event that this approach is exported from Iraq and the technique improved, it would not be unreasonable to anticipate attacks against chemical infrastructure generating significant numbers of civilian casualties. Over an even longer term, it is hard to foresee how the coming together of radical ideology, increasingly widespread knowledge, the acceptance of the instrumentality of violence, and further empowerment of individuals will play out.

NOTES

1. Javed Ali, Leslie Rodrigues, and Michael Moodie, *U.S. Chemical-Biological Defense Guidebook* (Alexandria, VA: Jane's Information Group, 1997), 21–22.
2. Russia's declared CW stockpile is located at seven sites: Gorny (Saratov oblast), Kambarka (Udmurt Republic), Kizner (Udmurt Republic), Leonidovka (Penza oblast), Maradikovsky (Kirov oblast), Pochep (Bryansk oblast), and Shchuch'ye (Kurgan oblast). John Hart, "Russia's Chemical Weapon Destruction Program: an Update," *ASA Newsletter*, Issue No. 111, December 9, 2005, http://www.asanltr.com/newsletter/05-6/articles/056b.html.
3. Some 7,500 tons of the original declared stockpile consist of blister agents, sulfur mustard, lewisite, and sulfur mustard–lewisite mixtures, and are/were located in bulk storage containers at Gorny and Kambarka. The remainder of the stockpile consists of three organophosphorus nerve agents—sarin, soman, and V-type gas—and are stored in approximately 4–4.5 million munitions. John Hart, "Russia's Chemical Weapon Destruction Program: an Update." December 9, 2005.
4. Major factors in the reduction of security concerns are improvements in the capacity of the Russian state to provide the resources required for adequate security combined with assistance from international aid providers such as the Global Partnership. The Global Partnership is assisting in CW destruction and in the provision of security improvements. http://www.dfait-maeci.gc.ca/foreign_policy/global_partnership/destruction-en.asp.
5. In 1993, the U.S. chemical weapons stockpile was stored at nine sites on U.S. territory: Aberdeen Proving Ground, MD; Anniston Army Depot, AL; Blue Grass Army Depot, KY; Pine Bluff Arsenal, AR; Pueblo Depot, CO; Newport Army Ammunition Plant, IN; Umatilla Depot, OR; Tooele Army Depot, UT; and Johnston Island, HI. As of September 2008, the stockpiles of CW agents and munitions held at Aberdeen Proving Grounds, Johnston Island, and Newport Army Ammunition Plan had been completely destroyed. http://www.cma.army.mil.
6. Filled bulk CW agent containers contain between 680 and 770 kilograms of liquid agent. Steven L. Hoenig, *Handbook of Chemical Warfare and Terrorism* (Westport, CT: Greenwood Press, 2002), 67.
7. Filled bulk CW agent containers weigh between 1315 and 1406 kilograms. Hoenig, *Handbook of Chemical Warfare and Terrorism*, 67.
8. Two U.S. facilities, both of which hold stockpiles of assembled chemical weapons that are fitted with fuzes and burster charges, extend the deadline significantly. Pueblo Chemical Depot (2,611 agent tons) should begin destruction operations in 2015, with a planned completion date of 2020. The Program Manager Assembled Chemical Weapons Alternatives (ACWA) Web site, accessed April 24, 2008, http://www.pmacwa.army.mil/co/project_stages.htm; Blue Grass Army Depot (523 agent tons) will not begin operations until 2017, with completion planned for 2023. Program Manager Assembled Chemical Weapons Alternatives (ACWA) Web site, accessed 24 April 2008, http://www.pmacwa.army.mil/ky/project_stages.htm.
9. David E. Kaplan, "Aum Shinrikyo," in Jonathan B. Tucker, ed., *Toxic Terror*, 216.
10. As an example, Tucker notes that the aluminum phosphorus complex (APC) process for the production of sarin creates an explosive hazard and produces large volumes of toxic by-products. The more traditional DMHP process requires the use of highly toxic and corrosive hydrogen fluoride gas. This is also the case with the production

of VX. Production of the key precursor transester (QL) requires working with chemicals that react violently to water and catch fire if exposed to moist air. The final reaction stage also involves an extremely energetic reaction. Jonathan B. Tucker, *War of Nerves: Chemical Warfare from World War I to al-Qaeda* (New York: Pantheon, 2006), 111, 134, 159.

11. Nadine Gurr and Benjamin Cole, *The New Face of Terrorism: Threats from Weapons of Mass Destruction* (London: I. B. Tauris, 2002), 51; Richard A. Falkenrath, Robert D. Newman, and Bradley A. Thayer, *America's Achilles' Heel: Nuclear, Biological, and Chemical Terrorism and Covert Attack* (Cambridge, MA: MIT Press, 1998), 107.
12. Office of Technology Assessment, *Technologies Underlying Weapons of Mass Destruction*, 1993, 30–31.
13. The important consideration to note here is that the person need not be a specialist who has already worked with CW agents. The important thing is that they have some familiarity with small batch production of chemicals.
14. Falkenrath et al., *America's Achilles' Heel: Nuclear, Biological, and Chemical Terrorism and Covert Attack*, 106.
15. *Planning Scenarios: Executive Summaries*, Scenario 8: Chemical Attack—Chlorine Tank Explosion, Homeland Security Council, 2004, 8-1–8-3.
16. John V. Parachini, "The World Trade Center Bombers" (1933), in *Toxic Terror*, ed. Johnathan B. Tucker, 185–201 (Cambridge, MA: MIT Press, 2000).
17. Chris Hastings, and David Bamber, "Terrorist nerve gas found in London raid," *Sunday Telegraph* (February 18, 2001):1.
18. Eric Croddy, Mathew Osborne, and Kimberly McCloud, *Chemical Terrorist Plot in Rome?*, March 11, 2002, http://cns.miis.edu/stories/020311.htm.
19. Sammy Salama, *Special Report: Manual for Producing Chemical Weapon to Be Used in New York Subway Plot Available on Al-Qaeda Websites Since Late 2005*, CNS Web site, http://cns.miis.edu/other/salama_060720.htm.
20. *The CBW Conventions Bulletin*, No. 72+73 (September 2006), 37.
21. Rose Nahmias, "Al-Aqsa Brigades: Chemical Warfare if Israel Invades Gaza," Ynet News.com (June 26, 2006).
22. Stahl, Julie, "Palestinian Threat to Use Biological, Chemical Weapons Just A Bluff, Expert Says." CNSnews.com (26 June 2006).
23. Ludwig F. Haber, *The Poisonous Cloud: Chemical Warfare in the First World War* (Oxford: Oxford University Press, 1986), 30–36. There were six attacks. One chlorine attack was anomalous and only involved the use of sixty cylinders containing 30 to 40 kilograms of chlorine each, for a total release of approximately one-quarter ton.
24. Lieutenant General Michal Maples, Curent and Projected National Security Threats to the United States. Statement for the record before the U.S. Senate Committee on Armed Services, Febuary 27, 2008, 8, http://www.dia.mil/pulibaffairs/Testimonies/statement_30.pdf. David Rising, "Al Qaeda in Iraq Beckons Nuclear Scientists," Associated Press, September 29, 2006, http://www.boston.com/news/world/articles/2006/09/29/al_qaeda_in_iraq_beckons_nuclear_scientists/.
25. Robert Carlson, "The Pace and Proliferation of Biological Technologies," *Biosecurity and Bioterrorism: Biodefense Strategy, Practice, and Science*, 1(3): 1–3, 2003.
26. Committee on Advances in Technolog and the Prevention of Their Application to Next Generation Biowarfare Threats. *Globalization, Biosecurity and the Future of the Life Sciences* (Washington, DC: National Academies Press, 2006), 48.

27. Ibid., 25.
28. See, for example, Gerald L. Epstein, *Global Evolution of Dual-Use Biotechnology,* A Report of the Project on Technology Futures and Global Power, Wealth, and Conflict (Washington, DC: Center for Strategic and International Studies, April 2005), 10.
29. Alexander Kelle, *The Changing Scientific and Technological Basis of the CBW Proliferation Problem*, Bradford Science and Technology Reports Number 7, University of Bradford, 2007, 7.
30. For example, Stanford University physical chemist Richard Zare commented, "To me, the big unanswered questions concern the chemistry of life processes." Philip Ball, "What Chemists Want to Know," *Nature* 442 (August 3, 2006), 501.
31. Epstein, Global Evolution of Qual-Use Biotechnology, 13.
32. Julie Fischer, *Dual-Use Technologies: Inexorable Progress, Inseparable Peril*, A Report of the Project on Technology Futures and Global Power, Wealth, and Conflict (Washington, DC: Center for Strategic and International Studies, April 2005), 3.
33. The NRC study notes, for example, that DNA synthesis technology is the equivalent of a matter compiler for genetic material. National Academy of Science, *Globalization, Biosecurity and the Future of the Life Sciences*, 56.
34. Tuan Nguyen, "Microchallenges of CW Proliferation," *Science*, August 12, 2005.
35. Ibid., 13.
36. James A. Russell and Christopher Clary, *Globalization and WMD Proliferation Networks: Challenges to U.S. Security*, Report of a Conference sponsored by the Naval Postgraduate School, June 29–July 1, 2005, 9.
37. Paul Bracken, "Sidewise Technologies: National Security and Global Power Implications," in *Technology Futures, and Global Power, Wealth, and Conflict,* edited by Anne G.K. Solomon, A Report of the Project on Technology Futures and Global Power, Wealth, and Conflict (Washington, DC: Center for Strategic and International Studies, May 2005), 91–100.
38. For more, see Gary A. Ackerman and Kevin S. Moran, "Bioterrorism and Threat Assessment," Paper No. 22, The Weapons of Mass Destruction Committee (The Blix Commission), November 2004, available at http://www.wmdcommission.org, 3.

CHAPTER 6

Jihadists and Biological and Toxin Weapons[1]

Cheryl Loeb

CONTENTS

INTRODUCTION

Throughout recorded history, humanity has faced widespread disease and death from scourges of emerging and reemerging infectious diseases. From smallpox to bubonic plague, these diseases evoke images of horror and suffering. Because of their ability to cause pervasive mortality, naturally occurring diseases have been used as weapons of war and terror for thousands of years.

Until recently, the biological weapons threat was largely attributed to nation-states and biological weapons being used as weapons of war on the battlefield. While there have been some nonstate actor cases of biological terrorism, such as the infamous 1984 poisoning of salad bars in The Dalles, Oregon, by the Rajneeshee cult, many experts believed that the scientific and technical requirements required for the development and deployment of biological and toxin weapons sophisticated enough to cause large numbers of human casualties were largely out of reach for most nonstate actors. The September 11, 2001 terrorist attacks against the United States and the following anthrax letter mailings against popular U.S. media establishments as well as the U.S. government, however, jarringly brought the specter of biological terrorism to the forefront of national and international security policy. With the 9/11 terrorist attacks came the awareness and understanding that jihadist terrorist organizations are both willing and capable of planning and carrying out successful mass casualty attacks against their chosen targets. Authorities have uncovered numerous plots, raw materials, equipment, and even small-scale laboratories dedicated to the development of weapons of mass destruction, including biological and toxin weapons, and numerous statements have been made by al-Qa'ida spokesmen as well as other jihadists justifying the use of weapons of mass destruction against their targets.

Key to countering future biological weapons terrorism is developing an understanding of the threat as it relates to jihadist terrorism. Advances in life sciences research have rapidly diffused the knowledge, equipment, and materials needed to produce even quite sophisticated biological weapons around the world, potenitally placing them in the hands of state and nonstate actors. The intersection of jihadist terrorism with this increasing revolution in life sciences only makes the threat more prevalent.

This chapter will provide a brief background on what biological and toxin weapons are and instances of their use throughout history. It will then examine the threat of jihadist terrorism vis-à-vis biological weapons in the context of capabilities and the minimum requirements for success. In addition, the chapter examines pathways to acquisition to procure biological weapons as well as known attempts by jihadists to embark down these pathways.

UNDERSTANDING BIOLOGICAL AND TOXIN WEAPONS

Biological weapons (BW) are produced from pathogenic microorganisms or toxic substances of biological origin, formulated in such a way that they are capable of disabling and/or killing people, crops, and livestock, and combined with an apparatus/method used to deliver the biological harm to the target population. Biological agents are the microorganisms and toxins that cause disease and could be used for manufacturing biological weapons. The biological agents that have been associated with weapons development can be divided into five key groups: bacteria, viruses, rickettsia, fungi, and toxins (bacteria, viruses, and toxins are the most well-known types of BW agents). Table 6.1 identifies some of the more well-known agents that have been associated with biological weapons development.

The difficulty in detecting biological terrorist attacks is that symptoms of illness do not appear immediately, as would occur in a chemical, nuclear, or conventional weapon attack. Because most biological weapons consist of living organisms, symptoms will occur only after an incubation period that may last days to weeks.[2] Many times, the initial symptoms could appear as a common cold or influenza and might be mistaken for a normal outbreak of infectious disease. Until large numbers of individuals report illness, the attack could go undetected. This is especially likely to be the case during annual cold and flu season. If the agent used can translate as a communicable disease, the infection could spread rapidly across a large population before health preventative measures

TABLE 6.1 Well-Known Agents Associated with Biological Weapons

Bacteria	*Bacillus anthracis*—Anthrax *Brucella melitensis, abortus, suis, and canis* —Brucellosis *Burkholderia mallei*—Glanders *Burkholderia pseudomallei*—Melioidosis *Vibrio cholerae*—Cholera *Chlamydia psittaci*—Psittacosis *Francisella tularensis*—Tularemia *Yersinia pestis*—Plague *Salmonella Typhi*—Typhoid fever *Shigella*—Shigellosis
Viruses	Ebola Hantaan virus Influenza Lassa fever Marburg Smallpox Venezuelan Equine Encephalitis (VEE)
Rickettsia	*Coxiella burnetii*—Q fever *Rickettsia prowazekii* —Epidemic typhus
Fungi	Coccidioides immitis Coccidioides posadasii
Toxins	Abrin Botulinum Ricin Staphylococcal Enterotoxin B Trichothecene [T-2] mycotoxins

are effectively put in place. Rapid growth in international travel further complicates the issue, allowing sick persons incubating disease to move around the globe, spreading the infection across multiple transit pathways and borders.

To provide but one example, an outbreak of smallpox could spread through a population quickly and might not be readily identified as a terrorist incident until several weeks after an attack. Smallpox, a deadly disease known for its high mortality rate and propensity to leave survivors with disfiguring facial and body scars, was eradicated in 1980 through a vigorous international campaign by the World Health Organization. When the World Health Assembly declared the disease eradicated countries halted their mandatory smallpox vaccination programs, thus leaving the current population highly susceptible to a release of smallpox, whether intentional or inadvertently. Shortly thereafter, all known stocks of the smallpox virus were consolidated at two repositories, one in Russia and one in the United States. Concerns, however, exist that some countries may still have undeclared samples of the virus.

Smallpox, which has no effective medical treatment once a person has been infected with the virus, has an incubation period of anywhere from seven to seventeen days (average of twelve days). After the initial incubation period, victims experience the onset of flu-like symptoms such as fever, malaise, body ache, and vomiting.[3] It is at the beginning of this stage that individuals become contagious. During the roughly two-week span between when a person has been infected until becoming contagious, infected individuals could have traveled anywhere in the world from the point of origin of attack. By the time an attack with smallpox is recognized by health authorities, the individuals initially infected through the terror attack could have traveled to multiple locations, thus precipitating outbreaks of disease worldwide. The impact of a bioterrorism attack of this magnitude cannot be overstated: smallpox has a mortality rate of about 30 percent (up to 90 percent for more severe forms including flat and hemorrhagic smallpox).

While toxins are produced by living organisms (such as bacteria, fungi, marine organisms, snakes, plants, or animals), they are different from viruses and bacteria in that they are nonliving agents and are neither infectious nor contagious. Toxin weapons nonetheless have pathologic effects on cells, tissues, organs and the systems of living subjects. Because of their inability to reproduce, toxins are unlikely to cause death in a wide target population (highly concentrated toxins are useful in targeting individuals). Toxins usually have a shorter incubation period than other types of biological agents, lasting from only a few hours to a few days.

The most common toxin that has been used for nefarious purposes, often in so-called 'biocrime' incidents, is ricin. Biocrimes differ from bioterrorism in that the biological agent is used for murder, revenge, extortion, and other limited aims not aligned with the common features of terrorism. Perhaps the most famous biocrime incident using the ricin toxin occurred in September 1978 when Bulgarian dissident Georgi Markov was stabbed in the leg with an umbrella gun and injected with a ricin pellet while waiting for a bus in London, England. He died four days after the incident.

DISSEMINATION AND DELIVERY OF BIOLOGICAL AND TOXIN WEAPONS

Biological and toxin weapons can be disseminated into target populations through a variety of different methods, depending on their form. The most effective means of disseminating an agent is in the form of a dry or wet aerosol—a cloud of solid particles suspended in the air. Dry aerosol mixtures are more difficult to produce than wet aerosol mixtures because, to cause illness, they typically have to be very small in particle size (1–10 microns) to be retained in the human respiratory tract (optimally, 1–5 microns). Dry aerosols are also more likely to be subject to the phenomenon of re-aerosolization after deposition, thus enabling them to potentially continue to infect target populations. Smallpox, for example, can survive up to twenty-four hours after release. Wet aerosol mixtures, on the other hand, are easier to produce but more difficult to deploy in a manner that will result in high levels of casualties, and they are unlikely to be subject to re-aerosolization.

Technical means of delivery include the use of cluster bombs, artillery shells, rockets, and sophisticated sprayers, but the use of such large-scale delivery systems is usually associated with military development of biological weapons. Nontechnical and cheaper modes of dissemination include using animal vectors (e.g., fleas and mosquitoes), improvised crop dusters designed for agricultural spraying purposes, backpack sprayers, and even purse-sized atomizers.

Another delivery method could include self-infection with a contagious agent, such as smallpox or plague. There are uncertainties with this method, of course, with serious and even fatal risks to the deliverer as well as the risk of indiscriminately infecting and even killing group members, leaders, followers, family, and friends.[4] Fanatical jihadists, however, may choose to accept the risks, believing that even in the "worst" case scenario, they will become martyrs. In one translation of a hadith (oral translations relating to the words and deeds of Prophet Muhammad, which are considered fundamental sources of Islamic theology), the Prophet said "Plague is the cause of martyrdom of every Muslim (who dies because of it)." Another hadith states that, "Five are regarded as martyrs: They are those who die because of plague, abdominal disease, drowning or a falling building etc., and the martyrs in Allah's Cause."[5] In extreme cases, such translations could provide religious justification for suicidal biological terrorism. (It should be noted, however, that alternate translations of a hadith may result in different meanings.)

The success of the delivery of a biological agent in the open air is dependent on meteorological and terrain conditions such as wind velocity, temperature, precipitation, and humidity, thereby making success difficult to predict. Other delivery methods include contamination of food and water supplies or agricultural products. While it may be easier from a technical perspective to contaminate food or water sources, this method is generally less effective than open-air aerosol dissemination because of the dilution of the agent in the food or water, quality control processes, and limited distribution of the agent. There has been much speculation and fear over the prospect of food supplies being contaminated with biological agents, however, achieving large-scale casualties with this method remains technically difficult and depends on the type of agent used and the method in which it is formulated and delivered. (Prepackaged foodstuffs are not always dependent upon such conditions.)

Other factors that can determine the effectiveness of a biological or toxin attack include the choice of agent, type of formulation, and the manufacturing process employed. Terrorists also have to contend with incremental degradation over time due to transporting materials from the point of acquisition or production to the point of use, not to mention ensuring a suitably virulent strain has been properly and effectively weaponized. The Japanese terror cult Aum Shinrikyo, which carried out the infamous March 1995 sarin nerve gas attack in the Tokyo subway, experimented with anthrax, botulinum toxin, cholera, and Q fever, and even attempted to obtain ebola during trips to Africa. On a number of occasions between 1990 and 1995, the cult attempted to release both botulinum toxin and anthrax on selected targets in Japan, but were unsuccessful in casuing casualties, mostly as a result of utilizing nonvirulent strains and unsophisticated delivery apparatuses.[6] In the 2001, anthrax attacks against the United States, the perpetrator chose to deliver the powdered anthrax spores through the U.S. postal system. One of the main reasons why more casualties did not occur is because the delivery method was extremely unsophisticated. These two examples amply demonstrate that even with a "working" biological weapon, if the delivery method is unsophisticated, or the terrorist group does not take into account important meteorological, terrain, and other factors, the outcome of the attack may be much less severe.

HISTORY OF USE

For centuries, biological agents have been used as weapons in war. One of the first recorded instances occurred in 1346 during the siege of Kaffa. Located on the Crimean Peninsula of the Black Sea, the invading Tartar forces experienced an outbreak of plague at this Genoese port city. The Tartar soldiers threw diseased corpses over the walls of the city to infect the defending forces within. The assault may have directly led to a devastating outbreak of disease in Kaffa that forced the defending forces to retreat, sailing to Venice in what they believed to be four untainted ships. These ships brought the Black Death to Italy, and from there the plague spread quickly throughout the Italian peninsula.[7] Centuries later, during the French and Indian War (1754–1767), British forces gave smallpox-contaminated blankets as "gifts" to the Native American Indians, causing a deliberate outbreak of disease that resulted in widespread death.[8]

During World War I, Germany used both anthrax and the equine disease glanders to infect livestock and animal feed scheduled for export to Allied forces.[9] During World War II, Japanese scientists conducted a wide-ranging offensive BW program from 1937 to 1945 in occupied Manchuria (China). The most famous research center of the Japanese program was known as Unit 731, located at Ping Fan, near Harbin, where scientists undertook warfare studies on anthrax, botulism, cholera, plague, and typhoid.[10] Japanese scientists used Chinese prisoners as experimental subjects, infecting them with biological agents to test dissemination patterns and times, infection rates, morbidity, and mortality, and, over the course of the program, killed an estimated 10,000 prisoners. By 1945, it is estimated that Japanese forces were able to produce 500 million plague-infected fleas per year and had stockpiled 400 kilograms of anthrax.[11]

The largest BW program ever known to exist was in the Soviet Union. According to Dr. Ken Alibek, a former senior official in the program, the Soviet BW program can be traced back to a secret decree issued in 1928 by the governing Revolutionary Military Council, which ordered research into the use of typhus as a weapon to be used on the battlefield.[12] After the initial decree, the Soviet program vastly expanded, eventually encompassing research on a wide range of biological agents, including anthrax, cholera, ebola, plague, tularemia, and smallpox. Even after signing and ratifying the 1972 Biological Weapons Convention, the Soviet Union continued to participate in an extensive offensive weapons program in flagrant violation of its international commitments. The program, partially run by the agency known as *Biopreparat*, aimed to develop, partially, a plethera of biological weapons, even attempting to create "chimera" weapons, such as genetically modifying ebola and smallpox into new biological weapons. The Soviet Union also attempted to create vaccine-resistant strains of tularemia and supervirulent strains of anthrax. The program was ostensibly halted in 1992 with the dissolution of the Soviet Union and the admittance by then-President Boris Yeltsin of the existence of the program.

There have only been a small handful of known terrorist attacks using biological agents as weapons (there have been numerous incidents involving ricin toxin, however, many of these were criminal rather than terrorist activities). One of the more famous incidents occurred in The Dalles, Oregon, in September 1984. In an effort to win control of the Wasco County Commission in the upcoming November 1984 election, members of the Rajneeshee cult poisoned salad bars at ten local area restaurants with *Salmonella Typhimurium*, which can cause severe gastroenteritis in humans. By the end of September 1984, over 751 cases had been reported to local health departments, although none of the cases resulted in fatalities.[13] As previously mentioned, the Japanese cult Aum Shinrikyo also experimented with biological weapons; however, despite numerous attempts to disperse a biological weapon, their activities never resulted in mortalities.

The most recent biological weapons attack occurred in the United States in 2001 and consisted of small amounts of powdered anthrax being disseminated through the U.S. postal service to news media outlets and two U.S. government senators' offices. The attack caused widespread fear and terror in a population already shaken by the September

11, 2001 terror attacks. The anthrax mailings resulted in a total of only five deaths and seventeen related causalities, but severely disrupted the U.S. economy and U.S. society.

MOTIVATIONS FOR USING BIOLOGICAL WEAPONS

For jihadists, or any other terrorist group, to successfully obtain and use a biological or toxin weapon, the group would likely have to display three key characteristics: sufficient motivation, an efficient organizational structure, and the requisite technical capability.[14] The September 11, 2001 attacks drove home the realization that jihadist attacks against populations have been increasing in intensity and severity over time. Based on jihadist strategists' statements (see Chapters 3 and 4) praising and legitimizing BW, as well as several confirmed reports of jihadists actually seeking biological weapons (see examples below), we know that a certain degree of motivation for at least acquiring a BW capability exists among jihadists.

Why would a terrorist group choose a biological weapon over other types of weapons, especially those known for their reliability and easy accessibility, like conventional explosives? Their ability to cause widespread death and disease, their indiscriminate nature, the shortage or complete lack of vaccines and therapeutics to treat many of the diseases caused by biological agents, their capability to invoke images of suffering and horror, and their similarity to apocalyptic biblical diseases and plagues, make them appealing to jihadist and other terrorist groups. Biological weapons are thus appealing to jihadists for many of the same reasons as chemical, radiological and nuclear weapons that have been thoroughly dealt with in other chapters of this volume, because they provide the opportunity to inflict serious physical, psychological, and economic harm on targets (see Chapter 3).

Another motivating factor for jihadist terrorist groups to pursue a BW capability relates to prestige or "bragging rights." Possession of a biological weapon (regardless of the degree of sophistication of the weapon), may provide a jihadist cell or group with respect and credibility within the jihadist community writ large. Such an elevation in status among other terrorist networks may not only boost morale but, more alarmingly, boost recruitment. Prestige may give the terrorist group access to more resources, such as funding, materials, and personnel, to include scientists and explosive experts. Finally, because biological weapons would theoretically enable a terrorist group to attack with low visibility - the targeted population would not begin to show symptoms of the attack until days or even weeks afterward—the group could potentially remain anonymous from authorities, providing them with the opportunity to carry out multiple attacks and then go into hiding before the onset of symptoms. Given the long incubation period of smallpox, for example, jihadists could have up to two weeks of undetected operational lead time before authorities caught up with them.

Biological and toxin weapons are almost universally viewed as immoral and inhumane weapons. Because biological weapons are viewed as abhorrent weapons, a jihadist terrorist will have to take into consideration a number of factors before they choose to deploy such a weapon. In particular, they will have to weigh the costs against the benefits, including potentially alienating their supporters and the high potential for fatal risks associated with indiscriminately infecting and even killing group members, leaders, followers, family and friends.

Assuming a terrorist group has overcome the ideological, political, technical, structural, and operational hurdles associated with obtaining or developing a biological or toxin weapon, the question then becomes how a group will choose to use BW. A number of factors will play into this decision, the most important being whether or not the strategic intent of the attack is to effect mass casualties or mass disruption.

Mass Casualty Weapons

Biological weapons are included under the rubric of weapons of mass destruction partly because of their potential to cause mass morbidity and mortality among target populations. As previously mentioned, biological weapons are derived from pathogenic microorganisms or toxic substances of biological origin. Throughout human history, these organisms have caused outbreaks of infectious disease and have resulted in hundreds of thousands of deaths. In *The History of the Peloponnesian War*, Thucydides wrote about a "plague" that laid waste to the Athenian armies in 430 BC, killing thousands of the population of the walled city of Athens, troops and civilians alike.[15] In 1367, the plague (better known by its popular term the "Black Death") spread like wildfire throughout Europe, killing as much as a quarter of the European population. But perhaps one of the deadliest and best-known pandemics in the twentieth century was the 1918-1919 outbreak of influenza, also commonly known as the Spanish Flu. At the end of World War I, the pandemic spread rapidly along trade lines and shipping routes causing severe numbers of fatalities; upwards of 50 million people died worldwide.[16]

Acquiring, developing, and successfully carrying out a mass casualty terrorist attack with a biological or toxin weapon requires vastly more technical sophistication and organization than an attack using conventional methods. While numerous studies have been undertaken to determine the number of casualties that might occur in the event of a successful attack with a biological weapon, perhaps the best indicator of mortality would be through looking at natural outbreaks of disease throughout human history. As the 1918 Spanish Flu demonstrated, infectious diseases are not only silent, but also deadly and effective killers.

Mass Disruption Weapons

As was demonstrated by the 2001 anthrax attacks, biological weapons can have an acute psychological effect on the target population. Though these attacks resulted in a low mortality rate - five deaths - fear of becoming infected with anthrax rippled disproportionately across the nation, frightening millions of Americans because of the indiscriminate nature of the weapon. A jihadist attack with a biological agent, regardless of sophistication of the weapon, would likely cause high-levels of anxiety, widespread fear, and perhaps even paranoia, resulting in self-isolation, withdrawal from social interaction and activities, and severe social disruption to civil society.[17] This would be further exacerbated if contagious agents such as plague and smallpox, which have long histories of causing widespread morbidity and mortality, are the weapons of choice. The specter of enforced quarantine, sensationalistic media reporting, and the lack of a discreet endpoint in a disease outbreak will only heighten the psychological effects on the targeted population.

Such an attack would also result in economic harm to a country. The 2001 anthrax attacks in the United States effectively shut down the nation's capitol, causing severe economic disruption to the country long after the last case of illness occurred. The attack caused severe economic damage not only from lack of business continuity, but also from the high cost of decontamination of buildings and other locations. Cleaning the Brentwood mail facility, located outside of Washington, DC, for example, cost a staggering $130 million and took 26 months to complete.[18] Since 2001, the United States (as well as other countries around the world) has spent billions of dollars on biodefense preparedness and countermeasures. Nevertheless, any terrorist attack involving biological weapons would still likely hamper the economy as a correlate of a host of associated factors including fear and uncertainty about possible follow-on or copycat attacks. The strain on the public health system in response to such an event as well as discontinuity in business operations and the high costs associated with clean-up and decontamination will be staggering.

If the costs outweigh the benefits, a terrorist group may choose to deploy a non-contagious biological weapon, such as anthrax or toxins like ricin or abrin, to ensure that the fatalities do not include the "innocent"—presumably members of the radical jihadist community that might be intermixed within the target population. The motivation for non-contagious BW use may thus be to cause psychological and economic harm against the target rather than mass casualties.

SUCCESS FACTORS

Organizational Structure

The importance that the organizational structure of a terrorist group plays in biological weapons production can not be underestimated or overstated. Internal organizational structure will determine if terrorists possess the requisite capabilities for not only procuring or indigenously developing biological weapons, but also to successfully carry out an attack. Particulars such as group size, mechanisms of leadership, and adaptability are all pivotal success factors. A number of subsequent questions can be formulated: Is the terrorist group able to obtain sufficient funding? Is it able to identify, track, detect, and interact with potential BW weapon suppliers? Is it able to recruit individuals who are capable of indigenously developing the weapon? Is it able to transship the weapon to the target without degradation or complete loss of function? Can the weapon successfully be released on the target population?

The global jihadist movement is not confined to specific geographies, regions, or states. Increasingly, growing numbers of terrorist groups and their affiliates have bases, operatives, and targets in multiple countries. While highly-organized jihadist groups such as the "core" al-Qa'ida may very well possess most or all of the abovementioned capabilities, an interesting issue in the current context is the capabilities possessed by smaller groups of jihadists. The structure and organization of terrorist groups have changed drastically since the 1990s. This is especially the case for jihadist terrorism, which, in addition to a core made up of large groups like al-Qa'ida, consists of loosely connected networks of cells located throughout the world. Many of these cells operate with complete autonomy, having limited or no interaction with other cells for direction or guidance. They often raise their own funding, recruit members, conduct training, choose targets, and carry out attacks of their own choosing independent of central control or leadership.[19] These cells are, however, inspired by radical jihadist ideology portrayed and reported on Internet Web sites, radio and television broadcasts, and publications (see Chapters 3 and 4 of this volume for examples). While not all jihadists are members of "core" al-Qa'ida, they tend to mimic and follow the propaganda and rhetoric espoused by Usama bin Ladin and jihadist religious clerics.[20]

It is possible, therefore, that the nature of dispersed jihadist terrorist cells, insofar as they operate independent of each other, diminishes their ability to obtain a biological weapon and subsequently carry out a successful attack. For example, even a very well-funded and organized terrorist group, like Aum Shinrikyo, which had at its disposal resources equaling over $1 billion; over 300 graduate-level scientists trained in biochemistry, medicine, genetic engineering, and biology; and state-of-the-art laboratories and equipment, repeatedly failed to release a biological weapon that resulted in human mortality.[21] It is questionable how a small, disaggregated jihadist cell could successfully obtain a biological weapon, whether through theft, purchase, indigenous development, or other methods.

On the other hand, because a jihadist cell acts independently from the larger group (read: al-Qa'ida), it benefits from the ability to "fly under the radar" of intelligence agencies, thereby increasing the probability that any BW procurement that does occur will escape detection. A large terrorist organization, like al-Qa'ida was in 2001, is vulnerable to penetration by law enforcement agents, defections by key members, and the arrest or killing of group leaders. The capture of Khalid Shaykh Muhammad in 2003, for example, provided investigators with detailed intelligence on production plans for biological weapons and also highlighted that al-Qa'ida was not as far along in the development or acquisition stage of BW as previously thought.[22] Yet, while a single jihadist cell may indeed be small in comparison to a large terrorist organization such as Aum Shinrikyo was, it can still benefit from an extremely large and wide-reaching jihadist network that may, over time, evolve and grow in sophistication and bestow some of the required capabilities even on disparate cells of jihadists. This will, thereby, will create complexities that make predicting their future capability especially troublesome.

Technical Capability

Perhaps the most important barrier to jihadist acquisition and use of biological weapons is technical capability. Until the 2001 anthrax letter attacks against the United States, many experts believed that the technical barriers were too difficult to surmount for most, if not all, terrorist groups. The example of Aum Shinrikyo amply demonstrates that even if a group has significant access to resources, developing a biological weapon and a sophisticated delivery method are extremely difficult undertakings. Considerable technical and scientific hurdles must be overcome if a terrorist is to successfully carry out a larger scale BW attack, which include

- Ensuring pathogenicity and virulence of the microbe
- Maintaining pathogen stability
- Calculating an infectious dose,
- Achieving optimal composition of the formulation (additives and their ratio)
- Dealing with the incremental degradation of the agent through transportation/shipment
- Ensuring survivability of the agent (replicability)
- Dealing with environmental complications such as terrain and meteorological conditions
- Ensuring the susceptibility of the target (whether humans, animals, or plants), since there are countermeasures and prophylaxis available for many agents.

More sophisticated weapons will require specialized knowledge (trained scientists and related experts) and materials, such as a seed stock of the desired pathogen, easily available growth media, and specialized equipment such as fermenters, lyophilizers, and centrifugal separators. If a dry mixture is created, specialized equipment will be needed for drying, milling, and stabilizing the mixture. Further, the terrorist group will need a facility where the production, storage, and even testing of a weapon can be conducted. If the agent is aerosolized, they will need specific equipment to ensure they do not infect their own group members or accidentally release the agent into their local population.

Recent advances in genetic engineering, biotechnology, vaccine production, and other life sciences research, however, are rapidly diffusing the knowledge, equipment, and materials needed to produce both crude and sophisticated biological weapons. Increased access to the Internet has expanded the availability of the knowledge and specialized equipment needed to produce biological weapons, such as seed stocks and culture collections, well beyond traditional scientific and technical communities (see Chapter 5 of this volume for additional information). Research once limited to national-level weapons programs can now be conducted in civilian settings.

A U.S. National Academies of Science report has identified four major categories of advances in the life sciences that will have high-impact consequences and alter the future of biological terrorism. These categories of activities include

- Technologies that seek to acquire novel biological or molecular diversity
- Technologies that seek to generate novel but predetermined and specific biological or molecular entities through directed design (e.g., synthetic biology, or genetic engineering)
- Technologies that seek to understand and manipulate biological systems in a more comprehensive and effective manner (e.g., RNA interference, systems biology, and genomic medicine)
- Technologies that seek to enhance production, delivery, and packaging of biologically active materials (e.g., mircroencapsulation technology and aerosol technology).[23]

As developments in life sciences continue to grow, jihadist terrorists will have increasing access to life sciences information and technologies, such as small fermenters capable of cultivating pathogenic microorganisms, protective and containment equipment, and other specialized materials, that could allow them to obtain the tools necessary to develop and carry out a biological weapons attack. The technical barriers are indeed significant, but increasingly becoming less so.

PATHWAYS TO JIHADIST ACQUISITION OF BW

There are a variety of avenues by which terrorists may obtain biological and toxin weapons, such as theft (from a state-run program), purchase (on the black market), and self-production. The potential to divert BW materials and supplies for sale on the black market is particularly strong in countries where former bioweapons scientists receive only a fraction of their previous salaries or are unable to find work in their fields (i.e., Russia, Libya, Iraq, and South Africa).[24] This is particularly relevant in the case of former weapons scientists from South Africa and the former Soviet Union. From 1981 to 1993, South Africa's apartheid-era chemical and biological weapons program, known as "Project Coast" collected hundreds of strains of microbes, including forty-five types of anthrax as well as strains of cholera, brucellosis, and plague. Dr. Wouter Basson, the former head of the project, is known to have traveled to China, Iraq, and Libya under the guise of business, and is believed to have sold cultures of these deadly pathogens, including genetically engineered varieties, on the black market for profit.[25] It is unknown how many other South African scientists have attempted to sell or have sold their materials and expertise on the black market.

Since the breakup of the Soviet Union in 1992, programs such as the Nunn–Lugar Cooperative Threat Reduction Program (CTR) have strived to keep former weapons scientists employed in their fields of expertise. There have, however, been cases where weapons scientists have either emigrated to suspected proliferant countries or have attempted to sell their knowledge and expertise on the black market. The government of Iran, for example, has attempted to recruit Soviet scientists to help it develop its biological weapons program and has hired several scientists once associated with institutes that were part of the Soviet Union's biological warfare program.[26] In 1973, *Biopreparat,* the organization responsible for the Soviet Union's biological warfare program, was created. *Biopreparat* was responsible for over 40 different organizations and upwards of 40,000 employees.[27] Considering the large size of the Soviet legacy program, the lack of post-1991 (after the breakup of the USSR) inventory of former Soviet BW facilities and their employees, and a high degree of Soviet-era security-induced compartmentalization, the exact number of facilities and personnel associated with the program are still unknown today.[28]

Today, over 1500 state-owned and commercial culture collections worldwide maintain, exchange, and sell samples of pathogens and toxins for research purposes. Many of these culture collections possess dangerous pathogens that are not adequately secured and controlled, making them vulnerable to theft or diversion.[29] This is particularly a concern in countries with underdeveloped infrastructures and weak regulations, such as the failure to have physical protection controls, access controls, materials accountability, and personnel screening, to name a few.

Analysts should be concerned with the potential for jihadists to exploit this instability and target such facilities for theft or even recruitment of employees who have access to specialized materials and resources. In 2002, for example, authorities in Almaty, Kazakhstan, arrested a man who entered the Scientific Center for Quarantine and Zoonotic Diseases with the apparent intent of stealing samples of BW pathogens. The intruder was arrested before penetrating the second layer of physical security and was not successful in his attempt.[30] Further compounding the issue is the fact that trade in microbial cultures is poorly regulated, both within countries and among them.[31]

Another potential avenue for the procurement of ready-made BW is through state sponsorship. Terrorists sponsored by a nation-state with a relatively sophisticated domestic life sciences capability could have access to funding, materials, training, and, at the extreme, ready-made BW. There is great debate, however, over the plausibility of state sponsorship of BW terrorism, in large part because the sponsoring state runs the risk of retribution if the country victimized in an attack could trace the biological materials to their origin.

Microbial forensics, the science of tracing the source of the causative agent to a specific individual or group, is a relatively new field and, since 2001, has rapidly developed. The field, however, is still subject to a number of limitations, including limited repositories of microbial reference strains as well as the scientific tools to analyze them. Any national or international microbial forensics capability will need to include databases on genomics, microbiology, forensics methods, associated materials and related evidence assays (including traditional forensic analyses such as fingerprints), bioinformatics, and standardized tools.[32]

One could infer that in the future, as microbial forensic capabilities improve, the probability of state sponsorship of terrorism will decrease. Of particular interest in the debate over state sponsorship of terrorism is the growing sophistication of Iran's biotechnology and pharmaceutical industries and the potential to divert dual-use agents and materials to terrorists. At a minimum, based on its biotechnology infrastructure, Iran has the capability to produce small quantities of offensive biological weapons. Some of the agents, which open-source reports have associated with Iranian research, include *Bacillus anthracis*, botulinum toxin, ricin, T-2 mycotoxin, and Variola virus, the causative agent of smallpox.[33] Iran is also known to encourage anti-Israel terrorist activity. Iran, which is Shi'i Muslim, might be expected to be more likely to assist a Shi'ite group like Lebanese Hezbollah; it has, however, also sponsored some Sunni groups such as Hamas and the Palestinian Islamic Jihad with extensive funding, training, and weapons.[34] While evidence does not indicate that Iran has supported jihadist terrorists with BW materials, equipment, or expertise, the threat exists that Iran, or any other nation with suspected BW programs (i.e., Pakistan, Syria, etc.) could become a state sponsor of BW terrorism, assuming the perceived benefits outweigh the risks of detection. Another possibility related to state sponsorship lies not in the government itself, but in rogue elements in a state's government or security forces that might sanction BW assistance to jihadists without such actions being official policy.

If terrorists are unable to procure ready-made weapons, another option is to manufacture or produce them indigenously. This introduces even more complications, including locating and extracting the correct microorganism in nature or in seed stocks, procuring the right equipment and growth media, avoiding contamination by other microorganisms, ensuring virulence during the production and weaponization stages and avoiding detection during the entire process. The production of an unrefined biological weapon is most likely within reach of dedicated, sophisticated, and highly organized jihadist terrorist groups. In sum, any jihadist group would not only have to overcome the technical difficulties associated with the production or procurement of an agent, but also the aforementioned difficulties associated with the transport and actual delivery or dissemination of the agent. It is important to note, for instance, that while the production of a crude agent is fairly difficult, producing an aerosolized agent is even more so.

JIHADISTS' QUEST FOR BW

Intelligence indicates that al-Qa'ida and other jihadist groups have actively been attempting to acquire biological and toxin weapons for a number of years. Authorities have uncovered numerous plots, raw materials, equipment, and even small-scale laboratories dedicated to the development of biological and toxin weapons.

In one of the few statements that elaborate on the jihadist desire to use BW—beyond mere mention of it along with other types of unconventional weapons—al-Qa'ida spokesman Suleiman Abu Gheith stated in 2002:

> We have the right to kill four million Americans, two million of them children...and cripple them in the hundreds of thousands. Furthermore, it is our obligation to fight them with chemical and biological weapons, to afflict them with the fatal woes that have afflicted Muslims because of their chemical and biological weapons.[35]

It is interesting to note that the justification here for using BW is to repay in kind for alleged U.S. bioweapons use. Indeed, numerous statements by al-Qa'ida members discuss the use of CBRN in the context of reciprocity, rather than first use. Another reason to use BW, as purported by Mustafa Setmariam Nasar (aka Abu Mus'ab al-Suri), is the use of CBRN as strategic weapons "if those engaged in jihad establish that the evil of the infidels can be repelled only by attacking them with weapons of mass destruction, they may be used even if they annihilate all the infidels."[36]

Open-source evidence, presented below, indicates that jihadist terrorists have been actively seeking out the resources, equipment, and technical know-how to obtain a biological weapon. There are numerous incidents that illustrate that jihadists have progressed beyond mere rhetoric when it comes to BW terrorism. The question remains, however, as to whether or not a jihadist group will successfully obtain and use a biological weapon as its choice tool of terror over other more proven methods, including conventional weapons.

On August 21, 1995, a handwritten statement from Abu Ahmad (aka Muhamad Salah), the head of the military wing of Hamas, indicated that the Islamic fundamentalist organization had attempted to recruit members in the United States with expertise in both biological and chemical weapons. According to Salah, who was arrested in 1993, the operation was initiated by Musa Abu Marzuq, the leader of the Muslim Brothers organization in the United States. Abu Ahmad was instructed by Marzuq to collect the names of Palestinians residing in the United States who had expertise in chemical materials, toxins, physics, military education, and knowledge of computers.[37] Approximately twenty-seven individuals were recruited by the group to manufacture weapons based on their field of expertise. It is unknown if the efforts were successful, however, as available interview transcripts with Salah do not indicate that the organization was successful in developing biological weapons.

In November 2001, the Kabul office of Pakistani scientist Dr. Bashir Mehmood was reportedly found to contain documents indicating an interest in anthrax, including calculations concerning the aerial dispersal of anthrax via balloons.[38] Mehmood, along with Pakistani scientist Abdul Majid, was accused of meeting with Usama bin Ladin in 2001 to share nuclear, biological, and chemical weapons information with al-Qa'ida.[39] While it is unlikely that any actual materials or equipment were ever transmitted to al-Qa'ida, technical information or information on possible sources of materials could have been transmitted. Mehmood is suspected of being a member of A. Q. Khan's vast underground WMD black market network.

In 2001 and early 2002, investigators in Afghanistan uncovered an abandoned laboratory under construction near Kandahar and numerous reference manuals and other equipment and materials related to biological weapons development, confirming fears that al-Qa'ida was indeed seeking WMD.[40] While the laboratories were dismantled, the discovery highlights the threat from jihadist bioterrorism and indicates that at least rudimentary BW knowledge and materials have fallen into the hands of jihadists.

On December 9, 2001, Malaysian authorities arrested suspected *Jemaah Islamiyya* (a Southeast Asia–based jihadist terror group) member Yazid Sufaat, an American-educated businessman and scientist who is believed to have been a key member of al-Qa'ida's biological weapons program. Sufaat, who has a bachelor's degree in biological sciences and a minor in chemistry, used his own company, Green Laboratory Medicine, as an al-Qa'ida front engaged in the development of biological weapons, especially Bacillus anthracis.[41] It is unclear what kind of success Sufaat achieved in developing anthrax for use as a weapon; however, it demonstrates that some reasonably technically proficient individuals are part of the global jihadist terrorist movement. Sufaat has been indefinitely detained under Malaysia's Internal Security Act.

On January 5, 2003, British authorities arrested six Algerian men at their London apartment on suspicion of attempting to produce ricin. Following the arrests, authorities discovered traces of ricin, castor oil beans, and equipment for crushing the beans in the London apartment. Those arrested are believed to be part of a terrorist cell known as the "Chechen network." Following the initial arrest of the six men, authorities expanded their search and arrested more individuals suspected of playing a role in the ricin incident.[42] Later reports were contradictory to the initial statement that the substance tested in the apartment was ricin. Technically, ricin is relatively easy to produce, and does not demonstrate a technical capability within jihadist terrorist groups to develop and distribute biological and toxin weapons capable of causing mass casualties. It does, however, demonstrate that terrorists are indeed seeking the capability.

Perhaps most illustrative of the threat of jihadist BW terrorism is a recent report on the status of al-Qa'ida's WMD program. On February 3, 2008, a *Los Angeles Times* article reported that al-Qa'ida member Abu Khabab al-Masri, formerly believed to have been deceased from a 2006 U.S. airstrike in Pakistan, was in fact alive and in charge of resurrecting al-Qa'ida's WMD program. While experts suppose that the research is currently focused on the development of cyanide, chlorine, and other poisons unlikely to cause mass casualties, the potential for simultaneous BW development cannot be ignored.[43] Intelligence reports indicate that Masri has begun to set up rudimentary labs in the mountains of Pakistan and has recruited some scientists to the cause.[44] Prior to the invasion of Afghanistan in 2002, al-Masri, who is a trained chemical engineer, wrote and distributed training manuals with information on the development of both chemical and biological weapons.

One of the greatest challenges facing analysts today is determining if and when jihadists could use biological and toxin weapons. Unquestionably, as the snapshot above shows, some jihadist terrorist groups have attempted to acquire, procure, and/or indigenously develop a biological or toxin weapons capability. We must proceed with caution, however, when measuring intent against progress towards actually obtaining and using a mass casualty biological weapon. One cannot assume that because a jihadist terrorist organization has stated that they desire to use WMD and have made rudimentary attempts to acquire BW that they will succeed in doing so or even proceed to choose a biological weapon as their favored method of attack. Serious questions, including whether or not their ideology (the perception and application of which may vary across jihadist cells) permits the indiscriminate use of the weapon (assuming it is a communicable agent), along with organizational factors, access to financial resources, and technical capabilities must be weighed carefully.

Still, the apparent resurrection of al-Qa'ida's WMD program, the number of uncovered plots to develop or obtain biological weapons by other jihadist terror groups, and the increasingly global availability of life sciences materials and technical know-how illustrate that the threat of jihadist bioterrorism cannot be ignored.

BIODEFENSE COUNTERMEASURES

Since 2001, the U.S. government has invested billions of dollars in biological weapon defense in an attempt to prevent and respond to a potential BW terrorist attack. In the United States, the Centers for Disease Control and Prevention (CDC) ranks bioterrorism agents and diseases under three categories—A, B, and C—for emergency preparedness and response purposes. The three categories are based on the ease of dissemination or transmission from person to person; the potential to result in high mortality rates and the potential for a major public health impact; the ability to cause public panic and social disruption; and the requirement for special action in terms of public health preparedness.[45] Category A agents, which are characterized by their high mortality rates and relative ease of dispersion, include anthrax, botulism, plague, smallpox, tularemia, and hemorrhagic fevers. These agents are classified in the highest category of importance because they require special action by public health preparedness.[46] Category B agents, including Brucellosis, Glanders, Meliodosis, ricin toxin, and Staphylococcal Enterotoxin B, are moderately easy to disseminate with lower mortality rates than category A agents. Category B agents require specific enhancements of the CDC's diagnostic capacity and enhanced disease surveillance. The last classification of bioterrorism agents is category C agents, which include emerging pathogens that could be engineered for mass dissemination in the future because of availability, ease of production and dissemination, potential for high morbidity and mortality rates, and major health impact.[47]

The creation of the Strategic National Stockpile (strategically placed stockpiles of large quantities of medical supplies, including vaccines for CDC category A and B agents, that will be delivered to any state in the United States within twelve hours in the event of public health emergencies such as a terrorist attacks or natural outbreak of disease), funding for disease early warning systems, and new medical countermeasures have all been put in place in an attempt to help protect the U.S. population. For example, in 2004 President George W. Bush signed into law Project Bioshield, which provides new tools to improve medical countermeasures against biological terrorism, such as

- 75 million doses of a second-generation anthrax vaccine
- New medical treatments for anthrax directed at neutralizing the effects of anthrax toxin
- A polyvalent botulinum antitoxin
- A safer second-generation smallpox vaccine.[48]

Other countries have also attempted to improve domestic disease surveillance and medical countermeasures since the 2001 anthrax attacks. In 2002, in anticipation of the possibility of another Gulf War, Israel carried out a program to vaccinate over 15,000 health care workers and other first responders against smallpox in just three months' time. Israel has in place plans to vaccinate the entire population for smallpox within four days of an imminent threat.[49]

Canada has also developed a robust biodefense program to counter biological weapons terrorism. The Canadian Department of National Defense has a number of different research facilities dedicated to chemical and biological weapons defense research. Canada also has a national counter terrorism technology center; is developing a chemical and biological forensic reference laboratory, composed of an All-Hazards Triage Facility (AHTF), a Biosafety Level 3 (BL-3) Laboratory, and a gamma irradiator;[50] and possesses a dedicated biological medical countermeasures program.

INTERPOL, which is the world's largest international police organization comprised of members from 186 countries, developed a dedicated bioterrorism program at its headquarters in Lyon, France, after the 2001 anthrax attacks to focus on building national and international capacities to counter biological weapons terrorism. The main focus of the multilateral program is to not only raise awareness of the threat among member states, but also to develop police training programs, strengthen efforts to enforce existing legislation, promote the development of new legislation, and encourage interagency cooperation on bioterrorism. INTERPOL has also created a bioterrorism incident preplanning and response guide.[51]

Regardless of the measures implemented, however, questions remain as to whether national and international countermeasures are adequate to deal with a BW terror incident. Critics have argued that U.S. biological defense countermeasures, such as novel vaccines and therapeutics, are not being developed rapidly enough to counter advances in life sciences. Vaccine development, however, is a time-consuming process and subject to rigorous controls and long testing procedures to ensure they do not result in wide-scale health complications. Other critics have argued that even though billions of dollars have been spent to shore up America's biodefense capabilities, the public health infrastructure will be unable to respond to a large surge capacity in demand from an outbreak of an infectious agent, such as smallpox or pandemic avian influenza.[52]

Optimally, the United States and other countries will continue to focus on developing robust national biodefense capabilities. At the same time, the best defense against bioterrorist attacks is prevention. Counterterrorism efforts need to address the threat of jihadist bioterrorism through intelligence capabilities coupled with an innate understanding of both the microbiology of BW as well as the ideology and psychology of jihadism (see Chapters 1 and 2, respectively, for in-depth discussions of both of these salient issues).

CONCLUSION

Despite evidence indicating jihadists' interest in biological terrorism, technical barriers still form a significant gap between the theoretical possibility and operational reality of a mass casualty attack involving biological weapons. The security environment, however, is changing. Accelerating advances in life sciences and the availability of materials, equipment, and technical know-how have vastly increased the playing field of actors who are capable of producing biological weapons; research once limited to national defensive or offensive weapons programs can now be conducted in civilian settings. When the confluence between motivation, intent, and technical capability merges, the question will become not if jihadist terrorists will carry out a biological weapons attack, but when.

NOTES

1 The views expressed in this article are those of the author and do not reflect the official policy or position of the National Defense University, the Department of Defense or the U.S. government.
2. Australia Group. Australia Group Common Control Lists, http://www.australiagroup.net/en/controllists.html (accessed March 18, 2008); USAMRIID, April 2005, *USAMRIID's Medical Management of Biological Casualties Handbook*, Sixth Edition, http://www.usamriid.army.mil/education/instruct.htm (accessed March 18, 2008).
3. Centers for Disease Control and Prevention, "Smallpox Disease Overview, http://www.bt.cdc.gov/agent/smallpox/overview/disease-facts.asp (accessed April 30, 2008).

4. See Adam Dolnik, "Die and Let Die: Exploring Links between Suicide Terrorism and Terrorist Use of Chemical, Biological, Radiological, and Nuclear Weapons," *Studies in Conflict and Terrorism* 26:1 (January–February 2003).
5. University of Southern California, Translation of Sahih Bukhari, Book 52: Fighting for the Cause of Allah (Jihaad), http://www.usc.edu/dept/MSA/fundamentals/hadithsunnah/bukhari/052.sbt.html#004.052.082 (accessed on March 11, 2008).
6. Kyle B. Olson, "Aum Shinrikyo: Once and Future Threat?" *Emerging Infectious Diseases,* Centers for Disease Control and Prevention, Special Issue, http://www.cdc.gov/ncidod/EID/vol5no4/olson.htm (accessed February 7, 2008).
7. Brown University Department of Italian Studies, "The Coming of the Plague to Italy," http://www.brown.edu/Departments/Italian_Studies/dweb/plague/origins/spread.shtml (accessed March 18, 2008).
8. Ibid., 18–19.
9. Center for Nonproliferation Studies, October 2001, "Chronology of State Use and Biological and Chemical Weapons Control," www.cns.miis.edu/research/cbw/pastuse.htm (accessed on February 13, 2008); George W. Christopher, Theodore J. Cieslak, Julie A. Pavlin, and Edward M. Jr. Eitzin, "Biological Warfare: A Historical Perspective," in *Biological Weapons: Limiting the Threat*, ed. Joshua Lederberg, (Cambridge, MA: The MIT Press, 1999)
10. John Norris, and Will Fowler, *NBC: Nuclear, Biological and Chemical Warfare on the Modern Battlefield*, (1997) Cambridge, MA: Brassey's Ltd., 29.
11. Ibid.; Federation of American Scientists, April 16, 2000, "Biological Weapons Program," http://www.fas.org/nuke/guide/japan/bw/ (accessed on February 13, 2008).
12. Ken Alibek, *Biohazard: The Chilling True Story of the largest Covert Biological Weapons Program in the World—Told from the Inside by the Man Who Ran It*, New York: Random House, Inc., (1999) 33.
13. Jonathan B. Tucker, "Historical Trends Related to Bioterrorism: An Empirical Analysis," *Emerging Infectious Diseases*, 5:4 (July–August 1999).
14. Nuclear Threat Initiative, "Characteristics of CBW Terrorists," http://www.nti.org/h_learnmore/bwtutorial/chapter01_05.html (accessed March 18, 2008).
15. Smith, Christine A., "Plague in the Ancient World: A Study from Thucydides to Justinian," http://www.loyno.edu/~history/journal/1996-7/Smith.html (accessed April 29, 2008).
16. Donald Thompson, Joel Swerdlow, and Cheryl Loeb, "The Bug Stops Here: Force Protection and Emerging Infectious Diseases," November 2005, *Defense and Technology Paper 21,* Washington, DC: National Defense University.
17. Stephen Prior et al., "Weathering the Storm: Leading Your Organization Through a Pandemic," November 2006, *Defense and Technology Paper 38,* Washington, DC: National Defense University.
18. Georgia Tech Research Institute, "New Decontamination System Kills Anthrax Rapidly," January 29, 2008, http://www.gatech.edu/newsroom/release.html?id=1687 (accessed April 29, 2008).
19. Dennis Pluchinsky, "The Global Jihad: Leaderless Terrorism," June 20, 2006, http://www.eisenhowerseries.com/pdfs/terrorism_06/final/final_2006-06-20.pdf (accessed February 9, 2008).
20. Ibid.
21. MIPT, 2007, Aum Shinrikyo/Aleph. http://www.tkb.org/Group.jsp?groupID=3956 (accessed March 11, 2008).

22. Center for Nonproliferation Studies, 2005, Chart: Al-Qa'ida's WMD Activities, http://cns.miis.edu/pubs/other/sjm_cht.htm (accessed February 3, 2008).
23. National Academies of Science, *Globalization, Biosecurity and the Future of Life Sciences*, Washington, DC: The National Academies Press, (2006).
24. Tucker, Jonathan, June 2003, "Preventing the Misuse of Pathogens: The Need for Global Biosecurity Standards," *Arms Control Today*, http://www.armscontrol.org/act/2003_06/tucker_june03.asp#notes (accessed on March 11, 2008).
25. Ibid.
26. Judith Miller, "Russian Biologist Denies Work in Iran on Germ Weapons," *The New York Times*, January 19, 1999, http://query.nytimes.com/gst/fullpage.html?res=9D00E7D91430F93AA25752C0A96F958260 (accessed March 17, 2008).
27. Federation of American Scientists, "Biopreparat," October 20, 1998, http://www.fas.org/nuke/guide/russia/agency/bw.htm (accessed April 30, 2008).
28. Nuclear Threat Initiative, "Russia Profile: Biological Overview," http://www.nti.org/e_research/profiles/Russia/Biological/index.html (accessed April 30, 2008).
29. Jonathan Tucker, June 2003, "Preventing the Misuse of Pathogens: The Need for Global Biosecurity Standards," *Arms Control Today,* http://www.armscontrol.org/act/2003_06/tucker_june03.asp#notes (accessed on March 11, 2008).
30. Ibid.
31. Ibid.
32. Bruce Budowle et al., "Building Microbial Forensics as a Response to Biological Terrorism," *Science*, 301 September 26, 2003.
33. Nuclear Threat Initiative. June 2007. "Iran Profile: Biological Overview," http://www.nti.org/e_research/profiles/Iran/Biological/index_2300.html (accessed on June 27, 2007).
34. U.S Department of State, April 30, 2007, "Country Reports on Terrorism: State Sponsors of Terrorism Overview," http://www.state.gov/s/ct/rls/crt/2006/82736.htm (accessed February 8, 2008).
35. Robert Wesley, "Al-Qaeda's WMD Strategy after the U.S. Intervention in Afghanistan," in *Unmasking Terror: A Global Review of Terrorist Activities Volume III,* ed. Jonathan D. Hutzley Washington, DC: The Jamestown Foundation, (2005) 20.
36. Ibid., 21.
37. Prepared Statement of Steven Emerson Before the Senate Judiciary Committee Subcommittee on Terrorism, Technology, and Government Information Subject-Foreign Terrorists in America: Five Years After the World Trade Center Bombing, Federal Information Systems Corporation (24 February 1998); http://www.geocities.com/CollegePark/6453/emerson.html (accessed March 13, 2008); In the Matter of the Extradition of Mousa Mohammed Abu Marzuq, United States District Court for the Southern District of New York, 8 May 1996, http://www.uniset.ca/other/cs5/924FSupp565.html (accessed March 13, 2008).
38. Center for Nonproliferation Studies, May 2005, Chart: Al-Qa'ida's WMD Activities, http://cns.miis.edu/pubs/other/sjm_cht.htm (accessed on March 13, 2008).
39. Ibid.
40. Ibid.
41. MIPT, 2007, "Key Leader Profile: Sufaat, Yazid," http://www.tkb.org/KeyLeader.jsp?memID=6345 (accessed February 12, 2008).

42. Center for Nonproliferation Studies, 2004, "Chronology of Incidents Involving Ricin," http://cns.miis.edu/pubs/reports/ricin_chron.htm (accessed February 12, 2008).
43. Josh Meyer, February 3, 2008, "Al-Qa'ida Said to Focus on WMDs," *Los Angeles Times,* http://www.latimes.com/news/nationworld/world/la-fg-khabab3feb03,1,1300705.story (accessed February 3, 2008).
44. IntelAnalysis, "Al-Qa'ida Said to Focus on WMDs," February 4, 2008, http://intelanalysis.org/2008/02/04/al-qaeda-said-to-focus-on-wmds/ (accessed May 1, 2008).
45. Centers for Disease Control and Prevention, "Bioterrorism Agents/Diseases By Category," http://www.bt.cdc.gov/agent/agentlist-category.asp#bdef (accessed April 30, 2008).
46. Ibid.
47. Ibid.
48. The White House, July 21, 2004, "Fact Sheet: Progress in the War on Terror," http://www.whitehouse.gov/news/releases/2004/07/20040721-9.html (accessed on February 12, 2008).
49. Cameron Brown, "Israel and the WMD Threat: Lessons For Europe," *Middle East Review of International Affairs*, 8:3 (September 2004).
50. Defence Research and Development Canada, "CB Forensic Reference Laboratory," http://www.dres.dnd.ca/Facilities/CB/DFS2002_01_FORLAB/index_e.html (accessed April 30, 2008).
51. INTERPOL, "Bioterrorism," http://www.interpol.int/Public/BioTerrorism/default.asp (accessed on March 12, 2008).
52. Senator Robert C. Byrd, May 23, 2006, "Biodefense and Pandemic Influenza," Hearing Before a Subcommittee of the Committee on Appropriations United States Senate, http://www.fas.org/irp/congress/2006_hr/biodefense.html (accessed on March 18, 2008).

CHAPTER 7

Radiological Weapons and Jihadist Terrorism

Charles D. Ferguson

CONTENTS

INTRODUCTION

Terrorists in general might choose to use a radiological weapon for one or more purposes: causing harm to human health through exposure to ionizing radiation, provoking psychological effects through stimulation of people's fears of radiation, as well as disrupting people's lives and livelihoods and causing significant economic damage through radioactive contamination of valuable property. Before trying to understand whether jihadist terrorists are motivated to use or capable of using radiological weapons, it is necessary to learn whether these terrorists could obtain the means to conduct a radiological attack by examining the characteristics, composition, and construction of these weapons.

Although radiological weapons can take many forms, the common ingredient required for success is radioactive material. This material emits ionizing radiation, which can knock electrons off atoms, thus creating ions. These ions, if present in large enough amounts in human tissue, can cause damage potentially leading to harmful health effects such as radiation sickness or cancer. For most scenarios involving radiological weapons, very few, if any, people near the scene of an attack would succumb to serious and immediate health effects. To experience these effects, people would have to receive relatively high exposures of ionizing radiation. Because radiological weapons are typically designed to disperse radioactive material over wide areas, the dispersed material would pose a far less potent health threat compared to concentrated amounts of radioactivity near a person. However, if people ingested or inhaled significant amounts of radioactive material, they might well develop serious health effects. Also, people exposed to even tiny amounts of excess radiation have a very small, but nonzero, increase in the probability of developing cancer. Nevertheless, because it could take several years to decades for cancer to develop, many people might live in fear of developing cancer after exposure to even small amounts of radiation in the aftermath of a radiological attack. Therefore, the psychological and social consequences of a radiological attack could linger for many years after the incident and dwarf the physical health effects.

A radiological weapon must not be confused with a nuclear weapon, and the effects of the two weapons differ greatly. For example, a radiological weapon cannot produce a nuclear chain reaction and will not, consequently, result in a massive explosion. The one characteristic common to nuclear and radiological weapons is that both employ radioactive material. A nuclear explosion through fission would produce massive amounts of radioactive material, whereas a radiological weapon cannot produce additional radioactive material than the amount that was originally contained in the weapon. Many experts, therefore, do not consider a radiological weapon to be a weapon of mass destruction (WMD); rather, they refer to radiological weapons as a different type of WMD: A weapon of mass *disruption*.[1] Massive disruption can stem from the economic, social, and psychological effects of a radiological attack alluded to above.

LOCATIONS OF RADIOACTIVE MATERIAL AND POSSIBLE PATHWAYS FOR TERRORIST ACQUISITION

The radioactive material in a radiological weapon can come from many sources. Nuclear power plants, research reactor facilities, hospitals, blood banks, universities, food irradiation centers, oil well sites, and shipbuilding and construction sites are many of the major places where radioactive materials are used and stored. Some of these places are more vulnerable than others to terrorists obtaining radioactive material.

Of the places listed above, nuclear power plants would probably have the most rigorous security and would have radioactive materials that are too radioactive to handle without thick shielding and too heavy to carry without special equipment. At nuclear power plants, spent nuclear fuel is highly radioactive and could give a lethal radiation dose in a few minutes without adequate shielding. Moreover, a spent nuclear fuel assembly at power plants typically weighs many tons.

Spent fuel from research reactors, on the other hand, may not contain nearly as much radioactivity as spent fuel from nuclear power plants because many research reactors operate at power levels much lower than nuclear power plants. Also, a spent fuel assembly at a research reactor can weigh much less than a spent fuel assembly at a power plant and thus might be more susceptible to transport by thieves. Of course, a terrorist group would have to surmount the barrier of finding out where the spent fuel is located within a facility. Reconnaissance and insider assistance could help provide this information.

At any location where radioactive materials are used, terrorists would have to determine how to gain access, identify where radioactive materials are situated, and figure out how to remove the materials. If removal proves too much of a problem, the terrorists could try to blow up the material in place. Such a scenario may or may not achieve the terrorists' intended objectives unless the location itself is considered to be of high enough tactical value to elicit the desired response from the terrorists' intended audience.

Certain locations where radioactive materials are used or stored appear more accessible than others relative especially to high-security nuclear power plants. For instance, hospitals and universities are designed to be open to the public. Thus, terrorist reconnaissance of these locations may not attract authorities' attention. But without specific information about where radioactive materials are located, the terrorists may not identify these locations without additional assistance from insiders or from external sources of information such as Web sites about the facilities. Thinking through potentially promising pathways for terrorists to try to acquire radioactive materials, security experts have identified—in addition to insider assistance and theft from facilities—alternative acquisition routes, including deliberate transfer by a government, unauthorized transfer by a government official or a facility custodian, looting during coups or other times of political turmoil, licensing fraud, organized crime, exploiting weaknesses in transportation links, sellers of illicitly trafficked radioactive material, and finding orphan radioactive sources (which have been lost, stolen, or fallen outside of regulatory control).[2]

Although national governments are not known to have deliberately transferred radioactive materials to terrorists, it is at least conceivable that some governments might attempt this. Virtually all states possess radioactive sources, and many governments own research reactors that can produce radioactive sources that could be useful in radiological weapons. (See the blocks labeled radioisotope production and source manufacture in Figure 7.1.) However, this threat is unlikely to occur because government leaders would fear retribution if the country that was the victim of the attack could trace the radioactive materials to its origin. While nuclear forensics and attribution pose considerable technical challenges, the United States has been working with partner governments and the International Atomic Energy Agency (IAEA) in developing and refining these methods. Thus, the transferring government would have to factor into its risk calculations the increasingly credible forensics capability available to many other governments.

Terrorists could try to recruit sympathetic government officials or custodians of facilities containing radioactive sources for unauthorized transfers. As of early 2008, however, there has been no evidence of such transfers. A terrorist group would face daunting challenges in exploiting this pathway. Possible exploitation techniques include extortion, other types of coercion, or perhaps cooption by winning officials or custodians over to the terrorists' cause. However, none of these methods is easy; terrorists would have to devote sufficient time and resources to open up this pathway and would face the risk of discovery by authorities.

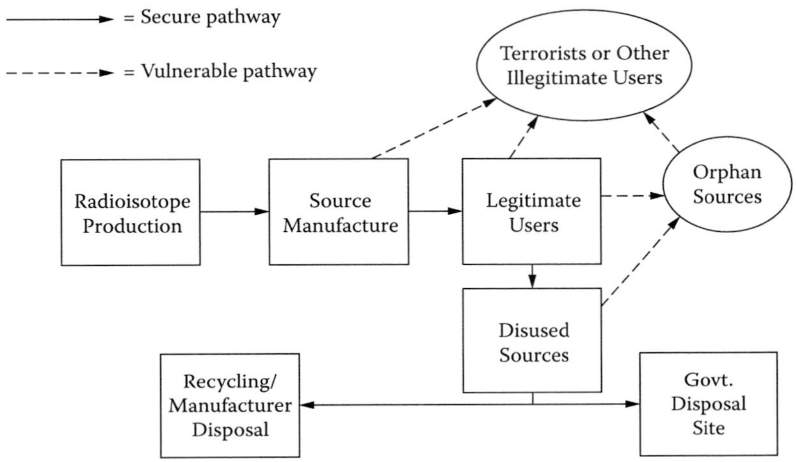

FIGURE 7.1 Radioactive source lifecycle.

National or local political turmoil such as the overthrow of a government could create opportunities for looting facilities containing radioactive sources. For example, looting broke out immediately after U.S.-led coalition forces toppled Saddam Hussein from power in Iraq in April 2003. Looters broke into the main Iraqi nuclear site at Tuwaitha, where they accessed barrels that contained uranium yellowcake. Fortunately, uranium yellowcake is weakly radioactive and is not suitable for use in radiological weapons. Nevertheless, if people had ingested significant amounts of uranium, they could suffer from toxic heavy metal health effects. More worrisome, the Tuwaitha site had more powerful radioactive sources than yellowcake. A subsequent IAEA investigation accounted for almost all of the uranium containers, but the status of some of the radioactive sources could not be determined. About a year later, in mid-2004, the U.S. Department of Energy helped secure many Iraqi high-risk radioactive sources; however, terrorists or other malicious people could have accessed some of these sources in the interim if they had known about vulnerabilities at Tuwaitha and other Iraqi facilities.

Instead of stealing sources from facilities or availing themselves of corrupt officials or insiders, terrorists might try to pose as legitimate buyers of sources. This is depicted by the dashed lines in Figure 7.1 leading from source manufacturers and legitimate users to illegitimate users. Terrorists could attempt, for instance, to file for licenses issued by nuclear regulatory authorities. Such licenses would entitle the holder to own potent radioactive sources. A related option is to create a fraudulent license. While not a terrorist, Stuart von Adelman, who exhibited deranged behavior on occasion, did just that in the 1990s on more than one occasion. Once he posed as a university physics professor and fraudulently obtained access to radioactive materials. Nonetheless, despite some episodes of irrational behavior, he did serve as a radiation safety officer at two universities and had also served as a licensing reviewer in a state radiation control program. Although he was never connected to terrorist activity, an assistant U.S. District Attorney stated that the radioactive material Adelman had obtained in Canada may have been used in a scam to earn money from terrorists. In 1996, he was arrested in the United States and pleaded guilty to charges of fraudulent acquisition of radioactive material. He received a five-year prison sentence.[3] In 2006, the U.S. Government Accountability Office showed that its researchers could use fake licenses to acquire radioactive materials.[4] Similarly, illicit buyers could misrepresent themselves on the Internet to try to purchase radioactive sources online. Regulating Internet commerce to guard against illicit radioactive material sales poses challenges.

Terrorists might also try to acquire radioactive materials through links to organized crime. While a nexus between terrorist and criminal groups for the transfer of such materials has not been publicly uncovered, in 2002 a criminal gang did steal five radioactive sources in Ecuador and held these sources for ransom. After paying the fee, the company that had owned the sources only received three of them back. According to the *Washington Post*, this "was the first known case of successful blackmail involving radiological material, and U.S. and UN experts fear the pattern could be repeated."[5]

Terrorists could link up with buyers of illicitly trafficked radioactive material. The IAEA's illicit trafficking database has shown many cases of opportunistic thieves trying to pawn off radioactive materials, with some cases involving relatively potent radioactive sources such as cesium-137.[6] However, this database should be treated with caution because countries are not required to report all incidents, the traffickers who are caught may not have been competent enough to find buyers (many of the traffickers were caught in sting operations), and it is uncertain whether there is a significantly large demand for these materials (unlike the issue of illicit drug trafficking). Analysis of the data does not indicate a convergence between terrorism and illicit radioactive materials trafficking.[7] Nonetheless, such a convergence in the future cannot be ruled out.

Finally, terrorists might try to find radioactive sources that have been abandoned, also known as "orphaned" sources. They might use radiation detectors such as Geiger counters to find these sources given some knowledge about where to look. For instance, within the former Soviet Union, there are estimated to be hundreds of orphan sources. The IAEA, the Russian Federation, other former Soviet republics, and the United States have been working together since the 9/11 terrorist attacks to track down these sources. While many have been found, many more are believed to still be orphaned because of the Soviet legacy production of large numbers of powerful radioactive sources.

HIGH-RISK RADIOISOTOPES

Different types of ionizing radiation vary in their ability to cause harm to human health depending on the energy content, the electromagnetic charge, and the penetrating capacity of the radiation. Commercially used radioactive sources emit four different types of ionizing radiation: alpha, beta, gamma, and neutron, each described below. Radioactive decay occurs because the radioactive substance is emitting energy to go from an unstable nuclear state to a more stable nuclear state. The end product of a radioactive decay chain is a stable nucleus; for example, the uranium decay chain eventually ends after several rounds of decay via different "daughter" elements to the stable nucleus of lead.

An alpha particle consists of a helium nucleus—two protons and two neutrons bound together. Because of the two protons, an alpha particle has a positive charge of two and thus can exert twice the electromagnetic force on an electron than a particle with only a single positive charge. Consequently, other characteristics being equal, alpha radiation has a greater ionizing power than singly charged particles. But alpha particles do not have great penetrating power. A sheet of paper or the outer dead layer of skin cells is thick enough to block alpha radiation from penetrating into the human body from external radiation sources. However, if people were to ingest or inhale significant amounts of alpha-emitting material that stayed resident inside the body for a significant period of time, harmful health effects could result. (The significant amounts of material and time of exposure depend on the type of radioactive material and the organs of the body exposed.[8]) Thus, alpha radiation is considered an internal health hazard but not an external hazard.

Beta radiation consists of an electron (or, more rarely, a positron, which is a positively charged electron) that is emitted from an unstable nucleus. Usually, the beta particle is moving at high speeds, although some nuclei emit relatively low energy or lower speed betas. A beta particle has a single electromagnetic charge, which exerts a force on other electrons, thus potentially causing ionization of atoms. Beta radiation has more penetrating power than alpha radiation; however, even thin sheets of aluminum can block most beta radiation. Concerning external exposure, a thick layer of clothing can offer shielding. Unshielded eyes, made of soft tissue, would likely be most at risk from external beta radiation sources. Like alpha radiation, beta radiation would also pose an internal health hazard if significant amounts of beta-emitting materials were ingested or inhaled and stayed resident in the body for a significant period of time.

Gamma radiation consists of high-energy light. People tend to be familiar with x-rays, another form of high-energy light that is also ionizing, because of medical and dental uses. Gamma radiation has even greater energy content than x-ray radiation; thus, gamma radiation has even greater penetrating power than x-rays and also greater penetration ability than alpha and beta radiation. Sheets of lead or relatively thick slabs of concrete or other dense shielding materials would be needed to block gamma radiation. Consequently, gamma radiation can pose an external health hazard as well as an internal health hazard. Unlike alpha and beta radiation, gamma radiation is uncharged, but it can ionize atoms by scattering off electrons and thereby stripping them off atoms.

Neutron radiation, like gamma radiation, is uncharged, and thus can easily penetrate nuclei without being repelled by the positively charged protons inside nuclei. A neutron, especially if it is moving at fast speeds (that is, it has a high energy content), can knock a proton out of a nucleus. The free proton can then interact with electrons, causing ionization and thus damaging living tissues. Neutrons can be emitted through spontaneous fission or can be produced when an alpha particle interacts with certain nuclei, for example, nuclei of beryllium, releasing a neutron.

Hundreds of radioactive substances or radioisotopes emit ionizing radiation. An isotope is a different nuclear form of an element. An element is the basic building block of chemistry. There are ninety-two naturally occurring elements from the lightest element hydrogen to the heaviest element uranium. In addition, scientists have been able to make about another dozen elements heavier than uranium, including americium, neptunium, and plutonium. Each element has unique chemical properties because of the number of protons in its nucleus. Different isotopes are formed by changing the number of neutrons in an element's nucleus. For example, hydrogen-1, which is nonradioactive, has only a single proton and zero neutrons. But hydrogen-2, which also is nonradioactive, has one proton and one neutron, and hydrogen-3, which is radioactive, has one proton and two neutrons. Thus, changing the number of neutrons changes the radioactive properties of the element hydrogen.

Scientists can make many different isotopes by adding neutrons to existing isotopes. Relatively few of the conceivable isotopes that exist or can be made are stable, that is, nonradioactive. The many that are radioactive have decay rates that vary from split seconds (nanoseconds) to billions of years. The rate of radioactive decay is measured by the time it takes for half a radioactive substance to decay, also known as "half-life." After seven half-lives have elapsed for a radioisotope, less than 1 percent of the original amount remains. The radioisotopes with short half-lives, of say an hour, would decay relatively rapidly and would not usually pose a security threat, since their levels of radiation would likely diminish below the danger threshold before they could be used to bring about prolonged exposure. On the other end of the decay scale, radioisotopes with very long half-lives, greater than a few thousand years, would usually not pose a security threat because these materials are emitting radiation at a relatively slow rate. To picture this concept, imagine standing next to a lump of a particular radioisotope. Over the course of a human lifetime, the very long-lived radioisotopes would emit very little of their radiation. In contrast, people could reduce their exposure to the short-lived radioisotopes by staying away from these substances and letting relatively rapid radioactive decay reduce the hazardous amounts of the radioisotope.

Because almost all of the radioisotopes have very short or very long half-lives, most radioisotopes do not pose significant security threats. Those radioisotopes that can present a security threat have intermediate-length half-lives from days to about a thousand years. Searching through the many hundreds of radioisotopes and selecting those with these intermediate half-lives, one finds a couple of dozen of significant concern. In addition to this criterion, one should ask how prevalently radioisotopes in this select group are used in a relatively large numbers of commercially available radioactive sources. After applying these selection criteria, one finds no more than a dozen radioisotopes of potential security concern. Table 7.1 lists these radioisotopes and their relevant nuclear properties.

Of this group, certain radioisotopes are more of a security concern than others. Those that occur in relatively large amounts in a radioactive source would tend to pose a greater threat than smaller amounts. Often in the literature of radiological terrorism, the term "large amount" is used. The actual mass of radioisotope in "large" radioactive sources is usually small as compared to the kilogram-sized quantities of fissile material dealt within nuclear weapons. To figure out how large an amount of radioisotope one would find in a radioactive source of security concern, look at the column labeled "Specific Activity" in Table 7.1. Activity quantifies the number of radioactive decays per second in a mass of radioisotope. Specific activity in turn refers to how much activity there is per unit mass, for example, per gram of material. For instance, consider cobalt-60, which has a specific activity of 40,700 GigaBecquerels per gram or, equivalently, 1,100 Curies per gram. (A Becquerel is the internationally recognized unit of activity, and it equals one decay per second. Giga equals one billion. Thus, one GigaBecquerel equals one billion decays per second. A Curie is the older unit of activity and is still predominantly used in the United States; it equals the amount of activity in one gram of radium, which equals 37 GigaBecquerels.) The amount of radioactivity in one gram of cobalt-60, which is a gamma emitter, is considered hazardous to someone near an unshielded source of this potency after an exposure of a few minutes. For internal exposures of some of the radioisotopes, such as polonium-210, in Table 7.1, microgram amounts can be fatal. Thus, gram-sized or even less massive quantities of certain radioisotopes can pose a safety and security threat.

COMMERCIAL RADIOACTIVE SOURCES

The radioactive materials of greatest security concern are commercial radioactive sources that contain relatively large amounts of ionizing radiation. Most of these sources are sealed in protective casings to prevent accidental exposure to the radioactive material. Sealed sources typically use double-encapsulated stainless steel to enclose the radioactive material. Thus, to access this material, terrorists would have to break open the seal. They would need some knowledge of radiation safety to perform this operation without inadvertently exposing themselves to lethal doses of radiation from the most powerful sources.

The IAEA has categorized radioactive sources in terms of potential harm to human health. Table 7.2 lists the definitions of each category from the highest health risk (category 1) to the lowest (category 5) and also mentions examples of types of sources in each category. Experts have reached a consensus that sources in categories 1 and 2 are truly high risk. However, it is important to note that there is an ongoing debate within the U.S. government, other governments, and the IAEA concerning whether this categorization makes sense from the perspective of security threats. For instance, a category 3 source may not cause much harm to human health but could lead to relatively significant economic damage if dispersed in an urban area with valuable property. Alternatively, dispersed lower level sources may not cause much contamination but may stimulate social and psychological effects. Consequently, the debate has centered on how to quantify contamination, social, and psychological effects from sources below category 2.

Social and psychological effects are related to the real and perceived health effects from radiation. Real effects are classified according to the received dose from radioactive material. Health physicists define two dose regimes: high dose and low dose. High

TABLE 7.1 Radioisotopes of Security Concern

Radioisotope	Half-Life	Specific Activity GBq/g (Ci/g)	High-Energy Alpha Emissions	High-Energy Beta Emissions	High-Energy Gamma Emissions
Americium-241 (Am-241)	433 years	125.8 (3.4)	Yes	No	Low energy
Californium-252 (Cf-252)	2.7 years	19,832 (536)	Yes	No	Low energy
Cesium-137 (Cs-137) [Barium-137m (Ba-137m)]	30 years [2.6 minutes]	3,256 [19,980 million] (88 [540 million])	N/A	Low energy [Low energy]	N/A [Yes]
Cobalt-60 (Co-60)	5.3 years	40,700 (1,100)	N/A	Low energy [Low energy]	Yes
Iodine-131 (I-131)	8.0 days	4.8 million (130,000)	N/A	Yes	Yes
Iridium-192 (Ir-192)	74 days	>16,650 (>450) std >37,000 (>1,000) high	N/A	Yes	Yes
Polonium-210 (Po-210)	140 days	166,500 (4,500)	Yes	Low energy	Low energy
Plutonium-238 (Pu-238)	88 years	636.4 (17.2)	Yes	No	Low energy
Plutonium-239 (Pu-239)	24,000 years	2.33 (0.063)	Yes	Low energy	Low energy
Radium-226 (Ra-226)	1,600 years	37 (1)	Yes	No	Low energy
Strontium-90 (Sr-90) [Yttrium-90 (Y-90)]	29 years [64 hours]	5,180 [20.35 million] (140 [550,000])	N/A	Yes [Yes]	N/A [Low energy]

doses can cause near-term (within minutes to weeks) health effects. These "deterministic" effects are clearly discernible, showing up as nausea, vomiting, and hair loss, for example, at the onset of the high-dose regime, that is, 75 to 100 Rad, or, equivalently, in international units, 0.75 to 1.0 Sieverts, of exposure. For even higher doses of 500 or more Rad (5 Sieverts or greater), death can result. But many radiological terrorism scenarios, especially those causing wide dispersal of radioactive material, would likely cause deterministic health effects in few, if any, people.

Many more people would receive low doses of radiation in these scenarios. Low-dose exposures, however, would not result in readily discernible deterministic health effects. Instead, over many years to decades, some members of the exposed population may develop cancer. But because potential cancer development is a complicated process involving not only the exposure to a carcinogen such as radiation but also the capabilities of a person's immune system, health physicists are not able to determine exactly who in that population will develop cancer. Thus, low-dose exposures are inherently probabilistic, like a roll of dice. Still, knowing the level of radiation exposure, experts can predict based on conservative modeling the fraction of people who would likely develop cancer. This modeling assumes that even very low amounts of radiation result in a nonzero probability of developing cancer. Some health physicists disagree about this modeling and instead believe evidence points to a threshold level of exposure below which people would not develop cancer. The paucity of reliable data in the low-dose regime has stymied resolution of this debate.

Concerning radioactive source categorization, experts also disagree about whether to include the probabilistic (what the literature calls *stochastic*) health effects from the low radiation levels someone might receive from categories 4 and 5 sources. Category 3 sources, as shown in Table 7.2, can lead to even higher levels of radiation exposure but would typically be expected to result in relatively low levels if dispersed in a radiological weapon. The IAEA categorization document excludes stochastic effects from consideration in the categorization criteria because "the deterministic effects resulting from an accident or malicious act are likely to overshadow any increased stochastic risk in the short term."[9] Although stochastic radiation doses may cause cancer in only a relatively small fraction of the exposed population, worries about stochastic effects could add to people's psychological burden.

Another issue in the debate over source categorization is how to factor in the ease of access to and transport of various sources. Devices containing sources with relatively high amounts of radioactivity tend to weigh much more than devices with lower level sources. For example, a research irradiator, which is a category 1 source, can weigh several hundred pounds including all of the lead shielding and metal casing of this device. In contrast, a brachytherapy device, which is a category 3 source, designed to be inserted in the body (for example, to treat prostate cancer), weighs much less than a pound and is only millimeters in length. Both types of sources can be found in hospital settings. Assuming terrorists could access a hospital that has these sources, they would have a far easier time carrying brachytherapy sources. If terrorists wanted the larger amount of radioactivity resident in the irradiator, they could try to cut into the device to remove the radioactive material. To be successful, they would need to know about the specific design of the device, possess the proper tools to break into the device, and need shielding to safely handle the radioactive material once they have removed it from the device. Even suicidal terrorists could not simply ignore the risk of radiation exposure as they would likely receive a deterministic and perhaps lethal dose of radiation if they did not shield a removed category 1 source within a few minutes. In sum, category 3 sources with

TABLE 7.2 Categorization of Radioactive Sources

Categories of Radioactive Sources	Definition and Types of Sources
Category 1	These sources, "if not safely managed or securely protected would be likely to cause permanent injury to a person who handled [them], or were otherwise in contact with [them] for more than a few minutes. It would probably be fatal to be close to this amount of unshielded material for a period of a few minutes to an hour." This category includes radioisotope thermoelectric generators, research and blood irradiators, and radiation teletherapy sources.
Category 2	These sources, "if not safely managed or securely protected could cause permanent injury to a person who handled [them], or were otherwise in contact with [them], for a short time (minutes to hours). It could possibly be fatal to be close to this amount of unshielded radioactive material for a period of hours to days." This category includes industrial radiography cameras and high-dose–rate and medium-dose–rate brachytherapy sources.
Category 3	These sources, "if not safely managed or securely protected could cause permanent injury to a person who handled [them], or were otherwise in contact with [them], for some hours. It could possibly be fatal to be close to this amount of unshielded radioactive material for a period of days to weeks." This category includes oil well logging sources and fixed industrial gauges using high activity sources and includes level gauges, dredger gauges, conveyor gauges, and spinning pipe gauges.
Categories 4 and 5	The sources in these categories contain relatively low activity materials and thus are generally not considered dangerous in the context of most radiological weapons, unless a large enough aggregate amount of these sources were collected and used. Examples of sources in these categories are smoke detectors and medical diagnostic sources.

relatively low levels of radioactivity might, under certain circumstances, pose greater security risks than higher activity category 1 or 2 sources.

Another contentious aspect of the debate is how to factor in the security risks of lower level sources that would not cause any appreciable, immediate threat to human health, but could still cause significant contamination. For example, a single category 3 source would likely not contain sufficient radioactivity to cause immediate health effects in a scenario in which the source's radioactive material were dispersed by a radiological weapon. Nonetheless, depending on where the material was dispersed, the contamination could result in significant property damage. Stepping back from the debate, the IAEA's source categorization excludes "socio-economic consequences resulting from radiological accidents or malicious acts [because] the methodology to quantify and compare these effects, especially on an international basis, is not yet fully developed."[10] Some independent security experts have recommended considering category 3 sources as high risk, especially when several of these sources are aggregated.[11] The IAEA's source categorization document also draws attention to aggregation of lower level sources resulting in a cumulative radioactivity amount that would be equivalent to a higher category source.[12]

Table 7.3 lists the most prevalently used sources in categories 1, 2, and 3, along with the typical amounts of radioactivity in each type of source. In addition to radioactivity, the chemical properties of a source can either increase or decrease the security risks. In particular, the chemical form strongly affects the ease or difficulty by which the substance can be dispersed. Cesium chloride tops the priority list of high-risk, easily dispersible radioactive sources because it is a talcum powder–like substance that could be spread just by blowing on it. In contrast, because cobalt-60 is in the form of metal pins or rods, it is much harder to disperse. Iridium-192 also typically exists in solid metallic form. In general, chemicals in the form of talcum- or salt-like substances can be more easily dispersed than chemicals that are solid or more tightly bound together.

Only a relatively small number of major manufacturers make the majority of radioisotopes used in commercial radioactive sources.[13] Governments tend to own the reactors

TABLE 7.3 High-Risk Radioactive Sources

Type of Source or Application	Radioisotope	Typical Radioactivity Level GBq (Ci)	Source Categorization
Sterilization and food irradiation	Cobalt-60	148 million (Up to 4 million)	1
	Cesium-137	111 million (Up to 3 million)	
Radioisotope thermoelectric generator (RTG)	Strontium-90	740,000 (20,000)	1
	Plutonium-238	10,360 (280)	
Research and blood irradiators	Cobalt-60	88,800-925,000 (2,400-25,000)	1
	Cesium-137	259,000-555,000 (7,000-15,000)	
Single-beam teletherapy	Cobalt-60	148,000 (4,000)	1
	Cesium-137	18,500 (500)	
Multi-beam teletherapy (gamma knife, e.g.)	Cobalt-60	259,000 (7,000)	1
Industrial radiography	Cobalt-60	2,220 (60)	2
	Iridium-192	3,700 (100)	
High- and medium-dose brachytherapy	Cobalt-60	370 (10)	2
	Cesium-137	111 (3)	
	Iridium-192	222 (6)	
Well logging	Cesium-137	0.74-74 (0.02-2)	3
	Americium-241/ Beryllium	0.74-74 (0.02-2)	
	Californium-252 (rare use)	37 (1)	
Level and conveyor gauges	Cobalt-60	0.74-74 (0.02-2)	3
	Cesium-137	0.74-74 (0.02-2)	

that are used to produce these radioisotopes. In particular, major radioisotope production occurs in reactors located in Argentina, Belgium, Canada, France, The Netherlands, Russia, South Africa, and the United States. Major source manufacturers in Belgium, Canada, Russia, South Africa, and the United States, to name the countries with the largest corporations, then place these radioisotopes in sealed sources, which are put in devices, such as irradiators, radiography cameras, and teletherapy machines. These corporations then sell the devices to thousands of users throughout the globe.

TYPES OF RADIOLOGICAL WEAPONS

Radiological weapons can take a variety of forms, from very crude explosive devices to sophisticated dispersal mechanisms. Unfortunately, the news media have latched onto the term "dirty bomb" to describe all types of radiological weapons, which conveys a very limited sense of the variety of these weapons. The popular image of a dirty bomb usually consists of conventional explosives, say dynamite, strapped to some type of radioactive material. When the explosives are ignited, the resulting blast disperses the radioactive material. The fact is that this dispersal mechanism may do a very poor job at effectively spreading out radioactive material in ways that can do serious harm to health or result in significant radioactive contamination that is hard to clean up. Based on studies done at Sandia National Laboratories by Fred Harper and colleagues, most dirty bombs would not produce significant amounts of aerosolized radioactive material and thus would not pose significant health risks for inhalation.[14]

To optimize the production of aerosolized material, terrorists would have to be skilled in conventional explosives and know how to choose the correct types and amounts of explosives depending on the chemical composition and amount of radioactive material present. They would also need to have knowledge of the chemistry and physical form of the radioactive source. In particular, they would need to know whether the source is a solid, liquid, or powder, and whether it is a metal or chemically bound to other elements. In sum, to move beyond a simple dirty bomb, a terrorist group would have to assemble experts with the correct skillsets and do their homework on the radioactive material they have accessed or are attempting to access.

If a terrorist group bent on using a radiological weapon had these skills, a larger palette of radiological weapons would be available to them. Radiological dispersal device (RDD) is the term in the literature, outside of press stories, that is used to describe many types of radiological weapons.[15] An RDD could use dissolved radioactive material in a liquid-like solution. In this chemical form, sprayers could disperse the solution. Similarly, radioactive materials already in a powdered form could be dispersed through such mechanisms. For example, conceivably, cruise missiles or unmanned aerial vehicles could disperse these solutions or powders by flying low over urban areas or other high-value targets.[16] But making the most hazardous-sized aerosolized particles, around one to a few microns in diameter, is far from easy to do.[17] Meteorological conditions can also significantly affect the ability to disperse hazardous clouds of radioactive materials with these methods.

Drawing upon some of these earlier studies about sprayers, James M. Acton, Brooke Rogers, and Peter M. Zimmerman in 2007 drew attention to "inhalation, ingestion, and immersion (I^3) attacks."[18] An inhalation attack would try to make victims breathe in and retain much of the radioactive material in their lungs; an ingestion attack would involve swallowing radioactive material; and an immersion attack would soak victims with the material in some type of solution or colloidal suspension of the material in a liquid. Acton et al. cautioned that radiological security experts have largely overlooked the seriousness of these types of radiological attacks. Instead, much more attention has been focused on dirty bombs and other explosive means of dispersing radioactive materials. They discussed two main reasons to be concerned about I^3 attacks. First, inhalation, ingestion, and immersion attacks would increase internal health hazards because these methods are designed to bring radioactive materials into the body. As the murder in November 2006 of former Russian spy Alexander Litvinenko with only micrograms of polonium-210 illustrated, "once inside the body, even a minute quantity of a radioactive material can be deadly."[19] Alpha-emitting materials such as polonium-210 are well suited for I^3 attacks because only a few hundredths of a Curie of internal alpha radiation exposure can cause serious health effects (when inhaled or ingested). Second, while the most effective I^3 attacks require significant technical skills, relatively simpler versions of these attacks are likely within the skillset of reasonably technically competent terrorists.

Examining other means of dispersal, terrorists might consider using incendiary devices to disperse radioactive materials. A radiological incendiary device (RID) would complicate firefighters' efforts at fighting a fire and rescuing people from a burning building while contending with radioactive contamination.[20] Even if the health risk from the radioactivity is not great, people who are experiencing the fire already have a tendency toward panic and may feel even more panicky if they knew that there was radioactive contamination as well.

Radiological weapons need not disperse radioactive materials to be useful instruments of terrorism. A radiation emission device (RED), for example, emits ionizing radiation from a stationary radioactive source. Thus, people closest to the source would receive the largest radiation dose. The intensity of this point source radiation is inversely proportional to the distance squared. For example, moving twice the distance away from the source would reduce the radioactivity intensity by a factor of four. Terrorists contemplating this simple type of radiological weapon would likely choose crowded locations such as urban train stations, concert halls, or sports arenas.

Terrorists' communication strategies would be critical in all radiological attack scenarios but perhaps even more so in an RID because of the fear associated with fire. For instance, the perpetrating group might contact the news media just before or soon after the attack started to increase the likelihood of stimulating people's anxieties. Alternatively, the group might decide to keep quiet and allow the authorities to find the radioactivity, leaving governments and citizens wondering and worrying about the next attack, if there will be one.

JIHADISTS' INTEREST IN RADIOLOGICAL WEAPONS

While security experts have shown intense interest in radiological terrorism, there have been relatively few examples of terrorists in general showing unambiguous interest in radiological weapons. Regarding security experts' views, in June 2005, Senator Richard Lugar released a survey in which more than eighty experts "judged the probability of a major radiological attack over the next five years to be greater than the probability of a biological, chemical, or nuclear attack over the same time period... 82% (68 of 83) [of the respondents] said that there was at least a 10% chance of a radiological attack that affects a major portion of a city."[21] Some experts had previously said that it would be all but inevitable for terrorists to do a radiological attack.[22] But the lack of such attacks to date and the paucity of data on terrorists' interest appear to point to the lack of security experts' understanding of terrorists' motivations. Similarly, the security experts have generally been disconnected from terrorism experts. As terrorism expert Jerrold Post has underscored, those "who study terrorist motivation and decision making" are "underwhelmed by the probability of such an event [nuclear or radiological terrorism] *for most—but not all*—terrorist groups."[23] Notably, jihadist groups are included in his area of concern.

The first reported incident of jihadists acquiring radioactive material and demonstrating this fact was in November 1995, when then-Chechen leader Shamil Basayev called a Russian television crew to tell them that there was a partially buried container of cesium-137 in Moscow's Ismailovsky Park. But the container was not blown up. Thus, Basayev may have only wanted to show that his group could carry out a radiological attack without actually following through, achieving a psychological effect on the Russian population without risking massive retribution from Russian authorities.

Although there are no known cases of al-Qa'ida or other Islamist terrorists actually dispersing radioactive materials using a dirty bomb or some other type of radiological weapon, the U.S. Central Intelligence Agency has warned, "Construction of an RDD is well within [al-Qa'ida's] capabilities as radiological materials are relatively easy to acquire from industrial or medical sources."[24] According to press reports in April 2007, British and other European counterterrorism officials have warned that a reenergized al-Qa'ida is determined to launch a spectacular attack. One press report on the British intelligence assessment referred to several foiled plots involving dirty bombs.[25] The known cases of al-Qa'ida's interest in radiological terrorism to date, however, indicate a relatively unsophisticated understanding of how to effectively use radioactive materials.

Al-Qa'ida's efforts at radiological terrorism first made a splash on the public's consciousness with the fanfare and doom-and-gloom presentation of the U.S. government's announcement of José Padilla's apprehension. In June 2002, then–U.S. Attorney General John Ashcroft announced that Padilla, aka Abdullah al-Mujahir, was under arrest for wanting to build a radioactive dirty bomb. Ashcroft gave the alarming and erroneous impression that Padilla could have killed and injured thousands of people. Since then, the U.S. government's case against Padilla as a dirty bomber has eroded, and information about his abilities and alleged intentions have cast doubt on the government's claims.[26] A former gang member, Padilla had converted to a radical form of Islam while serving time in prison in Florida. After release from prison, he made trips to the Middle East, where he is alleged to have met al-Qa'ida leaders, who asked him to go on a scouting mission to the United States. Immediately upon landing at Chicago's O'Hare airport in May 2002, he was arrested and subsequently charged with an attempt to make a dirty bomb. About two years later, the press reported that government investigators believed that Padilla wanted to use uranium in a dirty bomb.[27] But uranium is weakly radioactive and, consequently, would not make for a very potent dirty bomb. During Padilla's federal trial in 2007, federal prosecutors dropped the dirty bomb charges due to a lack of solid evidence. In January 2008, Judge Marcia Cooke sentenced him to seventeen years and four months in prison, a lenient sentence considering the U.S. government had sought life imprisonment. Explaining the lenient sentence, Judge Cooke said that the government had not presented evidence linking Padilla and his two co-defendants to specific terrorism acts.[28]

Other jihadist-related cases point to perhaps more serious interest in radiological attacks. In January 2003, British investigators reported that al-Qa'ida may have acquired radioactive materials and then constructed a dirty bomb near Herat, Afghanistan. However, an unnamed American official told the Associated Press that the report was unsubstantiated.[29] In 2004, an al-Qa'ida–affiliated group in London allegedly wanted to build dirty bombs. Dhiren Barot, aka Issa al-Hindi, a leader of one of the group's cells, had researched information about radioactive materials and concluded that his cell could safely handle the types of radioactive material found in smoke detectors. Based on a 2004 press report, he planned to acquire about 100 smoke detectors to make a dirty bomb.[30] During his trial, other reports indicated that Barot may have considered using upwards of several thousand smoke detectors. But such a radiological weapon would create little or no harm because only tiny amounts of radioactivity are in a smoke detector. More than one million smoke detectors would be needed to fuel a potent radiological weapon. The amount of time required to scrape off the tiny amount of americium-241 on each smoke detector—from thousands or millions of detectors—would likely exceed the resources and patience of almost all terrorist groups. Conceivably, though, if terrorists had access to a smoke detector factory, they might be able to acquire enough material.

An underreported and underanalyzed aspect of Barot's scheme is how he decided to focus on smoke detectors. During the time period of 2004 when he and his group were surveying potential targets, he had downloaded information on the Internet about radioactive sources. One of those downloaded reports was "Commercial Radioactive Sources: Surveying the Security Risks," published by the Monterey Institute of International Studies.[31] As the lead author of that report, I was contacted by the FBI before Barot's trial to confirm that he had copied paragraphs of text from the Monterey Institute report without attribution. Aside from showing that at least one terrorist had accessed useful information on the Internet about radioactive sources, this case illustrates that this terrorist was dissuaded from trying to acquire highly radioactive sources because of his concerns about ionizing radiation. Thus, terrorists may fear radiation as much as many members of the general public.

While the Padilla, Afghanistan, and Barot cases illustrate either possibly hyped government allegations or amateurish capabilities, there is other evidence that jihadist or jihadist-influenced or -affiliated groups are becoming more likely to use radioactive materials in an act of terrorism. For instance, Chechen rebels could become more radicalized by their association with al-Qa'ida–affiliated groups.[32] During the early years of fighting in the 1990s, Chechen rebels, who were trying to separate Chechnya from Russia, mainly targeted their attacks on the Russian military and other symbols of Russian authority. Since then they have widened their attacks to include harming more and more civilians, as shown by the takeover of a Moscow theater in October 2002 and the school siege in Beslan in September 2004, which ended up with 330 deaths, many of them children. This shift has correlated with Chechen rebels coming into closer contact with al-Qa'ida–affiliated Islamic extremists. Thus, the Chechen rebels' motivations for launching radiological attacks may have increased.

As early as the mid-1990s, the Chechen rebels showed they have the means for such attacks. As discussed earlier, Basayev had demonstrated acquisition of a radioactive source in November 1995 but did not disperse it. In December 1999, the Russian-supported Chechen Security Service stated that it had discovered and defused a container filled with radioactive materials and connected to an explosive mine. The container was located near a railway line. In September 1999, Chechen government officials reported that unidentified thieves had attempted to steal a container full of radioactive materials from a chemical factory in Grozny, Chechnya. In late December 2006, the U.S. National Academy of Sciences published a report that described three radiological incidents in the Grozny area from 2000 to 2002. In one of the incidents, an insurgent reportedly testified to authorities that he had helped organize the theft of a radioactive source from an inactive chemical plant.[33]

Since 2006, additional evidence has pointed to increasing interest and perhaps sophistication in the use of radioactive materials by jihadists. In March 2006, the Global Issues Report discussed instructions about making radiological weapons posted on the militant Islamic online forum AlGhorabaa.net.[34] The author of the instructions states that he wants to "make the experiment easy and available for you, my brother the mujahidin, as they say, in the kitchen." Thus, he goes on to discuss how to extract radioactive radium from luminescent industrial paint by using readily available chemicals, and he describes how to wrap the extracted radioactive material in aluminum foil for insertion into conventional explosives. The author of the instructions also appears confused about the actual effects of a dirty bomb when he writes about an "explosive chain reaction ... like the Hiroshima bomb." Further casting doubt on the seriousness of these instructions, the suggested advice about using radium watch dials would likely not result in jihadists obtaining significant amounts of radium for a potent radiological weapon. Decades ago, many watch dials, for example, were painted with radium so that they would glow in the dark. This practice has been discontinued, but in principle, someone could collect old watch dials to try to extract the radium. However, each dial contains tiny amounts of radium; therefore, a radiological terrorist would have to have dozens to thousands of old watches to have enough radium to do significant harm. Radium had been employed in numerous other applications until the use peaked in the 1950s, when artificially produced radioisotopes replaced naturally occurring radium in commercial products.[35] The United States and other governments have been rounding up several thousand disused radioactive sources, including hundreds of radium sources.

In September 2006, the leader of al-Qa'ida in Iraq, Abu Hamza al-Muhajir, better known as Abu Ayyub al-Masri or "Ayyub's Father the Egyptian," called for nuclear scientists and explosive experts to assist his organization in making biological and "dirty" radioactive weapons.[36] Al-Muhajir may have been motivated to consider radiological attacks because of his group's concerns that conventional attacks could fail to achieve the group's objectives. During the first three years of the Iraq War, terrorists and insurgents relied exclusively on improvised explosive devices and other conventional weapons in their attacks. But in early 2007, insurgents blew up a chlorine container in the town of Ramadi in al-Anbar province in Iraq. Since then, there have been several attacks in Iraq using chlorine. Although these attacks have not killed large numbers of people, hundreds have been injured. Perhaps more importantly from the terrorist perspective, the chlorine attacks demonstrate a tactical innovation that could also have the broader strategic objective of even more disruption of the Iraqi economy (see Chapter 5 on chemical weapons for a more detailed analysis).

As mentioned elsewhere in this volume, economic disruption appears to be a major goal of many jihadists, and certain radiological weapons could cause substantial financial damage. In a 2007 analysis of al-Qa'ida's own writings, Sammy Salama and David Wheeler concluded that al-Qa'ida's "target selection calculus is motivated by a far more ambitious, sophisticated and sinister motive: to destroy the economy of the United States and other Western powers by striking economic targets in the West and in the Muslim world."[37] Such targets include ports, densely populated urban areas, and financial centers. For example, the World Trade Center, a leading financial center, was destroyed in al-Qa'ida's 9/11 attacks on New York. Also, Barot, who had expressed interest in simple radiological weapons, reportedly had plans to attack financial institutions and major banks in London, New York, and Washington. While Barot's proposed radiological weapons using smoke detectors would have not caused significant economic harm, more sophisticated radiological attacks could. For example, according to a 2005 report by the Center for Risk and Economic Analysis of Terrorism Events that analyzed possible radiological attacks on the ports of Los Angeles and Long Beach, medium attack scenarios involving roughly several hundred Curies of radioactivity (see Table 7.3 for a list of possible radioactive sources) were estimated to cause upwards of $200 million in port shutdown and related business expenses, and high attack scenarios involving several thousand to tens of thousands of Curies of radioactivity were projected to cause upwards of $100 billion in these types of financial damages.[38] Moreover, actual radiological attacks on ports could lead to further economic harm due to authorities deciding to shut down several other ports in anticipation of additional attacks.

Radiological attacks and economic disruption are highlighted in a document on a prominent jihadist Web site, which states:

> The important thing is to disperse radioactive material in a large commercial area so the government is forced to shut down this area which will cause this country massive economic disruption due to the following reasons:

- The high costs of decontamination of radioactive areas
- The high economic losses in this large commercial area due to closure
- Subsequent unemployment and loss of jobs
- Stoppage of general life in that area
- Large compounded problems are to follow due to these losses

> Suggested cities: Las Vegas (the city of fornication and gambling that does not sleep)—New York—London—Sydney—Tokyo—Moscow—other large tourist cities—and commercial capitals of all infidel nations.[39]

Despite evidence indicating jihadists' interest in radiological terrorism, they confront significant barriers, including governments' and industry's increasing efforts at hardening targets, securing radioactive sources, replacing certain types of sources with nonradioactive alternative technologies, and deploying radiation detectors to increase the likelihood of interdiction. Hardened targets would likely dissuade many terrorists. For example, although Mohamed Atta, one of the lead al-Qa'ida operatives in the 9/11 attacks, expressed interest in attacking a nuclear power plant near New York City, this proposal received little support among the organizers of the 9/11 attacks because they "thought a nuclear target would be difficult because the airspace around [the nuclear power plant] was restricted, making reconnaissance flights impossible and increasing the likelihood that any plane would be shot down before impact."[40] In contrast, other settings have not appeared as hardened as nuclear power plants. For instance, many highly radioactive sources are used in hospitals and universities. However, as authorities have taken steps since 9/11 in improving security at these locations, jihadists may decide that their chances of being caught while attempting to access these sources is too high. While it is conceivable that terrorists could recruit insiders at these facilities, authorities are becoming more aware of this route and are instituting background checks on employees who have access to these materials. Nonetheless, these increased security measures have not covered all facilities in all countries, thus leaving open the possibility of terrorists exploiting this access route. Governments are also stepping up efforts to secure and track powerful radioactive sources. Moreover, governments and industry are considering significant risk reduction by replacing radioactive sources that use readily dispersible materials with radioactive materials that are less dispersible or with nonradioactive alternative technologies. Furthermore, the United States, along with some other governments, are deploying radiation sensors, which, although subject to false alarms, would still increase the chances that radiological terrorists could be interdicted. Although hardening, securing, replacing, and detecting measures are individually imperfect defenses, the combined effect of all of these measures would raise the barrier to radiological attack by jihadists. But the risk of radiological attack cannot and should not be reduced to zero because substantial benefits are received from using radioactive materials safely and securely. Also, this risk will remain as long as jihadists have motivations to consider and possibly use this means of attack.

NOTES

1. Among the first experts using this term were Henry Kelly, Steven Koonin, and Michael Levi. Henry C. Kelly, Testimony before the U.S. Senate Foreign Relations Committee, March 6, 2002; Steven E. Koonin, "Radiological Terrorism," *Physics and Society*, 31(2), 2002, 12–13; and Michael A. Levi and Henry C. Kelly, "Weapons of Mass Disruption," *Scientific American*, November 2002, 76–81.
2. For a fuller treatment of this pathway analysis, see Charles D. Ferguson and William C. Potter with Amy Sands, Leonard Spector, and Fred L. Wehling, *The Four Faces of Nuclear Terrorism* (New York: Routledge, 2005), 271–278.
3. Charles D. Ferguson and Joel O. Lubenau, "Securing US Radioactive Sources," *Issues in Science and Technology*, Fall 2003, 71.
4. U.S. Government Accountability Office, "Nuclear Security: Actions Taken by NRC to Strengthen Its Licensing Process for Sealed Radioactive Sources Are Not Effective," Testimony before the Permanent Subcommittee on Investigations, Committee on Homeland Security and Governmental Affairs, U.S. Senate, GAO-07-1038T, July 12, 2007.
5. Joby Warrick, "Smugglers Enticed by Dirty Bomb Components: Radioactive Materials are Sought Worldwide," *Washington Post*, November 30, 2003, A1.
6. International Atomic Energy Agency, Illicit Trafficking Database, information about it available at http://www-ns.iaea.org/security/itdb.htm (accessed on February 7, 2008).
7. Sonia Ben Ouagrham-Gormley, "An Unrealized Nexus? WMD-related Trafficking, Terrorism, and Organized Crime in the Former Soviet Union," *Arms Control Today*, July/August 2007.
8. See Argonne National Laboratory's radiological and chemical fact sheets for detailed information on the properties of the radioisotopes of concern, available at http://www.ead.anl.gov/pub/doc/ANL_ContaminantFactSheets_All_070418.pdf (accessed on January 29, 2008).
9. International Atomic Energy Agency, "Categorization of Radioactive Sources," IAEA-TECDOC-1344, July 2003, 4.
10. Ibid.
11. For example, Joel O. Lubenau and Charles D. Ferguson, "Security of Radioactive Sources in the United States," *NIS Export Control Observer*, July 2004, available at http://cns.miis.edu/pubs/nisexcon/pdfs/ob_0407e.pdf (accessed on January 29, 2008).

12. "Categorization of Radioactive Sources," op. cit., 9.
13. Charles D. Ferguson, Tahseen Kazi, and Judith Perera, Commercial Radioactive Sources: Surveying the Security Risks, Occasional Paper No. 11, Monterey Institute of International Studies, January 2003, and Gregory J. van Tuyle, Tiffany L. Strub, Harold A. O. Brien, Caroline F. V. Mason, and Steven J. Gitomer, *Reducing the RDD Concerns Related to Large Radiological Source Applications*, LA-UR-03-6664, Los Alamos National Laboratory, September 2003.
14. Frederick T. Harper, Stephen V. Musolino, and William B. Wente, "Realistic Radiological Dispersal Device Hazard Boundaries and Ramifications for Early Consequence Management Decisions," *Health Physics*, July 2007, 1–16.
15. Peter D. Zimmerman with Cheryl Loeb, "Dirty Bombs: The Threat Revisited," *Defense Horizons*, 28, January 2004.
16. Dennis M. Gormley, "Globalization and WMD Proliferation Networks: The Case of Unmanned Air Vehicles as Terrorist Weapons," *Strategic Insights*, 5(6), July 2006, available at http://www.ccc.nps.navy.mil/si/2006/Jul/gormleyJul06.pdf (accessed on January 28, 2008).
17. Steve Bowman and Helit Barel, "Weapons of Mass Destruction—the Terrorist Threat," *CRS Report for Congress*, December 8, 1999.
18 James M. Acton, M. Brooke Rogers, and Peter D. Zimmerman, "Beyond the Dirty Bomb: Re-thinking Radiological Terror," *Survival*, Autumn 2007, 152.
19. Ibid.
20. Joseph W. Pfeifer, *Improvised Incendiary Devices: Risk Assessment, Threats, Vulnerabilities, and Consequences*, Master's Thesis (Monterey: Naval Postgraduate School, September 2006).
21. Richard G. Lugar, "The Lugar Survey on Proliferation Threats and Responses," Office of Senator Richard G. Lugar, Chairman of U.S. Senate Foreign Relations Committee, June 2005.
22. Keay Davidson, "Dirty Bomb Called 'All But Inevitable,'" *San Francisco Chronicle*, September 5, 2004.
23. Jerrold M. Post, "Differentiating the Threat of Radiological/Nuclear Terrorism: Motivations and Constraints," Paper for IAEA Symposium on International Safeguards, Verification, and Nuclear Material Security, November 2, 2001.
24. Directorate of Intelligence, "Terrorist CBRN: Materials and Effects (U)," Central Intelligence Agency, May 2003.
25. Ian MacLeod, "Al Qaeda Plotting Radioactive Attack on West," *The Ottawa Citizen*, April 23, 2007.
26. Lewis Z. Koch, "Dirty Bomber? Dirty Justice," *Bulletin of the Atomic Scientists*, January/February 2004.
27. Charles J. Hanley, "Much Less to Padilla 'Dirty Bomb' Than Meets Feds' Eyes, Scientists Say," Associated Press, June 9, 2004.
28. Kirk Semple, "Padilla Gets 17 Years in Conspiracy Case," *New York Times*, January 23, 2008.
29. Associated Press, "BBC Says al Qaeda Produced a 'Dirty Bomb' in Afghanistan," *New York Times*, January 31, 2003.
30. Adam Zagorin and Elaine Shannon, "London's Dirty Bomb Plot," *Time*, October 3, 2004.
31. Ferguson, Kazi, and Perera, op. cit.

32. Jeffrey M. Bale, "The Chechen Resistance and Radiological Terrorism," NTI Issue Brief, April 2004, http://www.nti.org/e_research/e3_47a.html (accessed on February 6, 2008).
33. Committee on Opportunities for US-Russian Collaboration in Combating Radiological Terrorism, *US-Russian Collaboration in Combating Radiological Terrorism*, National Research Council (Washington, DC: The National Academies Press, 2007), 47.
34. Center for International Issues Research, "Dirty Bomb Instructions Posted on Hostile Web Forum," Global Issues Report, March 2, 2006.
35. Joel O. Lubenau, "A Century's Challenges: Historical Overview of Radiation Sources in the USA," *IAEA Bulletin*, 41/3/1999, 49–54.
36. Associated Press, "Zarqawi Successor Exhorts Scientists: Tape Urges Experts to Join Fight in Iraq," *Washington Post*, September 29, 2006, A15.
37. Sammy Salama and David Wheeler, "From the Horse's Mouth: Unraveling Al-Qa'ida's Target Selection Calculus," CNS Research Story, April 17, 2007.
38. Heather Rosoff and Detlof von Winterfeldt, "A Risk and Economic Analysis of Dirty Bomb Attacks on the Ports of Los Angeles and Long Beach," Center for Risk and Economic Analysis of Terrorism Events (CREATE), University of Southern California, October 2005.
39. Abu al-Usood al-Faqir, "Instances of Radiation Pollution from 1945–1987," *al-Farouq Jihadist Web site*, October 2005, as quoted and translated in Salama and Wheeler, op. cit.
40. National Commission on Terrorist Attacks, *9/11 Commission Report: Final Report of the National Commission on Terrorist Attacks Upon the United States* (New York: W. W. Norton and Company, 2004), 245.

CHAPTER 8

Jihadists and Nuclear Weapons

Charles P. Blair

CONTENTS

INTRODUCTION

On December 1, 2001, CIA Director George Tenet made a hastily planned, clandestine trip to Pakistan. Tenet arrived in Islamabad deeply shaken by the news that less than three months earlier—just weeks before the attacks of September 11, 2001—al-Qa'ida and Taliban leaders had met with two former Pakistani nuclear weapon scientists in a joint quest to acquire nuclear weapons. Captured documents the scientists abandoned as they fled Kabul from advancing anti-Taliban forces were evidence, in the minds of top U.S. officials, that a nuclear device was now "within reach" of al-Qa'ida.[1]

As Tenet's motorcade sped to a meeting with President Pervez Musharraf at Pakistan's Presidential Palace, present then were many of the elements that today have come together to form a possible nexus of jihadists and nuclear weapons, a nightmarish merging that, sadly, is more likely today than it was it was in 2001. Tenet's journey was in direct response to the attacks of 9/11; al-Qa'ida long battled the Soviets as well, and the subsequent collapse of that empire has left the world awash in potential sources of nuclear weapons and materials. Tenet's arrival coincided with the beginning of the battle of Tora Bora; Usama bin Ladin would escape, and, today, it is generally understood that al-Qa'ida has established a safe haven in Pakistan. Having "reconstituted its attack capability," al-Qa'ida undoubtedly continues its quest for nuclear weapons.[2] Tenet's convoy passed monuments to Pakistan's "great victory of building a nuclear bomb"; seven years later, its nuclear arsenal would make Pakistan, in the eyes of many experts, "the most dangerous country on earth."[3] Tenet's visit with President Musharraf solidified the seven-part agreement the United States had reached with Pakistan immediately after the attacks of 9/11; left intentionally unmentioned by both countries were the well-known proliferation activities of the A.Q. Kahn Network—deals that could portent nuclear transfers to terrorists.[4]

Thus, while the threat of nuclear terrorism has loomed for over half a century, current— that is, post-9/11—nuclear trepidation is indelibly intertwined with the publicly perceived paragons of terrorism: jihadists.[5] This chapter collectively examines the nexus of jihadists and nuclear weapons in four ways. The first section acquaints the reader with relevant nuclear weapon designs and the source of their explosive power—fissile materials. The second section presents a summary of intact nuclear weapons—specifically where jihadists might acquire them. The third section examines known jihadist activities and interests with regard to nuclear weapons. The fourth section looks at the overall likelihood of jihadists obtaining a nuclear capability. Finally, readers should be aware that the appendix to this chapter gives a brief history of the physics behind nuclear weapons. This section is placed as an appendix because it is not essential that the reader have an understanding of these principles in order to appreciate the potential merging of jihadists with nuclear weapons. However, it does offer the ability to approach the subject with a more nuanced understanding of how, in just fifty years, the field of nuclear physics went from innocuous x-rays to weapons of almost unimaginable fury.

While other chapters in this book deal in great depth with the calculus that determines jihadists' attitudes, proclivities, and strategic calculus toward chemical, biological, radioactive, and nuclear (CBRN) weapons in general, it is useful to consider what jihadists likely would hope to gain from a *nuclear* option. Jihadists' decisions to pursue a nuclear weapon would probably be informed by one or more of the following eight factors:

1. *Tactical concerns*: To achieve a first strike weapon or to forestall enemy action.
2. *Strategic concerns*: To help achieve military symmetry or superiority. Additionally, jihadists might perceive nuclear weapons as an effective political bargaining (blackmail) tool.
3. *Religious "duties"*: Usama bin Ladin has been widely quoted as saying that, "To seek to possess the weapons that could counter those of the infidels is a religious duty.... It would be a sin for Muslims not to seek possession of the weapons that

would prevent the infidels from inflicting harm on Muslims."[6] Some jihadists, moreover, have strong millenarian impulses; consequently, there is a strong psychological link between the kinds of destruction only imaginable with nuclear weapons and, what Robert Jay Lifton has deemed, "the relentless impulse toward world-rejecting purification."[7]

4. *The escalatory nature of some forms of terrorism*: Jihadists, in short, likely seek to outdo the destruction wrought by the attacks of September 11, 2001.
5. *Prestige*: A jihadist group publicly armed with a nuclear weapon (or having successfully detonated one, even one with a "fizzle" yield) would arguably enjoy enormous popularity in the Muslim world and could, consequently, garner greater financial and recruitment opportunities.
6. *Political advantages*: Some jihadists might perceive the acquisition of a nuclear weapon as a step toward formal international recognition and even statehood.[8]
7. *Opportunities*: The decision to attempt to procure intact nuclear devices or fissile materials might simply boil down to opportunity. If nuclear-armed governments collapse, and if general chaos ensues, jihadists might find procurement efforts well-rewarded.
8. *Revenge*: Usama bin Ladin's former official press spokesman, Suleiman Abu Gheith, asserted in 2002 that al-Qa'ida has the "right to kill four million Americans" in retaliation for, among other things, sanctions and enforcement of UN resolutions against Iraq ("1.2 million dead"), U.S. support of policies "against Palestinians" ("260,000 dead"), U.S. actions in Somalia ("12,000 dead"), and the U.S. war in Afghanistan ("12,000 dead").[9]

Jihadists seeking a nuclear capability have two broad options. First, they can attempt to indigenously build their own device. In this case, however, external procurement options still exist; they could, for example, theoretically fashion all the non-nuclear components of the warhead, turning then to external sources for the weapon's *nuclear* components, that is, fissile material. Second, jihadists could attempt to secure an *entire* nuclear device that has already been fabricated, either from a state or the putative nuclear weapons black market. The following two sections explore these two methods of fabrication and acquisition. [10]

IMPROVISED NUCLEAR DEVICES (INDs)

Nuclear weapons draw their explosive force from fission, fusion, or a combination of these two methods. The latter two of these weapon types are considered far too sophisticated for fabrication by contemporary jihadists, and, thus, this study only considers the production of fission-type nuclear weapons. Such weapons use fissile materials to generate their explosive properties. (See the appendix at the end of this chapter for a full accounting of the physics behind fission.) While over twenty fissionable isotopes exist (Table 8.1), most of them are only found in very minute—gram size or smaller—quantities. Moreover, many of these fissile materials have isotopic properties that make their use in an IND problematic. This chapter, therefore, mainly examines highly enriched uranium (HEU)[11] and plutonium—the most ideal isotopes with which to fuel an IND. Readers should be aware, however, that other isotopes likely pose a significant danger vis-à-vis INDs, most notably uranium-233, neptunium-237, and americium.[12]

TABLE 8.1 Fissioinable Isotopes

Isotope	Availability	Possible Fission Weapon Types	Bare Critical Mass
Uranium-233	LOW: DOE reportedly stores more than one metric ton of U-233.	Gun-type or implosion-type	15 kg
Uranium-235	HIGH: As of 2007, 1700 metric tons of HEU existed globally, in both civilian and military stocks.	Gun-type or implosion-type	50 kg
Plutonium-238	HIGH: A separated global stock, both civilian and military, of over 500 tons. Produced in military and civilian reactor fuels. Typically, reactor-grade plutonium (RGP) consists of roughly 60 percent plutonium-239, 25 percent plutonium-240, 9 percent plutonium-241, 5 percent plutonium-242, and 1 percent plutonium-238 (these percentages are influenced by how long the fuel is irradiated in the reactor). Large quantities found in spent nuclear fuel.	Implosion	10 kg
Plutonium-239		Implosion	10 kg
Plutonium-240		Implosion	40 kg
Plutonium-241		Implosion	10–13 kg
Plutonium-242		Implosion	89—-100 kg
Protactinium-231	VERY LOW: Produced in isotope production reactors. Very small quantities exist for research.	Gun-type or implosion-type	162 kg
Neptunium-236	VERY LOW: Very small amounts found in scientific research (it has no commercial use).	Implosion	7 kg
Neptunium-237	HIGH: An estimated 54 tons globally. Small amounts found in commercial and scientific applications. Large quantities found in spent nuclear fuel.	Gun-type or implosion-type	59–60 kg
Americium-241	HIGH: Total for all americium (241, 242m, 243) estimated to be 87 tons. Small amounts found in commercial and scientific applications. Larger quantities found in spent nuclear fuel.	Implosion-type	57 kg–100 kg
Americium-242m	LOW: Small amounts found in commercial and scientific applications. Large quantities found in spent nuclear fuel.	Implosion-type	9–18 kg
Americium-243	LOW: Small amounts found in commercial and scientific applications. Larger quantities found in spent nuclear fuel.	Implosion-type	50–155kg
Curium-243	VERY LOW: Available in milligram quantities only. Found in spent reactor fuels.	Gun-type or implosion-type	7–10 kg
Curium-244	VERY LOW: Available in milligram quantities only. Found in spent reactor fuels.	Implosion-type	30 kg

TABLE 8.1 Fissioinable Isotopes (continued)

Isotope	Availability	Possible Fission Weapon Types	Bare Critical Mass
Curium-245	VERY LOW: Available in milligram quantities only. Found in spent reactor fuels.	Implosion-type (possibly a gun-type candidate)	10–13 kg
Curium-246	VERY LOW: Available in milligram quantities only. Found in spent reactor fuels.	Implosion-type	39–84 kg
Curium-247	VERY LOW: Available in milligram quantities only. Found in spent reactor fuels.	Implosion-type (possibly a gun-type candidate)	7 kg
Berkelium-247	Has not yet been fabricated in an elemental form.	Implosion-type (possibly a gun-type candidate)	10 kg
Californium-249	VERY LOW: Very small bulk quantities found in spent reactor fuels.	Implosion-type	6 kg
Californium-251	VERY LOW: Very small bulk quantities found in spent reactor fuels.	Implosion-type (possibly a gun-type candidate)	9 kg

When fissile materials undergo fission, they release both energy and neutrons. These escaping neutrons can cause other nuclei to fission, releasing more energy and neutrons in what is termed a chain reaction. This cycle can repeat itself until either (1) the chain reaction dies out as all the neutrons escape due to a lack of fissile material or density—a subcritical mass, (2) there is a precise balance between neutrons lost and neutrons produced—a critical mass, or (3) the number of fissioning nuclei grows exponentially and ultimately releases an enormous amount of energy—a supercritical mass (a nuclear explosion). The goal for jihadists would be to utilize this last example: a rapidly achieved chain reaction that utilizes very large quantities of atomic nuclei. This objective could be met either by bringing two just-below critical masses rapidly together, or by changing the density of a subcritical mass into a supercritical configuration.

The weapon used on Hiroshima, Japan, in 1945 utilized technologies employing the former method. The mechanics of this kind of weapon, a so-called "gun-type" device, are quite basic; indeed, the first such mechanism was not even tested before it was employed against the Japanese. The design can include very few major components. Because of plutonium's relatively high rate of spontaneous neutron emission, use of it in a gun-type weapon would likely result in the device blowing apart before any substantial nuclear yield could occur; plutonium is therefore generally unsuitable for this type of weapon.[13] Thus, a gun-type device typically uses the barrel of a small artillery piece to fire one slug of just-below critical mass HEU into a mass of stationary just-below critical mass HEU. In addition to the gun's barrel and the HEU, a chemical explosive propellant is required to drive the HEU masses together. The final broad requirement is some kind of firing circuitry. Once the firing mechanism is triggered, the propellant drives one slug of HEU down the gun's barrel and toward the stationary mass of HEU. When the masses get to within 25 centimeters of one another, they become critical and, once they meet, they become supercritical.[14]

Utilizing approximately 60 kilograms (kg) of HEU, the gun-type weapon employed over Hiroshima had a yield of 16 kilotons, or 16,000 tons of TNT.[15]

The nuclear weapon detonated over Nagasaki, Japan, demonstrates the other type of fission weapon design that jihadists could plausibly use: a so-called "implosion-type" device. Rather than propelling two subcritical fissionable masses together, this weapon type *implodes* a single just-below critical mass of fissionable material, increasing, by a factor of two or more, the density of the mass into a supercritical configuration (i.e., only the *volume* of the plutonium changes, not the total *mass*). Because implosion-type devices compress the fissile mass extremely fast, either HEU or plutonium (or, theoretically, other fissionable isotopes) can be used to fuel the weapon—their relatively high neutron emission rates are not a complicating factor as they are in the gun-type device.

Implosion-type devices are much more complex than gun-type weapons. For example, they require the production of roughly 100 simultaneous explosions spread evenly over a subcritical mass of plutonium or HEU.[16] The arrangements of these explosives are called lenses, and their task is to perfectly compress substances of different size and density uniformly—an extremely challenging mission.[17] Properly employed, explosive lenses cumulatively produce pressures above 10 million pounds per square inch, compressing the subcritical mass into a supercritical nuclear explosion.[18] The implosion bomb used on Nagasaki, which employed 6 kg of weapons-grade plutonium, had a yield of 22 kilotons.[19]

Fissile Materials

With regard to fissionable materials, jihadists seeking to fabricate an IND have two acquisition possibilities. Jihadists might consider fabricating fissionable materials themselves, although, as detailed below, this is a highly unlikely route; they would be far more likely to look to external sources for their nuclear materials.

Indigenous Fissile Material Fabrication

Because of the enormous resources and technical sophistication needed for its production, production of HEU by nonstate actors has been generally dismissed as implausible for even the most sophisticated terrorists. (As noted below, plutonium is produced by irradiating uranium-238 in nuclear reactors; indigenous production of it by jihadists is extremely unlikely—they would obviously seek to develop HEU long before they considered plutonium options.) However, nonstate actors have pursued indigenous uranium enrichment alternatives in the past. Most notable among these groups was Aum Shinrikyo. This millenarian cult, best known for its infamous Tokyo, Japan, sarin gas attack in 1995, went as far as purchasing a sheep farm in Australia thought to be rich in uranium deposits.[20] The cult hoped to produce HEU by mining the uranium, converting it to uranium hexafluoride, and enriching it via laser isotope separation. Al-Qa'ida, during its time of sanctuary in Afghanistan from 1996 to 2001, reportedly looked into enrichment options as well.[21]

While experts do not foresee any changes in enrichment technologies that would allow for quick and easy production of enriched uranium, there exists a slim chance that such know-how could develop some time in this century.[22] Thus, it is conceivable that jihadists could secure uranium deposits and develop enrichment techniques at some point in the future if, as Graham Allison notes, "terrorist groups can rent a state [and secure] assistance from the international nuclear black market."[23] Given the fact that a nexus between state sanctuary and the alleged black market is presently unlikely, it is assumed that jihadists will be unable to plausibly pursue a nuclear weapon with the use of indigenously produced fissile materials for the foreseeable future. Thus, jihadists will have to turn to willing states, theft, seizure, or the putative nuclear black market to secure plutonium or HEU.

External Procurement of Fissile Materials

Current inventories of fissile materials are vast: As much as 2000 metric tons of HEU and 500 metric tons of separated plutonium, virtually all weapon-usable, exist globally.[24] As for the former, over 99 percent of the global HEU stockpile is in the custody of just seven states: Russia and the United States possess the vast majority, with France, the United Kingdom, and China having significant stores.[25] The amount of HEU in Pakistan and India is a fraction of the other nuclear weapon states, yet of all of the countries just mentioned, they are the only states that presently continue to produce HEU. The remaining global stockpile of HEU—less than 1 percent of the world's total—is spread out among 40 countries, in about 100 sites worldwide.[26] The vast majority of this HEU, as discussed below, is found in research reactors.

Two hundred and fifty metric tons of separated plutonium presently exist in military stockpiles with an additional 250 metric tons (separated as well) found in civilian stocks.[27] Over a dozen countries house these inventories, with Russia and the United States possessing the vast majority. France, Germany, and the United Kingdom all hold large stocks. Belgium, China, India, Israel, Japan, North Korea, Pakistan, and Switzerland also have inventories of separated plutonium.[28]

Jihadists could obtain HEU or plutonium in several forms and in a variety of settings. Notable among these are (1) weapons-grade plutonium or uranium, (2) oxide forms of uranium and plutonium, (3) plutonium found in spent nuclear fuels, and (4) HEU found in nonpower reactors, specifically research reactors.

Weapons-Grade Uranium and Plutonium

Metallic forms of uranium or plutonium would be the most ideal structure of fissionable materials for jihadists seeking to construct an IND. "Weapons-grade" material consists of either metallic uranium enriched to 90 percent or more uranium-235 or metallic plutonium containing 90 percent or more plutonium-239. In comparison to other forms fissionable materials might take, the purity and form of metallic weapons-grade material can substantially enhance the destructiveness, reliability, and deliverability of an IND.

Weapons-grade uranium can be employed in either a gun-type or an implosion-type IND, although more of it is needed when compared to weapons-grade plutonium (the bare critical mass of weapons-grade uranium is just over 50 kg. For weapons-grade plutonium the bare critical mass is around 11 kg).[29] Uranium's appeal is further bolstered by its relatively low signature—when compared to plutonium—vis-à-vis radiation detectors.

Although less weapons-grade plutonium is needed to fuel an IND compared to one utilizing uranium, jihadists would face several challenges with the material. Plutonium is "so unusual as to approach the unbelievable," wrote plutonium pioneer Glenn Seaborg in 1967. "Under some conditions it is as hard and brittle as glass; under others, as soft as plastic or lead. It will burn[30] and crumble quickly to powder when heated in air, or slowly disintegrate when kept at room temperature.... And it is fiendishly toxic, even in small amounts."[31]

In addition to plutonium's challenging physical properties described by Seaborg, jihadists would likely encounter three other difficulties in trying to utilize it in an IND. First, since there is no substitute for plutonium—chemically or in a metallurgical sense—jihadists would be unable to perform critical implosion tests prior to actual acquisition of the material (i.e., determining how best to utilize lenses so as to perfectly implode plutonium). In contrast, natural uranium can be used to simulate many of the properties of enriched uranium. Second, plutonium is usually much more detectable than uranium.[32] Finally, plutonium is extremely deadly and requires somewhat complicated handling capabilities; accidental inhalation, even by jihadists willing to sacrifice their lives in the fabrication of an IND, could lead to incapacitation via acute radiation poisoning.

Weapons-grade uranium and plutonium can be found in nuclear weapons, at nuclear weapons production and assembly/disassembly facilities, at nuclear laboratories, and on specific transportation links. Moreover, weapons-grade plutonium can be found at reprocessing facilities that are specifically designed to produce plutonium for nuclear weapons. The United States, for example, presently has weapons-grade materials spread among twelve Department of Energy (DOE) sites.[33] Security at some of these facilities has often been strongly criticized.[34] Furthermore, every year, two non-DOE sites handle tons of weapons-grade uranium for power reactors (the facilities blend the HEU into low enriched uranium—LEU) and U.S. Navy propulsion reactors. Security at these latter facilities has reportedly been sharply criticized in classified U.S. governmental reports.[35]

Oxide Forms of Uranium and Plutonium

If jihadists were able to acquire oxide forms of HEU and plutonium, they could theoretically use them to fuel an IND in one of two ways. In the first scenario, once jihadists obtained enough of the oxide—for example, from fuel fabrication facilities or civilian reprocessing plants—they would ideally convert it into metal. This would give the jihadists increased confidence that the weapon would successfully detonate with a reasonably high yield while enhancing delivery options by reducing the overall weight and bulk of the IND. While converting oxide to metal is considered by experts to be "within the reach of a dedicated technical team," it is still a complicated and time-consuming chemical operation.[36]

The other option is to use the oxide directly, with no post-acquisition processing. The drawback to this route, notes one nuclear weaponeer, is that it would require quantities "large enough to appear troublesome."[37] Still, if very well compacted, the critical mass of plutonium oxide is reportedly about "one and a half times as large" as that of metallic plutonium.[38] Other reports indicate that as little as 110 kg of uranium oxide and 35 kg of plutonium oxide (both at full crystal density) could function as bare critical masses for an IND.[39]

In addition to the disadvantage of having to grapple with copious amounts of oxide materials, there are two other general drawbacks, from a jihadist's perspective, to utilizing oxides. First, proper implosion of such quantities of oxide would likely require very large quantities of explosives, increasing the weight of the IND considerably.[40] Second, oxide-fueled INDs are likely to produce relatively small yields. With its longer neutron generation time, plutonium oxide, for example, would not likely produce a yield nearly the size of that generated by metallic plutonium.[41]

Plutonium Acquired from Spent Nuclear Fuels

Every year the world's nuclear reactors produce about 10,000 tons of spent nuclear fuel, 75 tons of which is plutonium.[42] Jihadists could theoretically fuel an IND with less than 15 kg of this so-called reactor-grade plutonium (RGP). RGP is fabricated in commercial nuclear reactors around the world. Global stockpiles of separated civil plutonium totaled, at the end of 2005, roughly 250 metric tons (enough for 40,000 nuclear weapons).[43] The process begins when the uranium-235 (contained in rods within the reactor) fissions, or "burns," bathing uranium-238 with neutrons (most fresh-fuel rods consist of 3–5 percent uranium-235 and approximately 95 percent uranium-238). Over time, some of the uranium-238 absorbs neutrons, becoming plutonium-239. The longer the plutonium stays in the reactor, however, the more neutrons it absorbs and, thus, significant amounts of plutonium-240, plutonium-241, and plutonium-242 are also fabricated.[44] Over time the fuel rods are removed and the so-called "spent" fuel can then be chemically separated via a process known as reprocessing. The broken down fuel typically consists of the unfissioned uranium-235 (about 1 percent), reactor-grade plutonium (about 1 percent), uranium-238 (about 93 percent), and fission fragments and other transuranics (totaling about 5 percent).

It is important to understand what exactly comprises the separated plutonium. Typically, RGP consists of roughly 60 percent plutonium-239, 25 percent plutonium-240, 6 percent plutonium-241, 5 percent plutonium-242, 1 percent plutonium-238,[45] and 3 percent americium-241 (these percentages are influenced by how long the fuel is irradiated in the reactor).[46]

All of these isotopes are fissionable. Indeed, nuclear weaponeer J. Carson Mark has noted, "that a bare critical assembly could be made with plutonium metal *no matter what its isotopic composition might be*."[47] Yet for decades the public was under the impression that, due to the properties of plutonium isotopes that were not plutonium-239 (e.g., isotopes with very high spontaneous neutron emission rates), a nuclear warhead could not be plausibly fueled with RGP. As Manhattan Project veteran Leona Marshall Libby explained, this erroneous belief began with the Los Alamos scientists themselves and their initial hope that RGP "might be spiked with so much plutonium-240 as to make stolen plutonium useless for clandestine bombs...."[48] However, in 1972 U.S. officials publicly acknowledged that by employing relatively simply design modifications, RGP could be used to successfully fuel a sizable nuclear yield.[49] "Clever bomb design," Libby noted a few years later, "has improved to the point that plutonium-240 can be made into an effective bomb. [...]What once was hoped to be a safeguard against clandestine terrorism is now little defense at all."[50]

HEU Acquired from Research Reactors

HEU is employed in over 130 research reactors around the world.[51] While most typical commercial power reactors are in the 3,000 megawatt (MW) range, research reactors vary in size from 1 MW to 250 MW.[52] Yet, despite their size, research reactors can possess significant quantities of HEU: As recently as 2004, 128 research reactors and their associated facilities possessed 20 kg of HEU or more.[53]

In addition to potentially possessing large amounts of HEU, research reactors have four other unique qualities that could make them of great interest to HEU-seeking jihadists. First, as noted in this book's radiological section (Chapter 7), research reactor fuels are often man-portable—the fuel rods are "often less than a meter long, several centimeters across, and weighing a few kilograms."[54] Second, separating HEU from other elements in the reactor fuel, while complex, is not an overwhelming task for a resourceful terrorist group.[55] Experts have noted that "the chemistry involved in converting opium poppies to heroin...is probably roughly as complex as the chemistry required to separate uranium from research reactor fuel...."[56] Third, irradiated research reactor fuels are very highly enriched. Indeed, whereas commercial nuclear power plants routinely have spent fuels that are 3 to 5 percent enriched, experts note with apprehension that "many fresh research reactor fuels are 90 percent enriched and are still more than 80 percent enriched after irradiation."[57]

Finally, jihadists might have a particular interest in research reactors because they are generally perceived to have lower security levels when compared to other potential sources of HEU and plutonium. Many countries have little to no security around their research reactors and "simply rely on the cavalry coming" in the event of some kind of terrorist incursion.[58] In Russia, for example, which has more HEU-fueled research reactors than any other country in the world, most civilian research reactor sites do not have the security to withstand a sophisticated assault by terrorists, nor are they likely immune to subterfuge by multiple insiders acting in unison.[59]

More Advanced Fission Weapon Designs: Initiators and Reflectors

Jihadists seeking to bolster the reliability and efficiency of the gun- and implosion-type INDs outlined above could attempt to enhance their weapons in two ways. First, they could employ a device that emits a burst of neutrons, at just the right time, to assist in triggering the chain reaction—a so-called "initiator." If a neutron initiator is not used, the IND must utilize background neutrons to trigger the chain reaction or the jihadists would risk a "fizzle yield." Yet, in order for a gun-type IND to work with only these background neutrons (i.e., without an initiator), the device's assembly must be crafted to "hold the bullet in place after it has been fired, for tens of millionths of seconds"—a significant engineering challenge.[60] Alternatively, jihadists could simply fit the IND with a "source that continually emitted neutrons"; however, this would dramatically decrease the yield of the device and might likely result in predetonation.[61]

The other enhancement jihadists might consider is a reflector: a device located around the bomb's fissile material that returns neutrons back into the fissioning mass during criticality.[62] As early as 1943 it was understood by physicists at Los Alamos that a reflector could serve, "not only to retard the escape of neutrons but also by its inertia to retard the expansion of the active material [...] thus giving the opportunity of the reaction to proceed further before it is stopped by the expansion."[63] Thus, the term *reflector* is a bit misleading; experts often use the expression *tamper* as well to describe this latter role of weakening or interfering with the expansion of the fissile core.[64] While the use of a reflector reduced the critical mass needed for the Nagasaki implosion weapon by 15 percent, far greater reductions of critical masses are presently possible with proper use of a reflector[65] (see Table 8.2).

TABLE 8.2 Effect of Reflector on Critical Mass[a]

Percentage of Uranium-235	Reflector Thickness (Utilizing Beryllium)		
	None	5 cm	15 cm
15%	1351.0 kg	758.3 kg	253.8 kg
30%	367.4 kg	171.2 kg	68.7 kg
45%	184.7 kg	80.5 kg	35.6 kg
70%	87.2 kg	36.5 kg	18.2 kg
93%	53.3 kg	22.3 kg	11.7 kg

[a] Alexander Glaser, "On the Proliferation Potential of Uranium Fuel for Research Reactors at Various Enrichment Levels," *Science & Global Security*, 14(1): 18, (2006), http://www.princeton.edu/~aglaser/2006aglaser_sgsvol14.pdf (accessed 03/01/08).

LIKELY IND CONSTRUCTION

The proceeding discussion implies that jihadists would have several options with which to design and fuel an IND. The reality, however, is that jihadists will likely have to design an IND based on whatever materials they are able to secure. Thus, one can look at an *ideal* weapon (if all of the above materials were available) and a *likely* weapon choice (if only the most probable fissile materials were available).

Initially, one might suppose that an implosion device might be ideal for jihadists. Such a device, especially one equipped with an initiator and a reflector, could be relatively light (adding to its deployability), reliable, and destructive (a yield of 10–20 kilotons).[66] It could theoretically utilize all of the fissile materials outlined above and in far fewer quantities than those needed for a gun-type device. However, there are several disadvantages to the implosion-type device. Most obviously, the required levels of technological sophistication necessary for its fabrication pose one engineering challenge after another, and, even after the device was completed, it would be less rugged and, thus, potentially more prone to malfunctions that a gun-type device. If jihadists wanted to enhance the reliability of their implosion weapon, the device would have to go through a series of tests, some of which would require plutonium. Moreover, use of impure fissile materials—reactor-grade plutonium, for example—could lead to a "fizzle yield." (Such a predetonation could still result in a yield as high as 2 kilotons.[67]) The North Korean nuclear test of 2006 is revealing in this regard. While some experts attribute the blast's relatively small yield—between 0.5 and 2 kilotons[68]—to the use of plutonium that was high in plutonium-240, it seems more probable that the yield was a likely result of an imperfect implosion design. "I don't think that it was a problem of the isotopics," observed former Los Alamos National Laboratory (LANL) director Dr. Siegfried Hecker. "The [North Korean] rudimentary design just didn't work; in the end it is difficult to get a perfectly spherical implosion."[69]

Because of easier fabrication requirements and a greater theoretical availability of HEU (which is also harder to detect than plutonium), a gun-type device would be a much more practical and likely design route for jihadists to take. (Although experts frequently assert that plutonium could not be used in a gun-type device, the reality is that use of plutonium could result in a "fizzle yield" resulting in widespread physical damage and enormous psychological harm over a wide target area.[70])

As already noted, the reliability and yield of a gun-type device could be augmented with the use of an initiator and/or a reflector. Fabrication of the former, while requiring technical sophistication, is not viewed by some experts as particularly difficult to design and manufacture.[71] Crude nuclear weapons have typically employed neutron initiators that utilized the neutrons produced when beryllium, or some other light element, is bombarded by alpha particles.[72] Thus, the acquisition of a suitable alpha emitter appears to be the biggest obstacle jihadists would likely face in fabricating and utilizing a neutron initiator.[73] The alternative, to forego a neutron initiator entirely, risks a fizzle yield or requires an IND engineered to extremely precise specifications.

Natural and depleted uranium can be used as a reflector for implosion weapons; however, these materials emit too many neutrons for use in a gun-type weapon.[74] Alternative reflector materials, suitable for both types of fission weapons, include beryllium, tungsten, and, possibly, iron.[75] As with an initiator, the greatest challenge jihadists likely face as they seek to employ a reflector is obtaining such materials.[76]

In sum, while ultimately the design of an IND would likely be determined by the fissile materials that jihadists are able to acquire, a gun-type device that utilizes uranium is the most plausible. Use of an initiator and/or reflector would dramatically enhance the reliability of the weapon while reducing the amount of fissile materials needed. However, the fabrication of an initiator and/or reflector would, in itself, add additional technical and resource hurdles that would likely be insurmountable to all but the most resourceful jihadists. Many observers have concluded, consequently, that any IND fabricated by terrorists would utilize a gun-type design that forgoes both an initiator and a reflector.[77] Such a device would be prone to predetonation and might likely "fizzle" when employed.

EXTERNAL PROCUREMENT OF INTACT NUCLEAR WEAPONS

For over fifteen years, there have been reports of jihadist groups attempting to procure intact nuclear devices. To date, these efforts are believed to have been unsuccessful, yet by all indications it appears that the quest continues. This section examines two sources from which jihadists might plausibly acquire an intact nuclear weapon: a state with an existing nuclear stockpile or the putative nuclear black market.

State Acquisition of an Intact Nuclear Weapon

Safety from Unauthorized Use

Nine states presently possess nuclear weapons: the United States, Russia, the United Kingdom, France, China, Israel, India, Pakistan, and North Korea. Experts generally foresee two to five new nations joining the nuclear club in the next ten years—most notably Iran.[78] While this section argues that willing state transfer of a nuclear weapon to jihadists is highly unlikely with all nuclear arsenals, there are deep and generally legitimate security concerns with regard to the Russian, North Korean, and Pakistani arsenals.

If jihadists were able to obtain an intact nuclear weapon, its detonation could be prevented by various technological barriers that have been employed by some nuclear-armed states. Most notable among these are so-called permissive action links (PALs):

a sophisticated combination of coded locks that block unauthorized detonation of the weapon.[79] "Bypassing a PAL," it has been noted, "should be about as complex as performing a tonsillectomy while entering the patient from the wrong end."[80] However, despite the technological security provided by PALs, "they are only effective if the codes for the locks are also kept secure," notes Zia Mian. "If anyone can have access to [or guess] the codes then PALs offer little if any restraint as command and control devices," Mian warns.[81] Moreover, if jihadists simply settled on accessing the nuclear materials within a PAL safeguarded weapon, they could eventually take the warhead apart. However, any warhead safeguarded with a PAL would not likely possess the *quantity* of nuclear material necessary to fuel an IND; jihadists would have to acquire and dismantle several such weapons.

States can also outfit their nuclear weapons with so-called safing, arming, fuzing, and firing (SAFF) features to prevent a weapon from detonating unless very specific requirements have been met.[82] These systems can be extremely complex, often employing barometric, temperature, and radar altimeter sensitive arming mechanisms; such arrangements can also be rather primitive, for example, the insertion of "mechanical devices into the pit (e.g., chains, coils of wire, bearing balls) to prevent complete implosion."[83] As opposed to PALs, it is highly unlikely that senior military and/or governmental officials could be of much assistance in defeating most complex SAFF procedures.[84] Again, jihadists might consequently be forced to abandon their quest to detonate the weapon and might simply settle on accessing the SAFF secured weapon's fissile materials.

United States

All U.S.-deployed nuclear weapons—3,575 strategic and 500 tactical warheads—are thought to utilize PALs and SAFF features.[85] Despite security mishaps, some of them quite serious, all U.S. nuclear weapons are generally viewed by experts as being "highly secure in all phases of their life cycle" and virtually immune to seizure by jihadists.[86] There are concerns that U.S. tactical nuclear weapons may not be as secure as their strategic counterparts, and some nuclear weapons experts have warned that tactical nuclear weapons "represent a particular concern from the standpoint of nuclear terrorism because of a combination of their physical properties and basing modes. Their relatively small size; portability; and....their forward deployment, make tactical nuclear weapons the likely weapon of choice for a nuclear terrorist organization."[87] Other experts note that U.S. tactical nuclear weapons are presently "as secure as strategic nuclear weapons."[88] It should be noted that the United States presently deploys several hundred tactical nuclear warheads in six different NATO countries, including Turkey.[89]

Russia

Even before the demise of the Soviet Union there were concerns over the security of nuclear materials and weapons in its Republics. In 1991 the United States began working with its allies to ensure that Soviet stocks of fissile materials and nuclear warheads were repatriated to the Russian Republic.[90] Even before these transfers were completed in 1994, however, it was evident that nuclear security within the newly independent state of Russia was deeply flawed.[91] Consequently, the United States made frantic efforts to assist Russia in securing and dismantling its nuclear infrastructure.[92] Presently, more than half of Russia's nuclear warhead sites have been cooperatively upgraded,[93] with one expert recently noting that "the difference between the security in place today and the security in place in 1994 is like night and day."[94]

As of early 2008, deployed Russian nuclear forces consist of approximately 3,113 strategic and 2,079 tactical warheads.[95] All of the former likely have PALs and employ SAFF features; however, there is debate over whether or not all of Russia's tactical nuclear weapons possess PALs.[96] Notwithstanding these technological safety features and ongoing physical security enhancements, profound concerns still exist over the security of Russian nuclear forces.

In large part these nuclear anxieties stem from widespread state corruption in Russia and a nuclear security culture perceived as lax. Moreover, fraud and nuclear negligence concerns are exacerbated profoundly with the existence of Russia's active and sophisticated jihadist networks.[97] Russia's Chechen jihadists, for example, have undertaken some of this decade's most audacious and tactically successful terrorist attacks.[98] The 2002 Dubrovka theatre incident and the 2004 Moscow subway and Beslan school attacks all reveal, notes one expert on Russian terrorists, that Chechen jihadists may have the operational capability to "take possession of ... Russian nuclear weapons and fuel sites."[99] The relative success of these and other terrorist operations reveals as well that Russia's nuclear security apparatus is frequently insufficient, careless, corrupt, and quite possibly willing to provide forms of insider assistance.[100]

As demonstrated in this book's radiological chapter, Russian jihadists have shown that they are intent on acquiring nuclear materials and weapons.[101] Russia is the only known nuclear weapon state to admit to having had its nuclear weapon storage facilities targeted and reconnoitered by terrorists.[102] Such potential nuclear insecurities, however, should not obscure the fact that all of Russia's nuclear weapons are presently under control and that, by all open-source accounts, no Russian nuclear device—strategic or tactical—has ever "made its way into the world's illegal arms bazaars," let alone into the hands of jihadists.[103]

United Kingdom, France, and China

On the one hand, the prevalence of terrorist groups in the United Kingdom—virtually every major jihadist group has had, at one time or another, a network operating within England—naturally leads to concerns over its nuclear arsenal. On the other hand, because of its size and deployment characteristics, the United Kingdom's nuclear arsenal is arguably the world's most secure: Its entire arsenal of active nuclear weapons, estimated to be about 185 warheads, is deployed on a fleet of nuclear-powered ballistic missile submarines (SSBNs).[104] Furthermore, all of the United Kingdom's operational warheads are believed to be equipped with PALs and possess SAFF features.[105]

French nuclear forces—estimated, in 2005, to be comprised of 348 active warheads[106] —are also widely seen as very secure despite the existence of several jihadist networks within that country. With the possible exception of France's submarine-launched ballistic missiles (SLBMs), all active warheads are thought to utilize PALs and SAFF features. [107]

China's nuclear arsenal is believed to possess about 200 warheads, 130 of which were thought to have been deployed in 2006.[108] There is no consensus on how many, if any, of these warheads are tactical. Experts agree that if China does have tactical nuclear weapons, they number less than twenty-five.[109] Various reports indicate that China likely has not yet incorporated PALs or critical SAFF features, or, according to one expert, "any other safety feature into its warheads."[110]

Little is known about potential jihadist threats to Chinese nuclear forces. Uighur separatists, active in Xinjiang Province, reportedly may have stolen radioactive sources from a Chinese nuclear facility in 1993.[111] In April 2008, the East Turkistan Islamic Movement (ETIM) allegedly plotted suicide attacks and kidnappings to disrupt the Beijing Olympics, perhaps portending an increase in sophisticated jihadist-related terrorist activity in China.[112] Nevertheless, even with restive native populations in Xinjiang, Tibet, and Inner Mongolia, and an arsenal that likely incorporates very few modern safety features, the domineering role of the Chinese Communist Party and the restrictive nature of Chinese society makes it highly improbable that jihadists could secure an intact Chinese nuclear weapon in the foreseeable future.

Israel

Despite its proximity to numerous jihadist groups and notwithstanding frequent terrorist attacks against it, the threat of jihadists seizing any of Israel's nuclear weapons is likely to be low. Little is known about Israel's undeclared arsenal—estimated to consist of between 75 and 200 warheads.[113] Many of these weapons are thought to be tactical.[114] The types and status of technological safeguards on Israeli nuclear weapons is unknown. A dated account suggests that, up until at least the early 1990s, some warheads were kept in a preassembled state in "special secure boxes that could be opened only with three keys, to be supplied by the top civilian and military leadership."[115] Recently, experts have advanced the idea that rather than relying strictly on PALs, Israel likely relies "on procedures and codes."[116]

India

India's nuclear arsenal is rapidly increasing. Its growth is constrained, according to a retired Indian vice admiral, "more by production capabilities than by international restraints."[117] While presently believed to have approximately "50–60 assembled warheads," India has announced plans to enhance this number many-fold—some Indian officials have given numbers as high as "300–400 fission and thermonuclear weapons" by 2010.[118] It is widely believed that India does not possess PALs technology.[119]

Several well-organized and resourceful jihadist groups are active in and around India.[120] Jaysh-e Muhammad (JEM), for example, conducted sophisticated attacks against the Kashmir State Assembly and the Indian Parliament in 2001 that again demonstrated JEM's very high operational capabilities.[121] Additionally, Lashkar-e-Taiba (LeT) has targeted Indian nuclear facilities in the recent past.[122] Arguably assuaging concerns over jihadist activities and India's potential lack of nuclear technological safeguards is the fact that India is unique among nuclear states in that its military does not have possession of India's nuclear arms.[123] In practice, this means that the physical authority of nuclear warhead cores resides with civilian authorities, while the military maintains possession only of the delivery vehicles for the warheads—a so-called "de-mated" posture.[124] Consequently it would be extraordinarily difficult for jihadists to secure an intact Indian nuclear warhead.

Pakistan

Pakistan is believed to have enough fissile material for 60 to 130 nuclear weapons.[125] The existence of jihadist groups on its soil (including a reconstituted al-Qa'ida in South Waziristan[126] and the Pakistani Taliban), internal political turbulence, jihadist influences in its military and intelligence services, and a disturbing history of nuclear technology and material transfers has led some observers to conclude that Pakistan's nuclear arsenal is profoundly insecure.[127] Indeed, since at least 1999, there have been calls for the United States and other countries to develop contingency plans to seize and "exfiltrate"

Pakistan's nuclear weapons to prevent them from falling into the hands of extremists in the event of widespread civil unrest or a governmental coup by Islamist forces.[128] In a thinly veiled recent reference to Pakistan, the U.S. Department of Defense (DoD) noted that, "although not necessarily hostile to the United States," certain states lack "effective governance" presenting opportunities for terrorists "to acquire or harbor WMD."[129] In contrast to these concerns, however, Pakistan consistently maintains that its arsenal is under "ironclad" control.[130] In addressing these seemingly contrary threat perceptions, four points can be made.

First, Pakistan's nuclear arsenal is widely believed to be stored in a "trifurcated" manner, that is, the nuclear core of the weapon, the non-nuclear components of the device, and the delivery vehicle are all kept separate.[131] Moreover, the nuclear components are said to be guarded by upwards of "10,000 troops."[132] Even during its extremely tense military standoff with India in 2001 to 2002, Pakistan is not believed to have mated its nuclear weapon components.[133] Consequently, it would appear to be virtually impossible for jihadists to overtly seize or steal an intact Pakistani nuclear device without considerable insider help. The greater threat, therefore, is of jihadists somehow acquiring weapons-grade fissile materials from a Pakistani source and subsequently employing them in an IND.

Second, while it is not clear whether or not Pakistan's warheads utilize PALs, the head of the Pakistani body that runs nuclear weapons operations has stated that the military utilizes both "enabling and authenticating codes" to safeguard its nuclear weapons.[134] Moreover, commentators frequently point to Pakistan's "two-man" or "three-man" rules and very tight selection process for vetting personnel involved with nuclear weapons—mirroring in many ways, some believe, the U.S. Personnel Reliability Program—as evidence that insider nuclear subterfuge, vis-à-vis an intact device, is a near impossibility.[135] Again it seems very likely that the extant threat lies in Pakistan's fissile materials.

Third, it can be argued that the threat of coup by extremists in Pakistan is very low. While those Islamic political parties that are most often linked to an Islamist political takeover (for example, Jama`at-i-Islami, Jami'at-i-Ulema-i-Islam, and Jami'at-i-Ulema-i-Pakistan) are the *loudest* groups that oppose Pakistani leadership, their political base is small, and they enjoy little backing from the key military and political coteries necessary to successfully take power.[136] Summing up this argument against the notion of an Islamist seizure of power, South Asian expert Frédéric Grare has noted that, "No Islamic organization has ever been in a position to politically or militarily challenge the role of the one and only center of power in Pakistan: the army."[137]

As for the Pakistani military, there are widespread concerns that significant elements of its ranks are linked to jihadist groups.[138] Consequently there is trepidation by some that radicalized elements of the military could collectively conspire to transfer an intact nuclear device to jihadists or, if they successfully seized power, directly assume control of Pakistan's nuclear assets.[139] Such scenarios are unlikely to transpire any time in the near future. President Musharraf and his regime are known to have mercilessly weeded out extremists from the Pakistani nuclear weapons complex.[140] Others argue that even if Islamists *did* occupy the upper echelons of military power, it is extremely unlikely that they would undertake or support nuclear transfers.[141] While acknowledging the military's loyalty and stability, however, there are still concerns among experts that growing civil unrest in Pakistan could distract the military "from its guard duties," rendering some of Pakistan's fissile materials more vulnerable to theft or direct seizure by jihadists.[142] In short, there is a strong sense by many informed analysts that the nexus between the Pakistani military and Islam is less political and more ideological and inspirational, and that Pakistan's army officers are "extremely sensitive to the corporate interests of the military."Moreover, it is still generally accepted that Pakistan's military sees its interests as being well-served by "enduring political, economic, technical, and military links with the United States," a perspective that would occlude any nuclear involvement with jihadists.[143]

Finally, there are acute concerns that transfers of nuclear technologies, materials, and know-how by Pakistan's top nuclear scientist, Dr. Abdul Qadeer Khan (commonly referred to as "A. Q. Khan"), pressage similar transfers to jihadists. Yet, despite claims that Pakistan has become the, "Wal-Mart for nuclear weapons shoppers," it is important to note what Pakistan has *not* stood accused of in the proliferation scandal that was publicly revealed in 2004.[144] Most importantly from the perspective of jihadists, the Khan Network transfers were to state entities (as opposed to nonstate actors), they did not involve intact nuclear warheads, and the nuclear material that was transferred was in the form of uranium hexafluoride—suitable for weapons use only *after* enrichment.[145] The bulk of what was apparently transferred—centrifuge technologies—would be of no present value to jihadists determined to acquire nuclear capability. Moreover, a nuclear weapon design, like the Chinese one that Dr. Khan allegedly gave to Libya, is not considered terribly difficult to come by, nor would jihadists need such a sophisticated blueprint.[146] In short, there is no evidence of a nexus between nuclear networks and terrorists, and the Khan Network, even as it existed at its apogee, would likely have been of little use to jihadists.

In sum, Pakistan is unique among all nuclear states with regard to the theoretical ability of jihadists to obtain nuclear weapons and materials. Its geographical proximity to, and, indeed, inclusion of jihadist groups is unparalleled. Additionally, Pakistan's nascent nuclear armory is unlikely to employ the same level of technical security sophistication that other arsenals possess. Amid a turbulent domestic venue that is punctuated by ongoing civil turbulence, including an insurrection in its federally administered tribal areas (FATA), coups, and assassinations, Pakistan's nuclear custodianship credibility is further tarnished by probable high-level state collusion with the A. Q. Khan nuclear network. While these factors have led some to speculate that Pakistan is the ultimate "nuclear nightmare," a more nuanced appraisal reveals a nuclear state with robust nuclear security arrangements collectively make it unlikely that intact nuclear weapons could end up in the hands of jihadists.[147] "Only if there's a complete breakdown in society, would there be an issue," notes Pakistani nuclear expert Leonard Spector, adding that, "Even then, I think you'll find a cadre, a very loyal military, who protect the assets because it's the patrimony of the country."[148]

North Korea

Having detonated its first nuclear weapon in October 2006, North Korea is the latest state to enter the nuclear club. Presently, North Korea is believed to have the nuclear materials to fabricate five to twelve warheads.[149] Three plausible scenarios exist linking North Korea's nuclear capability to jihadist acquisition of nuclear weapons. First, it is possible that should the present regime of Kim Jong-Il fall from power—from internal strife, military invasion, or a combination of the two—nuclear warheads might go missing in the ensuing disorder and could, presumably, end up in the hands of jihadists.[150] Second is the possibility that North Korea, already well experienced in missile sales to other countries, will begin to trade and sell its nuclear know-how with other states who, in turn, may supply warheads to jihadists.[151]

Third, and of greatest concern, North Korea could willingly provide nuclear weapons directly to jihadists. According to the U.S. State Department, North Korea maintains relations with various terrorist organizations, has supplied weapons to several terrorist groups including the Moro Islamic Liberation Front (a Sunni Islamist group), and allegedly provides "safe haven" to terrorists.[152] Moreover, coupled with missile sales to "states of concern," North Korea's involvement with drug smuggling and money counterfeiting are seen by some as proof positive "that Kim Jong-Il would be equally open to selling nuclear materials, technology, or weapons to terrorist groups."[153] A 2006 U.S. intelligence report to Congress—a "721 Report"—stated that in April 2005 Pyongyang warned that it "could transfer nuclear weapons to terrorists if driven into a corner."[154] As recently as December 5, 2006, a spokesperson for the National Nuclear Security Agency (NNSA) stated that the United States now has to consider "the possibility that the North Koreans...would be willing to either sell materials or sell a warhead to the highest bidder."[155]

Knowledgeable and responsible experts perceive the risk of North Korean nuclear transfers to terrorists as low.[156] Mindful that past behavior is often a key indicator of future actions, they stress that "no one has produced evidence to suggest that Pyongyang has ever attempted to sell nuclear materials to terrorist groups."[157] This fact would fall into line with the belief that North Korea views its nuclear arsenal not as a commodity to sell to terrorists but rather as a bargaining chip and a deterrent. During a visit to North Korea in 2006 by U.S. nuclear weapons experts, North Korean officials told Siegfried S. Hecker that North Korea "needs the deterrent; otherwise it can't defend its sovereignty," adding that North Korea would "not use nuclear weapons first, nor give them to terrorists like al Qaeda." The North Korean official went on tell Hecker that, "We make these expensive weapons to defend our right to survive."[158]

Significantly, at the time of this writing, it appears that North Korea is serious about dismantling its nuclear infrastructure.[159] The Six-Party talks, reenergized in February 2007, might ultimately lead to a completely de-nuclearized Korean Peninsula. In contrast, there are dramatic new allegations that North Korea helped Syria in building a nuclear reactor that was attacked by Israel in September 2007.[160] If true, such actions by North Korea will only fuel the erroneous argument that they would show no compunction in selling nuclear arms and materials to terrorists.

Iran

Because of its well-known support of groups that are on the U.S. State Department's list of foreign terrorist organizations and its ongoing nuclear program, Iran is perceived by some as a likely future source for jihadist acquisition of intact nuclear weapons. In a direct reference to Iran, for example, President Bush has warned of "outlaw regimes" supplying WMD to "their terrorist allies who would use them without hesitation."[161]

Despite "high confidence" assertions of the 2007 National Intelligence Estimate (NIE) that Iran likely halted nuclear weapons *development* in 2003 (and "moderate confidence Tehran had not restarted its nuclear weapons program as of mid-2007"), Iran undoubtedly continues to develop the technological *capability* to build nuclear weapons.[162] In doing so Iran will likely emulate the Japanese model of being a "virtual nuclear weapon state"—a technically *non*-nuclear weapon state with a robust civilian nuclear infrastructure that can be quickly modified with relative ease for nuclear weapons fabrication.[163] Accordingly, while certain geopolitical developments short of a foreign military occupation could convince Tehran to abandon its efforts,[164] it seems likely that within the next three to seven years Iran will have fully developed the ability to weaponize a nuclear device within months of a final decision to do so.[165]

Iran could produce a nuclear weapon using either plutonium or HEU. The former could theoretically be extracted from spent nuclear fuel rods taken from Iran's Bushehr reactor (or its Arak research reactor, due to be completed in 2009); the latter could be fabricated at Iran's Natanz facilities. Because all of Iran's declared nuclear facilities are presently under IAEA safeguards, the use of Bushehr or Natanz (or, in the future, Arak) to procure or produce fissile materials would instantly expose Iran's noncivil nuclear intentions to the international community. Consequently, some analysts postulate that Iran may be developing clandestine uranium enrichment facilities that could complement its efforts at Natanz. Conceivably, such a scenario would involve Iran fabricating LEU at Natanz and then "breaking out" by quickly enriching the uranium to HEU, ostensibly at a secret facility that, even if discovered, would not be as vulnerable as Natanz.[166] Such a route would seriously tax Iran's centrifuge capabilities and, if successful, would likely only initially yield a few nuclear devices annually.[167]

Iran is linked to several jihadist groups. Consequently there are deep, yet unfounded, concerns that, should Iran weaponize a nuclear capability, it would pass these weapons along to jihadists.[168] Created and largely funded by the Iranian Revolutionary Guard, Hizballah is the most frequently mentioned candidate as a potential Iranian nuclear proxy. Palestinian Islamic Jihad, although a Sunni group, is unique in its pro-Khomeini ideology and also enjoys backing from the Iranians. Hamas is also linked to Iran, yet it would be far less likely to be considered as a nuclear surrogate due to critical ideological incompatibilities between it and Tehran.[169] Finally, despite a widespread perception that Iran supports al-Qa'ida,[170] experts have recently reiterated that there are no indications that "Iran is supporting al-Qa'ida activities or harboring its members."[171]

Thus, of all potential jihadist groups, Hizballah and Palestinian Islamic Jihad are Iran's only plausible nuclear surrogates. Yet, despite their relationship with Iran, neither could usefully serve any purpose to Iran vis-à-vis nuclear weapons. Should Iran wish to attack, retaliate, or deter regional nuclear-backed threats, it could do so on its own with a nascent nuclear arsenal and ballistic missile capability. "Covert" use of a nuclear weapon against a nuclear region power (i.e., Israel) or U.S. forces would be suicidal for Iranian leadership. Iranian culpability of a nuclear strike using a proxy would almost certainly be established immediately,[172] and it is likely that Iran would suffer immediate and unimaginably destructive nuclear retaliation.[173] Contrary to popular perceptions, Iran's leadership is highly rational and, while it has made tactical and strategic miscalculations in the past, there is no evidence to suggest that the regime is suicidal or grossly delusional.[174]

In sum, Iran is moving toward a nuclear weapons capability. However, to go beyond being a "virtual nuclear weapon state"—to actually possess a weaponized nuclear arsenal—is a commitment that Iran would likely undertake only if it believed that it needed an immediate deterrent to some kind of massive military attack. Indeed, Iranian expert Trita Parsi has noted that, absent such dire circumstances, "The Iranians are well aware that a decision to weaponize would likely weaken rather than advance Iran's strategic position."[175] Subsequent transfers of nuclear warheads to jihadists are extremely unlikely and could only plausibly occur if Iran thought that its national existence was in jeopardy via a military invasion—a concern that would likely be obviated by the actual possession of nuclear weapons by Iran.

NUCLEAR BLACK MARKET

A 2005 survey of eighty-three experts in the field of CBRN security overwhelmingly concluded "black market purchase to be the most likely means through which terrorists would acquire nuclear weapons or weapons grade material."[176] While no one denies that nuclear trafficking and organized crime exist simultaneously in several regions of the world, no definitive proof has yet emerged linking the two. More importantly, "there is no compelling evidence of a solid nexus" among nuclear trafficking, organized crime, and terrorism.[177] In part, these uncertainties result from a lack of data collection and information sharing by various law enforcement agencies around the world and, obviously, by the fact that only known plots and incidents can be evaluated. In short, while there may be a robust nonstate nuclear black market in operation, one that ostensibly could supply jihadists with intact nuclear weapons, no known empirical evidence yet exists to support this fear.

Incidents of known nuclear trafficking are relatively widespread, but only a few of them involve fissile materials. The IAEA's Illicit Trafficking Database, for example, recorded only sixteen incidents from 1993 through 2006 that involved HEU or plutonium.[178] Only a few of these cases had "proliferation significant quantities" of materials (kilogram-level quantities of plutonium-239 or HEU) and none such cases have occurred since the 1990s.[179] Moreover, since at least 2001, only three cases are *potentially* linked to terrorists, and, according to one of the world's foremost nuclear trafficking experts, their actual connection to terrorism "really doesn't exist at this point."[180] Thus, the overwhelming motivation in all known cases of nuclear theft and smuggling appears to be profit and the market appears to be entirely supply-driven; there is almost no data to support any connections to terrorists or organized crime.

Still, such trafficking data generate more questions than they answer. Is the lack of recent cases involving fissile materials an indication that improved security measures in Russia and elsewhere are increasingly effective, or do they indicate that traffickers are simply more adept at not getting caught? Does the recent trend of cases involving small, as opposed to proliferation significant, quantities of fissile materials imply that smugglers are being forced to traffic less material due to enhanced security measures or less supply, or are the smaller quantities indicative of *samples* of larger quantities of materials that flow freely?[181] Finally, do these data simply represent underreporting? For example, one study has shown that only one-third of the smuggling incidents reported in the Russian media from 1993 to 2005 were "confirmed to the IAEA by the Russian Federation."[182] "This makes it difficult," the study concludes, "to rely for a comprehensive global assessment on nuclear trafficking on state-supplied information only."[183]

Complicating any analysis of the nuclear black market is the existence of proliferation networks that have supplied states with nuclear know-how and materials, specifically the aforementioned A. Q. Khan Network. The discovery of this network raised speculation that a similar subrosa system might exist, linking terrorists to nuclear materials. To date, however, there have been no credible reports linking the Khan Network to jihadist attempts to acquire a nuclear capability. This is not surprising given the nature of the Khan Network: profit-motivated operatives, dealing exclusively with states in enrichment technologies, typically engaging in transactions of several million dollars.

INCIDENTS OF JIHADIST INTEREST IN NUCLEAR WEAPONS AND WEAPONS-GRADE NUCLEAR MATERIALS

Despite no conclusive evidence of a nuclear black market servicing nonstate actors, jihadists have, since at least 1993, made serious attempts to acquire fissile materials and nuclear weapons. Several individuals linked to jihadist groups have been arrested or detained for plotting or attempting to acquire nuclear weapons or materials, yet to date there have been no confirmed incidents of a jihadist-linked individual or a jihadist group successfully obtaining fissile materials suitable for a nuclear weapon or an intact nuclear warhead.[184] In terms of technological know-how, this book (see Chapter 4) has already detailed how, to date, jihadists are thought to have secured mostly basic, often grossly inaccurate, information about nuclear weapons.[185]

Al-Qa'ida

Most active among jihadist groups seeking to acquire nuclear weapons and weapons-grade nuclear materials has been al-Qa'ida; according to the U.S. government, their determined efforts to acquire nuclear materials began "at least as early as 1992."[186] Jamal Ahmad al-Fadl, a Sudanese national and former Ibn Ladin associate, has testified that in late 1993 or early 1994 he observed the preliminary phases of a transaction between al-Qa'ida and various operatives for the purchase of uranium in Khartoum, Sudan.[187] It is not known if the actual transaction (reportedly for $1.5 million) ever took place, yet al-Fadl's testimony is generally considered to be credible. Throughout the 1990s there were numerous subsequent reports of al-Qa'ida unsuccessfully attempting to acquire uranium and nuclear warheads.[188]

Al-Qa'ida's efforts took a significant turn in 2000 and 2001, when Bin Ladin and Mullah Omar (Taliban's leader and Afghanistan's de facto head of state from 1996 to 2001) met with two former Pakistani nuclear scientists. One of them, Sultan Bashir-ud-din Mahmood, was a former chairman of the Pakistan Atomic Energy Commission (PAEC) and an expert in uranium enrichment and plutonium production.[189] Considered by Pakistan's Inter Services Intelligence (ISI) to be too politically and religiously radicalized for continued work as head of Pakistan's Khosab nuclear reactor complex, Mahmood was forced out of office in 1999 and subsequently founded the aid organization Ummah Tameer-e-Nau (UTN). Under the cover of UTN, Mahmood, along with Abdul Majid, another PAEC scientist, allegedly met with al-Qa'ida operatives and various Taliban state officials with the hopes of assisting them in the fabrication of nuclear weapons (documents seized in Kabul detail UTN's desire to undertake uranium mining in Afghanistan). Over a period of a few days, three weeks prior to the 9/11 attacks, Mahmood and Majid reportedly met with Bin Ladin and Ayman al-Zawahiri, around a "campfire in Kandahar," to discuss al-Qa'ida's quest for nuclear and radiological weapons.[190]

David Albright has written that Mahmood and Majid likely provided al-Qa'ida with "a blueprint for making nuclear weapons," while also providing al-Qa'ida or the Taliban with "classified information about producing nuclear weapons...or of facilitating access to others in the Pakistani nuclear program who had that knowledge."[191] With their vast experience in the Pakistani nuclear program, Mahmood and Majid, Albright adds, "could have provided important tips or direct assistance on managing and running a complex nuclear project."[192]

Following the demise of the Taliban in 2001, materials recovered by coalition military forces and the media shed more light on al-Qa'ida's nuclear enterprises while in Afghanistan.[193] While most of the documents revealed a relatively low level of understanding vis-à-vis nuclear weapons, some were reported to be of "higher quality," including, according to nuclear expert Matthew Bunn, "one fact about initiating a nuclear chain reaction that remains classified and could not simply have been downloaded from the internet."[194] Since 2002 there have been perennial reports of al-Qa'ida attempting to procure nuclear weapons and weapons-grade materials—none of which are believed to have been successful.[195] There are reports as well that al-Qa'ida has "at least one Central Asian nuclear weapons expert" presently working within its ranks.[196] Not surprisingly, there are reports that al-Qa'ida continues to maintain a strong desire to employ nuclear weapons against the United States and its allies.[197]

Altogether the documents recovered in Afghanistan, along with other reports of al-Qa'ida's nuclear activities, reveal a group that is serious about acquiring a nuclear capability. Al-Qa'ida has made several efforts to secure intact nuclear devices and fissile materials and has reportedly been prepared to pay many millions of dollars to do so.[198] While al-Qa'ida's technical grasp of nuclear weapons is thought to be nascent and occasionally bordering on the absurd, a caveat is in order. "History is replete with cautionary tales warning against basing threat assessments on static analyses of an opponent's motivations and capabilities," notes terrorism expert Gary Ackerman. "After all," he continues, "if their actions over the past decade have taught us anything, it is that terrorists are audaciously nimble operators who can adapt through reinvention and are prepared to persevere to attain their goals."[199] In this sense, al-Qa'ida and Taliban contact with nuclear scientists may be a harbinger of substantial jihadist nuclear expertise should they ever acquire enough fissile materials to fuel a nuclear weapon.

Russia's Chechen-Led Jihadists

Russia's Chechen jihadists, already noted as having a very high operational capability, have long been associated with nuclear materials acquisition and have made clear their intention to acquire nuclear weapons.[200] (Chechen militants have also been linked to attempts to *sell* fissile materials and entire nuclear warheads that they supposedly possessed.[201]) "Suspicious persons," allegedly linked to Chechen militants, scouted Russian nuclear warhead facilities in 2001.[202] In 2002 and 2003, suspected Chechen militants likely linked to jihadists attempted to break into one of Russia's facilities housing nuclear warheads.[203] Additionally, Chechen militants are suspected of conducting reconnaissance on Russian transport trains carrying nuclear weapons,[204] and they have been known to have obtained identification passes allowing them access to closed Russian nuclear facilities.[205] Warning that Chechens have insider knowledge of the location and security of Russia's nuclear weapons, Viktor Ilyukhin, a Russian Member of Parliament and deputy chairman of the Russian Parliament's security committee, has noted that "many Chechens served in the armed forces, in the interior ministry troops, and many have experience of guarding crucial [nuclear] facilities.... Their location is not in any way a secret for the Chechens."[206]

Nuclear-Related Threats and Attacks in India and Pakistan

Jihadists are publicly known to have plotted against India's civil nuclear infrastructure. In December 2005, Lashkar-e-Taiba (LeT)—a Sunni Islamist group—reportedly targeted an Indian nuclear power plant for attack. [207] In 2006 there were several security breaches at other nuclear power plants,[208] leading India's prime minister, Manmohan Singh, to conclude that terrorist targeting now includes "nuclear installations."[209] It is likely that such attacks would seek to disrupt the operations of the plant or cause them to malfunction. Such plots may herald future attacks on India's military nuclear infrastructure by jihadists seeking to acquire a nuclear capability.

In 2007, jihadists plotted, and in some cases actualized, attacks that targeted Pakistani military nuclear installations. While it appears that these strikes were tactically designed to inflict loss of life and generate mayhem, such attacks may by strategically intended to "erode the military's capacity to defend nuclear installations if the Taliban and al Qaeda can mount a raid to seize nuclear weapons."[210] Sargodha Air Force Base, which serves as the headquarters of the Central Air Command of the Pakistan Air Force (PAF) and likely houses "partially assembled air-deliverable nuclear devices," has been targeted by jihadists—allegedly linked to al-Qa'ida and the Taliban—on several occasions. [211] In November 2007, a suicide bomber killed eight and wounded twenty-seven in an attack at the air base.[212] Pakistan's Kamra Air Weapon Complex (AWC) has also been stuck by jihadist suicide bombers.[213] The facilities at Kamra are reportedly coupled with the "weaponization of Pakistan's nuclear devices."[214]

OVERALL LIKELIHOOD OF JIHADISTS OBTAINING NUCLEAR CAPABILITY

To date jihadists have been unsuccessful in all publicly known attempts to acquire fissile materials or intact nuclear weapons. These failures might be explained by tighter and more reliable security than is commonly presupposed at Russian and other nuclear facilities, a weak or nonexistent nuclear black market, or they could be attributable to a lack of resources by jihadists or, in the case of al-Qa'ida, "too many projects running simultaneously."[215]

Despite this unsuccessful history, however, there are no indications that serious interests by jihadists in acquiring a nuclear capability will abate in the near future. Whether or not they will succeed is one of the modern era's most daunting questions. Four broad factors will have a direct effect on any probable outcome. First is the quantity of global fissile materials, and the security associated with these stocks. As outlined above, present inventories are daunting: As much as 2,000 metric tons of HEU and 500 metric tons of separated plutonium, virtually all weapon-usable, exist globally. While the overall global stockpile of HEU is shrinking, production continues in Pakistan and India. Meanwhile, civilian stockpiles of separated plutonium are growing—they now likely exceed military stocks.[216] Global warming and concomitant dwindling oil reserves will likely be accelerating this trend, as states seek to secure carbon-free electricity.[217] While security over plutonium and HEU stocks continues to generally improve, Russia will remain as a source of great anxiety for many years to come, as well as fissile material stocks in other states.[218]

Second, global stockpiles of intact nuclear weapons and their security have an obvious bearing on the odds of jihadists successfully obtaining a nuclear capability. Inventories are declining in many states, yet they are growing in India, Pakistan, and China (and, perhaps, Israel). While overall security is arguably improving, concerns remain over the

Russian and Pakistani arsenals. Moreover, the nuclear weapons inventories of all other nuclear weapon states are not immune to all forms of nuclear subterfuge, with tactical nuclear weapons posing an especially acute threat.

Third, the spread of nuclear know-how and weapons to other states could dramatically alter any calculus used to determine the odds of jihadists being successful in their nuclear endeavors. A group of luminaries in the field of nuclear security recently concluded that, "the greatest danger to United States and indeed global security stems from the weakening or even collapse of the international consensus to prevent proliferation."[219] Foreseeable nuclear proliferation will likely occur in the world's least stable area—the Middle East.[220]

Finally, the number and sophistication of jihadist groups will likely have an enormous bearing on future developments. If their numbers remain the same or grow, it is very likely that their odds of eventual success will increase. If the conflict in Iraq significantly subsides, an exodus of jihadists is probable. They would likely take with them not only a fully militarized anti-Western ideology but also an increasingly sophisticated understanding of explosives and improvised explosive devices (IEDs). U.S. Director of National Intelligence, J. Michael McConnell, has addressed this possibility, noting that he is "increasingly concerned that as we inflict significant damage on al-Qa'ida in Iraq, it may shift resources to mounting more attacks outside of Iraq."[221] Such eventualities have already begun to transpire: The June 2007 London and Glasgow car-bomb attacks had alleged links to al-Qa'ida in Iraq and utilized a "technique previously employed in Iraq."[222]

In sum, the future will likely see the growth of fissile materials stockpiles and nuclear weapon arsenals in some of the world's least stable regions. It is very plausible that this dynamic will be bolstered by *new* nuclear states amid a post–Iraq exodus of increasingly well-trained jihadists. In December 2001, George Tenet believed that al-Qa'ida was on the verge of a nuclear capability; seven years later, jihadists are closer than ever.

NOTES

1. Ron Suskind, *The One Percent Doctrine* (New York: Simon and Shuster, 2006), 67.
2. "Combating Terrorism: The United States Lacks Comprehensive Plan to Destroy the Terrorist Threat and Close the Safe Haven in Pakistan's Federally Administered Tribal Areas," *Government Accountability Office (GAO), US Congress*, GAO-08-622, 2008, 9.
3. Joseph Cirincione, "Pakistanis under Musharraf and the Bush Doctrine," KGNU, Boulder, Colorado, April 8, 2008.
4. For the seven-part agreement, see Dan Balz, Bob Woodward, and Jeff Himmelman, "Afghan Campaign's Blueprint Emerges," *Washington Post*, January 29, 2002, available at http://www.washingtonpost.com/wp-dyn/content/article/2006/07/18/AR2006071800687_pf.html (accessed 03/21/08).
5. For a history of concerns around nuclear terrorism, see, for example, Micah Zenko, "Intelligence Estimates of Nuclear Terrorism," *The Annals of the American Academy of Political and Social Science* 2006; 607; 87, 93, available at http://ann.sagepub.com/cgi/reprint/607/1/87.pdf; and Central Intelligence Agency, National Intelligence Estimate (NIE) 31, "Soviet Capabilities for Clandestine Attack against the US with Weapons of Mass Destruction and the Vulnerability of the US to Such Attack," September 4, 1951, 3–6, available at http://www.fas.org/irp/threat/nieca1951.pdf (accessed 03/25/08).

6. As quoted in Michael Scheuer, *Through Our Enemies' Eyes: Usama bin Ladin, Radical Islam, and the Future of America* (Washington, DC: Potomac Books, Inc., 2002), 72.
7. Robert Jay Lifton, *Destroying the World to Save It: Aum Shinrikyo, Apocalyptic Violence, and the New Global Terrorism* (New York: Metropolitan Books, 1999), 204.
8. This would more likely be the goal of jihadists not wedded to the idea of the "restoration of the Caliphate"; for example, Hizballah and Hamas have a national goal, and "They have no global agenda or aspirations; they do not want to reestablish the Caliphate." Sammy Salama, "Islamist Organization in the 20th Century," *Monterey Institute of International Studies*, Monterey, CA, January 19, 2006.
9. " 'Why we fight America': Al-Qa'ida Spokesman Explains September 11 and Declares Intentions to Kill 4 Million Americans with Weapons of Mass Destruction," *Middle East Media Research Institute*, Special Dispatch Series, no. 388, June 12, 2002, available at http://memri.org/bin/articles.cgi?Page=archives&Area=sd&ID=SP38802 (accessed 08/03/07).
10. This study explores the acquisition of a single nuclear weapon by jihadists. It seems likely, however, that jihadists who have one nuclear weapon will have others as well. See, for example, Roger C. Molander, "Perspectives on Nuclear Terrorism," Testimony presented before the Senate Committee on Homeland Security and Governmental Affairs on April 15, 2008, available at http://hsgac.senate.gov/public/_files/041508Molander.pdf (accessed 04/18/08).
11. HEU is uranium with a content of 20 percent or more of the isotope uranium-235. Unless otherwise indicated, in this chapter it refers to uranium with an enrichment level above 80 percent uranium-235. See U.S. Congress, Office of Technology Assessment, *Technical Aspects of Nuclear Proliferation* (Washington, DC: Government Printing Office, 1993), 121.
12. See David Albright and Lauren Barbour, "Troubles Tomorrow? Separated Neptunium 237 and Americium," in David Albright and Kevin O'Neill, eds., *The Challenges of Fissile Material Control*, (Washington, DC: Institute for Science and International Security Press, 1999), 85–96, available at http://www.isis-online.org/publications/fmct/book/New%20chapter%205.pdf, and "US Nuclear Weapons Complex: Homeland Security Opportunities," *Project on Government Oversight*, May 2005, available at http://www.pogo.org/p/homeland/ho-050301-consolidation.html (accessed 04/02/08). See also "Evaluation of Nuclear Criticality Safety Data and Limits for Actinides in Transport," *Institut de Radioprotection et de Sûreté Nucléaire (IRSN)*, Département de Prévention et d'étude des Accidents, Service d'Études de Criticité, République Française, 2003, available at http://ec.europa.eu/energy/nuclear/transport/doc/irsn_sect03_146.pdf.
13. See Lillian Hoddeson, Paul W. Henriksen, Roger A. Meade, and Catherine Westfall, *Critical Assembly: A Technical History of Los Alamos During the Oppenheimer Years, 1943–1945* (New York: Cambridge University Press, 1993), 228–248; and Michael Levi, *On Nuclear Terrorism* (Cambridge, MA: Harvard University Press, 2007), 73.
14. See Jeremy Bernstein, *Plutonium: A History of the World's Most Dangerous Element*, (Washington, DC: Joseph Henry PRess, 2007), 112.
15. Robert W. Young and Geroge D. Kerr, eds. *Re-assesment of the Atomic Bomb Radiation Documentary in Hiroshima and Nagasaki* (Hiroshima, Japan: The Radiation Effects Foundation, 2005), 53.

16. Mason Willrich and Theodore B. Taylor, *Nuclear Theft: Risks and Safeguards: A Report to the Energy Policy Project of the Ford Foundation* (Cambridge, MA: Ballinger Publishing Company, 1974), 8.
17. One can imagine a drop of water hitting a pool of water. The shock waves go *out* uniformly. The idea of an implosion device is to have the water go *in* uniformly. No part of the inward-moving shock wave in an implosion device can reach the center before all the others. Author's personal communication with Dr. James A. McNeil, Professor, Colorado School of Mines Physics Department, March 22, 2008. For an excellent description of how lenses worked on the first two implosion devices, see Richard Rhodes, *The Making of the Atomic Bomb* (New York: Simon and Schuster, 1986), 575–578.
18. Willrich and Taylor, *Nuclear Theft,* 10.
19. Glasston and Dolan, *The Effects of Nuclear Weapons*, 36.
20. See Robert Jay Lifton, *Destroying the World to Save It: Aum Shinrikyo, Apocalyptic Violence, and the New Global Terrorism*; and Richard A. Falkenrath, Robert D. Newman, and Bradley A. Thayer, *American's Achilles' Heel: Nuclear, Biological, and Chemical Terrorism and Covert Attack* (Cambridge, MA: The MIT Press, 1998).
21. David Albright, "Al Qaeda's Nuclear Program: Through the Window of Seized Documents," *The Nautilus Institute Policy Forum On Line*, Special Forum 47, November 6, 2002, available at http://www.nautilus.org/archives/fora/Special-Policy-Forum/47_Albright.html (accessed 01/21/08).
22. For current trends in enrichment technologies, see M. D. Zentner, G. L. Coles, and R. J. Talbert, *Nuclear Proliferation Technology Trends Analysis,* PNNL-14480, *Pacific Northwest National Laboratory*, September 2005.
23. Graham Allison, *Nuclear Terrorism* (New York: Times Books, 2004), 98–99.
24. "Global Fissile Material Report," *International Panel on Fissile Materials*, 2007, 10.
25. See, ibid., 10–12.
26. Ibid., 12.
27. Ibid., 13.
28. Ibid., 17, 20.
29. A critical mass that does not utilize a reflector (explored below) is often called "the bare critical mass." Use of a reflector with a critical mass is often called "a reflected critical mass."
30. Plutonium can spontaneously ignite (it is pyrophoric) if not stored and handled correctly. For an excellent account of how plutonium's pyrophoric properties frequently wreaked havoc on U.S. military efforts to weaponize plutonium, see Len Ackland, *Making a Real Killing: Rocky Flats and the Nuclear West* (Albuquerque: University of New Mexico Press, 1999).
31. "The First Weighing of Plutonium," *Atomic Energy Commission Division of Technical Information,* Oak Ridge, TN, 1967, 4, available at http://www.osti.gov/accomplishments/documents/fullText/ACC0071.pdf (accessed 02/13/08).
32. Levi, *On Nuclear Terrorism*, 79–81.
33. "Global Fissile Material Report 2007," 21.
34. See, for example, "DOE Needs to Resolve Significant Issues Before It Fully Meets the New Design Basis Threat," *US General Accounting Office*, April 2004; and "US Nuclear Weapons Complex: Security At Risk," *Project on Government Oversight Report*, October 2001, available at http://www.pogo.org/p/environment/eo-011003-nuclear.html (accessed 04/02/08).
35. "Global Fissile Material Report 2007," 47, 54.

36. Paul Leventhal, Sharon Tanzer, and Steven Dolley, *Nuclear Power and the Spread of Nuclear Weapons* (London and New York: Brasseys, 2002), 236. See also Willrich and Taylor, *Nuclear Theft*, 14.
37. John McPhee, *The Curve of Binding Energy* (New York: Farrar, Straus and Giroux, 1973), 131.
38. Willrich and Taylor, *Nuclear Theft*, 14.
39. Mark, Taylor, et al., "Can Terrorists Build Nuclear Weapons?" 56–74
40. Michael Levi has estimated that the device's explosives, in such circumstances, might likely weigh more than the oxide itself. Levi, *On Nuclear Terrorism,* 83.
41. Willrich and Taylor, *Nuclear Theft*, 14.
42. "Global Fissile Material Report 2007," 13.
43. Ibid., 3
44. See, Bernstein, *Plutonium*, 159–160, and Garwin and Charpak, *Megawatts and Megaton*, 136–137.
45. Plutonium-238 is created when uranium-238 absorbs a neutron, becoming uranium-239, and then emits two neutrons. The resultant uranium-237 beta-decays into neptunium-237, which can become neptunium-238 after absorbing another neutron. This, in turn, can beta-decay into plutonium-238. Such circumstances occur if the plutonium is extracted from the rector after a relatively long period of time. See Bernstein, *Plutonium*, 159–160.
46. Richard L. Garwin and George Charpak, *Megawatts and Megaton: The Future of Nuclear Power and Nuclear Weapons* (Chicago: University of Chicago Press, 2001), 136–137; and, J. Carson Mark, "Reactor-Grade Plutonium's Explosive Properties," NPT/95, *Nuclear Control Institute*, August 1990, available at http://www.nci.org/NEW/NT/rgpu-mark-90.pdf (accessed 02/03/06). "Global Fissile Material Report 2007," 34.
47. Mark, "Reactor-Grade Plutonium's Explosive Properties" (emphasis added).
48. Leona Marshall Libby, *The Uranium People* (New York: Charles Scribner's Sons, 1979), 210.
49. Richard L. Garwin, "Reactor-Grade Plutonium Can be Used to Make Powerful and Reliable Nuclear Weapons," *Council on Foreign Relations*, August 26, 1998, available at http://www.fas.org/rlg/980826-pu.htm (accessed 05/25/05). It has been argued too that the relatively intense heat of reactor-grade plutonium, compared to that of WGP, would overheat "the thick high-explosive that surrounds the plutonium and any additional metal shells in a simple implosion weapon." However, it is now generally acknowledged that this development could be avoided by simply inserting the plutonium into the device just prior to detonation. Ibid.
50. Libby, *The Uranium People*, 210.
51. Matthew Bunn and Anthony Wier, *Securing the Bomb: 2007* (Cambridge, MA, and Washington, DC: Project on Managing the Atom, Harvard University/Nuclear Threat Initiative, 2007), vi.
52. The HEU that the Iraqis planned on using for their first few nuclear weapons—during the "crash program" of 1990—utilized the HEU from 5 megawatt and 40 megawatt research reactors. See Bukharin, Ficek, and Roston, "US-Russian Reduced Enrichment for Research and Test Reactors (RERTR) Cooperation."
53. "Nuclear Nonproliferation: DOE Needs to Take Action to Further Reduce the Use of Weapons-Usable Uranium in Civilian Research Reactors," *Government Accountability Office*, US Congress, GAO- 04-807, 2004, 28.

54. Matthew Bunn and Anthony Wier, "Terrorist Nuclear Weapon Construction: How Difficult?" *Annals of the American Academy of Political and Social Science* 607 (September 2006), 137.
55. Extracting HEU from research reactor fuel, noted James C. Warf, a nuclear specialist who headed the chemical processing program during the Manhattan project, "are not difficult procedures, particularly for someone intent on acquiring an atomic explosive; one might say, in fact, that they are not beyond the ability of most students in introductory chemistry classes at the college level." As quoted in Matthew Bunn and Anthony Wier, *Securing the Bomb: 2007*, 6.
56. Ibid., 138.
57. Ibid., 37.
58. Author's interview with Dr. Edwin Lyman, Senior Staff Scientist, Global Security Program, Union of Concerned Scientists, 02/27/08.
59. Bunn and Wier, *Securing the Bomb: 2007*, 78. Bunn and Wier conclude that Russian HEU-fueled civilian research reactor sites would "have great difficulty defending against a Beslan-scale attack (more than 30 well-trained attackers with automatic weapons, rocket-propelled grenades, and explosives, striking without warning)." Ibid.
60. Levi, *On Nuclear Terrorism*, 43.
61. Ibid.
62. For a detailed description of the technical parameters of reflectors, see "Military Critical Technologies List (MCTL) Part II: Weapons of Mass Destruction Technologies, Nuclear Systems Technology," *US Department of Defense*, 1998, Section 5, 58, available at http://www.fas.org/irp/threat/mctl98-2/p2sec05.pdf (accessed 02/02/08).
63. Robert Serber, *The Los Alamos Primer: The First LEctures on How to Build An Atomic Bomb,* (Berkeley, University of California Press: 1992), 43–44.
64. Jeremy Bernstein, *Nuclear Weapons: What You Need to Know* (New York: Cambridge University Press, 2007), 132.
65. Ibid, 133. See also Alexander Glaser, "On the Proliferation Potential of Uranium Fuel for Research Reactors at Various Enrichment Levels," *Science & Global Security,* vol. 14, no. 1 (2006), available at http://www.princeton.edu/~aglaser/2006aglaser_sgs-vol14.pdf (accessed 02/01/08).
66. For potential weapons' yield, see Ferguson and Potter, *The Four Faces of Nuclear Terrorism* (New York: Routledge, 2005), 112.
67. Mark, "Reactor-Grade Plutonium's Explosive Properties." See also Garwin and Charpak, *Megawatts and Megaton*, 315.
68. Richard L. Garwin and Frank N von Hippel, "A Technical Analysis of North Korea's Oct. 9 Nuclear Test, *Arms Control Today*, November 2006, available at http://www.armscontrol.org/act/2006_11/NKTestAnalysis.asp (accessed 05/06/07). The test reportedly utilized 6 kg of plutonium. See "North Korea Claims 30 Kilograms of Plutonium," *Global Security Newswire*, April 21, 2008, available at http://www.nti.org/d_newswire/issues/2008_4_21.html#30E487A0 (accessed 04/21/08).
69. Author's interview with Dr. Siegfried S. Hecker, co-director, Center for International Security and Cooperation, 03/10/08.
70. Author's interview, Dr. Louis Rosen, former Manhattan Project weaponeer and Los Alamos National Laboratory Fellow, 11/30/07.
71. See Richard. R. Paternoster, *Nuclear Weapon Proliferation: Indicators and Observables* (Los Alamos, NM: Los Alamos National Laboratory, 1992), 15, available at http://www.fas.org/sgp/othergov/doe/lanl/la-12430-ms.pdf (accessed 03/04/08).

72. U.S. Department of Defense, "Military Critical Technologies List (MCTL)," 60.
73. See Paternoster, *Nuclear Weapon Proliferation*, 14–15; and Levi, *On Nuclear Terrorism*, 43–44.
74. Bernstein, *Nuclear Weapons*, 132–133.
75. U.S. Department of Defense, "Military Critical Technologies List (MCTL)", 62; and Levi, *On Nuclear Terrorism*, 45–46.
76. Ibid.
77. See, for example, Robin Frost, "Nuclear Terrorism After 9/11," *Adelphi Papers*, December 2005, 45:378.
78. Richard Lugar, "The Lugar Survey on Proliferation Threats and Responses," June 2005, available at http://lugar.senate.gov/reports/NPSurvey.pdf (accessed 01/18/08).
79. See Peter Stein and Peter Feaver, *Assuring Control of Nuclear Weapons: The Evolution of Permissive Action Links* (Lanham, MD: University Press of America, 1987); Dan Caldwell and Peter D. Zimmerman, "Reducing the Risk of Nuclear War with Permissive Action Links," in Barry M. Blechman, ed., *Technology and the Limitation of International Conflict* (Washington, DC: SAIC, 1989), 149; and "Military Critical Technologies List (MCTL) Part II: Weapons of Mass Destruction Technologies, Nuclear Systems Technology," U.S. Department of Defense, 1998, Section 5, 68, available at http://www.fas.org/irp/threat/mctl98-2/p2sec05.pdf (accessed 02/02/08).
80. As quoted in Caldwell and Zimmerman, "Reducing the Risk of Nuclear War with Permissive Action Links," 159.
81. Zia Mian, "A Nuclear Tiger By the Tail: Problems of Command and Control in South Asia," in M. V. Ramana and C. Rammanohar Reddy, eds., *Prisoners of the Nuclear Dream* (New Delhi: Orient Longman, 2003), 107; see also Bruce Blair, "Keeping Presidents in the Nuclear Dark (Episode #1: The Case of the Missing Permissive Action Links)," Center For Defense Information, Bruce Blair's Nuclear Column, February 11, 2004, available at http://www.cdi.org/blair/permissive-action-links.cfm (accessed 03/21/2008).
82. See Gerald W. Johhnson, "Safety, Security, and Control of Nuclear Weapons," in Blechman, ed., *Technology and the Limitation of International Conflict*, 149.
83. "Nuclear Weapon Design," *Federation of American Scientists*, October 1998, available at http://www.fas.org/nuke/intro/nuke/design.htm.
84. For a study concluding that some modern SAFF systems can be overcome with "limited imagination," see Allison, *Nuclear Terrorism*, 90.
85. See, for example, Ferguson and Potter, *Four Faces of Nuclear Terrorism*, 66–67. For a discussion outlining the differences between strategic and tactical nuclear weapons, see Brian Alexander and Alistair Millar, eds., *Tactical Nuclear Weapons* (Washington, DC: Brassey's Inc., 2003), 6. For U.S. arsenal numbers, see, Robert S. Norris and Hans M. Kristensen, "US Nuclear Forces 2008," *Bulletin of the Atomic Scientists* (March/April 2008), 50–53, 58, available at http://thebulletin.metapress.com/content/pr53n270241156n6/fulltext.pdf (accessed 03/20/08).
86. Ferguson and Potter, *The Four Faces of Nuclear Terrorism*, 66–67. See also Michael Hoffman, "Nuclear Safety Slipped for Years Before Minot," *Air Force Times*, February, 26, 2008, available at http://www.airforcetimes.com/news/2008/02/airforce_250208_nukesafety/ (accessed 03/03/08). See also Scott D. Sagan, *The Limits of Safety: Organizations, Accidents, and Nuclear Weapons* (Princeton, NJ: Princeton University Press, 1993).

87. William C. Potter, "Book Review: Using Murphy's Law Against Nuclear Terrorist," *Arms Control Today*, April 2008, available at http://www.armscontrol.org/act/2008_04/BookReview.asp (accessed 04/20/08).
88. Joshua Handler, "The 1991–1992 PNIs and the Elimination, Storage and Security or Tactical Nuclear Weapons," in Brian Alexander and Alistair Millar, eds., *Tactical Nuclear Weapons*, 32.
89. See Robert S. Norris and Hans M. Kristensen, "US Nuclear Forces 2008," *Bulletin of the Atomic Scientists* (January/February 2008), 81, available at http://thebulletin.metapress.com/content/91n36687821608un/fulltext.pdf (accessed 03/20/08).
90. See Charles P. Blair and Jean P. du Preez, "Visions of Fission: The Demise of Negative Security Assurances on the Bush Administration's Pentomic Battlefield," *Nonproliferation Review*, March 2005, 41–42.
91. See, for example, John M. Shields and William C. Potter, eds., *Dismantling the Cold War* (Cambridge, MA: Harvard University Press, 1997).
92. For an overview of recent efforts, see Jennifer Lackie, Reported Accomplishments of Selected Threat Reduction and Nonproliferation Programs, By Agency, for Fiscal Year 2006, Partnership for Global Security, July 2007, available at http://www.ransac.org/Publications/Reports%20and%20Publications/Reports/index.asp (accessed 12/13/07).
93. See Bunn and Weir, *Securing the Bomb: 2007*.
94. Mathew Bunn Testimony, United States Senate Committee on Homeland Security and Governmental Affairs Hearing on "Nuclear Terrorism: Assessing the Threat to the Homeland," April 2, 2008, 7, available at http://hsgac.senate.gov/public/_files/040208Bunn.pdf (accessed 4/5/08).
95. Robert S. Norris and Hans M. Kristensen, "Russian Nuclear Forces, 2008," *Bulletin of the Atomic Scientists* (May/June 2008), 54–57, available at http://thebulletin.metapress.com/content/t2j78437407v3qv1/fulltext.pdf (accessed 04/29/08).
96. Russian nuclear weapon experts have reported an "absence" of PALS on older generation Russian tactical nuclear weapons. William Potter and Nickolai Sokov, "Tactical Nuclear Weapons: The Nature of the Problem," CNS Report, James Martin Center for Nonproliferation Studies, January 4, 2001, available at http://cns.miis.edu/pubs/reports/tnw_nat.htm (accessed 07/21/07). See also Ferguson and Potter, *Four Faces of Nuclear Terrorism*, 62.
97. Russia is considered one of the most corrupt countries in the world. See Transparency International, "Corruption Perceptions Index," 2007, available at http://www.transparency.org/policy_research/surveys_indices/cpi/2007 (accessed 04/01/08).
98. See Gordon M. Hahn, *Russia's Islamic Threat* (New Haven, CT: Yale University Press, 2007); Gordon M. Hahn, "The Jihadi Insurgency and the Russian Counterinsurgency in the North Caucuses," *Post-Soviet Affairs*, 2008, 24, 1; and, Gordon M. Hahn, "The New Caucasus Emirate?" *Russia Profile*, November 29, 2007, available at http://www.russiaprofile.org/ (accessed 03/12/08).
99. Hahn, *Russia's Islamic Threat*, 229.
100. See ibid.; Bunn and Weir, *Securing the Bomb: 2007*; and Simon Saradzhyan, "Russia: Grasping Reality of Nuclear Terror," International Security Program, Belfer Center for Science and International Affairs, 2003, 28, available at http://belfercenter.ksg.harvard.edu/files/saradzhyan_2003_02.pdf (accessed 03/24/08).
101. See, for example, Hahn, *Russia's Islamic Threat*, 229–230.
102. See Steve Gutterman, "Russia: Intruders Targeted Nuclear Site," AP June 22, 2005; "Terrorists Make Two Attempts on Russia Nuke Facilities," *Itar-Tass*, June 22, 2005; Andrew Osborn, "Chechen Militants Have Tried to Steal Nuclear Weapons

Twice, Says Russian Security Chief," *The Independent* June 24, 2005; National Intelligence Council, Annual Report to Congress on the Safety and Security of Russian Nuclear Facilities and Military Forces, December 2004, 6, available at http://www.dni.gov/nic/PDF_GIF_otherprod/russiannuke04.pdf (accessed 01/30/07). See also Bunn and Weir, *Securing the Bomb: 2007*, vi.

103. Robin M. Frost, "Nuclear Terrorism After 9/11," 8.
104. Robert S. Norris and Hans M. Kristensen, "British Nuclear Forces, 2005," *Bulletin of the Atomic Scientists* (November/December 2005), 81, available at http://thebulletin.metapress.com/content/k52425n3320m8644/fulltext.pdf (accessed 03/20/08).This assessment of the security of the United Kingdom's nuclear arsenal does not include the over 100 tactical U.S. nuclear weapons stationed at Lakenheath base in Suffolk, England. See also Shannon N. Kile, Vitaly Fedchenko, and Hans M. Kristensen, "World Nuclear Forces," in *SIPRI Yearbook 2006: Armaments, Disarmament and International Security* (Oxford: Oxford University Press, 2006).
105. See, for example, Ferguson and Potter, *Four Faces of Nuclear Terrorism*, 62.
106. Robert S. Norris and Hans M. Kristensen, "French Nuclear Forces 2005," *Bulletin of the Atomic Scientists* (July/August 2005), 73–75, available at http://thebulletin.metapress.com/content/n8rn0x5567572723/fulltext.pdf (accessed 03/20/08). See also "France to Reduce Nuclear Warheads," BBC News, 03/21/08.
107. Ferguson and Potter, *The Four Faces of Nuclear Terrorism*, 62, 99.
108. Robert S. Norris and Hans M. Kristensen, "Chinese Nuclear Forces 2006," *Bulletin of the Atomic Scientists* (May/June 2006), 60–63, available at http://thebulletin.metapress.com/content/1w035m8u644p864u/fulltext.pdf (accessed 03/08/08).
109. Hans M. Kristensen, Robert S. Norris, and Matthew G. McKinzie, "Chinese Nuclear War Forces and US Nuclear War Planning," The Federation of American Scientists and The Natural Resources Defense Council, November 2006, 98–104, available at http://www.fas.org/nuke/guide/china/Book2006.pdf (accessed 03/01/08). See also Charles D. Ferguson, Evan S. Medeiros, and Phillip C. Saunders, "Chinese Tactical Nuclear Weapons," in Brian Alexander and Alistair Millar eds., *Tactical Nuclear Weapons*, 110–126.
110. Jeffrey Lewis, *The Minimum Means of Reprisal: China's Search for Security in the Nuclear Age* (London: MIT Press, 2007), 38–39; see also Zia Mian, "A Nuclear Tiger By the Tail: Problems of Command and Control in South Asia," in Ramana and Reddy, eds., *Prisoners of the Nuclear Dream*, 105. See also Ferguson and Potter, *The Four Faces of Nuclear Terrorism*, 62.
111. See Nathan Busch, "China's Fissile Material Protection, Control, and Accounting: The Case for Renewed Collaboration," *Nonproliferation Review*, Fall/Winter 2002, 97–98, available at http://cns.miis.edu/pubs/npr/vol09/93/93busch.pdf.
112. See Ian Ransom, "China Says it Foils Plot to Kidnap Olympians," Reuters, April 10, 2008.
113. Robert S. Norris, Hans M. Kristensen, and Joshua Handler, "Israeli Nuclear Forces 2002," *Bulletin of the Atomic Scientists* (September/October 2002), 73–75.
114. See Nuclear Weapons: Israel, Federation of American Scientists, last update January 8, 2007, available at http://www.fas.org/nuke/guide/israel/nuke/index.html (accessed 02/04/08).
115. Seymour M. Hersh, *The Sampson Option* (New York: Random House, 1991), 216–217
116. Ferguson and Potter, *The Four Faces of Nuclear Terrorism*, 62.

117. Verghese Koithara, "Coersion and Risk-Taking in Nuclear South Asia," CISAC Working Paper, Center for International Security and Cooperation, March, 2003, 20.
118. Robert S. Norris and Hans M. Kristensen, "India's Nuclear Forces, 2007," *Bulletin of the Atomic Scientists*, July/August 2007, 74.
119. Koithara, "Coersion and Risk-Taking in Nuclear South Asia," 13.
120. See MIPT Terrorism Knowledge Base, "TKB Groups Page: India," available at http://www.tkb.org/Category.jsp?catID=221 (accessed 03/21/08).
121. See Gary Ackerman et al., *Assessing Terrorist Motivations for Attacking Critical Infrastructure* (Livermore CA: Lawrence Livermore National Laboratory, 2007), 56–61, available at https://e-reports-ext.llnl.gov/pdf/341566.pdf (accessed 03/22/08).
122. Terrorism Focus, The Jamestown Foundation, September 12, 2006, 3, available at http://www.jamestown.org/terrorism/news/article.php?issue_id=3852 (accessed 11/12/07). See also Andrew Prosser, "Nuclear Trafficking Routes: Dangerous Trends in Southern Asia," Center for Defense Information, November 22, 2004.
123. See Kerry Boyd, "India Establishes Formal Nuclear Command Structure," *Arms Control Today*, January/February 2003, available at http://www.armscontrol.org/act/2003_01-02/india_janfeb03.asp (accessed 07/10/08); and Gregory S. Jones, "From Testing to Deploying Nuclear Forces: The Hard Choices Facing India and Pakistan," Rand Issue Paper, Rand Corporation, Santa Monica, CA, 2000.
124. Sharon Squassoni, "Nuclear Threat Reduction Measures for India and Pakistan," Congressional Research Service, February 17, 2005, 9, available at http://digital.library.unt.edu/govdocs/crs/permalink/meta-crs-6185:1 (accessed 11/01/07). See also Koithara, "Coersion and Risk-Taking in Nuclear South Asia," 19.
125. See "Nuclear Notebook, Pakistan's Nuclear Forces 2007," *Bulletin of the Atomic Scientists*, May/June 2007, 71. See also Shaun Gregory, "The Security of Nuclear Weapons in Pakistan," Pakistan Security Research Unit (PRSU), Brief Number 22, November 18, 2007, 3, available at http://spaces.brad.ac.uk:8080/download/attachments/748/Brief_22finalised.pdf (accessed 04/05/08). See also Joseph Cirincione, Jon B. Wolfsthal, and Miriam Rajkumar, *Deadly Arsenals: Nuclear, Biological, and Chemical Threats* (Washington, DC: Carnegie Endowment for International Peace, 2005), 239; and David Albright and Kimberly Kramer, "Fissile Materials: Stockpiles Still Growing," *Bulletin of the Atomic Scientists*, November/December 2004, 14–16, available at http://www.isis-online.org/global_stocks/bulletin_albright_kramer.pdf (accessed 02/13/08).
126. See U.S. Congress, Government Accountability Office (GAO), *Combating Terrorism: The United States Lacks Comprehensive Plan to Destroy the Terrorist Threat and Close the Safe Haven in Pakistan's Federally Administered Tribal Areas*, GAO-08-622 (Washington, DC: GAO, 2008), 9.
127. For an overview of notable jihadist groups active in Pakistan, see Nicholas Howenstein, "The Jihadi Terrain in Pakistan: An Introduction to the Sunni Jihadi Groups in Pakistan and Kashmir," Pakistan Security Research Unit (PRSU), Research Report 1, February 5, 2008, available at http://spaces.brad.ac.uk:8080/download/attachments/748/Brief_22finalised.pdf (accessed 04/05/08).
128. See, for example, Jon B. Wolfsthal, "US Needs a Contingency Plan for Pakistan's Nuclear Arsenal," *Los Angeles Times*, October, 16, 2001; and Bruce G. Blair, "The Ultimate Hatred Is Nuclear," *The New York Times*, October 23, 2001; Seymour Hersh, "Watching The Warheads," *The New Yorker*, November 5, 2001; and John Barry, "Priority: Pakistan's Nukes," *Newsweek International*, November 12, 2001.

For pre-9/11 assessments that deal with Pakistan's nuclear guardianship, see Clayton P. Bowen and Daniel Wolvén, "Command and Control Challenges In South Asia," *The Nonproliferation Review*, Spring/Summer 1999; and Zafar Iqbal Cheema, "Pakistan's Nuclear Use Doctrine and Command and Control," in Peter R. Lavoy, Scott D. Sagan, and James J. Wirtz, eds., *Planning the Unthinkable* (Ithaca, NY, and London: Cornell University Press, 2000).

129. U.S. Department of Defense (DoD), *Report of the Quadrennial Defense Review* (Arlington, VA: DoD, 2006), 32, available at http://www.defenselink.mil/qdr/report/Report20060203.pdf (accessed 02/19/08).
130. See Paolo Cotta-Ramusino and Maurizio Martellini, "Nuclear Safety, Nuclear Stability and Nuclear Strategy in Pakistan," Landau Network—Centro Volta, January 2002, available at http://www.pugwash.org/september11/pakistan-nuclear.htm (accessed 01/25/07). See also, for example, Zafar Ali, "Pakistan's Nuclear Assets And Threats of Terrorism: How Grave Is The Danger?" The Henry L. Stimson Center, July 2007, http://www.stimson.org/southasia/pdf/PakistanNuclearAssets-070607-ZafarAli-FINAL.pdf (accessed 01/21/08).
131. See, for example, Paul Kerr and Mary Beth Nikitin, "Pakistan's Nuclear Weapons: Proliferation and Security Issues," CRS Report for Congress, Congressional Research Service, January 28, 2008, 4; and Gurmeet Kanwal, "Are Pakistan's Nuclear Warheads Safe?" Pakistan Security Research Unit (PRSU), Brief Number 27, November 18, 2007, 3, available at http://spaces.brad.ac.uk:8080/download/attachments/748/Brief27finalised.pdf (accessed 04/05/08).
132. "Pakistan Could Pose Nuclear Threat, Turkey Says," Global Security Newswire, March 3, 2008, available at http://www.nti.org/d_newswire/issues/2008_3_10.html#A14D244B (accessed 03/10/08).
133. Peter Lavoy, "Pakistan's Nuclear Posture: Security and Survivability," Paper presented to the Conference on Pakistan's Nuclear Future, Nonproliferation Education Center, Washington, DC, April 28, 2006, 10, available at http://www.npec-web.org/Frameset.asp?PageType=Single&PDFFile=20070121-Lavoy-PakistanNuclear-Posture&PDFFolder=Essays (accessed 03/19/08).
134. As quoted in Gregory, "The Security of Nuclear Weapons in Pakistan," 4. See also Kerr and Nikitin, "Pakistan's Nuclear Weapons." In a November 2006 speech, the Director General of Pakistan's Strategic Plans Division (SPD), Lt. Gen. Khalid Kidwai, stated that Pakistan had the "functional equivalent" of PALs. Robin Walker, "Paksitan's Evolution as a Nuclear Weapons State," Center for Contemporary Conflict, November 1, 2006, available at http://www.ccc.nps.navy.mil/news/kidwaiNov06.asp (accessed 03/23/08).
135. See, for example, Zafar Ali, "Pakistan's Nuclear Assets And Threats of Terrorism: How Grave Is The Danger?" The Henry L. Stimson Center, July 2007, available at http://www.stimson.org/southasia/pdf/PakistanNuclearAssets-070607-ZafarAli-FINAL.pdf (accessed 01/21/08); and Gregory, "The Security of Nuclear Weapons in Pakistan," 4.
136. See, for example, Frédéric Grare, "Pakistan: The Myth of an Islamist Peril," Carnegie Endowment for International Peace, Policy Brief , no 45, February 2006, available at http://www.carnegieendowment.org/files/45.grare.final.pdf (accessed 02/16/08).
137. Ibid.

138. See, for example, Subodh Atal, "Extremist, Nuclear Pakistan an Emerging Threat," Policy Analysis, No. 472, March 5, 2003, available at http://www.cato.org/pubs/pas/pa472.pdf (accessed 02/21/08); and Gregory, "The Security of Nuclear Weapons in Pakistan," 8.
139. See, for example, Atal, "Extremist, Nuclear Pakistan an Emerging Threat."
140. See, for example, Kanwal, "Are Pakistan's Nuclear Warheads Safe?"
141. Grare, "Pakistan: The Myth of an Islamist Peril," 3.
142. Cirincione, "Pakistanis under Musharraf and the Bush Doctrine."
143. See, for example, Andrew Koch and Kristin Rayhack, "Political Fallout—The Threat to Pakistan's Nuclear Stability," *Jane's Intelligence Review*, December 14, 2007; Kenneth N. Luongo and Brig. Gen. (Ret.) Naeem Salik, "Building Confidence in Pakistan's Nuclear Security," *Arms Control Today*, December 2007, available at http://www.armscontrol.org/act/2007_12/Luongo.asp (accessed 01/30/08); and Gaurav Kampani, "Safety Concerns About the Command & Control of Pakistan's Strategic Forces, Fissile Material, and Nuclear Installations," Center for Nonproliferation Studies, September 28, 2001, available at http://cns.miis.edu/research/wtc01/spna.htm (accessed 03/20/08).
144. For overview of the Khan Network see Gordon Corera, *Shopping for Bombs: Nuclear Proliferation, Global Insecurity, and the Rise and Fall of the A.Q. Khan Network* (Oxford: Oxford University Press, 2006); and William Langwiesche, *The Atomic Bazaar: The Rise of the Nuclear Poor* (New York: Faraar, Straus and Giroux, 2007).
145. See William J. Broad, David E. Sanger, and Raymond Bonner, "A Tale of Nuclear Proliferation: How Pakistani Built His Network," *New York Times*, February 12, 2004; and Michael Krepon, "Lessons from an Unpunished Crime in Pakistan," YaleGlobal Online, February 9, 2004, available at http://yaleglobal.yale.edu/display.article?id=3285 (accessed 02/21/08).
146. "Schematic drawings of fission explosive devices of the earliest types showing qualitative ways the principles used in achieving the first fission explosives are widely available." Taylor, Mark, et al., "Can Terrorists Build Nuclear Weapons?" in Leventhal and Alexander eds., *Preventing Nuclear Terrorism*, 58. See also William J. Broad, "Libya's Crude Bomb Design Eases Western Experts' Fear," *The New York Times*, February 9, 2004.
147. "U.S. has no good option in a Pakistan nuclear 'nightmare'," AFP, November 13, 2007, available at http://afp.google.com/article/ALeqM5h8fV0RNHzwjzr5ph0yDNZZl1fWMw (accessed 02/02/08). See also Pervez Hoodbhoy, "Letters to the Editor: 'Trust Us' Is Not Enough in Pakistan," Arms Control Today, March 2008, available at http://www.armscontrol.org/act/2008_03/Letter.asp (accessed 03/21/08).
148. "U.S. has no good options in a Pakistan nuclear 'nighmare'."
149. See David Albright, Paul Brannan, and Jacqueline Shire, "North Korea's Plutonium Declaration: A Starting Point for an Initial Verification Process," Institute of Science and International Security, January 10, 2008, 1, available at http://www.isis-online.org/publications/dprk/NorthKoreaDeclaration10Jan2008.pdf (accessed 03/10/08).
150. See Richard K. Betts, "Suicide from Fear of Death?" *Foreign Affairs*, January/February 2003.

151. For an inventory of North Korean missile sales see Greg Miller, "North Korea Threat Lies in Nuclear Sales," *Los Angeles Times*, October 21, 2006. See also Sharon A. Squassoni, "Weapons or Mass Destruction: Trade Between North Korea and Pakistan," CRS Report of Congress, RL31900, October 11, 2006, available at http://www.fas.org/sgp/crs/nuke/RL31900.pdf (accessed 12/02/07).
152. Emma Chanlett-Avery, "North Korea's Nuclear Test: Motivations, Implications, and US Options," CRS Report for Congress, RL33709, October 24, 2006, 11, available at http://www.fas.org/sgp/crs/nuke/RL33709.pdf (accessed 03/02/08).
153. Ibid. A recent report produced for the U.S. Congress stated that, "North Korea is an established exporter of ballistic missiles, and many observers, including the US government, equate North Korea's willingness to supply those items with a willingness to sell nuclear weapons or fissile materials." Ibid., 10.
154. Bill Gertz, "N. Korea Would Sell Nukes to Terrorists," *The Washington Times*, February 5, 2008.
155. "US to Boost Nuclear Forensics Funds, Official Says," Global Security Newswire, December 4, 2006, available at http://www.nti.org/d_newswire/issues/2006_12_4.html (accessed 12/05/2007).
156. Daniel A. Pinkston and Phillip C. Saunders, "Seeing North Korea Clearly," *Survival*, vol. 45, no. 3, Autumn 2003, 79–102.
157. Ibid.
158. Dr. Siegfried S. Hecker, "Report on North Korean Nuclear Program," Center for International Security and Cooperation, Stanford University, November 15, 2006. Emphasis added.
159. Author's interview with Dr. Siegfried S. Hecker, Co-Director, Center for International Security and Cooperation, 03/10/08.
160. See David Albright and Paul Brannan, "Syria Update III: New Information about Al Kibar reactor site," April 24, 2008, available at http://www.isis-online.org/publications/syria/SyriaUpdate_24April2008.pdf (accessed 04/24/08).
161. Bush, speech to the National Endowment for Democracy, October 6, 2005, available at http://www.whitehouse.gov/news/releases/2005/10/20051006-3.html (accessed 03/18/08).
162. See "National Intelligence Estimate: Iran's Nuclear Intentions and Capabilities," National Intelligence Council, Office of the Director of National Intelligence, November 2007, 6, available at http://www.dni.gov/press_releases/20071203_release.pdf (accessed 12/03/08). Emphasis added.
163. See Kurt M. Cambell and Tsuyoshi Sunohara, "Japan: Thinking the Unthinkable," in Kurt M. Campbell, Robert J. Einhorn, and Mitchell B. Reiss, eds., *The Nuclear Tipping Point: Why States Reconsider Their Nuclear Choices* (Washington, DC: Brookings, 2004), 243.
164. See Trita Parsi, *Treacherous Alliance: The Secret Dealings of Israel, Iran and the US* (New Haven, CT: Yale University Press, 2007).
165. Yaakov Katz, "IDF Developing Countermeasures to Iran's WMD Threat. Egypt Lends Israel Support for Efforts to Stop Teheran's Race to Nukes, 'Post' Learns," *Jerusalem Post*, September 19, 2006; "Iran is Judged 10 Years From Nuclear Bomb," *Washington Post*, August 2, 2005; and David Albright, "When Could Iran Get the Bomb?" *Bulletin of the Atomic Scientist*," July/August 2006.
166. See David Albright and Jacqueline Shire, "A Witches' Brew? Evaluating Iran's Uranium-Enrichment Progress," *Arms Control Today*, November 2007, available at http://www.armscontrol.org/act/2007_11/Albright.asp (accessed 12/01/2007).

167. See ibid.
168. See, for example, Gerald M. Steinberg, "Deterrence Instability: Hizballah's Fuse to Iran's Bomb," *Jerusalem Viewpoints*, No 529, April 2005, available at http://www.jcpa.org/jl/vp529.htm (accessed 02/21/08); and Ferguson and Potter, *The Four Faces of Nuclear Terrorism*, 319.
169. Author's interview with Dr. Jeffrey M. Bale, Director, Monterey Terrorism Research and Education Program, 03/19/08.
170. See, for example, "McCain Says It's 'Common Knowledge' That Iran Is Training Al Qaeda," Inforwars.net, March 16, 2008, available at http://infowars.net/articles/march2008/180308McCain.htm.
171. Sammy Salama and Elizabeth Salch, "Iran's Nuclear Impasse: Give Negotiations A Chance," James Martin Center for Nonproliferation Studies, CNS Research Story, June 2, 2006, available at http://cns.miis.edu/pubs/week/060602.htm (accessed 03/10/08).
172. Nuclear forensics would likely trace the blast back to Iranian uranium or plutonium. Charles P. Blair, "If Nuclear Terrorists Succeed: The Role of Post-Blast Forensics and Motivational Analysis in Determining Culpability," unpublished manuscript, Center for Nonproliferation Studies, 2005. See also Chris Schneidmiller, "More Nuclear Detectives Needed in Crisis, Groups Say," Global Security Newswire, February 20, 2008, available at http://204.71.60.36/d_newswire/issues/2008_2_20.html#D9445446 (accessed, 03/20/08).
173. Details of U.S. nuclear employment guidelines vis-à-vis Iran can be found in Hans Kristensen, "White House Guidance Led to New Nuclear Strike Plans Against Proliferators, Document Shows," November 5, 2007, available at http://www.fas.org/blog/ssp/2007/11/white_house_guidance_led_to_ne.php (accessed 04/01/08). See also Hans M. Kristensen, "US Strategic War Planning After 9/11," *Nonproliferation Review*, July 2007, available at http://cns.miis.edu/pubs/npr/vol14/142/142kristensen.pdf (accessed 04/01/08).
174. See, for example, Parsi, *Treacherous Alliance.*
175. Ibid., 269
176. Lugar, "The Lugar Survey on Proliferation Threats and Responses."
177. Sonia Ben Ouagrham-Gormley, "An Unrealized Nexus? WMD-Related Trafficking, Terrorism, and Organized Crime in the Former Soviet Union," *Arms Control Today*, July/August 2008, available at http://www.armscontrol.org/act/2007_07-08/CoverStory.asp (accessed 03/13/08).
178. Chris Schneidmiller, "Answers on Nuclear Smuggling Remain Elusive," NTI Global Security Newswire, February 19, 2008. See also "Incidents Involving HEU and Pu Confirmed to the ITDB, 1993–2006," IAEA Office of Nuclear Security, 2007, available at http://www.iaea.org/NewsCenter/Focus/NuclearSecurity/pdf/heu-pu_1993-2006.pdf (accessed 01/21/08).
179. See "Combating Illicit Trafficking in Nuclear and other Radioactive Material," *IAEA Nuclear Series,* no. 6 (Vienna: International Atomic Energy Agency, 2007), 126–135.
180. Author's interview, with Dr. Sonia Ben Ouagrham, Editor-in-Chief of the *NIS Export Control Observer*, March 13, 2008.
181. Ibid.
182. Lyudmila Zaitseva, "Organized Crime, Terrorism and Nuclear Trafficking," *Strategic Insights*, vol. 6, no. 5, August 2007, available at http://www.ccc.nps.navy.mil/si/2007/Aug/zaitsevaAug07.asp#references (accessed 01/30/08).

183. Ibid.
184. See, for example, *Commission on the Intelligence Capabilities of the United States Regarding Weapons of Mass Destruction, Report to the President* (Washington, DC: WMD Commission, 2005), 272, available at http://www.wmd.gov/report/wmd_report.pdf (accessed 02/18/08).
185. See also David Albright, "Al Qaeda's Nuclear Program: Through the Window of Seized Documents," *The Nautilus Institute: Special Policy Forum* 47, November 6, 2002, available at http://www.nautilus.org/archives/fora/Special-Policy-Forum/47_Albright.html (accessed 12/03/03). See also Anne Stenersen, "Al Qa'ida's Thinking on CBRN: A Case Study," in Magnus Ranstorp, ed., *Unconventional Weapons and International Terrorism* (New York: Routledge, 2009).
186. *United States of America v. Usama bin Ladin*, Indictment 98Cr., United States District Court Southern District of New York, 19, available at http://cns.miis.edu/pubs/reports/pdfs/binLadin/indict.pdf (accessed 02/13/08). See also Testimony of Mamdouh Mahmud Salim, as quoted in Peter Bergen, *The Usama bin Ladin I Know* (New York: Free Press, 2006), 339.
187. For an accounting of the 1993–1994 case and links to al-Fadl's testimony, see Kimberly McCloud and Matthew Osborne, "WMD Terrorism and Usama bin Ladin," *CNS Reports*, available at http://cns.miis.edu/pubs/reports/binLadin.htm (accessed 12/02/07). For al-Fadl's credibility, see Steve Coll, *Ghost Wars* (New York: Penguin Books, 2004), 367.
188. See, for example, Michael Scheuer, *Through Our Enemies' Eyes* (Washington, DC: Potomac Books, Inc, 2002), 71–74; "Al-Qa'ida's WMD Activities," *James Martin Center for Nonproliferation Studies*, May 13, 2005, available at http://cns.miis.edu/pubs/other/sjm_cht.htm (accessed 01/30/08). See also Sara Daly, John Parachini, and William Rosenau, "Aum Shinrikyo, Al Qaeda, and the Kinshasa Reactor: Implications of Three Case Studies for Combating Nuclear Terrorism," *RAND Project Air Force* (Santa Monica, CA: RAND Corporation, 2005), 29–33, available at http://www.rand.org/pubs/documented_briefings/2005/RAND_DB458.pdf (accessed 12/07/08).
189. For accounts of these meetings, see Bergen, *The Usama bin Ladin I Know*, 340–341; Suskind, *The One Percent Doctrine*, 27, 47; David Albright and Holly Higgins, "A Bomb for Ummah," *Bulletin of Atomic Scientists*, March/April 2003, 49; and Albright, "Al Qaeda's Nuclear Program: Through the Window of Seized Documents."
190. Suskind, *The One Percent Doctrine*, 27.
191. Albright, "Al Qaeda's Nuclear Program.
192. Ibid.
193. See ibid.
194. Matthew Bunn, "The Demand for Black Market Fissile Material," *Nuclear Threat Initiative*, last updated, June 16, 2005, available at http://www.nti.org/e_research/cnwm/threat/demand.asp#_ftnref16 (accessed 01/26/08).
195. See, for example, Max Delany, "Under Attack al-Qaeda Makes Nuclear Claim," *The Moscow News*, March 3, 2004; "N-Weapons May Be in US Already," *Daily Telegraph* (Sydney, Australia), November 14, 2001; Craig Whitlock, "Germany Arrests Two Al Qaeda Suspects," *Washington Post*, January 24, 2005; and "Iraqi Al-Qaeda Suspect held in Germany Sent by Bin Ladin," *Agence France Presse*, January 29, 2005.
196. Kanwal, "Are Pakistan's Nuclear Warheads Safe?" 6

197. See, for example, Frank Davies, "Pakistani Urged al-Qa'ida to Obtain Nuclear Weapons, Authorities Say," *Knight Ridder Washington Bureau*, February 11, 2005; "US Charges Pakistani With Urging al Qa'ida to Acquire Weapons," *Press Trust of India*, February 14, 2005; "Qaeda Wants to Smuggle N-material to US," *The Nation*, November 17, 2004; "Bordering on Nukes," *Time Magazine*, November 22, 2004.
198. See, for example, "Al-Qa'ida's WMD Activities," James Martin Center for Nonproliferation Studies.
199. Testimony of Gary A. Ackerman before the United States Senate Committee on Homeland Security and Governmental Affairs Hearing on "Nuclear Terrorism: Assessing the Threat to the Homeland," April 2, 2008, 7, available at http://hsgac.senate.gov/public/_files/040208Ackerman3.pdf (accessed 04/05/08).
200. See, for example, Hahn, *Russia's Islamic Threat*, 229–230.
201. See, for example, Gloria Steward, "My 3 Million Pound Deal for Deadly Plutonium w/ Chechnya's Ruthless Mafiosa," *The Express* (in English), June 28, 1999; and Rensselaer Lee, "Nuclear Smuggling, Rogue States and Terrorists," *China and Eurasia Forum Quarterly*, vol.. 4, no. 2 (2006), 25.
202. Saradzhyan, "Russia: Grasping Reality of Nuclear Terror," 28. See also Bunn, Testimony: United States Senate Committee on Homeland Security and Governmental Affairs Hearing on "Nuclear Terrorism: Assessing the Threat to the Homeland," 3.
203. Steve Gutterman, "Russia: Intruders Targeted Nuclear Site," *AP*, June 22, 2005; and "Terrorists Make Two Attempts on Russia Nuke Facilities." Andrew Osborn, "Chechen Militants Have Tried to Steal Nuclear Weapons Twice.
204. See Hahn, *Russia's Islamic Threat*, 229; and Saradzhyan, "Russia: Grasping Reality of Nuclear Terror," 28.
205. Saradzhyan, "Russia: Grasping Reality of Nuclear Terror,"20.
206. Osborn, "Chechen Militants Have Tried to Steal Nuclear Weapons Twice, Says Russian Security Chief."
207. Robert Wesley, "Let Threat to Indian Nuclear Facilities Remains a Serious Concern," *Terrorism Focus* vol. 3, no. 35 (September 12, 2006).
208. Ibid.
209. "Indian PM Warns of More Likely Terrorist Attacks," *Dawn*, September 6, 2006.
210. Bill Riggio, "Al Qaeda, Targeting Pakistani Nuclear Sites," *The Long War Journal*, December 11, 2007, available at http://www.longwarjournal.org/archives/2007/12/al_qaeda_taliban_tar.php (accessed 01/12/08).
211. Ibid. See also "Missile Facilities: Sargodha Air Force Base," *Nuclear Threat Initiative (NTI),* December 2003, available at http://www.nti.org/e_research/profiles/Pakistan/Missile/3294_3319.html (accessed 04/12/08).
212. Riggio, "Al Qaeda, Targeting Pakistani Nuclear Sites."
213. "North Pakistan Suicide Attack Injures Seven," *AFP*, December 10, 2007.
214. "Kamra; Air Weapon Complex (AWC); Pakistan Aeronautical Complex (PAC)," *Federation of American Scientists*, last updated June 2000, available at http://www.fas.org/nuke/guide/pakistan/facility/kamra.htm (accessed 04/12/08).
215. Daly, Parachini, and Rosenau, "Aum Shinrikyo, Al Qaeda, and the Kinshasa Reactor," 48.
216. International Panel on Fissile Materials, Global Fissile Material Report 2007, 7.
217. Harold, A. Feiveson, "Faux Renaissance: Global Warming, Radioactive Waste Disposal, and the Nuclear Future," *Arms Control Today*, May 2007, available at http://www.armscontrol.org/act/2007_05/feiveson.asp (accessed 04/05/08).

218. See, for example, Micah Zenko, "A Nuclear Site is Breached: South African Attack Should Sound Alarms," *Washington Post,* December 20, 2007.
219. "Toward True Security: Ten Steps The Next President Should Take To Transform US Nuclear Weapons Policy," *Federation of American Scientists, Natural Resources Defense Council, Union of Concerned Scientists*, February 2008, 11.
220. See Campbell, Einhorn, and Reiss, *The Nuclear Tipping Point.*
221. Annual Threat Assessment of the Director of National Intelligence for the Senate Select Committee on Intelligence, February 5, 2008, available at http://www.dni.gov/testimonies/20080205_testimony.pdf (accessed 04/17/08).
222. "Top 9 Risks of 2008: Terror Risks Remain High," *Eurasia Group*, January 10, 2007, available at http://www.eurasiagroup.net/publications/0801-10Top9RisksTerrorism.pdf (accessed 04/24/08). See also "Timeline: Failed Car Bomb Attacks," *BBC News*, July 6, 2007, available at http://news.bbc.co.uk/2/hi/uk_news/6260626.stm (accessed 04/24/08).

APPENDIX
TOWARD A NUCLEAR WEAPON: PRINCIPLES OF NUCLEAR ENERGY

Charles P. Blair

The idea of going beyond the limitations of chemical explosives—of somehow tapping into the energy contained within the atom—can be traced directly to the discovery of radium in 1898. Within just seventy years of that discovery, global stockpiles of nuclear weapons exceeded 38,000 and the threat of global nuclear genocide was at hand.[1] This appendix examines the principles of nuclear energy that make nuclear weapons possible. By understanding the physics behind nuclear weaponry, readers can better appreciate the avenues and barriers that both terrorists and states encounter as they seek pathways to the bomb.

Discovery of Radioactive Materials

The concept of an atomic structure goes back 2,500 years to ancient Greece and, if one examines the work of Hindu philosophers, to an even earlier age.[2] However, not until the nineteenth century was the atom transformed from a "somewhat vague reality to a material reality."[3] The sequence of discoveries leading to an understanding of atomic and nuclear structure began with the discovery of uranium in 1789. By 1869, uranium was the heaviest of all known elements cataloged in the "periodic table" created by Russian chemist Dimitri Mendeleev.[4] In 1895, German physicist Wilhelm Conrad Röntgen, working with cathode rays, discovered a mysterious beam that could penetrate matter and expose photographic film, revealing, among other things, the bones in his hand. Röntgen named these newly discovered rays "X" for mystery. When investigating Röntgen's work only a few months later, Frenchman Henri Becquerel discovered that uranium salts emitted another kind of "penetrating radiation"[5] that came "from inert matter unstimulated by rays or light."[6] Taking up Becquerel's discovery, Marie Curie coined the term "radioactivity" to describe the general phenomena of spontaneously emitted penetrating radiations. Together with her husband, Pierre, in 1898, Marie Curie identified the radioactive elements radium and polonium. In 1902, the Curies succeeded in isolating one-tenth of a gram of radium and illuminating the radioactive properties of radium.[7]

Divisibility of the Atom

English physicist Joseph John "J. J." Thomson studied cathode (electron) rays and, like Röntgen, his work laid the foundation for several critical discoveries that would ultimately make the development of an atomic bomb feasible. Working with cathode rays in 1897, Thomson demonstrated that negatively charged particles (electrons) could be "extracted" from atoms. The great physicist and cosmologist George Gamow observed that Thomson's discovery demonstrated that atoms are in fact divisible and made it clear that they are not, "as the Greek meaning of their name implies, indivisible constituent units of matter, but, quite to the contrary, rather complex systems formed by positively and negatively charged parts."[8] Of great significance, Thomson reasoned from his experimentation with electrons that since atoms were electrically neutral, an atom must contain just enough electrons to counterbalance the atom's positive charge.[9] Moreover, Thomson argued in 1904 that the positively charged substance could be distributed uniformly throughout the atom, with the negatively charged electrons imbedded so as to resemble "plums stuck randomly in a pudding"—the so-called *plum pudding* atomic model.[10]

Atomic Nucleus

One of J. J. Thomson's students, New Zealand–born Ernest Rutherford, identified three kinds of radioactive emissions: alpha, beta, and gamma; α, β, and γ, respectively. He used the α (alpha) radiation to investigate the plum pudding model of his mentor. Acting on a hunch in 1907, Rutherford instructed his young German assistant, Hans Geiger, to take a closer look into the matter. In an experiment that involved passing positively charged alpha particles through thin gold foils, Geiger expected to find that the alpha particles would pass through with little deflection, as predicted by Thomson's plum pudding model.[11] Shockingly, however, Geiger and another assistant, Ernest Marsden, reported to Rutherford that when passing alpha particles through a gold foil, "We were able to get some alpha-particles *coming backward*..."[12] Since alpha particles are thousands of times more massive than electrons, something else had to be responsible for the backward scattered alphas. Rutherford reasoned that the atom "contains a *massive* central charge distributed through a very small volume"—the atomic *nucleus*.[13] "It was the most incredible event that ever happened to me in my life," Rutherford later proclaimed.[14] Convinced that the nucleus of an atom consisted of positively charged protons surrounded by negatively charged electrons, Rutherford grappled with an explanation as to how such a nucleus, subject to the laws of electricity and magnetism, would not just fly apart. Rutherford proposed the existence of a new force in nature, strong enough to overpower the electrical repulsion of the protons. This was the *nuclear force*—the most powerful force in nature. It is this power that, 100 years after its identification by Rutherford, jihadists threaten to harness in a nuclear weapon.[15]

Discovery of Neutrons: A Pathway to the Nucleus

Following Rutherford's discovery, physicists puzzled over the difference between the atomic number of an element, which English physicist Henry Mosely had shown was related to the number of electrons in the atom, and the atomic mass expressed as a number of proton masses. One would expect a neutral atom to have an equal number of protons and electrons; the atomic mass (measured in proton masses) and atomic number should be the same. However, most atoms have an atomic mass at least twice the atomic number. In 1920 Rutherford suggested that the difference could be explained by electrons being trapped in the nucleus, thereby canceling the charge of some of the protons. However, quantum principles implied that such an electron would have an impossibly large kinetic energy and other properties could not be reconciled with Rutherford's trapped electron hypothesis. In 1932, French physicists Frédéric Joliot and Irène Curie (Marie and Pierre Curies' daughter), following up on earlier work by German physicists Walther Bothe and Herbert Becker, were able to create a new form of penetrating radiation by bombarding beryllium with alphas. English physicist James Chadwick, who had studied with Geiger and had been Rutherford's assistant at Cambridge, was able to demonstrate that this new form of radiation was the elusive neutron. The neutron opened up a whole new avenue to the study of the nucleus. Up until this point, the nucleus had only been scientifically

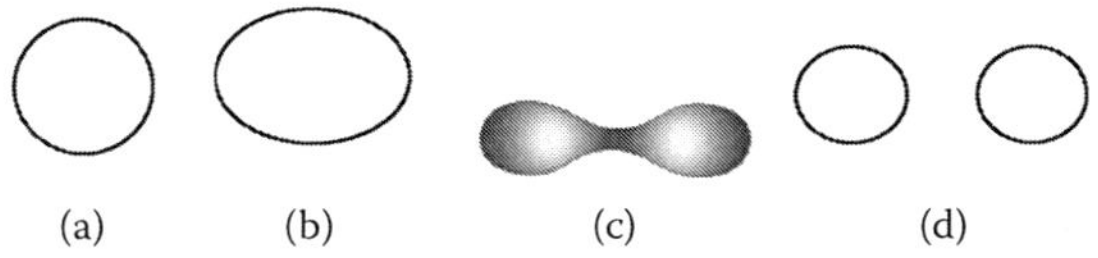

FIGURE 8A.1 Fission and Liquid Drop Analogy

probed with alpha particles. However, since the alpha particle and a nucleus both have positive charges, they repel one another, and there is a limit as to how close the alpha can get to the nucleus.[16] Thus, once discovered, scientists immediately recognized that with the neutral neutron one could truly probe the nucleus and, possibly, generate new isotopes and new elements.

Fission

Armed with this new knowledge, in 1934, Italian physicist Enrico Fermi and his team of scientists in Rome began to irradiate any element they could acquire with neutrons. Almost immediately the Rome University physics department came to believe that by using uranium (which, as mentioned earlier, has the highest atomic weight of all naturally occurring elements: 92) as a target of the neutron bombardment, they could create "transuranics"—elements with an atomic number *higher* than 92. Fermi's group did indeed create a transuranic, but they also created something else that they mistook for a transuranic.[17] In 1938 these other products of neutrons bombarding uranium were shown by two German scientists, Otto Hahn and Fritz Strassman, not to be transuranics but actually more familiar elements, like barium. Rather than create some new element, they had somehow fabricated familiar elements with a lower atomic weight. The two scientists were dumbfounded; they could not explain their results. Immediately following the test, Hahn communicated his findings to a former colleague, Lise Meitner. Working with her nephew, Otto Frisch, Meitner was able to show that Fermi, Hahn, and Strassman had actually *split* the atom, and barium, among other elements, comprised the fragments that resulted. Neutrons, it was now realized, could induce uranium atoms to split.

Up until the point of the Hahn–Strassman experiment, it had generally been accepted that when a nucleus captured a neutron, the result would temporarily be a "compound nucleus that would be left in an excited state."[18] Such reasoning concluded that the nucleus would then "decompose itself by emitting a particle such as a neutron or an alpha particle."[19] In contrast, Meitner and Frisch explained in early 1939 that the nucleus splits into two because, "the uranium nucleus has only small stability of form, and may, after neutron capture, divide itself into two nuclei of roughly equal size."[20] "On account of their close packing and strong energy exchange," the two went on to explain, "the particles in a heavy nucleus would be expected to move in a collective way which has some resemblance to the movement of a liquid drop: If the movement is made sufficiently violent by adding energy [i.e., by adding a neutron], such a drop may divide itself into two smaller drops." Meitner and Frisch called this process *fission*—a name Frisch had gotten from a colleague who had an interest in cell division.[21]

In sum, Meitner and Frisch explained that with nuclei containing many protons—the heavy elements—there is an inherent instability. Protons are similarly charged, and, since like charges repel, the more protons there are, the greater is the repulsive force.[22] By adding a neutron, the entire nucleus would oscillate and nuclear force (the strongest force in nature that keeps the nucleus together but only acts over extremely short ranges) would become subservient to the forces of electrical repulsion. Using the liquid drop analogy, the added neutron would cause the nucleus to elongate like a drop, weakening the short-range power of the nuclear force. Consequently, the electric force would create a nucleus with two bulbs, similar to the way drops form when separating from each other, with the nuclear force able to regain the lead within each one. They would thus be pulled into spheres by the consequent surface tension while, at the same time, the electrical repulsion divided the two spheres apart even further. Ultimately the two spheres would break apart, forming two nuclei smaller than the original nucleus[23] (see Figure 8A.1). Meitner and Frisch had succeeded in giving a *qualitative* explanation to the fission experiment. What was still needed, if fission was to have future military applications, was a *quantitative* theory.

Chain Reactions

In nature, uranium exists almost entirely (99.284%) with 146 neutrons—the isotope called uranium-238. Less than one percent of uranium (0.711%) has 143 neutrons—the isotope called uranium-235. For large nuclei, like uranium, the laws of electrostatic repulsion demand that it is always energetically favorable to "relax" in some fashion that reduces the electrostatic repulsion. There are many ways a nucleus can relax: beta decay, alpha decay, or fission. Normally, fission is the least likely decay process because the fragments must overcome a large energy barrier before they can separate. This barrier is much smaller for alpha particles, thus it is more common for large nuclei to undergo alpha decay. However, when uranium-235 captures a neutron to form uranium-236, the energy barrier is low enough that fission becomes the dominant decay mode. On the other hand, when uranium-238, the more abundant isotope, captures a neutron forming uranium-239, the barrier to fission is larger; therefore, only very energetic neutrons can cause uranium-238 to fission. Instead, the preferred decay mode of uranium-239 is beta decay, which forms the transuranic element plutonium-239. Things change rapidly, however, as plutonium-239 also readily captures neutrons to form plutonium-240, which, like uranium-236, does fission due to its low fission barrier.

These principles of element stability and energetics formed the basis of a quantitative theory for fission. Within just a few months of Meitner and Frisch's explanation of the Hahn–Strassman experiments, in a monumental paper published in June 1939, physicists Niels Bohr and John Wheeler speculated that the fission taking place in natural uranium occurred *entirely* in the rare uranium-235 nuclei.[24] Because of the lower level of electrostatic repulsion, smaller nuclei need fewer neutrons to maintain stability. Thus, when a large nucleus splits into two smaller ones, there is an excess of neutrons. These neutrons can do one of three things: (1) They can be captured by a nucleus; (2) they can escape from the nuclear matter; or (3) they can cause other nuclei to fission, which in turn releases two or more neutrons. Realizing this third principle, that dividing nuclei can yield more neutrons, Bohr and Wheeler speculated that a self-sustaining chain reaction with uranium-235 was theoretically possible.[25]

Although Bohr and others doubted that a chain reaction could be brought about using the technical means at their disposal (their studies had only considered natural uranium), others immediately grasped the military implications of fission and sought out to utilize them. The products of fission, that is, the masses of the resulting nuclei, are less than the mass of the parent nucleus. The difference, illustrated by Einstein's equation $E = mc^2$, is found in the fission fragment's kinetic energy.[26] In the case of the fission of uranium-235, the excess energy available after the fission is approximately 200 million electron volts (MeV), an enormous quantity compared with the 1 electron volt of energy released in a typical chemical reaction.[27] In a runaway chain reaction, the number of fissions in each successive generation of neutrons grows exponentially, releasing an enormous amount of energy. Thus, fissioning 1 kilogram of uranium (U-235) will release the energy equivalent to *seventeen thousand tons* (17kt) of TNT.[28]

Armed with the knowledge that fissioning uranium-235 could cause other nuclei to fission, possibly causing a chain reaction of fissioning isotopes, research turned to the challenge of separating uranium-235 isotopes from uranium-238 isotopes—so-called "enrichment." Alarmed by the rapidity of technical developments vis-à-vis realizing a chain reaction, physicist Leo Szilard and Einstein crafted a letter to President Roosevelt (signed by Einstein only) that urged the president to secure uranium ore supplies, increase research funding, and warned of German interest in uranium. Meanwhile, in Great Britain, Otto Frisch reentered the picture, as did James Chadwick, when the two met in Liverpool, in 1939, to develop the idea of a "cascade" to produce uranium-235. Together with Rudolf Peirels, Frisch worked on the challenges of initiating a chain reaction (a so-called "initiator" described elsewhere in this chapter) and determining the critical mass of uranium-235.

By 1940, just forty-five years after Röntgen's discovery of x-rays, the race was on to build a weapon of almost unimaginable fury. Many of the vital players in the discoveries of nuclear physics examined in this section—Fermi, Frisch, Bohr, Wheeler, Peirels, and other luminaries in the field—soon found themselves in Los Alamos struggling to overcome the theoretical and practical challenges necessary to build the world's first atomic bombs. They were, of course, successful. The question is, will the modern incarnations of the weapons they built somehow find their way into the hands of jihadists?

Notes

1. Table of Global Nuclear Weapons Stockpiles, 1945–2002, Natural Resources Defense Council, 2002, available at http://www.nrdc.org/nuclear/nudb/datab19.asp (accessed 12/12/07).
2. Samuel Glasstone, *Sourcebook on Atomic Energy* (Canada: D. Van Nostrand Company Inc., 1958), 1.
3. Ibid.
4. Jeremy Bernstein, *Plutonium: A History of the World's Most Dangerous Element* (Washington, DC: Joseph Henry Press, 2007), 3.
5. Catherine Caufield, *Multiple Exposures: Chronicles of the Radiation Age* (Chicago: University of Chicago Press, 1989), 22.
6. Richard Rhodes, *The Making of the Atomic Bomb*, New York: Simon and Schuster, 1986, 41.
7. Caufield, *Multiple Exposures*, 22–23.
8. George Gamow, *Thirty Years That Shook Physics: The Story of Quantum Theory* (New York: Dover Publications, 1966), 29–30.
9. Jeremy Bernstein, *Nuclear Weapons: What You Need to Know* (Cambridge: Cambridge University Press, 2007), 16.
10. Ibid. See also, Gamow, *Thirty Years That Shook Physics*, 30.

11. Glasstone, *Sourcebook on Atomic Energy*, 93.
12. Bernstein, *Nuclear Weapons*, 9–20. Italics added.
13. Glasstone, *Sourcebook on Atomic Energy*, 94. Italics added. George Gamow provided the following analogy: "If we throw an iron ball at a piece of coal it will bounce off it at an odd angle, perhaps breaking the coal into several pieces. But if we grind the same piece of coal into fine powder and throw the same ball through the resulting coal dust cloud, it will pass through without any deflection. The observed very large deflection in Rutherford's scattering experiments definitely proved that the positive charge (associated with most of the mass) of the atom is not distributed all through its body, as in the previous example of the coal dust cloud, but is concentrated, like the solid piece of coal, in a little hard nut—the nucleus. Gamow, *Thirty Years That Shook Physics*, 37. Rutherford revealed his finding in 1911. See E. Rutherford, "The Scattering of α and β Particles by Matter and the Structure of the Atom," *Philosophical Magazine*, Series 6, vol. 21, May 1911, available at http://www.lawebdefisica.com/arts/structureatom.pdf (accessed 12/13/07).
14. Bernstein, *Nuclear Weapons*, 20.
15. Ibid.
16. Ibid., 34.
17. Fermi had assumed that the neutron would penetrate the uranium nucleus, with the temporary result being a new uranium isotope (an isotope is an element whose nucleus has the same number of protons but a different number of neutrons. For example, polonium has 34 isotopes, all of which have 84 protons but neutrons of various numbers). The new uranium isotope, Fermi assumed, would convert the neutron into a proton when it decayed. The addition of a proton would alter the uranium's atomic number. In short, Fermi believed that he had created an unknown element. Per F. Dahl, *From Nuclear Transmutation to Nuclear Fission, 1932–1939* (London and New York: Taylor and Francis, 2002), 180–181.
18. Bernstein, *Plutonium*, 52.
19. Ibid.
20. Lise Meitner and Otto R. Frisch, "Disintegration of Uranium by Neutrons: A New Type of Nuclear Reaction," *Nature*, 143, Feb. 11, 1939, 239–240, available at http://www.atomicarchive.com/Docs/Begin/Nature_Meitner.shtml (accessed 12/06/07).
21. Bernstein, *Nuclear Weapons*, 49.
22. Indeed, Meitner and Frisch discovered that the reason that no element heavier than uranium exists naturally in the world is because the two forces would eventually cancel each other out.
23. Rhodes, *The Making of the Atomic Bomb*, 258–259.
24. Niels Bohr and Archibald Wheeler, "The Mechanism of Nuclear Fission," *Physical Review*, 56, September 1939.
25. The Hungarian theoretical physicist Leo Szilard grasped the potential for a nuclear chain reaction in 1933, and in the following year he filed a patent application for "the concept of using neutron-induced chain reactions to liberate energy." "If the thickness is larger than the critical value," Szilard's application noted, "I can produce an explosion." Awarded the patent, Szilard could technically claim to be the atomic bomb's inventor. Charles R. Loeber, *Building the Bombs: A History of the Nuclear Weapons Complex* (Albuquerque, NM, and Livermore, CA: Sandia National Laboratories, 2002), 5.

26. The mass (m) loss is converted into energy (E). Because the speed of light (c) is a large number (300,000,000 meters/second), c squared is a massive number. Stan Ulam commented about $E = mc^2$ that, "What the whole [Manhattan] Project was working on depended on those few little signs on paper." S. M. Ulam, *Adventures of a Mathematician* (New York: Charles Scribner's Sons, 1976), 157.
27. Glasstone, *Sourcebook on Atomic Energy*, 390.
28. According to physicist Jeremy Bernstein, "Each fission would produce roughly 10^{-11} joule of energy. This means that 10^{24} fission [that number of fissions that would occur after eighty generations] would produce about 10^{13} joules of energy. So we get out about 10^{13} joules per kilogram from the fission of uranium-235. Compare this to TNT, which produces about a million—10^{6}—joules per kilogram." Bernstein, *Nuclear Weapons,* 65.

SECTION III

Countering the Threat

CHAPTER 9

Early Warning and Prevention of Jihadist WMD Terrorism

Law Enforcement and Intelligence

Randall S. Murch and Jeremy Tamsett

CONTENTS

INTRODUCTION

In general, the ideal way to counter any particular terrorist threat is to identify it long in advance and to act to prevent it from materializing, thus obviating the need for mitigating its effects or cleaning up the mess after an attack has occurred. Clearly, this is not always possible, which is why we must attempt to structure the environment so that the threat becomes infeasible (see Chapter 11), as well as harden potential targets and prepare to respond to attacks (see Chapter 12). Yet, one of the primary—and arguably the most effective—means of countering the jihadist use of weapons of mass destruction (WMD) is through early warning and prevention (in the sense of tactical or operational interdiction or disruption), which falls mainly within the purview of the intelligence and law enforcement domains. Although their missions are in some ways symbiotic, there has historically more often than not been a functional gap between law enforcement[1] and intelligence institutions,[2] where each set of actors has developed a distinctive, and not always compatible, culture and set of standard operating procedures.

It is manifestly clear, however, that the current constellation of diffuse transnational threats exemplified by jihadist WMD use presents new challenges for both law enforcement and intelligence agencies. On the one hand, these threats represent a departure from the monolithic, state-centric intelligence activities of the past and, on the other, a challenge for law enforcement, which has historically been more comfortable with investigating crimes after the fact and bringing the guilty parties to justice than preventing surprise attacks. The deficiencies of both intelligence and law enforcement in preventing jihadist terrorism have been well-documented publicly,[3] as have the difficulties of intelligence agencies in detecting illicit WMD programs.[4] We contend, however, that by further erasing boundaries between law enforcement and intelligence domains (for example, by involving local law enforcement in the intelligence collection process) and enhancing analytical and operational tradecraft in both communities, the prospects are increased for successfully identifying and preventing such threats as that posed by jihadists using WMD.

The purpose of this chapter is to establish a conceptual framework by which to explore some of the prominent challenges and opportunities concerning the early warning and prevention of jihad-inspired WMD terrorism. We begin by introducing some basic intelligence and warning concepts, including a discussion of the intelligence cycle and the continuum of prevention and warning in the context of the interrelationship between time and risk. Next, we explore the challenges presented to law enforcement and national intelligence operations, both generally in the current global threat environment and specifically in the domain where jihadism and WMD intersect. Building upon these ideas, we examine ways for both intelligence and law enforcement agencies working together to more creatively engage the global threat space to better target the gray areas where jihadist terrorist groups operate. In so doing, we offer some observations and insights that we feel are essential for success in the threat environment where jihadist terrorist activity converges with WMD acquisition and use.

PREVENTION AND EARLY WARNING: THE INTELLIGENCE CYCLE AND CONTINUUM

The ideal position, in terms of prevention and early warning, would be to have the capacity to identify all harm and prevent it before it happens. It is a truism to state that achieving a perfect predictive capability in intelligence is ultimately impossible (see Chapter 14 for more detail); nonetheless, we can and should strive to continually improve our technological proficiency and analytic competency in these areas so that we can better interpret, evaluate, and, hence, understand our adversaries' capabilities and intentions. Before explaining how we might do this, it is necessary to present some of the basic elements of intelligence and how they relate to prevention and early warning.

The traditional view of intelligence is reflected in the so-called "intelligence cycle," as shown in Figure 9.1. In its most simple form, this is a process consisting of five main stages, each of which leads to the next in a closed loop. These stages are (1) *direction*, where a decision-maker issues requirements to answer a specific question or achieve a specific objective; (2) *collection*, where available sources and methods are employed to collect raw data; (3) *processing*, where the collected raw data are organized, for instance, by collating or translating; (4) *analysis*, where the raw data are considered relative to existing knowledge and are embodied with meaning; and (5) *dissemination* to decision-makers of the results, which in turn generates actions in the outside world, and ultimately feedback that starts the cycle anew by producing new and refined direction.

The efficacy of this traditional construct has been criticized recently as being too linear and allowing for a diffusion of accountability, with a more network-oriented approach being suggested.[5] So, while intelligence in the classic paradigm has predominantly been thought of as a national-level activity carried out by specialized agencies, in recent years we have seen a shift toward integration across intelligence domains (the so-called INTs[6]) and to provide more timely and meaningful information and intelligence for all levels of decision-makers not just those at the national level.[7] Intelligence informs decisions at each of these levels in different ways, from the method of collection and analytic tools employed to the ways in which people interact with the intelligence once it is disseminated. In addition, not all intelligence flows upward along hierarchies to the highest levels of government, nor would that be desirable. There are many diverse consumer-sets, ranging from military commanders on the battlefield to national policymakers. Additional

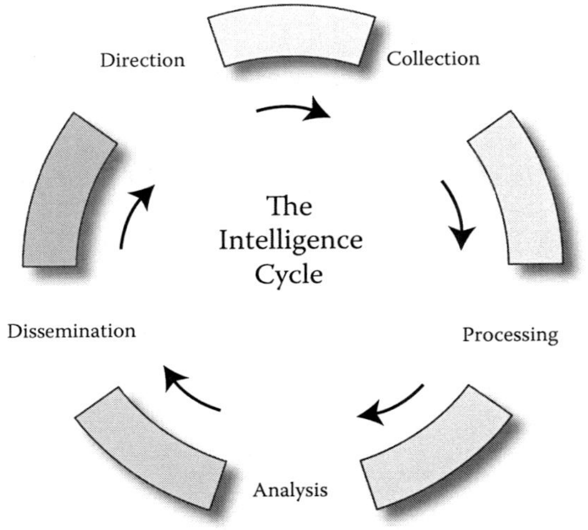

FIGURE 9.1 The intelligence cycle.

oft-overlooked consumers are state and local officials, police chiefs, emergency responders, and other key leaders within local communities.

The role of intelligence and law enforcement agencies in threat prevention can be situated along a continuum, which measures risk reduction relative to the time when the agencies intervene to deal with an attack. Though it is not usually thought of in such a manner, risk prevention and management, together with the tradeoffs these activities involve, are, in fact, implicit in the law enforcement and intelligence functions. "Actionable" intelligence thus becomes intelligence that can be used to inform decisions and actions to reduce risk. This is depicted in Figure 9.2 in the form of what we refer to as the "risk management continuum," with "anticipation" at one end (achieved by attaining constant knowledge of an adversary's intentions, plans and capabilities) being the ultimate objective and the other end being recovery (from surprise by an adversary's attack or actions), clean-up, finger-pointing and, hopefully, lessons learned.

While anticipation is the goal, several of the earlier chapters in this volume have shown that it is often a difficult and complicated task to discern and comprehend intent with respect to the most sophisticated and, consequently, dangerous of adversaries such as al-Qa'ida. Short of anticipating every move by an adversary, interdiction and disruption of plots in progress are in practice worthwhile objectives. Yet, even this is complicated by the fact that the most worrisome adversaries invest intellectual, experiential, and resource capital to protect key persons, information, assets, and processes using various dynamic means. One of the primary challenges for law enforcement and intelligence, therefore, becomes overcoming these defensive measures and moving as early as possible to learning the plans of the adversary, either directly or indirectly.

This difficulty is compounded by the fact that, irrespective of the actions of terrorists, there are also inherent limits—both cognitive and technological—to information collection, synthesis, and analysis, which preclude intelligence agencies from always achieving

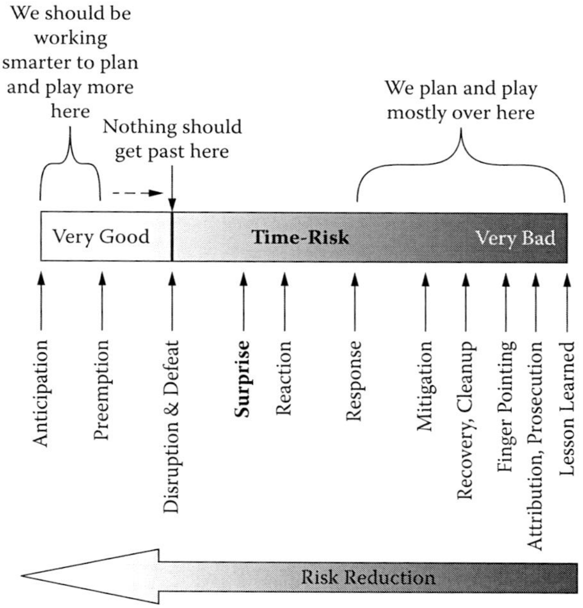

FIGURE 9.2 The risk management continuum.

anticipation. The difficulty of sorting or filtering collected data, for example, hinders our ability to accurately predict threats all of the time. Placing information into context so that it becomes "knowable"[8] is a perennial challenge that requires more research and study, especially in the cognitive sciences.[9] Properly assessing and anticipating when, where, and how adversary intent decussates with capabilities is a fundamental challenge for early warning and prevention.

Unfortunately, it seems as if much of the activity during the last decade with respect to terrorism in general and WMD terrorism in particular has occurred near the opposite end of the continuum from anticipation. If law enforcement and intelligence authorities operate predominantly in this area of the continuum, their contributions are mainly limited to responding to and recovering from harm (i.e., pursuing attribution and prosecution of perpetrators) as well as perhaps being called to answer for intelligence "failures." They are also more likely to operate in a perpetual reactive mode. This suggests that while some resources must be devoted to this end of the continuum, prevention and early warning (the left-hand side of Figure 9.2) should be the prime objective.

Where along the risk management continuum law enforcement and intelligence activities fall is somewhat contextual: It depends not only on the nature of the threat (severity and type of event, e.g., mass casualty attack), its timing and environmental circumstances (political climate and societal perception), but also on the authorities and capabilities of the agencies involved to effectively organize and coordinate their actions. Achieving successes in this regard is not universal or uniform; it requires tailored approaches along with authorized and agile access to utilize the right people, information, places, tools, and processes when and where needed. The ability to significantly influence an adversary's environment and behavior increases the likelihood of favorable outcomes, but this is not an inconsequential or trivial endeavor.

CHALLENGES TO PREVENTION AND WARNING IN THE CONTEXT OF JIHADISM AND WMD

The threats occurring at the intersection of jihadism and WMD present a host of challenges for intelligence and law enforcement agencies. Some of these challenges stem from the changing nature of national security threats in general; others are unique to the domains of WMD or jihadism. Some of the more salient challenges are briefly described below.

Current Asymmetric Threats Require Both Breadth and Depth of Expertise

One of the interesting features of the Cold War is that it both required and allowed for analysts within the intelligence community to develop a deep level of expertise on specific, well-defined targets of intelligence collection. For example, in the United States, silos of expertise were developed around enduring problem sets that permitted analysts time to ruminate over long-term strategic estimates of issues like Soviet industrial capacity and analyses of political leadership within the walls of the Kremlin (analysts who acquired such specialized knowledge were known as "Kremlinologists"). While there is undeniable value in developing expertise and specializing in one critical area or domain (i.e., developing strategic insights that provide contextual frameworks for understanding complex events), it is also necessary to apply gradations of new and diverse knowledge to address increasingly complex asymmetric problem sets such as the threat posed by jihadist WMD terrorism.

This is illustrated in Figure 9.3. Imagine that all possible threats—both known and unknown—are transposed onto a three-dimensional geometric plane that demarcates the jihadist threat space. Threats that are known and understood within this geometric plane are represented by bounded silos of knowledge, a condition often referred to as "stovepiping." Every potential threat or threat event that occurs outside of this silo of knowledge is either not recognized or recognized but not understood; hence, it is *gray matter.* Unfortunately, this is where much of the threat markers for jihadists using WMD are likely to fall.

Knowledge of Language and Culture in the Jihadist Threat Space

To better understand the nebulous environment in which jihadist terrorists operate, it is necessary first and foremost that we understand the adversary. This requires both deep theological knowledge of jihadism, as well as the ability to rapidly and accurately process and comprehend raw information available in languages and dialects spoken throughout the Muslim world, including not only Arabic, but also Urdu, Farsi, Pashto, Bahasa Indonesia, Uzbek, and so forth. It is widely recognized that intelligence and law enforcement agencies lack sufficient numbers of analysts and practitioners with either the required depth of knowledge or level of language skills to properly address the new threats. Current analysis is therefore rendered partially impotent because of a lack of systemic and comprehensive knowledge of jihadism and the languages in which it is expressed.

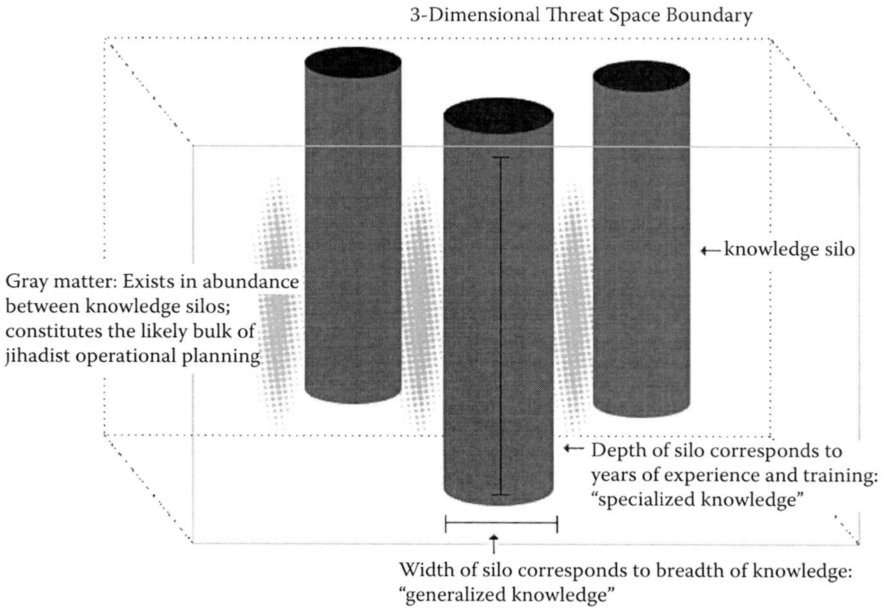

FIGURE 9.3 Jihadist WMD terrorism is gray matter within the threat space.

Signal to Noise and Value to Cost Ratios

The intelligence and law enforcement communities, like any public agencies, must almost always operate within the constraints of limited resources. Any activities (for example, adding new analysts or engaging in additional training) must be carefully evaluated in the context of uncertain long-term benefits, unintended consequences, and often considerable costs. At the same time, the amount of raw data that is available from both open and classified sources is growing at a tremendous rate, which makes it more and more difficult to detect the relatively few important items (which constitute the genuine "signal") within increasing volumes of superfluous data ("noise"). This leads to an overall decrease in the signal to noise ratio.

The "Gray–Green" Divide

When the focus of the intelligence mission changed in the post–Cold War era (the target of the mission for the better part of fifty years largely evaporated), the intelligence community experienced a "brain drain" of highly skilled and talented veteran analysts. Very few held on to their posts and braced for the challenges of the new millennium. The U.S. intelligence community suffers what the Deputy Director of National Intelligence for Analysis, Thomas Fingar, calls the "gray–green divide," where "roughly 55 percent of all analysts in the intelligence community joined after 9/11."[10] One serious consequence of this so-called divide is the lack of deep expertise in critical national security arenas like counterterrorism and WMD. At the same time, among the pre 9/11 veterans that remained, few have any significant counterterrorism experience since Cold War-era analysis focused on state-level threats.

Information Sharing

The imperative for intelligence sharing has never been more acute for the ever widening array of intelligence customers engaged in the war on terrorism. It has long been recognized, however, that there are barriers to information sharing among intelligence agencies, let alone between intelligence and local law enforcement officials. Some of the challenges facing collaboration and integration between local, state, national, and international police forces include the following: different legal and cultural environments, competing resources and unequal assets, disparate training methods, diffuse missions, varying datasets, incompatible technology, and disaggregated collection sources. In the United States, the poor state of collaboration, coordination, and information sharing between (and even within) various elements of the U.S. intelligence community has been associated with some of the biggest intelligence failures of recent decades. In fact, members of the WMD Commission stated that "the 15 intelligence organizations are a 'community' in name only and rarely act with a unity of purpose."[11] Resistance to sharing information not only happens horizontally across agencies and departments within the same national-level intelligence bodies, but also vertically among local, state, and federal law enforcement and intelligence agencies. Coordination of the vertical flow of intelligence, however, is challenged by the need to protect sources and methods, which requires security clearances obtained through a corresponding level of classification, and the need to get intelligence to the right customer at the right time, which entails a security risk. Furthermore, different security procedures are in place for different agencies and organizations.

Information sharing must be evaluated not just in terms of quantity, but also its quality and "actionability"—the value proposition of operational intelligence. While intelligence must, in the end, include information-sharing prerogatives, additional value and meaning are derived from creating the intelligence collectively.

Strategies designed to encourage agencies with different mission scopes and functions to communicate and work with each other have traditionally relied on mandates and the secondment of personnel to staff "joint" centers. The deficiency of such mandated or directed action is that it doesn't necessarily engender much-needed proactive collaboration. For example, geographic colocation of analysts under one roof is not always feasible and does not necessarily ensure that they will share information with each other in a way that is meaningful and constructive.[12] It is not sufficient, therefore, to simply add more people to the room—if people are only brought together on the basis of surface-level functional expertise, there may be little connectivity. Emphasis should be placed, therefore, on a multidimensional model of coproduction in the team buiilding environment versus a one-dimensional model of colocation.

Increased Scale and Scope of Jihadist Behavior

Jihadists have demonstrated a propensity and willingness to engage in behaviors and acts on a scale that has rarely been seen in the annals of terrorism. These include large-scale, indiscriminate attacks, often involving suicide tactics against a wide range of targets and vulnerable populations. Jihadists seem to seek "spectacular" attacks that transcend previous levels of violence (see Chapters 2 and 3 for greater detail), which means that any errors by intelligence and law enforcement agencies that result in even a single attack piercing a country's defenses can have extremely deleterious consequences. Moreover, the jihadist threat has manifested itself worldwide. Previous eras of terrorism have been dominated by "locally" oriented activity, where most of the time a single nation was targeted by a single group. However, driven by its globalistic ideology, a transnational strain of jihadism has emerged, which identifies much of the world's governments and peoples as its enemy and the entire globe as its area of operations. This complicates intelligence and law enforcement efforts because success depends on cross-national cooperation between sovereign governments, which introduces multiple kinds of friction.

Jihadist Operational Advantages and the Difficulties of Infiltration

Jihadists have proven themselves to be highly capable planners and operatives. Jihadists, like many types of criminal, terrorist, and intelligence enterprises that survive for any length of time, have developed ways to protect their plans, resources, capabilities, and operations. Jihadists in embedded, distributed organizations and networks are difficult to fully characterize, gain access or proximity to, and effectively neutralize, especially in unstable societies or under weak governments that may be heavily influenced by sympathetic views or apathetic authorities. Jihadists are adept at leveraging ethnicity, tribalism, language, religion, and culture as natural shielding or control barriers to prevent intrusion from the outside. In addition, it is likely that communities in which jihadists operate will also be self-policed. This is especially likely to be true in the Middle East, where the roles of family, tribe, clan, and ethnic group often take precedence over government control.

Essentially, HUMINT is a long-term collection process ideal for targeting jihadist cells that are difficult to or cannot be sufficiently targeted by technical means such as signals or imagery intelligence (SIGINT and IMINT, reprectively). HUMINT involves the use of a number of direct or indirect methods and techniques which are employed to collect intelligence from and on human targets by human assets. SIGINT involves the collection and exploitation of electronic, voice, and data signals for interlligence purposes. IMINT involves the imaging of the intelligence targets from ground, air, and space systems and interpreting those images for intelligence purposes. An existential challenge inherent to HUMINT is the long recruitment cycle of foreign agents coupled with the long training cycle of clandestine HUMINT officers, both of which can be anachronistic to the demands of policymakers and the public for expedient results. Generally, law enforcement or intelligence services from outside of a targeted country or society in which jihadists are operating will have substantial operational and practical challenges to overcome if they wish to accomplish infiltrations, especially in culturally homogenous societies and locales where it is easy for the enemy to spot the presence of anything outside of the ordinary in their environs. In the case of police, investigative, and intelligence services trying to penetrate a target group, it is often necessary to either recruit those who are already well-placed or can be inserted near enough to access the best sources of information or who are able to blend in and be accepted by those communities in which jihadists are likely to operate. Moreover, jihadists have established networks in several Western countries. Those networks exploit civil liberties and legal restrictions that protect the practice of religion and right of assembly, as well as restrictions on government intrusion without justification or legal countenance.

WMD Terrorism Requires Specific Technical Expertise

In the case of WMD terrorism, it is vitally important to be able to identify precursor materials, equipment, and behaviors that point toward a burgeoning WMD capability. This constitutes a new and esoteric sphere of knowledge for many, at least in law enforcement. Differences between chemical, biological, radiological, and nuclear (CBRN) weapon types are as important as they are nuanced (see the four chapters on CBRN weapons in Section II, "Agents of Harm" of this book). Here, the scale and scope of complexity inherent in any one weapon type may significantly alter the motivations, goals, and expectations of an adversary, depending on their relative technical capacities and available resources (e.g., financing, access to raw materials, scientists, and specialty equipment). Therefore, intelligence collectors and analysts are required to gain expertise in not one, but many technical areas in order to adequately identify threat indicators.

For CBRN threats, intelligence and law enforcement agencies must consider a wide range of science and technology indicators. Examples include monitoring potential facilitators working in dual-use fields such as nuclear weapons and nuclear energy infrastructure; those who legitimately acquire, use, regulate, and transfer radiological materials (such as for medical purposes and research); and the development, production, use, storage, movement, safety, and regulation of hazardous chemicals across research, industry, and military sectors. This requires developing finely tuned capabilities to unpack and discern "dual use," that is, accurately discriminating between what is being done for legitimate purposes and what is not.

The challenges described above leave us with a number of questions. How best to detect and address threats in complex, dynamic, and open societies as early as possible using effective and legally permitted approaches, while protecting sources and methods? How best to apply constrained resources across all policing and investigative programs? How should police agencies collaborate with intelligence agencies to optimize the allocation of scarce resources? How does law enforcement and domestic security individually or together alter the balance of an extremist "signal" against societal "noise" to increase the probability of detection and enable action when it is appropriate? Although there are no easy answers to these questions, the following section offers some preliminary recommendations.

Example of a Prevention Challenge: Crime and Terrorism

The potential for criminal activity to converge with terrorist activity is one growing area of concern where law enforcement and intelligence should increase focus and investment. The potential for collaboration between transnational criminal groups and jihadist terrorist networks where shared interests overlap pose significant security challenges. Money laundering, drug trafficking (to raise money), and other types of financial support networks, are examples where cross-cutting cleavages may exist between crime and terrorism.[13] Other nodes where criminal and terrorist interests are likely to converge may at least be partially driven by geographies where illicit activities flourish in the absence of state controls or, worse still, where their actions are supported or tolerated for a variety of reasons. The Tri-Border Region in South America, the Pakistan–Afghanistan border, and other "black spots"[14] are potential safe havens for jihadists and transnational criminal groups to co-mingle and take advantage of local populations and resources for their own ends. A range of criminal networks and drug cartels have a monopoly on lines of communication in these unsavory and lawless areas. This is an example of niches that are attractive to terrorist groups seeking information, financing, and possibly even support to smuggle people, narcotics, or even WMD across porous borders.[15]

These imprecise and difficult-to-measure transaction seams require more study and more coordination between agencies in the United States (as well as between the United States and foreign government intelligence and law enforcement agencies). In particular, the Federal Bureau of Investigation (FBI), the Department of Treasury, the Drug Enforcement Administration (DEA), the Department of Homeland Security (DHS), and the Department of Defense all have a role to play in intelligence collection, investigation, and interdiction. Where jurisdictions and missions overlap or even collide, information sharing can become problematic as data move across organizational boundaries and into different processes and cultures.

In the case of intelligence sharing, each of these agencies may engage in intergroup competition and, accordingly, seek to be viewed as the preeminent agency. The pressure to build intraorganizational identity may in some instances, therefore, exceed any perceived incentive to work toward common goals with fellow agencies. On the other hand, beyond the inherent competitiveness, sometimes an agency's "turf" is constructed by organizational culture and priorities, which may differ from one agency to another—this is especially likely to be the case between local law enforcement and national intelligence entities, for example. Different bureaucratic cultures may also play a role in shaping both processes and outcomes. The end goal should be to build an "enterprise identity" in which each member of the team (whether intraagency or multijurisdictional) can see and pursue common responsibilities and goals while still working within a system that enables individual team members to pursue their own goals and missions.

ESSENTIALS FOR SUCCESS AGAINST JIHADISTS AND WMD

Success against jihadists seeking to acquire and use WMD requires that whenever and wherever feasible, law enforcement and intelligence communities should collaborate and leverage all assets possible to acquire timely information and intelligence. Here, it is as important to focus investment on the *process* as it is to focus on the *content* of intelligence. Additionally, it is not just oversight, but leadership, mentorship, and sound management that are essential to ensure that the goals are achieved.

Expanding our Knowledge of the Jihadist-WMD Threat Space

It is on the outer fringes of bounded knowledge,[16] where information is fragmented, that jihadist cells pose potentially the greatest threat—insofar as their operations are unknown or are not properly understood (in other words, the "dots" are there, but they remain unconnected). Increasing our knowledge of the threat space has value, but actionable intelligence in the dangerous universe of jihadist WMD terrorism is crucial. But how do we increase surveillance and enhance our competency within the threat space?

We could increase our understanding of the gray areas of the jihadist threat space by systemically recruiting, training, and hiring more analysts and collectors with diverse knowledge and skillsets. This means that in addition to encouraging intelligence analysts to delve deeper into their specializations, we should be looking to incorporate a broader sphere of analytic knowledge built upon what could be considered ancillary and even esoteric disciplines of study. In theory, by inserting more knowledge into the threat space, we reduce uncertainty and diminish the overall volume of the unknown gray matter within the threat space.

Populating analyst teams with single-issue subject matter experts as well as experienced generalists could add considerable value to hypothesis testing by examining problem sets from nontraditional perspectives. The anticipated outcome of this arrangement is that intelligence could be considered creatively from different and competing perspectives to hedge against overly narrow definitions and assumptions. The key is that validated (credible and reliable) information must be integrated or at least related to an existing knowledge base to become meaningful intelligence. The context will vary depending on the type of knowledge and how the specialized or generalist analysts relate incoming data to that knowledge. It is important to note, however, that having *all* analysts become generalists could dilute necessary specialization and reduce the effectiveness of reach-back—a means of applying lessons learned to current or ongoing problem sets.

With respect to *process*, intelligence analysts also need to work more closely with consumers to develop a better understanding of requirements, and they need to work cohesively and innovatively with collectors to continually improve and refine the process.

We must also promote innovation in the way in which information is perceived and contextualized—retooling of existing methodologies and introduction of new analytic techniques are needed. At the same time, expertise acquired through academic study is not a perfect substitute for experience; veteran analysts should be encouraged to systematically mentor and train new generations of analysts to impart insights and context that cannot be gleaned from study alone. The value and importance of experience should not be lost.

With respect to *content*, law enforcement and intelligence need to be able to fully characterize jihadist groups and networks of groups organizationally (structure) and functionally (operational behaviors). These characterizations need to be dynamically identified, processed, and updated. Just because a group falls into one category today, doesn't mean that it will tomorrow. In addition, we must establish taxonomies of supporting networks (to include transnational criminals and gangs) to map linkages for future attribution and disruption (including, ideally, prosecution). Key nodes (including persons with specialized expertise) and linkages (by which the highest priority transfers occur) should be the subject of appropriate law enforcement and intelligence attention, action, exploitation, and manipulation. Linkages between "strategic" criminal groups (e.g., transnational gangs like Mara Salvatrucha [MS-13]) and jihadist terrorist groups in particular present a dynamic challenge that requires an equally dynamic response.

Risk Intelligence

Technology is changing the perspective of the geographic space in which threats are traditionally characterized. There has been a shift in intelligence from threat-centric targeting to future-oriented risk mapping, an enterprise that we call risk intelligence. Risk intelligence is a process of minimizing uncertainty by creating taxonomies of that which is known and accepting the uncertainty that remains as an inherent fixture in the equation that must be accounted for (not discounted). One of the benefits of risk intelligence is that by anticipating and accounting for uncertainty, intelligence analysts are empowered to overcome natural ontological insecurities about the threat environment. As Roberts highlights in Chapter 12 of this volume, government risk equations quite often "understate the uncertainty of the terrorist threat."

So how do we effectively risk map and track the threat of jihadist WMD terrorism? Formal risk assessment should include modeling of the topology (capacities and resources, threats, vulnerability, and consequences) on both sides. Threats tend to be dynamic—they are always in motion; therefore, we need to develop capacities to be more proactive in our approach to counter and mitigate them. Critical path maps[17] and other models can be developed and adjusted over time to enable visualization and effective intelligence requirements, planning, collection, analysis, sharing, and use.

This should result in a more structured way to identify, understand, and manage risk, and produce an adaptive, agile "toolkit" available to both intelligence and law enforcement professionals, which should be vigorously evolved and updated through positive and negative experiences (application of lessons learned). Any proposed solution set must contain an integrated and agile set of strategies, techniques, and procedures that focus on the time–risk continuum prior to the manifestation of surprise by the adversary. Such solutions will likely have to be tailored to geographic regions, countries, societies, and demographics, over and above specific characteristics and vulnerabilities of known jihadist targets. To be comprehensive, solutions must also include analysis and assessment of the nature and level of intent and sophistication of capabilities (which is a measurement of technical maturity delimited by the product of knowledge acquired over time).

Creativity and Imagination

The 9/11 Commission Report claimed that one of the principal deficiencies of the U.S. intelligence community in not foreseeing the attacks by al Qa'ida on the homeland was a lack of imagination. The commission did not cite "lack of information" as a problem; rather, the report refers to the lack of imagination about the possible meanings and extrapolations of the information gathered.

The collector and the analyst must infuse imagination into the analytical process and be agressive in their efforts to engage the aforementioned fragmented data in the jihadist–WMD threat space creatively. Viewing data from diverse perspectives may provide unconventional insights into ill-defined threats such as jihadist intentions and capabilities with respect to WMD. By increasing our creative observation space, more data points are encompassed, which could lead to a well-rounded picture of the emerging threat before it becomes a reality. In this conceptual milieu, it is important to develop a deeper understanding of the necessity for creativity to be appropriately intermixed in the intelligence process. Sometimes novel, creative, and imaginative ways of thinking about asymmetric problem-sets, like jihadist terrorist tactics and targeting (see Chapter 3 for a detailed discussion of this particular topic), are necessary to formulate and develop effective strategies for countering such adversaries.

Overcoming Obstacles to Information Sharing: Fusion Intelligence

Prevention and early warning of jihadist terrorism with respect to WMD is in many ways a "wicked"[18] problem whose solution will encompass the transformation of personnel, policies, and institutions and will necessarily involve the fusion of intelligence at the tactical, operational, and strategic levels. This requires innovation and creativity—fusion centers, joint task forces, and regional working groups are great steps forward in the right direction, but much more needs to be done to foster a new culture and mindset of effective partnering at the local and national levels. This means that not only should Department of Homeland Security and Federal Bureau of Investigation officials work with local law enforcement in regional centers, but law enforcement should also send officers to receive hands-on training at the National Counterterrorism Center (NCTC), for example.[19]

Fusion intelligence is a term we use to describe the integration between law enforcement and national intelligence both in terms of process and outcome. The idea behind fusion intelligence, essentially, is to enhance situational awareness so that officials at the local, state, and federal levels can better understand and, hence respond to, threats in local communities that may affect national security. This involves fusing or merging data from a variety of sources to produce a synergy of effective and actionable intelligence products for consumers. Fusion intelligence may, therefore, range from suspicious activity reports collected and compiled by police in a local community to HUMINT collected from undercover Drug Enforcement Administration (DEA) agents stationed abroad.

The perceived need for intelligence collected from disaggregated sources across jurisdictions and agencies prompted the Department of Homeland Security in the United States to work with state governors and law enforcement agencies to create "intelligence fusion centers." In theory, fusion centers are intended to act as conduits to share information and circumvent the traditional "stovepipe" approach to intelligence collection and dissemination where national intelligence is classified, compartmentalized, and rarely, if ever, shared with the law enforcement community. While DHS continues to struggle with funding the creation and continuity of these centers ($254 million was appropriated in 2004–2007), only thirty analysts from the DHS Office of Intelligence and Analysis will be deployed to work in one or more of fifty-eight fusion centers dispersed throughout the United States by the end of fiscal year 2008.[20]

To be effective, fusion centers must comprise not only of representatives from multijurisdictional agencies, but also of multidisciplinary teams with sufficiently diverse knowledge sets, based on a combination of experience and expertise. Ultimately, it is essential that strong, interdependent relationships are built among members of a fusion intelligence team to ensure effective and efficient collaboration. These relationships must be built on the recognized value of the mission as well as recognition and appreciation of individual contributions, which leads to mutual confidence and trust. A critical success factor for fusion centers is shaping the culture of intelligence from a "need to know" to a "responsibility to provide" mindset, which is espoused as one of four strategic goals in the February 2008 U.S. Intelligence Community Information Sharing Strategy. Education in this regard must be targeted to not only describe the benefits of information sharing but, in a very practical sense, it must also teach analysts *how* to recognize the information that should be shared and how to create the organizational culture and protocols to share information effectively and appropriately.

National, Regional, and Global Law Enforcement and Intelligence Collaboration Models

The line between foreign and domestic intelligence collection is increasingly irrelevant. Local law enforcement constitutes a critical layer in identifying, developing, and tapping tactical criminal intelligence sources that can be useful for both domestic and foreign intelligence enterprises. Many large metropolitan jurisdictions in the aftermath of 9/11 established, for example, their own individualized intelligence efforts, optimized for local conditions and perceived community needs.[21] Subsequently, local and state law enforcement intelligence analysis has expanded to include both counterterrorism and assorted threats to national security, including WMD. While federal law enforcers and investigative services like the FBI, U.S. Secret Service, U.S. Customs (now U.S. Customs and Border Patrol [CBP]), and other criminal investigative agencies have been conducting global criminal intelligence for decades, ultimately, the counterterrorism process should include both federal and local law enforcement, as well as international law enforcement agencies like Interpol and Europol.[22]

Today, major metropolitan law enforcement police units can easily and readily move in and out of local, national, or even international jurisdictions and domains. The New York City Police Department (NYPD) is an example of a local, municipal law enforcement agency that has formed partnerships with federal law enforcement and the intelligence community and has participated in international investigations. The department has police liaisons in ten cities around the world. Through its Joint Terrorism Task Force (JTTF)'s partnership with the FBI, for example, the NYPD has access to national-level classified intelligence, which enables the department to work with the FBI on international terrorism investigations. But it also enables the NYPD's counterterrorism and intelligence divisions to gather, analyze, and disseminate intelligence through both open-source and classified channels to city, state, and federal law enforcement and intelligence agencies.[23]

Police in major metropolitan areas will increasingly need to acquire skills in global affairs and undergo language and culture training. More research, study, and innovation of emerging models and paradigms for "global policing"[24] as applied to the jihadist–WMD threat are needed.

Maximizing HUMINT by Involving Law Enforcement

Local law enforcement has a significant but untapped role to play in the counterterrorism HUMINT mission. Because law enforcement agencies are uniquely positioned to best understand the threat environment of their local communities, they are well-suited to implement "a preventive style of policing that focuses on building local relationships to solve community problems."[25] The idea here is to leverage knowledge that does not need to be created; it already exists on the street. Police departments have access to criminal intelligence data that provide them with the ability to detect emerging threats within their jurisdictions.

The Los Angeles Police Department's (LAPD) Counter-Terrorism and Intelligence Bureau provides one example of how local law enforcement has taken steps to incorporate reporting of "potential terrorist related activity" as part of conventional duties related to crime prevention. Such proactive grassroots endeavors have led to the creation of a "National Counter-Terrorism Academy (NCTA) for state and local law enforcement," which could become a model for other municipalities and jurisdictions.

Local law enforcement (wherever "local" may be, ranging from Los Angeles to New York or Paris to Islamabad) is also in the position of being able to develop community awareness, human access, and targeted collections against identified or suspected threat actors or their co-optees. Such efforts are currently being carried out by law enforcement officers that receive special training to become Terrorism Liaison Officers (TLO). In addition to identifying, collecting, and providing suspicious activity reports (SAR) and major criminal activity reports to state and regional fusion centers, TLOs also conduct critical infrastructure vulnerability assessments in close cooperation with federal and state agencies.

From a statistical perspective, there are approximately 20,000 special agents, investigators, and field-ready personnel from the FBI, DEA, Marshals, and ATF. With the advent and subsequent (some might say perpetual) enlargement of the Department of Homeland Security, approximately 100,000 federal law enforcement personnel from Customs and Border Patrol (CBP), Immigrations and Custom Enforcement (ICE), and the Transportation Security Administration can be added to the quantity of the federal government field agents on the ground. By way of comparison, there are well over 700,000 sworn local enforcement officers in the United States serving in a variety of capacities ranging from municipal police, sheriffs, and highway patrol. In essence, the law enforcement community could be the country's 5th column, so-to-speak or "first preventers" of terrorism. It is law enforcement, after all, that best understand the dynamic threats facing their local communities—they are familiar with neighborhoods and people on the street. As Los Angeles Chief of Police William J. Bratton stated at the 2008 National Fusion Center Conference in San Francisco, CA, "We are the eyes and ears of our country's communities."

In sum, intelligence agencies require proper technical capabilities and intellectual capacities to address the information requirements of decision-makers in a timely and effective fashion. To properly seize opportunities presented or created by early warning of probable terrorist activity requires being positioned at the right place and at the right time with the right tools. Mission success requires integration of all source intelligence in efficient and effective ways to address key questions and complications as they arise. In addition, law enforcement and intelligence agencies need to operate in a collaborative, cooperative, and adaptive fashion from the strategic to the tactical as threats and conditions change. This will require a complex "system of systems" perspective and approach in a campaign undertaking. Wherever possible, this has to be done on a global scale with full participation and buy-in from international partners.

Countering Collaboration

Effective counterterrorism strategies must prevent terrorists from socializing with criminals (and vice-versa) in blackspots and other safe havens where technology and knowledge transfers are possible and even probable. If we can reverse incentivize potential nodes of collaboration, we might be able to undermine trust not only between terrorist and criminal groups (inter-group relationships), but also trust between terrorists and criminal members (intra-group relationships). Creating an environment of discord and disharmony and exacerbating long-standing political, social, and cultural sensitivities through subversion and disinformation could provide a foundation for exploitation by local law enforcement, counterterrorism, and intelligence agents. Specifically, the level of social cohesion in the relationship between the two organizations affects the willingness of the source organization to commit itself to make the knowledge exchange successful.

CONCLUSION

WMD in the hands of those who routinely demonstrate indiscriminate destruction and harm to persons they perceive as their enemy and zealously express religious justification for doing so, should be among the very top priorities for law enforcement and intelligence agencies. Though all societies face public safety and security challenges, it is difficult to imagine anything more important from the strategic perspective than the catastrophic potentiality of WMD. It is also doubtful that any one measure or initiative alone can be successful in today's security environment, which is marked by complexity and uncertainty.

The fact remains that jihadism is an evolving, complex phenomenon in which our competence is still very limited. To develop a better understanding of the jihadist WMD terrorism threat and, thereby, to improve our early warning and prevention capabilities, a combination of multi-disciplinary approaches is necessary, starting with more engagement and collaboration between law enforcement and intelligence. The relationships between national, state, and local law enforcement and intelligence agencies need to become increasingly integrated and fluid in their operations to more cogently address the threat of jihadist-WMD terrorism.

We surmise that jihadist intentions and motivations are unlikely to change dramatically in the near future, even though their tactics, methods, and relative capabilities will be adversely affected as scrutiny of their activities and communications increases the likelihood of detection by counterterrorism intelligence agencies.

NOTES

1. Law enforcement refers to the core function of post-incident criminal investigation; this definition encompasses national and international police agencies, but unless otherwise specified, we use the term to mean local or community-based police forces.
2. Intelligence incorporates the core functions of collection and analysis at the national level targeted primarily against foreign actors, and encompasses both civilian and military intelligence-related activities.
3. "The 9/11 Commission Report," http://www.gpoaccess.gov/911/pdf/fullreport.pdf.
4. "Commission on the Intelligence Capabilities of the United States Regarding Weapons of Mass Destruction," Washington, DC, March 13, 2005, available at http://www.wmd.gov/report/.
5. This view is articulated in more detail in Robert M. Clark, *Intelligence Analysis: A Target-Centric Approach* (Washington, DC: CQ Press, 2007), 13–23.
6. There are many disciplines of intelligence categorized generally along the different collection types including signals intelligence (SIGINT), human intelligence (HUMINT), and imagery intelligence (IMINIT), to name a few.
7. Ibid.
8. Just because information is knowable does not, however, mean that it is known; see Jack Davis, "Tensions in Analyst-Policymaker Relations: Opinions, Facts, and Evidence," Sherman Kent Center for Intelligence Analysis, Occasional Papers, 2:2 (January 2003), available at https://www.cia.gov/library/kent-center-occasional-papers/vol2no2.htm.
9. For ground-breaking work in this area, see David Snowden, "Complex Acts of Knowing: Paradox and Descriptive Self-Awareness," *Journal of Knowledge Management*, Spring 2002, available at http://www.kwork.org/Resources/snowden.pdf.
10. "Remarks and Q&A by the Deputy Director of National Intelligence for Analysis and Chairman, National Intelligence Council, Dr. Thomas Fingar," Council on Foreign Relations, March 18, 2008.
11. WMD Commission, 5.
12. These sentiments are echoed by the U.S. WMD Commission Report, "Information Sharing Still Depends too Much on Physical Co-Location and Personal Relationships as Opposed to Integrated, Community-Wide Information Networks," from "Report on the Commission on the Intelligence Capabilities of the United States Regarding Weapons of Mass Destruction," March 31, 2005, available at http://www.wmd.gov/report/wmd_report.pdf, 14.
13. For an excellent overview of this topic see Daveed Gartenstein-Ross and Kyle Dabruzzi, "The Convergence of Crime and Terror: Law Enforcement Opportunities and Perils," Policing Terrorism Report, No. 2, Center for Policing Terrorism, Manhattan Institute, June 2007.
14. The concept and definition of "black spots" is best articulated by Bartosz H. Stanislawski and Margarat G. Hermann, "Transnational Organized Crime, Terrorism, and WMD," Prepared as a discussion paper for the Conference on Non-State Actors, Terrorism, and Weapons of Mass Destruction, University of Maryland, October 15, 2004, available at http://www.cidcm.umd.edu/carnegie/papers/stanislawski_hermann.pdf.

15. See Marc Sageman, *Understanding Terror Networks* (Philadelphia: University of Pennsylvania Press, 2004); and especially Kimberley L. Thachuk, ed., *Transnational Threats: Smuggling and Trafficking in Arms, Drugs, and Human Life* (Westport, CT: Greenwood, 2007).
16. Bounded knowledge is an epistemological concept with broad application and expansive history; see Michael J. Wichura, *The Emergence of Probability: A Philosophical Study of Early Ideas About Probability Induction and Statistical Inference* (Cambridge: Cambridge University Press, 2006).
17. Critical path analysis (CPA) was developed in the 1950s to more effectively map dependencies between key nodes within complex systems and is widely used to manage high technology and defense projects. See "Critical Path Method," in Wikipedia, May 19, 2008, available at http://en.wikipedia.org/w/index.php?title=Critical_path_method&oldid=213429957.
18. First enunciated by Rittel and Weber in H. Rittel and M. Webber, *Dilemmas in a General Theory of Planning, Policy Sciences*, Vol. 4, No. 2 (Amsterdam: Elsevier Scientific Publishing Company, Inc., 1973), 155–169.
19. For example, one argument is that there is no blueprint for how federal agencies should interact with state, local, and law enforcement agencies; see "Interview with John Brennan, The Enemy Within," presented by "Frontline" (PBS), June 3, 2006, available at http://www.pbs.org/wgbh/pages/frontline/enemywithin/interviews/brennan.html.
20. Director of National Intelligence, February 22, 2008, 2.
21. "State and Local Fusion Centers," U.S. Department of Homeland Security, April 25, 2008, available at http://www.dhs.gov/xinfoshare/programs/gc_1156877184684.shtm.
22. See, for example, K. Jack Riley et al., "State and Local Intelligence in the War on Terrorism," RAND, (Santa Monica, CA: RAND Corporation, 2005); and "Intelligence-Led Policing: The New Intelligence Architecture," U.S. Department of Justice, September 2005.
23. A good discussion of counterterrorism policing in Europe is found in Mathieu Deflem, "Europol and the Policing of International Terrorism: Counter-Terrorism in a Global Perspective," *Justice Quarterly*, vol. 23, no. 3, September 2006, available at http://www.cas.sc.edu/socy/faculty/deflem/zeuroterror.pdf.
24. New York Police Department Web site, available at http://www.nyc.gov/html/nypd/html/administration/counter_terrorism_units.shtml.
25. "Global policing" holistically integrates national and metropolitan police, intelligence agencies, nongovernmental organizations (NGOs), and private/corporate security entities. See John P. Sullivan, "Global Terrorism and the Police," Unpublished paper presented at 49th Annual ISA Convention, San Francisco, CA, March 29, 2008.

CHAPTER 10

Deterrence and WMD Terrorism

Calibrating Its Potential Contributions to Risk Reduction

Brad Roberts

CONTENTS

INTRODUCTION

What can deterrence contribute to reducing the risks of terrorism by jihadists using weapons of mass destruction (WMD)?[1] In the months after 9/11, there was sharp despair that deterrence might contribute anything at all to the challenges posed by militant Islamist extremists. The *National Security Strategy* issued by the U.S. government in that period summarized the prevailing view as follows:

> Traditional concepts of deterrence will not work against a terrorist enemy whose avowed tactics are wanton destruction and the targeting of innocents; whose so-called soldiers seek martyrdom in death and whose most potential protection is statelessness.[2]

Over the next few years, however, thinking shifted at senior levels of the Bush administration. In September 2006, the administration issued a revised version of its *National Strategy for Combating Terrorism,* which clearly stated that deterrence is a primary objective. This theme was echoed in other guidance as well.[3] If "traditional concepts" are out, what new concepts should inform counterterror planning and operations? What role might deterrence already be playing? What more can reasonably be asked of deterrence against such a diffuse and motivated enemy? How can its contributions to risk reduction be enhanced in the course of a "long war"?

Some preliminary thinking on facets of these questions has already been done at senior levels of government. This is illustrated in the 2006 *National Strategy for Combating Terrorism*:

> A new deterrence calculus combines the need to deter terrorists and supporters from contemplating a WMD attack and, failing that, to dissuade them from actually conducting such an attack. Traditional threats may not work because terrorists show a wanton disregard for the lives of innocents and in some cases for their own lives. We require a range of deterrence strategies that are tailored to the situation and the adversary. We will make clear that terrorists and those who aid or sponsor a WMD attack would face the prospects of an overwhelming response to any use of such weapons. We will seek to dissuade attacks by improving our ability to mitigate the effects of a terrorist attack involving WMD—to limit or prevent casualties, economic disruption, or panic. Finally, we will ensure that our capacity to determine the source of any attack is well-known, and that our determination to respond overwhelmingly to any attack is never in doubt.[4]

Similarly, the academic community has explored different facets of these questions from various perspectives and with varied methodologies.[5] But there appears not to have been a systematic exploration of these questions that builds on the cumulative insights gathered in the period since 9/11.

This chapter aims to help fill this gap. It is a first cut at building a new analytical deterrence structure on the foundations of recent work done in the academic and policy communities. Its view is comprehensive, though, for reasons of space availability, it cannot be fully systematic. This chapter proceeds as follows: The first section establishes the scope of inquiry with some framing arguments about the nature of the WMD terrorism threat and the functions of deterrence. A key argument here is that the militant Islamist extremist WMD terrorism threat is not monolithic and that there is analytical value in disaggregating the threat by exploring distinct components of the terrorist network/movement. The following section of the chapter explores the current and potential contributions of deterrence to the effort to influence the behaviors of those specific components. The chapter then derives some conclusions of a more general kind about the impact of deterrence on the prospects for WMD terrorism. It then turns to an exploration of how that impact can be strengthened and outlines a series of policy recommendations. A primary purpose of this chapter is to stimulate further work that can be helpful to future policy formulation. It is essentially an interim assessment based on a body of analytical work done by a larger community that remains in development, with the hope that it can help focus some next steps useful for a deepening understanding of how "the new deterrence calculus" can be brought together in the coming years.[6]

SCOPE OF INQUIRY

To help focus this analysis, this chapter proceeds with the following understandings about the nature of the WMD terrorism threat and the functions of deterrence.

First, let us begin with a definition of "WMD." This label masks substantial differences between chemical, biological, and nuclear weapons in terms of their lethality and other impacts, in their ease of acquisition and use, and in their potential appeal to individuals with specific motivations. It also obscures the ways in which the precursor materials to these weapons might be used to poison a place or a population but in a way that does not seek to exploit the full lethal potential of the actual weapons. But the label also reflects the important similarities among these weapons. If developed and employed with a high level of technical skill, they can create effects quite distinct from those created with the "bombs and bullets" associated with traditional terrorist operational art. Their effective employment could generate casualties on orders of magnitude larger than the more conventional tools. The prospect of a campaign of attacks with such weapons would have a potent effect on the targeted societies far in excess of the potential impact of campaigns of more conventional attacks. In a manner consistent with the remainder of this volume, this chapter utilizes the shorthand "WMD" because of these similarities and effects. As useful along the way, it highlights ways in which distinctions between the weapon types may be important from the perspective of the functioning of deterrence.

Second, which actors matter in characterizing the WMD terrorist threat? Varied nonstate actors have shown an interest in WMD or their precursor materials, including cults (recall the Rajneeshees and Aum Shinrikyo), the American militia movement (recall Larry Wayne Harris), loners (recall the Alphabet Bomber), and even the occasional national separatist movement (recall the Tamil Tigers).[7] Moreover, many types of actors have shown an interest in attacks that kill indiscriminately in very large numbers and thus might find WMD appealing.[8] But the focus here is on militant Islamist extremists who have enlisted in "jihad" against the so-called near and far enemies. One good reason for embracing the term *WMD*, as argued in the preceding paragraph, is that these extremists have embraced the term; the moral case for mass casualty attacks on noncombatants is set out in a *fatwa* entitled "A Treatise on the Legal Status of Using Weapons of Mass Destruction on the Infidels."[9]

Militant Islamist extremists evidently share a set of beliefs aligned in an ideological construct that motivates terrorist acts on behalf of jihad.[10] But the network and movements of which they are a part consists of many actors other than the individual perpetrators of terrorism and movement leaders. As the *National Strategy for Combating Terrorism* argues,

> The enemy we face today in the War on Terror is not the enemy we faced on September 11. Our effective counterterrorist efforts, in part, have forced the terrorists to evolve and modify their ways of doing business. Our understanding of the enemy has evolved as well. Today, the principal enemy confronting the United States is a transnational movement of extremist organizations, networks, and individuals—and their state and non-state supporters—which have in common that they exploit Islam and use terrorism for ideological ends. This transnational movement is not monolithic. Although al-Qaida functions as the movement's vanguard and remains, along with its affiliate groups and those inspired by them, the most dangerous manifestation of the enemy, the movement is not controlled by any single individual, group, or state. What united the movement is a common vision, a common set of ideas about the nature and destiny of the world, and a common goal of ushering in totalitarian rule.[11]

As Paul Pillar has argued, the suppression of the al-Qa'ida structure as it existed on 9/11 has magnified the challenges of dealing with a diverse and adaptive adversary.[12]

For purposes of this analysis, this larger movement is disaggregated into the following main components:

- jihadist footsoldiers
- the terrorist professionals who sometimes provide training and other logistical guidance and support
- the leaders of al-Qa'ida
- groups affiliated by ideology and aspiration (so-called franchisees)
- operational enablers (financiers, etc.)
- moral legitimizers
- state sponsors
- passive state enablers (generally weak states that are unable or unwilling to prevent terrorists from exploiting their territory or other assets)

Although these are disparate elements of a movement that is in fact far more multifaceted and complex, they must also operate as a network if acts of WMD terrorism are to be enabled and sustained. For purposes of shorthand in the remainder of this chapter, the term "movement/network" will be used to refer to the larger whole of which the elements are a part, recognizing that no single term accurately captures the complexity of the phenomenon. This taxonomy guides the next section of this chapter, which explores the potential impact of deterrence on these different components. A key question for this analysis is the extent to which these components have a shared risk-taking propensity. Do their ideological affinities render irrelevant the differences of interest and stake that might otherwise influence their willingness to run risks?

The third question about scope relates to the definition of deterrence. Thomas Schelling has defined deterrence as "persuading a potential enemy that he should in his own interest avoid certain courses of activity."[13] Schelling goes on to say, "By 'deterrence' I mean...inducing an adversary or a victim *not* to do something, to continue not doing something. The word takes the preposition 'from.'"[14] Glenn Snyder provided some useful elaboration with his argument that there are two modes of deterrence.[15] One is deterrence by the threat of punishment, which compels the adversary to try to calculate whether the potential benefits of action are outweighed by the potential costs. The credibility of the threat to impose those costs is of course key to this mode of deterrence, as a threat that is not seen as credible may be dismissed by the adversary even if the capability or will to enforce it is actually in place. The potential costs of inaction are also a part of this decision calculus and with them so too the adversary's understanding of the balance between the known costs of inaction and the unknown costs of action.[16] The other mode of deterrence is deterrence by denial. This mode relies on denying the adversary the perceived benefit of action.[17]

It is important to distinguish deterrence from other forms of influence, as Paul Davis, Brian Jenkins, and others have done in prescribing policies for dealing with the militant Islamist extremist threat. As Davis and Jenkins argued,

> Even when we stretched definitions of deterrence, the concept was too narrow to use as an organizing principle...the *influence* component of counterterrorism provides a better framework [emphasis in original].[18]

What else lies along this influence spectrum? Schelling elaborated a key distinction between deterrence and compellence:

> By "compellence" I mean inducing a person *to do* something through fear, anxiety, doubt, etc. "Compel"' takes the preposition "to..."' Deterrence is simpler. The command to do something requires a date and a deadline; to keep on not doing something is timeless.[19]

Dissuasion also lies along this continuum. As noted above, the *National Strategy for Combating Terrorism* makes a distinction between deterring terrorists from contemplating a WMD attack and dissuading them from actually doing so.[20] Persuasion and inducement have their own places on this spectrum.[21]

The focus of this chapter is on deterrence by threat of punishment and by denial of success. It attempts to calibrate the relative weight of these two modes of deterrence in the larger influence spectrum. It also attempts to characterize the sources of self-restraint that may inhibit WMD actors or enablers from developing and employing WMD. These are largely speculative tasks, intended to help calibrate in an approximate way the specific functions of deterrence.

Jihadist Footsoldiers

Jihadist footsoldiers have accepted what they understand to be a call to martyrdom.[22] This simple fact calls into question any potential contribution of deterrence. Someone who has chosen to give his or her life to jihad seems an unlikely target for any deterrence strategy because they are unlikely to be motivated not to do something by the threat of a severe punishment, even death.

But this important insight apparently does not exhaust the topic. Let us consider two additional key insights. Not all jihadist footsoldiers are suicide bombers. And suicide bombers have to contend with the possibility that they may not be successful in the intended act of martyrdom.

Consider the possible implications of the fact that not all jihadist footsoldiers are suicide bombers. Of the approximately 11,000 terrorist attacks in 2005, only 360 were suicide bombings—roughly 3 percent.[23] As a recent study by the National Academy of Sciences has pointed out, "terrorists value their own lives."[24] Terrorists not motivated by an immediate desire to commit suicide may be amenable to influence strategies in a way that suicidal terrorists are not. A task force of terrorism experts argued just this point in June 2002: "deterrence theory should be applicable against individual terrorists most of the time, but it will not be applicable against all individuals all of the time."[25] Indeed, there is evidence to suggest that this is so. Social science research has demonstrated a striking commonality in the risk-taking propensity of individuals involved in illicit and potentially fatal activity: A low level of perceived risk is an enticement, but the expectation of both mission failure and significant risk of a significant penalty can influence behavior patterns. These findings are drawn from the drug trade, other transnational criminal activities, terrorism of the 1970s, and even the suicide attacks of 9/11.[26] A study from the mid-1970s found that "increasing the certainty of punishment acts as a better deterrent than increasing the severity of punishment."[27] A more recent study concluded in 2007 that "even the most cost and risk acceptant terrorists can be deterred in a predictable fashion from specific actions."[28]

It is important to note that studies available in the social sciences sometimes point to contradictory insights and conclusions. One study, drawing on British experience in trying to deter the Irish Republican Army, illustrates the ways in which deterrence policies generated acts of defiance by some even as it succeeded in gaining acquiescence by others.[29] In a classic study of deterrence, Alexander George and Richard Smoke have defined this problem as follows: "Reinforcement of deterrence in a crisis may succeed in deterring the opponent, but at the cost of hardening his conviction that the defender is unresponsive to the legitimate interests that lie behind his effort to obtain a change in the situation. As a result, the initiator may resolve to prepare more effectively."[30]

There is even some limited evidence to suggest that suicide bombers can be influenced by perceptions of operational risk. As Robert Anthony has concluded from a statistical review of terrorist operations, "even suicide terrorists are willing to delay their attack until they are convinced that they have a 'good' chance of success."[31] Some appear to be influenced by the desire to strike at targets where the prospect of success is good and thus turn away from "hard" targets to softer ones. The move to softer targets by militant Islamist extremists has been striking in recent years, as has the shift from logistically complex operations to less demanding ones.[32]

There may also be some prospect of deterring suicidal bombers by increasing the perceived risk that their operation will fail in a way that results not in their martyrdom but in their incarceration. As a National War College study has concluded, "a terrorist may be willing to die for his cause but be unwilling to spend the rest of his life in the unglamorous, isolated, largely forgotten role of prisoner."[33] Prolonged imprisonment may pose a particular worry for jihadists, who might fear a loss of faith over time. Al-Qa'ida's training manual includes prescriptions for life in prison with an emphasis on "upholding religion" and team work to enable righteousness and piety.[34] The potential deterrence value of enhancing operational risk for suicidal terrorists seems born out in the Israeli experience. One study, drawing on Israeli experience in the second Palestinian intifada between 2000 and 2004, concludes: "Israeli authorities have prevented more than 340 suicide bombings from advancing beyond the planning stages...the right mix of threats in at least some instances challenges the conventional wisdom that suicide bombers are undeterrable."[35]

In sum, evidence suggests that jihadist footsoldiers are influenced by both modes of deterrence. Deterrence by denial seems to play a role vis-à-vis those individuals who attach importance to success in the operational sense. Deterrence by the threat of punishment seems also to play some role, if the prospect of getting caught is significant enough and the sanction severe enough (for that fraction of the jihadist recruit population willing to commit suicide, the severest sanction may be the denial of martyrdom).

As important as these insights may be, they should not be construed to suggest that deterrence can play a highly significant role in influencing the behavior of jihadist footsoldiers. The available social science research suggests that footsoldiers are generally not amenable to influence strategies of any kind. Persuasion, dissuasion, and inducement seem to offer little promise in shaping the behaviors of individuals committed to militant extremism. But among the tools of influence, deterrence should not be completely written off, given its various potential contributions so far noted.

Terrorist Professionals

Although some jihadist footsoldiers form cells and plan and conduct operations entirely on their own, many such soldiers and cells receive assistance from others who have made terrorism a profession and career. Such individuals run training camps. They help plan operations. They facilitate operations by linking cells to needed resources. They sometimes lead specific operations. Their ideological affinity with jihad and their propensity to run risks and even to commit suicide may be no different from that of the jihadist footsoldiers, and thus they may be susceptible in only very marginal ways to deterrence strategies. But here, too, some alternative propositions should be considered.

First, the infrequency with which terrorist professionals give their own lives in such operations suggests that martyrdom is not highly valued by them in the accomplishment of any single operation. As a general proposition, they seem to be in it for the campaign, the cause, or the money, but not apparently for martyrdom, at least in the short term.

Second, perceptions of operational risk are at least as important for the professional as for the footsoldier, if not more so. Professionals build reputations on delivering results. Success matters. Success for them is defined in terms of operational goals, as opposed to more fundamental ones.[36] Planners have shown themselves to be influenced by perceptions of operational risk. Speaking from the perspective of his experience with operatives of the Irish Republican Army, a senior British counterterror official has observed that "deterrence [of specific operations] is possible with overt activity aimed at reconnaissance, preparation, attack, and escape phases."[37] Davis and Jenkins echo this theme with the observation that "the empirical record shows that even hardened terrorists dislike operational risks and may be deterred by uncertainty and risk."[38]

But the available social science suggests that there is an analogue here to the "defiance response" noted in the preceding discussion of footsoldiers. Measures that enhance operational risk in attacks on specific targets may not reduce the threat; they may simply displace it onto another target. A study from 1993 argues as follows:

> substitutions...must be accounted for, along with indirect effects.... [T]he unintended consequences of an antiterrorism policy may be far more costly than intended consequences, and must be anticipated. In the case of metal detectors, kidnappings increased; in the case of embassy fortification, assassinations became more frequent.[39]

This suggests that the terrorist professional, like the jihadist footsoldier, can be influenced by the two forms of deterrence. Deterrence by denial of operational success influences their target selection and mode of operation. Deterrence by threat of being captured or killed seems also to play an important role (but here the evidence is not well developed). Persuasion, dissuasion, and compellence seem again to have little or nothing to contribute to influencing the behavior of these actors.

Leaders

The leaders of al-Qa'ida, like the jihadist recruits, are also inspired to martyrdom—but not their own, at least in the short term. Rather, they seek a movement of martyrs. Al-Qa'ida leaders have "raised Islamic martyrdom to the status of a principle of faith."[40] Many observers of al-Qa'ida equate the leadership's commitment to acquire WMD with a commitment to employ it once acquired—otherwise, why expend the effort and resources? Here, too, some alternative propositions merit consideration.

First, success at the operational level matters to those interested in success vis-à-vis more fundamental goals. That any individual operation be successful may matter less to the leadership of al-Qa'ida than to the professionals responsible for organizing it, but failures will become important if their cumulative impact is to undermine achievement of fundamental goals. That leadership is interested in utilizing violence to re-write the grand historical narrative in ways it considers right and necessary; violence that is ineffective toward this end or, worse, clumsy and generates unwanted reactions, is unlikely to be long tolerated. For example, some jihadists have criticized al-Qa'ida's senior leadership for the 9/11 attacks because they led to the loss of Afghanistan. Successful operations also help at the more prosaic level of generating jihadist volunteers and the other resources needed to sustain operations.

Second, al-Qa'ida's leaders themselves say that the U.S. failure to punish in substantial and meaningful ways fueled the belief that the United States could be bent to al-Qa'ida's will. As RAND scholar Jonathan Schachter has described it, "September 11 represents first and foremost a failure to deter." Referencing cruise missile attacks on al-Qa'ida camps in Afghanistan in the late 1990s, Schachter argues further as follows:

> Cruise missiles hold a special mystique in the American perspective. Their combination of destructive power...accuracy and range mean that specific targets can be hit without endangering American personnel. But this virtue in the eyes of American citizens, soldiers, and decision-makers is an indication of weakness to our al-Qa'idah adversaries. Not only were the response attacks largely ineffective...they were seen as another small and cowardly step by a wounded tiger.[41]

Of course it is not possible to go back and seize the opportunities for deterrence that might have been there a decade ago. But the fact that deterrence failed suggests the possibility that it might have succeeded had there been more attention to its requirements. Might the threat of retaliation make a difference to the strategic calculations of the al-Qa'ida leadership? Some analysts believe so: "Al-Qa'ida has shown a pragmatic side," argues Jerry Mark Long, and "it realizes that indiscriminate use of WMD would likely bring devastating retaliation, and Afghanistan is a case in point."[42] Others observe that the threat of retaliation can be quite meaningless: "In the perceptions of the terrorists and their supporters, they may have little, if anything, to lose from a defender's retaliation."[43] Some worry that the leaders of al-Qa'ida even welcome very dramatic forms of retaliation, on the argument that this would help to "clarify the historical narrative" by reinforcing the image of the enemies of Islam as hugely evil. But the publicly available evidence on any of these propositions is scant.

These observations suggest that the two modes of deterrence contribute little to restraining al-Qa'ida leadership from seeking to develop and employ WMD. Yet their restraint seems to have been significant—so far. That leadership has not invested in WMD in the way that it has invested in other operational modes. This is not an observation about the scale of investment, but rather about scale relative to the challenge. Al-Qa'ida leadership has invested for success in multiple modes of attack and to create the infrastructures to enable such modes. But it has not so far scaled its investment in WMD toward this end—or so the record of nonattack suggests. What accounts for this perceived restraint? If the restraint is not imposed through mechanisms of deterrence or other means, then it must be a self-imposed restraint. How might we understand these potential sources of self-restraint—and manipulate them? The available analysis of the leadership's self-restraint points to a number of potential sources.

Because movement leaders concern themselves above all with fundamental goals, as opposed to operational ones, they must concern themselves with how the acquisition and use of WMD might advance or retard those goals. Their potential value in advancing those goals seems well understood by those who seek to deter WMD terrorism, but this does little to explain the pattern of restraint. How might the leadership of al-Qa'ida perceive WMD acquisition and use as retarding their fundamental goals? That leadership has been painstaking in its effort to develop an operational code of jihad. That code depicts jihadist tactics as just within their own moral construct—a construct that is self-defined as defensive and discriminate. One thorough review of this operational code comes to the blunt conclusion that "when we turn to al-Qaeda's doctrine of WMD doctrine, the most salient factor is that there is none....Significantly, manuals like *Military Studies in the Jihad against the Tyrants* fail to mention them at all."[44] The use of WMD has not been "normalized" within this construct. Apparently, it remains controversial.[45] WMD employment might inflame this controversy in ways that would be unhelpful for the leadership. How?

First, such employment could deepen disaffection within the leadership group among those who opposed it. Historically, concerns about such potential disaffection have constrained terrorist leaders from employing controversial tactics, largely out of a concern to sustain a high level of trust among the inner core. The occasional defector has proven crippling to terrorist organizations.[46]

Second, Muslims drawn to jihad but not al-Qa'ida's brand may be more willing after an act of WMD terrorism than before to compromise al-Qa'ida operations or individuals of whom they are aware because of a sense of moral outrage. Winning the "hearts and minds" of Muslims is clearly an objective of the al-Qa'ida leadership, and utilization of tactics that a wide majority of Muslims deem unacceptable would work against this goal. The loss of support occasioned by extremely violent al-Qa'ida actions in Iraq led to a significant effort by al-Qa'ida leadership to adopt tactics less offensive to Muslims.[47]

Third, the leadership has a few resources that are particularly scarce when measured against the requirements of a very long campaign, and it may wish not to squander them in any particular attack, however spectacular in its short-term effect, or in any prolonged research and development effort, however potent the capability it may produce at some future time. These resources could be understood as including the "vanguard"—the special cadre of "'professional revolutionaries' possess[ing] both the intellectual capacity and the fighting spirit to blaze the trail of revolution."[48] As one study argues, "Marxist-Leninist-Maoist revolutionary doctrine is critical to understanding jihadi strategy," and that doctrine puts strong emphasis on a vanguard that catalyzes the larger revolution and must be preserved even as soldiers in the field are expended.[49] Another scarce resource is the tolerance and support of those key individuals in a position to use personal or institutional assets to advance al-Qa'ida's cause. Their will to enable may be reduced and with it key operational assets lost.

The longer term influence of these and potentially other sources of self-restraint on al-Qa'ida's WMD intentions is a matter of conjecture. Some experts see evidence that they are eroding.[50] But the leaders of such groups and movements must contend with the fact that "members have different goals and objectives, and preferred strategies for achieving them. Preferences and commitment level vary across specific roles performed within the organization and among sub-group leaders."[51] This challenge will endure.

Affiliate Groups

These are groups that have sprung up in response to al-Qa'ida's call to militant jihad or that previously existed but have sought association with al-Qa'ida for reasons of ideology or expedience. Assuming adherents of such groups share the ideological zeal for martyrdom of their counterparts in the core al-Qa'ida elements, there ought be nothing unique or distinct about deterrence of them. But some alternative possibilities should be considered.

Shared goals do not necessarily equate with identical goals. Fundamental goals may overlap but also diverge in significant ways. Consider, for example, Islamist groups that have employed terrorist tactics in traditional ways for traditional purposes, as, for example, to replace a local government with one more aligned ideologically with their views. Such groups may share one of al-Qa'ida's fundamental goals: to renew Islam's place in global affairs. On the other hand, they may see some of al-Qa'ida's objectives vis-à-vis the "far enemy" as unhelpful to their cause. Examples of this phenomenon can be found in Southeast Asia, where some Islamist resistance groups also resist some local al-Qa'ida initiatives. Operational goals may also overlap but not fully converge. Local groups sympathetic to al-Qa'ida may desire to strike the same targets as the al-Qa'ida leadership, but they may be concerned about local reactions to attacks deemed excessive in a way that the al-Qa'ida leadership may not. After all, they are competing for local legitimacy. Such factors seem to account for some of the backlash against al-Qa'ida among militant Islamist groups in Malaysia and Indonesia.[52] One recent academic study observes that "groups that are primarily focused on local concerns can be coerced into denying sanctuary (and other assistance) to members of more dangerous groups."[53]

"Jihadi-on-jihadi tension has historically run high," argues one report, as "seen in the conflict between the 'Afghan Arabs' and the Afghan mujahedeen, as well as in other jihadi combat experiences."[54] That study also reports that al-Qa'ida subgroups "need to be very careful about who they hit in order to avoid losing...critical support."[55] If the available social science literature is an accurate reflection, these tensions remain little studied by Western experts. How and why coalitions with al-Qa'ida weaken and collapse seem to be as little studied as the more general question of why terrorist groups and movements collapse; the available literature focuses almost entirely on what causes movements, groups, and coalitions to coalesce. But there ought to be valuable lessons in what causes them to disintegrate.[56]

These arguments suggest that affiliate groups may have sources of self-restraint above and beyond the restraints of movement components more closely aligned with al-Qa'ida's fundamental and operational goals. What does this line of argument imply about deterrence? The sources of disharmony may be a vulnerability that can be exploited. The local vulnerabilities of such groups, including their need to sustain some popular support and some room for maneuvering in the targeted state, may be targetable in the sense that public and governmental responses can intensify in the wake of actions deemed particularly egregious. This may have a deterrent effect within the movement as such, by increasing pressure from the affiliate groups on al-Qa'ida leadership to moderate behaviors globally that are unhelpful locally.

Operational Enablers

These are individuals who provide money, documents, safe houses, weapons, communications, and other operational assets. Their ranks also include some dupes or individuals willing to turn a blind eye to an attack in preparation or execution. These individuals may conceive themselves as called to jihad, but they have not made the commitment to self-sacrifice. Many extend support to extremists under the cover of legitimate ongoing economic, social, or political activity. In this case, they have not even chosen to sacrifice their public face in the name of jihad.

As Davis and Jenkins have rightly argued, "Bin Laden may feel he has nothing to lose, but at least some of his financiers live comfortably with wealth, family, and prestige. Obviously, they do have something to lose."[57] This proposition seems broadly applicable to the group of enablers more generally. Accordingly, many studies have concluded that deterrence by threat of punishment ought to be effective against enablers seeking to act covertly in their own societies.[58] The evidence to support or contradict this conclusion is not generally available. It is difficult to conceive that deterrence by defeat would play any role in shaping the incentives of these actors.

One particular type of operational enabler deserves separate scrutiny—transnational criminal organizations. They deserve such scrutiny because contradictory expectations have formed within the expert community about their susceptibility to deterrence strategies. On the one hand, it seems plausible that criminal organizations would conduct business with terrorists just as they would with any other entity where there is money to be made. After all, a successful act of nuclear terrorism might seem especially lucrative to those enablers with materials, technologies, or expertise. The concern about criminal trafficking in Russian nuclear weapons and materials is particularly acute.[59] Because such groups already operate effectively despite whatever sanctions the state places on them, goes the argument, they are unlikely to be deterred from seeking such profits by the threat of punishment. On the other hand, criminal organizations are essentially parasites. They depend on the health of the organism from which they extract wealth. Cooperating with terrorists can be bad for business. Indeed, there is some evidence illustrating a willingness of such organizations to cooperate with law enforcement officials to eliminate people who are bad for business. This line of argument suggests that the threat of additional punishment may be a significant barrier to criminal organizations enabling WMD terrorism.[60] The available evidence is too sparse, unfortunately, to prove definitively one or the other hypothesis.

Moral Legitimizers

These individuals are enablers, but of a particular kind. The assets they provide to militant extremists are not operational but theological. They define a moral context within which jihadist terror is deemed legitimate, indeed sacred. They operate within a religious tradition that establishes ethical limits on the use of force[61] and participate in an ongoing exploration of and debate about how specific actions correspond with the dictates of Islamic jurisprudence.[62] Sometimes their work is deeply rooted within this jurisprudential context; at others, their work draws on that context in convenient ways to make an argument of expedience in the cloak of morality. These are individuals in the mosques, schools, and media who have made the commitment to jihad and who also operate quite overtly and thus are not potentially subject to the penalties that offer some leverage over those operating covertly.[63]

The permissions given by such authorities to employ terrorist tactics, including the use of WMD, are critical enablers. But it is important to also recognize the flip side of this proposition: Jurisprudential concerns are also an important source of restraint within the militant community. Historically, many terrorists groups have had to concern themselves with finding the right dividing line between killing "enough" and killing "too many," which is to say with finding the threshold at which they could motivate desired change without generating a crippling backlash from the state or the people on whose behalf they perceive themselves as fighting. The fact that the moral legitimizers of terrorism have concerned themselves with this threshold may yet prove to be a significant barrier to the full exploitation of the lethal potential of WMD. In other recent experience, religious leaders have ended up playing an important role in shifting the moral debate in a way that has constrained terrorist violence.[64]

But the means for influencing the moral legitimizers seem to be few. They are not open to persuasion, except perhaps by members of their own religious tradition, who are likely to be the only ones to have the credibility to challenge the moral standing of the legitimizers within their own community. They do, however, need to concern themselves with their own legitimacy and the possibility of a backlash against their moral vision generated by acts of violence widely deemed egregious violations of Islamic norms. Those who are in it not for religious conviction but expedience of one kind or another may be amenable to influence strategies, however, such as imprisonment or other forms of direct, personal punishment.

State Sponsors

State sponsors of terrorism provide various goods and services to those whom they sponsor, including sanctuary, political support, weapons, intelligence, and logistics. The Department of State designates the following states as sponsors of terrorism: Cuba, Iran, North Korea, Sudan, and Syria.[65] Conspicuously, four of the five are also suspected of seeking nuclear, biological, and/or chemical weapons (Sudan is the exception).[66]

This facet of the terrorist threat seems readily amenable to deterrence by threat of punishment. As a National Academy of Sciences study concluded, "the facts that the Taliban lost control of Afghanistan and al-Qa'ida was wounded no doubt constitute a credible warning to other states harboring terrorists...that the United States is willing to act and that it has a destructive capacity."[67] The prospective deterrent effect of such U.S. actions was evidently valued by President Bush, who reportedly argued shortly after 9/11: "Let's hit them [the Taliban] hard. We want to cause other countries like Syria to change their views."[68] The prospect of such punishment is credited by many experts with inducing the leaders of terrorism sponsoring states not to open their WMD arsenals (or developmental processes) to those whom they sponsor.

But there are some potential problems with this line of argument. One is that a case study widely used as a reference point in this discussion is interpreted by analysts in contradictory ways. The case study is Libya and its response to the bombing of Tripoli authorized by President Ronald Reagan in 1984. Some analysts conclude that the bombing induced Muammar Qaddafi to curtail his support to terrorism, including specifically attacks on American targets. In the words of one study, "the findings support the conclusion that the application of the principle of deterrence to international terrorism was at least partially successful in this instance."[69] Others survey the historical record and conclude that "the retaliatory raid on Libya appeared to increase terrorism in the near term, but did not have a significant long-run impact, good or bad."[70] There is a similar debate about what factors actually induced Qaddafi to abandon his WMD programs and capabilities two decades later.[71]

A second problem is that the WMD restraint so far observed by state sponsors may have explanations other than deterrence. One plausible explanation is that the leaders of these states typically maintain tight control so as to be safe from internal and external enemies and are averse to losing control of powerful means that might be turned back against the regime or its interests. Another plausible explanation is that weapons development programs have not reached a point where the arsenal of available weapons or materials is sufficiently ample to allow diversions to other than central military purposes of the regime.

A third problem is that the credibility of the threat to punish a state sponsor of WMD terrorism seems to require that the sponsor believe that such sponsorship can be attributed to him. A growing appreciation of the gaps in these attribution capabilities has spurred high-level efforts to strengthen capabilities with the hope that this will enhance deterrence.[72] The degree to which capability gaps undermine the functioning of deterrence is a matter of conjecture. As Michael Quinlan has argued, "a state may not be sure of being found out; but equally it cannot be sure of not being found out."[73] That uncertainty may be a sufficient deterrent if the expected penalty associated with discovery is very high.

A final problem with the view that states can be deterred from sponsoring WMD terrorism is that it depends on a threat to put the survival of the regime at risk. But what if the regime already perceives itself to be at risk? Or what if it perceives that the threats are not meant to deter but are merely a ruse to justify the use of pre-emptive force against it? Deterrence might well fail in such instances, if the regime in power genuinely feels itself to be in jeopardy and if it has developed strong relations with terrorist organizations.[74]

These problems imply that deterrence may not be as reliable in inducing restraint by the leaders of terrorism sponsoring states as we might believe or hope. The historical record is nonetheless quite striking in that for decades now the state sponsors of terror have not opened their WMD toolkits to those whom they sponsor.

An interesting additional question arises about the possibility of exerting deterrence influence over terrorist organizations through their state sponsors. Can state sponsors be induced to do more than exercise self-restraint? Can they be induced to also impose their will on terrorists not to seek, acquire, or use WMD? Some analysts are hopeful that this might be so. Michael Quinlan argues:

> There is naturally now...a further strand of concern about the willingness of individuals to give their lives...in order to carry out terrorist attacks. What can deterrence, in the strict sense, do about these? In immediate terms, nothing. But they scarcely ever, if indeed ever, exist and operate in isolation from organizations, and these organizations rarely in isolation from states; and deterrence can be brought to bear by that route.[75]

Other analysts are skeptical. Alexander George, for example, argued as follows: "Efforts to coerce a non-state actor indirectly by persuading states friendly to the non-state actor to exert pressure against it may work sometimes, but such efforts of indirect coercion are often difficult and may be counterproductive."[76]

Passive State Enablers

Passive state enablers are a component of the terrorism threat network distinct from state sponsors in a dimension critical to deterrence: intent. Sponsors are states that support terrorist groups as a matter of policy. Enablers reject such support and indeed have policies supporting counterterrorism but tolerate terrorist activities within their borders because they cannot prevent them. By one count, there are nearly four times as many enablers as sponsors, most of them weak and collapsing states.[77] As Daniel Byman has noted, "the greatest contribution a state can make to a terrorist cause is by not acting. A border not policed, a blind eye turned to fundraising, or even toleration of recruitment all help terrorists build their organizations, conduct operations and survive."[78] Weak or failing states may be especially lucrative as venues to acquire unconventional weapon capabilities.[79]

What is the potential role of deterrence in motivating restraint by state enablers? If individuals throughout the state structure are indeed committed to countering terrorism, they need no such motivation—they already have it. In that case, they may simply need help. But the commitment to countering terrorism may not be as broad or deep as to motivate the necessary cooperation to curtail enabling actions. In this case, "outside governments should try to raise the costs to regimes of tolerating passive support," argues Daniel Byman, who notes further that "simple embarrassment [has] proved highly effective."[80] Additional motivation may be useful in the form of enhanced international efforts to define clearly and precisely the obligations of sovereign states vis-à-vis activities within their jurisdiction deemed in violation of international laws and norms. As the *National Strategy for Combating Terrorism* argues, "States that have sovereign rights also have sovereign responsibilities, including the responsibility to combat terrorism."[81] The commitment made there to "update and tailor international obligations to meet the evolving nature of the terrorist enemies and threats we face" should be helpful in enhancing this mode of influence over states whose commitment to the cessation of enabling actions is less than complete.[82]

ASSESSING THE CONTRIBUTIONS OF DETERRENCE TO RISK REDUCTION

What conclusions about the contributions of deterrence to reducing the risks of WMD terrorism follow from the preceding review of the terrorist network/movement by component?

First, deterrence is not irrelevant to the effort to combat terrorism and to reduce the risks of WMD terrorism. The shift in national guidance from 2001 to 2005 makes good sense because the record suggests that deterrence has played a more important role in shaping the risks of terrorism than was understood in the immediate aftermath of 9/11. But nor is the role of deterrence foundational to strategy in the way that it was in the Cold War. Deterrence is but one of many tools of influence and sometimes not the most promising one.[83]

Second, deterrence, like other tools of influence, is a strategy for creating disincentives in an adversary's mind to courses of action he might otherwise adopt. But sometimes those disincentives already exist. As this review has shown, there are many sources of self-restraint within the network/movement of militant Islamist extremists. Sometimes the primary goal of an influence strategy might be simply to reinforce those existing restraints.

Third, both modes of deterrence are relevant—deterrence by the threat of punishment and deterrence by denial. But they operate differently across elements of the network/movement, sometimes in combination, sometimes only one or the other. Deterrence by threat of punishment seems especially promising vis-à-vis state sponsors and operational enablers. Deterrence by denial seems especially promising vis-à-vis footsoldiers, professionals, and leaders.

Fourth, the cumulative effect of deterrence on the WMD terrorism threat is nearly impossible to predict. It seems highly unlikely that deterrence and other influence strategies could be employed so successfully as to ensure that all of the operational and leadership elements of the militant Islamist extremist movement see WMD as too risky to acquire and use. It seems equally implausible that these strategies could be employed so poorly that all leaders and sponsors connive to develop WMD, the senior most planners prepare, and footsoldiers execute spectacular campaigns with WMD that reap the full lethal potential of those weapons. Such a result would also require a complete collapse of all of the sources of self-restraint within the movement, which is also implausible.

If these extreme results are unlikely, is there a more plausible set of possible results? Three are suggested here:

1. Deterrence may succeed in lowering the lethality of individual attacks with WMD, by inhibiting the cooperation of those most capable of developing and employing WMD in ways that reap their full lethal potential. Especially if state sponsors and critical operational enablers can be deterred from facilitating such attacks, small cells and others operating with limited training and skills seem unlikely to be able to master all of the technical and operational requirements of successful WMD attacks.
2. Deterrence may succeed in curtailing campaigns of attacks. Such campaigns are the most certain way to reap the full lethal potential of WMD and seem particularly plausible with biological weapons.[84] Deterrence by denial may show such campaigns to be ineffective in achieving their intended results.[85] Deterrence by punishment may inhibit the continued cooperation of the enablers and others who were willing to accept the risks of a spectacular blow but not the costs of sustained retaliation by those being attacked. Both modes of deterrence may drive the residual networks attempting campaign-style attacks to untried developmental and delivery methods with the associated increased risks to operational security.
3. Deterrence may induce the leadership of al-Qa'ida to utilize nuclear weapons, when and if they acquire them, only for purposes of deterrence and defense as they conceive them rather than for purposes of aggression and terrorism. It may induce caution of the kind that has been induced in all new acquirers of these capabilities.

A final closing observation is necessary: These conclusions are of course speculative. Scholarship on deterring terrorism remains underdeveloped. To be sure, there is a steadily growing base of sound analytical work generating useful policy-relevant insights being done by a diverse group of social scientists and others. The relative paucity of materials of the 1980s and 1990s has given way to a growing wealth of materials. But the work is not comprehensive. And there are few signs that it is cumulative. Some of it is deeply rooted in a solid evidentiary base; much of it is little more than theory-building and even, occasionally, wishful thinking.

RECOMMENDATIONS FOR ENHANCING DETERRENCE

How can contributions of deterrence to WMD risk reduction be enhanced? To enhance the future performance of deterrence by denial, a great deal of capability and capacity development is already underway in the United States. The protection of high-value targets inside and outside of the United States is already much enhanced after 9/11, and more is being done to protect critical civilian and military infrastructures, political symbols, and power projection capabilities. The lesson from the British experience cited above has been taken, meaning that protection also extends to overt policing activities in each of the realms where militant Islamist extremists might prepare attacks on high-value targets: reconnaissance, preparation, attack, and escape.

It is impossible, naturally, to protect all of the hard and soft targets in the United States and elsewhere that might be attacked by terrorists. Studies typically recommend better intelligence on terrorist cells—a platitude surely not already lost on any counterterror policymaker. What would be useful for targeting U.S. protection investments and also potentially knowable is how leaders in al-Qa'ida and other jihadists understand—or debate—centers of gravity in the United States. The fact that Marx, Lenin, and Mao have been influential in the development of al-Qa'ida leadership thinking may provide a focal point for such investigation. Very little analytical work has been done along these lines but much is possible, especially if the U.S. government were to make publicly available to scholars the enemy captured and open-source documents available to it.

To enhance the future performance of deterrence by threat of punishment, capability and capacity development is already well launched. The stand-up of the National Counter-Terrorism Center (NCTC) under the auspices of the Director of National Intelligence has catalyzed a higher level effort to bring together the analytical and operational planning elements to develop options for collapsing terror cells and operations. Its linkage to the National Counter Proliferation Center should prove helpful in enabling successful interdictions of the linkages between state sponsors with WMD and terrorists seeking those WMD. The ongoing process of strengthening forensic capabilities to attribute nuclear and biological attacks in the United States should also prove helpful to the future performance of deterrence by threat of punishment.

Essential to the effective functioning of deterrence by threat of punishment is the credibility associated with the threat. The desire to enhance the credibility of U.S. threats is a major driver of the effort to strengthen capacities in the Department of Defense and elsewhere in the U.S. government for strategic communication. It also motivates continued pursuit of clearer and more precise declaratory policies as elaborated at the most senior levels of government. Both sets of initiatives have been widely embraced in the studies done post-9/11. Alas, the work surveyed for this study suggests that policymakers should have only very modest expectations about the likely result of such efforts in enhancing the credibility of U.S. threats. Why?

First, the targets of U.S. threats already have well-formed views of the United States and of how and why it behaves on the global scene. As argued above, the targets in the terrorist network/movement potentially susceptible to deterrence by threat of punishment are state sponsors, operational enablers, affiliated groups, and perhaps also to a very limited degree leaders and footsoldiers. Typically, these individuals have been thinking about the United States as an enemy for at least a decade or longer. Many see the United States as a paper tiger or at least heavily constrained not to use violence in ways that cause collateral damage, especially when the media eye can be brought to bear. And as

Robert Jervis has observed, "One of the basic findings of cognitive psychology is that images change only slowly and are maintained in the face of discrepant information. This implies that trying to change a reputation of low resolve will be especially costly."[86] This suggests that public policy statements aimed at enhancing a U.S. reputation that it makes good on its threats will have little or no impact on this problem at this time. More likely to be influential in shaping U.S. reputation will be what it does over the course of what the Pentagon called "the long war" in the *Quadrennial Defense Review,2006*.[87] The deterrence value of U.S. threats may be enhanced over time if the United States can better understand how its signals are received by the target audiences (and others). This, too, can be facilitated by a greater openness with enemy documents.

Second, whatever is said now to these actors in the way of clarified U.S. threats will be sifted through their views of the lessons of U.S. military action in Iraq. A result there that they interpret as defeat of and retreat by the United States would likely erode the credibility of future U.S. threats to intervene to remove a regime that has provided egregious assistance to a terrorist WMD capability. As this is an outcome that many of those actors desire (i.e., they wish the United States to retreat a broken power, as the Soviet Union retreated from Afghanistan), they are likely to find confirmatory evidence of their views no matter what the actual results on the ground in Iraq might be. The continuation of Robert Jervis' argument above adds an important dimension to this discussion, however. In meeting the challenges of changing a reputation for low resolve, he argues, "only the running of what is obviously a high risk or engaging in a costly conflict will suffice."[88] The war in Iraq may yet persuade the specific targets of deterrence by threat of punishment strategies that U.S. threats are credible because it is willing to run high risks and pay high costs.

Third, the credibility of the deterrence threat must attach also to a promise of restraint. Recall the theory of deterrence as synopsized at the beginning of this chapter: to have a restraining influence, a threat to punish must include not just an expectation of successful punishment (because the means and will exist) but also a promise that if restraint is exercised by the object of the deterrence threat, restraint will be exercised by the one who issued the threat. This promise of restraint may well be plausible to state sponsors and operational enablers, but it seems likely to be less plausible to leaders and footsoldiers. They may believe that the United States is already doing all that it can to locate and punish them, especially after 9/11, and would be deeply skeptical of any promise to do less. It is conceivable, however, that they may take a different view of reluctant partners of the United States in the global counterterror effort. A campaign of WMD attacks on the United States (and others) could catalyze a much higher degree of cooperation among the major powers to defeat militant Islamist extremism. Potentially more significantly, it could catalyze greater cooperation from those "front-line" states that have so far been reluctant to engage fully with the United States in its efforts to confront and collapse terrorist networks. Indeed, if they become the targets of such attacks, these states might well demand a much higher level of punitive action—and even attempt to catalyze it.

It is useful to note that strategic communication also has a role to play in enhancing the performance of deterrence by denial. Its function is not to lend credibility but to lend doubt. Those targets potentially amenable to deterrence by denial include footsoldiers, professionals, and leaders. If their WMD assets are few, they are unlikely to be willing to risk them in unviable operations. They will want to be able to calibrate the likely effectiveness of U.S. protection capabilities. Deterrence is well served by confounding their ability to gain confidence in such assessments. They should be concerned that they cannot adequately calibrate specific risks and also persuaded that U.S. protection capabilities are good enough to put their potential operations at risk.

Here again many studies offer platitudes about the value of better intelligence, this time for effective strategic communication. What would be useful to know and might actually be knowable?

Leadership assessments of the endgame in Iraq potentially meet these two criteria. Do they find confirmatory evidence of prior beliefs that the United States is a paper tiger and that it will soon go the way of the Soviet Union when it was driven from Afghanistan, or are they drawing different conclusions?

Also useful and potentially knowable is how to influence the so-called willingness function of terrorists. As previously noted, this term relates to the willingness of individuals to run risks as informed by the prospect and severity of punishment.[89] This function has been well explored in various criminal fields (e.g., drug trafficking) and explored on only a preliminary basis in the terrorism realm. More work could fruitfully be done here that would be useful in calibrating threat communication strategies and observable performances of protection capabilities.

Three further recommendations for enhancing the future performance of deterrence follow from this analysis. First, accelerate the development of deterrence capacities within the U.S. government and also their integration. The 2006 *National Strategy for Combating Terrorism* argues in its second paragraph that "the paradigm for combating terrorism now involves the application of all elements of our national power and influence."[90] The application of those elements of power seems further advanced in the realm of defeating terrorism than of deterring it. The U.S. military has done some path-breaking thinking in the Joint Operating Concept (JOC) on Deterrence about how to employ military tools for the deterrence of nonstate actors, and the concept is being utilized to inform the development of operational plans for combating terrorism by the combatant commanders. Similarly path-breaking conceptual work and operational integration are not evident across the U.S. government more generally. As a starting point, there ought to be some exploration of how the concepts in the JOC can be supported by "all elements of our national power and influence."

Second, refresh national guidance on deterrence. The ideas on deterrence set out in the 2006 combating terrorism strategy were broad and brief. Greater specificity is now possible. In revising guidance, it would be useful to align the distinctions between deterrence and dissuasion, as elaborated in the strategy, with the distinctions used elsewhere in the government and consistent with the usages developed in this chapter. The 2006 strategy argues as follows: "a new deterrence calculus combines the need to deter terrorists and supporters from contemplating a WMD attack and, failing that, to dissuade them from actually conducting an attack."[91] Logically, dissuasion relates to the formation of the intent and deterrence to inhibiting action in fulfillment of the intent. In the Department of Defense, dissuasion is a "shaping function" employed in "Phase Zero" to prevent the emergence of challenges of deterrence (Phase Two) and crisis and war operations in later phases. Being clearer about the different functions of deterrence and dissuasion can help to motivate actions tailored for each.

Third, explore alternative future deterrence contingencies. How might the character of the long war change over time? What new deterrence challenges might emerge that have not so far captured our attention? We can hope that the *National Strategy for Combating Terrorism* is successful in containing, shrinking, and ultimately extinguishing the terrorist threat for militant Islamist extremists. But what if it is not, at least in the short or medium term? What if al-Qa'ida's strategy proves more successful, in the sense that extremists are successful in gaining political control over the holy sites in Arabia; reconstituting a caliphate; and then, under a nuclear umbrella, pursuing revolutionary war to cast out apostate governments, re-make borders in and around the *umma*, and potentially conduct further aggressions against the Far Enemy? This would present a deterrence challenge of a quality and character not so far considered in this analytical review.

NOTES

1. This chapter was originally prepared as a research paper of the Institute for Defense Analyses under contract to the Department of State and was released as Paper P-4231 in June 2007. This updated version was finalized in early 2008. The author has benefited significantly from a critique of earlier drafts by Alexis Blanc and Mark Stout of the Institute for Defense Analyses and Sina Lehmkuhler of the Department of Defense. The author alone is responsible for the final contents of this chapter. The views expressed here are his personal views and should not be attributed to the Institute for Defense Analyses or any of its sponsors.
2. *National Security Strategy of the United States of America, September 2002*, from Chapter 5.
3. *National Strategy for Combating Terrorism, September 2006*, 14. Also the national strategy for defense against biological threats, *Biodefense for the 21st Century*, section on attribution and deterrence.
4. Ibid.
5. The work of the analytic community on deterring terrorism can be divided into three main clusters. One cluster is composed of work from the 1970s and 1980s done by social scientists to explore the ways in which patterns of terrorism were influenced by state responses. A second cluster emerged in the year or so after 9/11, when various study teams, generally associated in one way or another with the federal government, explored first-order questions about how deterrence might be applied to the newly revealed challenges. A third cluster is the much more diffuse work done in a wide variety of institutions in the last two to three years that explores specific mechanisms or targets of deterrence. Work from all three clusters is cited liberally in the body of this chapter.
6. For a discussion of Defense Department thinking about the challenges of tailoring deterrence to new security requirements, see M. Elaine Bunn, *Can Deterrence be Tailored?* Strategic Forum No. 225 (Washington, DC: National Defense University, Institute for National Strategic Studies, 2007).
7. Jonathan B. Tucker, ed., *Toxic Terror: Assessing Terrorist Use of Chemical and Biological Weapons* (Cambridge, MA: MIT Press, 2000).
8. One study compiled data on 34 terror events from 1970 to 2003 that killed 100 or more people and characterized the primary motivation of the perpetrators, concluding that those motivations included leftist, rightist, religious, ethno-nationalist, state, narco-terror, and others, including some in combination. See Victor Asal and Andrew Blum, "Holy Terror and Mass Killings? Reexamining the Motivations and Methods of Mass Casualty Terrorists," *International Studies Review*, vol. 7, 2005, 153–158. They note also that only 3 groups have initiated more than one such attack.
9. Robert Wesley, "Al-Qaeda's WMD Strategy After the U.S. Intervention in Afghanistan," *Terrorism Monitor* (Jamestown Foundation), vol. 3, no. 20, 2005.

10. For one of many excellent explorations of this topic, see Jerrold M. Post, "Killing in the Name of God: Osama Bin Laden and Al Qaeda," in Barry R. Schneider and Jerrold M. Post eds., *Know Thy Enemy: Profiles of Adversary Leaders and Their Strategic Cultures* (Maxwell Air Force Base, AL.: USAF Counterproliferation Center, 2002), 17–40.
11. *National Strategy for Combating Terrorism,* 5.
12. Paul Pillar, "Counterterrorism after Al Qaeda," *Washington Quarterly,* vol. 27, no. 3, Summer 2004, 101–113. See also Bruce Hoffman, "Al Qaeda and the War on Terrorism: An Update," *Current History* December 2004.
13. Thomas Schelling, *The Strategy of Conflict* (Cambridge, MA: Harvard University Press, 1960), 9.
14. Thomas Schelling, "Thinking about Nuclear Terrorism," *International Security,* vol. 6, no. 4 (Spring 1982), 72.
15. Glenn H. Snyder, *Deterrence and Defense: Toward a Theory of National Security* (Princeton, NJ: Princeton University Press, 1961).
16. As Gary Schaub has argued, "Many adversaries do not view inaction as a neutral outcome; rather they believe inaction will result in some sort of loss." Schaub, "Deterrence, Compellence, and Prospect Theory," *Political Psychology*, vol. 25, no. 3, 2004, 406.
17. For further elaboration of these concepts, including as they apply to nonstate actors, see *Deterrence Operations Joint Operating Concept*, U.S. Department of Defense, 2006.
18. Paul Davis and Brian Jenkins, *Deterrence and Influence in Counterterrorism: A Component in the War on Al Qaeda* (Santa Monica, CA: RAND Corporation, 2002), 9. See also Davis and Jenkins, "The Influencing Component of Counter-Terrorism," background paper prepared for a joint RAND-IDA project on deterring terrorism, July 2002.
19. Schelling, "Thinking about Nuclear Terrorism," 72.
20. *National Strategy for Combating Terrorism*, 14.
21. Davis and Jenkins, *Deterrence and Influence in Counterterrorism*, 10–24.
22. Robert Pape, *Dying to Win: The Logic of Suicide Terrorism* (New York: Random House, 2005).
23. *Country Reports on Terrorism 2005, Statistical Annex,* National Counterterrorism Center, April 7, 2006, v.
24. The study concludes that terrorists "value their own lives, except under the condition of the decision, made on their own terms, that suicide is justified by the overriding importance of personal salvation or group." See Neil J. Smelser and Faith Mitchell, eds., *Discouraging Terrorism: Some Implications of 9/11*, Panel on Understanding Terrorists in Order to Deter Terrorism, Center for Social and Economic Studies, National Research Council, National Academy of Sciences, 2002, 12.
25. *Tailored Deterrence: Restructuring Deterrence for the 21st Century,* Final Report prepared by the Special Task Force on Terrorism and Deterrence for the Defense Advanced Research Project Agency, 2002, 27.
26. Robert Anthony, "A Calibrated Model of the Psychology of Deterrence," *Bulletin on Narcotics,* vol. LVI, nos. 1 and 2, 2004; Anthony, *Deterrence and the 9/11 Terrorists*, D-2802 (Alexandria, VA: Institute for Defense Analyses, 2003); and Laura Dugan, Gary LaFree, and Alex R. Piquero, "Testing a Rational Choice Model of Airline Hijackings," *Criminology,* vol. 43, no. 4, 2005, 1031–1059.

27. Robert Chauncey, "Deterrence: Certainty, Severity and Skyjacking," *Criminology* (1975) 12:447–473.
28. Lee E. Dutter and Ofira Seliktar, "To Martyr or Not to Martyr: Jihad is the Question, What Policy is the Answer?" *Studies in Conflict & Terrorism,* (2007) 30:431. In drawing this conclusion, the authors are explicitly drawing on a large number of studies in the academic world.
29. Gary LaFree, Raven Korte, and Laura Dugan, "Deterrence and Defiance Models of Terrorist Violence in Northern Ireland, 1969 to 1992," unpublished research paper, June 2006.
30. Alexander George and Richard Smoke, *Deterrence in American Foreign Policy* (New York: Columbia University Press, 1974) 579.
31. Robert W. Anthony, *Deterrence and the 9-11 Terrorists*, Document D-2802 (Alexandria, VA: Institute for Defense Analyses, 2003), 9. Anthony's work draws on a long-running exploration of the willingness function of criminal actors—defined as their will to act in the face of what they understand about the likelihood and severity of punishment. This work begins with the observation that "with the threat of lethal force, an 8–12 per cent interception rate held down trafficking to less than 15 per cent of former levels, causing a collapse of the Peruvian cocaine trade. Less severe consequences worked at higher interception rates in the transit zone to the United States." See Robert Anthony, "A Calibrated Model of the Psychology of Deterrence," *Bulletin on Narcotics,* vol. 56, no. 1, 2004. Anthony argues in the first work cited above that initial investigations support the hypothesis that terrorist activities are susceptible to similar intervention strategies.
32. *National Strategy for Combating Terrorism,* 13. See also Todd Sandler and Walter Enders, "September 11 and Its Aftermath," *International Studies Review,* (2005) 7:167.
33. *Combating Terrorism in a Globalized World,* Report by the National War College Student Task Force on Combating Terrorism, National War College, (2002) 44.
34. *The Al Qaeda Training Manual*, as published in *Military Studies in the Jihad Against the Tyrants*, Jerrold M. Post, ed., (Maxwell Air Force Base, AL: USAF Counterproliferation Center), 169–172.
35. Doron Almog, "Cumulative Deterrence and the War on Terrorism," *Parameters*, Winter 2004–2005, 4. See also Daniel Byman, "Do Targeted Killings Work?" *Foreign Affairs* (March/April 2006) 95–112.
36. Dutter and Seliktar have defined the distinction between these two sets of goals as follows: "Fundamental goals are the basic, long-term objectives of the initiators of terrorist acts, as well as supporters and sympathizers in their 'host' population. These include objectives such as the radical restructuring or replacement of the economic, political, social, and/or territorial status quo in a state or region. On the other hand, instrumental or operational goals are short-term, transient objectives, the achievement of which can be viewed as logistical successes and which terrorists perceive as relevant to the achievement of one or more fundamental goals." See Dutter and Seliktar, "To Martyr or Not to Martyr," 431.
37. David Veness, "Low Intensity and High Impact Conflict," *Terrorism and Political Violence* (Winter 1999) 14.
38. Davis and Jenkins, *Deterrence and Influence in Counterterrorism,* xii.
39. Walter Enders and Todd Sandler, "The Effectiveness of Antiterrorism Policies: A Vector-Autoregression-Intervention Analysis" *American Political Science Review*, (1993) 87:842–843.

40. "The organization adopted suicide as the supreme embodiment of global jihad and raised Islamic martyrdom to a principle of faith." Yoram Schweitzer and Sari Goldstein Ferber, *Al-Qaeda and the Internationalization of Suicide Terrorism,* Memorandum no. 78 (Tel Aviv: Tel Aviv University, Jaffee Center for Strategic Studies, November 2005) 26.
41. Jonathan Schachter, "Understanding al-Qa'idah: Power, Perception, and the Powell Doctrine," unpublished research paper, RAND Corporation, 2002.
42. Jerry Mark Long, "Strategic Culture, al Qaeda, and Weapons of Mass Destruction," paper prepared by SAIC for the Advanced Systems and Concepts Office of the Defense Threat Reduction Agency, November 20, 2006, 24.
43. Dutter and Seliktar, "To Martyr or Not to Martyr," 437.
44. Long, "Strategic Culture, al Qaeda, and Weapons of Mass Destruction," 21. See also Lewis A. Dunn, *Can al Qaeda Be Deterred from Using Nuclear Weapons?* Occasional Paper No. 3 (Washington, DC: Center for the Study of Weapons of Mass Destruction, National Defense University, 2005).
45. For more on the internal debate, see Sammy Salama and Lydia Hansell, "Does Intent Equal Capability? Al-Qaeda and Weapons of Mass Destruction," *Nonproliferation Review,* vol. 12, no.3, November 2005, 615–653. See also Long, "Strategic Culture, al-Qaida, and Weapons of Mass Destruction," 22–23, who describes a "vigorous deliberation within the al-Qaida's shura about the utility of WMD" and cites various internal accounts.
46. See J. Tucker, "Lessons From the Case Studies," *Toxic Terror,* 249–270.
47. Fawaz Gerges, "Buried in Amman's Rubble: Zarqawi's Support," *Washington Post,* December 4, 2005. See also David Ignatius, "Are the Terrorists Failing?" *Washington Post,* September 28, 2004; and "Unfamiliar Questions in the Arab Air, Special Report, Arab World, Iraq, and al-Qaeda," *Economist,* (November 26, 2005) 29–31.
48. *Harmony and Disharmony: Exploiting al-Qa'ida's Organizational Vulnerabilities,* Combating Terrorism Center, Department of Social Sciences, United States Military Academy (February 14, 2006) 49. This is a seemingly unique resource, as the work is based directly on captured al-Qa'ida documents.
49. Ibid.
50. Salama and Hansell, "Does Intent Equal Capability?" See also Michael Scheuer, "Al-Qaeda's Completed Warning Cycle—Ready to Attack?" *Jamestown Foundation News,* March 3, 2005. Scheuer argues that "After 9/11 bin Laden received sharp criticisms from Islamist scholars that dealt with the al Qaeda chief's failure to satisfy several religious requirements pertinent to waging war. The critique focused on three items: (1) insufficient warning; (2) failure to offer Americans a chance to convert to Islam; and (3) inadequate religious authorization to kill so many people." Scheuer recounts subsequent efforts by Bin Laden to address these concerns and concludes that the religious requirements had been fully met by the winter of 2005.
51. Various studies have explored the ways in which consensus is an important value for the leadership core of terrorist movements. See, for example, *Harmony and Disharmony,* 3.
52. Azhar Ghani, "JI Changes Goals," *Straits Times,* November 17, 2006, 6. See also Derwin Pereira, "Sharp Drop in Support for Terrorism in Indonesia," *Straits Times,* November 18, 2006, 4.
53. Robert Trager and Dessislava P. Zagorcheva, "Deterring Terrorism: It Can Be Done," *International Security,* vol. 30, 3, Winter 2005/06, 120.
54. Ibid., 50.

55. Ibid., 46.
56. A valuable exception to this general proposition is Audrey Kurth Cronin, "How Al Qaeda Ends: The Decline and Demise of Terrorist Groups," *International Security* vol. 31, no. 1, Summer 2006, 7–48. See also David Cook, *Paradigmatic Jihadi Movements,* Combating Terrorism Center, United States Military Academy, West Point (undated); and Gary Ackerman, "WMD Terrorism Research: Whereto from Here?" *International Studies Review,* vol. 7, 2005, 140–143.
57. Davis and Jenkins, *Deterrence and Influence,* 15.
58. See for example, *Combating Terrorism in a Globalized World,* 47–49; and Gordon Drake, Warrick Paddon, and Daniel Ciechanowski, *Can We Deter Terrorists from Employing WMD in the US Homeland?* National Security Program Discussion Paper Series, Kennedy School of Government, Harvard University, 2003.
59. See, for example, Jessica Stern, *The Ultimate Terrorists* (Cambridge, MA: Harvard University Press, 1999), Chapter 6, "The Threat of Loose Nukes," 87–106.
60. See Phil Williams, "Terrorism and Organized Crime," in Brad Roberts ed., *Hype or Reality? The 'New Terrorism' and Mass Casualty Attacks* (Alexandria, VA: Chemical and Biological Arms Control Institute, 2000), 117–146; and Williams, "Transnational Criminal Networks," *Networks and Netwar,* RAND MR-1382-OSD, RAND Corporation, Santa Monica, CA, 2002.
61. James Turner Johnson, "Jihad and Just War," *First Things,* No. 124, June/July 2002. See also Johnson and John Kelsay, eds., *Just War and Jihad* (New York: Greenwood Press, 1991).
62. See, for example, Muhammad Khalid Masud et al., eds., *Islamic Legal Interpretations: Muftis and their Fatwas* (Cambridge, MA: Harvard University Press, 1996).
63. See Youssef H. Aboul-Enein and Sherifa Zuhur, *Islamic Rulings on Warfare* (Carlisle Barracks, PA: Strategic Studies Institute, U.S. Army War College, October 2004).
64. Writing about "the troubles" in Northern Ireland in the late twentieth century, Michael Quinlan has argued that "The Roman Catholic clergy there were not all as immediate, as outspoken, as unequivocal and as unanimous in their condemnation of Republican terrorism as Christian ethics truly required and as they themselves mostly later became; but significant change did take place, and progressively played a part in making community attitudes less tolerant of terrorism." See Sir Michael Quinlan, "Deterrence and Deterrability," *Contemporary Security Policy*, vol. 25, no. 1, April 2004, 16.
65. In addition, it has deemed Venezuela as "not fully cooperating with U.S. counterterrorism efforts." See *Country Reports on Terrorism, 2007*, Office of the Coordinator for Counterterrorism, Department of State, April 30, 2007.
66. George Tenet, "Worldwide Threat 2004—Challenges in a Changing Global Context," Statement of the Director of Central Intelligence to the Senate Armed Services Committee, March 9, 2004.
67. J. Melser and Mitchell, *Discouraging Terrorism*, 32.
68. As cited in Bob Woodward, *Bush at War* (New York: Pocket Books, 2003), 98.
69. Henry W. Prunchkun, Jr., and Philip B. Mohr, "Military Deterrence of International Terrorism: An Evaluation of Operation El Dorado Canyon," *Studies in Conflict and Terrorism*, vol. 20, 1997, 278.
70. Enders and Sandler, "The Effectiveness of Antiterrorism Policies," 843.
71. Bruce W. Jentleson and Christopher A. Whytock, "Who 'Won' Libya?" The Force-Diplomacy Debate and Its implications for Theory and Policy," *International Security,* vol. 30, no. 3, Winter 2005/2006, 47–86.

72. See Linton F. Brooks, "Countering Nuclear Terrorism," administrator, National Nuclear Security Administration, remarks to Chatham House, London, United Kingdom, September 21, 2006. See also John R. Harvey, "Countering Nuclear Terrorism," remarks to the Center for International Security and Arms Control, Stanford University, Stanford, CA, February 20, 2007. Harvey is a senior advisor at the National Nuclear Security Administration. See also Caitlin Talmadge, "Deterring a Nuclear 9/11," *Washington Quarterly*, vol. 30, no. 2, Spring 2007, 21–34. The national biodefense strategy also highlights the importance of attribution in deterring sponsorship. See *Biodefense for the 21st Century.*
73. Quinlan, "Deterrence and Deterrability," 15.
74. Jasen J. Castillo, "Nuclear Terrorism: Why Deterrence Still Matters," *Current History* no. 102, December 2003, 431.
75. Quinlan, "Deterrence and Deterrability," 15.
76. Alexander George, "The Need for Influence Theory and Actor-Specific Models of Adversaries," unpublished research paper, 2001.
77. John Parachini, "Putting WMD Terrorism into Perspective," *Washington Quarterly*, vol. 26, no. 4, Autumn 2003, 37–50.
78. Daniel Byman, "Passive Sponsors of Terrorism," *Survival*, vol. 47, no. 4, Winter 2005–06), 117.
79. Parachini, "Putting WMD Terrorism into Perspective."
80. Byman, "Passive Sponsors of Terrorism," 138.
81. *National Strategy for Combating Terrorism, September 2006*, 19.
82. Ibid.
83. The basic finding that deterrence is relevant but not foundational in combating terrorism is echoed repeatedly in studies done by varied institutions and individuals in recent years. See, for example, *Discouraging Terrorism: Some Implications of 9/11;* Quinlan, "Deterrence and Deterrability"; Davis and Jenkins, *Deterrence and Influence in Counterterrorism; Combating Terrorism in a Globalized World;* Trager and Zagorcheva, "Deterring Terrorism: It Can Be Done"; Dunn, *Can al Qaeda be Deterred from Using Nuclear Weapons?;* Kurt M. Campbell and Richard Weitz, *Non-Military Strategies for Countering Islamist Terrorism: Lessons Learned from Past Counterinsurgencies* (Princeton, NJ: Princeton Project Papers, 2006); James M. Smith and William C. Thomas, "Deterring WMD Terrorism," unpublished research paper, *United States Air Force Institute for National Security Studies*, 2006; Daniel Whiteneck, "Deterring Terrorists: Thoughts on a Framework," *Washington Quarterly*, vol. 28, no. 3, Summer 2005; and Sina Lehmkuhler, *Combating WMD Terrorism: Is Deterrence Relevant?* Master's Thesis, George Washington University, May 2002.
84. Thomas Schelling argued nearly three decades ago that "a campaign is what they [terrorists with nuclear weapons] will plan, not an episode." See Schelling, "Thinking about Nuclear Terrorism," 65. See also Richard Danzig, "From MAD to SAD: An Axiom and Six Hypotheses About Instrumental Terrorists Non-Use and Use of Pathogens as Weapons of Mass Killing," unpublished research paper, September 2006; and Brad Roberts, "Terrorist Campaigns: Defining the Challenges of Campaign-level Responses to Campaign-style CBW Terrorism," unpublished research paper, Institute for Defense Analyses, 2005.

85. For a discussion of the particular benefits of passive defenses in de-motivating continuing attacks with pathogenic materials, see Danzig, "From MAD to SAD"; and Michael J. Powers, *Deterring Terrorism with CBRN Weapons: Developing a Conceptual Framework* (Alexandria, VA: Chemical and Biological Arms Control Institute, 2001).
86. Robert Jervis, "Deterrence and Perception," *International Security,* vol. 7, no. 3, Winter 1982/83, 9.
87. *Quadrennial Defense Review, 2006* (Washington, DC: Department of Defense, 2006).
88. Ibid.
89. Anthony, "A Calibrated Model of the Psychology of Deterrence."
90. *National Strategy for Combating Terrorism,* 1.
91. Ibid., 14.

CHAPTER 11

Global and National Efforts to Prevent Jihadist Access to WMD

Brian Finlay and Jeremy Tamsett

CONTENTS

INTRODUCTION

In February 2001, Usama bin Ladin was tried *in abstentia* in the U.S. District Court, Southern District of New York, for his role in the American embassy bombings in Kenya and Tanzania in 1998. The revelations of the U.S. government's star witness in this case, a Sudanese al-Qa'ida defector named Jamal Ahmad al-Fadl, shocked the national security community. He testified that, as early as 1993, he was involved in al-Qa'ida's unsuccessful attempts to purchase uranium in Sudan. According to al-Fadl, al-Qa'ida had been willing to pay $1.5 million for an unknown quantity of bomb-grade material.[1] Seven months later, three thousand people would die at the hands of that same terrorist organization in a coordinated series of attacks on the American homeland. The collective and historic sense of America's imperviousness was shattered on that tragic September morning. Then, on October 11, 2001, just one month after the collapse of the twin towers, President Bush was notified that a covert CIA agent (code-named Dragonfire) had obtained evidence that al-Qa'ida terrorists had acquired a ten-kiloton Russian nuclear warhead. Reportedly, the weapon already had been smuggled onto American soil and was awaiting use in New York City. Dragonfire's intelligence tracked with a report from a Russian general who claimed that Moscow had lost a similarly sized weapon. A panicked search ensued that was led by the Department of Energy's Nuclear Emergency Search Team (NEST). In the end, NEST teams found nothing.[2] While investigators ultimately concluded that the intelligence provided by Dragonfire was incorrect, no one presumed that the scenario was implausible.

While the possibility of catastrophic terrorism using chemical, biological, radiological, or nuclear (CBRN) weapons of mass destruction (WMD) had long pre-dated the attacks of September 11, 2001, it was not until the World Trade Center fell that the American public became sensitized to this real and growing threat. While al-Fadl's Sudanese purchase was unsuccessful, it reaffirmed the intelligence community's contention that jihadists had been seeking to acquire materials of mass destruction for almost a decade. Thus, preventing the world's most dangerous individuals from acquiring the world's most dangerous weapons became an instant *cause célèbre* for the Bush administration, for Congress, and for U.S. allies around the world as part of America's new "Global War on Terror."

Although efforts to preclude the illicit acquisition of WMD by rogue states and terrorist organizations were longstanding, going back even as far as the mid-1990s, the emphasis given to the proliferation threat was generally state-centered and often schizophrenic. For example, in 1995, a Presidential Decision Directive/NSC-39 stated that, "The acquisition of weapons of mass destruction by a terrorist group, through theft or manufacture, is unacceptable. There is no higher priority than preventing the acquisition of this capability or removing this capability from terrorist groups potentially opposed to the US."[3] Meanwhile, in a report prepared by the Pentagon, the secretary of defense noted that, "[m]ost terrorist groups do not have the financial and technical resources necessary to acquire nuclear weapons, but could gather materials to make radiological dispersion devices and some biological and chemical agents. Some groups have state sponsors that possess or can obtain NBC [nuclear, biological and chemical] weapons. Nations such as Iran and Libya have backed numerous groups over the years, but no sponsor has yet demonstrated a willingness to provide such groups with NBC weapons, perhaps a testament to the looming and certain threat of retaliation should the state be identified as the supplier."[4]

Just one year later, the tenor of reporting had shifted rather remarkably. The Defense Department began reporting that "[t]he increased availability of...technologies, coupled with the relative ease of producing chemical or biological agents, has increased concern that the use of chemical or biological weapons may become more attractive to terrorist groups intent on causing panic or inflicting large numbers of casualties.... Threats from terrorism and the lack of security of nuclear material in the states of the former Soviet Union are two issues that greatly concern the United States and its allies. In addition, the proliferation of such weapons raises the possibility that some states or entities within these states could provide chemical, biological, or radiological weapons to terrorists."[5]

By 1998, warnings to the Clinton administration by the U.S. intelligence community had reached a fever pitch, concluding that the threat had not only been tied to a specific return address, but had become a virtual certainty: "Sooner or later, Bin Ladin will attack U.S. interests, perhaps using WMD."[6] Throughout the rest of that year, U.S. officials were "worriedly discussing ... reports that Bin Ladin's associates thought their leader was intent on carrying out a 'Hiroshima.'"

Today, concern over WMD terrorism has not abated, and preventing the acquisition of weapons, materials and expertise of mass destruction rightly remains a central objective of the United States and other world governments.

CHOKING SUPPLY TO COUNTER THE THREAT: A HISTORY OF NONPROLIFERATION EFFORTS

Supply-side efforts to prevent the diffusion of weapons of mass destruction to hostile states or terrorist organizations are nothing new. Committed governments around the world, often led by the United States, have been working to prevent wider proliferation since the dawn of the nuclear age. The earliest nonproliferation efforts were essentially counterespionage operations designed to prevent Cold War enemies from acquiring the atomic secret. Only after the nuclear code was broken by the Soviets was heightened attention given to the seriousness of wider proliferation.

On December 8, 1953, President Dwight Eisenhower stepped to the podium at the United Nations General Assembly in New York City. The nuclear arms race was in full swing. The United States had already produced nearly 1,500 warheads.[7] The Pentagon was equipping all of the military services with nuclear weapons for a wide range of missions. The Soviet Union and Great Britain were both testing and deploying atomic weapons. In his speech, the president gave voice to America's rapidly evaporating nuclear hegemony cautioning that, "the knowledge now possessed by several nations will eventually be shared by others—possibly all others." He went on to warn the assembly about the perils of proliferation: "Let no one think that the expenditure of vast sums for weapons and systems of defense can guarantee absolute safety for the cities and citizens of any nation. The awful arithmetic of the atomic bomb does not permit any such easy solution."[8]

Eight years later, the nuclear club expanded yet again as France conducted its first nuclear test, leading Senator John Kennedy to sharply criticize then–Vice President Richard Nixon for his inattentiveness to the growing proliferation threat. Kennedy asserted that, "there are indications, because of new inventions, that ten, fifteen, or twenty nations will have a nuclear capacity—including Red China—by the end of the presidential term in 1964."[9] As it turned out, China would indeed go nuclear in that year, and Italy, Sweden and other wealthy industrialized European countries were actively pursuing weapons programs. Fears of rampant proliferation across the Northern Hemisphere pervaded national security literature. A new international effort to stymie proliferation was necessary.

The cornerstone of the current global nonproliferation regime was laid in 1968 with the conclusion of the Nuclear Nonproliferation Treaty (NPT). The so-called "grand bargain" was struck whereby non-nuclear states pledged not to seek atomic weapons, while the nuclear states (by definition, those states that had manufactured and exploded a nuclear weapon prior to January 1, 1967, which included the United States, Russia, China, France, and the United Kingdom) agreed to move toward total and complete disarmament. The lion's share of effort and resources focused on curbing the spread of CBRN weapons, technology, and know-how to additional states beyond the permanent five (P5) members of the Security Council. Throughout the decades of the 1960s, 1970s, and 1980s, new regional nuclear weapons free zones, limitations on nuclear testing, and technology control agreements and measures grew in support of the objectives of the NPT.

National governance over WMD materials and technologies, coupled with little upward pressure on breakout to additional countries because of superpower suasion, meant that the proliferation challenge was largely manageable. With a limited number of nuclear states, know-how and materials under the near-exclusive control of P5 governments, a growing and nonpermissive global regime, and downward pressure from the superpowers on their allies against going nuclear, proliferation prevention translated into restriction of supply. One analyst best describes this strategy in the doctrine of the "three no's": No unsecured weapons and materials and no new domestic capabilities to enrich uranium or reprocess plutonium meant no expansion of the nuclear club.[10]

The entry-into-force of the NPT tempered the overt pursuit of the bomb beyond the original permanent five members of the UN Security Council for the next decade, but did nothing to stem proliferation between the two superpowers whose arsenals chased one another up the ladder of escalation. By the 1980s, proliferation experts were again sounding alarms: The nonproliferation regime was under siege. This time, the locus of concern was not on the developed states of the north, but on developing states in the Southern Hemisphere. Up to 18 developing countries were thought to be harboring nuclear ambitions including Argentina, Brazil, Syria, Iraq, Nigeria, and Libya. By the time that President Clinton assumed office, Israel, Pakistan, India, and South Africa were being joined by Iran, North Korea and Taiwan as potential breakout states. By the end of the administration, the Pentagon was warning that, "In virtually every corner of the globe, the United States and its allies face a growing threat from the proliferation and possible use of nuclear, biological, and chemical weapons and their delivery systems."[11]

Though the future seemed to be terrifying, the apocalyptic projections of 18 to 20 new nuclear-armed states in the 1980s proved false.[12] Vertical proliferation (intrastate stockpiling and production) in the twentieth century was rampant, but the restriction of nuclear states to eight at the turn of the millennium was testament to the relative stability in global political and economic relations wrought by the tepid peace of the Cold War. The same was considered to be true of chemical and biological weapons as regimes similar to the NPT grew up around the Chemical Weapons Convention (1997) and the Biological and Toxin Weapons Convention (1975). Though generally criticized, the nonproliferation regime withstood the opposition and held up remarkably well. Despite this largely positive track record, however, gathering global dynamics were threatening to unleash a new era of proliferation.

By the new millennium, the U.S. government had established an impressive track record in executing just such a preventive strategy with a suite of collaborative programs in the states of the former Soviet Union. Subsumed under the moniker of Cooperative Threat Reduction (CTR) or "Nunn-Lugar" (so named for the two U.S. senators that introduced legislations for CTR, namely Sam Nunn and Richard Lugar), the programs had already developed an astonishing record of success: Thousands of former Soviet nuclear warheads had been deactivated; more than 500 intercontinental ballistic missiles once pointed at the United States and its allies were dismantled; dozens of nuclear submarines that once prowled the world's oceans waiting to deliver their atomic payloads on the West were destroyed; hundreds of tons of highly enriched uranium from dismantled warheads were blended down and burned in civilian power reactors; and thousands of former weapons experts were redirected into sustainable civilian employment.[13] These activities were instituted beginning in 1992 and grew incrementally for a decade. In 2002, the program contributors expanded when the G8 Partners pledged matching dollars to deal with the post–Soviet Cold War legacy. These efforts were intended as a complement to, but not a replacement of, the preexisting global nonproliferation regime. Still however, the focus remained on state-based efforts to choke off supply as the principal means to prevent their wider diffusion.

But as the United States government began considering new geographical boundaries for the expansion of Nunn–Lugar preventive activities, the security calculus was again undergoing a radical transformation. For years, the global intelligence community harvested rumors that nuclear scientist and father of the Pakistani bomb, A.Q. Khan, was proliferating critical technologies and expertise abroad—to China, North Korea and across the Muslim world. When news of the size and scope of the Khan network finally came to light, the national security community was again rocked. The U.S. director of Central Intelligence asserted that Khan had done more damage to the security of the United States than Usama bin Ladin had ever dreamed. For more than a decade, Khan's black market in nuclear technologies spanned the globe, providing one-stop shopping to dozens of customers from North Korea and Iran to Libya. The success of the network demonstrated the ease in which existing measures to prevent proliferation have been challenged by the globalization of technology.

In response, supply-side efforts to prevent terrorism incidents involving WMD were redoubled and layered with new approaches that were ostensibly devised as a fail-safe against technology leakage. The multilateral treaty regime and Cooperative Threat Reduction programs were paired with the Proliferation Security Initiative, the Global Partnership, the Global Initiative to Combat Nuclear Terrorism, and other coalitional instruments of prevention and detection. Counterproliferation, interdiction, and securing the raw materials and the essential components necessary to manufacture, create, and build chemical, biological, radiological weapons at their source formed the centerpiece of a layered strategy to prevent the ultimate nightmare scenario: A terrorist attack with WMD.

FRAYING FORCES OF MODERATION

The end of the Cold War is commonly held up by national security experts as the turning point from a predictable world order to one characterized today by uncertainty. While the collapse of the superpower standoff was certainly an important factor in eroding relative stability generally and the nonproliferation regime specifically, it was not the only factor. Globalization, privatization, technological innovation, the ease of international communication and transportation, free trade, financial liberalization, the rise of the nonstate actor, and the advent of the "virtual world" all collided to challenge the authority, effectiveness, and resiliency of the nonproliferation regime. The role of states both as potential proliferators and as bulwarks for the preventative nature of the nonproliferation regime increasingly came under scrutiny and question as an array of irrepressible forces became more and more prominent in driving human interactions. New substate actors emerged—including private companies with access to and control over sensitive weapons technologies, underemployed individuals with critical competencies, and terrorist groups intent on acquiring weapons of mass destruction—and acted to challenge the traditional state sovereignty. Governmental controls over CBRN, while necessary, became insufficient in a globalized economy where states could no longer be reasonably expected to exercise total authority over their territories. The massive transfer of equipment and technologies, once under the exclusive control of national governments, transitioned to private hands around the globe. Innovation drove new dual-use and commercial off-the-shelf technologies to the marketplace. In addition to (some might argue because of) systemic changes in the marketplace, jihadist terrorist networks were also beginning to show an interest in acquiring CBRN as scientific know-how, advanced high technology, precursor materials, and equipment were becoming increasingly available and accessible. Concurrently, the biotechnological revolution broadened the availability of dual-use equipment and expanded exponentially the number of individuals with the knowledge necessary to engage in nefarious weapons research (see Chapter 6 for a more detailed treatise of this premise).

ROAD AHEAD: KEEPING WMD OUT OF THE HANDS OF JIHADISTS

When considered alongside the portentous prognosis of some two-dozen nuclear-armed states in the 1980s and the rising awareness of the dangers posed by the potential nexus between jihadists and WMD, existing preventive measures have been miraculously effective. But while the illicit acquisition of weapons, bomb-grade materials, and know-how are critical elements of any prevention strategy, they are ultimately short-term measures. As Adam Smith reminds us, provided that demand remains high, there will always be supply. A. Q. Khan's distribution network revealed yawning gaps in the ability of existing treaties, agreements, programs, and initiatives to effectively address the role that individuals and nonstate actors motivated by radical ideology may play in undermining global nonproliferation objectives. It also further highlighted the limitation of supply-side restrictions in an era of globalization.

The next section of this chapter maps out the logical steps that a terrorist must take to develop a CBRN capacity. While an entire section of this volume is dedicated to underscore the possible corollary relationships between jihadists and WMD ("Agents of Harm"), we include a brief overview of the pathways to WMD here to frame the context for exploring existing measures—which fall almost exclusively on the supply side—to prevent the proliferation of weapons of mass destruction to terrorists. Second, we identify critical gaps in existing strategies that could be exploited by nonstate actors and other terrorist organizations in their continuing drive to obtain a WMD capability. Finally, we presents a series of recommendations aimed at closing existing programmatic gaps, breaking down policy stovepipes, instituting a layered strategy to address the supply and demand sides of the proliferation challenge, and ultimately, preventing catastrophic jihad-inspired terrorism with respect to WMD.

In a world where the state is competing with the dynamic forces of globalization, communications, and transportation, the law of averages favors the terrorist. At the macrolevel, we find that additional emphasis should be placed on surmounting the emerging and ever-growing obstacles to state control over weapons and technology, as well as on supporting sustainable programs and initiatives that encourage international and nonstate actor buy-in to the nonproliferation regime and thus address the growing demand for WMD weapons and technologies.

UNDERSTANDING THE JIHADISTS' PATH TO WMD

Congruent with motivations and intent, a terrorist organization's technical savvy and scientific know-how play a pivotal role in determining whether it possesses the capability to manufacture, acquire or use CBRN. The rhetoric emanating out of the al-Qa'ida camp reveals that their intent to use CBRN remains stable and persistent.[14] Moreover, the barriers to accessing fissile materials, equipment, and the related technology needed for such weapons grow increasingly porous. The unclassified version of the U.S. National Intelligence Estimate (NIE) released in July 2007 states that: "We assess that al-Qa'ida will continue to try to acquire and employ chemical, biological, radiological, or nuclear material in attacks and would not hesitate to use them if it develops what it deems is sufficient capability."[15]

Nuclear Weapons

While the probability of terrorists successfully acquiring and using a nuclear weapon is low relative to chemical, biological or radiological weapons (for a more detailed treatment of jihadists' pursuit of nuclear weapons, see Chapter 8 of this volume), the devastating impact of such an attack anywhere in the world is the very definition of mass destruction. There is no evidence to suggest that the threat of this form of terrorism has abated since 9/11. Conversely, the enabling forces that present committed terrorists with the opportunities and means to acquire a catastrophic weapon continue to intensify—often unchecked.

If we view risk as the output of likelihood times consequence, we can state with certainty that nuclear terrorism poses one of the greatest risks to the global community today, followed closely by biological terrorism. Using this equation, consequence is best viewed as a constant, where the damage incurred is proportional to the square of the explosion (yield) of a nuclear weapon. The unique aspect of nuclear weapons is that very small yields are capable of producing enormous damage. Because the consequences of even a low-yield nuclear detonation are well known, the variable that is the subject of much of this edited volume is the degree to which the threat is likely to increase and be realized, thereby affecting the level of risk presented by potential nuclear-armed terrorists.

In the wake of 9/11, and with the realization that the prevailing instruments of nonproliferation were being increasingly challenged, governments and outside analysts agreed that the most comprehensive, cost-effective means to prevent a "nuclear 9/11" was to consolidate, secure, monitor, and eliminate excess weapons and weapons-usable materials at their source. As one former senior U.S. Energy Department official noted, "Acquiring weapons and materials is the hardest step for the terrorists to take, and the easiest step for us to stop. By contrast, every subsequent step in the process is easier for the terrorists to take and harder for us to stop. Once they gain access to materials, they've completed the most difficult step."[16] As a result, any layered strategy to prevent nuclear terrorism must logically proceed from the central goal of securing weapons and materials before they proliferate.

It is unlikely, although not implausible, that terrorists could procure an intact nuclear weapon from a state. For example, jihadists could capitalize on political and civil unrest, or even a *coup d'état* in a nuclear-armed state like Pakistan, and seize a weapon. The point of acute vulnerability is during transport, which may be more likely to occur during a crisis where consolidation of armaments may be viewed as a method of control.[17] In other circumstances, dire working and living conditions, coupled with extreme cuts in defense spending, could create an unstable environment of corruption that is ripe for security officers and related personnel to be blackmailed or otherwise coerced into working with a terrorist group—or they could be bribed into just looking the other way at the right time.

The availability of weapons-usable uranium around the world is unreasonably high—more than 100 research reactors still use weapons-grade highly enriched uranium (HEU).[18] Efforts are underway (as discussed below) to convert these reactors to use low-enriched uranium (LEU) instead of HEU, but for now, the civilian market remains awash in bomb-grade uranium that could be diverted for terrorist use.

Unlike the procurement or manufacture of conventional explosives, nuclear fabrication is an extraordinarily technical and, therefore, costly endeavor. Hence, access to adequate funding is critical. Two nuclear specialists estimated that, for $2 million, a terrorist group could acquire the necessary equipment, personnel, nonfissile material, and transportation support to build a crude nuclear device. For an additional $8 million, they speculated that enough bomb-grade material could be acquired.[19] While not inconsequential, it is by no means beyond the realm of possibility that a terrorist group of reasonable size would leverage such resources for a nuclear project. Modern terrorist movements like Aum Shinrikyo in the 1990s and al-Qa'ida more recently, have had this level of resources at their disposal.

Jihadists intent on building a nuclear weapon from scratch would also need access to scientists and technicians with the requisite knowledge to properly assemble the device. Popular assumptions that the Internet has democratized plans for nuclear weapons fail to recognize that specialized expertise obtained through practical, hands-on work and direct interactions with other scientists is critical for weapon development. As one nuclear analyst pointed out, "Soviet scientists encountered significant problems replicating the US design and production process obtained from Soviet spy Klaus Fuchs, even though they already had an active nuclear program with knowledgeable scientists and engineers. The British encountered similar problems, even though their scientists contributed to the Manhattan Project."[20] Therefore, this knowledge is still difficult, though not impossible, to come by.

If the know-how to build a nuclear weapon is sought by terrorists, then there is also the potential for the recruitment of sympathetic, underpaid or unemployed scientists and technicians to aid in this effort. Undoubtedly, some individuals with scientific and technological expertise may be sufficiently motivated, or at least sympathetic, to a particular extremist movement; however, this need not be the case for successful recruitment by terrorist organizations. For example, scientists may be motivated by a range of factors that mutually align with terrorist intentions, including the age-old incentives of money, revenge and perhaps the incarnation or restoration of national or personal glory.

The scientific capacity is but one node of human capital necessary for fabrication and development of a nuclear device. One of the most important aspects of nuclear terrorism, aside from building or acquiring the device itself, is making sure that it reaches its target. Building a reliable pathway to ensure that the improvised nuclear device (IND) or other such weapon ends up where it is intended would be a critical component of any terrorist's strategy (see Chapter 8). As a result, support cells, unscrupulous middlemen, and transportation networks would be needed as well. In fact, in the final delivery phase, resilient and perhaps redundant support cells, adequate funding, and reliable transportation and communication links are essential.

There would be a substantial risk of detection if nuclear materials were to be transported across international boundaries. Fissile source materials that might be used in a nuclear weapon are much less radioactive than the materials that might be found in a radiological weapon. Nevertheless, even with moderate to heavy shielding, the prospect of detection is likely to dissuade all but the most sophisticated and risk-prone terrorist groups. In general, it is logical to assume that the greater the distance from the point of acquisition of the radioactive materials to the target, the greater the likelihood of detection by intelligence and law enforcement agencies (see Chapter 9).

Since September 11, 2001, there have been no reported cases of theft of any radioactive sources above more than a few grams. A recent attempt was disrupted in November 2007 when two Hungarians and a Ukrainian were arrested for peddling weapons-grade materials thought to be from the former Soviet Union.[21] According to the International Atomic Energy Agency (IAEA), there have been 15 known instances of individuals or groups engaged in illegal trafficking—including possessing, selling, and smuggling across national borders—of either highly enriched uranium or plutonium between January 1993 and December 2006.[22] These numbers pale in comparison to the 332 cases involving theft or loss of nuclear or radioactive sources during the same time period. In 2006 alone, 85 incidents of either theft or loss were reported, in addition to 51 instances of finding orphan or abandoned sources whose whereabouts were previously unknown. A staggering 67% of cases involving lost or stolen materials have not been recovered to date (for more detailed information about potential theft and seizure of radiological and nuclear materials, see Chapters 7 and 8 of this volume, respectively).

Pathways to Chemical Terrorism

Like the nuclear threat, jihadists have two main pathways to unleash a chemical attack (see Chapter 5 of this volume for an in-depth analysis of chemical weapons): Development of an indigenous capability to manufacture chemical weapons and/or procurement of ready-made chemical weapons (developed by states for military purposes). Chemical weapons designed by states for the purpose of warfare possess the capacity to kill or maim large numbers of people. While many states around the world have sanctioned chemical weapons programs, including South Korea, North Korea, India, Syria, Iraq, Iran, and especially Russia, it is unlikely that these states would provide terrorists with these types of weapons because the extraordinary damage to the state's reputation in the international community would far exceed the nominal damage that could be incurred by an act of chemical terrorism.

An indigenous chemical weapon manufacturing capability would require jihadists to have access to certain precursor and dual-use chemical equipment, which could be procured through legitimate back channels, theft, or purchase on the black market. Certain chemicals, like chlorine, phosgene, and hydrogen cyanide, can be readily found in bulk quantities around the globe and serve a variety of industrial uses. Jihadist terrorist groups would have little difficulty in using improvised, nonmilitary toxic chemicals as weapons. On the other hand, while nerve agents are extremely lethal in small doses and are thus appealing to terrorist groups, they are difficult to produce and require sophisticated equipment and advanced scientific know-how. While it is likely that improvised chemical agents would pose less of a direct threat, they would still have the potential to cause severe disruption and widespread panic.

Like radiological and nuclear weapons, the use of chemical agents against civilians would likely cause mass hysteria in the target population. The effectiveness of terrorism incorporating chemical weapons depends on the toxicity and type of selected chemical, the manner in which it is disseminated, the physical characteristics of the location in which the chemical is released, and local environmental factors such as wind, humidity, and temperature.

Pathways to Biological Terrorism

Biological pathogens and toxins are inexpensive, readily accessible in nature and, if weaponized effectively, particularly dangerous (see Chapter 6 for a more detailed discussion of bioterrorism). While the effects of biological weapons are often not properly distinguished in news reports and casual analyses from that of chemical, radiological, and nuclear weapons, there are fundamental and important differences. The implications of the divarication between biological and other weapon types are tremendous: while the damage caused by a chemical or nuclear weapon, for instance, would be a singular event causing immediate damage, release of a lethal biological pathogen could spread from victim to victim over time, creating a cascade of catastrophic disease that could threaten the entire global population.[23] Biological and nuclear weapons, although more effective for higher death counts, are much more difficult to procure, manufacture, and employ than chemical or radiological weapons.

Like chemical weapons, biological weapons are most effective when properly weaponized to optimize delivery, penetration, and lethality in the target population. The effect of a biological attack is determined to a large extent by how well the agent has been prepared for delivery. The most effective way to disseminate biological agents is in the form of an aerosol, which is a suspension of microscopic particles or droplets in the air. Because victims of a bioterrorist attack may not exhibit symptoms for several days or weeks, biological agents have the potential to affect a large number of people beyond the geographical point of introduction.

Unlike chemical weapons, biological agents like viruses and bacteria are more difficult to procure and use, but the prestige associated with possessing a biological capability (second only to possession of a nuclear weapon) makes this type of weapon attractive to certain jihadist groups like al-Qa'ida. For example, U.S. troops discovered an abandoned laboratory in Kandahar, Afghanistan in March 2002, where it is believed that members of al-Qa'ida were planning to develop biological weapons. Al-Qa'ida is also believed to have recruited a Pakistani microbiologist to help them manufacture botulinum toxin and anthrax.[24]

Jihadists may be able to develop an indigenous capability to manufacture and weaponize primitive pathogens and toxins, but these efforts would be complicated because of the difficulty in maintaining the purity and virulence of the agent as compared with state-backed biological programs designed for military purposes. Furthermore, jihadists would need to ensure that any agent they sought to use was weaponized to the extent that it would be able to resist any environmental changes and to withstand long periods of time at different temperatures.

Pathways to Radiological Terrorism

One key distinction between radiological and nuclear weapons is that a radiological dispersal device (RDD—commonly referred to as a "dirty bomb"—does not involve a nuclear reaction and hence, there is no nuclear explosion (Chapter 7 of this volume contains comprehensive information about jihadists with respect to different types of radiological weapons). Jihadists might choose to pursue development of a radiological weapon for a variety of reasons including relative ease of acquisition, development, and use vis-à-vis nuclear and biological weapons in particular. A radiological attack would likely result in immediate panic, some casualties, and possibly extensive economic damage. This option would also be attractive for jihadists seeking to gain notoriety, prestige, or power through a high-profile attack. Thus, radiological devices are best viewed as strategic weapons with a premium on psychological impact and social disruption, rather than as tactical modes for accomplishing limited ends.

Despite the increasing likelihood of RDD acquisition and use by terrorists, radiological weapons have relatively benign consequences. This means that their overall impacts are less than those posed by nuclear terrorism and as a result, they receive only marginal treatment in this section. Nevertheless, terrorists who lack extensive technical and scientific expertise may find the option of using a "dirty bomb" very attractive. Unlike nuclear weapons, a radiological weapon could be assembled in a process that is not much more demanding than that required to assemble the improvised explosive devices (IEDs) currently being employed by insurgents in Iraq. Terrorists are likely to at least consider the possibility of manufacturing a radiological weapon for this reason.

Sources that emit a high level of gamma radiation and could be potentially used in a radiological weapon are: thorium-230 and 232, radium-224, 226 and 228, radon-222, cobalt-60, barium-137m, and iodine-129 and 131. These radioactive materials are used widely around the world for diagnosing and treating illnesses, sterilizing equipment, and inspecting welding seams. Gamma-emitting materials, such as cobalt-60, cesium-137, and iridium-192, are all found in cancer therapy hospitals and clinics, industrial radiography, industrial gauges, food irradiation equipment, oil well logging, nuclear reactors, and spent-fuel reprocessing plants.

The availability of radioactive resources in the former Soviet Union (FSU) is equally abundant, especially in remote locations where security protocols cannot be assumed to be as stringent as those that might be used in urban locations. Examples of radioactive materials in the FSU that could be potentially used by terrorists in a radiological dispersion device include radioisotope thermal generators (RTGs) and Gamma-Kolos seed irradiators.[25]

The manufacture of radiological dispersal weapons (RDDs) would pose little problem for a terrorist group that has access to radioactive material. Because a dirty bomb is essentially radioactive material wrapped around a conventional explosive, little or no additional scientific technical expertise is required to make the jump from a conventional weapon to an RDD. Of course, the more effective the terrorists wanted to be in dispersing radioactive residue, the more precise they would have to be in selecting the proper type of radioisotope; in addition, both quality and quantity matter. The size of the conventional explosive used to distribute the radioactive material is similarly important—the larger the yield, the larger the area in which the radioactive material is spread. Besides RDDs, radiological weapons could even consist of a stationary source that is hidden and emits gamma rays to an unsuspecting target.

SURVEYING THE PREVENTION TOOLKIT: GLOBAL AND MULTILATERAL NONPROLIFERATION EFFORTS

We define global multilateral nonproliferation efforts as undertakings that are open to the entire international community and, to the extent that is possible, are participated in by a predominant number of states. During the twentieth century, numerous global multilateral treaties, agreements, and institutions were founded, including the aforementioned Chemical Weapons Convention, Biological and Toxin Weapons Convention, and Nuclear Nonproliferation Treaty. Consensus for these and other treaties are typically initiated by one or more states and are largely negotiated through the United Nations in the General Assembly. There are existential limitations to all international agreements, namely, that national interests and perspectives change over time. As priorities shift, so do state interests and budgets in response to a variety of domestic and foreign pressures and competing causes. Consequently, maintaining a sense of priority and urgency to perpetuate such a mission offers political challenges that need the utmost consideration and that quite often, receive the least attention.

As a result, supplementary initiatives were designed to help complement and bolster the existing nonproliferation regime, while carefully filling any key gaps that it left exposed. These ad hoc agreements bypassed the protocols and processes associated with treaties in the United Nations. For example, the Global Initiative to Combat Nuclear Terrorism and the Proliferation Security Initiative are international in scope, but are organized informally as coalitional approaches to mitigate the enduring threat of proliferation.

Global and Multilateral Efforts to Prevent CBRN Terrorism

Nuclear Nonproliferation Treaty (NPT)[26]—The NPT is widely viewed as the most important weapons treaty ever negotiated and is the only binding commitment by the nuclear-weapon states to a goal of eventual nuclear disarmament. The treaty also promotes the peaceful uses of nuclear energy and obligates nuclear weapon states as recognized by the treaty (known as the P5, which are all permanent members of the UN Security Council) not to assist non-nuclear weapon states in any way to acquire a nuclear weapon capability. Furthermore, the NPT requires states parties to comply with robust safeguards systems under the auspices of the International Atomic Energy Agency. These safeguards are designed to prevent diversion of nuclear weapons-usable material, and to ensure equal access to nuclear technology for peaceful purposes. The NPT opened for signature in 1968 and entered into force in 1970; there are a total of 188 states party to the treaty and in 1995, at the NPT Review and Extension Conference held at the United Nations, these States agreed to extend the treaty indefinitely.

Chemical Weapons Convention (CWC)[27]—The Chemical Weapons Convention represents the first disarmament agreement that contains provisions to eliminate an entire category of WMD. As a comprehensive treaty, it bans the development, production, acquisition, stockpiling, transfer, and use of chemical weapons. The mechanisms of the convention are verified through the Organization for the Prohibition of Chemical Weapons (OPCW) in The Hague. The convention requires states parties to the treaty to destroy chemical weapons stockpiles and production facilities within 10 years after entry into force, which occurred in 1997. The tenth anniversary of the convention in 2007 came and went without full compliance to key provisions of the treaty by states parties despite the OPCW's mandate to enforce the Treaty and to help states with implementation. There are over 180 States Parties to the CWC.

Biological Weapons Treaty (BWC)—The BWC, known formally as the Biological and Toxin Weapons Convention and ratified in 1972, is widely viewed as a complement to the 1925 Geneva Protocol banning the use of chemical and biological weapons in warfare (but not their production, stockpiling or transfer).The fundamental weakness of the BWC is that it lacks formal inspection, verification, and compliance mechanisms to enforce the treaty. One of the greatest challenges facing states party to the convention involve protection of confidential business information related to biopharmaceutical trade secrets, particularly among U.S. companies. The burden is upon private and public stakeholders to strike an amicable agreement to minimize costs and burdens to implement key provisions while ensuring international competitors do not gain an unfair advantage from increased scrutiny that would accompany verification and compliance.

UN Security Council Resolution 1540—The 9/11 Commission called upon the international community to "develop laws and an international legal regime with universal jurisdiction to enable the capture, interdiction, and prosecution of such smugglers [in reference to the A. Q. Khan nuclear smuggling network] by any state in the world."[28] Since 2004, the U.S. Government has worked diligently toward this objective, although in some cases, the necessary follow-through has been lacking. In April 2004, at the urging of the United States, the UN Security Council adopted Resolution 1540. The resolution requires states to enact and enforce national, legal and regulatory measures to prevent proliferation of weapons of mass destruction, their delivery systems, and related materials to nonstate actors, as well as to establish financial controls to prevent the financing of such transactions.

International Convention for the Suppression of Acts of Nuclear Terrorism—The International Nuclear Terrorism Convention, adopted in April 2005 by the 59th UN General Assembly, is significant in that it is the first antiterrorism convention adopted and completed since the September 11, 2001 terrorist attacks on the United States. The convention entered into force in July 2007 after Bangladesh became the required 22nd state to submit its instrument of ratification. Essentially, the convention seeks to criminalize specific threats and acts of terrorism involving the unlawful and intentional possession or use of nuclear and radioactive materials.[29] On July 12, 2007, President George Bush transmitted the text of the convention to the U.S. Senate for its advice and consent to ratification.[30] He simultaneously submitted a report by the State Department that included various assumptions and reservations of the administration. The President indicated that the administration would submit to Congress separately the recommended legislation necessary to implement the convention.[31]

1980 Convention on the Physical Protection of Nuclear Materials—This Convention, which entered into force in 1987, is primarily concerned with the appropriate use, storage, and transport of nuclear materials and provides a legal framework for state parties to ensure that nuclear materials are not diverted from legitimate, peaceful nuclear uses.[32] In July 2005, a Conference of State Parties adopted an amendment to expand the convention's jurisdiction to make it legally binding upon states parties to protect domestic use, storage, and transport of nuclear materials, as opposed to strictly international control. The 2005 amendment requires two-thirds of the 130 States Parties to submit their instrument of ratification before it enters into force. The amendment would criminalize nuclear smuggling and nuclear sabotage.

Evaluation Global and Multilateral Efforts to Prevent WMD Terrorism

Since the dawn of the nuclear era, the global nonproliferation regime has rested on the foundation of a broad series of multilateral treaties. For reasons both domestically driven and internationally imposed, that regime has suffered a series of significant setbacks during the past decade. Senator Richard Lugar said it best when he noted that, "There is growing concern, both in the United States and abroad, that U.S. non-proliferation and arms control policies lack a unifying consensus on how to pursue U.S. strategic interests. As contradictions in American policy have emerged, confidence in U.S. leadership on nonproliferation and arms control has eroded and U.S. commitment is being questioned in foreign capitals."[33] The continuing stalemate regarding the conclusion of a Fissile Material Cutoff Treaty, the U.S. failure to complete ratification of the International Atomic Energy Agency (IAEA) Additional Protocol, funding shortfalls to the Organization for the Prohibition of Chemical Weapons, the inability to reach agreement with Russia on an extension to the Strategic Arms Reduction Talks (START) Treaty verification regime, and funding cuts to the Comprehensive Test Ban Treaty's monitoring system may have all served to dampen a robust global commitment to pursuing collaborative counterterrorism and nonproliferation efforts.

Even core administration initiatives whose *modus operandi* is the promotion of a coordinated global effort to prevent proliferation have suffered. Despite early attention, UN Security Council Resolution 1540 has neither received the consistent support of the United States, nor the sustained commitment from the international community requisite to move the resolution from a multifaceted directive to an effective instrument of nonproliferation. The Security Council Committee responsible for monitoring the implementation of 1540 is both overwhelmed and underresourced—its mandate restricted to monitoring without detailed analysis or comparison of correlated needs and resources. Many countries have even questioned the legitimacy of the resolution itself, resulting in uneven implementation and a loss of prioritization. To date, only 136 of the 192 member states of the United Nations have undertaken the first stage of implementation by submitting a mandatory report on their national execution of the resolution. As a result of all of these factors, the global multilateral arms control and disarmament regime seems to be in no small amount of trouble.

Coalitional Efforts to Prevent CBRN Terrorism

G8 Global Partnership Against the Spread of Weapons and Materials of Mass Destruction—The Global Partnership was created at the 2002 G8 Kananaskis Summit and is focused, *inter alia*, on securing fissile materials and dismantling nuclear submarines in the Russian Federation and Ukraine.[34] The United States pledged $10 billion—matching an aggregate international contribution of $10 billion for a total commitment goal of $20 billion dollars—to combat nuclear terrorism over 10 years (by 2012). To date, the initiative has secured $18.2 billion from about 20 countries; nevertheless, much more needs to be invested by more states in future years to build and sustain the Global Partnership.

Proliferation Security Initiative (PSI)—Launched in 2003, the PSI has grown from the 11 original participants to 86 as of November 2007.[35] The purpose of PSI is to stop the flow of weapons of mass destruction, their delivery systems, and related materials while in transport at sea, in the air, or on land. To date, the PSI has played a key role in helping to interdict more than thirty shipments, including the interdiction of centrifuge parts that helped encourage Libya to abandon its chemical and nuclear weapons programs.[36] Roughly two-dozen successful interdiction missions were carried out by PSI partners between 2005 and 2006.[37] The United States views the PSI as an informal organization and consequently, does not refer to participants as members. All PSI activities are conducted within the bounds of international law and PSI does not confer new laws or rights on any participating nation. There is no established funding for PSI. Despite its successes, however, the Proliferation Security Initiative continues to encounter legal challenges to its legitimacy. The PSI countries are concerned about the circumstances in which they might be legally justified in interdicting a WMD or missile shipment and are thus interested in clarifying the relevant legal bases for action. Indeed, their first order of business was to assess their own authorities and export control regimes in the context of intercepting suspect cargoes within their own territorial waters, land, and air space. In and of itself, the PSI has been helpful in bringing additional rigor to the export regimes of partner countries—even if the principles it has adopted are far from universal.

Global Initiative to Combat Nuclear Terrorism—This effort was launched jointly by the United States and Russia in 2006 at the G8 Summit in St. Petersburg, where both countries invited other like-minded nations to participate.[38] Today, more than 67 countries have joined the Initiative as partners, where the IAEA and EU hold observer status. The Global Initiative seeks to protect and control civilian facilities where radioactive/nuclear materials are stored. It also creates and improves information sharing networks among member nations to detect and prevent illicit trafficking of such materials.[39] The overarching aim of the Global Initiative is to promote the full implementation, in the United States, of numerous other WMD-related anti-terrorism measures including UNSCR 1540[40] and the Physical Protection of Nuclear Materials Convention, as well as its 2005 amendment.[41] Eight core commitments for participating member nations are outlined in the Global Initiative, but the Statement of Principles does not include a specific plan for action and accountability that could actually stifle the PSI's long-term sustainability and effectiveness.[42]

Evaluating Coalitional Efforts to Prevent WMD Terrorism

Beyond the core nonproliferation treaties and the supplemental and direct bilateral programming under Nunn–Lugar, additional programming efforts have sprung up. The legacy arrangements most closely associated with the coalitional export control regime are informal and consensus-based and thus have no official enforcement mechanism. They also have proven to be critically important consensus building tools, forging common definitions and approaches to preventing the proliferation threat and promoting domestic legislative enforcement mechanisms. These mechanisms have also proven to be organic, that is, capable of growing and evolving based upon changing technology and a changing threat environment.

For example, a promising attempt to legalize PSI-like interdiction efforts is the 2005 amendment to the Convention for the Suppression of Unlawful Acts Against the Safety of Maritime Navigation (SUA Convention). Article 4 of the amendment criminalizes the transportation of WMD, WMD material, and any dual-use technology intended to create WMD.[43] The amendment also creates a "comprehensive set of procedures and protections designed to facilitate the boarding of a vessel" that eliminates "the need to create time-consuming ad hoc boarding arrangements when facing the immediacy of ongoing criminal activity."[44] While 144 states have ratified the original SUA Convention, only two countries have ratified the amendment. Full ratification and entry into force will likely take years.[45]

Unfortunately, inconsistent implementation, inadequate state-based capacity, a lack of universality, enforcement, and verification continues to challenge the efficacy of these export control arrangements.[46] Perhaps the best illustration of such shortcomings is the A. Q. Khan network and its proliferation success. Many new and emerging supplier states, such as Malaysia, do not participate in informal export control arrangements and are therefore not bound by their guidelines. Lacking the legal status of treaties and the threat of enforcement, the role of these arrangements in identifying clandestine programs like Khan's and preventing proliferation is quite limited. Recognizing these shortcomings, the U.S. government has led the way in developing additional coalitions of like-minded governments that are intent on recognizing the changing nature of the proliferation threat, identifying gaps, and then backfilling these holes within the existing regime. National prioritization of the terrorist threat is not symmetrical and thus, these coalition-driven efforts have been initiated by a comparatively small number of countries—with the United States offering the lion's share of funding.

National and Bilateral Efforts to Prevent CBRN Terrorism

International Materials Protection, Control, and Accounting—The MPC&A program seeks to secure nuclear weapons and weapons-usable nuclear materials by upgrading security at nuclear sites, by consolidating these materials at sites where installation of enhanced security systems has been completed, and by improving nuclear-smuggling detection capabilities at international borders. Despite numerous successes, in 2005 approximately one-half of the nuclear materials in the FSU lacked adequate security protection because of so-called "access disputes,"[47] a situation that improved only marginally by the end of 2006.[48] According to the U.S. General Accounting Office, the effectiveness of the program is further hindered because the Department of Energy "lacks a management information system to track the progress made toward its goal of providing Russia with a sustainable MPC&A system by 2013."[49]

Global Threat Reduction Initiative (GTRI)—Russia and the United States jointly launched the GTRI in 2004 to remove and secure HEU from research facilities around the globe. From mid-2004 to late 2007, GTRI secured 575 radiological sites in 40 countries with physical protection upgrades and removed 5,150 at-risk radiological sources from within the United States.[50] As of September 2007, GTRI had returned to Russia more than 410 kilograms of HEU in 13 shipments and converted 12 research reactors worldwide that formerly operated with HEU—which can be diverted for use in a nuclear weapon—to LEU.[51] More than 90 countries have joined the GTRI effort since its inception.[52]

Cooperative Threat Reduction (CTR) Program—Founded in 1991, the CTR program is managed by the Department of Defense and seeks to fulfill four objectives: Dismantle FSU WMD and associated infrastructure; consolidate and secure FSU WMD and related technology and materials; increase transparency and encourage higher standards of conduct; and support defense and military cooperation with the objective of preventing proliferation.[53] Since 2005, CTR has implemented security enhancements at 11 Russian nuclear weapon storage sites and performed security upgrades at more than 70 nuclear warhead and storage material sites. In addition, 75% of buildings in the FSU that contain nuclear materials have undergone "rapid upgrades" and 54% have undergone "comprehensive upgrades."[54] Since 2005, positive changes in the CTR program have included repeal of annual congressional certification requirements to ensure that money continues to be available for essential work. A $50 million funding cap, however, still prevents implementation of CTR programs outside the FSU.

Evaluating National and Bilateral Efforts to Prevent WMD Terrorism

In the fifteen years since inception, the bilateral Cooperative Nonproliferation Programs (CNP) operated from the U.S. Departments of Defense, Energy and State have been an unparalleled foreign policy success.[55] No other effort has done more to reduce the likelihood that weapons, materials, or expertise of mass destruction will fall into the hands of a terrorist organization. Since the inception of these programs in 1992, more than 6,800 former Soviet nuclear warheads have been deactivated. Twelve of twenty-four Russian nuclear weapons storage sites have received critical security upgrades. Also, 885 nuclear air-to-surface missiles have been eliminated and 104 of 380 priority border crossings, airports, and seaports around the world have been outfitted with radiation detection equipment. In addition, Russian and other former Soviet facilities storing 260 tons of fissile material have received either comprehensive or rapid security upgrades and 262 metric tons of HEU from dismantled nuclear weapons has been blended down to non-weapons-usable LEU for burning in civilian power reactors. Finally, innovative new partnerships developed to promote peaceful joint U.S.-Russian research at forty-nine former biological weapons facilities are ongoing.[56]

Despite an impressive roster of accomplishments, the nonproliferation programs as they are currently configured are neither providing the maximum return on government investment, nor accomplishing their goals at a pace commensurate with the urgency of the threat. Much of the blame for these inefficiencies can be laid on the doorsteps of the host government states that have often proven to be fickle partners. The lack of a sense of urgency regarding the nature of the threat, enduring Cold War hostilities, and a variety of unrelated issues have all conspired to frustrate seamless progress toward achieving the ultimate objective of the nonproliferation programs. Like its foreign partners, however, the United States government has unwittingly contributed its own internal barriers to success. A recent study by the Henry L. Stimson Center in Washington, DC has grouped the major impediments into four broad categories: lack of interagency collaboration, unrealistic expectations, inefficient congressional oversight, and overly burdensome restrictions over program implementation.[57] Although the resource levels committed to these programs from both budgetary and human resource perspectives have flat-lined since 2005, a large infusion of financial resources would likely be counterproductive until the core organizational challenges are overcome.

Continued Challenges to Implementation of National Nonproliferation Efforts

Interagency collaboration—The Departments of Defense, Energy and State all suffer under significant programmatic impediments resulting from unclear lines of authority between agencies or from discontinuities in the interagency process. Furthermore, a definite need exists for increased information-sharing among agencies regarding their respective programs and activities in the field. It is common for multiple agencies to simultaneously plan and pursue similar opportunities on the ground in the FSU, only to learn of one another's efforts there from their host partners. The impact of agency parochialism has resulted in delays in the execution of programs, redundancies in efforts, unrealized potential to build synergies within or between agency efforts, and a potential for program efforts to work at cross-purposes with, or to be impeded by, other foreign policy objectives. As the geographic reach of these programs expands, this problem is likely to grow.

Unrealistic expectations—An enduring need exists for more planning, building of consensus, and a stronger sense of clarity in regard to procedures between the United States and host countries in the early stages of program development. This balancing and tempering of expectations would help to avoid misunderstandings down the line and the potential souring in relations because of program changes midstream or simply confusion regarding the underlying assumptions of the agreements. U.S. efforts to ensure sustainability will benefit from a more solid foundation if they work to build consensus regarding the host country's needs and objectives. Without this foundation at the outset, U.S. efforts will likely meet with resistance in program implementation and find that the ultimate transition to an exit strategy to be very difficult. As one worrisome example, program managers point to Russia's lack of priority attention to HEU protection as a case of how U.S. investments may not endure after U.S. funding sunsets. The Russian government is far more preoccupied with the threat presented by "dirty bombs" and has thus prioritized its domestic funding on that basis.

Inefficient oversight—All three executive agencies are under the strain of cumbersome congressional oversight activities—reporting requirements, nonsensical earmarks, lack of nuance in metrics for progress, and an insufficient understanding of the programs themselves. The complexity of the programs, their dispersion among multiple agencies, the limited personnel responsible for executing them, and the relatively small budgets afforded them all suggest that finding a more effective and less time-consuming means for informational exchanges between the agency actors and their congressional counterparts would be very beneficial and lead to fewer legislative restrictions on implementation and thus an expedited pace of success.

Overly burdensome restrictions—As the cooperative nonproliferation programs expanded in a piecemeal fashion across the Departments of Defense, Energy, and State, Congress applied an array of requirements and restrictions on program activities. Over time, many of these have outgrown their utility and are creating obstacles to effective implementation of the programs today. Certification requirements on host government compliance with arms control agreements, legislative ceilings on annual maximum allowable increases to Defense Department budget lines, and legislative restrictions that unnecessarily restrict Department of Energy funding in the areas of program implementation and in-country execution funds create an inflexibility that has led to inefficient implementation of programs and a failure to capitalize upon changing opportunities on the ground.

Financial resources—Topline nonproliferation funding has remained largely static since 2005, increasing only marginally from $1.25 billion in 2005 to $1.4 billion in 2007. While it is clear that more money could translate into faster progress in select programs, big boosts to targeted initiatives in the past have oftentimes not been expended efficaciously. In addition to the obstacles to effective implementation described above, budgetary increases have been seldom matched by additional personnel capacity at the agency to efficiently execute enhanced funding. Although additional across-the-board funding would signal heightened political attention for these programs and increase the leverage of the implementing agencies over their host country sponsors, until programs are successfully adjusted to effectively use the additional resources, then budgetary increases could prove counterproductive.

CONCLUSION

National and bilateral nonproliferation and related preventive efforts have gained additional traction in the wake of the 9/11 attacks. Additional—if ultimately insufficient—attention has been afforded the Nunn-Lugar program and massive new resources have been funneled into border protection and other second and third line of defense activities. However, these bilateral and unilateral actions ultimately produce short-term answers to enduring systemic threats. A lack of comprehensive buy-in from many states of proliferation concern, coupled with a lack of willingness to pay the costs of implementing the agenda, threaten the viability of the regime.

Across the board, the global nonproliferation community needs to embrace a more holistic, multifaceted, and coordinated strategy to prevent WMD terrorism. To do so in the most strategic and effective way, we believe that the following three steps should be pursued: First, we need to engage the international community in mutually agreeable and collaborative efforts that are tangible, sustainable, and to the extent possible, quantifiable. In the near term, this requires working globally to ensure that raw materials suitable for use in CBRN weapons are secured. This means the global expansion of Nunn-Lugar to secure at their source excess weapons and materials, as well as the expertise to turn the latter into the former. While the success of the Cooperative Threat Reduction and associated nonproliferation programs has been significant, the long term reach of these programs remains unknown. Without sustained host country engagement, nonproliferation programs could be short lived in an environment where demand remains high.

Accelerating these supply-side efforts will require increased funding and oversight of key programs in the United States, like CTR. Funds are needed to increase staff and invest in future leadership, but such measures are only effective if there is a coherent strategy that articulates outcomes against realistic objectives. Staff must be better aligned with goals of programs and be trained to focus on results, not budgets or only near-term deliverables. Program managers must be given the tools necessary to accomplish their missions and internal and interagency bureaucratic encumbrances must be eliminated.

Second, a successful strategy to prevent proliferation requires the development of innovative new strategies that take advantage of the changing global realities and that fill the gaps created by the inability of states to prevent proliferation. While the existing bilateral, coalitional, and multilateral arrangements surveyed in this chapter are all critical elements of a unified regime, an inviolable nonproliferation strategy will not be possible without continual and rapid reactions to the changing forces that generate new proliferation routes to terrorists. The involvement of new nonstate actors such as private industry, which increasingly controls critical know-how and technologies, will be critical for the long-term success of preventive programs. Relevant stakeholders need to be defined, identified, and informed so that they have a responsibility in accounting for and tracking materials and capacities.

And finally, in the long-term, we must work toward establishing the preconditions that mitigate the demand-side of the proliferation threat. More needs to be done with respect to understanding the root causes of terrorism by incorporating literature and research outside of the traditional hierarchy of security studies (see Chapter 9 for a discussion of this concept within the context of intelligence early warning and prevention). A variety of factors and variables should be assessed across the economic, political, social, and religious contexts with an eye toward identifying areas for joint action on a global level to better understand how to neutralize and prevent terrorism in the first place. Existing efforts related to global development, public health, education, and other "soft" security challenges must be incorporated into a unified strategy to promote sustainable development and global nonproliferation. Bureaucratic and policy stovepipes that have prevented U.S. federal agencies from closer collaboration must be eliminated in order mitigate the desire and ultimately prevent the world's most dangerous weapons from falling into the hands of the world's most dangerous terrorists.

NOTES

1. Testimony of Jamal Al-Fadl, *United States vs. Usama bin Ladin et al.*, trial transcript, Day 2, Feb. 6, 2001.
2. Massimo Calabresi and Romesh Ratnesar, "Can We Stop the Next Attack?" *Time* magazine, March 11, 2002, 24–37.
3. Presidential Decision Directive 39, *US Policy on Counterterrorism*, June 21, 1995.
4. "Proliferation: Threat and Response," Office of the Secretary of Defense, U.S. Department of Defense, April 1996, available at http://www.fas.org/irp/threat/prolif96/index.html.
5. "Proliferation: Threat and Response—1997," Office of the Secretary of Defense, U.S. Department of Defense, November 25, 1997, available at: http://www.fas.org/irp/threat/prolif97/index.html.
6. "Information Paper on Usama Bin Ladin," February 12, 1998, as cited in *The 9/11 Commission Report: Final Report of the National Commission on Terrorist Attacks Upon the United States—Authorized Edition* (New York: W. W. Norton & Company, July 22, 2004, paperback edition).
7. "Archive of Nuclear Data, Table of US Nuclear Warheads 1945-75," Natural Resources Defense Council, available at: http://www.nrdc.org/nuclear/nudb/datab9.asp.
8. Address by Dwight D. Eisenhower, President of the United States of America, to the 470th Plenary Meeting of the United Nations General Assembly, December 8, 1953, available at: http://www.iaea.org/About/history_speech.html.
9. "Face-to-Face, Nixon-Kennedy," Vice President Richard M. Nixon and Senator John F. Kennedy, Third Joint Television-Radio Broadcast, John F. Kennedy Presidential Library and Museum, October 13, 1960, available at: http://www.jfklibrary.org/Historical+Resources/Archives/Reference+Desk/Speeches/JFK/JFK+Pre-Pres/Third+Presidential+Debate+101360.htm.
10. Graham Allison, "How to Stop Nuclear Terror," *Foreign Affairs*, January/February 2004.
11. "Proliferation: Threat and Response," Office of the Secretary of Defense, U.S. Department of Defense, January 2001, 1.
12. Lewis A. Dunn, *Beyond Nonproliferation: US Policy in a Proliferating World* (Washington, DC: Twentieth Century Fund, 1981).
13. Brian Finlay and Elizabeth Turpen, "Cooperative Nonproliferation: Getting Further, Faster," The Henry L. Stimson Center, January 2007, 1.

14. We chose to rely on using al-Qa'ida throughout this chapter as a jihadist typology of the "lowest common denominator." Al-Qa'ida, for example, makes their operational information and objectives readily available to other jihadist terrorist groups to enhance the global jihadist movement and the operational capability of jihadist cells worldwide. Al-Qa'ida is not protective of their operational information as demonstrated by the conventional manuals that are authored by some of their foremost operatives (see Chapter 4 of this volume for more information). In the end, we assume that al-Qa'ida is trying to launch a global jihadist revolution, and it relies on other jihadist cells for operational momentum.
15. National Intelligence Estimate, "The Terrorist Threat to the US Homeland," Director of National Intelligence, July 17, 2007, available at: http://dni.gov/press_releases/20070717_release.pdf.
16. See http://www.globalsecurity.org/military/library/congress/2002_hr/curtis2.pdf
17. One of the most egregious examples of the potential vulnerability of a state's nuclear arsenal occurred in 1991 during the coup in the Soviet Union.
18. "Improving Security at World's Nuclear Research Reactors," International Atomic Energy Agency, June 7, 2006, http://www.iaea.org/NewsCenter/News/2006/heu_symposium.html.
19. Peter D. Zimmerman and Jeffrey G. Lewis, "The Bomb in the Backyard," 2006, available at: http://www.ksg.harvard.edu/ksgnews/Features/opeds/122006_lewis.html.
20. Sonia Ben Ouagrham-Gormley, "Nuclear Terrorism's Fatal Assumptions," *The Bulletin Online*, available at: http://www.thebulletin.org/columns/sonia-ben-ouagrham-gormley/20071023.html.
21. "Slovak Uranium Arrests Reveal Shadowy Market," MSNBC, available at: http://www.msnbc.msn.com/id/22022256/.
22. "International Atomic Energy Agency Illicit Trafficking Database Releases Latest Aggregate Statistics," *IAEA*, September 11, 2007, available at: http://www.iaea.org/NewsCenter/News/2007/itdb.html.
23. John D. Steinbruner, "Biological Weapons: A Plague Upon All Houses," *Foreign Policy Magazine*, Winter 1997-98, 85-96.
24. "BW Terrorism Tutorial," *Center for Nonproliferation Studies*, available at: http://www.nti.org/h_learnmore/bwtutorial/chapter01_06.html.
25. Peter D. Zimmerman and Cheryl Loeb, "Dirty Bombs: The Threat Revisited," *Defense Horizons*, no. 4, January 2004, 3, available at: http://www.hps.org/documents/RDD_report.pdf.
26. Information from this section draws upon the Nuclear Threat Initiative's (NTI) educational *WMD 411* web portal available at: http://www.nti.org/f_wmd411/.
27. Ibid.
28. 9/11 Commission Report, 381.
29. "International Convention for the Suppression of Acts of Nuclear Terrorism," United Nations, April 2005, available at: http://untreaty.un.org/English/Terrorism/English_18_15.pdf.
30. See "International Convention for the Suppression of Acts of Nuclear Terrorism," Inventory of International Nonproliferation Organizations and Regimes, James Martin Center for Nonproliferation Studies, October 22, 2007, available at: http://www.cns.miis.edu/pubs/inven/index.htm.
31. "Message to the Senate of the United States," Office of the Press Secretary, White House, July 13, 2007, http://www.whitehouse.gov/news/releases/2007/07/20070713-4.html.

32. "Convention on the Physical Protection of Nuclear Material," United Nations Office on Drugs and Crime, http://www.unodc.org/unodc/terrorism_convention_nuclear_material.html.
33. See: http://lugar.senate.gov/press/record.cfm?id=291477&&.
34. The Global Partnership also provides international assistance to help Russia meets its obligations under the Chemical Weapons Convention (CWC).
35. "Proliferation Security Initiative Participants," Bureau of International Security and Nonproliferation, U.S. Department of State, current as of November 9, 2007, available at: http://www.state.gov/t/isn/c19310.htm.
36. Robert G. Joseph, Undersecretary for Arms Control and International Security, "The Global Initiative to Combat Nuclear Terrorism: A Comprehensive Approach to Today's Most Serious National Security Threat," Remarks to the Capitol Hill Club, Washington, DC, July 18, 2006, available at: http://www.state.gov/t/us/rm/69124.htm.
37. Sharon Squassoni, "Proliferation Security Initiative (PSI)," *CRS Report for Congress*, September 14, 2006.
38. "Global Initiative to Combat Nuclear Terrorism: Joint Fact Sheet," Official Web Site of the G8 Presidency of the Russian Federation in 2006, available at: http://en.g8russia.ru/docs/7.html.
39. Fact Sheet, "Partner Nations Endorse Global Initiative to Combat Nuclear Terrorism Statement of Principles," Bureau of International Security and Nonproliferation, US State Department, November 7, 2006, http://www.state.gov/t/isn/rls/fs/75845.htm.
40. UNSCR 1540 calls on states to enforce domestic controls over WMD and WMD-related materials in production, use, storage, and transport, to maintain effective border controls, and to develop national export and trans-shipment controls over such items.
41. Office of the Spokesman, "U.S.-Russia Joint Fact Sheet on the Global Initiative to Combat Nuclear Terrorism," U.S. State Department, July 15, 2006, available at: http://www.state.gov/r/pa/prs/ps/2006/69016.htm.
42. Matthew Bunn, *Securing the Bomb: 2007* (Cambridge, MA and Washington, DC: Project on Managing the Atom, Harvard University and the Nuclear Threat Initiative, September 2007), 8
43. International Maritime Organization, *Protocol of 2005 to the Convention for the Suppression of Unlawful Acts Against the Safety of Maritime Navigation*, November 1, 2005, available from the IMO Library.
44. "International Conference Amends Maritime Treaties on Unlawful Acts," U.S. Department of State, 27 October 27, 2005.
45. The two ratifying countries are the Cook Islands and St. Kitts and Nevis. See: "Status of Conventions by Country," International Maritime Organization, available at: http://www.imo.org.
46. For a complete critique see Jacob Blackford, "Multilateral Nuclear Export Controls After the A.Q. Khan Network."
47. *Report on the Status of 9/11 Commission Recommendations, Part III: Foreign Policy, Public Diplomacy, and Nonproliferation*, November 14, 2005, 5.
48. By the end of FY06, comprehensive upgrades were completed for an estimated 55% of all the buildings in the FSU containing weapons-usable nuclear material. Rapid upgrades had occurred at an additional 15% of those sites for a total of 70% with at least rapid upgrades. Security upgrades were completed at roughly half of the nuclear warhead sites in Russia. M. Bunn, *Securing the Bomb: 2007*, September 2007.

49. "Progress Made in Improving Security at Russian Nuclear Sites, but the Long-term Sustainability of U.S.-Funded Security Upgrades Is Uncertain," Government Accountability Office, February 2007.
50. "GTRI: More Than Three Years of Reducing Nuclear Threats," *NNSA Fact Sheet*, September 2007.
51. Ibid.
52. "Past and Current Efforts to Reduce Civilian HEU Use," *Nuclear Threat Initiative*, available at: http://www.nti.org/db/heu/pastpresent.html#gtri.
53. "Cooperative Threat Reduction Annual Report to Congress Fiscal Year 2008," U.S. Department of Defense, 1.
54. Office of the Press Secretary, "Statement by President Bush on 15th Anniversary of the Cooperative Threat Reduction Program," The White House, August 29, 2007.
55. Throughout this document, the term "Cooperative Nonproliferation" (CNP) will be used to refer to the entire suite of nonproliferation programs operated across all U.S. federal agencies. Cooperative Threat Reduction (CTR) refers only to programs managed by the Department of Defense. For a more comprehensive scorecard of nonproliferation successes, see the Henry L. Stimson Center Web site at: http://www.stimson.org/ctr/?SN=CT20050804895.
56. For a comprehensive scorecard of cooperative nonproliferation successes, see the Henry L. Stimson Center Web site at: http://www.stimson.org/cnp/?SN=CT20050804895.
57. Brian Finlay and Elizabeth Turpen, "Cooperative Nonproliferation: Getting Further, Faster."

CHAPTER 12

When Prevention Fails
Mitigation as Counterterrorism Strategy

Patrick S. Roberts

CONTENTS

INTRODUCTION

Experience teaches that mitigation is an important part of preparing for disaster. Governments once devoted most of their resources to response and recovery from disasters in an ad hoc fashion. Eventually, they learned that devoting some resources to protection and vulnerability reduction before disaster strikes can save lives and property in the long run. These activities are forms of mitigation, and they promise to be an important part of countering the threat of jihadist terrorism just as they are an important part of preparing for natural disasters.

In the United States, the Department of Homeland Security (DHS) is developing a comprehensive risk assessment to guide efforts to mitigate the consequences of disaster. The terrorist threat, however, poses particular challenges because it falls within the realm of uncertainty rather than simply probability. Therefore, it is more difficult to assess the risk of attack than the risk of floods or other natural events. The best solution to coping with uncertainty is to expand the all-hazards approach to natural disasters to include terrorism, where feasible. The all-hazards concept was developed in emergency management during the 1990s. It holds that plans and procedures that can be used for one kind of disaster should, as much as possible, be used for others. Because the number of potential terrorist targets is vast, DHS should emphasize mitigation, prevention, and its underexploited intelligence function, and a minimum capacity for response to chemical, biological, radiological, and nuclear (CBRN) events as well as associated pandemic disease. Though this chapter focuses on the policy options of the DHS, other countries face similar political environments. Jihadists that possess the potential to use CBRN weapons pose special challenges, but these challenges can be addressed as part of a comprehensive strategy that appropriately weighs risks and resources.

MITIGATION STRATEGY AT DHS

The Department of Homeland Security is charged with preparedness for catastrophic events.[1] Mitigation, which is any activity intended to reduce the consequences of disaster, is a crucial but often neglected part of preparing for catastrophic disasters. It is related to what some planning documents refer to as protection or strengthening potential disaster sites to resist hazards. It also includes activities such as dispersing targets like chemical plants or information storehouses, so that a single event does not devastate an entire economic sector. Mitigation is different than preparing to respond to an incident, which includes training and funding personnel and equipment that travel to a disaster site after an event. Mitigation is one of a number of strategies that make up disaster preparedness, but the federal government's current policy documents governing emergency management, primarily the National Incident Management System (NIMS) and Homeland Security Presidential Directives (HSPD) 7 and 8, do not mention mitigation. Instead of mitigation, these documents, crafted in the wake of September 11, use the terms preparedness, prevention, protection, response, and recovery to frame emergency management. In practice, the department engages in mitigation, even if the activities are casually referred to as prevention. For example, many fire and flood prevention programs reduce the effects of an event rather than preventing it from occurring. Prevention technically refers to measures that stop an event from occurring, as when law enforcement agencies apprehend potential terrorists.

The way in which federal emergency management institutions have grown over time, however, has led to a system that favors response and, to some extent, recovery over prevention and mitigation. The federal government has intervened in major disasters since the early days of the republic, but usually only in an ad hoc fashion, providing relief after a major catastrophe.[2] Requests for aid from localities directly affected by a disaster along with neighboring regions, combined with the spectacle of a major catastrophe, put pressure on the federal government to act to relieve suffering and restore order to disaster-stricken communities. The rise of the twenty-four–hour news cycle has only amplified pressure for the government to increase involvement in relief, though not necessarily in mitigation.[3] As a result, in recent decades the national government played a greater role in policy domains, such as emergency management, that were once the sole responsibility of states and localities. Disaster organizations at all levels of government have, over time, added more programs to aid response than they have supported mitigation. National granting programs such as the Emergency Management Performance Grant program provide states and localities with resources to purchase response equipment but not to invest in activities to reduce the consequences of disasters.[4]

The nation engages in limited activities under the name of "mitigation," but these are uncoordinated and minor compared to investments in other types of emergency management support. To date, mitigation activities largely concern natural hazards and not terrorism. Through the Department of Homeland Security, the federal government provides grants to states and localities for mitigating the effects of disasters through exercises, though this is essentially preparing to respond rather than strengthening structures or dispersing material in order to make sites less vulnerable to disaster. The Army Corps of Engineers and other agencies build structures to reduce the effects of flooding, but, as Hurricane Katrina showed, some of their structural mitigation efforts may have done more harm than good in the long run because they have not lived up to the aims associated with them.[5] Efforts to set structural standards for resistance to fires, earthquakes, and floods have been more successful, but localities have the final say on such standards.

In the end, the resources and attention given to mitigation and preventative activities before a disaster occurs pale in comparison to those given to response and recovery. Nevertheless, authorities are more likely to devote resources to relieving damage after the policy "window" opens following a catastrophic event than to invest in the mitigation of an event that may never occur.[6] Politicians and agencies suffer blame when they are perceived to respond poorly to a disaster, but they are less often blamed for failing to anticipate and reduce the consequences of a disaster before it happens. Therefore, there is a greater incentive for public officials to prepare to respond to disasters rather than to attempt to reduce disaster losses over time through means other than response.

Though some mitigation programs might not be worth the cost, studies have shown that, on average, money spent on mitigation before a disaster saves much more money than would be spent after the disaster, even without considering the possible loss of life and suffering. Critics have accused mitigation programs for being, at best, wasteful and, at worst, programs to reward powerful politicians.[7] Measuring the value of mitigation programs is difficult because it requires accounting for nonevents, but in this respect it is no different than regulating for other safety and security measures. Recent attempts to document the value of mitigation show that well-thought-out programs, such as those espoused by the Federal Emergency Management Agency (FEMA), reduce the damage caused by inevitable fires, floods, earthquakes, and other disasters.[8] The most comprehensive study, by the National Institute of Building Sciences Multihazard Mitigation Council, found that, on average, a dollar spent by FEMA on hazard mitigation provides about $4 in future benefits while also saving lives.[9] To the extent that mitigation promotes a sustainable or resilient natural environment, it has benefits that are not adequately evaluated by economic measures. For example, preventing severe drought preserves wildlife, fish, forests, and natural ecosystems that might otherwise be damaged.[10] Mitigation should remain an important part of a homeland security policy that seeks to protect the nation against catastrophes of many kinds (see Table 12.1).

TABLE 12.1 Phases of Disaster Preparedness

Mitigation	
To reduce the consequences of an event to lives and property.	
Prevention	
To stop an event from occurring through interdiction or deterrence.	
Protection	
To strengthen a community's or single asset's defenses through hardening targets or building redundancy.	

RISK VERSUS UNCERTAINTY

Mitigation policy typically assumes a world of risk, in which people can calculate the frequency and severity of a particular type of event and adopt a strategy to increase their ability to withstand its effects. This kind of reasoning suits disasters that occur periodically. For example, flood mapping identifies the rate at which floodwaters will reach a particular height.[11] Policymakers designate floodplains and either restrict construction in those areas or warns their occupants that they should purchase insurance and be prepared to evacuate when flooding occurs.

Assuming that hazards occur in a world of risk and that the history of a particular hazard can be used to predict the frequency of future events serves people well most of the time. Our understanding of probability has allowed us to cope with fluctuations in natural disasters and financial turmoil in ways not imagined by societies that lacked an appreciation of probability.[12] Some risks, however, are subject to extreme uncertainty. The concept of uncertainty was best expressed by John Maynard Keynes in 1937:

> By "uncertain knowledge".... I do not mean merely to distinguish what is known for certain from what is only probable. The game of roulette is not subject, in this sense, to uncertainty.... The sense in which I am using the term is that in which the prospect of a European war is uncertain, or the price of copper and the rate of interest twenty years hence, or the obsolescence of a new invention.... About these matters there is no scientific basis on which to form any calculable probability whatever. We simply do not know![13]

Uncertainty has at least two meanings. First, uncertain threats are those for which the distribution of the underlying probability is unknown. Scientists have a theory predicting the causes of floods, and they have data about the history of floods. By comparing the theory about how floods occur through a combination of rainfall and the features of the built environment with historical patterns, scientists can predict the likelihood of future floods. Automobile fatalities and even crime are understood in a similar way. Experts can predict the number of automobile fatalities in a large population over time with some accuracy and, therefore, recommend that automobile drivers wear seatbelts in order to reduce fatalities. After seatbelt laws go into effect, scientists can verify whether the recommendation proved successful (it did).

We have no such understanding of the terrorist—and, in particular, the jihadist—threat, in part because it is so rare and also because it is not very well understood, at least not in probabilistic terms. Scientists do not understand the causes of terrorism as well as they do the causes of floods, and there have not been enough terrorist events in the United States for history to reveal concrete patterns. Some countries, such as Israel, have enough experience with a single type of terrorism that they can develop protection measures that will reduce the damage caused by attacks.[14] Israel's adversaries have favorite targets and methods, and over time Israel has developed measures to prevent and protect against attacks. The United States does not yet have such experience, and the methods and targets of jihadist terrorists may vary greatly because of the networked and decentralized nature of these groups.

The magnitude of the consequences of terrorist attacks is also subject to uncertainty, which makes deciding how much to spend in defense against attack a particularly difficult task. Disaster losses may have what statisticians call fat tails.[15] In so-called normal distributions, events that are five or more standard deviations from the mean are considered extremely rare, and twice that distance from the mean is virtually impossible. In disasters, however, events that occur with a frequency and with consequences five or more standard deviations from the mean are the ones that matter most. Large disasters cause immediate damage and have reverberations for politics and society that extend years into the future. Scientists simply cannot predict when and how these extreme events will occur with accuracy. For example, the 1994 Northridge, California, earthquake was so destructive that it sent insurance markets into turmoil.[16] Risk estimation and probability analyses did not predict the magnitude of the event. Consider that scientists understand the terrorist threat far less well than the threat of earthquakes, even though they still cannot predict the timing and magnitude of earthquakes with accuracy.

The magnitude of the consequences of catastrophic disasters demands that the federal government prepare for them through mitigation, with the assistance of state and local governments and private organizations. Improving response and recovery alone will never be sufficient because catastrophic disasters, by definition, are more extreme than expected and can overwhelm any economically or politically feasible level of response. Governments cannot afford massive teams of responders waiting for the worst case.

Even given uncertainty about terrorist intentions, critical infrastructures remain an important class of target to defend. Jihadists have expressed interest in attacking targets of economic and symbolic importance worldwide, which includes most facilities that fall under the term critical infrastructure.[17] (The term critical infrastructure is of U.S. origin and is rarely used in some countries.[18]) Right-wing militias and environmental insurgents may have different objectives, but intelligence about jihadist strikes on critical infrastructures can help determine what sites and functions are most vulnerable. Carefully targeted mitigation activities hold the promise of reducing the damage caused by disasters more than improvements in response and recovery could accomplish alone—a conclusion that is perhaps even truer for terrorism than for natural hazards because of the uncertain nature of the terrorist threat.

UNCERTAINTY AND TERRORISM

A central challenge to mitigating terrorist attacks, or protecting against them, is that terrorist intentions, capabilities, and most-desired targets are not well understood. In addition, terrorists (unlike natural hazards) are strategic adversaries, and they may adjust their strategies in response to attempts to defend against particular targets.[19] Even considering captured al-Qa'ida documents and members of al-Qa'ida in custody, government officials struggle to determine the group's objectives and in particular what targets it wants to attack. Most likely, the preferred targets change, and there is disagreement among al-Qa'ida leaders over the most desirable targets. Even if the intentions of terrorist groups were clear, leaders at the top of a hierarchy do not always have the power to constrain the behavior and choices of group members who carry out attacks.[20] There will always be some element of uncertainty in what targets terrorists will select, and government plans should reflect the variability. To date, however, government guidelines understate the uncertainty of the terrorist threat. The fiscal year 2007 Homeland Security Grant Program (HSGP) guidance defines a threat as "the likelihood of an attack occurring," and vulnerability and consequence as "the relative exposure and expected impact of an attack."[21] While these are reasonable definitions, grant guidance could take into account the relative uncertainty about the terrorist threat by allocating resources toward many kinds of threats or by establishing a minimal level of preparedness capabilities throughout the United States, both strategies that do not rely on precise information about terrorist groups.[22]

ALL HAZARDS AND DUAL USE

Given that we know very little about jihadists' intentions and that terrorists are strategic adversaries, the best strategy to prepare for attacks is to devote resources to mitigation and protection applicable to a number of hazards. Combining mitigation strategies for multiple threats makes sense given the diverse responsibilities of homeland security organizations and the tendency for political pressure to emphasize preparation for the last major disaster (which may leave terrorism to be neglected after the next big disaster strikes).[23] The task of defending against terrorism is complicated by the obvious fact that the government's resources are limited and spending time and money defending against terrorism necessarily sacrifices some other worthy public aim. Using the same resources to prepare for multiple hazards is more efficient than having multiple plans for each hazard.

Protecting physical structures from high-impact events by, for example, strengthening building codes or erecting barriers around a building can protect a structure from floodwaters, fire, and terrorist attack at the same time. These structural improvements will not prevent disaster, but they may reduce its effects. Structural mitigation prevented the attack on the Pentagon on September 11 from being worse than it was. Investing in stronger buildings and dispersing concentrations of valuable targets will reduce the damage caused by many types of hazards.[24]

In the age of homeland security, federal, state, and local governments are preparing for disasters under the mantra of "all hazards," which means that resources should be allocated to activities that support preparedness for all kinds of disasters.[25] DHS has experimented with a variant of "all hazards" language as a way to diffuse contests between factions favoring preparation for either terrorist attack or natural disasters. The language of dual use has its roots in the Cold War, when local civil defense programs were allowed to also engage in preparation for natural disasters. Today, dual use refers to using resources intended for terrorism to prepare for natural disasters. The Bay Area SUASI (Super Urban Area Security Initiative), which received $20 million from DHS, recently expanded the allowable scope of program activities to include planning for natural disasters and pandemic disease "provided that these activities also build capabilities that relate to terrorism."[26] As in the Cold War, allowing federal resources to be used for multiple hazards increases the buy-in to federal programs by local managers who are usually most concerned with the natural disasters that routinely strike their communities.

In addition to strengthening structures, mitigation can be achieved by reducing the concentration of vulnerable sites. Concentrations have increased in at least three areas: (1) energy products in the industrial storage and process industries; (2) populations in risky areas subject to compound disasters, such as those affected by ruptured oil storage tanks in Katrina or the propane tanks in St. Louis that were nearly set on fire by flooding; and (3) economic power for efficiency gains, whether in technology as in Microsoft's Windows products or the beef and milk industries, each of which is made more vulnerable to disruption because of concentration.[27] These concentrations are likely terrorist targets, and as they become more dense their safety decreases without additional protection. Private industry controls many of these concentrations, so dispersing or protecting these sites requires coordinated action. Limiting U.S. government reinsurance would ensure that property owners would not count on the federal government to compensate them for the loss of property built in high-risk areas. Policymakers should re-examine the federal policy of reinsuring property against avoidable risk. Nevertheless, federally financed insurance can improve individual behavior. The federal flood insurance program encourages private landowners to purchase flood insurance before floods materialize, thereby reducing the moral hazard problem inherent to government involvement in disaster recovery.[28]

The challenge for disaster planners in the twenty-first century is to fold responsibility for mitigating terrorist attacks into the all-hazards system that gives DHS and emergency managers at all levels of government responsibility for many different kinds of disasters. Dense concentrations of hazardous materials and vulnerable people are in danger of terrorist attacks as well as natural and industrial disasters. For example, improving the surge capacity of a hospital in case of terrorist attack strengthens the nation's public health system to address many kinds of epidemics and disasters. Natural, industrial, and terrorist hazards have enough in common to share resources, ideas, and especially a timeline that includes mitigation as well as response and recovery.

CAN INTELLIGENCE IMPROVE MITIGATION?

While recognizing the uncertainty inherent to the terrorist threat, the Department of Homeland Security could improve mitigation and prevention by better organizing its intelligence capabilities to support federal, state, and local decision-makers responsible for making day-to-day decisions about what to protect and how much to spend. Though not formally an intelligence collection agency, DHS acquires information about terrorist threats through its more than 180,000 employees.[29] The department has important collection resources in border and customs authorities, the Transportation Security Administration, the Secret Service, and the Coast Guard. The department also has close ties with state and local authorities that may provide data. The department must exploit this information not only for prevention—catching terrorists before they strike—but also, where possible, for mitigation, or identifying and reducing vulnerabilities. To date, DHS has connected intelligence to mitigation strategies in the following two areas.

Mapping

The National Geospatial-Intelligence Agency (NGA) has formed support teams to work with DHS to provide imagery and geographic information to be used in disaster response and recovery.[30] In 2007, the Director of National Intelligence expanded the range of federal, state, and local agencies that could gain access to intelligence satellites so that they could be used to map structural and geographic vulnerabilities as well as, potentially, terrorist hideouts. The Department of Homeland Security now must work to make sure this information can be easily and quickly interpreted by its agencies and state and local partners in, for example, monitoring border activity.

Risk Assessment

DHS has begun the difficult task of producing a risk assessment comparing the magnitude and consequences of various dangers to homeland security.[31] The October 2007 National Strategy for Homeland Security mandates a threat and vulnerability assessment as an essential tool to guide resource allocation. The strategy defines risk as a function of threats, which include terrorism as well as natural and industrial hazards; vulnerabilities to those threats; and their consequences. It calls for the creation of a risk framework to "identify and assess potential hazards ..., determine what levels of relative risk are acceptable, and prioritize and allocate resources among all homeland security partners."[32] The DHS Intelligence Enterprise research plan was a first step toward a department-wide risk analysis. It is not yet clear what this DHS intelligence analysis product will look like, but according to Charles Allen, the DHS Undersecretary for Intelligence and Analysis, the scope is broad:

> The most critical and overarching threat to the Homeland remains terrorism—transnational and domestic—and much of the IC's [Intelligence Community] resources are devoted to this issue. I believe, however, that my Office adds unique value by viewing terrorism through the prism of threats to the Homeland. This holistic perspective allows us to make connections—if and where they exist—between terrorism and other illicit transnational criminal activities. Moreover, these other illicit activities often constitute serious threats to the Homeland, and we must address these as well to support our Departmental mission and to help secure the Nation.[33]

Allen raises two emerging issues: To reduce the threat of terrorism, homeland security must address the threat of criminal networks that fund terrorism and illicit weapons sales. In addition, criminal and terrorist networks are international. Therefore, homeland security is not just a domestic issue; rather, it is quite multifaceted and broad in scope (see Chapter 9 of this volume for more detailed discussion of these issues).

DHS risk assessments are to be distributed in some form to federal, state, and local agencies and will map threats and vulnerabilities across the country for several years into the future. The department's threat assessment has begun to include a broader range of threats, including infectious diseases, such as avian flu, that could spread to humans, and animal diseases that could devastate the economy and food supply. As the assessment develops, the department will face the challenge of how to limit what might constitute a threat to the homeland—is it any hazard for which DHS does not have formal responsibility, or any hazard that poses a loss of life above a certain minimum threshold within a particular length of time? Disaster researchers have addressed similar questions about what constitutes a disaster.

INTELLIGENCE

Despite the promise of untapped intelligence resources in DHS and taking into account the observations offered in Chapter 3 of this volume, a homeland security mitigation strategy should, nevertheless, assume that government at all levels will have very little precise information about jihadists' targeting intentions and attack modalities.[34] Therefore, the government should protect the nation's highest value targets, no matter what jihadists' intentions might be. Doing so might forego efficiencies that result from mapping intelligence about the intentions and capabilities of particular groups onto protection strategies, but it makes sense to develop a mitigation plan without assuming perfectly accurate knowledge of jihadist strategies. The Homeland Security Advisory Council critical infrastructure task force has made strides toward this goal by mapping critical infrastructure.[35]

Intelligence remains a vital part of homeland security, as long as it takes into account uncertainty about the terrorist threat. Intelligence analysis can identify the existence of a threat and what classes of targets terrorist groups signal they will pursue.[36] If a jihadist group is ideologically drawn toward certain targets (or away from others), as Chapter 3 of this volume suggests, intelligence can guide resource allocation and strategies.[37] Ecoterrorists, for example, favor businesses that have a large impact on nature. Jihadist intentions are more difficult to discern, in part because of the diversity of these groups.[38] Nevertheless, research shows that jihadists want to inflict economic damage and enact a psychological toll (see Chapter 3 for more information). Symbolic facilities, therefore, may be targeted for reasons other than their economic value.

In addition, intelligence can shed light on probable means of attack. Jihadists have expressed interest in using CBRN weapons, and mitigation and protection strategies must take into account the consequences of a CBRN attack (see Chapter 4 of this volume). Building shelters, for example, may be an appropriate strategy to defend against some CBRN weapons. Securing fissile material, an important component of nuclear material, becomes increasingly important if jihadists express interest in using nuclear weapons. Intelligence may not provide information about terrorist intentions that can be calculated quantitatively (with accuracy), but it can provide information about what classes of targets and what classes of attacks hostile groups favor.[39]

HARDENED TARGETS

The primary means of defending against terrorist attack has been to harden targets. This is usually referred to as protection, and it is also a form of mitigation because it reduces the consequences of an attack. For example, the 2006 Buffer Zone Protection Program in the United States provides funds to "implement preventive and protective measures that make it more difficult for terrorists to conduct surveillance or launch attacks within the immediate vicinity of high-risk critical infrastructure assets."[40] Making surveillance more difficult raises the cost of learning about a target, which may be sufficient to deter an attack.[41] Jihadists, in particular, are known to perform extensive surveillance. A buffer zone also minimizes damage from an attack to the surrounding region. Thus, some grant programs may contribute to both mitigation and prevention.

Some programs to harden targets against terrorist attacks grew out of programs to mitigate against natural disasters. FEMA has long been involved in working with states and localities to develop structural codes. The agency has few sticks, but it has at times used its carrots wisely to show other governments and private entities that structural mitigation is in their best interest. Vulnerable sites are routinely hardened to protect against natural disasters.[42] Because California has adopted strict building codes, minor earthquakes cause little or no damage and do not take lives. Constructing levees and barriers accomplishes a similar end.

Soon after 9/11, FEMA incorporated terrorism into its mitigation programs. In January 2002, FEMA issued a paper stating that terrorism is just another hazard and therefore can be mitigated like any other. Of course it is not *exactly* like any other hazard, but FEMA found authority in the Stafford Act to provide mitigation for fire, floods, and explosions, regardless of their cause. One way FEMA can engage in terrorism mitigation is to encourage the adoption of building standards that can protect against earthquakes and floods while also providing defense against car bombs.[43] To fully incorporate terrorism mitigation into other mitigation programs, more people with security clearances who have access to threat information need to be involved in mitigation. An all-hazards approach to mitigation requires breaking down barriers between managers with top secret knowledge and managers without security clearances who are responsible for dealing with natural disasters.

Hardening targets requires some technical knowledge to determine, for example, how hard a target must be to adequately mitigate damage from an attack. Such calculations are beyond the capacity of most state and local governments.[44] DHS could assist state and local governments by providing information about mitigation and protection strategies. The Homeland Infrastructure Threat and Risk Analysis Center (HITRAC) identified sixteen benchmark threats, such as a suicide bomber or vehicle-borne explosive, to assist planning.[45] HITRAC has reportedly assessed the likelihood that each of the sixteen types of attacks would be initiated against the seventeen categories of critical infrastructure.[46] It is not clear that policy analysts can calculate the precise quantitative risk of damage from attack to a particular infrastructure because there are so little data about terrorist attacks in the United States. Nevertheless, tying estimations of risk to infrastructure could help decision-makers allocate resources to the greatest threats.

PROTECTING INFRASTRUCTURE

DHS must secure the critical functions of networks in addition to protecting single (sometimes called "point") targets. For all their regrettable destruction, disasters rarely cause macroeconomic consequences in the United States.[47] In other words, a single disaster does not pose a vital threat to the United States. Disasters are more likely to have macroeconomic consequences for developing countries and therefore threaten the stability of countries with low state capacity.

The U.S. economy, on the other hand, depends on the functioning of critical networks, such as power generation and transmission, communication, and food supply and distribution. Some nodes are more vital to the health of networks than others, and a national (or international) homeland security strategy should make protecting the function of essential networks a primary goal.[48] DHS incorporates networks in its strategy for critical infrastructure protection, but a comprehensive strategy would recognize the multiple means for mitigating the consequences of attack to critical infrastructures. The 2004 *Guidelines for Identifying National Level Critical Infrastructure and Key Resources* include criteria that relate to sites' contributions to networks, but the DHS Office of the

Assistant Secretary of Infrastructure Protection (IP) appears to have focused on making these sites more secure as stand-alone entities rather then as members of a network.

Closer attention to the properties of networks reveals that some types provide better defense against terrorism than others. Scale-free networks have nodes that are not randomly or evenly connected, such as the World Wide Web or human social networks. These are more robust than random networks in case of random node failures such as disasters but more brittle in case of international attacks because some nodes are more critical than others.[49]

Researchers have begun to investigate ways in which technology could make networks more efficient as well as less vulnerable to attack.[50] Systems that have traditionally required extensive written protocols and hierarchical control are vulnerable to attack whether scale-free or not, because their links and movements are predictable. Power generation and transmission fall into this category. Researchers investigating swarm intelligence want to apply the self-organizing properties of bee and ant swarms to computers and human institutions. A swarm system might generate and transmit power by relying on actions among individual agents that would react more rapidly to changing conditions than a hierarchical system.

MITIGATION BEYOND HARDENING TARGETS

Mitigation, moreover, includes strategies other than hardening a target. It may be more efficient to replace or duplicate a target's functions than to harden the site against many different means of attack.[51] Recall that mitigation strategies should assume minimal knowledge of jihadists' intentions and capabilities. Electrical substations, for example, can be easily replaced or duplicated, but the cost of protecting them against attack is high. Redundant systems may be less expensive than hardening targets through structural improvements and security procedures. Losing an electrical grid for a time will cause less damage if critical facilities such as hospitals and mobile phone towers have backup generators.

Similarly, hospital surge capacity can be increased without building expensive new facilities by performing triage in parking lots, provided sufficient personnel are available.[52] Mitigation efforts that involve redundancy or plans for reducing the consequences of disasters may be more sensible than protective measures usually seen as "hardening." The Internet and communication networks already offer some redundancy in case of attack to a single point, although their reliance on common operating systems such as Microsoft Windows renders them more vulnerable to hackers.[53] Jihadists engaged in multiple simultaneous attacks at different locations as on September 11, in Madrid in March 2004, and in London in July 2005. Redundancy ensured that these attacks did not disable transportation and communication infrastructure for long.

MITIGATION AND THE PRIVATE SECTOR

Many critical functions and valuable targets are in the hands of the private sector. They may be privately owned, but their successful function is a public concern. The government has begun to consider these privately owned sites of public importance as critical infrastructures, but the government's power to mandate mitigation is limited.

Before the homeland security era, government reports narrowed the definition of "infrastructure" to exclude sites such as rail service, schools, public housing, and toxic waste sites owned and operated by private entities.[54] Some of the planning for Hurricane Katrina was frustrated by the government's inability to require action by private firms.[55] Defending against terrorist attacks poses similar difficulties. Some important sites and networks may be privately owned yet still merit consideration as critical infrastructure.

The method of protecting sites in private hands will be different than the methods used to protect government-owned sites, but they need not be less effective. Private entities and state and local governments often resist "partnering" with the federal government in efforts to reduce vulnerability unless they are provided with significant economic incentives.[56] Even then, they may be loathe to cede authority. Given the power of industry lobbying against security standards perceived to be onerous, it is unclear whether regulations or even legislation would be successful.[57] For privately owned sites, DHS should establish regular communication channels with critical industries and private firms and, when necessary, make public the dangers posed by attacks on certain sites. Publicity would encourage the owners of private firms to protect their sites. The federal government already provides rather exhaustive vulnerability reduction for earthquakes and floods, including both financial incentives and mandates (for example, requiring a certain level of mitigation as a condition of federal disaster assistance). A similar set of incentives could be produced for terrorist hazards.

Sharing information about vulnerabilities can provide incentives for private companies to increase mitigation and prevention activities. In 2003, Homeland Security Presidential Directive/HSPD-7 called for the creation of a venue to share information across the public and private sectors about terrorist threats and vulnerabilities. The venue, the World Wide Information Sharing and Analysis Center, groups information about threats, vulnerabilities, and solutions into fourteen types of critical infrastructure, including financial services, energy, and surface transportation.[58] Membership in the center is voluntary, but many organizations find it worthwhile to join in order to share ideas about low-cost mitigation and prevention activities as well as sharing metrics and benchmarking data.

Nevertheless, there are barriers to greater public–private cooperation. Companies are unlikely to share trade secrets or operating formulas that could endanger their competitive position.[59] These formulas may be necessary to find consensus about how much the government should pay for security regulation and how much of the cost should be borne by the private sector. Should airlines pay for Transportation Security Administration (TSA) screeners or for the space used by screeners in airports? The airline industry provides a good example for how the government might weigh regulatory intervention. If airlines were to develop a cost model and share it with the TSA, the agency could forecast what happens if, for example, it doubled the number of airline screeners. The agency needs access to proprietary information to develop accurate cost models to predict the impact of regulation on an industry's financial health. Many private companies, however, do not trust the government with proprietary information.

There is often an investment gap between what businesses think is cost-effective to spend on protection and prevention and what the public thinks is necessary. The government can either provide tax incentives to encourage greater protection and investment or it can regulate. Sometimes, once companies do their homework, they recognize vulnerabilities and change on their own. "Soft" regulation, by working with companies to identify vulnerabilities and encourage smart practices to reduce vulnerability can be effective. For example, the TSA persuaded airlines that installing security cameras in baggage handling areas would pay for itself by reducing theft.

Intelligence about jihadist objectives and tactics can help determine what security vulnerabilities are most important, even while recognizing uncertainty about which targets terrorists prefer. While this discussion has primarily concerned the United States, there is no reason why similar approaches to risk and mitigation cannot be adopted internationally. The Information Sharing and Analysis Center is worldwide, as the name suggests. Building trusted networks and sharing sensitive information becomes more difficult internationally when a greater number of governments are involved.

RESOURCE ALLOCATION

While making use of science, the process of risk allocation is inevitably political because it requires judgment about what the nation values. With some fanfare, the Department of Homeland Security has made a risk-based strategy of resource allocation central to its goals, but determining what "risk-based" means in practice is a difficult task.

There are multiple competing strategies for resource allocation that could be legitimately called "risk-based." One approach to risk reduction focuses on defending against the most catastrophic threats, which include smallpox, anthrax, botulinum toxin, nuclear radiation, and pandemic flu.[60] Another risk reduction strategy funds a minimal level of preparedness across the United States and allocates funding beyond that level on the basis of risk to specific jurisdictions and the mix of potential targets within them. Most disaster researchers agree that all regions, including those designated "low risk," must attain at least a minimum capacity for response and recovery in order to provide a "surge capacity" for other areas in times of disaster. Beginning in 2004, the U.S. Congress, through the DHS, created Project Bioshield to purchase vaccines and other countermeasures against anthrax, smallpox, and other CBRN agents. Stockpiling vaccines ensures a minimal level of preparedness. A CBRN event could still inflict damage, but the presence of vaccines on hand makes it less likely that the event would cause massive causalities. It is difficult to know, however, whether the $5.6 billion spent on Project Bioshield over ten years is an optimal amount. The government has few tools to weigh tradeoffs in resource allocation across hazards. (Project Bioshield is a joint effort between the DHS and the Department of Health and Human Services.)

To date, the DHS has engaged in two major strategies to allocate resources to mitigation and preparation for terrorism given uncertainty about terrorist and jihadist intentions in particular.

Allocate to the Worst Case

At its inception, the Department of Homeland Security adopted a form of worst-case analysis known as capabilities-based planning (CBP) to organize its preparation for disasters. The premise of CBP is that information about threats is poor, so planners should develop capabilities based on a set of plausible scenarios rather than on detailed evaluations of specific threats.[61] DHS planners borrowed the idea from similar efforts in the Pentagon and applied it to all hazards, whether terrorist, industrial, or natural. In CBP, planners imagine worst-case scenarios; define the tasks needed to prepare for, respond to, and recover from those scenarios; and determine the most cost-effective means to carry out those tasks. A DHS working group identified a "dozen possible attacks considered most plausible or devastating," including the detonation of a nuclear bomb in an urban area, a sarin gas attack, and an attack involving "terrorists filling a truck with an aerosolized version of anthrax and driving through five cities over two weeks spraying it into the air."[62] The scenarios also include a major hurricane and earthquake, though most of the disasters involve deliberate attack, which historically is less likely than natural or industrial disasters.

Worst-case planning has its virtues.[63] It can stimulate thinking, especially in a previously neglected domain such as domestic terrorist attack. Sometimes worst cases are probable, or at least likely enough to warrant attention. The White House recommends that planners "not shy away from exercising worst-case scenarios that 'break' our homeland security system."[64] Probabilistic thinking, in contrast, can be used to justify dangerous behavior. Proponents of nuclear power stress the very small chance of a nuclear meltdown, but in the eyes of people living near the plant the chance may be large enough that they demand protection without which the potential costs of disaster are unbearable.[65] People who must bear the risk of the disaster are more concerned with potential consequences than with probabilities. For some preventable, high-consequence disasters, failure is not an option.

Worst-case planning has drawbacks, though. Imagining nightmare scenarios can divert attention from other, more frequent scenarios that cause more damage over time. In addition, the publicity given to nightmare scenarios can frighten citizens and shore up public support for efforts at prevention, even if these scenarios are unlikely.[66] One emergency manager who helped develop the national planning scenarios defended their use as a long-term planning tool, but cautioned that worst cases were not suitable in all situations. "This is not a document you can decipher when you are on a scene," said Gary C. Scott, chief of the Campbell County Fire Department in Gillette, Wyoming. "It scared the living daylights out of people."[67] Worst-case analysis may also lead to overcautiousness. Engineers once designed weapons to operate under the worst possible combination of conditions even though the odds of a perfect storm of bad conditions were small. Worst-case analysis in weapons design added enormous costs and provided few benefits (in addition to contributing to the arms race).[68]

The department's resource allocation is still driven by worst-case thinking in some cases. The 2007 homeland security funding request provides $2 billion more than the previous year for port security, because a terrorist attack against a U.S. port could be "economically devastating"—regardless of how likely it is.[69] The Office of Management Budget publication, in which these data appear, however, makes no mention of tradeoffs involved in funding port security as compared to other security measures.

Allocate to the Greatest Risks

Since the Second Stage Review in 2005, homeland security programs have moved from a largely "worst-case" analysis toward greater attempts to allocate resources according to risk. Proponents of a risk-based approach enjoy the support of politicians and their appointed representatives, which bodes well for attempts to further integrate risk into planning. During his confirmation hearing, DHS Secretary Michael Chertoff advocated a risk-based approach, and since then he has repeated the term *risk-based* like a mantra. Chertoff has proclaimed that "DHS must base its work on priorities driven by risk."[70]

The department's primary tools to reduce risk are grant programs to state and local agencies.[71] These programs incentivize and support efforts to prepare for all kinds of disasters. After charging that initial grant programs were more general revenue sharing than true risk-based allocation, critics proposed ways in which DHS could take into account risk factors. The 9/11 Commission, for instance, recommended that the department consider "population, population density, vulnerability, and the presence of critical infrastructure within each state."[72]

Hurricane Katrina—and the associated perceived government failures—spawned recommendations that DHS allocate resources according to risk. The White House Report, *The Federal Response to Hurricane Katrina: Lessons Learned*, recommends that the goal of national preparedness "must be to achieve and sustain risk-based target levels of capability to prevent, protect against, respond to, and recover from major natural disasters, terrorist incidents, and other emergencies."[73] The White House recommendation builds on the department's own Second Stage Review, issued in July 2005, which concluded that a higher percentage of grant monies should be spent on the basis of risk than were being so allocated at the time. The department adopted a formula that defined risk as vulnerability multiplied by threat plus consequences [risk = vulnerability * (threat + consequences)].[74] The review, however, did not substantially increase the department's policy planning staff even though issuing credible risk assessments requires a substantial staff because of the complexity and diversity of risk in homeland security. Neither the White House report nor the review takes a position on the relative risk of terrorist attack as compared to natural disasters and other hazards.

A serious consideration of how to allocate resources begs the question of what counts as homeland security. Homeland security, like all public policy, has a political rather than purely administrative element. Social scientists have shown that the definition of a policy area can attract or repel various constituencies, and homeland security is a new term ripe for definition and redefinition.[75] For example, Republicans reframed a debate over what was once termed "estate tax" as a battle over "death taxes" and, in doing so, tapped a network of principled anti-tax conservatives for support.[76] Future homeland security officials will have to negotiate political debates over what counts as a potential catastrophe and a threat to security.[77] Law professor Richard Posner advocates extending the definition of catastrophe to include global warming and other threats not traditionally considered part of homeland security (though he does not address whether these events should be addressed by DHS). Sociologist Gary Kreps summarizes the scholarly consensus on the definition of disaster as "nonroutine events in societies or their largest subsystems (e.g., regions, communities) that involve social disruption and physical harm. Among the key defining properties of such events are (1) length of forewarning, (2) magnitude of impact, (3) scope of impact, and (4) duration of impact."[78] Homeland security, like disaster and catastrophe, is a potentially capacious term, and it will be up to deliberations among elected politicians, their staff, and agency bureaucrats to either extend or limit the definition.

STATES AND LOCALITIES

For all the pledges of risk-based resource allocation, the implementation of mitigation and protection strategies requires the active participation of state and local governments. To date, states and localities have struggled to formalize risk-based mitigation strategies. Subnational governments lack analytic capacity in general and terrorism expertise in particular. Even after September 11, only the largest cities and states had staff devoted solely to preparing for terrorism. One review of the government's capacity for analyzing the threat of terrorism in 2002 noted that: "Currently, however, the U.S. government's departments and agencies are in no position to make optimal use of available modeling and simulation technologies to support the creation of an overall strategy for their counterterrorism activities."[79] Since then, the federal government's capacity has improved, but state and local governments lack a strategy connecting knowledge about terrorism to decisions about protection and mitigation made at the state and local levels. DHS could assist mitigation by providing subnational governments with information to help them decide how to allocate resources among possible projects to prepare for disaster.

Whether state and local governments have hazard mitigation plans is a good test of their analytic capacity and ability to allocate resources based on risk. States and localities are required to have approved hazard-mitigation plans, which may include risk assessments, in order to be eligible for certain funds such as the Hazard Mitigation Grant Program, according to the Disaster Mitigation Act of 2000. But since there is no single risk assessment accrediting body, the character of these mitigation plans varies. Some governments use FEMA's HAZUS as a model. This is GIS-based software that provides a probabilistic estimate of damage, including loss of life, and provides a template for risk assessment.[80] The models in HAZUS are still in development, however, and require more historical data and local mapping of critical infrastructure.

To date, states and localities have not widely adopted formal risk and vulnerability assessments, which can guide resource allocation. In the last major review of local mitigation plans, conducted in August 2005, jurisdictions representing only 37.44 percent of the nation's population had adopted plans. Thomas Lyons Carr speculates that the low adoption rate may be caused by "multiple philosophies [about mitigation and risk], misinterpretations, or limited local capacity, capability, competence, or support...."[81] Even among the groups with plans, few have well-developed risk assessments because much of the Hazard Mitigation Grant program guidance focuses on pre-disaster mitigation projects without regard to the relative risks of different disaster types.

Performing a comprehensive risk assessment requires more resources than most communities can muster. It requires the time and skills of several staff members, but rural counties usually have only a single emergency management coordinator or give the job to a fire or police chief.[82] Even some large jurisdictions assign integration of emergency management preparation to administrators with other, more particular responsibilities. In Minneapolis, a city with more than 300,000 residents, the fire chief serves as the emergency director. Traditionally, state and local emergency management planning has focused on warning, response, and evacuation, not mitigation.[83]

If the federal government is to support state and local planning efforts, it will need to devote more resources to assessing and comparing risk and long-term strategy. It is not clear whether the federal government puts many resources into assessing hazards such as unconventional methods of attack not explicitly tied to homeland security and emergency management grant programs.[84] At present, neither DHS nor its overseers in the White House, Congress, or other agencies have a method to compare the efficacy of a dollar invested in inspecting shipping containers at U.S. ports with a dollar invested in securing nuclear material abroad.[85] It is likely that a dollar invested in securing nuclear material abroad is, up to a point, more efficacious, but there exists insufficient evidence for policymakers to make arguments about such tradeoffs and no easy way to transfer money from one activity to another, especially if the activities are part of different departmental budgets or under the jurisdiction of different congressional committees. Even within DHS, most agency budgets receive incremental increases from year to year rather than reflecting tradeoffs between homeland security policy choices.[86] The DHS Performance Assessment and Evaluation Office devotes most of its resources to performance assessment and accountability measures required by the executive branch, not long-term planning across mission types. The next administration will face the challenge of aligning budgets with policy priorities. Budget scholar Cindy Wiliams advocates a White House–led Quadrennial Homeland Security Review to publicize the link between strategic protection priorities and resource allocation. At present the DHS secretary leads the review, but he or she cannot mandate budget priorities for other cabinet-level agencies.

SUMMARY

Adopting a mitigation strategy for terrorism requires the politically sensitive admission that not all attacks can be prevented. Nevertheless, a strategy for mitigating the effects of attacks when they occur has the potential to save lives and protect property. Existing programs to mitigate natural and industrial disasters can be expanded to include terrorism. In some cases, policymakers might consider terrorism-specific mitigation and protection programs. Terrorism, however, does not fit a risk-based model of resource allocation as easily as other hazards because it is characterized by uncertainty about the intentions of jihadists and other groups.

Given the uncertainty about terrorist intentions, the government should protect the nation's most valuable infrastructure and functions. Calculating what is most valuable and how to mitigate damage requires significant analytic capacity. In some cases it may be more efficient to provide for redundant or easily replaceable systems than to protect sites from attack. DHS could assist states and localities in calculating the most efficient means to mitigate disasters of all kinds and provide information about specific terrorist threats when it is available.

ACKNOWLEDGMENTS

The author would like to thank members of the working group on homeland security at the Center for International Security and Cooperation at Stanford University for many of the insights developed in this chapter. Members of the group included Lynn Eden, Michael May, Charles Perrow, and Jacob Shapiro.

NOTES

1. "Department Six-Point Agenda," Department of Homeland Security, Washington, DC, July 2006, available at http://www.dhs.gov/xabout/history/editorial_0646.shtm.
2. E. L. Quarantelli, ed., *Disasters: Theory and Research* (Beverly Hills, CA: Sage Publications, 1978); Kathleen J. Tierney, Michael K. Lindell, and Ronald W. Perry, *Facing the Unexpected: Disaster Preparedness and Response in the United States* (Washington, DC: Joseph Henry Press, 2001); Philip L. Fradkin, *The Great Earthquake and Firestorms of 1906* (Berkeley: University of California Press, 2005).
3. Thomas A. Birkland, *Lessons of Disaster* (Washington, DC: Georgetown University Press, 2006); Peter J. May, *Recovering from Disasters: Federal Disaster Relief Policy and Politics* (Westport, CT: Greenwood Press, 1985).

4. The EMPG grants fund "Evacuation Planning; Logistics and Resource Management; Continuity of Operations (COOP) / Continuity of Government (COG) Planning; and Recovery Planning," but not explicitly mitigation, prevention, or protection. See DHS, FY07 Emergency Management Performance Grants Program Guidance, November 2006, available at http://www.ojp.usdoj.gov/odp/docs/fy2007empg.pdf; Patrick S. Roberts, "Shifting Priorities: Congressional Incentives and the Homeland Security Granting Process," *Review of Policy Research*, no. 4, July–August 2005.
5. U.S. Army Corps of Engineers, *Performance Evaluation of the New Orleans and Southeast Louisiana Hurricane Protection System: Draft Final Report of the Interagency Performance Evaluation Task Force* (USACE, 2006), available at https://ipet.wes.army.mil/ accessed (June 8, 2008) 14 November 2007; Raymond Seed et al., *Investigation of the performance of the New Orleans flood protection systems in Hurricane Katrina on August 29, 2005* (Berkeley: University of California, Berkeley, 2006), also available at http://www.ce.berkeley.edu/~new_orleans/; Brig. Gen. Stuart Leavenworth, "Will We Ever Learn?" *Sacramento Bee,* July 2, 2006.
6. John Kingdon, *Agendas, Alternatives, and Public Policies*, 2nd ed. (Upper Saddle River, NJ: Pearson, 1997); Birkland, *After Disaster: Agenda Setting, Public Policy, and Focusing Events* (Washington, DC: Georgetown University Press, 1997); George J. Busenberg, "Learning in Organizations and Public Policy," *Journal of Public Policy* 21(2), 173–189.
7. Rutherford H. Platt and Claire B. Rubin, "Stemming the Losses: The Quest for Hazard Mitigation," in *Disasters and Democracy: The Politics of Extreme Natural Events,* ed. Rutherford Platt, (Washington, DC: Island Press, 1999), 69–110.
8. *Measuring Mitigation: Methodologies for Assessing Natural Hazard Risks and the Net Benefits of Mitigation* (Geneva, Switzerland: International Federation of Red Cross and Red Crescent, 2004); Hank Jenkins-Smith and Howard Kunreuther, "Mitigation and Benefits Measures as Policy Tools for Siting Potentially Hazardous Facilities: Determinants of Effectiveness and Appropriateness," *Risk Analysis* 21, April 2001, 371–382.
9. "Natural Hazard Mitigation Saves: An Independent Study to Address the Future Savings from Mitigation Activities," Multihazard Mitigation Council, National Institute of Building Sciences, Washington, DC, 2005, available at http://www.nibs.org/MMC/mmcactiv5.html.
10. Peter H. Gleick and Linda Nash, *The Societal and Environmental Costs of the Continuing California Drought* (Berkeley, CA: Pacific Institute for Studies in Development, Environment and Security, 1991).
11. Kris Wernstedt and Robert Hersh, "Climate Forecasts and Flood Planning under the Reign of ENSO," *Natural Hazards Review*, vol. 5, no. 2, May 1, 2004, 97–105.
12. Peter L. Bernstein, *Against the Gods: The Remarkable Story of Risk* (New York: John Wiley and Sons, 1998).
13. John Maynard Keynes, "The General Theory," *Quarterly Journal of Economics* 51 (1937), 209–233; Frank H. Knight, *Risk, Uncertainty, and Profit* (Boston: Houghton Mifflin, 1921); Mark Blyth, "Great Punctuations: Prediction, Randomness, and the Evolution of Comparative Political Science," *American Political Science Review* 100, November 2006, 493–498.
14. Yonah Alexander, *Combating Terrorism Strategies of Ten Countries* (Ann Arbor: University of Michigan, 2002); Alexander, *Palestinian Religious Terrorism: Hamas and Islamic Jihad* (New York: Transnational Publishers, 2002).

15. Nicholas Nassim Taleb, *The Black Swan: The Impact of the Highly Improbable* (New York: Random House, 2007); Nassim Nicholas Taleb, "Scaring Us Senseless," *New York Times*, July 24, 2005.
16. "Earthquakes: Risk and Insurance," Insurance Information Institute, November 2006; Frank Nutter, "Financing Catastrophe Risk and the Role of Government," in *Earthquake Insurance: Public Policy Perspectives from the Western United States Earthquake Insurance Summit* (San Francisco, CA: Reinsurance Association of America, 1998), 159–163.
17. *The Jericho Option: Al-Qa'ida and Attacks on Critical Infrastructure* (San Jose, CA: Center for Terrorism and Intelligence Studies, June 2006), xxiii.
18. Gary Ackerman, Jeffrey M. Bale, and Kevin Moran, "Assessing the Threat to Critical Infrastructure," in *Homeland Security: Protecting America's Targets, Volume III: Critical Infrastructure,* ed. James J. S. Forest (Westport, CT: Praeger, 2006).
19. Jacob Shapiro, "Terrorist Organizations' Vulnerabilities and Inefficiencies: A Rational Choice Perspective," in *Terrorism Financing and State Responses: A Comparative Perspective*, eds. Jeanne K. Giraldo and Harold A. Trinkunas (Stanford, CA: Stanford University Press, 2007), 56–71; Michael May, Lynn Eden, Patrick Roberts, and Jacob Shapiro, "An Analytic Approach to Preparedness for Homeland Security," Center for International Security and Cooperation, Freeman Spogli Institute for International Studies, Stanford University, 2007.
20. One of the strongest empirical regularities in terrorist groups is that when leaders seek to take a less radical approach, more extreme members often spin off and continue to commit politically counterproductive attacks. For a theoretical explanation of this phenomenon see Ethan Bueno de Mesquita, "Conciliation, Counterterrorism, and Patterns of Terrorist Violence," *International Organization*, vol. 59, no. 1, 2005, 145–176. I thank Jacob Shapiro for suggesting this point.
21. DHS, FY2007 Homeland Security Grant Program, Washington, DC, January 2007, available at http://www.ojp.usdoj.gov/odp/docs/fy07_hsgp_guidance.pdf.
22. On DHS strategy of capabilities-based planning, see Thomas Goss, "Building a Contingency Menu: Using Capabilities-Based Planning for Homeland Defense and Homeland Security," *Homeland Security Affairs* 1, Summer 2005; Sharon L. Caudle, "Homeland Security Capabilities-Based Planning: Lessons from the Defense Community," *Homeland Security Affairs* 1, Fall 2005.
23. Birkland, *After Disaster.*
24. Perrow, *The Next Catastrophe* (Princeton, NJ: Princeton University Press, 2006).
25. David Alexander, *Principles of Emergency Planning and Management* (New York: Oxford, 2002); ed. Claire B. Rubin *Emergency Management: The American Experience, 1900–2005* (Fairfax, VA: Public Entity Risk Institute, 2007).
26. The SUASI URL is http://www.bayareasuasi.org/intranet/login.asp.
27. Perrow, *The Next Catastrophe*, 7; Brad Allenby and Jonathan Fink, "Toward Inherently Secure and Resilient Societies," *Science* 309, August 12{**AU: year?**}, 1034–1036; Stephen Flynn, *America the Vulnerable: How Our Government is Failing to Protect Us from Terrorism* (New York: HarperCollins, 2004).
28. Dennis S. Mileti, *Disasters by Design: A Reassessment of Natural Hazards in the United States* (Washington, DC: Joseph Henry Press, 1999); Ian Burton, Robert W. Kates, and Gilbert H. White, *The Environment as Hazard*, 2nd ed. (New York: Guilford Press, 1993).
29. On DHS' role in intelligence collection, see Richard A. Best, Jr., "Homeland Security: Intelligence Support," Congressional Research Service, February 23, 2004.

30. Jeff J. Leonard and Lynn Mueller, "Commercial Imagery Strategy Focused on End-user," *Directions Magazine*, November 8, 2007, available at http://www.directionsmag.com/article.php?article_id=2607&trv=1.
31. Patrick Roberts, "Toward a National Hazards Risk Assessment," *Journal of Homeland Security and Emergency Management*, vol. 4, no. 3, 2007, available at http://www.bepress.com/jhsem/vol4/iss3/9.
32. White House, *National Strategy for Homeland Security*, Washington, DC, October 9, 2007, available at http://www.whitehouse.gov/infocus/homeland/.
33. Statement of Charles E. Allen, Under Secretary for Intelligence and Analysis, Department of Homeland Security, Before the Subcommittee on Intelligence, Information Sharing, and Terrorism Risk Assessment, February 14, 2008, available at http://www.dhs.gov/xnews/testimony/testimony_1203028466025.shtm.
34. I thank Jacob Shapiro for suggesting this point.
35. See the National Infrastructure Protection Plan, available at http://www.dhs.gov/xprevprot/programs/editorial_0827.shtm; also see Agenda and Executive Summary, "2007 Critical Infrastructure Partnership Advisory Council Plenary Session," Capital Hilton, Washington, DC, July 19 2007. Minutes available at http://www.dhs.gov/xprevprot/committees/editorial_0843.shtm.
36. Jeffrey M. Bale and Gary A. Ackerman, "How Serious is the 'WMD Terrorism' Threat?" in *Terrorist Motivations and Capabilities for Using Chemical, Biological, Radiological, and Nuclear (CBRN) Weapons,* Center for Nonproliferation Studies, Monterey Institute of International Studies, Monterey, CA, forthcoming. 3–5.
37. I thank Gary Ackerman for suggesting this point.
38. Bruce Hoffman Testimony before Congress, Combating Terrorism Center, February 14, 2007, available at http://ctc.usma.edu/Hoffman_ Testimony021407.pdf.
39. For the argument that terrorists have broadly similar motivations and strategies across time and place, see Martha Crenshaw, "Introduction: Thoughts on Relating Terrorism to Historical Contexts," in *Terrorism in Context* (State College: Pennsylvania State University Press, 1994); Crenshaw, "'New' versus 'Old' Terrorism," *Palestine-Israel Journal of Politics, Economics and Culture* 10(2003:48–53.
40. DHS, *FY 2006 Infrastructure Grant Programs*, 28. I thank Paul Stockton for making this point.
41. Robert Powell, "Defending Against Terrorist Attacks with Limited Resources," American Political Science Review vol. 101 (2007): 527–541; Ethan Bueno de Mesquita, "Political and the Suboptimal Provision of Counterterror," International Organization, 61, no. 1 (Winter 2007): 9–36.
42. After September 11, FEMA made minor adjustments to accommodate new concerns about terrorism, forming working groups on the subject and hiring of emergency managers with some terrorism experience. For instance, Shawn Fenn was a graduate student at the University of Florida researching how to integrate terrorist threats into urban planning when terrorists struck on 9/11. He soon found that his research was a hot commodity and after working for the state of Florida, he joined FEMA's mitigation division in order to integrate counterterrorism into federal, state, and local "all-hazard" mitigation programs. "There's a mitigation posture in the (emergency management) community right now," Fenn said. "How do you fold terrorism into that? That's the challenge."

    In January 2002, FEMA issued a paper stating that terrorism is just another hazard and therefore can be mitigated like any other. Of course it is not exactly like any other hazard, but FEMA found authority in the Stafford Act to provide mitigation for fire, floods, and explosions, regardless of their cause. One way FEMA can engage in terrorism mitigation is to encourage the adoption of building standards that can protect against earthquakes and floods while also providing defense against car bombs. But terrorism will take some time to be included into the mitigation division, Fenn says, because few people in his division have security clearances or are in contact with national security personnel who have access to threat information.

Examples of publications advising risk management for terrorism, published in December 2003, include: FEMA 426, *Reference Manual to Mitigate Potential Terrorist Attacks Against Building;* FEMA 427, *Primer for Design of Commercial Buildings to Mitigate Terrorist Attacks;* FEMA 428, *Primer to Design Safe School Projects in Case of Terrorist Attacks;* FEMA 429, *Insurance, Finance, and Regulation Primer for Risk Management in Buildings. See* http://www.fema.gov/fima/rmsp.shtm.

43. Examples of publications advising risk management for terrorism, published in December 2003, include: FEMA 426, *Reference Manual to Mitigate Potential Terrorist Attacks Against Building;* FEMA 427, *Primer for Design of Commercial Buildings to Mitigate Terrorist Attacks;* FEMA 428, *Primer to Design Safe School Projects in Case of Terrorist Attacks;* FEMA 429, *Insurance, Finance, and Regulation Primer for Risk Management in Buildings. See* http://www.fema.gov/fima/rmsp.shtm.
44. Roberts, "Toward a National Hazards Risk Assessment."
45. "Risk Management: Further Refinements Needed to Assess Risks and Prioritize Protective Measures at Ports and Other Critical Infrastructure," Government Accountability Office, December 2005.
46. Stewart A. Baker, Robert B. Stephan, and Gregory Garcia, Statement Before the United States House of Representatives Committee on Homeland Security, Subcommittee on Transportation Security and Infrastructure Protection, Washington, DC, March 23, 2007.
47. Ilan Noy, "The Macroeconomic Consequences of Disasters," University of Hawaii Department of Economics Working Paper, February 2007, available at http://www.economics.hawaii.edu/research/workingpapers/WP_07-7.pdf; Douglas Holtz-Eakin, "Macroeconomic and Budgetary Effects of Hurricanes Katrina and Rita," Congressional Budget Office Testimony before the Committee on the Budget of the U.S. House of Representatives, Washington, DC, October, 6, 2005.
48. For examples of critical nodes, see Ted G. Lewis, *Critical Infrastructure Protection in Homeland Security* (Hoboken, NJ: Wiley, 2006).
49. Jean-Loop Guillaume, Matthieu Latapy, and Clémence Magnien, "Comparison of Failures and Attacks on Random and Scale-free Networks," in *Lecture Notes in Computer Science* (Heidelberg, Berlin: Springer, 2005): 186–196. L. K. Gallos and P. Argyrakis, "Scale-Free Networks Resistant to Intentional Attacks," *Europhysics Letter*, vol. 80, no. 5, 2007, 58002--05.
50. Eric Bonabeau and Guy Theraulaz, "Swarm Smarts," *Scientific American*, vol. 282, no. 3, March 2000, 82–90.
51. May et al., "An Analytic Approach to Preparedness for Homeland Security."
52. For example, the Veterans Administration plans to employ parking lot triage during a pandemic flu, effectively extending the number of patients who can be treated at a particular hospital. See Ceci Connolly, "US Plan for Flu Pandemic Revealed," *Washington Post*, April 16, 2006.
53. May et al., "An Analytic Approach to Preparedness for Homeland Security."

54. U.S. Congressional Budget Office, *New Directions for the Nation's Public Works*, September 1988, xi–xiii; Moteff and Parfomak, "Critical Infrastructure and Key Assets," 2.
55. "The Federal Response to Hurricane Katrina: Lessons Learned," White House, February 2006.
56. Platt and Rubin address these questions in Rutherford H. Platt and Claire B. Rubin, "Stemming the Losses: The Quest for Hazard Mitigation," in *Disasters and Democracy*, Platt ed. (Washington, DC: Island Press, 1999), 72.
57. See, for example, industry's effective campaign to prevent the District of Columbia from limiting HAZMAT shipments through the National Capital Region. For a summary see Carol D. Leonnig, "Judge Upholds Hazmat Rail Ban," *Washington Post,* April 19, 2005, B02; Carol D. Leonnig, "Judge Demands To View Rail Plan; D.C. Hazmat Cargo Ban At Issue in CSX Lawsuit," *Washington Post*, September 22, 2005, B01.
58. http://www.wwisac.com.
59. Ideas from the next two paragraphs were stimulated by discussions at a Center for International Security and Cooperation conference at Stanford University, "Homeland Security after the Bush Administration: Next Steps in Building Unity of Effort," August 23, 2007, Stanford, CA.
60. Lawrence M. Wein, "Face Facts," *New York Times*, October 25, 2006.
61. Thomas Goss, "Building a Contingency Menu: Using Capabilities-Based Planning for Homeland Defense and Homeland Security," *Homeland Security Affairs* I, Summer 2005; Sharon L. Caudle, "Homeland Security Capabilities-Based Planning: Lessons from the Defense Community," *Homeland Security Affairs* I, Fall 2005.
62. Eric Lipton, "U.S. Lists Possible Terror Attacks and Likely Toll," *New York Times*, March 16, 2005; David Howe, Senior Director for Response and Planning, "Planning Scenarios," The Homeland Security Council, Washington DC, July 2004.
63. Lee Clarke, *Worst Cases: Terror and Catastrophe in Popular Imagination* (Chicago: University of Chicago Press, 2005).
64. "The Federal Response to Hurricane Katrina: Lessons Learned," White House, February 2006, 73.
65. Risk analysis shows that scientists and engineers think about risk differently than does the mass public. Most people fear new and unproven technologies such as nuclear power more than do scientists, who rely on evidence of catastrophic losses to declare a technology unsafe. Paul Slovic, "Perception of Risk," *Science,* 236, (1987) 280–285.
66. Ian Lustick, *Trapped in the War on Terror* (Philadelphia: University of Pennsylvania Press, 2006).
67. Eric Lipton, "U.S. Lists Possible Terror Attacks and Likely Toll," *New York Times*, March 16, 2005.
68. John S. Hammond, Ralph L. Kenney, and Howard Raiffa, "The Hidden Traps in Decision-making," *Harvard Business Review*, January 2006, 126.
69. U.S. Office Management and Budget, *Analytical Perspectives* (Washington, DC: U.S. Government Printing Office, 2007), Table 3-7.
70. "Homeland Security Sectary Michael Chertoff Announces Six-Point Agenda for Department of Homeland Security," Press Release, Office of the Press Secretary, U.S. Department of Homeland Security, July 13, 2005; Secretary Michael Chertofff, U.S. DHS Second Stage Review Remarks, July 13, 2005, available at http://www.dhs.gov/xnews/speeches/speech_0255.shtm: "We must make tough choices about how to invest finite human and financial capital to attain the optimal sate of preparedness.

Our risk analysis is based on these three variables: threat, vulnerability, and consequences. These variables are not equal. For example, some infrastructure is quite vulnerable, but the consequences of an attack are relatively small; other infrastructure may be much less vulnerable, but the consequences of a successful attack are very high, even catastrophic." Michael Chertoff, Remarks by Secretary Michael Chertoff at a Press Conference Announcing DHS Fiscal Year 2008 Budget Request," February 5, 2007; Warren D. Morningstar, "Chertoff Wants More 'Risk Based' Security on GA 2007," cited November 6, 2007, available at http://www.aopa.org/advocacy/articles/2007/071106customs.html.

71. For a list of grant programs, see Shawn Reese, "Homeland Security Grants, Evolution of Program Guidance and Grant Allocation Methods," Congressional Research Service, CRS RL 33583, August 7, 2006.
72. National Commission of Terrorist Attacks Upon the United States, *The 9/11 Commission Report: Final Report of the National Commission of Terrorist Attacks Upon the United States* (New York: W. W. Norton and Company 2004), 396.
73. "The Federal Response to Hurricane Katrina: Lessons Learned," White House, February 2006, 68.
74. Todd Masse, Siobhan O'Neil, and John Rollins, "The Department of Homeland Security's Risk Assessment Methodology," Congressional Research Service, CRS RL33858, February 2, 2007, 14; DHS FY2007 Homeland Security Grant Program: Program Guidance and Application Kit, January 2007, 8.
75. George Lakoff, *Moral Politics* (Chicago: University of Chicago Press, 1996); Erving Goffman, *Frame Analysis: An Essay on the Organization of Experience* (New York: Harper & Row, 1974).
76. Michael J. Graetz and Ian Shapiro, *Death by a Thousand Cuts* (Princeton, NJ: Princeton University Press, 2005).
77. E. L. Quarantelli, "Catastrophes are Different from Disasters: Some Implications for Crisis Planning and Managing Drawn from Katrina," Social Science Research Council, September 26, 2005, available at http://understandingkatrina.ssrc.org/Quarantelli/.
78. Gary A. Kreps, "Disaster as Systemic Event and Social Catalyst," in *What is a Disaster?,* ed. E. L. Quarantelli (London: Routledge, 1998), 34.
79. James Thorp, "Complex and Interdependent Systems," in *Making the Nation Safer: The Role of Science and Technology in Countering Terrorism*, ed. Alberts and Wulf, eds (Washington, DC: National Academy of Sciences Press, 2002), 287–312; Yacov Haimes, "A Roadmap for Modeling the Risks of Terrorism to the Homeland," *ASCE Journal of Infrastructure Systems,* vol. 8, no. 2, June 2000.
80. See http://www.fema.gov/plan/prevent/hazus/index.shtm.
81. Thomas Lyons Carr III, "A Study of Local Governments Participating in the Pre-disaster Mitigation (PDM) Program and Populations Served," *Journal of Homeland Security and Emergency Management*, vol. 4, no. 2, 2007.
82. Personal interview with county emergency manager, March 18, 2007.
83. Peter J. May and Walter Williams, *Disaster Policy Implementation: Managing Programs under Shared Governance* (New York: Plenum Press, 1986).
84. Cindy Williams, "Strengthening Homeland Security: Reforming Planning and Resource Allocation," IBM Center for the Business of Government, 2008, 20, available at http://www.businessofgovernment.org/pdfs/CindyWilliamsReport.pdf.

85. Ibid., 20; Henry H. Willis, "Risk Informed Resource Allocation at the Department of Homeland Security," Testimony before the House Appropriations Committee, Subcommittee on Homeland Security, February 7, 2007; Todd Masse, Siobhan O' Neil, and John Rollins, "The Department of Homeland Security's Risk Assessment Methodology: Evolution, Issues, and Options for Congress." Congressional Research Service, February 2, 2007.
86. Williams, "Strengthening Homeland Security."

SECTION IV

The Once and Future Threat

CHAPTER 13

Islamist Use and Pursuit of CBRN Terrorism

Victor H. Asal and R. Karl Rethemeyer

CONTENTS

INTRODUCTION

The prospects of politically violent nonstate actors utilizing chemical, biological, radiological, or nuclear (CBRN) weapons has captured the imaginations of not only public officials and the news media, but also a sizeable group of scholars who have sought to better define and characterize this apparent threat. Except for a few alarmist examples, most of the scholarship on CBRN use by terrorist groups has endeavored to replace anecdote and sensationalism with analytical consideration of both the motivations and capabilities required for nonstate regime opponents to succeed in brandishing such fearful arsenals (Ferguson et al. 2004; Palfy 2003: 82, 87; Cameron 2000: 164, 167, 169; Roberts 1997).

Concurrently, a growing group of scholars have hypothesized that extremist Islamic ideologies—especially those that have accepted the potent but canonically questionable concept of jihad-as-holy war—motivate the most lethal organizations (Zimmerman 2004; Quillen 2002; Johnson and Russell 2005). Many of these groups have also sought or used CBRN weapons. While only 3.2 percent of non-Islamist terrorist groups active between 1998 and 2005 sought or used CBRN weapons, nearly 13 percent of Islamist groups active during this same period sought or used such weapons (authors calculations). This observation immediately begs the question: What factors drive Islamist organizations to seek the most feared of weapons?

Other chapters within this volume have attempted to answer this and related questions from a variety of perspectives, including strategic, historical, and psychological approaches. However, all of these analyses have been qualitative in nature. Indeed, we are unaware of any study that has treated Islamic groups as a separate subcategory and attempted to model their pursuit or use of CBRN capabilities quantitatively.

This undoubtedly reflects the general paucity of statistical studies in analyses of terrorist behavior, which is to a large degree the consequence of a lack of comprehensive and consistent data on terrorist incidents. The good news is that dataset collection efforts over the past seven years have begun to remedy this situation. The relative rarity of incidents involving CBRN materials has enabled the development of a comprehensive, open-source database of such incidents, known as the Monterey WMD Terrorism Database.[1] The far more onerous task of providing a comparison dataset of conventional terrorist incidents has been undertaken by the Memorial Institute for the Prevention of Terrorism (MIPT), which since 1998 has collected data on both domestic and international terrorist incidents and organizations as part of its Terrorism Knowledge Base (TKB) (MIPT 2006). The TKB has more recently been joined by the Global Terrorism Database (GTD), developed by the National Consortium for the Study of Terrorism and Responses to Terrorism at the University of Maryland.

These data, limited though they may be, allow us to undertake a preliminary analysis of assertions and hypotheses concerning CBRN terrorism among Islamically inspired terrorist organizations. Although this volume is focused on Islamist use of WMD, that is, weapons that are capable of causing massive casualties or socioeconomic disruption, two factors prevent us from performing a quantitative analysis of the use of WMD at this time: (1) the absence of any true WMD attacks by terrorists (and thus no empirical record), and (2) the difficulties associated with inferring from plots to use CBRN the scale of the planned attack. It is for this reason that we offer here an analysis of Islamist use and attempted use of the broader category of CBRN weapons in the hope that this might lead to a greater understanding of Islamist proclivities for using WMD.

Below, we examine several hypotheses concerning the factors related to such organizations' decision to pursue or use CBRN weapons by applying quantitative methods to incident and organization data between 1998 and 2005. Specifically, the available data allow us to examine the effects of state sponsorship, organizational size and age, the organization's linkage to allied peers, its "experience" with terrorist acts, and a set of contextual factors regarding the country in which the organization is based. The first section of this chapter lays out our hypotheses and variables. The second reviews the myriad of data sources we leverage for the study. The third presents our findings. We conclude with a brief discussion of what our findings mean for those who study or attempt to thwart use of the world's most deadly weapons.

VARIABLES AND HYPOTHESES

The choice of variables for investigation was driven by two concerns—data availability and a desire to examine a range of factors. For this preliminary analysis we selected variables in three broad categories, each reflecting a different level of analysis. These categories are (1) "environmental" variables, which include contextual historical, cultural, economic, and other sociopolitical factors in the wider milieu of the "host country" within which the terrorist organization operates (meaning the country in which their primary leadership, resources, and personnel are found); (2) "organizational" variables that deal with the structure and functional dynamics of the organization itself and its immediate "organizational environment"; and (3) "affective" variables, which manifest the ideological, aspirational, and psychological aspects of the organization.[2]

Environmental Variables

Within this category, we selected five variables: whether or not the Islamist organization received sponsorship for its activities from a state; the level of the host state's technological development, as proxied by energy consumption per capita; the degree to which the host country is embedded in the global economy and Western culture; and the regime type of the country that serves as the organization's base of operations.[3]

State sponsorship. Regarding state sponsorship for terrorist organizations, this does not refer to the issue of direct provision of CBRN weapons since there are no reported instances of such transfers ever having occurred.[4] Rather, it refers to the notion that a terrorist organization backed by the resources of a state, whether this takes the form of funding, sophisticated weaponry, or logistical or technical support, will have greater latitude to engage in CBRN terrorism. This could arise from two possible effects: The organization would possess a higher level of resources and technical expertise than it would otherwise be able to muster, while at the same time its strategic calculus would be less constrained by the need to maintain the support of a wider popular constituency.[5] The archetypical examples here would be the relationship between the Sudanese and Taliban governments, respectively (and sequentially), and al-Qa'ida. It is arguable, for instance, whether al-Qa'ida would ever have been able to set up its chemical and biological weapons "laboratories" in Afghanistan, or pursue its nuclear ambitions while in Sudan, were it not for the hospitable environment provided by the anti-Western governments of these states (Center for Nonproliferation Studies 2005).

Technological development. Our second variable focuses on the level of technological development in the countries in which these organizations are based. One might expect that the higher the base level of technological development in the society from which the organization draws its members, the more likely the organization will be to possess the requisite knowledge, skills, materials, and equipment (whether these be in physics, chemistry, engineering, or biology) to produce and deliver viable CBRN weapons. In recent years, the United Nations Conference on Trade and Development (UNCTAD) has developed an index of technological development (United Nations Conference on Trade and Development 2002); however, the index is not available for several key countries in this study, including Afghanistan, Sudan, and Iraq. Nevertheless, the UNCTAD index is highly correlated (0.86) with energy consumption per capita. Thus we have settled on this widely available measure as an appropriate proxy for the technological level of the terrorist organization's home state.

Embedding in Western economic and cultural institutions. Creation of CBRN weapons requires access to bodies of knowledge that have largely been the product of Western science and research. While much of this knowledge is published and available on the Internet or in public and academic libraries, it still requires access to training and research institutions to be effectual. Moreover, much of the knowledge that is needed to develop CBRN capabilities may be "impacted" in the heads of scientists and engineers in the host countries (Gulati 1998; Powell 1990; Powell, Koput, and Smith-Doerr 1996). Integration into the knowledge flows and institutions of the developed world may be essential because terrorist organizations need adherents that possess the requisite skills. The probability of finding a skilled adherent can be expected to increase the more integrated the host country is into the "invisible colleges" (Price and Beaver 1966) of the sciences.

Additionally, creation of weaponized chemical, biological, radiological, or nuclear devices often requires access to devices and materials not generally available from suppliers in less developed countries. For instance, it is well known that more sophisticated nuclear devices require high-speed switches (i.e., krytrons) to detonate properly (Pasley 1996). Thus integration of the terrorist organization's host country into the global economy through trade may be essential. Greater flows of trade offer more opportunities for terrorist groups to hide shipments of parts and materials among legitimate cargos. Greater trade with the developed world makes it more likely that local, licit organizations will have the materials needed on hand—either because they manufacture for export to the developed world or because they import such materials from developed countries.

While trade captures a measure of economic integration with the West, it does not necessarily capture cultural integration into a world economy that may give nonstate actors a stronger awareness of what might be achievable—or what might be considered a gross violation of generally accepted norms of behavior the world over. In the same way that Boli and others argue that there is a growing normative "world culture" encouraging human rights (Boli and Thomas 1997; Meyer et al. 1997), we argue that the penetration of Western cultures is having an impact as well. This connection, which goes beyond raw trade numbers and energy consumption, is important as well for how nonstate actors think about unconventional means of terror. We choose to measure this hard-to-operationalize concept by making concrete Barber's (1992) metaphor of "McDonaldization" of the world by using the presence of McDonald's restaurants in a country as a way of capturing a country's link to this larger world culture.

Regime type. The regime type of the terrorist's home country may contribute to its capability or motivation to engage in CBRN terrorism through their different security postures. Terrorists might find it more difficult generally to operate in an autocratic environment where the state can exert greater police powers than is possible in a democracy,[6] *ceteris parabis* decreasing its ability to dabble in the relatively experimental realm of CBRN weapons. However, this effect may be ameliorated by the availability of state sponsorship: If a terrorist group is sponsored by its host country, the general effect of autocracy may be reduced. Our model controls for each separately to account for this possibility.

Civil war. Finally, civil conflict (either solely internal or internal and internationalized) may play a role in the pursuit and use of CBRN capabilities. Civil wars often create zones with little effective central authority—or better still, zones where authority is wielded by the terrorist organization or its political wing—making it easier to assemble the materials, knowledge, and technology needed to pursue CBRN weapons. On the other hand, civil strife may absorb the time and attention of the organization, denying it the relative calm usually needed to pursue sophisticated science and engineering. We believe both perspectives could be correct and have no a priori reason to favor either perspective. To sort this empirical question, we include a control for the number of years the host country experienced internal or internal and internationalized conflict during our study period.

Organizational Variables

The "organizational" category is represented by five variables: The size of the terrorist organization (in terms of its estimated number of members), the organization's age (in other words, the number of years that the organization has been in operation), the amount of "experience" an organization has at committing terrorist acts, the degree to which it is connected to and/or embedded in terrorist "syndicates," and the organization's control over territory.

Organizational membership. In order for an organization to embark upon a concerted CBRN program, it would arguably need to devote substantial resources to the acquisition, production, and, in some cases, testing of their weapon.[7] While plentiful funding is not a sufficient condition for successful CBRN weapons deployment, it is arguably a necessary—or at least a facilitative—factor, both for the acquisition of raw materials, equipment, or expertise and to enable the organization to "buy their way out of technical difficulties" (Cameron 1999). Unfortunately, we are not aware of any dataset that provides a comprehensive measure of financial resources available to terrorist organizations appropriate for use in a quantitative analysis. A weaker proxy for all available resources is organizational membership. Membership reflects the depth of financial resources currently and potentially available (by donations or mobilizations by members) and the scope of the "talent pool" from which organizational leadership may find needed skills and expertise. Thus, the size of a terrorist organization could potentially be correlated with the use of CBRN weapons (Zanders 1999: 30).

Organizational age. A second organization-specific factor to consider is the organizational age of the terrorist group. While organizational age may impact many of the same capability-related requirements for CBRN weapons as organization size, an older organization that has survived prolonged counterterrorism campaigns and consistently maintained a support base through "an almost Darwinian principle of natural selection" (Hoffman 1992: 5) is more likely to have a larger pool of funds and to possess a well-developed and efficient logistical network. In an environment where an established terrorist organization might have to compete for support and attention with upstart competitor organizations, where there is a risk that the intended audiences for its violence may become desensitized if the same tactics are repeated, and where counterterrorist operations adapt over time to the organization's *modus operandi*, incentives might accumulate as the organization ages for it to innovate tactically—see Jackson (2001: 185), McCormick (2003: 480), and Hoffman (1997: 4). This innovation may take the form of an escalation in the scale and lethality of attacks, but might also manifest in a desire to embrace new forms of weaponry, including the psychologically potent CBRN variety. Additionally, there is the notion that in most cases CBRN attacks will require an "R&D" phase, including the absorption of both tacit and explicit knowledge and a learning curve (Jackson 2001: 188–203), leading to longer attack incubation periods than conventional attacks. These longer preparation periods may be more suited to well-established, older terrorist organizations than newer organizations eager for action.

Age may eventually mitigate against the pursuit of CBRN capabilities. As organizations age, they become increasingly institutionalized and headed by leaders who may wish to be accepted as "statesmen." Yasser Arafat's career and the evolution of Al Fatah would be one example. Use of CBRN agents is one pathway to delegimitzing both the leadership and organization forever. As organizations age—provided they exist long enough to age—there may be a strain toward the use of conventional, "accepted" practices rather than deviant, abhorred options. For this reason, we test age using a quadratic specification.

Inexperience. Most terrorist organizations do not attempt CBRN attacks, and most certainly would not attempt such an attack as a first resort. Instead, we hypothesize that organizations generally only seek a CBRN capability after they have some experience with other forms of attack. There are several interlocking reasons for this. First, as noted with respect to age, there is much explicit and tacit knowledge to gain experientially (Jackson 2001: 188–203). Second, the use of CBRN weapons crosses a threshold. States are likely to be much more vigilant in seeking to uproot organizations that are known to seek or use CBRN. Finally, because the achievement of CBRN capabilities could be substantially facilitated with the help of "peers" or state sponsors, terrorists may need to establish their *bona fides* with like-minded organizations and sponsors by demonstrating proficiency with other forms of violence. There are of course counterexamples where groups pursue CBRN weapons from the start, especially when CBRN weapons form part of a group's intrinsic belief systems or the group's leaders develop a fascination with CBRN. However, organizations that evidence apocalyptic tendencies are relatively uncommon among terrorist organizations and differ substantially from most "peers" in several respects.[8] Probabilistically, then, we expect a group's operational experience to be associated with a greater likelihood of CBRN weapons pursuit.

After experimenting with several thresholds for "inexperience" with terrorism, we have found in this and other work (Asal and Rethemeyer 2008) that perpetrating three or fewer attacks is a sensible cutoff, which we will use here as well.

Alliances. Like most modern organizations, those with a terrorist bent engage in relationships with other organizations in their environment to secure needed resources. There is a growing literature in the study of social movements that underlines the value of social networks to social movement organizations (SMOs) (Diani and McAdam 2003; Khagram, Riker, and Sikkink 2002; Arquilla and Ronfeldt 2001; Klandermans and Oegema 1987). The advantages that networks bring to other types of SMOs should accrue to terrorists as well (Asal and Rethemeyer 2006). Through relationships, terrorist organizations spread out mobilization tasks, diversify the risks inherent in mobilizing resources (of detection in particular), and even build the basis for a division of labor between organizations.

When organizations pursue a CBRN capability, network connections are likely to be very useful in overcoming the knowledge and materials barriers. Any given organization may lack the expertise or parts needed to build a weapon, but within a larger set of organizations both knowledge and materials are more likely to be available. There are multiple ways to measure network size and participation (see Wasserman and Faust 1994). We focus on what Granovetter terms social "embeddedness" (Granovetter 1985). The concept of embeddedness focuses not simply on the number of connections an individual or group possesses, but also on the degree to which those connections lead to people or groups who are themselves quite thoroughly connected. For instance, being connected to a set of friends who socialize with no one else may not be nearly as useful as having friends with lots of other friends (some of which you may not know). The measure of centrality that we use to capture "embeddedness"—eigenvector centrality—captures this notion through a recursion: My "embeddedness score" depends on the embeddedness score of all my contacts that are in the network, which in turn depends on my own score.

Control of territory. Finally, control of territory may also contribute to the pursuit and use of CBRN weapons.[9] Control of territory is one of the characteristics of state sovereignty (Morgenthau and Thompson 1985: 329–330); it provides a variety of resources and can make an important "contribution to a state's perceived power and security" (Hensel 2000: 59). In the context of insurgency, Mao argued that the same is true—that building bases and holding territory is an important developmental stage through which a successful movement must progress (Ford 2005: 57). We believe the argument can be extended to terrorist organizations.

Specifically, researchers have argued that "black holes" (Makarenko 2004: 138) existing in weak or failing states can provide valuable resources and shelter from military or civilian authorities seeking to disrupt terrorism (Stanislawski 2005: 159). For instance, Hamas' partial control of the Gaza Strip has historically allowed it to smuggle in a variety of deadly weapons (Inbar 2006: 829). Control of territory allows organizations to "accommodate entire training complexes, arms depots, and communications facilities" (Takeyh and Gvosdev 2002: 98) and access to recruits. Makarenko suggests that al-Qa'ida's base in the "black hole" of Afghanistan was central to its rise as a security threat to the United States (Makarenko 2004: 139). We hypothesize that controlling territory will make it easier to pursue or use CBRN capabilities because the authorities are less likely to discover and, thus, disrupt the long development cycle implicit in such complex weaponry.

Other Variables

We have considered affective variables, including the possibility that Shi'i and Sunni organizations may pursue CBRN capabilities differentially. However, our modeling failed to find any support for differences in professed variants of Islam. To simplify our model, we have not included these variables in the findings that follow.

In sum, the idea is that, generally speaking, a very young, inexperienced, relatively small terrorist organization with no territory to call its own will be more likely to husband its (presumably scarce) resources and focus on the least risky and most reliable tactical mode of attack. Obviously there are exceptions—for instance, when an organization displays a fetishistic relationship toward CBRN weapons and pursues these irrespective of the opportunity costs involved. In general, though, we expect only larger, established, and well-connected organizations to attempt this form of terrorism.

The following hypotheses about the pursuit of CBRN capabilities by Islamist organizations are thus suggested by the above discussion:

- Organizations known to receive some form of state sponsorship will be more likely to engage in CBRN terrorism.
- The higher the level of technological development (as proxied by energy consumption) in the organization's host country, the greater the likelihood of pursuing a CBRN capability.
- The more authoritarian the host country, the lower the likelihood that an organization will pursue a CBRN capability.
- The more embedded an organization's host country is in the world economy (as proxied by exports to the United States) and Western culture (as proxied by the

presence of McDonald's restaurants), the more likely the organization will pursue a CBRN capability.

- The more members a terrorist organization possesses, the more likely it will be to pursue CBRN weapons.
- The longer an organization has continually been active, the more likely it will be to pursue CBRN terrorism.
- Inexperienced organizations are less likely to pursue a CBRN capability.
- The more embedded an organization is in the web of global terrorist alliances, the more likely it is to pursue a CBRN capability.
- Organizations hosted by countries experiencing civil conflict may be more or less likely to pursue CBRN capabilities.
- Organizations that control territory are more likely to pursue CBRN capabilities.

Data and Methodology[10]

To test our hypotheses, we leveraged two data sources. The Monterey WMD Terrorism Database provided us with data on the use and attempted use of CBRN materials for destructive purposes. This database is widely regarded as the most comprehensive unclassified data source on the use of CBRN agents by nonstate actors.[11] We married the Monterey data to information found in the National Memorial Institute for the Prevention of Terrorism's (MIPT) Terrorism Knowledge Base (TKB), as supplemented by our own extensive coding efforts on terrorist organizations. The MIPT data is the only dataset of domestic and international terrorist organizations that is comprehensive and global in nature.[12] TKB is complete for the years 1998 to 2005, which was the focus of this study.

We adopt the MIPT's definition of terrorism: "Terrorism is violence, or the threat of violence, calculated to create an atmosphere of fear and alarm. These acts are designed to coerce others into actions they would not otherwise undertake, or refrain from actions they desired to take...."[13] We then define CBRN terrorism as terrorism involving chemical, biological, radiological, or nuclear materials. Terrorism can be undertaken by a range of actors, including covert state forces, insurgents, small groups of radicals, and even aggrieved individuals. We restrict our discussion to nonstate terrorism, and define a terrorist organization as any group of individuals acting in concert that employs terrorism as one of its primary activities.

An important caveat in this regard is the role of lone actors and small, ad hoc bands of extremists who have embraced the use of CBRN weapons. The majority of these people act from purely criminal motives[14] (such as extortion or spousal murder) and their behavior is not analyzed here. Nevertheless, a sizeable number of individuals or tiny "entities" who are not identified as belonging to any recognized "terrorist organization" have engaged, or attempted to engage, in attacks that employ CBRN agents for political or ideological reasons. Data on such entities are limited to the consideration of those terrorist groups identified as such by the TKB and the results of our analysis, therefore, pertain only to the actions of these types of relatively structured organizations.

As of January 17, 2006, MIPT had identified 499 organizations that had committed at least 1 incident between 1998 and 2005. Of these, we identified 108 as being motivated by some variant—however unorthodox—of Islam. To make that designation, we relied upon the MIPT data pages, Internet searches for information on the group, various published and unpublished sources, and general knowledge of the "organization space" in which these entities operate. For each of these organizations, we married the MIPT data to the Monterey CBRN data on use or attempted use. The dependent was set to "1" if the organization had used or attempted to develop a CBRN capability during the period 1998 to 2005.

Though we believe the MIPT list of terrorist organizations to be as comprehensive as possible over our study period, it is important to note that "unknown" accounts for 72.1 percent of the incidents, 46.7 percent of the injuries, and 47.5 percent of the fatalities caused by all types of terrorist attacks during this period. Why these attacks are unclaimed is itself unknown. Many of these acts may be committed by entities (individuals, small groups, temporary splinter groups, etc.) that would not fit the generally accepted definitions of "organization." Juergensmeyer (2003) suggests that religious organizations may also tend to leave their acts unclaimed because they wish to avoid attention. If so, our dataset may not contain all of the Islamist groups.[15] Nevertheless, we may still be missing some organizations from our dataset.

Once the organizations were identified we undertook extensive efforts to independently confirm the existence of each in order to remove observations that were aliases, covers, or temporary fronts for other members of the dataset. Eventually, five "alias/fronts" were removed, for a total of 395 observations.

For each organization, we had coders read the organization's MIPT data page and extract information on its size (in terms of number of members), date of founding, ideology (which MIPT calls "classification"), sources of state sponsorship (defined as financial transfers), the organization's "host" or "home-base" country,[16] and the number of connections to other terrorist organizations (reported in MIPT's "related groups" pages). If information in the page was contradictory or if the MIPT's data were contradicted by other sources, we sought independent confirmation from academic, Internet, and print media resources before assigning a final code or value for a variable.

In an effort to increase the number of organizations for whom a size estimate was available, we asked a panel of experts at the Monterey Terrorism Research and Education Program at the Monterey Institute of International Studies (MIIS) to provide a best estimate of size based on a series of intervals. Our coders also sought additional information from Internet sources as we compiled the dataset. Just over half of the organizations were recoded through our and MIIS' efforts. After combining data from MIPT, MIIS, and our own coding there were still seventy-seven organizations for which we had "low-confidence" size data. Those organizations were coded as having size "0." Table 13.1 presents our coding scheme for size.

To capture the effect of organizational alliances, we coded TKB's twenty-two–item "related groups" system into six codes that ranged from "target" to "affiliated wing." We then used the software package UCINET 6 (Borgatti, Everett, and Freeman 2002) to calculate the eigenvector measure of centrality developed by Bonacich (1972). This measure sets the centrality of each node i to $c_i = \alpha \Sigma A_{ij} c_j$, where A_{ij} is the sociomatrix for

TABLE 13.1 Size of Organizational Membership

Size intervals	Code	N
0–100 and low confidence	0	261 77: low confidence 184: 0–100
100–1000	1	74
1000–10,000	2	45
10,000 or more	3	12

the organizational network and c_j is the centrality of node j. The measure is recursive, so the parameter α must be selected to create a nontrivial result. The solution is to set α to the reciprocal of an eigenvalue. The centralities are the corresponding eigenvector. This approach makes the centrality of any node depend on the centrality of those nodes to which it is connected, rather than simply the count of local ties. The highest value is achieved as nodes are connected to other, highly central nodes. As implemented in UCINET 6, the measure is based on the largest eigenvalue calculated for the matrix.

We calculated organizational age as the number of years (in whole numbers) that have elapsed between the year of founding and 2005, inclusive of the year of founding. The square of this term was also included to account for the possible quadratic relationship between age and pursuit/use of CBRN weapons. Organizational experience with terrorism was based on the number of attacks of all types perpetrated by the group between 1998 and 2005.

To control for environmental effects, we connected each organization to a set of measures from the POLITY IV (Marshall and Jaggers 2003) and Correlates of War (COW) (Correlates of War II 2004; Singer 1988) datasets to characterize the nature of the country in which the organization is based (which in most cases is also the country that is most often attacked) using the three-digit country code (or "CCODE") system (used to uniquely identify each country from 1815 to present) available in both datasets. To assure that the relationship between environmental variables and organizational behavior is causal, we used data from 1997—the year preceding the beginning of our study interval. We used the POLITY2 variable for regime type, which varies from 10 (strongly democratic) to -10 (strongly autocratic).[17] From COW, we used measures of energy consumption and total population to construct an energy consumption per capita measure as a basic control for the level of economic development and wealth of the country in which the organization is based.

Data on the number of McDonald's restaurants were coded from financial statements prepared by the corporation. The spreadsheets contain a count of restaurants in each country for 1998, 2001, and 2003. We used the 1998 data because they are most parallel to our choice to use 1997 for the country environment data, though there is some small chance that terrorist behavior could influence the number of restaurants found in a given country in 1998.

The U.S. bilateral trade data were derived from work by Robert C. Feenstra at the National Bureau of Economic Research and available from www.internationaldata.org (Feenstra 1996, 1997, 2004, 2004). We used trade statistics for the year before our dataset began, 1997.

Data on the presence of civil strife (either isolated to the country or internationalized) was extracted from the Uppsala Conflict Data Program / International Peace Research Institute, Oslo (UCDP/PRIO) Armed Conflict Dataset, 1946–2005 (Harbom, Högbladh, and Wallensteen 2006; Uppsala Conflict Data Program [UCDP] and Research Institute—Oslo [PRIO] 2006; Gleditsch et al. 2002). Our variable counts the number of years of civil strife reported in the UCDP/PRIO dataset (type 3 and 4 conflicts) for our study period.

There are eleven organizations that appear in the Monterey WMD Terrorism dataset but are not available in the MIPT data and thus are not part of this analysis. Of these, only the Hausa militants and possibly the shadowy "September 11" organization are Islamically inspired. Neither organization was active (i.e., they did not perpetrate attacks with either conventional or CBRN weapons) during the period 1998 to 2005.

Table 13.2 lists the fourteen Islamist organizations in our dataset that have used or pursued CBRN capabilities from 1998 to 2005. Ten organizations considered and pursued

TABLE 13.2 Islamic Organizations That Have Used or Tried to Use CBRN Terrorism 1998–2005

Organization	Used Pursued 1998–2005	Org. Age	Members	McD.	Alliance Centrality	Civil War	Three or Fewer Attacks	Log Exports to the United States
al-Qa'ida	Pursued	19	2	3	88.62	0	0	21.090
Ansar al-Islam	Pursued	5	1	0	25.06	2	0	19.471
Armed Islamic Group	Pursued	14	1	0	20.83	8	0	21.615
East Turkistan Liberation Organization	Used	4	1	382	13.16	0	1	24.860
Hamas	Used	19	3	65	8.24	8	0	22.715
Hizballah	Pursued	24	3	2	15.38	0	0	18.169
Jaish-e-Mohammad (JeM)	Pursued	6	1	3	19.46	0	0	21.090
Jamiat ul-Mujahedin (JuM)	Pursued	16	1	3	2.92	0	0	21.090
Jemaah Islamiya (JI)	Pursued	13	1	67	13.52	8	1	22.942
Lashkar-e-Jhangvi (LeJ)	Pursued	10	1	3	19.37	0	0	21.090
Lashkar-e-Taiba (LeT)	Used	6	1	3	20.96	0	0	21.090
Palestinian Islamic Jihad (PIJ)	Pursued	29	1	65	4.40	8	0	22.715
Riyad us-Saliheyn Martyrs' Brigade	Used	4	1	45	14.09	7	0	22.180
Tawhid and Jihad	Pursued	9	0	0	21.57	2	0	19.471
Average, Users & Pursuers		12.71	1.29	45.79	20.54	3.07	0.14	21.399

TABLE 13.3 Description of Variables

Variable	N	Mean	Std. Dev.	Min	Max
Use/attempted use of CBRN (dependent)	108	0.13	0.337	0	1
State sponsorship	108	0.139	0.347	0	1
Technology development (energy per capita)	108	1.606	1.622	0.004	6.972
Democracy (POLITY2)	108	-0.935	7.639	-10	10
Cultural embeddedness (McDonald's)	108	40.981	108.434	0	927
Econmic embeddedness (log exports to US)	108	20.482	2.978	0.001	24.859
Organizational membership	108	0.62	0.806	0	3
Organizational age	108	9.759	11.071	1	65
Organizational age squared	108	216.667	503.476	1	4225
Inexperience (three or fewer attacks)	108	0.713	0.454	0	1
Alliance embeddedness	108	7.449	11.268	0	88.619
Years internal or external civil war	108	3.315	3.24	0	8
Control of territory	108	0.13	0.337	0	1

to some degree CBRN terrorism but were unsuccessful in actually perpetrating an attack. Four organizations tried and succeeded at least once in deploying CBRN materials in a terrorist attack. None of these attacks killed a large number of people, and actual cases of attempted use were fairly rare. As noted above, our key dependent variable for this chapter then could not be lethality but attempted and actual use. Table 13.2 also includes the values for key variables for each of the CBRN using or pursuing organizations.

Table 13.3 provides descriptive statistics for all of our variables across all 108 Islamic organizations in our dataset.

Because the dependent variable was a simple qualitative variable, we used a standard logit model, though we did use a cluster correction for the standard errors to account for any dependence among organizations based in the same host country (Rogers 1993). Table 13.4 contains our results.

FINDINGS

The logistic regression results tell a compelling story. Six of our ten identified factors have a significant relationship with the choice to pursue or use CBRN capabilities. The model is able to explain an impressive 65.1 percent of variation (using the pseudo-R^2 statistic as the standard), though the relatively small sample size of 108 does suggest that the findings should be taken as suggestive but not conclusive. The model correctly predicts 93.5 percent of all cases (101/108), using as a standard a predicted probability of greater than 0.50 as evidence that the group would pursue or use CBRN capabilities during the period 1998 to 2005. Of the cases not predicted correctly, there were three false positives (rate: 3/94 = 3.2%) and four false negatives (4/14 = 28.6%). As is usually the case, the model does better with the more common outcome than the rare one. Nonetheless, the results suggest that the model has captured the character of the existing data rather well.

The results are interesting in both the stories that are confirmed and those that are not. Starting with the confirmed drivers of behavior, there is strong evidence that both cultural

TABLE 13.4 Logit Regression—Pursuit/Use of CBRN Capabilities, Islamist Terrorist Organizations

CBRN	Pursuit/Use
State sponsorship	0.591
	(1.765)
Technology development (Energy/pop)	0.340
	(0.306)
Democracy (POLITY2)	-0.126
	(0.087)
Cultural embeddedness (McDonald's)	-0.011**
	(0.004)
Economic embeddedness (Log exports to US)	2.276*
	(0.952)
Organizational membership	0.425
	(0.782)
Organizational age	0.748*
	(0.338)
Organizational age squared	-0.021*
	(0.009)
Inexperience (three or fewer attacks)	-5.911*
	(2.833)
Alliance embeddedness	0.166*
	(0.083)
Years internal or external civil war	-0.653*
	(0.277)
Control of territory	1.690
	(2.104)
Constant	-53.269*
	(21.648)
N	108
Pseudo R^2	0.651
Log-likelihood	-14.542
χ^2	1203.444

* $p<0.05$; ** $p < 0.01$
Standard errors in parenthesis.

and economic embedding matters, but in different directions. Cultural embeddedness, as proxied by our McDonald's variable, tends to reduce the probability of CBRN pursuit or use, while economic embeddedness is strongly related to increased pursuit or use. This suggests a nuanced interpretation of the earlier hypotheses. Greater involvement in the global "cultural mainstream" may generate two "innoculative" effects. First, organizations and their members may be exposed to the global norm that use of CBRN weapons is, normatively speaking, "unthinkable." Second, engagement with global culture makes it far more difficult to view "the enemy" as an "other" worthy of destruction by means generally abhorred by most global citizens. Nine of fourteen pursuer/user organizations reside in countries with three or fewer McDonald's. It is interesting to note that more than 60 percent of the Islamist groups are based in countries with three or fewer restaurants. Slightly less than 15 percent of non-Islamic groups reside in countries that have so little contact with the Golden Arches. If the presence of a McDonald's is innoculative (even minimally so), then most of the Islamic-inspired host countries have missed their vaccination.

By contrast, embedding in the global economy is a significant contextual factor that enables pursuit of CBRN capabilities. In fact, the Islamic users/pursuers were hosted by countries that did about 2.5 times as much trade with the United States as the mean organizations in our dataset. Only three organizations resided in countries that did below-average trade with the United States; none of those organizations attempted to use CBRN capabilities—they pursued only. Islamist users and pursuers are not hosted in the most disconnected and backward host countries. On average, users and pursuers were hosted in countries doing nearly $2 billion of trade with the United States. Trade may provide both the conduit for parts and expertise as well as a potential flashpoint for discontent over the economic intrusion of the West.

Turning to the organizational variables, age and inexperience were significant predictors, with age exhibiting the quadratic relationship that was hypothesized. As organizations reach their midteens, the quadratic term begins to turn the relationship from positive to negative, as we will discuss below. It seems that there may be an "institutionalization" effect at work, as leaderships and organizations become sufficiently established that they seek to join the "legitimate" world of politics rather than resort to weapons that inspire horror and near universal condemnation. Separate from age, inexperience also has a large negative effect, as expected. Young, inexperienced organizations do not use or pursue CBRN capabilities. Older organizations have a mixed set of factors. Older organizations may be seeking access to legitimate political activity, but their experience with terrorism may better prepare them to seek and use CBRN weapons.

Alliance connections, as hypothesized, have a positive effect on the probability of CBRN pursuit and use by Islamist organizations. The coefficient is not particularly large, but it is quite significant. This finding accords with the nature of the groups that pursue and use CBRN. Users and pursuers have, on average, 2.75 times as many connections or ties to other terrorist groups as those Islamist groups that do not pursue or use CBRN. In fact, *all* Islamist groups have a much higher average connectivity than those that adhere to other ideologies. The Islamist average eigenvector centrality is more than *57 times* higher than for the other 279 organizations for which the MIPT has information. A defining feature, then, of Islamist groups is their tendency to ally and connect. If we are correct that alliance connections help to convey critical resources for CBRN pursuit and use (among other bad behaviors), then this tendency toward cooperation may be one of the defining risk factors for all Islamist groups. In general, *every* Islamist group may be more prone to CBRN pursuit and use because they tend to create alliances and connections so much more frequently and extensively than other types of terrorist organizations.

Finally, civil strife in the host country is negatively related to the pursuit or use of CBRN weapons with a coefficient that is relatively large. Civil strife may both consume the concentration and focus of terrorist organizations while denying scientists and engineers the peace and calm needed to pursue their work. An allied interpretation may be that it is harder to recruit high-skill members during a civil war as such people are usually engaged in safeguarding their family and accumulated wealth. The recent civil war in Iraq, for example, resulted in a severe brain drain that removed potential CBRN technicians from the operating area of the terrorist organizations in Mesopotamia.

Turning now to the variables for which our modeling failed to find support, we find no evidence that state sponsorship is a primary driver of pursuit or use of CBRN capabilities. Of the fourteen organizations that have pursued or used CBRN, four have some form of state support—Hamas, Hizballah, Palestinian Islamic Jihad, and the East Turkistan Liberation Organization. Of these four, only one—Hamas—has actually used CBRN weapons. Seven other organizations enjoyed some form of state support but were not known to have pursued CBRN capabilities.

Why does state support not tend to promote CBRN pursuit or use? The literature on the nature and implications of state support has been decidedly mixed in its conclusions. Much of the terrorism literature argues that lethality is highly correlated with all forms of external support but especially state support (Byman 2005: 49; Quillen 2002: 285). State support is sometimes viewed as having a "force multiplying effect (Hoffman 1999, 15). However, Simon and Benjamin suggest that "state sponsors have typically wanted [organizational] acts of terror to" preserve their clients' eligibility for a place at the bargaining table and thus "have calibrated these acts to avoid retaliation or war" (Simon and Benjamin 2001: 5). Our results suggest Simon and Benjamin have it right. In fact, our work on lethality (Asal and Rethemeyer 2008) has also failed to find a link between state sponsorship and the *intensity* of killing. However, we have found that the *choice* to kill is related to state sponsorship. State sponsors are permissive of killing, provided that it is not too extravagant.

The use of CBRN weapons in some sense represents the ultimate violation of existing norms of behavior among states, whether directly or by proxy. State sponsors must take into account the possible "blowback" that might result from a proxy's choice to use CBRN agents or methods. The case that proves this point is the September 11 attack and the subsequent U.S. invasion of Afghanistan.

Turning next to the technology and democracy indices, neither variable proved to be statistically significant. On average, the countries that host Islamist terrorist organizations tend to be somewhat authoritarian in nature (the average POLITY2 score is -0.93). By contrast, the non-Islamic groups are, on average, located in solidly democratic host countries (POLITY2 average: 7.42). Nonetheless, there is no evidence in the current analysis or the analysis of the entire universe of terrorist organizations (not reported here) to suggest that the regime type of the host country matters to the pursuit or use of CBRN capabilities. Motivation seems to reside in other factors. Similarly, the hypothesis that technologically advanced host countries tend to promote pursuit or use is also not borne out. Instead it is probable that organizations may pursue technical and scientific knowledge through other avenues outside the host country: connection to like-minded groups and collection of talent through recruiting of scientifically trained members.

Organizational membership was also found to be statistically insignificant. One reason for this may be the strong tendency for Islamist organizations to ally. Organizations may not need to have a particularly large membership if they can draw upon a network of like-minded organizations for financing, expertise, materials, and access to places and

TABLE 13.5 Probability of CBRN Use/Pursuit

	Values	P (CBRN Use or Pursuit)
Probability at means:		0.0034
McDonald's		
Min	0	0.0054
Mean	40.98	0.0034
+1 Std. Dev.	149.41	0.001
Max	927	0
Economic embeddedness (Exports to US)		
Min	0	0
Mean	20.48	0.0034
+1 Std. Dev.	23.46	0.7488
Max	24.83	0.9854
Inexperience		
Three or fewer	1	0.0006
Four or more	0	0.1865
Alliances		
Max	0	0.001
Mean	7.45	0.0034
+1 Std. Dev.	18.72	0.0214
+2 Std. Dev.	29.98	0.1238
+3 Std. Dev.	41.25	0.4771
Max	88.62	0.9996
Civil War		
Min	0	0.0287
Mean	3.31	0.0034
+1 Std. Dev.	6.55	0.0004
Max	8	0.0002
Organizational age		
Min	1	0
Mean	9.76	0.0034
+0.50 Std. Dev.	15.29	0.0122
+0.75 Std. Dev.	18.06	0.0145
+1 Std. Dev.	20.83	0.0126
+1.5 Std. Dev.	26.37	0.0037
+2 Std. Dev.	31.9	0.0003
Max	65	0

knowledge. There may be a trade-off between network connections and membership, though we would need longitudinal data to test that proposition rigorously.

Finally, control of territory did not generate a statistically significant relationship with the pursuit or use of CBRN capabilities. The coefficient is positive and fairly large—but so is the standard error. Five of the fourteen pursuers and users control territory, but the effect may have been accounted for primarily by other country-context variables like civil strife and exports to the United States.

To get a sense of the size of effects, we simulated the probability of pursuing or using CBRN capabilities using our logit model—see Table 13.5. Unless otherwise noted, the change in probability is found by varying the status variables from 0 to 1 and holding all other values of the independents at their means.[18]

The "average" organization in the dataset—defined as a mythic organization whose values for the independent variables are all set to the mean of the 108 organizations in the dataset—is extremely unlikely to pursue CBRN capabilities. Our simulations suggest the probability is about one-third of 1 percent. Why this discrepancy when we know that nearly 13 percent of the Islamist organizations pursued or used CBRN capabilities? It is because the users and pursuers tend to have relatively extreme values for the factors in the model. On average, users and pursuers were much more connected, hosted in countries with much more trade with the United States, were somewhat older (but not too old), had fewer McDonald's, and had somewhat fewer years of civil war.

To look at specific variables, experience, high values of economic embeddedness, and relatively extreme values of alliance connectivity radically increased the probability of pursuing or using CBRN capabilities. Conversely, having committed three or fewer attacks, experiencing multiple years of civil war, being very young, having no alliances, having many McDonald's, and having no trade with the United States lead to a probability of pursuit or use that is, for all practical purposes, zero. Organizational age has a modest effect that peaks at about eighteen years of existence and declines thereafter. The McDonald's effect, while statistically significant, is relatively small.

CONCLUSION

While acknowledging that the historical behavior of terrorist organizations is at best an imperfect indicator of the nature and likelihood of their future actions,[19] the empirical record of Islamist CBRN terrorist events can provide insight into which factors (besides their Islamist ideology) are most relevant in an organization's decision to employ these weapons. It is important to reiterate the key caveat about our findings: They are based on a limited temporal dataset and are constrained like all analyses by the inability to code unclaimed attacks. Yet for all this they have yielded several insights that either have not been mentioned in the extensive literature on CBRN terrorism or have remained uncorroborated. We feel that the most important of these results are the lack of significance of several environmental variables—including state support, regime types and level of technological development—and the apparent ascendancy of organizational variables such as alliance connections, inexperience, and age.

Paired with our analytic findings are other, descriptive characteristics of Islamist organizations that bear more scrutiny. First, Islamist organizations tend to be far more heavily connected to one another. This study confirms other work that we have done (Asal and Rethemeyer 2008) regarding the importance of alliance connections as a correlate of bad behavior. Our understanding of why Islamist groups are so thoroughly connected is still incomplete. One hypothesis is that al-Qa'ida acts as a giant "Schelling point": Places or institutions through which people who are wholly unknown to one another but share an ideology and a motive for violence may "congregate," virtually and/or actually (Smith 1993; Schelling 1978, 1960). Al-Qa'ida may also serve as an inspiration and point of convergence around ideology and tactics that carry into alliance relations. To nail down these questions, longitudinal network data are essential, but very difficult to construct.

Second, Islamist organizations *on average* tend to be very unlikely to pursue or use CBRN capabilities. Nevertheless, it is somewhat common for Islamist organizations to acquire the bundle of characteristics that are correlated with the pursuit or use of weapons of mass destruction. Why is this the case? One potential explanation may rest with the nature of leadership and the way leaders use mosques to "spread the word" about their organizations and recruit new members. Islamist leaders may be particularly good at manipulating the institutions and icons of religion in the service of their goals. Concomitantly, large, sophisticated terrorist groups like al-Qa'ida or Hamas cannot continue to operate in the absence of management talent. For whatever reason, the leadership cadre has the managerial flair needed to build a big operation. Our understanding of the management and construction of such enterprises is still poor, yet managerial talent may be a key ingredient that is missing from the modeling we have done here.

Islamist organizations represent just over 27 percent of all terrorist organizations active between 1998 and 2005, yet they represent more than 60 percent of the organizations that have pursued or used CBRN capabilities. Our modeling provides a first set of clues regarding why these organizations pursue and use CBRN capabilities. The key is not their Islamist character per se, but the set of characteristics that Islamic organizations tend to acquire over time. Experienced, connected, "middle-aged" organizations operating in countries relatively free of civil strife that are outside the Western cultural mainstream but part of Western economic flows are the most dangerous organizations, at least over the period 1998 to 2005. Many Islamist organizations tend to possess these organizations' characteristics and operate in country environments that make it more likely they will pursue and attempt to use the deadliest of weapons.

APPENDIX

COMPARISON OF ISLAMIST, NON-ISLAMIST, AND ISLAMIST USERS/PURSUERS AVERAGE CHARACTERISTICS

	Org. Age	Members	McDonald's	Alliance Centrality	Years Civil War	Inexperi-ence	Log Exports to United States
Non-Islamists (279 orgs.)							
Mean	11.7	0.48	164.19	0.13	2.56	0.76	21.46
Std. Dev	12.56	0.81	368.32	1.23	3.55	0.43	2.45
Max	87	3	2852	19.67	8	1	25.52
Min	1	0	0	0	0	0	0
Islamist (108 orgs.)							
Mean	9.76	0.62	40.98	7.45	3.31	0.71	20.48
Std. Dev.	11.07	0.81	108.43	11.27	3.24	0.45	2.98
Max	65	3	927	88.62	8	1	24.86
Min	1	0	0	0	0	0	0
Islamist CBRN pursurers (14 orgs.)							
Mean	12.71	1.29	45.79	20.54	3.07	0.14	21.4
Std. Dev.	7.88	0.83	100.61	20.67	3.73	0.36	1.68
Max	29	3	382	88.62	8	1	24.86
Min	4	0	0	2.92	0	0	18.17

NOTES

1. See the Monterey Weapons of Mass Destruction Terrorism Database (Monterey Terrorism Research and Education Program 2006). As of March 2006, the database lists over 1,350 cases of CBRN incidents perpetrated by nonstate actors.
2. This schema is far from unique and merely intended to draw attention to the differences between the variables we have selected. Compare this to the schema used in Post, Ruby, and Shaw (2002). In the schema offered above, Post, Ruby, and Shaw's triggering events and key actors would be included in one of the aforementioned categories.
3. We coded base of operations using the primary designation from the MIPT dataset (2006). We then had coders check the primary location of each organization using other sources.
4. There is a debate amongst scholars concerning the likelihood of such an eventuality ever occurring. There are those who believe it to be highly unlikely that any state would ever facilitate the acquisition of CBRN weapons by a terrorist organization for fear of both the targeted state's retribution and international opprobrium, together with the fact that most states would be reluctant to place control of such powerful weapons in the hands of a substate organization, no matter how strong the ideological ties between them. The contrary position avers that in cases in which leaders feel a sense of desperation, or if they believed they could conceal their contribution, then

some degree of assistance to terrorists with obtaining a CBRN capability would be possible—see, for instance, Tucker and Sands (1999); Cordesman (2001: 37); and Stern (2001: 49).

5. This follows from the ideas of Jenkins (1986: 778). On the matter of greater technological prowess on the part of state-sponsored organizations, see Jackson (2001: 199).
6. See, inter alia, Wilkinson (2000). While liberal democracies may be more vulnerable to terrorist attacks in the tactical sense, Wilkinson argues that they are more robust against terrorist campaigns succeeding strategically.
7. Indeed, one proffered reason for the preponderance of the use of conventional weapons over CBRN in terrorist attacks is that most terrorist organizations follow a form of Occam's Razor—operations must be as far from the maximum level of complexity as possible in order to secure the highest probability of achieving desired outcomes. See Palfy (2003: 87).
8. Moreover, the presence of allusions to CBRN agents in their ideology makes these groups fairly easy to identify and is an obvious indicator of intent.
9. We are indebted to an anonymous reviewer of our previous work for this insight.
10. Some materials in this section have been previously published in Asal and Rethemeyer, 2008.
11. Since the Monterey WMD Terrorism Database (2006) contains any substate use of CBRN weapons, we restrict our data selection to those cases that the database defines as "Type I: Politically or Ideologically motivated," which roughly corresponds to what we are using as our definition of terrorism.
12. There are several other datasets of terrorist incidents, such as the U.S. State Department's Patterns of Global Terrorism (2004) and the ITERATE dataset (Mickolus 2004). However, none of these systematically include "domestic" incidents, namely, those incidents involving the citizens of the same country or territory. The only other datasets that include both "domestic" and "international" instances of terrorism are the National Counterterrorism Center's (2007) Worldwide Incident Tracking System, which only includes incidents from 2004, and the Global Terrorism Database (2007), which has only recently become partially available. The MIPT data were thus felt to be the most comprehensive available dataset as of the time of writing.
13. Given the importance of definitions it is worth citing the full definition as well as the explanation provided. The full MIPT definition of terrorism is: "Terrorism is violence, or the threat of violence, calculated to create an atmosphere of fear and alarm. These acts are designed to coerce others into actions they would not otherwise undertake, or refrain from actions they desired to take. All terrorist acts are crimes. Many would also be violation of the rules of war if a state of war existed. This violence or threat of violence is generally directed against civilian targets. The motives of all terrorists are political, and terrorist actions are generally carried out in a way that will achieve maximum publicity. Unlike other criminal acts, terrorists often claim credit for their acts. Finally, terrorist acts are intended to produce effects beyond the immediate physical damage of the cause, having long-term psychological repercussions on a particular target audience. The fear created by terrorists may be intended to cause people to exaggerate the strengths of the terrorist and the importance of the cause, to provoke governmental overreaction, to discourage dissent, or simply to intimidate and thereby enforce compliance with their demands" (MIPT 2006).

14. According to the Monterey WMD Terrorism Database (2006) there have been 204 incidents involving CBRN agents where lone actors acted from purely criminal motives, while only 86 incidents involved lone actors who were politically or ideologically motivated.
15. We are indebted to Brian Lai (University of Iowa) for this insight.
16. This is not the same as the "base of operations" MIPT lists in the page; in some cases, organizations may operate from one country but target another.
17. POLITY2 is probably the most widely used measure of regime type. Created by subtracting the "autocracy" score from the "democracy" score in the POLITY IV dataset, the resulting measure provides a good index of a given country's tendency toward democracy or autocracy overall. For more information, see http://www.cidcm.umd.edu/polity/.
18. Since we used the quadratic specification, we used the square of the average age as the value in our simulations (unless we were manipulating age itself) rather than the average of the squared age.
19. Dan Verton (2003) expresses this sentiment well: "we judge the future of terrorism solely on the basis of…historical examples at our own peril...we cannot disregard the use of new and innovative tactical measures that are designed to augment the psychological and even physical impact of traditional violent terrorist attacks."

REFERENCES

Arquilla, John, and David Ronfeldt. 2001. *Networks and Netwars: The Future of Terror, Crime, and Militancy*. Santa Monica, CA: RAND Corporation.

Asal, Victor H., and R. Karl Rethemeyer. 2008. The Nature of the Beast: Organizational Structures and the Lethality of Terrorist Attacks. *Journal of Politics*.

Asal, Victor, and Karl Rethemeyer. 2006. Researching Terrorist Networks. *Journal of Security Education* 1 (4):65–74.

Barber, Benjamin. 1992. Jihad vs. McWorld. *Atlantic Monthly* 269 (3):53–65.

Boli, John, and George M. Thomas. 1997. World Culture in the World Polity: A Century of International Non-Governmental Organization. *American Sociological Review* 62 (2):171–190.

Bonacich, Phillip. 1972. Factoring and Weighting Approaches to Status Scores and Clique Identification. *Journal of Mathematical Sociology* 2:113–120.

Borgatti, S. P., M. G., Everett, and L. C. Freeman. 2002. UNICET 6 for Windows: Software for Social Network Analysis (Version 6.102). Harvard, Massachusetts: Analytic Technologies.

Byman, Daniel. 2005. *Deadly Connections: States that Sponsor Terrorism*. New York: Cambridge University Press.

Cameron, Gavin. 1999. Multi-Track Microproliferation: Lessons from Aum Shinrikyo and Al Qaida. *Studies in Conflict & Terrorism* 22 (4):277–309.

———. 2000. WMD Terrorism in the United States: The Threat and Possible Countermeasures. *Nonproliferation Review* 7 (1):162–179.

Center for Nonproliferation Studies. 2006. *Chart: Al-Qa'ida's WMD Activities*. Monterey Insitute of International Studies, May 13, 2005 [cited March 17, 2006].

Cordesman, Anthony H. 2001. *Defending America: Asymmetric and Terrorist Attacks with Radiological and Nuclear Weapons*. Washington, DC: Center for Strategic and International Studies.

Correlates of War II. 2004. *National Material Capabilities* (v3.01), March 26, 2004 [cited November 20, 2004]. Available from http://cow2.la.psu.edu/.

Diani, Mario, and Doug McAdam, eds. 2003. *Social Movements and Networks: Relational Approaches to Collective Action*. Oxford, England: Oxford University Press.

Feenstra, Robert C. 1996. U.S. Imports, 1972–1994: Data and Concordances. Cambridge, MA: National Bureau of Economic Research.

———. 1997. U.S. Exports, 1972–1994, With State Exports and Other U.S. Data. Cambridge, MA: National Bureau of Economic Research.

———. 2004. US Exports: National Bureau of Economic Research (NBER).

———. 2004. US Imports: National Bureau of Economic Research (NBER).

Ferguson, Charles D., William Potter, Amy Sands, Leonard Spector, and Fred Wehling. 2004. *The Four Faces of Nuclear Terrorism*. Monterey, CA: Center for Nonproliferation Studies.

Ford, Christopher M. 2005. Speak No Evil: Targeting a Population's Neutrality to Defeat an Insurgency. *Parameters* 35 (2):51–66.

Gleditsch, Nils Petter, Peter Wallensteen, Mikael Eriksson, Margareta Sollenberg, and Håvard Strand. 2002. Armed Conflict 1946–2001: A New Dataset. *Journal of Peace Research* 39 (5):615–637.

Granovetter, Mark. 1985. Economic Action and Social Structure: The Problem of Embeddedness. *American Journal of Sociology* 91 (3):481–510.

Gulati, Ranjay. 1998. Alliance and Networks. *Strategic Management Journal* 19 (4):293–317.

Harbom, Lotta, Stina Högbladh, and Peter Wallensteen. 2006. Armed Conflict and Peace Agreements. *Journal of Peace Research* 43 (5):617–631.

Hensel, Paul R. 2000. Theory and Evidence on Geography and Conflict. In *What Do We Know About War*, edited by J. A. Vasquez. Lanham, MD: Rowman & Littlefield Pub., Inc.

Hoffman, Bruce. 1992. *Terrorist Targeting: Tactics, Trends, and Potentialities*. Santa Monica, CA: RAND.

———. 1997. *The Modern Terrorist Mindset: Tactics, Targets, and Technologies*. St. Andrews, Scotland: Center for the Study of Terrorism and Political Violence, St. Andrews University.

———. 1999. Terrorism Trends and Prospects. In *Countering the New Terrorism*, edited by I. O. Lesser, B. Hoffman, J. Arquilla, D. Ronfeldt and M. Zanini. Santa Monica, CA: RAND.

Inbar, Efraim. 2006. Israel's Palestinian Challenge. *Israel Affairs* 12 (4):823–842.

Jackson, Brian A. 2001. Technology Acquisition by Terrorist Groups: Threat Assessment Informed by Lessons from Private Sector Technology Adoption. *Studies in Conflict* Jenkins, Brian M. 1986. Defense Against Terrorism. *Political Science Quarterly* 101 (5):773–786.

Johnson, Thomas H., and James A. Russell. 2005. A Hard Day's Night? The United States and the Global War on Terrorism. *Comparative Strategy* 24 (2):127–151.

Juergensmeyer, Mark. 2003. *Terror in the Mind of God: The Global Rise of Religious Violence*. 3rd ed. Berkeley: University of California Press.

Khagram, Sanjeev, James V. Riker, and Kathryn Sikkink, eds. 2002. *Restructuring World Politics: Transnational Social Movements, Networks, and Norms*. Minneapolis: University of Minnesota Press.

Klandermans, Bert, and Dirk Oegema. 1987. Potentials, Networks, Motivations, and Barriers: Steps Towards Participation in Social Movements. *American Sociological Review* 52 (4):519–531.

Makarenko, Tamara. 2004. The Crime-Terror Continuum: Tracing the Interplay Between Transnational Organised Crime and Terrorism. *Global Crime* 6 (1):129–145.

Marshall, Monty G., and Keith Jaggers. 2004. *POLITY IV*. Center for International Development and Conflict Management 2003 [cited September 1 2004]. Available from http://www.cidcm.umd.edu/inscr/polity/.

McCormick, Gordon. 2003. Terrorist Decision Making. *Annual Political Science Review* 6:473–507.

Meyer, John W., John Boli, George M. Thomas, and Francisco O. Ramirez. 1997. World Society and the Nation-State. *American Journal of Sociology* 103 (1):144.

Mickolus, Edward F., Todd Sandler, Jean M. Murdock, and Peter Flemming. 2004. *International Terrorism: Attributes of Terrorism Events (ITERATE), 1968–2003*. Dunn Loring, VA: Vinyard Software.

MIPT. 2006. *MIPT Terrorism Knowledge Base*. National Memorial Institute for the Prevention of Terrorism, Jan. 8, 2006 2006 [cited January 29, 2006]. Available from http://www.tkb.org/Home.jsp.

Monterey Terrorism Research and Education Program. 2006. Monterey Weapons of Mass Destruction Terrorism Database: Monterey Institute of International Studies.

Morgenthau, Hans J., and Kenneth W. Thompson. 1985. *Politics Among Nations: The Struggle for Power and Peace*. 6th ed. New York: Knopf.

Palfy, Arpad. 2003. Weapon System Selection and Mass-Casualty Outcomes. In *Terrorism & Political Violence*. Frank Cass & Company Ltd.

Pasley, John. 2007. *Pulse Power Switching Devices—An Overview*. The Federation of American Scientists, May 8, 1996 1996 [cited September 23 2007]. Available from http://nuclearweaponarchive.org/Library/Pasley1.html.

Post, Jerrold M., Keven G. Ruby, and Eric D. Shaw. 2002. The Radical Group in Context: An Integrated Framework for the Analysis of Group Risk for Terrorism. *Studies in Conflict & Terrorism* 25 (2):73–100.

Powell, Walter W. 1990. Neither Market nor Hierarchy: Network Forms of Organizations. In *Research in Organizational Behavior*, edited by B. M. Staw and L. L. Cummings. Greenwich, CT: JAI Press.

Powell, Walter W., Kenneth W. Koput, and Laurel Smith-Doerr. 1996. Interorganizational Collaboration and the Locus of Innovation: Networks of Learning in Biotechnology. *Administrative Science Quarterly* 41 (1):116–146.

Price, Derek J. De Solla, and Donald Deb Beaver. 1966. Collaboration in an Invisible College. *American Psychologist* 21 (11):1011–1018.

Quillen, Chris. 2002. A Historical Analysis of Mass Casualty Bombers. *Studies in Conflict & Terrorism* 25 (5):279–292.

Roberts, Brad. 1997. Has the Taboo Been Broken? In *Terrorism with Chemical and Biological Weapons: Calibrating Risks and Responses*, edited by B. Roberts. Alexandria, VA: Chemical and Biological Arms Control Institute.

Rogers, William H. 1993. Regression Standard Errors in Clustered Samples. *Stata Technical Bulletin* 13:1923–1928.

Schelling, Thomas C. 1960. *The Strategy of Conflict*. Cambridge, MA: Harvard University Press.

———. 1978. *Micromotives and Macrobehavior*. New York: Norton.

Simon, Steven, and Daniel Benjamin. 2001. The Terror. *Survival* 43 (4):5–18.

Singer, J. David. 1988. Reconstructing the Correlates of War Dataset on Material Capabilities of States, 1816–1985. *International Interactions* 14 (2):115–132.

Smith, Mark A. 1993. *Voices from the WELL: The Logic of the Virtual Commons* [WWW Page]. University of California—Los Angeles 1993 [cited April 27, 1999]. Available from http://www.sscnet.ucla.edu/soc/csoc/papers/voices/.

Stanislawski, Bartosz H. 2005. Transnational Organized Crime, Terrorism, and WMD. *International Studies Review* 7 (1):158–160

Stern, Jessica. 2001. *The Ultimate Terrorists*. Cambridge, MA: Harvard University Press.

Takeyh, Ray, and Nikolas K. Gvosdev. 2002. Do Terrorist Networks Need a Home? *The Washington Quarterly* 25 (3):97–108.

Tucker, Jonathan B., and Amy Sands. 1999. An Unlikely Threat. *Bulletin of the Atomic Scientists* 55 (4):46–52.

UCINET 6 for Windows: Software for Social Network Analysis 6.102. Analytic Technologies, Harvard University, Cambridge, MA.

United Nations Conference on Trade and Development. 2002. Indicators of Technology Development. Geneva: United Nations.

Uppsala Conflict Data Program (UCDP), and Research Institute—Oslo (PRIO). 2006. UCDP/PRIO Conflict Dataset Codebook. Oslo: Uppsala Conflict Data Program (UCDP) & International Peace Research Institute, Oslo (PRIO).

Verton, Dan. 2003. *Black Ice: The Invisible Threat of Cyber-Terrorism*. Emeryville, CA: McGraw-Hill/Osborne.

Wasserman, Stanley, and Katherine Faust. 1994. *Social Network Analysis: Methods and Applications*. Cambridge: Cambridge University Press.

Wilkinson, Paul. 2000. *Terrorism Versus Democracy; The Liberal State Response*, *Cass Series on Political Violence*. London: Frank Cass.

Zanders, Jean Pascal. 1999. Assessing the Risks of Chemical and Biological Weapons Proliferation to Terrorists. *Nonproliferation Review* 6 (4):17–34.

Zimmerman, John C. 2004. Sayyid Qutb's Influence on the 11 September Attacks. *Terrorism & Political Violence* 16 (2):222–252.

CHAPTER 14

The Future of Jihadists and WMD
Trends and Emerging Threats

Gary Ackerman

CONTENTS

INTRODUCTION[1]

> For man does not even know his hour: like fish caught in a fatal net, like birds seized in a snare, so are men caught in the moment of disaster when it falls upon them suddenly.
>
> **Ecclesiastes 9:12**

Even were one to concede that the jihadists of today lack the will or capability to engage in large-scale acts of terror using chemical, biological, radioactive, and nuclear (CBRN) weapons, this says very little about the jihadists of tomorrow. After all, if their actions over the past decade have taught us anything, it is that jihadists are audaciously nimble operators who will adapt to survive and are prepared to persevere *sine die* to attain their goals. At the same time, the global system in which they operate is not standing still—the political, rhetorical, and, perhaps most important, technological landscape is continually reshaping itself into novel and unexpected topologies that might present both obstacles and opportunities for the purveyors of jihad. The future relationship between jihadists and weapons of mass destruction (WMD) is thus a crucial issue, albeit one that forces the unwary analyst to venture onto the treacherous terrain of forecasting. The prudent commentator might wish to demur on such matters, yet the alternative to a judicious inquiry into the problem is to sit on the sidelines with a smug fatalism and provide hollow critiques after disaster has struck. Indeed, it is arguably the moral obligation of all those who study the domains of jihadism or WMD to explore the nebulous horizons of WMD terrorism—no matter how difficult this may prove—in pursuit of insights that might assist in preventing or planning for the unthinkable.

The future nexus of jihadists and WMD is a topic of some controversy. On the one side are those who view the use by al-Qa'ida and other jihadists of WMD as all but "inevitable."[2] These observers generally point to jihadists' demonstrated capacity for mass casualty attacks, their evolving capabilities, eroding technical constraints, and the increased availability of the raw materials with which to produce WMD.[3] On the other side are those who take a more skeptical approach, highlighting persistent technical obstacles to the efficient weaponization of CBRN agents, as well as the lack of sufficient incentives (based on both "pragmatic and jurisprudential reasons"[4]) for jihadists to expend serious efforts on attaining WMD relative to more conventional weapons.[5]

In either case, it is very seldom that commentators offer anything beyond addressing the basic issues of whether (and occasionally when) jihadists might use WMD. If the discourse is to rise above the level of the sound byte and provide usable policy direction, we must consider additional details, such as where an attack might occur, which weapons are likely to predominate, and what means of delivery might be used. We also need to contextualize the threat of jihadist WMD attacks within the broader concerns of jihadist violence and WMD terrorism, respectively. For instance, are jihadists the most likely actors to use WMD, or will the first WMD attacks come from a different quarter? Moreover, there remains a need to address what I have elsewhere termed "second-order questions,"[6] which relate to the rate of change in the likelihood of WMD terrorism over time. In this regard, one might ask whether an initial WMD attack by jihadists would spark a string of copycat events and further escalations, which would represent the ascendancy of nonstate power, or alternatively whether the victim's retribution and the international outcry in the wake of the attack would reassert state power and dissuade follow-on attacks?

While several of the previous authors in this volume have touched upon the future prospects of jihadists successfully using WMD, this chapter will explicitly address the question and seek to attend to it in greater detail. The chapter will begin with a discursion outlining the impediments to anticipating future threats in general and to predicting jihadist WMD use in particular, with the objective of setting the problem context. This will be followed by a brief survey of a variety of forecasting methodologies and the justification of the selection of expert elicitation using the Delphi Method. After bounding the problem with best- and worst-case scenarios, the format and content of the Delphi study that was performed on the threat of jihadists and WMD will be detailed. The results of the study will be analyzed at some length and compared with the bounding scenarios, after which tentative conclusions will be drawn regarding the nature of the future convergence of jihadists and WMD.

PERILS OF PREDICTION[7]

> Prediction is very difficult, especially about the future.
>
> **Niels Bohr (1885–1962)**

The future is an "undiscovered country," one that lies forever beyond the horizons of our perception and our present toils. It should be immediately apparent to all but the most solipsistic or fatalistic among us that uncertainties abound as we look further ahead in time, with myriad possibilities presenting themselves at each moment. While this should not be viewed as grounds for quiescence in the matter of trying to anticipate the threat of jihadists acquiring WMD, it is only by better understanding the impediments—both conceptual and practical—to accurate prediction of jihadist behavior that we can begin to address them and approach the threat more judiciously. The most important of these impediments are discussed below, separated into three types, reflecting different levels of specificity: (1) general obstacles to accurate forecasting, (2) problems inherent in anticipating human behavior, and (3) particular complications in the context of jihad and WMD terrorism.

Before turning to these impediments, two preliminary notes are warranted. First, it is important to draw a distinction between two generic types of prediction that occupy opposite ends of a continuum. "Strategic prediction" seeks to describe general trends and the existence and magnitude of future threats, whereas "point prediction" focuses on the precise nature of future events, such as their exact timing and location or the identities of the individuals involved. Generally speaking, while even strategic prediction is often extremely problematic, the closer one moves toward seeking point predictions, the more difficult the enterprise of anticipation becomes.

Second, it is almost axiomatic that as one extends the temporal range of one's forecast, there is a greater level of uncertainty and prediction is more complicated.[8] It is important, therefore, to select the range of our forecasts with care, so that we maximize the utility of a forecast by looking as far ahead as practically possible, while at the same time minimizing the attendant uncertainties by not seeking to gaze too far into the future. In light of these considerations, this chapter will focus on the more strategic aspects of the threat of jihadists acquiring and using WMD over the short to medium term (at most twenty-five years from the time of writing). It will leave the task of immediate, tactical-level threat anticipation and prevention to intelligence and law enforcement agencies, and the realm of the far future to the applications of futurists and other creatively prescient minds, although it will hopefully yield insights that can inform the work of both. Besides practical considerations, the key reason for this choice is that one of the broader purposes of this volume is to guide policy, and it is not always necessary to expend a large amount of resources on attaining point predictions, or exploring the long-distant future, when strategic predictions of the medium term will suffice to guide a particular policy direction.

General Forecasting Complexities

Fundamental Unpredictability of Certain Classes of Events

Most of us are aware of the basic epistemic distinction, highlighted recently by former U.S. Secretary of Defense Donald Rumsfeld, between "those things we know that we don't know" and "those things we don't know that we don't know," and we intuitively recognize that the latter present more of a problem than the former. However, both laypersons and policymakers often fail to realize that, when dealing with certain domains and systems, there are also things that we absolutely cannot know. At least since the work of Kurt Gödel,[9] philosophers and mathematicians have known that a complete description of some systems cannot be attained. Such concepts have only recently, however, begun to enter the social sciences and policy community, with notions of formal complexity[10] and "wicked" problems.[11] In this regard, Cynthia Kurtz and David Snowden[12] describe both the complex domain, in which patterns can emerge and be perceived but cannot be predicted, and the chaotic domain, which is devoid of cause and effect. If a threat or potential threat is situated in one of these domains, the best strategy is not to attempt to predict the specifics of an outcome, but rather to ameliorate the threat through a process of probing[13] or actions designed to restructure the environment in which the threat might arise. Jihadist terrorism, with its myriad interacting causes, dynamics, and effects, has many elements of a complex or wicked problem. We must remain open to the possibility, then, that at least parts of the threat we are considering may not even be forecastable in the traditional sense.

The Past as an Imperfect Indicator of the Future

Most attempts at the anticipation of future threats are based either implicitly or explicitly on extrapolations from past events. There is a variety of opinions on the utility of relying on past observables as indicators of future probabilities, ranging from viewing the past as an indispensable guide to the future to believing that concentrating on past experiences is, to quote the philosopher Nassim Nicholas Taleb, like "drivers looking through the rear view mirror while convinced they are looking ahead,"[14] so that we are blind to substantial future changes. The objective state of affairs probably lies somewhere in between.

On the one hand, the philosophers Thomas Hobbes and David Hume resolutely demonstrated the inherent perils of induction (deriving general rules from a finite number of observations). In this regard, every innovation in terrorist operations or tactics—for example, the advent of suicide bombers—can be viewed as disrupting a previous trend, thereby frustrating those who had extrapolated from tactics seen prior to the innovation. Then there is the added complication of large, sudden, and unexpected shocks to the system, what have been described variously as "black swans"[15] or "wild cards." New information, for example, that South Africa's former nuclear weapons program had produced more intact weapons than previously known and that these weapons had disappeared would represent a radical departure from previous expectations and necessitate a complete re-evaluation of the dynamics and probability of nuclear terrorism, as would the discovery of a (heretofore undreamt of) cheap and simple method of enriching uranium. A further complicating factor in relying on past experience is that recorded history is an imperfect guide—we often place undue reliance on past *observables*; that is, we impute causation to those factors that we are able to measure and for which we have data. Since many less tangible aspects of past cases of terrorism are not recorded (for instance, a deceased terrorist leader's true motivation for selecting CBRN over conventional weapons as opposed to what he told his followers), standard empirical analysis can lead to the development of false trend models and erroneous expectations of future events. Taking into account these caveats, it is no wonder that Brian Jenkins has argued that historical analysis provides no reliable basis for forecasting catastrophic terrorism involving WMD.[16]

On the other hand, while one would be foolish to view terrorism as in any way deterministic, it would be equally unwise to dismiss the lessons of our past experience completely. There are many social and behavioral trends that are both observable and consistent, and which can serve as a guide to anticipating future threats. Indeed, several behavioral disciplines, ranging from political science to criminology, rely heavily on the notion that the past bears some relevance to the future. While technologies and tactics might change prodigiously, many of the broader strategies, motivations, and operational requirements of terrorists remain essentially the same as those of the past. The so-called "new terrorism" that was much touted after 9/11 should therefore be regarded more in evolutionary as opposed to revolutionary terms, an argument championed by Martha Crenshaw.[17]

The difficulty arises in discerning—prior to employing either quantitative or qualitative inductive techniques—between those aspects of the past record of jihadist terrorism or CBRN materials that can be extrapolated and those that are no longer likely to apply. For those areas where the past is unlikely to offer any useful guidance, we need to explore the use of new, nonfrequentist, and nondeterministic methods of analysis.[18] In sum, past and present events can serve as one (not the only) guide to anticipating future terrorist attacks. Paying attention to current trends, while remaining sensitive to outlying possibilities and nonlinear dynamics, is thus a prudent strategy.

Signal versus Noise

The shrinking ratio of relevant signal to irrelevant noise is a more practical, although no less problematic, impediment to anticipating future threats. The maturation of the information revolution has not only meant that more information is available than ever before,[19] but also that new developments, be they propaganda videos from a remote terrorist hideout or maps of new genomes, can spread virally, and almost instantaneously, around the globe. The sheer volume of information makes it impractical for any individual to monitor every possible information source to detect early signs of impending disaster, even if we knew what signs to look for. Those seeking to predict future threats therefore must rely on information sharing, extensive collaboration, and automated tools. Unfortunately, none of these activities, whether alone or in combination, has thus far been implemented in a manner that would comprise a robust method for finding the needle of true threat in the haystack of superfluous data. Please see Chapter 9 for a more detailed discussion about these and other related issues.

Impediments to Forecasting Human Behavior

The obstacles to anticipating the future mentioned above can apply to all events, whether those brought about intentionally or disasters that are "naturally" occurring. There are, however, several aspects of intentional acts by human beings that make behavioral prediction especially difficult and that come into play in any consideration of terrorism. First, human threats are even more dynamic than natural processes (in the sense of being nonstochastic), in that human beings can adapt their behavior instantaneously, can strategize to avoid defenses, and can concentrate their efforts on vulnerabilities. Second, human beings display an exquisite diversity of action rarely observed in the natural world, with innovation a common occurrence among human adversaries. Lastly, while many natural processes are quite well understood and at least relatively well defined, the study of human mental processes is in many ways still a rather nascent endeavor, with few well-defined features and hardly any predictive tools with general application.

Added Complexity of Predicting Jihadist Terrorism Using WMD

In addition to the standard impediments to accurate forecasting, the threat of jihadists using WMD might present unique challenges to the predictive endeavor, since this threat lies at the nexus of two subjects—jihadist terrorism and weapons of mass destruction—that are both characterized by high levels of dynamism. To begin with, extreme behavior of any sort serves to exacerbate the baseline difficulties of predicting human behavior. Indeed, fewer actors demonstrate more extreme behavior than the current crop of jihadists who are driven by recondite interpretations of Shari'a and who must engage in constant organizational reinvention as a matter of survival. Their future intentions and actions are thus likely to prove more difficult to gauge than those of the majority of law-abiding citizens. Another obvious (though no less serious) complication related to jihadists stems from the fact that terrorists and many other dangerous actors, by their very nature, operate clandestinely, thus making proactive identification of one's subjects and subsequent data collection more difficult, say, than studying the prospective response of consumers to the addition of a new ingredient in laundry detergent.

Then there are the singular dynamics associated with the technologies underlying weapons of mass destruction. Many of these technologies are growing and maturing[20] at an exponential rate.[21] This is particularly noticeable in the life sciences, but similar breakthroughs are being made almost daily in fields as diverse as metallurgical engineering (including nano-assemblers and rapid prototyping) and chemical engineering (such as microreactors that can combine chemicals on a platform not much larger than the size of a microchip). If the rapid rate of technological development might result in future capabilities that look very different from those of today, we must be careful not to act like the proverbial generals fighting the last war by preparing to confront only past (or indeed present) threats. Just because no terrorist has ever synthesized a pathogen from scratch, this does not mean that it will not happen sometime in the near future.

Last, when looking at the threat of jihadists using WMD, the sample size of previous events is (thankfully) zero, which means that any extrapolations cannot even be based on the same dependent variable, but must rely on proxy measures, such as past unsuccessful jihadist plots involving WMD or past terrorist use of small-scale CBRN weapons. We must be especially cautious about using similar events as proxies, since the nonlinearity of the behaviors of interest means that the variance of outcomes presaged by indicators that differ only in seemingly minor aspects can be substantial.

It might appear that, with impediments such as undependable proxies that may or may not be indicative of future threats and the possibility of unforeseen factors that we do not or even cannot discern, the entire enterprise of attempting to forecast the behavior of jihadists involving WMD is stillborn. Yet this is hardly so. A diverse array of techniques has emerged in recent years to assist planners and policymakers in assessing the future, several of which will be noted in the following section. In fact, following Confucius' dictum that "real knowledge is to know the extent of one's ignorance," we are now far better equipped to engage in that activity of forecasting, so long as we bear the following in mind:

1. We should not ignore current trends, but must approach them judiciously by admitting the possibility of outliers and maintaining a healthy index of suspicion regarding rapid changes.
2. We need to meticulously monitor the dynamics of our adversaries, looking for early indicators of change in patterns of behavior. For instance, we need to pay more attention to prevailing currents of jihadist ideology for signs of major shifts in the permissibility or appeal of certain tactics.
3. Once we come to terms with the fact that uncertainty is a pervasive element in any predictive effort, we can manage the uncertainty by incorporating it into our strategies and policies, rather than attempting to minimize or eliminate it.

EXPERT ELICITATION AS A FORECASTING TOOL AND THE DELPHI METHOD

While none of the methods that have been devised to forecast future events succeed in completely overcoming the obstacles described in the previous section, several of these methods have attained high levels of forecasting accuracy in certain circumscribed contexts. The skill is to be found in selecting which of the variety of methodologies is most appropriate for a given forecasting domain.[22] Extant methods can be divided into three major categories: quantitative methods, judgmental methods, and forecast simulations,[23] and the initial selection must be between these broad categories.

Generally speaking, quantitative methods (such as multivariate regression and extrapolation of time-series data) are preferred to the more qualitative judgmental methods (including expert opinions, profiling, and analogy by case study) since they have historically provided greater accuracy, either alone or in conjunction with judgmental methods, than judgmental methods alone.[24] However, the use of quantitative methods is predicated on the availability of sufficient empirical data. As mentioned above, we are fortunate that there have not been any true WMD attacks by jihadists, but this also means, in the language of the statistical sciences, that we have no variation on our dependent variable. The most we can analyze statistically is attempts to use CBRN weapons (not necessarily WMD) by jihadists, a task ably carried out by Asal and Rethemeyer in this volume (Chapter 13) and therefore not attempted here. Moreover, such analyses do not take into account future discontinuities that might diverge significantly from past experience.

Simulations include a variety of computational-based approaches such as neural networks or agent-based models. Although computational models of terrorist behavior have received significant attention in the past five years,[25] using computationally based simulations for forecasting—as opposed to theory-building or other purposes—is the most challenging application of such simulations and is still in the early stages of development and validation.

This leaves only judgmental methods. In selecting which of the many judgmental forecasting techniques to employ, emphasis was placed on the principle[26] that structured methods generally are to be favored over unstructured methods.[27] Of the structured judgmental methods, only three are candidates for use: formal expert elicitation, simulated interactions (a structural form of role-playing or red-teaming), and judgmental bootstrapping.[28] Judgmental bootstrapping, a promising technique that involves modeling the choices of experts to ensure greater consistency, is inapplicable here because it requires multiple forecasts by each expert on the same dependent variable in order to build the models, which is not practical in the case of analyzing prospects for an extremely rare event like the use by jihadists of WMD. This chapter will leave simulated interactions and similar role-playing methods for further research. This means that the method selected for this preliminary exploration of the future direction of the threat of jihadists using WMD was formal expert elicitation, specifically the Delphi Method.

The Delphi Method, first developed by the RAND Corporation in the 1950s,[29] is a structured process for eliciting, refining, and combining the opinions of groups of experts. Its main features are anonymity of participants, iterated response and feedback, and statistical aggregation of expert responses.[30] Although there are many variants, the Delphi process generally involves having participant experts provide answers to a structured survey and then distributing the results (without attribution) to all the participants in order to expose the experts to a diversity of opinions and inputs. Each expert then completes the survey again, with the option of amending her answers and the process is repeated until a predefined stability criterion between rounds is reached. The Delphi Method enables experts in several different disciplines or specialties to contribute to a forecast whose problem area is "much broader in scope than the knowledge that any one of the individuals possesses,"[31] while at the same time avoiding many of the deleterious group dynamics (such as groupthink) that can pervade in-person discussions. While comparisons with traditional methods can be difficult, research into the accuracy of the Delphi Method has revealed that it proved a superior method of forecasting to single-round surveys or statistical groups in twelve studies but worse in two and was shown to be more accurate over traditional group meetings of experts in five studies to one with two ties.[32]

The only recent related study surveying experts was a single-round (non-Delphi) survey conducted under the auspices of Senator Richard Lugar in 2005,[33] which polled eighty-five nonproliferation and international security experts on their estimates regarding nonproliferation-related issues within the short and medium terms.[34] While the survey was concerned with large-scale CBRN attacks by terrorists, it did not distinguish among potential perpetrators (and consequently did not include separate estimates for jihadists) and was focused on nonproliferation issues—primarily the means by which terrorists could acquire these weapons—rather than on how the weapons would be used. Nonetheless, several of the items in the Lugar survey are sufficiently similar to the survey described below so as to allow for comparison and will be mentioned in the discussion of the results of the Delphi survey.

POINTS OF REFERENCE

Prior to describing the Delphi survey that was conducted to address the question of the likelihood of jihadists using WMD, it is necessary to create a context within which we can orient any results we obtain. This will be accomplished by constructing two extreme hypothetical scenarios[35] extending forward a quarter of a century into the future, which represent extremely pernicious and sanguine pictures, respectively, of developments involving jihadists and WMD. In order to create a plausible narrative, each scenario (for convenience labeled "Worst-Case" and "Best-Case") will be written in the form of a retrospective account set in 2032. It is important to note that at this stage I am not suggesting that either of these scenarios is at all likely, merely that they can be used as reference points highlighting salient aspects of jihadist WMD terrorism against which the results obtained from the expert elicitation can be compared.

Worst-Case Scenario: The Wasteland of WMD Jihad

Dateline: December 12, 2032

It is difficult to imagine the world as it was at the turn of the twenty-first century. Our hopes were rooted in technological progress; a prosperous, globalized world; and, above all, trust in the robustness of our way of life. How arrogant that now seems. Little did we know that the shocking attacks of September 11, 2001 would turn out to be merely a prelude to a relentless assault on ourselves and our society. As the fever of jihadism spread inexorably throughout the first two decades of the twenty-first century, more and more of our own countrymen were drawn to that hateful path, joining millions of alienated and angry fanatics who had come to believe that only by utterly destroying the infidel and his way of life could salvation for the Ummah be achieved. Soon it was not only the dispossessed and the destitute who made up the majority of jihadist ranks, but also those raised and educated in the cream of our institutions of higher learning. And these highly skilled recruits had much raw material upon which they could focus their technical expertise in pursuit of a global caliphate. A combination of inadequate safeguards, institutional inertia, and willful ignorance to the magnitude of the threat meant that the political and corporate leaders of the world did far too little to secure the most dangerous materials, allowing toxic chemicals, harmful biotechnology, and even fissile materials to fall into the hands of the jihadists. Petty politics and bureaucratic bungling meant that our defenses proved woefully inadequate. In hindsight it seems almost inevitable that our implacable enemies would soon succeed in visiting death and destruction upon us on a previously undreamt of scale. The first attacks by homegrown extremists involving the release of noxious gases from our chemical plants were both simple and brutally effective, poisoning thousands. No sooner had we acted to secure these facilities than we were struck by campaigns of radiological terrorism in 2012 that destroyed our economy and rendered some of our most productive city centers uninhabitable. Although the initial few bioattacks were crude contaminations that were more of a nuisance than anything else, our enemies were getting better at their game all the time and the pneumonic plague epidemic that ravaged our northwest in 2019 took even our vaunted intelligence agencies by surprise. Our clumsy attempts at retribution only inflamed the jihad further. Yet still we managed to somehow limp along, despite the riots, the detentions without trial, and the states of emergency. That was until last month, when Yusif al-Libi and his followers detonated their "al-Rasul" weapon, a gun-type HEU bomb that destroyed most of the Hague. We are still trying to come to grips with the idea that the jihadists have successfully launched a nuclear attack and are now promising to "rain fire upon the heads of the Great Satan" in a final push to destroy us. Fear is almost palpable and nobody believes the assurances of the government that they can protect us. How much more can we take before the nation breaks apart at the seams and we descend into anarchy? Perhaps we should just give up and accept their terms.

Best-Case Scenario: WMD Jihad Confined

Dateline: December 12, 2032

Vigilance. It is a guiding principle that has served us well as we enter the second third of the twenty-first century. Yes, there have been setbacks and sacrifices, and we are not out of the woods yet, but we have largely succeeded in containing the first major challenge to international security of the third millennium. The jihadist attacks of September 11, 2001 were a tragic wakeup call, and it took us almost another decade to rethink our strategies, but the prospect of our enemies inflicting massive death and destruction on our society spurred our leaders and ourselves toward confronting the threat head-on. After a shaky start, our intelligence and law enforcement agencies in collaboration with their international counterparts spearheaded major counterterrorism successes, apprehending the leadership of al-Qa'ida and routing its followers from Pakistan. When we subsequently discovered their reconstituted CBRN weapons programs, the world's leaders vowed never again to allow the jihadists to ensconce themselves in ungoverned spaces and instituted the largest international development campaign in history to deprive the jihadists of safe havens. At the same time, a massive ideological effort was underway to counter the tide of radicalization, enlisting the assistance of several prominent Islamic theologians. We realized, however, that the more fanatic of our enemies would be frustrated by their reversals and would attempt to even the score asymmetrically by stepping up their efforts to acquire CBRN weapons. This is why the global initiative to secure all dangerous CBRN materials was devised, completely rewriting old nonproliferation regimes to the extent that the new term of "deproliferation" was coined to describe the dramatic reduction in fissile material, orphan radiological sources, and chemical weapons that was achieved by 2015. By that time, our national laboratories had developed a new suite of technologies to detect and counter unconventional weapons of all types, and within a few years these sentinels were positioned in a multilayered defense surrounding the homeland. Our enemies did not give up, of course—they attempted to launch a number of disruptive chemical and radiological attacks. However, each of these was an abject failure, either being interdicted at an early stage or causing fewer casualties than a simple suicide bomber. The fact that our society had been working at becoming more resilient also helped to blunt their efforts. Many jihadists abandoned the cause and those that persevered were reduced to using homemade explosives in attacks that were little more advanced than those of a century earlier. While we must remain watchful, it seems that the threat of jihadists launching a devastating WMD attack is on the wane; they are losing support everywhere and by giving them little room for maneuver, the fanatics are unlikely to have the luxury of being able to pursue WMD seriously. Even if they somehow got lucky and stumbled across a viable weapon, they would still have a daunting task of getting through the multiple layers of passive and active detection we have established. The world can now get on with the task of ushering in a new era of prosperity and global harmony.

The above passages may seem fanciful, but that is the point. They provide the parameters for a continuum of possible futures along which we can situate the results of the Delphi study, which represents the experts' estimates of what we are most likely to face in terms of jihadists and WMD.

FUTURE OF JIHADISTS AND WMD DELPHI STUDY

Once Delphi was selected as the most appropriate method by which to elicit expert opinion about the future of the jihadist WMD threat, it was necessary to enunciate the goals of the study, to determine the nature and identities of the participants, and to develop the survey instrument. The goals of the Delphi study were fairly straightforward:

- To assess current expert opinion in a structured manner regarding the probability of jihadists using WMD in the future
- To delve more deeply into the motivational and capability-related drivers of these probabilities
- To determine the anticipated method of attack (agent used, means of delivery, location, and target type)
- To situate all these answers within the larger contexts of nonstate WMD use and the threat posed by jihadism
- To include methodological checks for consistency and bias amongst responses.

In selecting participants, the literature on Delphi recommends using between five and twenty experts as well as participants whose expertise is sufficiently heterogeneous so as to cover all the dimensions of the problem space.[36] The most logical participants were the set of authors who had contributed to this book, because they had spent time and effort researching and thinking about the problem of jihadists and WMD from a variety of perspectives. However, in order to ensure as broad a diversity of opinions as possible, a number of additional participants with expertise in this area who were not involved in the current project were invited. The final set of respondents reflected expertise in both the jihadist terrorist threat and the technical aspects of CBRN weapons and represented a variety of academic disciplines, including political science, international relations, history, social psychology, physics, chemistry, and biology. It also included experts from both the research and practitioner communities dealing with terrorism and WMD. Thirty experts were invited to participate and twenty persons participated in at least one round. The first round received nineteen responses and the second round fourteen responses, with thirteen participants taking part in both rounds. A complete list of participants and their affiliations at the time of writing is given in Appendix 1.[37]

As a structured elicitation method, the formulation of a Delphi survey instrument is central to the success of the exercise. Decades of use of the Delphi Method have led to the development of a number of principles in this regard, as many as possible of which were incorporated into the survey development process. The survey itself consisted of a set of instructions (see Appendix 2) and twenty-five items designed to address the above goals (see Appendix 3). Several of the questions were variants of previous questions addressing different time periods. These questions utilized three time horizons, which I loosely refer to as the "short term" (from the present to five years' time), the "medium term" (five to ten years' time), and the "longer term" (ten to twenty-five years' time). While it would have been optimal to cover each time period for each question and to ask participants to provide separate responses for each CBRN weapon type where applicable, there was a need to balance comprehensiveness against the time constraints of the participants, many of whom are prominent scholars or officials with limited time to participate in such an exercise. Therefore, the decision was taken to cover successive time periods only for those items whose temporal dynamics were believed to be key elements of the analysis. Other items were either presented without a temporal dimension or sought estimates on the initial attack occurrence only. In addition, for weapon-specific items, participants were instructed to supply answers relating to the weapon type with which they were most familiar, rather than having each participant provide responses for each weapon type. This had the obvious result of providing a smaller sample size for each weapon type for these items.

Delphi scholars have emphasized the need to properly establish the problem context, in order to provide reference points against which participants can orient their responses.[38] This was accomplished in the survey via three mechanisms. First, the instructions given to participants provided explicit definitions of terms used in the survey in order to avoid ambiguity or the problem of different participants answering the same question in different ways. Second, the initial items in the survey sought probabilities for related events, such as general WMD terrorist attacks, smaller scale jihadist CBRN uses, and general mass casualty attacks by jihadists, in order to provide a relative mental context for the key question of jihadist WMD use. Third, items were included that specifically prompted respondents to reconsider and expand upon their previous responses from different perspectives.[39]

Another important aspect is the elicitation of subjective probabilities, a task that many participants (particularly those coming from a more qualitative background) might find difficult.[40] The survey instructions thus included examples of how such subjective probabilities can be construed. Furthermore, participants were requested to provide rationales for all of their estimates, which has been argued to increase the effectiveness of Delphi surveys.[41] Since it is important to avoid framing effects and to ensure that the questions are posed unambiguously,[42] the questions were stated as succinctly as possible, giving explanations as necessary. The survey was also pretested by two volunteers (who were not participants) in order to illuminate any items that required modification or descriptions that required clarification. Lastly, a number of checks were built into the survey[43] so that internal inconsistencies and bias could be detected within the responses. For example, if the participant responded consistently, the probability supplied for item 6 must be less than or equal to the probability supplied for item 1. Also, it was possible to detect (although not prove) signs of potential bias by comparing the relative probability rankings of weapons types supplied in item 10 with the weapon type with which the participant stated they were most familiar (extracted from items 20 through 24).[44]

The Delphi study was carried out between January and March 2008 using Delphi Decision Aid, an online tool developed by J. Scott Armstrong and supported by the International Institute of Forecasters[45] that administers the surveys and aggregates results. The survey instructions were sent to all participants and these instructions set a deadline for the completion of the first round. Once the first round was complete, the results were aggregated and both the aggregate and anonymized individual results were distributed to participants, along with all comments provided by participants (also anonymized). Participants were given the opportunity to review the first-round results and retake the survey, making any modifications they deemed necessary to their previous estimates. Six experts who participated in round 1 chose not to participate in the second round, whereas one new expert who had been unable to participate in the first round, joined the study in round 2. After the second round, the results of both rounds were compared and, despite the participant changes, there were no appreciable differences in the aggregate results.[46] Taking this into account, as well as the time constraints of participants and the observed rate of attrition between the first two rounds, it was therefore decided to terminate the study after two rounds and utilize the results of the second round.

In keeping with standard Delphi practice,[47] each expert's estimates were weighted equally and aggregated for each item. At the same time consistency and bias checks were performed on each individual's responses and on the aggregate estimate. Of the 320 total responses given, there were only three responses displaying clear-cut logical inconsistency and six suspect responses that may or may not have been inconsistent. There were no obvious signs of respondent bias detected. These results give a certain degree of confidence that participants offered reasoned, coherent responses and that the exercise possesses at least some internal validity. The descriptive statistics and frequency distributions of second-round responses for each question are presented in Appendix C.

DISCUSSION OF RESULTS

Broader Jihadist and WMD Terrorism Contexts

On the question of a WMD attack (irrespective of the identity of the perpetrator) within the next ten years, the experts were split almost evenly into three groups. One group generally rated the possibility of a genuine WMD attack as low (between 0% and 20%), with members referencing a high cost-to-benefit ratio, including a lack of sufficient incentives relative to other weapons, as well as increased attention by security forces worldwide after 9/11. At the other end of the scale, a second group placed the probability at 90 percent or more, implying that the past history of CBRN use and strong motivation mean that at least one terrorist group will likely succeed in attaining and using a weapon that will cause mass disruption, if not necessarily mass casualties. The members of the third group occupied the middle ground and estimated this probability to be close to half, citing global security uncertainties and technological diffusion coupled with the relative ease of producing certain mass effect weapons. Unsurprisingly, therefore, both the mean (53%[48]) and median (50%) probabilities hovered about the midpoint, with a comparatively large standard deviation. This distribution of estimates also reflects in many ways the ongoing debate and uncertainty within both scholarly and policy circles about prospects for witnessing WMD terrorism in the medium term. The median and mean values are somewhat higher than the results for any of the CBRN weapon types in the Lugar survey,[49] although the Lugar survey dealt with each type of attack separately. It is worthwhile to note that in the Delphi study only one expert placed this probability at under 5 percent. Even a one in twenty chance of an attack within the next decade translates into a huge risk[50] when one accounts for the tremendous physical, social, and/or economic consequences of a WMD attack. So, a near consensus amongst a variety of experts lends some credence to the argument that WMD terrorism is a sufficient threat so as to warrant considerable investment in prevention, protection, and response.

There is far more convergence when one looks at estimates of the most likely perpetrators of a WMD attack. The participants overwhelmingly rated Sunni jihadists as the biggest threat within a ten-year period (ranked number one out of thirteen possible perpetrator types by almost three-quarters of participants), followed by apocalyptic cults, Shi'i jihadists, and "lone wolves" (idiosyncratic, disgruntled, or mentally ill individuals). These top four ranked perpetrator types did not change across rounds. The prominence of Sunni jihadists in threat estimates for WMD appears to reflect an appreciation within respondents' comments of the general threat of terrorism stemming from this ideological front, the Sunni jihadists' avid interest in WMD, and the purported disincentives for WMD use amongst secular groups who calibrate their actions to achieve limited political goals and to avoid alienating their social constituencies. One respondent observed that opportunity might play a large role, so that were almost any type of actor to "stumble" upon a WMD capability, they would entertain the possibility of using WMD, thus lending even more uncertainty to the future of the threat. It is also interesting to note that the likelihood of WMD use taking the form of an overt attack by a state (i.e., the traditional military use of WMD) was on average ranked quite low (ninth on the list), which mirrors the results (given for nuclear weapons only) in the Lugar survey.[51]

The focus of the survey next moved to considering the context of jihadist actions exclusively. Setting aside the question of what kinds of weapons might be used and focusing on the physical scale of the attack, the experts' estimates of any mass casualty attack by jihadists evidence a plurality of opinion and break down into similar groups to those seen for the general WMD question. However, in this case, the mean (67%) and median (80%) are far higher, signifying that more experts are confident that there will be at least one attack by jihadists within the next ten years that results in more than 1,000 casualties. This reflects the widely held belief that, despite the best efforts of counterterrorist forces, there is sufficient motivation and capability among jihadists that they will very likely succeed in their mass casualty ambitions (over the two rounds, there were five instances where this was rated as a certainty!). The vulnerability of populations, especially in less-developed areas of the world, was noted as a factor in generating an estimate. Nonetheless, at least one expert viewed the September 11 attacks as an exceptional event unlikely to be repeated on the same scale. When exploring the complementary case—CBRN use by jihadists within a decade, irrespective of the scale of the attack—with the exception of two outliers, the majority of participants estimated this probability as very high, with a large mean (75%) and median (80%). This accords with the past interest in and numerous attempts to develop CBRN weapons by jihadists, even though some observers believe that their capability will not reach the WMD level.

Future Jihadist Use of WMD

Respondents were asked to estimate the probability of at least one genuine WMD attack committed by jihadists within first a five-year, then a ten-year, and finally a twenty-five–year period. Figure 14.1 shows the means and medians of respondent estimates for each of these periods. These results are illuminating. First, the majority of respondents foresee at least an appreciable probability of jihadists succeeding in perpetrating a WMD attack in the short term (only one respondent rated the probability as less than 5%). Second, as is apparent from many of the individual chapters in this volume, there is almost unanimous consent that the threat will continue to grow over time. Lastly, while the estimates exhibit a fair degree of diversity, no estimate for the five- or ten-year period exceeded 75 percent, whereas more than half of the estimates within the twenty-five–year period were greater than 80 percent (a right-skewed distribution). While this undoubtedly reflects in part the unequal intervals of the different periods, it also shows that most experts expect the probability of a jihadist WMD attack to rise dramatically between ten and twenty-five years' time. Some of the factors that the experts considered might add to the probability of jihadists using WMD were progression up the learning curve in terms of capabilities, the success of the "global war on terror" forcing jihadists into new modes of attack, the rate of technology diffusion, the observation that al-Qa'ida is prepared to bide their time for long periods between major attacks, the continued spread of jihadist ideology, and instability within states that possess CBRN materials or weapons. The factors that were

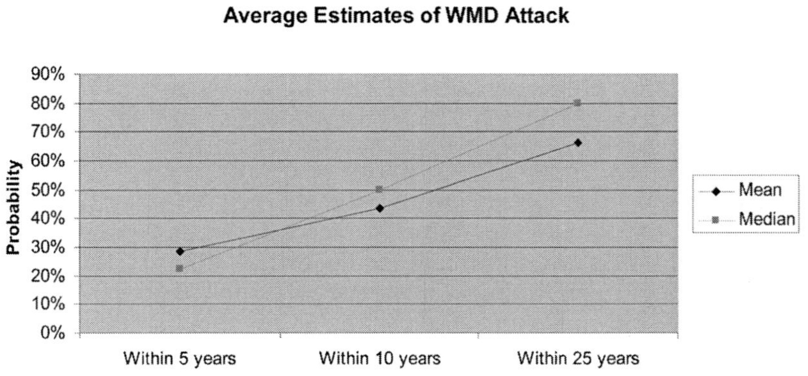

FIGURE 14.1 **Estimates of probabilities of jihadist WMD attacks.**

listed as decreasing the probability of WMD attack included persistent technical obstacles, strategic disincentives for using WMD, the continuation of propaganda benefits that have accrued to jihadists after the 9/11 attacks, and the possibility of moderation within the jihadist movement over time.

In an attempt to address the black swan problem and introduce the possibility of radical departures from current trends, participants were requested to list those events that—despite the participant's belief that the events would not occur[52]—would either substantially increase or decrease the probabilities of jihadists launching a WMD attack within the given timeframes. The suggestions for events that would increase the baseline probabilities fell into three categories: (1) events related to the actions of the jihadists themselves or new evidence about their activities (such as the catalytic influence of a successful WMD attack or near-successful attempt, evidence of close collaboration with international organized crime, or evidence of the successful recruitment of highly competent scientists); (2) events related to the actions and status of governments, particularly the decisions of the United States (such as a U.S. invasion of Iran or occupation of any more Islamic lands, state collapse in Pakistan or North Korea, or the complete breakdown of nonproliferation regimes); and (3) events related to the global physical, technological, and social environment (for example, faster-than-expected diffusion of advanced biotechnologies to the developing world or global economic depression). Participant suggestions for unlikely but "game-changing" events that would lessen the probability of a successful WMD use by jihadists fell into the same three categories: (1) events related to the actions of the jihadists themselves or new evidence about their activities (such as an ideological moderation within the jihadist movement, evidence of repeated jihadist failures to make WMD work, or a set of high-profile *fatwas* by respected clerics denouncing the use of WMD); (2) events related to the actions and status of governments, particularly the decisions of the United States (including a complete U.S. withdrawal from the Middle East, a sudden reduction in global stockpiles of nuclear arms and fissile material or the complete annihilation of the jihadist leadership); and (3) events related to the global physical, technological, and social environment (including scientific and technical breakthroughs in CBRN countermeasures that negate the danger of these weapons, increased societal resilience to WMD, or successful programs preventing radicalization globally). It must be reiterated that none of these events, whether those increasing or decreasing the baseline probabilities, were believed to be likely to occur by the participants; hence their appearance would be regarded as unexpected and discontinuous.

Another set of questions attempted to broach second-order effects by asking the respondents to estimate the number of WMD attacks by jihadists within the next five years, between five and ten years, and between ten and twenty-five years, respectively.[53] Answers were given on an ordinal scale and the median across experts for all three periods was between one and ten WMD attacks. However, for the second five- to ten-year period, there were fewer experts who believed that no attacks would occur, and for the ten- to twenty-five–year period, there were four experts who believed that there would be between ten and fifty WMD attacks by jihadists. Participant comments stressed two important ideas in this regard. First, that in the longer term, jihadists will likely have accumulated sufficient know-how and materials to be able to competently conduct at least large-impact chemical, biological, and radiological attacks, although achieving the level of a WMD will always remain a fairly difficult endeavor. Second, that the total number of attacks over the entire twenty-five–year period is very much dependent on the outcome and repercussions of the first true WMD attacks by jihadists. On the one hand, there will almost certainly be a tremendous reaction by the targeted state, both in terms of retribution against the jihadists and in terms of its own defensive posture, both of which might make further attacks more difficult. On the other hand, if the initial attacks are perceived by jihadists to fulfill their tactical and strategic goals, then copycat actions may be stimulated, increasing the motivation to conduct WMD attacks, at the same time as learning effects, as well as knowledge and material proliferation, increase jihadist capabilities, leading to a rise in the number of WMD attacks.

Tactical and Operational Choices

One of the most important questions for policymakers and those responsible for defending against WMD attacks is how to apportion preventative, defensive, and response resources to different manifestations of the WMD threat, and a large portion of the survey was designed to elicit such operationally useful details. The most obvious point of departure is to rank the relative likelihood of attack using the different weapon types (biological, chemical, nuclear, and radiological) over the short (0–5 years), medium (5–10 years), and longer (10–25 years) terms. For the first and second five-year periods, on average chemical weapons were believed to be the most likely to be used, followed by radiological weapons, biological weapons, and lastly nuclear weapons.[54] Over three-quarters of the experts ranked a chemical attack as the most likely for the next ten years, especially the dangers of jihadists releasing toxic industrial chemicals (TICs). Participants stated that they had arrived at the relative rankings by considering a combination of the availability of weapons materials and the technical knowledge and infrastructure required to weaponize the agents. Several experts believe that biological weapons will become more practicable over a ten-year period as a result of improvements in biotechnology, but that chemical weapons attacks would still predominate. Between ten and twenty-five years, however, the ranking changes: Chemical weapons are still ranked first, but now bioterrorism is ranked before radiological weapons, which might have become too rudimentary an attack for sophisticated jihadists by that stage. The use of nuclear weapons, although still ranked last overall, was ranked higher by certain experts than in the earlier periods. The overall distribution for the longer term period was a lot "flatter," signifying a greater level of disagreement among the estimates.

Two items were included to explore the earlier stages in the attack chain prior to the actual use of WMD. The first asked participants to select whether, for the weapons type with which the participant was most familiar, they believed jihadists would be more likely to procure a ready-made weapon or to manufacture their own weapon within the next ten years. The estimates were overwhelmingly in favor of terrorists manufacturing their own weapons in the case of chemical weapons and also showed a preference for indigenous production of radiological, biological, and nuclear weapons,[55] although each of these latter weapons types were addressed by only one or two participants. The general consensus seemed to be that ready-made weapons reduced the chances of interdiction or disruption of the plot and allowed for greater reliability from the terrorists' point of view. Similarly, a second item queried whether, within a ten-year timeframe, jihadists would be more likely to procure or manufacture a weapon in the same country as the intended target, or to procure or manufacture the weapon somewhere else and then transport it across international borders into the target country. Here opinions varied considerably across weapon types. For chemical weapons, the majority of experts believed that it was simpler for jihadists to utilize the chemical precursors or the toxic industrial chemicals available within the target country to constitute their weapon. On the other hand, the ease of concealing biological agents was believed to make it more likely for the attackers to develop and test the weapon in a safe haven and then to transport it to the target state, although the dissemination mechanism might be constructed within the target state. For radiological weapons, experts were more uncertain, but came down on the side of acquisition inside the target country within a ten-year period. Opinions related to nuclear weapons were evenly split.

The next operationally relevant variable upon which estimates were elicited was the location of the first WMD attack by jihadists. The region viewed by the greatest number of experts as the most likely target of an initial attack was Western Europe, followed by Eastern Europe (including Russia) and the Middle East. Many experts felt that although most jihadists would like to attack the United States first, it would present a more difficult target to attack and that a combination of easier access to materials, easier delivery routes, and larger indigenous Muslim populations would make Western Europe a more likely first target than the United States. The animosity of the Chechens toward Russia and the poor security of Russian weapons stocks were cited as reasons for selecting Eastern Europe as the second most likely target.

In terms of the delivery mechanism most likely to be used in a WMD attack by jihadists, this is obviously not independent from the weapon type each expert believed was most likely. Delivery via an explosion was favored by most experts. Besides explosives being the only delivery method for a nuclear weapon and the optimal means of disposing radiological material (in the form of an RDD), experts pointed to motivational factors, such as jihadists' purported desire for a "big bang" and the fact that they are already familiar with explosives. The next most commonly selected delivery mechanisms were aerosol release (especially from an attack involving TICs) and the contamination of food, water supplies, or consumer products, which was described as being relatively easy to accomplish.

Experts were requested to rank the types of targets that they believed would be most likely to be chosen by jihadists for an initial WMD attack. Transportation systems, with their previous track record as a favorite target of jihadists, their decentralized vulnerabilities, their importance as an infrastructure in daily life, and their inherent ability to disperse the harm caused by a chemical, biological, or radiological weapon over a large area, were ranked as the most likely target, followed by an enclosed area and then defined open areas. It was asserted by several participants that widespread locales were an unlikely target for an initial attack since a more sophisticated capability is required in order to deliver chemical or biological agents effectively over large, open areas. A few experts argued that it was the symbolic or political value of a particular target that would drive target selection rather than any practical concerns associated with the delivery of the weapon, and consequently that the type of target would vary according to this criterion rather than any single target type being generally preferred.

Evolving Nature of Motivation and Capabilities

In order for a threat—in the sense of the intentional infliction of harm[56]—to exist, there must be at least one human actor who is both willing and able to inflict the type of harm under consideration. Although we have already discussed experts' assessments of the overall risk[57] in terms of the probability of a successful jihadist attack with WMD, the survey delved more deeply into the constituent parts of the threat in an attempt to gain greater insight into how jihadist actions might evolve over the next quarter-century. The matter of motivation was addressed by asking participants for their belief as to whether the number of jihadists willing to use WMD would increase, decrease, or remain the same over a ten-year period. More than two-thirds of the participants believed that there would be more jihadists motivated to use WMD in ten years' time, less than a third believed that the number would remain the same as at present, and no participants believed that the number would decrease. A few experts declined to offer an opinion owing to the large amount of uncertainty involved. Some of the participants who advocated an increasing number of jihadists willing to use WMD based their decision on an increase in the number of jihadists overall as radicalization spreads, with one participant identifying third- and fourth-generation jihadists as particularly virulent and less cautious. Others raised the argument that, irrespective of changes in the total number of jihadists, as jihadists begin to realize that existing methods of attack are not able to fulfill their broader objectives, frustration will lead more jihadists to look toward WMD. Part of the reasoning of those choosing the "remain the same" option was the idea that the number of jihadists willing to use WMD is dependent on fundamental factors in the political, economic, and religious environment that are unlikely to change much within ten years.

Capabilities were approached differently. Within a milieu as closely networked as that of jihadists, capabilities are likely to take on a threshold character, meaning that once a certain capability has been attained, it is likely to persist and diffuse throughout the movement. This makes it less useful to ask participants to estimate the probability that a particular capability threshold will be breached within a given period—we are more interested in how long it will be before the threshold is reached. Therefore, participants were asked to supply a date by which time they believed that it was more likely than not (i.e., a probability of over 50%) that jihadists would attain a certain capability. As noted previously, participants were only asked to supply data for the weapon type with which they were most familiar.

The first capability threshold described was that of successful access to the required raw materials and equipment needed to construct a weapon that would qualify as a WMD. The raw materials and equipment for radiological weapons were estimated to be available right now. Those for chemical weapons were estimated to become available sometime between now and 2010, especially in the case of toxic industrial chemicals, which already exist in large quantities in industrial facilities. Estimates for the likely availability of materials and equipment for biological weapons were also concentrated over the next few years, while the materials for nuclear weapons were felt to be the most difficult to acquire, becoming more likely than not to be available to jihadists only after 2015.

In terms of the technical skills and personnel required to produce viable WMD, in the case of radiological weapons, the experts again felt that jihadists are likely to already possess this capability. For chemical weapons, the experts estimated a latest date of 2010, if not earlier, and on average the biological weapons skills and personnel were estimated as likely becoming available sometime within the next five years. The largest obstacle to producing a nuclear weapon is believed to be the acquisition of fissile material, with many commentators believing that jihadists could conceivably construct a working weapon today if they had the requisite material.[58] In any event, the experts in the survey believed by 2015 jihadists would be more likely than not to have this capability.

The last area of jihadist capabilities investigated in the study was the broader logistical infrastructure (including funding) required to ensure that a WMD would be successfully constructed, stored, and transported to its target. For chemical, biological, and radiological weapons, the participants generally agreed that the support structures are likely to be in place within the next few years, if they are not in place already. The infrastructure to support the construction of a nuclear weapon might take a few years longer, but also might already be in place. In short, many of the experts believed that as long as jihadists maintain their safe havens in Pakistan, Southeast Asia, and elsewhere, the logistical requirements for WMD are likely to be met, although there was some mention that successful counterterrorist activities, especially in these regions, might decrease the jihadists' logistical capabilities.

Two points related to the estimates of probability for jihadist capabilities are worth mentioning. The first is that participants were only asked to estimate by what date jihadists would likely be able to produce their own weapon. Jihadists might also be able to acquire intact WMDs through theft, gift, or purchase, the probability of which is extremely difficult to estimate and thus was not put to participants. Nonetheless, all the date estimates for capability acquisition described above could be brought forward considerably if terrorists succeed in acquiring an operational weapon from an external source. The second point relates to the interdependence between motivations and capabilities. Even though, for the purposes of this study, they were presented as separate items in the survey, we should not forget that not only can motivation drive the acquisition of the required capabilities to engage in WMD terrorism, but that capabilities can in turn influence motivation. If, for example, technological developments make it substantially easier to produce certain biological weapons, this might make such weapons more attractive to jihadists, or if jihadists happen to stumble upon an intact chemical or nuclear weapon, this would certainly affect their choice of which weapon they are likely to use in a WMD attack.

Mortality and Morbidity

Although the actual consequences of a jihadist WMD attack would involve numerous uncertainties that were not elucidated in this study, the participants were asked to estimate the total number of physical casualties (including fatalities and injuries) that they believed would result from jihadist WMD attacks within the next twenty-five years. Their responses can be viewed to some degree as a proxy for their perceptions of the overall seriousness of the threat. The median response was the range between 5,000 and 25,000 casualties, with three respondents each selecting the 1 to 5,000 interval and the 25,000 to 100,000 interval. Only one respondent believed that jihadists would inflict no casualties using WMD over this period. So, while no participants viewed the jihadist threat as existential for the West in a physical sense, most believed that the threat from this quarter would result in significant numbers of dead and wounded.

CONCLUSION

The results of the Delphi study are sobering. A panel of experts participating in a structured elicitation has collectively estimated that the probability of jihadists successfully perpetrating a WMD attack within the next twenty-five years is substantial, and that this probability will increase as time passes. Jihadists are perceived as already having the motivation and either presently or in the near future will likely have the capability to engage in at least some forms of WMD terrorism. Moreover, the majority of experts believe that there will likely be more than one WMD attack by jihadists over the next twenty-five years and that at least several thousand people will be harmed in these attacks. This would seem to put the forecast of experts far closer to the worst-case scenario described above than to the best-case end of the spectrum.

The study also revealed new information that could potentially be utilized to better counter the threat. It yielded several operational insights, from the ranking of the most likely types of weapons jihadists might use (chemical, followed in second place by radiological in the near term and biological in the longer term), to at least a partial consensus on the most likely location (Western Europe) and type (transportation system) of the initial target. It has also revealed that most of the experts agree that jihadists are more likely to manufacture their own weapons than to attempt to purchase or steal them.

Lastly, by making explicit the assumptions underlying the expert judgments as well as identifying factors that would increase or decrease the threat of WMD terrorism by jihadists, the forecast has provided us with a set of potential loci around which to concentrate policy. By paying attention to both the trends and the black swans that have emerged from the Delphi study, we can attempt to structure the external environment and our actions within it to make the negative trends and discontinuities less likely and the positive ones more so. For example, understanding the role that might be played by *fatwas* outlawing the use of WMD might allow us to prioritize our counter-WMD efforts.

It must be emphasized that the Delphi study represents only a preliminary attempt to investigate the future relationship between jihadists and WMD and should be supplemented by other methods. Moreover, the domain in which this problem rests is highly dynamic, and this necessitates a constant re-evaluation of any estimates, so at the minimum the study needs to be repeated periodically. Nonetheless, the results thus far indicate a certain momentum attached to the future threat of jihadists using WMD, which is likely to continue to grow in the absence of any countervailing developments.

APPENDIX 1

EXPERTS PARTICIPATING IN DELPHI SURVEY

Gary Ackerman, National Consortium for the Study of Terrorism and Responses to Terrorism (START), University of Maryland

Victor Asal, Rockefeller College, University at Albany–SUNY

Jeffrey M. Bale, Monterey Terrorism Research and Education Program (MonTREP), Monterey Institute of International Studies

Charles Blair, Center for Terrorism and Intelligence Studies (CETIS)

Seth Carus, Center for the Study of Weapons of Mass Destruction, National Defense University

David Cleaves, Noblis, Inc.

Eric Croddy, Department of Defense

Mark Dechesne, Center for Terrorism and Counterterrorism, University of Leiden–Campus The Hague

Charles D. Ferguson, Council on Foreign Relations

James Forest, Combating Terrorism Center, United States Military Academy

David Hamon, Defense Threat Reduction Agency (DTRA)

Bruce Hoffman, Georgetown University

Keith Keener, Federal Bureau of Investigation (FBI)

Cheryl Loeb, Center for Technology and National Security Policy, National Defense University

Magnus Normark, Center for Asymmetric Threat Studies, Swedish National Defense University

R. Karl Rethemeyer, Rockefeller College, University at Albany–SUNY

Sammy Salama, Combating Terrorism Center, United States Military Academy

Jeremy Tamsett, Henley-Putnam University; Center for Terrorism and Intelligence Studies

Jonathan Tucker, James Martin Center for Nonproliferation Studies, Monterey Institute of International Studies

Daniel Uyesugi, Noblis, Inc.

APPENDIX 2

DELPHI EXERCISE INSTRUCTIONS: THE FUTURE OF WMD AND JIHADISTS: TRENDS AND EMERGING THREATS

Thank you very much for agreeing to participate in the Delphi Exercise relating to future developments involving jihadists and WMD. We anticipate that this will be an enlightening process for all participants, with possibly some surprises in store for what we each believe to be conventional wisdom. We understand that this domain is associated with a high degree of uncertainty, so all we ask for is that you supply your best estimate based on your expertise.

One of the strengths of the Delphi Method is that it leverages the different expertise of its participants. We have selected participants from a variety of backgrounds, so do not be concerned if you are more comfortable answering some questions than others—all we ask is for you to answer each question to the best of your ability. We would also like to remind you that your answers will not be used individually in the final analysis—only composite measures across all participants will be utilized, and individual scores will be anonymous.

1. The following are two important definitions used in the exercise, since they apply to all of the questions and an incorrect understanding of the terminology can jeopardize the exercise:

   WMD (weapons of mass destruction): While there is some degree of controversy surrounding the scope of this term, for the purposes of this exercise, we are restricting the definition of "WMD" to chemical, biological, radiological, and nuclear (CBRN) weapons with the potential to inflict catastrophic casualties, widespread social disruption, OR devastating economic consequences. Although it is difficult to put precise numbers on the scale of casualties, disruption, or economic damage, we are discussing attacks at least as deadly, destructive, or disruptive as the effect of the multiple attacks of September 11, 2001. Smaller scale CBRN attacks or attacks using high explosives are not included, unless mentioned explicitly.

   Jihadist: We are focusing in particular on the motives and behavior of jihadists (violent Islamist) actors. Jihadists are those Islamists who believe that waging armed struggle against unbelievers (*jihad bi-al-sayf*, i.e., "jihad of the sword") is the only path to victory over the forces of "unbelief." By "Islamism" we are referring to a radically anti-Western Islamic political ideology with both revolutionary and restorationist elements. Also, although al-Qa'ida is the most prominent example of jihadists at the moment, please do not limit your thinking to this organization, or indeed to any specific subgroup of the jihadist movement. (For example, Shiite jihadist groups should be considered in addition to Sunni-based groups.)

2. A note on estimating probabilities: Many of the questions ask for you to supply a numerical probability. In this case, we are asking for a number between 1 and 100 (i.e., a percentage). For some participants, thinking in terms of numerical probabilities is not difficult at all; others can find it quite confusing. One alternative way of selecting a probability (which some people find easier to conceptualize) is to think of it in relative, contextual terms. For example, if I were

to ask you: "What is the probability of a terrorist using Widget X in at least one attack in the next ten years?" one (and not necessarily the best) way of reasoning out the probability might be the following: "Since I think that Widget X is still quite difficult to manipulate, and most terrorists lack the practical skills, the probability is fairly low. In fact I think that around 1 in 25 (or 4 in 100) terrorist attacks are likely to use Widget X. Therefore, if there are 1,000 attacks per year, around 4 percent of these are likely to involve Widget X. The probability of at least one use of Widget X over a ten-year period is thus 40 percent. But since I think that terrorists will get more proficient with equipment of the type of Widget X near the end of the ten-year period, I am going to raise this slightly to 45 percent... etc."

3. No matter what method you use to come to a probability, score, or ranking, one element that is integral to the Delphi Method is to provide explanations/justifications for your choices. These can be short (one or two brief bullet points) or long (a detailed explanation listing various causal variables), depending on your preference, but the comments should be sufficient to allow any reader to understand how you made your estimate and what assumptions were involved. We therefore ask that—unless otherwise stated—you supply at least some explanation for every comment field in the questionnaire.

4. One last reminder—Please take careful note of the timeframe and weapon type a particular question is referring to, since some of the questions are similar but refer to different time periods or weapon types.

Thank you once again for participating in this study.

APPENDIX 3
DELPHI SURVEY RESULTS

Question 1.) What do you estimate the probability of a WMD terrorist attack overall (anywhere, by any non-state actor) within the next 10 years to be?

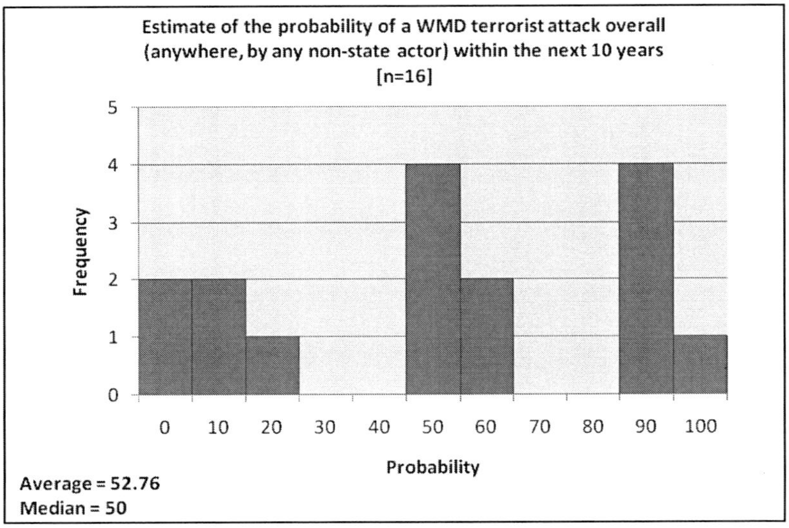

Question 2.) Please rank the following (from most likely to least likely) in terms of which type of actor you believe would be a likely perpetrator of a WMD attack within the next 10 years?

Ranking of the most likely perpetrator (in terms of actors) of a WMD attack within the next 10 years [n=15]

Rank	Group	Avg. Rank	Best	Worst	No. of times ranked 1
1	Sunni Jihadists	3	1	11	11 (73%)
2	Apocalyptic Cult	3.5	1	12	3 (20%)
3	Shi'i jihadists	4.3	2	8	0
4	Idiosyncratic/disgruntled/mentally ill indiv.	4.9	2	12	0
5	Non-Islamic religious extremists	6.4	3	10	0
6	Right-wing	6.7	3	10	0
7	Left-wing	7.9	5	11	0
7	Single-issue actor	7.9	3	12	0
9	Ethno-nationalist group	8.1	4	12	0
9	State (covert)	8.1	3	11	0
11	State (overt as warfare)	8.2	2	12	0
12	Criminal Group	9.1	1	13	1 (7%)
13	Other	12.9	12	13	0

Question 3.) What do you estimate the probability to be of ANY mass-casualty attack (with either conventional OR unconventional weapons) by JIHADISTS within the next 10 years? Mass-casualty refers to more than 1,000 casualties (either injured or dead).

Estimate of the probability of any mass-casualty attack (with either conventional or unconventional weapons) by jihadists within the next 10 years [n=15]

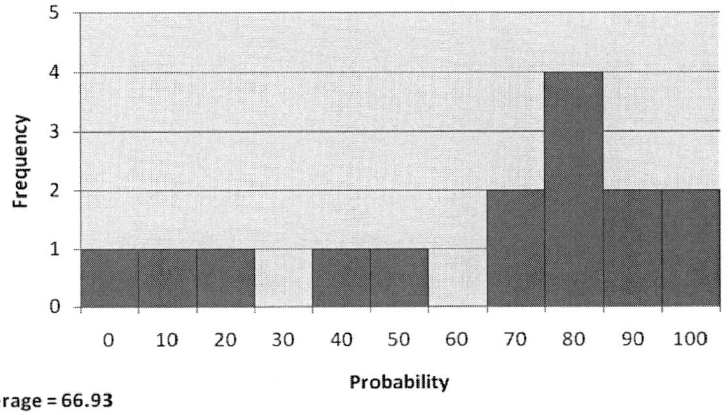

Average = 66.93
Median = 80

Question 4.) What do you think the probability is of there being a low-level attack using chemical, biological, or radiological agents by JIHADISTS within the next 10 years (i.e. an attack that results in less-than-catastrophic casualties, socio-economic disruption, or physical destruction, etc.)?

Estimate of the probability of a low-level attack using chemical, biological, or radiological agents by jihadists within the next 10 years [n=15]

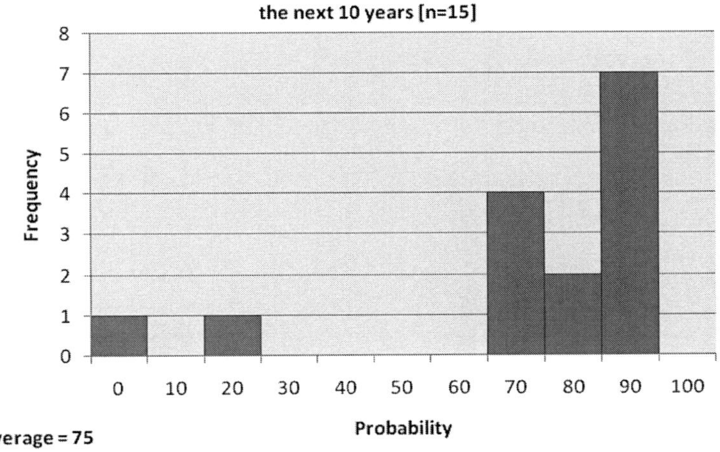

Average = 75
Median = 80

Question 5.) Based on what you currently know and think is going to happen in the next 5 years, what do you estimate the probability to be of AT LEAST ONE (catastrophic level) WMD attack by JIHADISTS within the next 5 years?

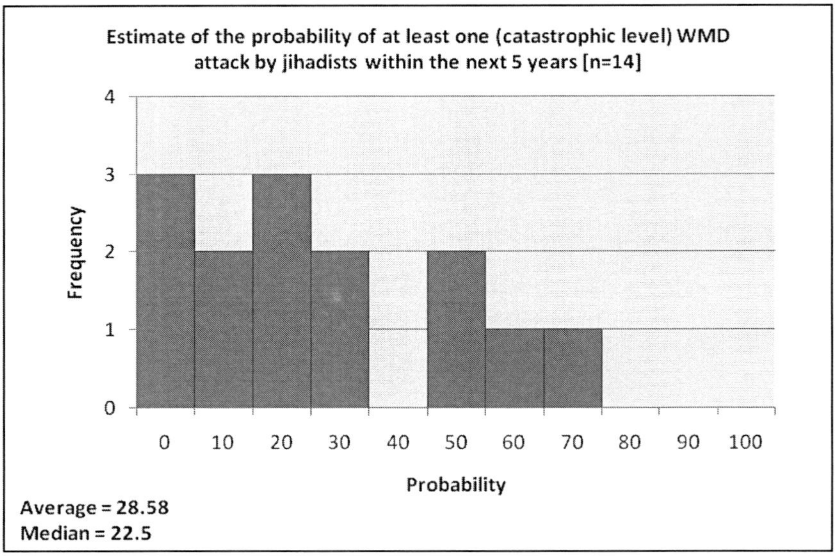

Question 6.) Based on what you currently know and think is going to happen in the next 10 years, what do you estimate the probability to be of AT LEAST ONE (catastrophic level) WMD attack by JIHADISTS within the next 10 years?

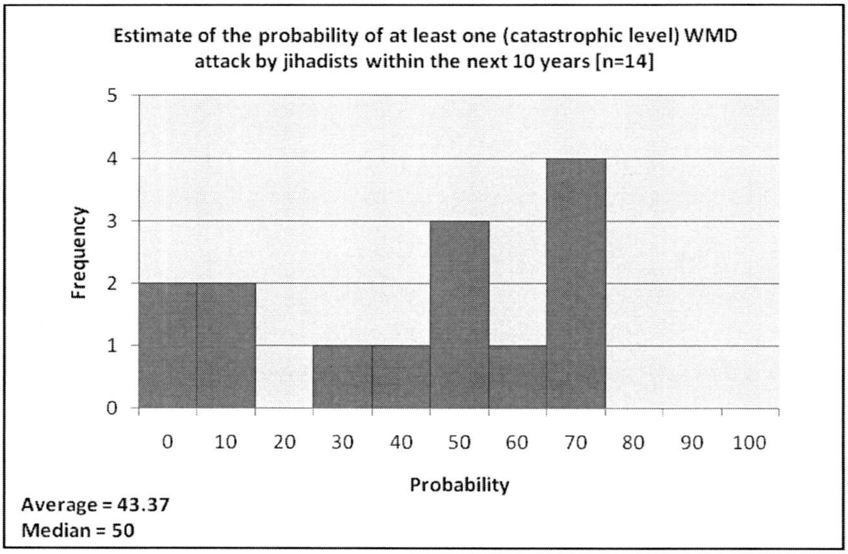

Question 7.) Based on what you currently know and think is going to happen in the next 25 years, what do you estimate the probability to be of AT LEAST ONE (catastrophic level) WMD attack by JIHADISTS within the next 25 years?

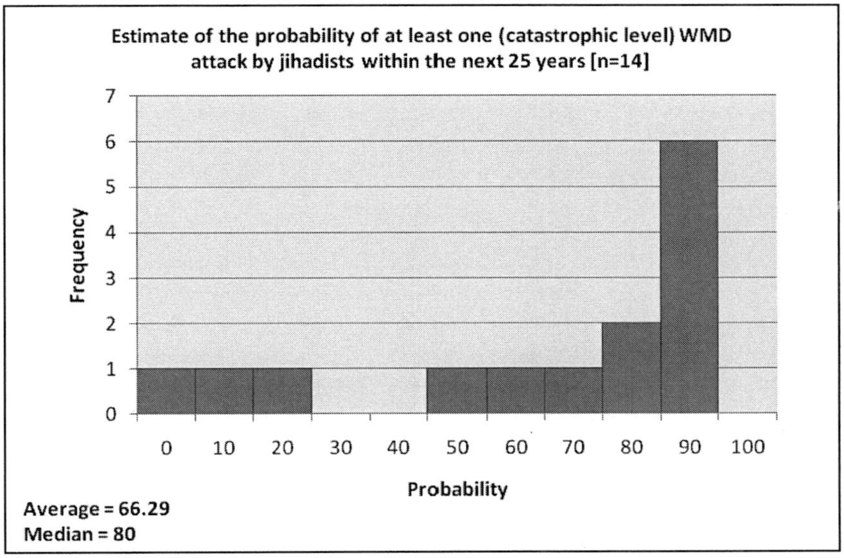

Question 10.) Rank order (from most likely to least likely) the weapons type likely to be used by jihadists in a WMD attack (as defined) within the next 5 years.

Ranking of weapon type from most likely to least likely to be used by jihadists in a WMD attack within the next 5 years [n=14]

Rank	Weapon Type	Avg. Rank	Best	Worst	No. of times ranked 1
1	Chemical Weapons	**1.3**	1	3	11 (79%)
2	Radiological Weapons	**2**	1	3	3 (21%)
3	Biological Weapons	**2.7**	2	3	0
4	Nuclear Weapons	**4**	4	4	0

Question 11.) Rank order (from most likely to least likely) the weapons type likely to be used by jihadists in a WMD attack (as defined) within the next 10 years.

Ranking of weapon type from most likely to least likely to be used by jihadists in a WMD attack within the next 10 years [n=14]

Rank	Weapon Type	Avg. Rank	Best	Worst	No. of times ranked 1
1	Chemical Weapons	**1.4**	1	3	11 (79%)
2	Radiological Weapons	**2.1**	1	3	3 (21%)
3	Biological Weapons	**2.5**	2	3	0
4	Nuclear Weapons	**4**	4	4	0

Question 12.) Rank order (from most likely to least likely) the weapons type likely to be used by jihadists in a WMD attack (as defined) within the next 25 years.

Ranking of weapon type from most likely to least likely to be used by jihadists in a WMD attack within the next 25 years [n=14]

Rank	Weapon Type	Avg. Rank	Best	Worst	No. of times ranked 1
1	Chemical Weapons	**1.6**	1	3	7 (50%)
2	Biological Weapons	**2**	1	3	4 (29%)
3	Radiological Weapons	**2.4**	1	4	3 (21%)
4	Nuclear Weapons	**3.9**	3	4	0

Question 13.) Based on what you expect to occur within the next 5 years, how many genuine WMD attacks perpetrated by jihadists are likely to occur WITHIN 5 YEARS? Select an option between 1 and 4 from the list below: none, between 1 and 10, between 10 and 50, and more than 50 attacks.

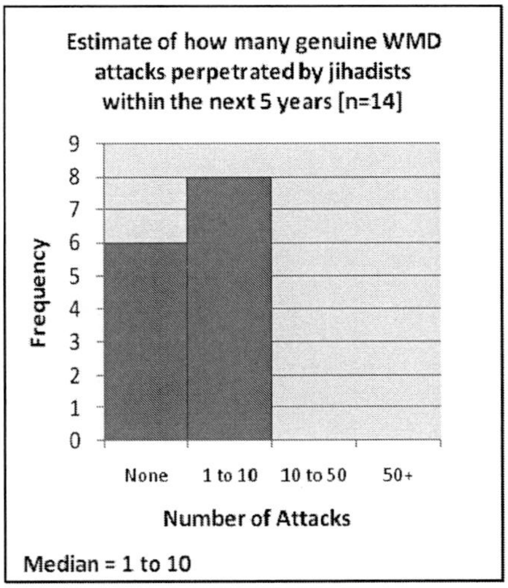

Question 14.) Based on what you expect to occur within the next 10 years, how many genuine WMD attacks perpetrated by jihadists are likely to occur WITHIN 10 YEARS? Select an option between 1 and 4 from the list below: none, between 1 and 10, between 10 and 50, and more than 50 attacks.

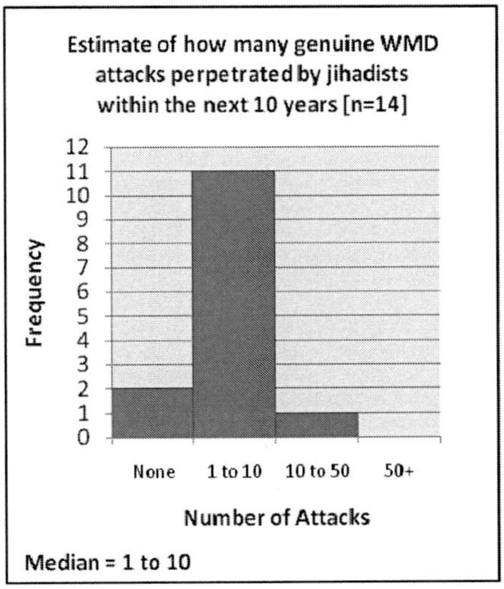

Question 15.) Based on what you expect to occur within the next 25 years, how many genuine WMD attacks perpetrated by jihadists are likely to occur WITHIN 25 YEARS? Select an option between 1 and 4 from the list below: none, between 1 and 10, between 10 and 50, and more than 50 attacks.

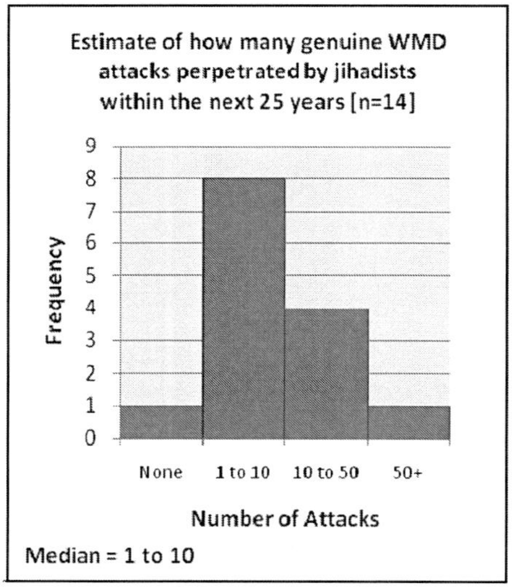

Question 16.) Where do you think the FIRST jihadist WMD attack will take place? Select from Africa, Asia (including Australasia), Eastern Europe, Central or South America, Middle East, United States, Other North America, Western Europe.

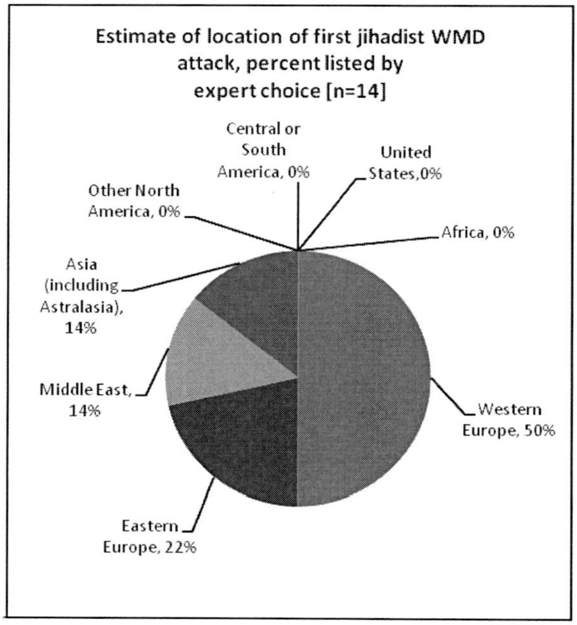

Question 17.) What delivery mechanism ismost likely to be used in an initial WMD attack by jihadists? Select from aerosol delivery, contamination (of food, water supplies, or other consumer product), explosion, single source contagion (bio-weapon only), and other.

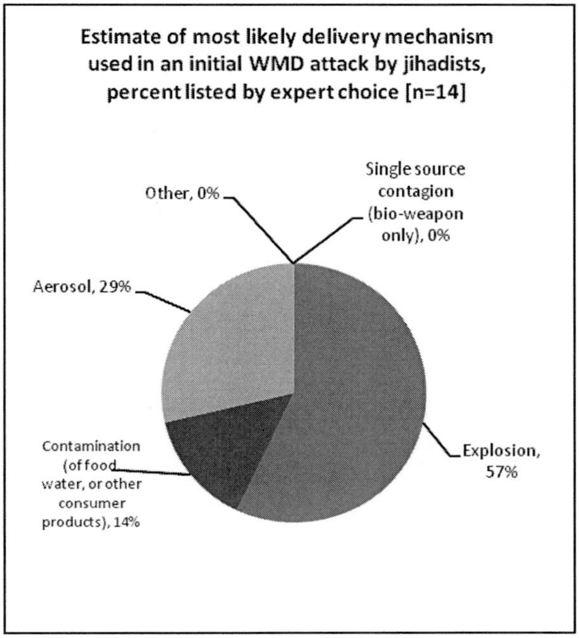

Question 18.) Please rank possible jihadist targets of an initial WMD attack, putting the most likely first: widespread locales (e.g. entire commerical district of a city, water supply of a town); defined open areas (e.g. sports stadium, marketplace, Times Square); transportation system; enclosed area (e.g. concert hall, commercial building, government agency headquarters); other.

Expert ranking of possible jihadist targets of an initial WMD attack [n=14]

Rank	Jihadist Target	Av. Rank	Best	Worst	No. of times ranked 1
1	Transportation System	**1.9**	1	4	6 (43%)
2	Enclosed Area	**2.2**	1	4	5 (36%)
3	Defined open areas	**2.7**	1	4	1 (7%)
4	Widespread locales	**3.6**	1	5	1 (7%)
5	Other	**4.5**	1	5	1 (7%)

Expert specified other as a "symbolic target"

Explanation of Jihadist Targets:
Widespread locales (e.g. entire commercial district of a city)
Defined open areas (e.g. sports stadium, marketplace, Times Square)
Transportation system
Enclosed area (e.g. concert hall, commercial building, government agency headquarters)
Other (if other selected, asked to specify in comment section)

Question 19.) Within the next 10 years, do you believe that the number of jihadists willing to use WMD will increase, decrease, or remain the same?

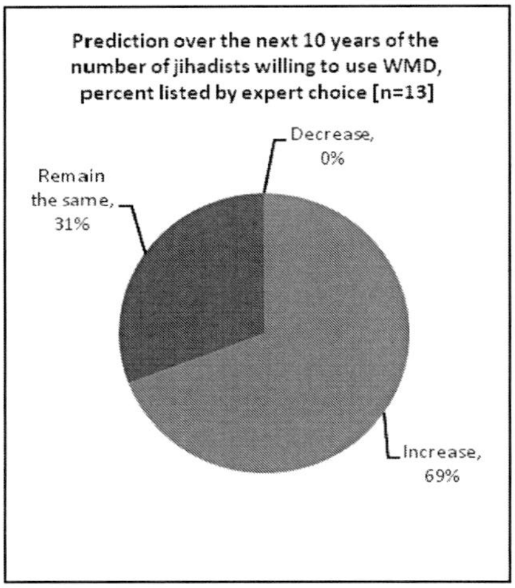

Question 20.) For the weapon type (chemical, biological, radiological, or nuclear) with which you are most familiar, please state by which year you believe there is a greater than 50% chance that jihadists will succeed in obtaining the required access to the RAW MATERIALS and EQUIPMENT needed to construct a weapon that would qualify as a WMD.

Year when experts predict that there is greater than 50% chance that jihadists will succeed in obtaining required access to *Raw Material and Equipment* needed to construct a WMD [n=9]

Weapon Type (grouped)	Year	Average Year (by Weapon Type)
Chemical	2008	2009.33
	2010	
	2010	
Biological	2010	2010.5
	2011	
Radiological	2008	2008
Nuclear	2015	2015
(Weapon type not specified)	2008	
	2028	

Average year by weapon type, when experts predict a greater than 50% chance that jihadists will succeed in obtaining required access to *Raw Materials and Equipment* needed to construct a WMD [n=9]

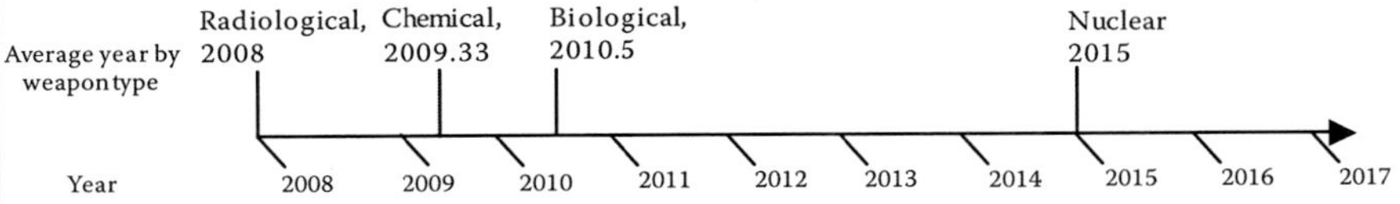

Question 21.) For the weapon type (chemical, biological, radiological, or nuclear) with which you are most familiar, please state by which year you believe there is a greater than 50% chance that jihadists will succeed in obtaining the required access to the SCIENTIFIC AND TECHNICAL SKILLS AND PERSONNEL needed to construct a weapon that would qualify as a WMD.

Year when experts predict that there is greater than 50% chance that jihadists will succeed in obtaining required access to *Scientific and Technical Skills and Personnel* needed to construct a WMD [n=9]		
Weapon Type (grouped)	**Year**	**Average Year (by Weapon Type)**
Chemical	2008 2010 2010	2009.3
Biological	2012 2015	2013.5
Radiological	2008	2008
Nuclear	2012	2015
(Weapon Type not Specified)	2008 2012	

Average year by weapon type, when experts predict a greater than 50% chance that jihadists will succeed in obtaining required access to Scientific and Technical Skills and Personnel needed to construct a WMD [n=9]

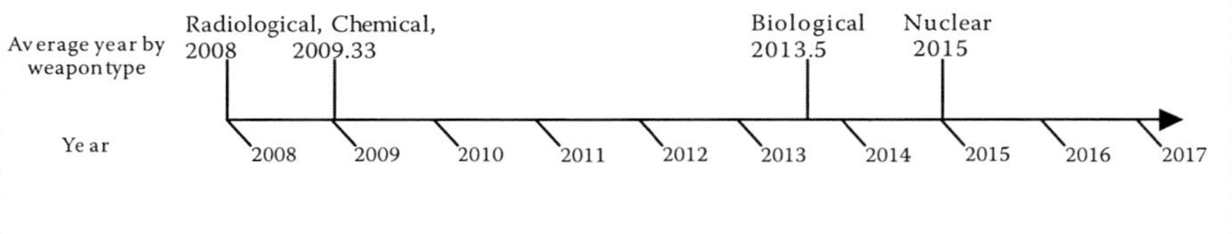

Question 22.) For the weapon type (chemical, biological, radiological, or nuclear) with which you are most familiar, please state by which year you believe there is a greater than 50% chance that jihadists will succeed in obtaining the required access to the FUNDING and SUPPORT INFRASTRUCTURE needed to construct a weapon that would qualify as a WMD.

Year when experts predict that there is greater than 50% chance that jihadists will succeed in obtaining requiredaccess to Funding and Support Infrastructure needed to construct a WMD [n=9]

Weapon Type (grouped)	Year	Average Year (by Weapon Type)
Chemical	2010	2010.67
	2010	
	2012	
Biological	2009	2010.5
	2012	
Radiological	2008	2008
Nuclear	2015	2015
(Weapon Type not specified)	2009	
	2012	

Average year by weapon type, when experts predict a greater than 50% chance that jihadists will succeed in obtaining required access to Funding and Support Infrastructure needed to construct a WMD [n=9]

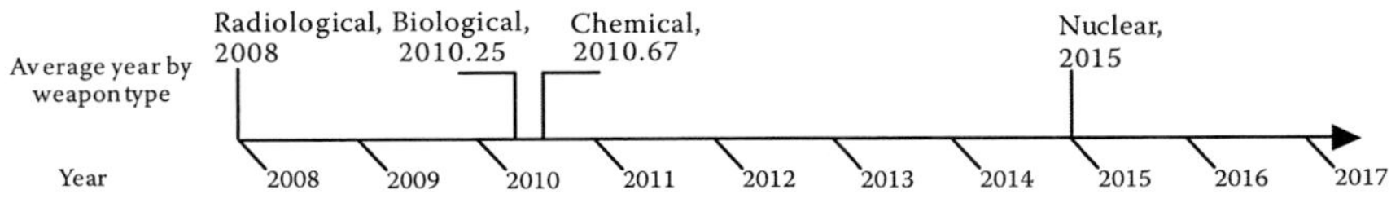

Question 23.) For the weapon type (C, B, R, or N) with which you are most familiar, do you believe that within the next 10 years, jihadists are more likely to PROCURE (through gift, purchase or theft) a "ready-made" weapon, or to MANUFACTURE a weapon themselves?

Expert prediction on procurement (through gift, purchase, or theft) a ready-made CBRN weapon or manufacture a CBRN weapon in the next 10 years themselves [n=9]

Weapon Type: Manufacture/Ready-made	Frequency
Chemical Weapon - Ready-made	0
Chemical Weapon - Manufacture	5
Biological Weapon - Ready-made	0
Biological Weapon -Manufacture	2
Radiological Weapon - Ready-made	0
Radiological Weapon - Manufacture	2
Nuclear Weapon - Ready-made	0
Nuclear Weapon - Manufacture	1

Question 24.) For the weapon type (C, B, R, or N) with which you are most familiar, do you believe that within the next 10 years, jihadists are more likely to procure / manufacture a weapon in the same country as their target (i.e. DOMESTICALLY), or to procure / manufacture the weapon external to the target country and then transport it TRANSNATIONALLY?

Expert prediction on procurement/manufacture CBRN weapon domestically in target country, or transnationally and then transport into target country, in the next 10 years [n=9]

Weapon Type: Domestic/Transnational	Frequency
Chemical Weapon - Domestic	4
Chemical Weapon - Transnational	1
Biological Weapon - Domestic	0
Biological Weapon - Transnational	1
Radiological Weapon - Domestic	1
Radiological Weapon - Transnational	0
Nuclear Weapon - Domestic	1
Nuclear Weapon - Transnational	1

Question 25.) Taking into account that there is a large degree of uncertainty, how many total physical casualties do you estimate will result from WMD attacks by jihadists over the next 25 YEARS? Select 0; 1 to 5,000; 5,000 to 25,000; 25,000 to 100,000; 100,000 to 1,000,000; more than 1,000,000.

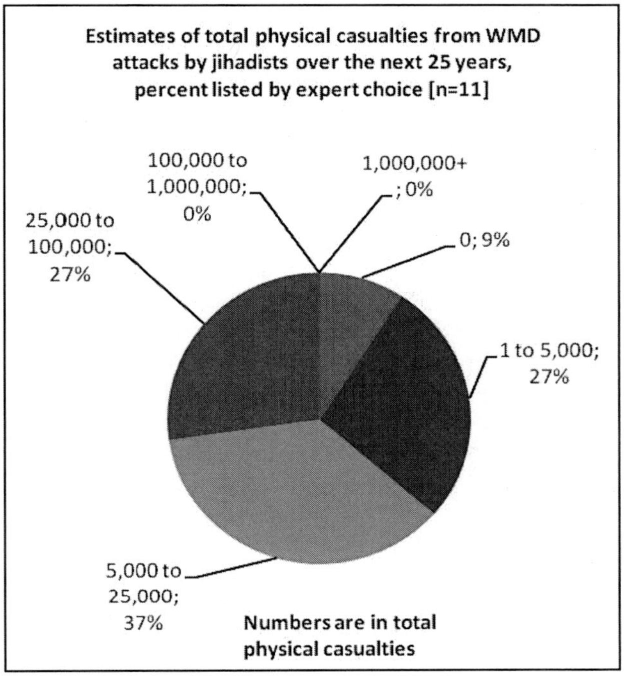

NOTES

1. I would like to thank Matthew Rhodes for his invaluable assistance in conducting the Delphi study and his astute comment on earlier drafts. I would also like to thank J. Scott Armstrong, Kesten Green, and the International Institute of Forecasters for their guidance and for enabling individual researchers to conduct ambitious forecasts, as well as Simon Galperin at SkyTech Systems for providing copies of the raw data collected during the survey. Lastly, I would like to thank all those who graciously gave of their time to participate in the Delphi exercise.
2. See Tiina Tarvainen, "Al-Qaeda and WMD: A Primer," *Jamestown Terrorism Monitor,* vol. 3, no. 11, June 2, 2005. Graham Allison has stated that the probability of a nuclear terrorist attack is greater than 50% within the next decade; Graham Allison *Nuclear Terrorism: The Ultmate Preventable Catastrophe* (New York: Holt Paperworks, 2005). Among others, uberinvestor Warren Buffet also subscribes to this view: "Warren Buffett Warns on Terror Risk," *BBC News*, Monday, 6 May 2002.
3. This echoes many of the arguments surrounding WMD terrorism more generally, espoused for almost a decade by such scholars as Bruce Hoffman, "Terrorism and WMD: Some Preliminary Hypotheses," *Nonproliferation Review*, vol. 4, no. 3, 45, 51; Richard A. Falkenrath, Robert D. Newman, and Bradley A. Thayer, *America's Achilles' Heal: Nuclear, Biological, and Chemical Terrorism and Covert Attack* (Cambridge, MA: MIT Press, 1998), 213; and Nadine Gurr and Benjamin Cole, *The New Face of Terrorism: Threats from Weapons of Mass Destruction* (London: I. B. Tauris, 2002), 41.
4. Jerry Mark Long, *Strategic Culture, Al-Qaida, and Weapons of Mass Destruction.* Science Applications International Corporation report prepared for Defense Threat Reduction Agency, November 2006, 24.
5. Others have even propounded the argument that, at least in the realm of chemical and biological weapons, the increasing salience of international norms of nonproliferation (and consequent greater vigilance by suppliers) will make it more difficult for terrorists to legitimately acquire needed outside sources of equipment and raw materials—see Jean Pascal Zanders, "Assessing the Risk of Chemical and Biological Weapons Proliferation to Terrorists," *Nonproliferation Review,* vol. 6, no. 4, Autumn 1999, 33.
6. This is discussed in greater detail in Gary Ackerman, "WMD Terrorism Research: Whereto from Here?" *International Studies Review,* vol. 7, no. 1, March 2005, 142.
7. Much of this section is drawn from Gary Ackerman, "It is Hard to Predict the Future: Evolving Nature of Threats and Vulnerabilities" in *Preparedness of Veterinary and Public Health Services in Responding to Accidental and Provoked Biological Disasters*, ed. Martin Hugh-Jones *OIE Scientific and Technical Review*, vol. 25, no. 1, April 2006; and Gary Ackerman, "Defining Knowledge Gaps Within CBRN Terrorism Research," in ed. Magnus Ranstorp *Unconventional Weapons and International Terrorism* (New York: Routledge, 2009).
8. This is true at least within a human frame of reference, but it might not be so over extremely long periods of time. For example, while it might be more difficult to predict events in 2050 than in 2015, we are relatively certain that in approximately 5 billion years' time our sun's core will collapse and likely destroy anything unlucky enough to still be living on earth.

9. Gödel's so-called Incompleteness Theorem was one of the first formal representations of this idea. See Kurt Gödel, "Über formal unentscheidbare Sätze der Principia Mathematica und verwandter Systeme, I" (Over Formally Undecidable Sets of the Principia Mathematica and Related Systems), *Monatshefte für Mathematik und Physik*, vol. 38, 1931, 173–198.
10. For a general, nontechnical introduction to complexity, see Mitchell M. Waldrop, *Complexity: The Emerging Science at the Edge of Order and Chaos* (New York: Simon and Schuster, 1992); and for a recent application of these concepts to the realm of terrorism, see Nancy K. Hayden, "The Complexity of Terrorism: Social and Behavioral Understanding Trends for the Future," in *Mapping Terrorism Research: State of the Art, Gaps and Future Direction* ed. Magnus Ranstorp (New York: Routledge, 2007).
11. For a definition of wicked problems, see H. Rittel and M. Webber; "Dilemmas in a General Theory of Planning," *Policy Sciences*, vol. 4, 1973, 155–169.
12. C. F. Kurtz and D. J. Snowden, "The New Dynamics of Strategy: Sense-Making in a Complex and Complicated World," *IBM Systems Journal*, vol. 42, no. 3, 2003, 462–483.
13. Akin to the echolocation of a bat, "probing" involves taking positive action within a system with the express purpose of observing the reactions of other elements of the system and thus of gaining information that is not otherwise obtainable. An example within the realm of our discussion would be to covertly "leak" or inject a distinctive recipe for creating a nerve agent into jihadist circles. Even though the recipe might not be genuine, it could be constructed to seem plausible and particularly easy to make and to provide specific signatures (such as a peculiar ingredient or process) that could be observed in the broader system. Counterterrorism authorities could then trace the movement of the recipe through jihadist virtual and physical networks, thus increasing their information about the dissemination of this CBRN knowledge, and also identify any would-be CBRN terrorists who might try to follow the recipe.
14. Nicholas Taleb, *The Black Swan: How the Improbable Rules the World and Why We Don't Know It* (New York: Random House, 2007).
15. Ibid.
16. Brian Jenkins, "The WMD Terrorist Threat—Is There a Consensus View?" in *Hype or Reality?: The "New Terrorism" and Mass Casualty Attacks*, ed. Brad Roberts (Alexandria, VA: Chemical and Biological Arms Control Institute, 2000), 242, 245.
17. Martha Crenshaw, "Have Motivations for Terrorism Changed?" in *Tangled Roots: Social and Psychological Factors in the Genesis of Terrorism*, ed. Jeffrey I. Victoroff (Amsterdam: IOS Press, 2006).
18. For several examples of how to approach such a task, see J. Scott Armstrong ed, *Principles of Forecasting* (New York: Springer-Verlag, 2001).
19. For example, the NetCraft Web Server Survey, one of the most widely cited measures of the size of the Internet, reported in February 2008 the existence of 158,209,426 Internet sites — see http://news.netcraft.com/archives/web_server_survey.html, accessed on March 14, 2008. An estimate published in 2003 put the total amount of information on the Internet at over half a million terabytes of data. (Peter Lyman and Hal R. Varian, *How Much Information?*, 2003, retrieved from http://www.sims.berkeley.edu/how-much-info-2003 on March 16, 2008.)
20. Here I am referring to the time it takes a new technology to transition from a laboratory experiment to something that is mass produced and available in COTS (commercial off-the-shelf) applications.

21. Ray Kurzweil, *The Singularity Is Near: When Humans Transcend Biology* (New York: Penguin, 2006).
22. The most comprehensive survey of the characteristics, selection, and efficacy of forecasting methods is Armstrong, op. cit.
23. The first two categories are presented explicitly in Armstrong, op. cit., passim. Simulations used for forecasting purposes, which I have added as a third category, contain elements of the other two categories but can be viewed separately because they seek to provide an observable platform for experimenting with a variety of inputs by attempting to replicate real-world dynamics and generate forecasts of future states of the world.
24. J. Scott Armstrong, "Selecting Forecasting Methods," in Armstrong op. cit., 373.
25. For a promising example, see Edward MacKerrow, "Understanding Why?—Dissecting Radical Islamist Terrorism with Agent-Based Simulation," *Los Alamos Science*, no. 28, 2003, accessed at http://library.lanl.gov/cgi-bin/getfile?28-27.pdf on March 17, 2008.
26. Armstrong, op. cit., 373.
27. Many of the authors in this volume have included in their analyses considerations of future developments, thus implicitly employing unstructured forecasting. While unstructured qualitative analysis is valuable for exploring the current situation relating to jihadists and WMD, it is felt that an explicit consideration of future events would be better examined through a more structured approach.
28. The other major methods, conjoint analysis and intentions data, require the participation of the subjects of the forecast and, since in this case that would mean the jihadists themselves, these methods are not feasible, at least not in the open sources.
29. An early description of the Delphi Method can be found in Bernice B. Brown, *Delphi Process: A Methodology Used for the Elicitation of Opinions of Experts* (Santa Monica, CA: RAND Corporation, September 1968). The seminal text describing Delphi is Harold Linstone and Murray Turoff, eds., *The Delphi Method: Techniques and Applications* (London: Addison-Wesley, 1975).
30. Gene Rowe and George Wright. "Expert Opinions in Forecasting: The Role of the Delphi Technique" in Armstrong, op. cit., 126.
31. Ian Mitroff and Murray Turoff, "Philosophical and Methodological Foundations of Delphi" in Harold Linstone and Murray Turoff eds., op. cit., 27.
32. Gene Rowe and George Wright. "The Delphi Technique as a forecasting tool: Issues and analysis," *International Journal of Forecasting*, vol. 15, 1999, 353–375.
33. Richard J. Lugar, *The Lugar Survey On Proliferation Threats and Responses*, June 2005. http://lugar.senate.gov/reports/NPSurvey.pdf (accessed on March 18, 2008).
34. Most questions requested both five- and ten-year estimates.
35. For more on the use of scenarios, see Peter Schwartz, *The Art of the Long View: Planning for the Future in an Uncertain World* (New York: Doubleday Business, 1996).
36. Gene Rowe and George Wright, op. cit.,128; and Nancy Goldstein, "A Delphi on the Future of the Steel and Ferroalloy Industries," in Linstone and Turoff, op. cit., 220.
37. All participants took part in their personal capacity and their views did not represent the opinions of their employers or affiliated institutions.
38. D. Sam Scheele, "Reality Construction as a Product of Delphi Interaction," in Linstone and Turoff, op. cit., 62.
39. Items 8 and 9. For a discussion on the use of examples to set context, see ibid., 43.

40. See Rowe and Wright, op. cit., 133–134; and John Ludlow, "Delphi Inquiries and Knowledge Utilization," in Linstone and Turoff, op. cit., 102–103.
41. Rowe and Wright, op. cit., 129.
42. Ibid., 132.
43. Ibid., 135.
44. For a detailed listing of the coherence checks and their results please contact the author.
45. The Delphi Decision Aid can be accessed at http://armstrong.wharton.upenn.edu/delphi2/ or through the Principles of Forecasting Web site at http://www.forecasting-principles.com.
46. The optimal number of rounds in a Delphi study has not been determined, but the general notion is to cease polling participants when successive rounds show reasonable stability, although there is no consensus as to what exactly constitutes stability (see Rowe and Wright, op. cit., 131). In the current exercise, owing to the large degree of uncertainty involved in the topic, it was decided to continue successive rounds until the mean of responses to an item in a given round showed a change of less than 10% from the mean in the previous round. Categorical and ranked-order variables would be handled on an item-by-item basis. After two rounds, eight questions had a difference in means of less than 10% with Question 1 having a decrease in mean value of 11.2% and Question 7 showing an increase in mean of 13.6%. As for the rank-order questions, Questions 10, 11, 12, and 18 showed no change between rounds; Question 2 retained the top four ranked actors in order; Question 16 retained the same top three ranked regions; and for Question 17, the second and third (aerosol and contamination) and fourth and fifth rankings (single-source contagion and other) traded places between the two rounds. For those questions with categorical variables, overall results of Question 19 remained unchanged, while Question 23 changed for nuclear weapons only, from having one response each for manufactured and ready-made nuclear weapons to a single response for manufacturing nuclear weapons. Similarly, Question 24 changed in respect to radiological weapons only, from two votes to one for transnational over domestic acquisition to one vote to none for domestic acquisition. Questions 20 to 22 showed no major differences between rounds. Therefore only two questions out of ten exceeded the mean criterion we had set for ourselves (and then only moderately), and the differences between rounds for the ranked-order and categorical variables were relatively minor.
47. Ibid., 131.
48. Throughout this discussion, statistical measures will be rounded off, often to the closest percentage, in order not to mislead the reader into believing that there is more precision than actually exists when dealing with subjective probability estimates.
49. Lugar, op. cit., 17–23.
50. This follows the basic risk equation of Risk = Likelihood × Consequence.
51. In the Lugar survey, 79% of respondents believed that terrorists as opposed to a government would be the most likely perpetrator if a nuclear weapon were to be used within a ten-year period. Lugar, op. cit., 15.
52. If the participants believed the events would occur, they were advised to include these events as assumptions in their previous probability calculations.
53. Note that, unlike the general probability of a jihadist WMD attack, this set of questions dealt with each time period discretely.

54. This differed from the Lugar study, in that there the most likely type of WMD attack was judged to be radiological. However, over a ten-year period, the means for each weapon type in the Lugar study were somewhat closer together (ranging between 29.2% and 39.8%). Lugar, op. cit., 14, 18–23.
55. In the nuclear weapons case, the fissile material would still be sourced externally, but the weapon components would be fabricated by the group.
56. This is to be distinguished from a hazard, which includes the natural and accidental infliction of harm, as well as a risk, which is a combination of threat, vulnerability, and consequence.
57. Items 5 through 7 of the survey implicitly required respondents to consider all aspects of risk simultaneously. The threat component was alluded to by asking for the possibility of an attack, and the use of the terms *WMD* and *catastrophic* implied a successful attack (and thus alluded to vulnerability) with a minimum scale of consequences.
58. The Presidential Commission on the Intelligence Capabilities of the United States Regarding Weapons of Mass Destruction reported in March 2005 that by October 2001 the U.S. intelligence community assessed al-Qa'ida as being capable of producing at least a "crude" improvised nuclear device (IND) if it secured access to highly enriched uranium (HEU) or plutonium. Commission on the Intelligence Capabilities of the United States Regarding Weapons of Mass Destruction, Report to the President (Washington, DC: WMD Commission, 2005), 267, 71, 92.

CHAPTER 15

Conclusion

Jeremy Tamsett and Gary Ackerman

CONTENTS

> The catastrophic threat at this moment in history is...the threat posed by Islamist terrorism—especially the al Qaeda network, its affiliates, and its ideology.
>
> **9/11 Commission Report, 2004**[1]

> The nexus of weapons of mass destruction (WMD) and terrorism poses one of the gravest potential risks to the national security of the United States and its global partners. A successful major WMD terrorist attack could result in mass casualty events and produce far-reaching economic and political consequences that would affect all members of the international community.
>
> **U.S. State Department, 2008**[2]

The above two statements encapsulate two of the key security concerns facing the Western world at the beginning of the twenty-first century. In this volume we have endeavored to explore the extent to which they intersect by using different various approaches to analyzing the putative nexus between jihadist terrorists and weapons of mass destruction. In so doing, we have learned much about both the jihadists themselves and the frightening weapons it is feared that they will use. We now attempt to provide a brief summary of the book's findings within the framework of the four questions posed in the introduction.

First, we invoke our editorial privilege to offer two thoughts in order to lay out a broader historical canvas for the discussion that follows. To begin with, for most of the recorded history of social conflict, those outside the corridors of power who were seeking to change the status quo by force had, generally speaking, a set formula for doing so.[3] This involved raising an army of like-minded (or at least mercenary) compatriots and using this force to establish territorial control over the village, city, or state in question, assuming that they were victorious over any opposing forces. In certain cases, this may have required going as far as directly removing the incumbant regime from power. Most important, the leaders of the rebellion, insurrection, or conquest had to convert or otherwise mobilize to their cause sufficient numbers of combatants to match and eventually overcome the scale of the anticipated opposition.

Today, this somewhat simple scenario no longer applies. On the one hand, traditional military power has become so concentrated in the hands of governments, at least in the developed world, that it is almost inconceivable that fanatical and sectarian non-state actors could succeed in rallying sufficient numbers of armed supporters among their purported "brethren" to seriously challenge the existing government by force, at least in the absence of support from another state or a serious eroson of regime legitamacy. This is all the more true for ideologies whose adherents seek control of large portions of the globe, if not the entire world. So, whereas in the seventh and eighth centuries the first wave of Muslims, driven by the zeal of a newly born faith, were able to conquer large swathes of Eurasia, the zealots of today, to the extent that they are even slightly pragmatic, must realize that their immediate prospects of repeating such exploits using traditional military power are slim to nonexistent. This leaves those with grandiose visions little choice other than to pursue their aims asymmetrically, which usually translates into applying what little force they have against civilians and other "soft" targets. It also means leveraging the new opportunities provided by the information revolution for disseminating their message, both to potential converts and to a worldwide audience through media outlets. The apparent lack of success in achieving their long-term objectives can thus be expected to precipitate the use of ever more asymmetric means by the purveyors of armed jihad, including the adoption of tactics and weapons with which a small number of the faithful hope to wreak a massive blow against their enemies.[4] The central question then becomes: At what point do conventional means no longer suffice?

This brings us to a consideration of the weapons themselves.[5] For thousands of years, the harm potential of a single act by an individual or small group unsupported by a broader political entity was limited to the range of a sword, spear, or bow.[6] The invention first of gunpowder and then TNT, eventually expanded the scale of destruction to the hundreds; whereas the insidious stratagem of using the enemy's own infrastructures against him, as on September 11, 2001, boosted the harm capacity even further. Yet, at no previous time in human history has a relatively small cabal of hateful fanatics had the ability, absent support from a state, to devastate economies, disrupt the functioning of entire countries, or kill and injure hundreds of thousands in a single attack. Weapons of mass destruction, were they to end up in the hands of terrorists, would offer them such a possibility. In a sense, then, the acquisition by terrorists, jihadist or otherwise, of WMD would represent the apogee of the firepower arc and would signal the true "consumerization" of military force.

It is in this context that we now turn *seriatim* to the framing questions posed in the introductory chapter.

HOW SERIOUS IS THE THREAT OF JIHADISTS USING WMD, REALLY?

To answer this question, we should be a little more formal about what we mean by threat. There are several conceptions of threat, but one of the most widely used is to view a threat as the likelihood of an actor intentionally acting to bring about harm. Threat, thus, becomes part of the overall risk equation:

$$\text{Risk} = \text{Likelihood of Adverse Event} * \text{Consequences of the Adverse Event}^{7}$$

which can be abbreviated as

$$\text{Risk} = \text{Threat} * \text{Consequences}$$

Each of the elements on the right-hand side of the equation can be disaggregated to yield an extensive form of the risk equation:

$$\text{Risk} = \underbrace{(\text{Intent} \text{ ¤ } \text{Capability})}_{\textit{Threat}} \ast \underbrace{(\text{Vulnerability} \text{ ¤ } \text{Effect})}_{\textit{Consequence}}$$

However, the above equation, while concise, does not convey the interrelationships between its constituent factors. To clarify, we refer to Figure 15.1.

Two important points should be noted about Figure 15.1. First, the various risk elements do not act independently since the nature of some of these elements can affect and be affected by several others as indicated in the diagram by the arrows between elements. If we regard the constituents as being mutually exclusive, we might miss synergies that can reduce risk. One obvious example: by reducing vulnerability to a specific biological pathogen through widespread vaccination, we make an attack using that agent less attractive to the terrorists. Second, the intention of the attacker is not necessarily dependent on objective measures of the effects of the weapon or the vulnerabilities of the target, but rather on the attacker's *subjective perception* of those effects and vulnerabilities,

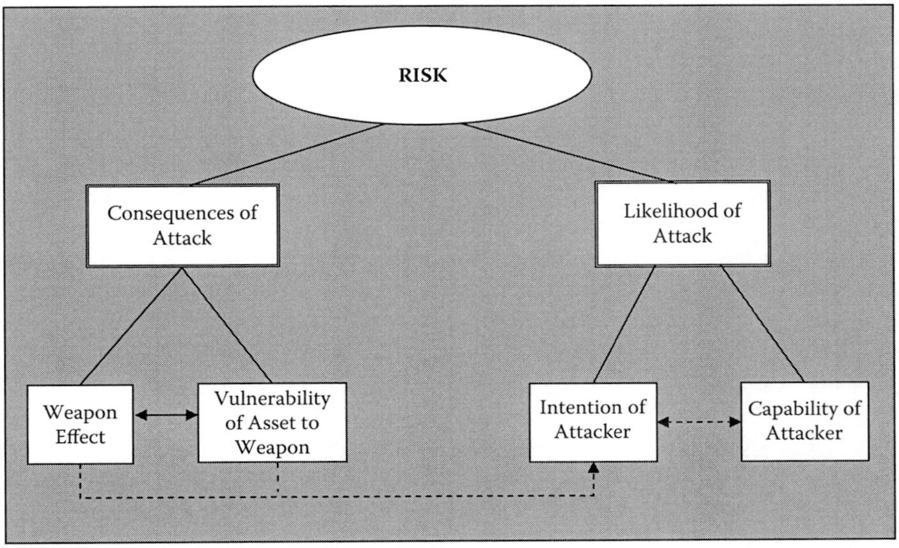

FIGURE 15.1 The risk tree.

which may or may not conform to their objective measures (perception is indicated by the broken arrows in Figure 15.1). Understanding this subtlety can lead to the development of additional policy options that otherwise might go unnoticed. For example, it may very well be impossible to reduce the true vulnerability of civilian populations to a specific CBRN weapon, but it might be feasible to attempt to alter the perception of this vulnerability held by terrorists. If terrorists do not perceive a target to be vulnerable, they will desist from attacking it, irrespective of its true level of vulnerability.

Throughout the discussion that follows, we will use the above construction.[8] It follows that to establish the level of threat of jihadists employing WMD, we need to determine both their intentions and capabilities, as well as help to clarify the sort of interplay between them.

Intentions

James Forest and Sammy Salama point out that most nonstate actors refrain from pursuing WMD as the use of these weapons would be counterproductive in terms of achieving their ultimate objectives. The interest and activities of jihadists in doing just this, on the other hand, means that we must take a closer look at both their ideology and strategy as a means of discovering their underlying motivation and intention. Jeffrey Bale highlights the importance of ideology and makes a forceful case that many jihadists, particularly members of al-Qa'ida, although not necessarily apocalyptic in the narrowest, most traditional sense of that term, are nonetheless at their core less motivated by rational, strategic concerns and more influenced by "delusional, utopian, and nonnegotiable goals" stemming from "a theologically-based and fanatical fantasy ideology" than is often presumed. Therefore, although they can be extremely calculating and brutally effective at the operational level, Bale contends that their penchant for carrying out spectacular, mass casualty attacks, their willingness to disrupt and confound their enemies, and their desire to eradicate the purportedly "evil" forces against which they strive means that, in practical terms, there will be few, if any, scruples that would seriously serve to inhibit them from employing WMD.[9]

Mark Dechesne echoes Bale's emphasis on ideology, particularly as it is espoused by an organization's leadership, but introduces additional factors to explain the appeal of WMD for jihadists, namely, the urge for tactical extremeness, the presence or absense of alternative strategic options, and components of the decision-making process. Dechesne identifies the presence or absence of ideological themes revolving around issues of control, revenge, identity, and truth as encouraging a higher level of risk, and maintains that themes of identity and truth are especially relevant because these concepts can give rise to aims that are less likely to be achieved through resort to weapons other than WMD. Dechesne sees current developments involving globalization—pertaining to promulgation of both Western values and the jihadist struggle agsinst those values—as particularly worrisome in this regard, as this has led to an increased emphasis on Islamic identity, which, when added to the theme of revenge, might increasingly lead to the consideration of WMD use as the only means by which the jihadists believe that they might substantially transform reality.

Forest and Salama draw our attention back to the different types of actors that comprise the jihadist movement and argue that both the desire to use WMD and the choice of tactics and targets are likely to depend on whether the actors involved are "locally-oriented, regionally-affiliated, or directly linked with al-Qa'ida central," as well as their understanding of the strategic and tactical utility of CBRN weapons.

Capabilities

In contrast to their evaluation of jihadist intentions, the contributors to this volume are far more skeptical about current jihadist capabilities, especially those required to engage in larger scale and greater impact CBRN attacks. The most important point to note is that despite clear and numerous indications of attempts to acquire a mass casualty CBRN capability, there is no evidence that al-Qa'ida or any other jihadist group has thus far been at all successful in their pursuits.

As has been detailed by each of the authors in the "Agents of Harm" section, there are several failure points on the path to launching a successful WMD attack. The significance of each barrier differs, however, according to the type of weapon being pursued. For example, as Charles Blair has noted in the case of nuclear weapons, the primary obstacle is the availability of fissile materials, while Markus Binder and Michael Moodie identify delivery mechanisms as the largest barrier preventing jihadists from causing mass casualties using chemical weapons. Jihadist acquisition is further complicated by government efforts to secure or detect dangerous materials (see, for example, the chapter by Charles Ferguson on radiological weapons) and successful delivery can also be thwarted by target hardening and preparedness measures.

There is little evidence that the technical sophistication required to produce a working WMD is widespread among jihadists. Sammy Salama and Edith Bursac's analysis of online jihadist materials related to CBRN weapons reveals that the instructions presented therein are not suitable for the production of true WMD, but instead would result in crude weapons that would be useful for small-scale poisoning or, at most, disruptive attacks. Of course, while online materials offer some insight into the general state of knowledge within the jihadist community, the extent of jihadist technical sophistication cannot be measured only by information found online. It remains possible that jihadists could obtain the necessary information on WMD by gaining access to ideologically sympathetic or purely mercenary scientists and technicians, although this is arguably unlikely to be a common occurrence.

Furthermore, neither external acquisition nor internal development takes place in a vacuum. The lead times needed to assemble the requisite raw materials, scientists, technicians, equipment, and funding are long and the process tenuous; the possibilities for detection increase as the amount of time and effort devoted to pursuing a CBRN project grows. Also, in general, the farther the intended target is from the source of the weapon, the more complicated the planning and logistics need to be, which in turn requires the involvement of more people to ensure that the operation is carried out with a degree of success, thereby increasing relevant risk factors like detection and defection. As Salama and Bursac observe, "there are relatively few groups or individuals with the requisite combination of both tactical competence and strategic freedom to actually benefit from investing the time, money, manpower and effort into a WMD attack."

Interplay between Intent and Capability

It is clear that there are many elements of the jihadist milieu that have no moral qualms about using WMD. Some may, in fact, regard WMD as an important, if not crucial, factor in inflicting retribution and achieving final victory over their enemies. While we should not underestimate the intentions of jihadists, we must at the same time recognize the obstacles that an adversary must surmount in order to achieve his desired goals. And obtaining a viable WMD is no easy task, even for the most sophisticated of jihadists. So, while no author in this volume completely dismisses the possibility, at the time of writing most are extremely doubtful that any jihadists possess a true WMD capability. The current threat equation is therefore somewhat lop-sided: The intent is medium to high, but the requisite capability is relatively low, making the overall threat situation of WMD use at most a low to medium threat and certainly far less than that of the threat of conventional weapons or small-scale CBRN attacks.

It is important to note in closing that neither the jihadists themselves nor the environment in which they operate is static. In the biotechnology sector, for example, Cheryl Loeb has indicated that research once limited to national defensive or offensive biological weapons programs can now be conducted in civilian settings. Moreover, one should not dismiss the ingenuity of at least the more proficient jihadists nor fail to heed the truism that "where there's a will, there's a way." The future threat picture might thus look very different from that of today.

WHICH ASPECTS OF THE WMD TERRORISM PROBLEM ARE SPECIFIC, AND CONSEQUENTIALLY SO, TO JIHADISTS?

If jihadist behavior with respect to WMD did not differ in any significant way from that of any other nonstate actor who might use WMD, then there would be little value in taking the analysis beyond determining whether or not jihadists pose a threat in the above regard. In many respects it is true that once intentionality has been established, the requirements for acquiring WMD and launching a successful attack are based more on physical realities than ideology or strategy. After all, as detailed in Section II of this volume, a working C, B, R, or N weapon depends on a confluence of the correct raw materials and certain basic (but precise) principles of physics, biology, or chemistry that must be mastered irrespective of whether the user is a state, an ethno-nationalist group seeking independence, or a religiously motivated jihadist.

Organization

There are, however, certain characteristics that are either unique to the jihadist movement or exist within this movement on a scale or in a form not witnessed elsewhere, which are salient in terms of how the WMD threat from these actors might materialize. The first of these relates to the singular organizational structure characteristic of the movement as a whole, which seems to be able to exploit the best of all organizational worlds. On the one hand, the jihadist milieu (at least on the Sunni side) possesses a strong, symbolic figurehead in the core al-Qa'ida organization. Al-Qa'ida not only provides the ideological leadership and inspiration to the broader movement, but also serves as the hub of a much larger logistical network,[10] providing channels through which expertise, equipment, and raw materials can flow from one affiliate to another. Moreover, the senior strategists and operational commanders of al-Qa'ida central have always been early adopters, and they seem to be ideally situated in their current safe haven along the Afghan–Pakistani border to continue to pursue innovation and improvisation. Indeed, Victor Asal and Karl Rethemeyer's chapter highlights this very aspect: the connectedness of a jihadist group as the key factor in its pursuit of CBRN weapons.

The other end of the organizational scale is also prevalent with the jihadist milieu—the proliferation of diffuse cells of self-radicalized, entrepreneurial jihadists throughout the globe, who can be regarded as part of a network insofar as they remain conjoined by the virtual ideological connections between them. These networks, if they are managed efficiently, are extremely difficult to detect and infiltrate, yet are able to expeditiously proselytize, exchange information, distribute *fatwas*, and recruit new members with the click of a mouse. To the extent that they can operate without the direct support of a distinct external leadership, these groups make up what Marc Sageman calls "leaderless jihad."[11] Although most analysts believe that the greater resources and capabilities available to the more established networks dominated by al-Qa'ida central make a genuine WMD attack more likely to arise from that part of the milieu, there need not be an overarching plan to acquire WMD for the threat to manifest itself. Once a small cell of jihadists has been ideologically primed to desire mass destruction, WMD may be utilized as a much sought after weapon of opportunity if the group discovered a weapon susceptible to interception or recruited the right type of insider. Furthermore, diffuse cells may even be more desirous of using WMD than the often-prudent strategists of al-Qa'ida central. As Dechesne notes in Chapter 2, after 9/11, when the United States "had reduced the control of al-Qa'ida executive command...small pockets of jihadists, isolated from the central leadership, began to formulate their own version of the struggle, which often lead to more non-specific and much more radical intentions."

Technology and Recruitment

Jihadists of all stripes, from al-Qa'ida and Hizballah to unnamed cells in Western countries, have often recognized and exploited new modes of technology. With increased access to and use of the Internet to facilitate communication, jihadists are no longer dependent upon a geographic base of operations from which to plan, coordinate, or otherwise carry out attacks. Technology such as Web sites, chat rooms/forums, wikis, blogs, video, telecommunications, and other amalgamations of innovation that comprise what is known as "Web 2.0" make it easier for jihadists to cloak their locations, intentions, and plans in an ocean of data that is difficult for even the most advanced intelligence agencies and professionals to collect and analyze. While the accuracy of information concerning CBRN materials disseminated over these media is still subpar, this burgeoning digital infrastructure makes it more likely that any technical, CBRN-related breakthroughs that do occur will be quickly disseminated across the jihadist community.

One aspect of the jihadist movement that is not shared by many other types of extremists is the dramatic growth in members over the past decade. Working from a base established during the Afghan conflict against the Soviets, the jihadist movement planted seeds throughout the Middle East, North Africa, South and Southeast Asia, and even in sub-Saharan Africa during the 1980s and 1990s. The dispersal of al-Qa'ida and Taliban fighters in 2001 and the role of the war in Iraq as a locus of recruitment, along with other factors, led to an upswing in the radicalization of Muslims in Europe and North America as well. Despite operational setbacks since 2001, the jihadist movement has succeeded magnificently in the propaganda sphere, and the global pace of radicalization shows no sign of abating any time soon. The more people that join the jihad against the West, the greater the probability that personnel with the appropriate scientific education or technical expertise to produce or work with WMD will enter the jihadist fold. As a whole, therefore, the jihadist movement is global, with several interconnecting layers, which makes it more resilient and places the network in a good position to exploit any opportunities that may arise for the acquisition or use of WMD.

Another distinguishing characteristic of jihadists has been their proclivity for martyrdom that is unrivalled by almost any other modern terrorist group, except perhaps for the Tamils in Sri Lanka. By extolling martyrdom as the ultimate sacrifice, one that will yield copious rewards in the hereafter, jihadist leaders have ample access to a cadre of willing footsoldiers who are difficult or impossible to deter, at least by normal threats of punishment, as Brad Roberts has described in detail. Essentially being able to muster a cohort of "human smart bombs," this affords jihadist planners an incredibly wide tactical latitude in all types of attacks,[12] including the delivery of WMD should the movement ever succeed in acquiring these weapons.

Which Weapon Type Are Jihadists Most Likely to Pursue?

The question of which weapons type is most likely to be pursued by jihadists is a complex one. As noted above, jihadists have not proven themselves adept at effectively using even the crude chemical weapons and toxins that they have acquired. At the opposite end of the CBRN spectrum, jihadists have repeatedly evinced a desire for a nuclear capability. The gap between their intent and current capabilities must be obvious even to the most fanatic jihadist, and the probability of being able to successfully acquire and weaponize a particular agent will, therefore, weigh heavily in the selection process, together with motivational factors such as the "expressive" or strategic benefit of any particular attack. Moreover, it is difficult to generalize about jihadists' choice of weapon because (1) in cases where a particular target is selected first, the specific circumstances surrounding the intended target (including levels of protection and the likelihood of interdiction) will determine the most efficacious weapon type; (2) at least for chemical and biological agents, both the effects and the ease of acquisition and production vary considerably between the various chemicals or pathogens; and (3) opportunism may play a major role; for instance, if a jihadist stumbles across an orphan radiological source, this might steer him toward the use of an agent he had not previously considered. When it comes to weapon selection, the devil, as they say, is truly in the details.

Nonetheless, it is possible to make some preliminary observations about likely weapons choices. Bearing the above caveats in mind, Table 15.1 presents a summary of the benefits and costs of the various weapon types *when used as WMD*, if one assumes that all other factors are equal.[13] These estimates have been derived from the four chapters in Secion II and represent the situation as it is believed to exist at the time of writing. The relative advantage of each motivational factor is denoted by the number of "+" signs and, since the acquisition of a WMD capability is presumed to incur some costs, the relative disadvantage imposed by each capability factor is denoted by the number of "–" signs. While these familiar symbols have been used to illustrate advantages and disadvantages, this is not meant to imply any algebraic formulation. Rather, the table is only meant to provide an overall picture of the relative attractiveness to jihadists of each weapon type in a general sense.

Table 15.1 accords with the relatively short-term (within five years) forecast explicated by Gary Ackerman in Chapter 14, which ranked the most likely types of weapons jihadists might use as chemical, followed in second place by radiological, then biological, and lastly nuclear. Ackerman's chapter also forecast that within the next ten years at least, jihadists are more likely to manufacture their own weapons than to attempt to

TABLE 15.1 General Attractiveness to Jihadists of CBRN in a WMD Context

	Chemical	Biological	Radiological	Nuclear
Motivation-Related				
Massive casualty potential	+ + +	+ + + +	– –	+ + + + +
Economic damage potential	+	+ + +	+ + +	+ + + + +
Massive disruption (psychosocial effects)	+ + +	+ + + +	+ + + +	+ + + + +
Legitimacy to followers	+ + + + +	+ + +	+ + + +	+ + +
Capability-Related				
Access to raw materials	–	– –	– –	– – – – –
Access to technical expertise	– –	– – –	– –	– – – –
Cost (money; manpower)	– –	– – –	– –	– – – – –
Difficulty of weaponization (delivery system)	– – –	– – – – (noncontagious) – – (contagious)	– –	– – – –
Safety hazard	– – –	– –	– – –	– –

purchase or steal them. An important observation is that Table 15.1 may inadvertently suggest a static representation, whereas changes in the relative attractiveness of different weapons might occur very rapidly, for instance, following a successful attack with one weapon type or technology breakthroughs that relate to either the offensive or defensive aspects of a particular weapons type.

WHICH MEASURES ARE LIKELY TO BE EFFECTIVE IN COUNTERING OR PREVENTING WMD ATTACKS BY JIHADISTS AND WHICH ARE NOT? HOW DO THESE RELATE TO CURRENT COUNTERTERRORISM TOOLS AND PRACTICES?

We have seen that WMD terrorism in general is a very complex problem, involving a host of factors ranging from esoteric ideological precepts to the finer points of chemical and nuclear engineering. It is perhaps to be expected, then, that the avenues we must proceed along to counter this problem will be just as complex. Section III of this volume has already provided lengthy discussions of specific approaches to combating the use of WMD by nonstate actors but it remains necessary to situate these approaches relative to one another and explore how they interact.

Defense

The currently prevailing paradigm under which countering WMD terrorism (as well as several other security threats) is conceptualized is generally referred to as "layered defense" (sometimes also called "defense-in-depth"). At its core, layered defense presupposes that no single defensive measure will be sufficient to counter the actions of a dedicated, adaptable adversary[14] and that by implementing several (often intersecting) layers of defenses, the probability is increased of preventing or interdicting the threat. It is essentially a strategy of multiple redundancy. Figure 15.2 displays a graphical depiction of the various layers that are currently deployed in one or more nations to counter WMD terrorism. Each defensive layer is represented by a box, with arrows indicating how some of the layers are connected to one another, although most layers serve an independent function as well. The various defensive layers have been grouped according to which component of the risk equation they most directly address. It is proposed that each layer of the defense be viewed as part of a feedback loop that intersects with both our threat estimates and the calibration of every other layer. Layered defense can then be analyzed in terms of a dynamic system of interdependent components that can incorporate second- and higher order effects such as the strategic actions of jihadists to our counterterrorism efforts. It is within this framework that we should discuss those elements for which the distinctive aspects of the jihadist threat bear the most relevance.

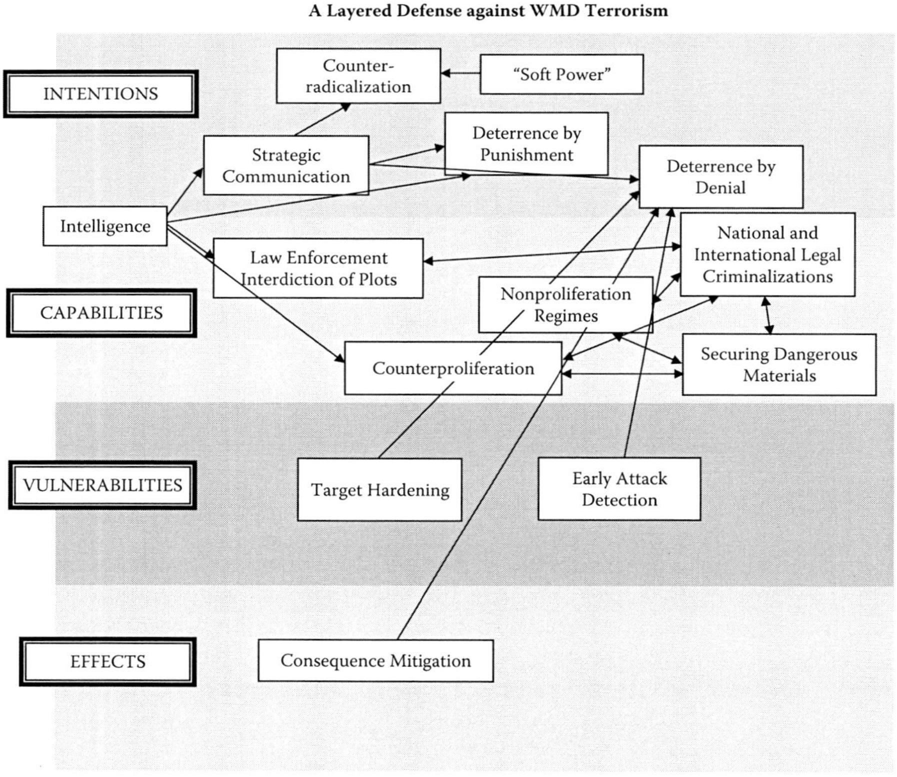

FIGURE 15.2 A layered defense against WMD terrorism.

Soft Power

The most basic, and in many ways also the most vital, element in preventing the use of WMD by jihadists is to arrest the growth of the jihadist movement by preventing the radicalization of Muslims and attempting to persuade the less committed that continuing along the path of jihad is not in their best interests. Accordingly, measures to prevent radicalization include counterpropaganda, as well as the use of "soft power" efforts to address development, public health, education, and other challenges facing the Muslim world. The need for a structured approach in this regard has been discussed extensively elsewhere,[15] but it is important to note that little progress has been made thus far. To counter the WMD threat in particular, one option may be to carry out a program of covert or overt de-legitimization of CBRN weapons from a theological standpoint, although previous, often crude efforts at delegitimizing jihadist behavior by governments in the Middle East and elsewhere have proven mostly unsuccessful.

Deterrence

Deterrence of jihadists is problematic, above all due to ideological factors. As Bale observed, what is particularly intractable about jihadist Salafism and other religiously inspired ideologies is the "stubborn maintenance of faith that their agendas and actions are 'divinely-sanctioned,' even in the face of looming defeat and disaster." Such an ingrained outlook obviously complicates attempts at deterrence. Brad Roberts concedes that deterrence, especially in the context of the threat of punishment, is not always feasible when dealing with jihadists, but he maintains that deterrence has a definite role to play in preventing their use of WMD. For example, while threats of punishment are most likely to be effective only against state sponsors and operational enablers of jihadist activities, for the jihadists themselves—including footsoldiers, operational professionals, and leaders—deterrence by denial (i.e., convincing would-be attackers that an attack is unlikely to succeed or to yield the benefits they seek) is a more promising approach. This type of deterrence is influenced by the overall protective and preparedness posture of the target (as seen in Figure 15.2) and is likewise tied to enhancements in the efficacy of intelligence, target hardening, and mitigation. Because jihadists place a premium on success, by introducing uncertainty into their calculations through a robust defense, it might be possible to deter them, although this will likely be on a case-by-case basis. In any event, it seems highly unlikely that deterrence and other influence strategies could be employed so successfully as to ensure that all of the operational and leadership elements of the violent Islamist movement see WMD as too risky to acquire and use.

Nonproliferation and Counterproliferation

If convincing jihadists not to pursue a WMD capability is not successful, the next step is to prevent them from gaining this capability. This necessitates initiating a range of so-called "supply-side" measures aimed at keeping the raw materials, equipment, and expertise required to produce or use WMD out of jihadist hands. The global, transnational nature of the jihadist movement, together with its myriad network connections built up over decades, implies that a weak link in safeguarding dangerous materials or expertise almost anywhere in the world could pose a threat to the jihadists' proclaimed enemies. This state of affairs calls out for a concerted global approach to prevent jihadists from gaining access to WMD capabilities. Moreover, the involvement of new non-state actors such as private industry, which increasingly controls critical know-how and technologies, will be critical for the long-term success of preventive programs. However, as Brian Finlay and Jeremy Tamsett have pointed out, the tempo of international innovation and participation in nonproliferation and counterproliferation efforts has been uneven at best.

Intelligence

Perhaps the most well-worn target of criticism in the current struggle against jihadism has been the intelligence community. While intelligence agencies have exhibited a multitude of deficiencies, especially prior to September 11, 2001—including stovepiping of information, a lack of cultural and language capabilities, and so forth[16]— it must be acknowledged that the intelligence community is faced with an admittedly daunting task.[17]

The first challenge, is that "Exhortations to the intelligence community to penetrate terrorist groups are useless if the groups that need to be penetrated have not even been identified."[18] Identifying perpetrators and monitoring their activities remain vital to countering jihadist attempts to procure WMD. Randall Murch and Jeremy Tamsett offer recommendations for overcoming some of these obstacles, especially those involved with gaining human intelligence (HUMINT) in culturally homogenous and often lawless regions of the world, like the Federally Administered Tribal Areas (FATA) in Pakistan. Recruitment of foreign agents and operatives is critical to mission success in such areas, which—as the authors point out—is further complicated by the prevalence of Islamist or otherwise radical extremist sympathizers in these areas. In such cases, anyone appearing from without the community is likely to be quickly identified and assessed as an "outsider" and, therefore, treated as such. Murch and Tamsett also advocate incorporating local police units in the HUMINT mission, as they are in a position to best understand the communities in which they live and operate and, hence, are better positioned to spot anomalies or disruptions in normal activity. If local police around the world were trained to recognize CBRN weapons-related materials and jihadist activities, this may constitute a powerful new strategic intelligence asset.

Finally, new approaches to intelligence need to be adopted to counter new threats like jihadists acquiring WMD. For example, there has been a shift in intelligence from threat-centric targeting to future-oriented risk mapping, which is a process of minimizing uncertainty through proper categorization of knowledge as well as accepting the uncertainty that remains as an inherent fixture in the equation that must be accounted for (rather than being ignored). While we do not propose to go into detail here about new analytical methods, we need to bring all methods in the social and physical sciences to bear on the problem of jihadists and WMD (social network analysis and agent-based modeling are but two potentially useful techniques).

Mitigation

If prevention fails, early detection, together with prompt and efficient response and mitigation are essential. Patrick Roberts notes that in the presence of uncertainty about threat, a prudent mitigation strategy for terrorism must be as robust to all forms of threat as possible. In addition, there should be closer integration between those studying the intentions and capabilities of the jihadist adversary and those designing and implementing mitigation strategies, so that new findings by the former (such as the tactical preferences inferred by Forest and Salama) can be incorporated into the planning and prioritizations of the latter.

Final Thoughts about Counterterrorism Strategy

A parallel can be drawn between the demonstrated adaptability of many jihadist opponents and some of the more apparently paradoxical results from quantum theory,[19] which suggest that jihadist behavior cannot be understood in isolation from what counter terrorism forces are doing, if we hope to ascertain their intentions, determine their capabilities, and counter their actions. Whichever measures are taken, in formulating and developing counterterrorism strategies and plans in the context of jihadist WMD terrorism, policymakers and operators must be aware of the possibility of cocreating the threat with the enemy. For example, as Patrick Roberts notes, "...terrorists (unlike natural hazards) are strategic adversaries, and they may adjust their strategies in response to attempts to defend against particular targets." Actions to counter the jihadist WMD threat must, therefore, always be viewed through two lenses: first, the initial action focused on countering the extant threat and, second, the adversary's attempt to blunt, thwart, or circumvent that (counter) action as much as possible. Above all, states must take care not to create through their actions a more deleterious threat condition than the status quo.[20]

Jihadists have demonstrated a penchant for both tactical and organizational innovation. In order to keep abreast of the threat, a clear awareness is needed regarding what is and what is not known at any given point in time about jihadist activities. This threat awareness must be supported by methods to measure and manage uncertainty. Sustained, continual re-evaluation of the threat space (see Murch and Tamsett, Chapter 9) and special attention paid to the so-called "black swans" discussed by Ackerman are thus crucial for successful future prevention efforts. Ultimately, the more adaptive, responsive, and flexible counterterrorism strategies are, the more marginalized the effects of alterations in the operational tempo of the enemy will become.

WHAT DOES THE FUTURE HOLD FOR THE PROSPECTS OF WMD USE BY JIHADISTS?

We have established that the current threat of WMD use by jihadists is not very high, primarily owing to their rather lackluster demonstrated capabilities to acquire and weaponize CBRN agents. Yet, in a highly dynamic global environment that is seemingly dominated more by revolution than evolution in many spheres of activity, we would be remiss in failing to consider possible developments that may lie just over the horizon. The perils of prediction are well known and have been set out in Chapter 14. Bearing these in mind, we offer a preliminary assessment of the future of the jihadist threat.

With regard to jihadist ideology and grand strategy, we do not expect any dramatic changes, at least not in the short to medium term. We believe, however, that the manifestation of these motivational foundations in the form of the desire to use WMD at an operational level is likely to increase. First, jihadist networks can only ensure their durability and relevance as a viable global ideological movement if they can "stay in the news:

elbowing [themselves] into the limelight through dramatic and bloody attack, thereby promoting [their] continued relevance as the defenders and avengers of Muslims everywhere."[21] At some point in time, they become victims of their own success, and conventional attacks and eventually even small-scale CBRN strikes exhaust the psychological *frisson* that al-Qa'ida and other elements of the jihadist movement require to continue to inspire Muslims worldwide and fuel their jihad. At this point, escalatory pressures may mount and a highly publicized attack involving "exotic" weapons like WMD might begin to seem more and more attractive. Paradoxically, even success on the counterterrorism front could potentially increase jihadists' desire to use WMD. This would relate mainly to that portion of the jihadist movement that some experts have asserted are presently feeling somewhat constrained with respect to using WMD out of concern for alienating potential supporters. If these members of the movement begin to feel backed into a corner by counterterrorism forces or come to believe that their constituency is beginning to perceive them as weak, they may very quickly join their more ardent brethren in extolling the virtues of WMD.

It is in the realm of jihadist capabilities with respect to procuring or producing WMD that we are likely to witness the most rapid and significant changes in coming years. On the positive side, it is likely that as the scrutiny of jihadist activities and communications increases, so will the likelihood of detection by counterterrorism intelligence operations, which will hamper any WMD procurement or development plans and necessitate changes in tactics, methods, and corresponding logistics. Yet these new obstacles are likely to be outweighed by the tremendous facilitative effects of advances in science and technology, combined with the worldwide diffusion and commercial exploitation of these new technologies as a result of increased globalization. The consequences of this combination, particularly for the empowerment of individuals, small groups, and existing network operations, will undoubtedly play to the jihadists' advantage. Facilitative technologies are already under development in the chemical, biological, and engineering fields, but are more speculative in the nuclear domain. At the same time as these broader breakthroughs are occurring, the technical pedigree of jihadist personnel will likely increase. The information revolution has crossed the entire globe, which means that disaffected youths in even the most underdeveloped countries can now enroll in technical courses online. In addition, the effects of the increasing radicalization that is occurring within the developed world may become significant given that the latest technology and institutions of higher learning are more widely available there. This is best summed up by Binder and Moodie in the case of chemical weapons, but their words apply equally to the other weapons types: "The indirect recruitment or inspiration of individuals from developed societies possessing technical skills could rapidly transform the jihadist CW equation from one in which repeated demonstrations of incompetence cease to be the norm."

When the above developments are set against Finlay and Tamsett's contention that comprehensive nonproliferation efforts with respect to keeping WMD materials out of the hands of terrorists are a chimera and that even the viability of the entire nonproliferation regime is in question, the outlook becomes bleaker still. In short, all indications are that, in the absence of substantial changes in international policies and practice (changes that would in many cases be counterproductive if they end up obstructing the development of new technologies), the threat of WMD use by jihadists is likely to increase substantially. It is thus no surprise that in the Delphi study, the assembled experts viewed the probability of jihadists successfully perpetrating a WMD attack within the next twenty-five years as substantial. How this affects the larger risk equation is not yet clear, since the increase in the threat could conceivably be offset by substantial investments in decreasing the vulnerabilities to and impact of CBRN weapons. Yet, such efforts are unlikely to be able to offset the threat entirely, and, in any case, the political and financial costs of implementing them may not be feasible.

CONCLUDING REMARKS

This volume has sought to explore the dangerous nexus between jihadists and WMD as comprehensively as possible. It is hoped that the information contained herein has served in some small way to increase understanding of the nature of this nexus. However, we are under no illusions that this is the final word on the subject. Rather, we view the present work as no more than a springboard or guidepost to future research on this topic. Topics for further research that we have already identified include looking at how the morphology of global jihad might evolve in the future from the current al-Qa'ida plus dispersed cells structure, more detailed analysis of the problem from a formal complex systems perspective, viewing jihadist WMD activity as a form of swarm intelligence, assessing the efficacy of ideological de-legitimization strategies for WMD, and exploring detailed policy options for dealing with advances in technology. We are certain that there are many more that we have not even considered.

The threat of jihadists successfully using WMD, in the sense of large-scale, mass impact CBRN attacks, is admittedly quite limited at present, especially when compared to their demonstrated capabilities with conventional explosives. All of the indications are, however, that the situation is unlikely to remain so indefinitely. Of course, WMD are not the only threat we face; emerging infectious disease and climate change are also potentially catastrophic risks. Neither do jihadists constitute the only threat to peace and stability on the world stage; millions of people are still plagued by civil war and uncivil dictators. Yet, the nexus between jihadists and CBRN weapons can be compared to the proverbial snowball rolling down a mountainside: Initially it is rather far away, moving slowly and awkwardly and is dwarfed by more current concerns. Nevertheless, as time passes, the snowball gathers speed and grows in size, so that by the time it eventually reaches us, it has become a paradigm-shifting WMD.

Although there are no easy solutions, the jihadist threat is not wholly intractable. Unfortunately, it will require our protectors—and ourselves—to adopt postures that are every bit as adaptive and dynamic as those of our jihadist opponents, a shift in which our current bureaucratic institutions of national security have not, thus far, shown themselves adept. Technology is transforming the geographic space in which threats have traditionally emerged, and we will need to engage both the jihadists and the weapons they covet on a host of new battlefields, not just in the caves and villages of Waziristan, but also on the blogs where the *ulama* debate what is acceptable, in the *banlieues* of Europe with their disaffected Muslim youth, and the hi-tech laboratories where they may seek materials and expertise. Above all, we must continue to bear in mind that just because the jihadists' worldview might be anachronistic and fantasy-driven, this does not mean that their methods will not be innovative and future-oriented.

From a larger historical perspective, the nexus between jihadists and WMD portends a more menacing nexus—that occurring where small groups of violent dissenters from the status quo, driven by solipsistic and uncompromising ideologies, become capable of repeatedly unleashing the most devastating weapons known to humanity and are, thus, able to present themselves as credible rivals to the state's curent monopoly on military power. We must do all we can to extend the period before this nexus materializes, for it will usher in an entirely new and even more dangerous world.

NOTES

1. *Report of the National Commission on Terrorist Attacks Upon the United States*, Chapter 12, 362.
2. "The Global Challenge of WMD Terrorism," *Country Reports on Terrorism* (2007), Chapter 4, U.S. State Department, April 30, 2008.
3. Those nearer to the seats of power had at their disposal even more tools, including assassination.
4. These ideas are not too dissimilar to those propounded by advocates of the notion of Fourth-Generation Warfare (4GW), including John Boyd, "Destruction and Creation" (1976), available at http://www.goalsys.com/books/documents/DESTRUCTION_AND_CREATION.pdf; and William Lind et al. "The Changing Face of War: Into the Fourth Generation," *Marine Corp Gazette* (October 1989).
5. The following idea is drawn from Testimony of Gary Anthony Ackerman, Research Director, National Consortium for the Study of Terrorism and Responses to Terrorism (START), "Nuclear Terrorism: Assessing the Threat to the Homeland," United States Senate Committee on Homeland Security and Governmental Affairs, April 2, 2008.
6. Poisoning or contamination were fairly common tactics in antediluvian warfare, but their efficacy was usually limited to a single food or water source, and even then often relied on a fair amount of luck or the assistance of pathogenic microorganisms.
7. In the following, "*" and "¤" are used to denote that the two elements are combined, without specifying the nature of the operation (for instance, addition versus multiplication).
8. There are numerous alternative constructions, for example, the one cited by Patrick Roberts in Chapter 12 and employed by the Department of Homeland, that is, Risk = Vulnerability * (Threat + Consequences), although we feel that the one we have suggested is a little easier to conceptualize.
9. This contrasts with the views of some other scholars, such as Jeffrey Mark Long, 23–24, who argue that the question of the legitimacy of WMD within the jihadist world has not been entirely settled.
10. This would make the central leadership invaluable to the movement even if it played no other role. As Daveed Gartenstein-Ross and Kyle Dabruzzi observe, "even if the central leadership's role is limited to connecting terrorist nodes—pairing skill sets, financing, and operatives—it can transform terrorist groups from disunited regional problems into cohesive adversaries capable of threatening Western societies." Daveed Gartenstein-Ross and Kyle Dabruzzi, "Is Al-Qaeda's Central Leadership Still Relevant?" *Middle East Quarterly*, Spring 2008, 27–36.
11. Marc Sageman, *Leaderless Jihad: Terror Networks in the Twenty-First Century* (Philadelphia: University of Pennsylvania Press, 2008).
12. For more on this idea, see Jeffrey W. Lewis, "Precision Terror: Suicide Bombing as Control Technology," *Terrorism and Political Violence* 19:2 (June 2007).
13. For each weapon type, the maximum scale of event believed to be feasible at the current time was used to generate the estimates. For example, the envisaged chemical event could be a large-scale release of toxic industrial chemicals (TICs) in an inhabited area or the aerosol dissemination in a contained space (such as a sports stadium) of a nerve agent.

14. Thomas D. Lehrman, Acting Office Director, Office of Weapons of Mass Destruction Terrorism, Department of State, "Building a Layered Defense to Combat Weapons of Mass Destruction (WMD) Terrorism," Remarks to the NPT Conference, Washington College of Law, American University, Washington, DC, February 9, 2006, available at http://www.state.gov/t/isn/rls/rm/61383.htm.
15. See, for example, Daniel Benjamin and Steve Simon, *The Next Attack: The Failure of the War on Terror and the Strategy for Getting it Right* (New York: Macmillan, 2005).
16. For an instructive analysis, see the 9/11 Commission Report, available at http://www.9-11commission.gov/report/911Report.pdf; and the Commission on the Intelligence Capabilities of the United States Regarding Weapons of Mass Destruction, available at http://www.wmd.gov/report/index.html.
17. For information about "wicked problems," see Nancy Kay Hayden, "Terrifying Landscapes: A Study of Scientific Research Into Understanding Motivations of Non-State Actors to Acquire and/or Use Weapons of Mass Destruction," Advanced Systems and Concepts Office, Defense Threat Reduction Agency, June 22, 2007.
18. Paul Pillar, "Counterterrorism after Al Qaeda," *Washington Quarterly* (2003), as cited in James F. Hoge, Jr. and Gideon Rose, eds., *Understanding the War on Terror* (New York: Foreign Affairs, 2005), 367–381.
19. Specifically Heisenberg's Uncertainty Principle, which basically asserts that the greater accuracy with which one determines the location of a particle, the less accuracy with which one can determine its momentum, and vice versa.
20. In many ways, this makes the threat of jihadist terrorism a "wicked problem"; Hayden, "Terrify Landscapes."
21. Bruce Hoffman, "Combating Al Qaeda and the Militant Islamic Threat," Testimony presented to the House Armed Services Committee, Subcommittee on Terrorism, Unconventional Threats and Capabilities, February 16, 2006, available at http://www.rand.org/pubs/testimonies/2006/RAND_CT255.pdf.

Postscript

As this volume was going to press [December 2008], a major U.S. government report was released that, although arrived at independently from the authors in this volume, echoed many of their findings. The *Report of the Commission on the Prevention of WMD Proliferation and Terrorism* (appropriately entitled "World at Risk") describes jihadists as key threats for using WMD and in its opening paragraph states that: "unless the world community acts decisively and with great urgency, it is more likely than not that a weapon of mass destruction will be used in a terrorist attack somewhere in the world by the end of 2013."[*] This sober assessment not only underscores the need for those researchers and scholars who study this phenomenon to continue to examine the possibility of such an attack, but demands heightened vigilance and dynamism by global intelligence and counterterrorism agencies in the face of this very real threat.

[*] Bob Graham, Jim Talent, et. al. *World At Risk: Report of the Commission on the Prevention of WMD Proliferation and Terrorism*. (New York: Vintage Books, 2008), xv.

Appendix A
Al-Qa'ida's CBRN Activities

Compiled by Erin McNerney and Matthew Rhodes

*Based on an earlier version covering the years 1997 through 2004 from the Weapons of Mass Destruction Terrorism Research Program at the James Martin Center for Nonproliferation Studies**

* The following table is meant as a comprehensive open-source information resource containing reports of incidents linking al-Qa'ida with chemical, biological, radiological, and nuclear weapons from 1997 to the present. A number of the sources for these incidents are of questionable reliability, however, and by including them, we make no assertions as to their validity

Estimated Date of Incident	CBRN	Incident	Date First Reported	Source(s)	Citations
Unspecified	Nuclear	A leaked intelligence report stated that bin Ladin allegedly paid over 2 million British pounds to a middle man in Kazakhstan for a "suitcase" bomb.	8/16/1998	Israeli military intelligence sources	Marie Colvin, "Holy War with US in his Sights," *Times* (London), 16 August 1998
Unspecified	Nuclear	Bin Ladin supposedly engaged in a comprehensive plan to acquire nuclear weapons and reportedly gave a group of Chechens $30 million in cash and two tons of opium in exchange for approximately 20 nuclear warheads.	11/1998	"Secret reports" that have reached the U.S. National Security Council from "several sources," including the Russian FSB	Riyad 'Alam al-Din, "Report Links Bin Ladin, Nuclear Weapons," *Al-Watan al-Arabi*, 13 November 1998; Emil Torabi, "Bin Laden's Nuclear Weapons," *Muslim Magazine* (Winter 1998)
Unspecified	Biological	Associates of bin Ladin were reported to have bought anthrax and plague from arms dealers in Kazakhstan.	6/4/2000	Unspecified "intelligence sources"	Paul Daley, "Report Says UBL-linked Terrorist Groups Possess 'Deadly' Anthrax, Plague Viruses," *Melbourne Age*, 4 June 2000
Unspecified	Nuclear/ Radiological	Bin Ladin allegedly sent envoys to several Eastern European countries to purchase enriched uranium. These efforts reportedly were both unsuccessful and very costly for the organization.	12/24/2000	"Arab security sources"	"Arab Security Sources Speak of a New Scenario for Afghanistan: Secret Roaming Networks that Exchange Nuclear Weapons for Drugs," *Al-Sharq al-Awsat*, 24 December 2000

Estimated Date of Incident	CBRN	Incident	Date First Reported	Source(s)	Citations
Unspecified	Nuclear / Radiological	Bin Ladin allegedly obtained seven enriched uranium rods, which were supposedly U.S.-made, from mafia connections.	11/2001	Italian anti-organized crime office, according to a "French expert"	Uthman Tizghart, "Does Bin Ladin Really Possess Weapons of Mass Destruction? Tale of Russian Mafia Bosfs Simion Mogilevich Who Supplied Bin Ladin With the Nuclear 'Dirty Bomb,'" *Al-Majallah (London)*, 25 November 2001
Unspecified	Biological	The Kabul office of Pakistani scientist Mehmood was reportedly found to contain documents indicating an interest in anthrax, including calculations concerning the aerial dispersal of anthrax via balloon. Also, an Associated Press photo showed something at the anthrax vaccine laboratory described as "anthrax spore concentrate."	11/28/2001	*The Economist*	"Sketches of Anthrax Bomb Found in Pakistani Scientist's Office," *Rediff.com*, 28 November 2001
Unspecified	Biological	U.S. forces discovered a BW laboratory under construction near Kandahar that was abandoned by al-Qa'ida. It was allegedly being built to produce anthrax, but no biological agents or traces thereof were found in the facility.	3/22/2002	U.S. Government	Dominic Evans, "US Troops Found Afghan Biological Lab," Reuters, 22 March 2002; Michael R. Gordon, "US Says it Found Qaeda Lab Being Built to Produce Anthrax," *New York Times*, 23 March 2002
Unspecified	Chemical/ Biological	The 11th volume of al-Qa'ida's 5,000-page *Encyclopedia of Jihad* was devoted to instructions on constructing CBW.	6/23/2002	Al-Qa'ida text: *Encyclopedia of Jihad*	"Osama Bin Laden's Bid to Acquire Weapons of Mass Destruction Represents the Greatest Threat that Western Civilization has Faced," *Mail on Sunday* (London), 23 June 2002

Estimated Date of Incident	CBRN	Incident	Date First Reported	Source(s)	Citations
Unspecified	Chemical	CNN correspondent Mike Boettcher reported that coalition intelligence agencies detected several recent purchases of cyanide by al-Qa'ida operatives.	7/31/2002	"Coalition intelligence agencies"	"Wolf Blitzer Reports," CNN, 31 July 2002.
Unspecified	Nuclear	At some point before September 11, 2001, bin Ladin allegedly bought 48 "suitcase nukes" from the Russian mafia.	9/8/2002	An unnamed French anti-terrorism expert	"Al-Majallah Obtains Serious Information on al-Qa'ida's Attempt to Acquire Nuclear Arms," *Al-Majallah* [London-based Saudi weekly], 8 September 2002
Unspecified	Chemical	CNN released videotapes, allegedly made by al-Qa'ida before September 11, 2001, showing dogs being killed by unidentified toxic chemicals (experts believe either a crude nerve agent or hydrogen cyanide gas was used).	8/19/2002	Al-Qa'ida videotapes	"Insight," CNN, 19 August 2002
Unspecified	Radiological	British intelligence discovered documents in western Afghanistan which suggested that al-Qa'ida members built a dirty bomb in Afghanistan. British officials also claim that the Taliban provided medical isotopes to al-Qa'ida members to help construct the bomb. U.S. officials cannot substantiate this claim.	1/30/2003	British Government	Ed Johnson, "Report: al-Qa'ida Made Bomb in Afghanistan," Associated Press, 30 January 2003

Estimated Date of Incident	CBRN	Incident	Date First Reported	Source(s)	Citations
Unspecified	Chemical/ Biological	With the capture of Khalid Shaykh Muhammad, investigators uncovered detailed information about production plans for chemical and biological weapons. According to captured documents, certain members of al-Qa'ida had plans and the requisite material to manufacture cyanide and two biological toxins, and were close to producing anthrax bacteria.	1/30/2003	British Government	Barton Gellman, "Al-Qa'ida Near Biological, Chemical Arms Production," *Washington Post*, 23 March 2003
Unspecified	Biological	Al-Qa'ida operatives allegedly planned to poison U.S. troops stationed in Afghanistan and Kuwait. Afghan terrorists allegedly delivered an "unspecified poison" to Afghan nationals who were hired as cooks for U.S. forces in Afghanistan. The incident has been tied to the January 2003 arrest of 11 al-Qa'ida suspects in Britain who were reportedly in possession of the biological toxin ricin. Some sources also indicate that the group Ansar al-Islam was involved in this plot to use ricin against U.S. troops.	2/1/2003	U.S. Government	James Gordon, "Feds Find Poison Plot vs. Gulf Troops," *Daily News*, 10 February 2003; Mike Toner, "Humble Bean Produces a Deadly Toxin," Cox News Service, 20 March 2003
Unspecified	Chemical	U.S. Government officials announced that a group of al-Qa'ida members along with al-Zarqawi had established a weapons lab in Kirma, Iraq. The lab was to be used to produce ricin and cyanide.	3/2/2004	U.S. Government	"Program Transcript—Terrorist Attacks in Iraq," *NBC Nightly News*, 2 March 2004

Estimated Date of Incident	CBRN	Incident	Date First Reported	Source(s)	Citations
Unspecified	Nuclear/ Biological/ Chemical	According to the 9/11 Commission, al-Qa'ida operatives in Afghanistan prior to the 9/11 attacks were considering ways of using WMD, including mustard and cyanide, against Jews in Iran, "forcing Russian scientists to fire a nuclear-armed missile at the U.S.," and using air conditioning systems in buildings to pump poisonous gas.	6/16/2004	U.S. Government; 9/11 Commission	"Al-Qaeda Operatives Discussed WMD Attacks While Training Prior to 9/11, Report Says," Global Security Newswire, 16 June 2004
Unspecified	Chemical/ Biological	French Interior Minister Dominique de Villepin claimed that al-Qa'ida affiliates had produced chemical and biological weapons in Georgia's Pankisi Gorge. De Villepin told members of a bioterrorism conference in Lyons, France, that after the fall of the Taliban, al-Qa'ida cells moved to the Pankisi Gorge in order to continue efforts to produce anthrax bacteria, ricin, and botulinum toxin.	1/3/2005	French Government	"Al-Qaeda Made Biological Weapons in Georgia—French Minister," *Moscow News*, 3 January 2005
Unspecified	Nuclear	Pakistani businessman Saifullah Paracha allegedly told al-Qa'ida operatives that he knew where to obtain nuclear weapons that could be used against U.S. troops and urged al-Qa'ida leaders to procure 50 of them. Paracha denied the allegations but admitted to meeting Usama bin Ladin in 1999 to discuss business deals. Paracha was the owner of an import company in New York.	2/11/2005	U.S. Government	"Pakistani Told al-Qaeda Operatives to Acquire Nuclear Weapons, U.S. Investigators Say," Nuclear Threat Initiative, 11 February 2005; Frank Davies, "U.S. Alleges Pakistani Businessman Urged al Qaeda to Acquire Nuclear Weapons," *Miami Herald*, 11 February 2005

Estimated Date of Incident	CBRN	Incident	Date First Reported	Source(s)	Citations
1993-1994	Nuclear/ Radiological	Jamal al-Fadhl claimed that, on behalf of bin Ladin, he investigated purchasing uranium for nuclear weapons.	2/2001	Al-Qa'ida operative Jamal al-Fadhl, a witness at a U.S. trial	Kimberly McCloud and Matthew Osborne, "WMD Terrorism and Usama bin Ladin," *CNS Report,* 20 November 2001, at http://cns.miis.edu/pubs/reports/binladen.htm
1996-1998	Chemical	Bin Ladin allegedly purchased CW over a two-year period prior to 1998 from European states and from the former Soviet Union. This information was allegedly provided by a jihadist leader while he was in custody (he was arrested on 20 August 1998 in Baku, Azerbaijan) during the April 1999 "Trial of the Returnees from Albania" in Egypt.	4/1999	Ahmad Salama Mabruk (in custody during his trial in Egypt)	Muhammad Salah, "Bin Ladin Front Reportedly Bought CBW From E. Europe," *Al-Hayah*, 20 April 1999; idem, "US Said Interrogating Jihadist Over CBW," *Al-Hayah*, 21 April 1999
1997 - 1998	Chemical/ Biological	Islamic extremists, including al-Qa'ida members, were allegedly trained in secret camps near Baghdad on how to use CW and BW by instructors from the secret Iraqi military intelligence, Unit 999.	7/14/2002	"Abu Muhammad," a former colonel in Saddam Husayn's Fidayin militia	Gwynne Roberts, "Militia Defector Claims Baghdad Trained Al-Qaeda Fighters in Chemical Warfare," *Sunday Times* (London), 14 July 2002
10/1997	Chemical / Biological	A meeting was held in Sudan between Bin Ladin, Ayman al-Zawahiri, and Hasan al-Turabi, leader of Sudan's National Islamic Front regime, about the construction of a CBW factory.	10/1997	Unspecified report received by a Western or Arab security agency	Jihad Salim, "Report on Bin Ladin, Zawahiri, 'Afghans,'" *Al-Watan al-Arabi*, 16 February 2001

Estimated Date of Incident	CBRN	Incident	Date First Reported	Source(s)	Citations
1998	Nuclear	On 8 February 2004, the Egyptian newspaper *Al-Hayat* reported that al-Qa'ida had purchased tactical nuclear weapons from the Ukraine in 1998 and was "storing them for possible use." Al-Qa'ida allegedly purchased the bombs in Kandahar after a visit from Ukrainian scientists. The Ukrainian government denied that the transaction had taken place, stating that all nuclear weapons stored in the Ukraine had been transferred to Russia as of 1996.	2/8/2004	*Al-Hayat* newspaper (Egypt)	"Al-Qaida Said to Possess Nuclear Arms," Associated Press, 9 February 2004; "Al-Qaida May Have Nuclear Weapons," Al Jazeera.net, 8 February 2004; "Al-Qaida Does Not Have Our Nuclear Bombs Insists Ukraine," *The Scotsman*, 11 February 2004; Sokov, Nikolai, "Suitcase Nukes: Permanently Lost Luggage," CNS,13 February 2004; Jane Macartney, "Al-Qaeda Unlikely to Have Attained Nuclear Know-How," Reuters, 6 February 2004
1998	Nuclear/ Radiological	Russian intelligence allegedly blocked a deal in which a Pakistani firm controlled by bin Ladin attempted to purchase Soviet-origin uranium.	9/19/2001	A "former Russian intelligence official"	Earl Lane and Knut Royce, "Nuclear Aspirations? Sources: Bin Laden Tried to Obtain Enriched Uranium," *Newsday*, 19 September 2001

Estimated Date of Incident	CBRN	Incident	Date First Reported	Source(s)	Citations
1998	Chemical/ Biological	A reporter purchased two computers from a looter in Kabul, Afghanistan, that had been found in an abandoned al-Qa'ida office. The U.S. government confirmed the existence of the computers. One of the computers allegedly contains a file describing "plans to launch a chemical and biological weapons program." Bin Ladin's deputy, al-Zawahiri, reportedly created computer documents describing his CW and BW program, code-named "Curdled Milk," which included work on a pesticide/nerve agent that used a chemical to increase absorption and was tested on rabbits and dogs. He was assisted by Midhat al-Mursi/Abu Khabbab, a chemical engineer.	12/2001	Al-Qa'ida computers	Alan Culluson and Andrew Higgins, "Computer in Kabul Holds Chilling Memos," *Wall Street Journal*, 31 December 2001; "Report: Al Qaeda Computer Had Plans for Bio-Weapons," Reuters, 21 December 2001
5/1998	Chemical/ Biological	Bin Ladin's group reportedly purchased three CBW factories in the former Yugoslavia and hired a number of Ukrainian chemists and biologists to train its members.	7/1998	"Arab sources"	Guido Olimpio, "Islamic Group Said Preparing Chemical Warfare on the West," *Corriere della Sera*, 8 July 1998; Yossef Bodansky, *Bin Laden: The Man Who Declared War on America* (Roseville, CA: Prima, 2001), 326

Estimated Date of Incident	CBRN	Incident	Date First Reported	Source(s)	Citations
8/1998	Chemical	The United States charged that al-Qa'ida was producing chemical weapons at the al-Shifa pharmaceutical factory in Khartoum, Sudan. As a result, the United States bombed the factory on 20 August 1998.	8/1998	U.S. Government	Michael Barletta, "Chemical Weapons in the Sudan: Allegations and Evidence," *The Nonproliferation Review* (Fall 1998), 115–136
8/1998	Chemical	John Gannon, chairman of the National Intelligence Council, revealed that the CIA had discovered that bin Ladin had attempted to acquire unspecified CW for use against U.S. troops stationed in the Persian Gulf.	8/1998	U.S. Central Intelligence Agency	Barry Schweid, "US Suggests Iraq Got Weapons from Sudan," *The Record* (New Jersey), 27 August 1998
9/1998	Nuclear/ Radiological	A bin Ladin aide, Mamduh Mahmud Salim, was arrested in Munich, Germany, on charges of trying to obtain nuclear materials (allegedly for al-Qa'ida), including highly enriched uranium.	9/26/1998	German Government	Benjamin Weiser, "US Says Bin Ladin Aide Tried to Get Nuclear Weapons," *New York Times*, 26 September 1998
9/1998	Chemical	Wadi al-Hajj, a Lebanese national, was arrested in Arlington, Texas, for perjury. The FBI contended that he had lied about his affiliation with bin Ladin in 1997 and 1998 court testimonies. A grand jury investigated al-Hajj's possible activities in procuring CW for bin Ladin.	12/20/1998	U.S. Government	CNN, 20 December 1998
1999	Chemical	Local Afghan sources said that bin Ladin was using a plant in Charassiab, a district 30 kilometers south of Kabul, to produce CW.	12/1999	(Afghan) Northern Alliance	"Afghan Alliance—UBL Trying to Make Chemical Weapons," *Parwan Payam-e Mojahed*, 23 December 1999

Estimated Date of Incident	CBRN	Incident	Date First Reported	Source(s)	Citations
4/1999	Biological	Bin Ladin and his followers allegedly obtained BW substances through the mail from countries of the former Soviet Union (the Ebola virus and salmonella bacterium), from East Asia (anthrax-causing bacteria), and from the Czech Republic (botulinum toxin).	8/1/1999	Various defendants in the Egyptian "Trial of the Returnees from Albania"	Al J. Venter, "Elements Loyal to Bin Laden Acquire Biological Agents 'Through the Mail'," *Jane's Intelligence Review* (August 1999); Khalid Sharaf al-Din, "Bin Ladin Men Reportedly Possess Biological Weapons," *Al-Sharq al-Awsat*, 6 March 1999
6/1999	Chemical/ Biological	Usama bin Ladin reportedly constructed "crude" CBW laboratories in Khost and Jalalabad, Afghanistan, and acquired ingredients for CW and BW from former Soviet states.	6/1999	Unspecified intelligence sources	John McWethy, "Bin Laden Set to Strike Again?" *ABC News*, 16 June 1999
7/1999	Chemical / Biological	An Islamist lawyer stated that bin Ladin's organization had CBW and would likely use such weapons against the United States.	7/1999	Muntasir al-Zayyat, lawyer defending Islamists in Egypt	"Islamist Lawyer on Bin Ladin, Groups," *Al-Sharq al-Awsat*, 12 July 1999
2/2000	Chemical	An apparent plot by nine Moroccans to poison the water supply of the U.S. embassy in Rome using a cyanide compound was foiled by Italian police.	2/2002	Various media reports	Eric Croddy et al., "Chemical Terrorist Plot in Rome?" *CNS Research Story*, 11 March 2002
2/2/2000	Chemical/ Biological	CIA Director George Tenet told the U.S. Senate that bin Ladin had shown a strong interest in CW and that his operatives had "trained to conduct attacks with toxic chemicals or biological toxins."	8/19/2002	CIA Director George Tenet	Pamela Hess, "Al Qaida may have chemical weapons," UPI, 19 August 2002

Estimated Date of Incident	CBRN	Incident	Date First Reported	Source(s)	Citations
Late 2000	Nuclear	The intelligence agency of an unnamed European country reportedly intercepted a shipment of approximately 20 nuclear warheads—originating from Kazakhstan, Russia, Turkmenistan, and the Ukraine—intended for bin Ladin and the Taliban regime of Afghanistan.	12/24/2000	"Arab security sources"	"Arab Security Sources Speak of a New Scenario for Afghanistan: Secret Roaming Networks that Exchange Nuclear Weapons for Drugs," *Al-Sharq al-Awsat*, 24 December 2000
2001	Biological	Various reports describe Muhammad Atta, the leader of the September 11 hijackers, meeting in Prague with an Iraqi intelligence agent, who allegedly gave him a vial of anthrax. This claim, originally made by foreign intelligence sources, was later contested by the Czech government.	10/20/2001	Israeli or Egyptian intelligence officials; denied by Czech intelligence chief Frantisek Bublan	"FBI Overlooks Iraq's Connections to Anthrax Attacks," Newsmax; Kriendler & Kreindler 9/11 lawsuit; "Prague Discounts an Iraqi Meeting," *New York Times*, 21 October 2001; "Czechs retract Iraq terror link," UPI, 20 October 2001.
2001	Biological	Documents found in Afghanistan ostensibly revealed that al-Qa'ida was researching the use of botulinum toxin to kill 2,000 people.	1/1/2002	Al-Qa'ida documents	"Al Qaeda Tested Germ Weapons," Reuters, 1 January 2002
2001	Chemical	Ahmad Rassam (an al-Qa'ida terrorist who pleaded guilty to plotting to bomb Los Angeles International Airport) claimed in court in 2001 that he had witnessed the gassing of a dog with cyanide by jihadis.	8/19/2002	Al-Qa'ida operative Ahmad Rassam, in U.S. custody	Pamela Hess, "Al Qaida May Have Chemical Weapons," *UPI*, 19 August 2002

Estimated Date of Incident	CBRN	Incident	Date First Reported	Source(s)	Citations
2001	Biological	In December 2001, Yazid Sufaat was arrested in Malaysia for terrorist activities as a member of Jemaah Islamiyah. According to subsequent interrogations of two captured terrorists, Khalid Shaykh Muhammad of al-Qa'ida and Hambali of Jamaah Islamiyah, Sufaat was part of a plan to obtain and weaponize biological warfare agents. Jamaah Islamiyah maintains close ties to al-Qa'ida.	12/1/2001	Malaysian authorities	Maria Ressa, "Reports: Al Qaeda Operative Sought Anthrax," CNN, 10 October 2003; Judith Miller, "U.S. Has New Concerns About Anthrax Readiness," *New York Times*, 28 December 2003; "Yazid Sufaat," The Open Source Threat Network Database, 26 January 2004
2/2001	Chemical	The United States allegedly aborted a planned air strike against Afghanistan for fear of a retaliatory chemical attack by al-Qa'ida, after receiving warnings from an Arab embassy in Islamabad, Pakistan.	2/2001	"Arab sources"	Sa'id al-Qaysi, "US Said Aborted Planned Attack on Bin Ladin for Fear of 'Chemical Strike,'" *Al-Watan al-Arabi*, 16 February 2001
2/2001	Chemical	Bin Ladin's elite 055 Brigade was supposedly reorganized under the leadership of Midhat al-Mursi, aka Abu Khabab, an Egyptian and an expert in sarin gas production.	2/2001	"Sources in Afghanistan"	Sa'id al-Qaysi, "US Said Aborted Planned Attack on Bin Ladin for Fear of 'Chemical Strike'," *Al-Watan al-Arabi*, 16 February 2001
4/2001	Nuclear/ Radiological	Ivan Ivanov claimed he met bin Ladin just over the Pakistani border in China and discussed setting up an environmental company to buy nuclear waste. Ivanov was then approached by a Pakistani chemical engineer interested in buying nuclear fuel rods from the Bulgarian Kozlodui reactor.	10/14/2001	Bulgarian businessman Ivan Ivanov and ex-Bulgarian Defense Minister Velizar Shalamanov	Adam Nathan and David Leppard, "Al-Qa'ida's Men Held Secret Meetings to Build 'Dirty Bomb,'" *Sunday Times* (London), 14 October 2001

Estimated Date of Incident	CBRN	Incident	Date First Reported	Source(s)	Citations
Summer 2001	Chemical/ Biological/ Nuclear	Starting in the summer of 2001, Iraqi military instructors allegedly trained al-Qa'ida fighters in northern Iraq on the use of CBW agents, and possibly also on the handling of nuclear devices. Between 150 and 250 al-Qa'ida trainees purportedly passed through the training facilities.	8/20/2002	DEBKA [an online newsletter relying heavily on hawkish Israeli intelligence sources]	"Abu Nidal's Nemesis," DEBKA File [Jerusalem], 20 August 2002
8/2001	Nuclear/ Biological/ Chemical	Two Pakistani scientists allegedly shared nuclear, biological, and chemical weapons information with bin Ladin, and thereby learned of radiological material given to him by the Islamic Movement of Uzbekistan. They told bin Ladin that there was insufficient material for use as a weapon.	11/12/2001	Pakistani scientists Sultan Bashir ul Din Mehmood and Abdul Majid; Pakistani government contests their level of nuclear knowledge	Toby Harnden, "Rogue Scientists Gave bin Laden Nuclear Secrets," *Daily Telegraph* (London), 13 December 2001; Peter Baker, "Pakistani Scientist Who Met Bin Laden Failed Polygraphs, Renewing Suspicions," *Washington Post*, 3 March 2002; Susan B. Glasser and Kamran Khan, "Pakistan Continues Probe of Nuclear Scientists," *Washington Post*, 14 November 2001

Estimated Date of Incident	CBRN	Incident	Date First Reported	Source(s)	Citations
11/2001	Nuclear	Al-Qa'ida reportedly acquired a Russian-made suitcase nuclear weapon from Central Asian sources. The device was reported to weigh 8 kg and to possess at least 2 kg of fissionable uranium and plutonium. The report said the device, with a serial number of 9999 and a manufacturing date of October 1998, could be set off by a mobile phone signal.	11/14/2001	"Reports from Pakistan"	"N-weapons May be in US Already," *Daily Telegraph* (Sydney, Australia), 14 November 2001
11/2001	Nuclear/ Chemical/ Radiological	A *Times* (London) reporter discovered a blueprint for a "Nagasaki bomb" in an abandoned al-Qa'ida house in Kabul, Afghanistan. Also discovered were studies of missiles, chemical devices, and nuclear devices.	11/19/2001	Al-Qa'ida files; *Times* reporter	"Nuke Plans Found; Brit Paper Discovers Details of Weapons in Kabul Safe House," *Toronto Sun*, 15 November 2001; Hugh Dougherty, "Afghan Nuclear Weapons Papers 'May Be Internet Spoofs,'" Press Association, 19 November 2001
Late 2001	Biological	U.S. operatives in Afghanistan allegedly discovered evidence indicating that one or more Russian scientists were helping al-Qa'ida weaponize anthrax.	12/9/2001	A "well-placed" U.S. intelligence source	Jeffrey Bartholet, "Terrorist Sleeper Cells," *Newsweek*, 9 December 2001
Late 2001	Biological	Reports claim that al-Zawahiri's home in Kabul tested positive (perhaps falsely) for traces of anthrax, as did five of nineteen al-Qa'ida labs in Afghanistan.	12/10/2001	U.S. Government	"Al-Qaeda: Anthrax Found in al-Qaeda home," Global Security Newswire, 10 December 2001; Judith Miller, "Labs Suggest Qaeda Planned to Build Arms, Officials Say," *New York Times*, 14 September 2002

Estimated Date of Incident	CBRN	Incident	Date First Reported	Source(s)	Citations
Late 2001	Biological	John Walker Lindh allegedly told interrogators that battlefield rumors suggested that a biological attack was expected to be a "second wave" al-Qa'ida attack.	10/3/2002	"American Taliban" John Walker Lindh, citing "battlefield rumors"	"US biological attack imminent—Taliban," iafrica.com, 12 December 2001; "Walker Lindh: Al Qaeda Planned More Attacks," CNN, 3 October 2002
2002	Chemical	One of the facilities of Ansar al-Islam, a radical Islamist group operating in northern Iraq with ties to al-Qa'ida and Iran, produced a form of cyanide cream that kills on contact.	8/25/2002	Unnamed U.S. interrogators	William Safire, "Tying Saddam to Terrorist Organizations," *New York Times*, 25 August 2002
First half of 2002	Biological	Ansar al-Islam was reported to have been experimenting with ricin, a deadly toxin, including on at least one human being. This report was denied by Ansar spokesman Muhammad Hasan Muhammad.	8/20/2002	U.S. Government	"US Knew of Bioterror Tests in Iraq," BBC News, 20 August 2002; "US Monitors Kurdish Extremists," Fox News, 21 August 2002; Isma'il Zayir, "Ansar al-Islam Group Accuses [Jalal] Talabani of Spreading Rumors About Its Cooperation with al-Qa'ida," *Al-Hayah*, 22 August 2002
1/2002	Nuclear	Diagrams of U.S. nuclear power plants were found in abandoned al-Qa'ida camps and facilities in Afghanistan.	1/31/02	Al-Qa'ida document cache	Bill Gertz, "Nuclear Plants Targeted," *Washington Times*, 31 January 2002; John J. Lumpkin, "Diagrams Show Interest in Nuke Plants," Associated Press, 30 January 2002

Estimated Date of Incident	CBRN	Incident	Date First Reported	Source(s)	Citations
2/2002	Nuclear	No evidence was discovered in Afghanistan that al-Qa'ida possessed nuclear weapons, raising the question of whether al-Qa'ida might have been tricked into buying metal containers with phony nuclear symbols, but filled with worthless material.	2/26/2002	U.S. analysts	Thom Shanker, "US Analysts Find No Sign bin Laden Had Nuclear Arms," *New York Times*, 26 February 2002
5/2002	Radiological	U.S. citizen Abdullah al-Muhajir (formerly José Padilla) was arrested in Chicago and alleged to be involved with al-Qa'ida in planning to perpetrate a radiological bomb attack in the United States.	6/11/2002	U.S. Government	Dan Eggen and Susan Schmidt, "'Dirty Bomb' Plot Uncovered, US Says: Suspected Al Qaeda Operative Held as 'Enemy Combatant,'" *Washington Post*, 11 June 2002
5/2002	Chemical	Among the items seized during the arrest of Sami Uthman, a Lebanese national who moved to the United States and became an Imam at a Islamist mosque in Seattle, were papers by London-based al-Qa'ida recruiter Shaykh Abu Hamza al-Masri, firearms, military manuals, and "instructions on poisoning water sources."	7/13/2002	Confidential "investigative document"	Patrick J. McDonnell and Josh Meyer, "Links to Terrorism Probed in Northwest," *Los Angeles Times*, 13 July 2002
6/3/2002	Radiological	Al-Qa'ida allegedly attempted to acquire 11 pounds of radioactive thallium from measuring devices on decommissioned Russian submarines, but Russia's Federal Security Service claims to have blocked the attempt.	6/3/2002	Russia's Federal Security Service	"Insider Notes," UPI, 3 June 2002

Estimated Date of Incident	CBRN	Incident	Date First Reported	Source(s)	Citations
7/18/2002	Biological	Stephen Younger, director of the Defense Threat Reduction Agency, claimed that al-Qa'ida's interest in BWs was focused mainly on anthrax.	7/18/2002	Stephen Younger	"Weapons Worries," CBS News, 18 July 2002
9/13/2002	Chemical/ Biological	Pentagon officials admitted that lab equipment found near Kandahar, Afghanistan, supported the assessment that al-Qa'ida might have acquired what it needed for "a very limited production of biological and chemical agents."	9/14/2002	U.S. Government	Judith Miller, "Lab Suggests Qaeda Planned to Build Arms, Officials Say," *New York Times*, 14 September 2002
10/2002 or 11/2002	Chemical	The Islamist group Asbat al-Ansar, a Lebanon-based Sunni organization affiliated with al-Qa'ida that is currently operating in northern Iraq, reportedly obtained the nerve agent VX from the Iraqi regime.	12/12/2002	U.S. Government	Barton Gellman, "US Suspects Al Qaeda Got Nerve Agent From Iraqis," *Washington Post*, 12 December 2002
11/9/2002	Chemical	British security officials arrested three men reportedly plotting a cyanide attack on the London subway.	11/18/2002	Unnamed sources	Hala Jaber and Nicholas Rufford, "MI5 Foils Poison-Gas Attack on the Tube," *Sunday Times* (London), 17 November 2002.
Early 2003	Radiological	After the 2003 Casablanca bombings, a police roundup of Salafia Jihadia exposed a plot by 'Abd al-'Aziz ibn Laysh to attack a French nuclear power plant at Cap de la Hague. Additional evidence indicated that members of al-Qa'ida trained Salafia Jihadia for this mission.	6/7/2003	Moroccan authorities	Martin Arostegui, Terrorism in Morocco Deeper Than Imagined," UPI, 7 June 2003; "Frenchman on Trial in Morocco Over Suicide Bombings," AFP, 25 August 2003

Estimated Date of Incident	CBRN	Incident	Date First Reported	Source(s)	Citations
1/5/2003	Biological	Six Algerians were arrested in London and charged with plotting to produce ricin. Authorities discovered traces of ricin and equipment used to process castor beans in the apartment. According to news sources, the group was plotting to attack a British military base by poisoning the food. Later reports indicated that the substance tested in the apartment was not ricin, however.	1/9/2003	British Government	Jeffrey Bale, Anjali Bhattacharjee, Eric Croddy, and Richard Pilch, MD, "Ricin Found in London: An al-Qa'ida Connection," Center for Nonproliferation Studies, 23 January 2002, available at http://cns.miis.edu/iiop/cnsdata?Action=1Concept=0&Mime=1&collect
3/1/2003	Radiological	On 20 March 2003, the FBI announced that they were searching for Adnan al- Shukrijuma in connection with the Jose Padilla case. Padilla was arrested May 2002 for plotting to obtain materials in Canada for a dirty bomb. Shukrijuma was identified from documents obtained in connection with the 2002 arrest of Ramzi bin al-Shib, a key 9/11 architect.	3/1/2003	FBI	Bill Gertz, "Al Qaeda Pursued a Dirty Bomb," *Washington Times*, 17 October 2003; A1; Entity Record: "Adnan El Shukrijumah," Sentenial TMS Records: Tracking the Threat, 25 November 2003. Available online at http://www.trackingthethreat.com/db/ENT1706.htm (accessed 20 May 2004); Katherine Wexler, "Father Denies Son Linked to Terror," *St. Petersburg Times*, 22 March 2003; Scott Wheeler, "Evidence Points to Dirty-Bomb Plot," *Insight Magazine*, 29 October 2003

Estimated Date of Incident	CBRN	Incident	Date First Reported	Source(s)	Citations
2004	Radiological	Reports indicated that an al-Qa'ida affiliate named Midhat Mursi may have been constructing a "dirty bomb" in early 2004. Mursi was reportedly in contact with Ayman al-Zawahiri and was suspected of managing al-Qa'ida chemical labs in Afghanistan. Mursi allegedly uses the name "Abu Khabab."	1/1/2004	U.S. Government	Muhammad Wajdi Qandyl, "Searching for Weapons of Mass Destruction and Al-Qa'ida," *Al-Akhbar* (Cairo), 18 January 2004
1/23/2004	Chemical	U.S. forces found 3 kg of cyanide at the Baghdad house of Ahmad Fadhl Nazzal al-Khalayila, an aide to al-Zarqawi. The cyanide was to be placed in construction bricks and used against coalition troops. Troops also uncovered a document thought to be written by al-Zarqawi asking al-Qa'ida for aid.	2/7/2004	U.S. Government	John Lumpkin, "U.S. Forces in Iraq Find Some Cyanide," AP, 7 February 2004; Douglas Jehl, "U.S. Aids Report Evidence Tying Al Qaeda To Attacks," *New York Times*, 10 February 2004
3/1/2004	Chemical	British authorities announced they had thwarted a possible chemical attack tenuously linked to al-Qa'ida. The plot, which was in an early planning stage, involved the use of conventional explosions enhanced with osmium tetroxide in London's shopping centers, railway stations, and the Underground.	4/5/2004	British authorities	"Deadly Chemical Planned for Use in Potential British Bomb Plot," AFP, 26 April 2004; "Osmium Tetroxide: A New Chemical Terrorism Weapon," *CNS Research Story of the Week*, 13 April 2004; available at http://cns.miis.edu/pubs/week/040413.htm

Estimated Date of Incident	CBRN	Incident	Date First Reported	Source(s)	Citations
4/20/2004	Chemical	The Jordanian Intelligence Service seized six trucks wired with explosives containing 20 tons of an unknown chemical. The trucks were reportedly part of a plot by al-Zarqawi and a number of al-Qa'ida members to destroy Jordan's Intelligence Department, Prime Minister's office, and the U.S. embassy.	4/21/2004	Jordanian Government	"Qaeda-Linked Chemical Attack in Jordan Could Have Killed 80,000," AFP, 26 April 2004; "Confessions of Group Planning Jordan Chemical Attack," *BBC Monitoring,* 26 April 2004; Interview with Mahmud Al-Kharabsha, Member of the Jordanian Parliament
6/1/2004	Chemical/ Radiological	Eight men were arrested in Britain and charged with conspiracy to murder after they were discovered with information on chemicals, explosives, and radiological materials. Also in their possession were plans of the New York Stock Exchange, the Citigroup Building in New York, the International Monetary Fund in Washington, and the Prudential Building in New Jersey. The arrests occurred two weeks after a series of 13 arrests of men allegedly affiliated with the al-Qa'ida network. The men were identified as Dhiren Barot, Omar Abdur Rehman, Zia ul Haq, Abdul Aziz Jalil, Nadeem Tarmohammed, Moammed Naveed Bhatti, Quaisar Shaffi, and Junade Feroze.	8/2004	British Government	Ben English, "Britain Charges Eight over US 'Terror Campaign,'" *The Advertiser*, 18 August 2004

Estimated Date of Incident	CBRN	Incident	Date First Reported	Source(s)	Citations
08/2004	Nuclear/ Radiological	When U.S. officials arrested Sharif al-Masri, an Egyptian al-Qa'ida operative in Pakistan, he claimed that al-Qa'ida had been working to move nuclear materials from Europe to Mexico in order to launch attacks on the United States. Al-Qa'ida members previously arrested indicated that the group viewed Mexico as a good place to acquire and assemble chemical, biological, and radiological materials.	11/15/2004	U.S. Government	"Mexico Link in Qaeda Nuke Plot," *The New York Post*, 15 November 2004; "Bordering on Nukes," *Time* magazine, 22 November 2004; "Qaeda Wants to Smuggle N-Material to US," *The Nation*, 17 November 2004
11/2004	Nuclear / Radiological	A German citizen of Iraqi descent, Ibrahim Mohammad K., allegedly attempted to purchase 48 grams of enriched uranium from a group in Luxembourg, and he and his brother, Yasser Abu S., were arrested by the German police. Ibrahim was a veteran of al-Qa'ida's terrorist camps and was believed to have been in close contact with Usama bin Ladin and Ramzi bin al-Shibh.	1/23/2005	German Government	Craig Whitlock, "Germany Arrests 2 Al Qaeda Suspects," *Washington Post*, 24 January 2005, pg. A12; Mark Lander, "German Arrest 2 on Suspicion of Planning Suicide Blast," *The New York Times*, 24 January 2005, A11; "German Authorities Detain Two Suspected Al-Qa'ida Members," *BBC Monitoring*, 23 January 2005
2005	Chemical	Abu Musab al-Zarqawi was reportedly planning a chemical attack in Europe, according to German intelligence services.	3/30/2005	German Federal Intelligence Service	"Zarqawi Planning Chemical Attack in Europe: German Press," AFP, 30 March 2005

Estimated Date of Incident	CBRN	Incident	Date First Reported	Source(s)	Citations
2005	Chemical	A French Al-Qa'ida cell led by Said Arif purportedly planned to "unleash an unspecified chemical agent" on a U.S. naval base in Rota, Spain.	5/3/2005	French authorities	"Spain: Al Qaida Planned Chemical Attack," UPI, 3 May 2005; "Qaeda Eyed Chemical Hit on U.S. Base in Spain-Paper," Reuters, 3 May 2005; "Zarqawi Planned Chemical Attack on US Base in Rota," *The Spain Herald*, 4 May 2005
9/12/2005	Chemical	Jaysh al-Ta'ifa al-Mansoura (Army of the Victorious Community) issued a statement claiming that it had used chemical weapons in mortar attacks in Baghdad's Green Zone. The claim was unsubstantiated and U.S. and Iraqi spokespersons later refuted the claim, announcing that two mortar shells had exploded in an empty parking lot, causing no casualties. Jaysh al-Ta'ifa al-Mansoura claimed to be linked to al-Qa'ida, but an al-Qa'ida spokesperson denied any connection with this bombing.	9/13/2005	U.S. and Iraqi Governments	"Al-Qaeda-linked Group Says it Fired Chemical Arms at Baghdad," AFX International Focus, 13 September 2005

Estimated Date of Incident	CBRN	Incident	Date First Reported	Source(s)	Citations
11/20/2005	Chemical	Authorities in Morocco arrested 17 members of the Salafist Group for Preaching and Combat who were suspected of links to al-Qa'ida and who were allegedly in the process of renaming their group "al-Qa'ida Organization in the Arab Maghreb Countries." In the process of these arrests, authorities discovered diagrams for the construction of a bomb employing toxic gas.	11/30/2005	Moroccan authorities	"Paper Says Moroccan Terrorist Cell Planned to Produce Toxic Gases," *Al-Ahdath al-Maghribiyah*, 30 November 2005; MoroccanAuthorities Foil Terrorist Cell Pursuing Chemical Weapons," *WMD Insights*, February 2006, available at http://www.wmdinsights.com/Old_Africa/Feb06/12_AF1_Moroccon.htm
1/28/2007	Chemical	A suicide bomber drove a dump truck filled with explosives and a chlorine tank into an Emergency Response Unit (ERU) compound, northwest of Ramadi, Iraq. The attack killed 16 people and injured 52, but according to U.S. officials, there were no indications that any of the casualties were the result of the release of chlorine gas.	1/30/2007	U.S. Government	"Emergency Response Unit Compound in Ramadi Attacked by SVBIED," Multi-National Force—West PAO, 30 January 2007; 1st Lieutenant Shawn Mercer
2/20/2007	Chemical	Insurgents suspected to be from the group al-Qa'ida in Iraq detonated a crude chlorine bomb outside a restaurant in the village of al-Taji, Salahuddin Province, Iraq. During the attack, two chlorine tanks were thrown from a vehicle and began to leak gas into the surrounding area, killing 6 and injuring over 130 due to gas exposure.	2/21/2007	U.S. Government	Christian Berthelsen, "The Conflict in Iraq: Bomber Targets Funeral," *Los Angeles Times*, 21 February 2007; Borzou Daragahi, "The World: Another Chlorine Gas Bomb Attack in Iraq," *Los Angeles Times*, 22 February 2007; "Blood Flows in Terror Day," *Northern Territory News*, 21 February 2007

Estimated Date of Incident	CBRN	Incident	Date First Reported	Source(s)	Citations
2/21/2007	Chemical	During a raid on two suspected car bomb factories in the Al-Garma district east of Fallujah, Iraq, U.S. and Iraqi forces seized conventional weapons and chemical weapons including chlorine and "a glycerin substance." Four Iraqi citizens were arrested, and several vehicles intended for use as VBIED were also seized, one containing three canisters filled with an unidentifiable chemical. The factories were believed to belong to or be linked with al-Qa'ida in Iraq.	2/22/2007	U.S. and Iraqi Government	"Chemical Weapons network Captured in Iraq," *Al-Sharq al Awsat*, 27 February 2007; "Chlorine Cylinders Found in Iraq Bomb-Making Factory: General," AFP, 22 February 2007; "Joint Iraqi-US Operations Result in Death of 'Scores' of Terrorists," *Al-Ittihad*, 25 February 2007
3/16/2007	Chemical	The first of a series of three suicide attacks using chlorine gas, suspected to be perpetrated by al-Qa'ida in Iraq, occurred at 4:11 pm, northeast of Ramadi, Anbar Province, Iraq. The driver of a pickup truck carrying an explosive device attached to pressurized chlorine gas containers detonated his vehicle at an Iraqi security force checkpoint northeast of Ramadi, Iraq. One U.S. soldier and one Iraqi civilian were wounded in the attack.	3/18/2007	U.S. and Iraqi Government	Ibon Villebeitia, "Decapitated Bodies of Nine Police Found in al-Qa'ida Area of Baghdad," *The Independent*, 19 March 2007; Kim Gamel, "Chlorine-Laden Suicide Truck Bombs Strike Anbar Province, Sickening Hundreds," AP, 18 March 2007; Kirk Semple, "Suicide Bombers Using Chlorine Gas Kill 2 and Sicken Hundreds in Western Iraq," *New York Times*, 18 March 2007; Tina Susman and Christian Berthelsen, "Chlorine Bomb Attacks in Iraq Kill 2, Sicken 350," *Los Angeles Times*, 18 March 2007

Estimated Date of Incident	CBRN	Incident	Date First Reported	Source(s)	Citations
3/16/2007	Chemical	The second of a series of three suicide attacks using chlorine gas, suspected to be perpetrated by al-Qa'ida in Iraq, occurred at roughly 7:00 pm, near Amariya, Anbar Province, Iraq. The driver of a dump truck carrying an explosive device attached to chlorine gas tanks detonated his vehicle when he was blocked at an Iraqi checkpoint. Two Iraqi police officers were killed in the explosion, while close to 100 were treated for symptoms of chlorine gas exposure.	3/18/2007	U.S. and Iraqi Government	Ibon Villebeitia, "Decapitated Bodies of Nine Police Found in al-Qa'ida Area of Baghdad," *The Independent*, 19 March 2007; Karin Brulliard, "Chlorince Blasts Kill 8; 6 Troops Also die in Iraq," *Washington Post*, 18 March 2007; "Chemical Weapons in Iraq," Kommersant.com (in English), 19 March 2007, available from FBIS, document identification number CEP20070319950035; Kirk Semple, "Suicide Bombers Using Chlorine Gas Kill 2 and Sicken Hundreds in Western Iraq," *New York Times*, 18 March 2007; Tina Susman and Christian Berthelsen, "Chlorine Bomb Attacks in Iraq Kill 2, Sicken 350," *Los Angeles Times*, 18 March 2007

Estimated Date of Incident	CBRN	Incident	Date First Reported	Source(s)	Citations
3/16/2007	Chemical	The third of a series of three suicide attacks using chlorine gas, suspected to be perpetrated by al-Qa'ida in Iraq, occurred at 7:13 pm in the Albu Issa tribal region of Anbar Province, Iraq. The driver of a dump truck carrying an explosive device attached to a tank holding "at least 900 liters" of pressurized chlorine gas detonated his vehicle near the home of Khamis al-Hasnawi, a Sunni tribal leader. Two civilians were killed and up to six were wounded in the attack. Additionally, a U.S. military spokesperson claimed that about 250 civilians had been exposed to the gas, some of whom needed treatment.	3/18/2007	U.S. and Iraqi Government	"Chemical Weapons in Iraq," Kommersant.com (in English), 19 March 2007, available from FBIS, document identification number CEP20070319950035; Ibon Villebeitia, "Decapitated Bodies of Nine Police Found in al-Qa'ida Area of Baghdad," *The Independent*, 19 March 2007; Karin Brulliard, "Chlorince Blasts Kill 8; 6 Troops Also die in Iraq," *Washington Post*, 18 March 2007; Kim Gamel, "Chlorine-Laden Suicide Truck Bombs Strike Anbar Province, Sickening Hundreds," AP, 18 March 2007; Kirk Semple, "Suicide Bombers Using Chlorine Gas Kill 2 and Sicken Hundreds in Western Iraq," *New York Times*, 18 March 2007; Tina Susman and Christian Berthelsen, "Chlorine Bomb Attacks in Iraq Kill 2, Sicken 350," *Los Angeles Times*, 18 March 2007

Estimated Date of Incident	CBRN	Incident	Date First Reported	Source(s)	Citations
4/6/2007	Chemical	In Ramadi, Iraq, a truck driven by a suicide bomber swerved into an apartment building and exploded. The truck had approached a security checkpoint at a high speed and the security officers had opened fire on it. The vehicle was suspected to have been carrying chlorine gas canisters, and it is unknown if the gunfire, the collision, or detonation by the driver caused the explosion. Twelve Iraqi civilians were killed and 43 were injured in the explosion, though it is not known how many of the casualties were due to the explosion and how many were due to the chlorine gas. It is unclear as to whether the casualties were caused by the explosives or by the release of the chlorine gas.	4/7/2007	U.S. and Iraqi Governments	Alissa J. Rubin, "Chlorine Gas Attack by Truck Bomber Kills Up to 30 in Iraq," *New York Times*, 7 April 2007; Karin Brulliard, "Gas Bomb Explodes in Ramadi," *Washington Post*, 7 April 2007; Multi-National Force—West PAO, "Suicide Vehicle Detonates Outside Police Checkpoint," No. 20070406-34, 6 April 2007, available online at http://www.mnf.iraq.com, accessed on 13 May 2007; Ned Parker, "U.S.-Iraqi Raids Target Sadr Militiamen," *Los Angeles Times*, 7 April 2007

The CNS researchers that contributed to the earlier version of this table include Lindsey DeFazio, Matthew Osborne, Benjamin Heath, Kimberly McCloud, Gary A. Ackerman, Jeffrey M. Bale, Praveen Abhayaratne, Lauren Harrison, and Lydia Hansell. The CNS WMD Terrorism Database was a valuable information source for completion of this table through 2007.

Appendix B
Selected Jihadist Statements and Discussion on WMD[1]

Compiled by Erin McNerney

Date of Statement	Person Making Statement	Provenance	Source of Statement	Main Points	Selected Quotes
Unspecified	Unidentified member of Islamic Jihad		Post, Jerrold M., Sprinzak, Ehud and Denny, Laurita M. (2003) "The Terrorists in Their Own Words: Interviews with 35 Incarcerated Middle Eastern Terrorists," Terrorism and Political Violence, 15:1, 171-184, pp. 180-181.	We (Islamic Jihad) were not interested in WMD. The use of WMD is forbidden under Islamic law because it damages the land and living things	"As for the question of weapons of mass destruction or non-conventional weapons, the question never arose. All I wanted was a pistol. But we did discuss the subject once. Islam wants to liberate, not kill. Under Islamic law, mass destruction is forbidden. For example, chemical, biological or atomic weapons damage the land and living things, including animals and plants, which are God's creations. Poisoning wells or rivers is forbidden under Islam."
Unspecified	Unidentified members of Izz a-Din al-Qassam		Post, Jerrold M., Sprinzak, Ehud and Denny, Laurita M. (2003) "The Terrorists in Their Own Words: Interviews with 35 Incarcerated Middle Eastern Terrorists," Terrorism and Political Violence, 15:1, 171-184, 180.	We (members of Izz a-Din al-Qassam) would not hesitate to use WMD. WMD would make Izz a-Din al-Qassam stronger.	We would like the organization to have any kind of weaponry "that is necessary to defeat the enemy and to liberate our lands and can inflict damage to the enemy."

Date of Statement	Person Making Statement	Provenance	Source of Statement	Main Points	Selected Quotes
March 1998	Usama bin Ladin	Leader of al-Qa'ida	*Interview*: "Interview with bin Laden Reported," March 31, 1998, FBIS document no. FTS1998033100479. As cited in Sara Daly, John Parachini, and William Rosenau, *Aum Shinrikyo, Al Qaeda, and the Kinshasa Reactor: Implications of Three Case Studies for Combating Nuclear Terrorism*, Washington DC: RAND Corp., 2005.	The United States should be annihilated, and every Muslim must struggle to achieve this.	"The United States is the biggest terrorist and rogue and it is the duty of every Muslim to struggle for its annihilation."
May 1998	Usama bin Ladin	Leader of al-Qa'ida	*Televised interview broadcast on ABC*: http://www.pbs. Org/wgbh/pages/frontline/shows/binladen/who/interview.html .	Americans can only be stopped through retaliation in kind with a nuclear weapon.	"Those who threw atomic bombs and used the weapons of mass destruction against Nagasaki and Hiroshima were the Americans. Can the bombs differentiate between military and women and infants and children? America has no religion that can deter her from exterminating whole peoples. Your position against Muslims in Palestine is despicable and disgraceful. America has no shame. ... We believe that the worst thieves in the world today and the worst terrorists are the Americans. Nothing could stop you except perhaps retaliation in kind."

Date of Statement	Person Making Statement	Provenance	Source of Statement	Main Points	Selected Quotes
December 1998	Usama bin Ladin	Leader of al-Qa'ida	*Interview*: John Miller, "Terror Suspect: an Interview with Osama bin Laden," ABC News, December 22, 1998.	It is a religious duty for Muslims to acquire the weapons needed (including WMD) to protect themselves and others.	"Acquiring weapons for the defense of Muslims is a religious duty. If I indeed have acquired these weapons I am carrying out a duty. It would be a sin for Muslims not to try and possess weapons that would prevent the infidels from inflicting harm on Muslims. But how we would use these weapons if we possessed them is up to us."
December 1998	Usama bin Ladin	Leader of al-Qa'ida	*Al Jazira interview*: Bruce Lawrence, ed., *Messages to the World: The Statements of Osama bin Ladin*, London: Verso, 2005, 65–94.	Christians and Israel have nuclear weapons. Muslims have nuclear weapons too (Pakistan).	"America knows today that Muslims [i.e., Pakistan] are in possession of such a weapon."
April 15, 1999	Ayman al-Zawahiri	Senior member of al-Qa'ida's shura council; described as second in command to Usama bin Ladin	*E-mail to Muhammad Atif*: Alan Cullison, "Inside Al-Qaeda's Hard Drive," *The Atlantic Monthly*, September 2004.	Biological weapons could be very useful tools for global jihad. Westerners themselves helped us [al-Qa'ida] discover the utility of such weapons through their constantly expressed concerns. The best way to obtain a biological weapons capability would be to recruit a specialist with knowledge of biological pathogens.	a) "The enemy started thinking about these weapons [biological weapons] before WWI. Despite their extreme danger, we only became aware of them when the enemy drew our attention to them by repeatedly expressing concerns that they can be produced simply with easily available materials ..." b) "The destructive power of these weapons is no less than that of nuclear weapons."

Date of Statement	Person Making Statement	Provenance	Source of Statement	Main Points	Selected Quotes
					c) "A germ attack is often detected days after it occurs, which raises the number of victims." d) "Defense against such weapons is very difficult, particularly if large quantities are used … I would like to emphasize what we previously discussed—that looking for a specialist is the fastest, safest, and cheapest way [to embark on a biological weapons program]."
September 1999	Abu Mus'ab al-Suri	Prominent al-Qa'ida–linked strategist	*Lecture series that was audio-recorded*: From transcript of "Jihad Is the Solution," Audiofile No. 37, Tape No. 10b, 06:28 – 16:00, muntada al sawt, www.saowt.com/forum/showthread. Php?t=16158. Cited and translated in Brynjar Lia, *Architect of Global Jihad*, New York: Columbia University Press, 2008, 310–312.	Nuclear weapons and radioactive materials can be bought relatively easily in Central Asia.	"Weapons of mass destruction are nuclear. They are quick and easy and can be obtained from most mafias in the world. This is a strategic weapon. Nuclear weapons have become mafia merchandise. They are sold… in Uzbekistan and Pakistan. It is a beautiful and fantastic thing that the uranium sources in the world are located in the region in which we are now moving. Understand? The reservoirs of uranium in the world are in Central Asia."

Date of Statement	Person Making Statement	Provenance	Source of Statement	Main Points	Selected Quotes
November 5, 1999	Abu Mus'ab al-Suri	Prominent al-Qa'ida–linked strategist	Umar 'Abd al-Hakim (Abu Mus'ab al-Suri), "The Muslims in Central Asia and the Coming Battle of Islam," Kabul: The Ghuraba Center for Islamic Studies, November 5, 1999. Translated passages in Brynjar Lia, *Architect of Global Jihad*, New York: Columbia University Press, 2008.	Muslims must acquire WMD to restore the balance of power between them and the West, and for the purpose of deterrence. The Central Asian region has developed factories and possesses the raw material needed for WMD acquisition or production.	"The difference in armament and number between Muslims and their enemies, between the oppressed and the strong, has never been larger…Military logic shows us that it is almost absurd to launch a classical confrontational war to restore the balance of power… [Hence] the renascent Islamic forces in…Central Asia…must attempt to acquire weapons of mass destruction (nuclear, biological, bacteriological) in exactly the same way as the aggressive, oppressive world represented by the Jews and the West possesses these weapons. One has to threaten with them [these weapons] and deter the enemy exactly like they [the enemy] have been doing…The Central Asian region has developed factories, and they have raw material for these weapons, which has made a base and a hope for Muslims to acquire these weapons.…This is a strategic goal which is within reach, but only Allah knows."

Date of Statement	Person Making Statement	Provenance	Source of Statement	Main Points	Selected Quotes
November 17, 1999	Shaykh Muhammad Tantawi	Grand Shaykh of the al-Azhar mosque; prominent Sunni leader	Original at http://islamonline.net/iol-arabic/dowalia/alhadath-17-11/alhadath2.asp, November 17, 1999. Translated passage from Shmuel Bar, "Jihad Ideology in Light of Contemporary Fatwas," Hudson Institute, Series No. 1, Paper No. 1, August 2006, 14, available at http://www.futureofmuslimworld.com/docLib/20060906_ SBarJihad.pdf.	To draw an analogy from the ruling of Caliph Abu Bakr, if the enemy uses a nuclear bomb, it is the duty of Muslims to use it as well.	"Had Abu Bakr lived today he would have said to Khaled ibn Al-Walid: 'If they fight you with a nuclear bomb, fight them with a nuclear bomb.' Strength is [one] of the traits of good and wise people who know their obligation towards their God and towards their homeland, and they use this strength in order to defend their faith and their homeland. This is the Sunna that was known to the forefathers of all times, and is known to us as well."
2001	Ahmad Rassam	Al-Qa'ida member; contributor to alleged plot to bomb Los Angeles International Airport	*Testimony while in U.S. custody*: "Bin Laden's Biological Threat," BBC, 28 October 2001.	Bin Ladin is personally interested in using low-flying aircraft to dispense BW agents.	
November 2001	Usama bin Ladin	Leader of al-Qa'ida	*Interview with Pakistani journalist*: Hamid Mir, "Osama Claims He Has Nukes: If US Uses N-Arms It Will Get Same Response," *Dawn* [Karachi], November 10, 2001, available at www.dawn.com/2001/11/10/top1.htm.	We [Usama bin Ladin and his followers] have chemical and nuclear weapons and will use them as a deterrent.	"I wish to declare that if America used chemical or nuclear weapons against us, then we may retort with chemical and nuclear weapons. We have the weapons as [a] deterrent."

Date of Statement	Person Making Statement	Provenance	Source of Statement	Main Points	Selected Quotes
April 2002	Abu Zubaydah	Purportedly head of al-Qa'ida's operations and recruiting at time of his arrest	*Interrogation in U.S. custody*: Jamie McIntyre, "Zubaydah: Al Qaeda Had 'Dirty Bomb' Know-How," CNN, 22 April 2002.	Al-Qa'ida is interested in producing a dirty bomb and knows how to do it.	
June 2002	Sulayman Abu Ghayth	Al-Qa'ida spokesman	*Article published on website*: MEMRI Special Report No. 25, January 27, 2004, available at www.memri.org/bin/articles.cgi? Page=archives&Area=sr&ID=SR2504#_edn21.	Muslims have the right to kill four million Americans, including children, and to use chemical and biological weapons to accomplish this.	"The [number of Americans] killed in the World Trade Center and the Pentagon were no more than fair exchange for the ones killed in the Al-'Amiriya shelter in Iraq, and are but a tiny part of the exchange for those killed in Palestine, Somalia, Sudan, the Philippines, Bosnia, Kashmir, Chechnya, and Afghanistan. We have not reached parity with them. We have the right to kill four million Americans—two million of them children—and to exile twice as many and wound and cripple hundreds of thousands. Furthermore, it is our right to fight them with chemical and biological weapons, so as to afflict them with the fatal maladies that have afflicted the Muslims because of the [Americans'] chemical and biological weapons."

Date of Statement	Person Making Statement	Provenance	Source of Statement	Main Points	Selected Quotes
November 21, 2002	Usama bin Ladin	Leader of al-Qa'ida	"Statement from Abdallah Usama Bin Ladin to the Peoples of the Countries Allied to the Tyrannical U.S. Government," AlNeda.com, November 21, 2002.	The use of WMD against Americans is a legitimate response to their current and past killings of Muslims.	"This is an unfair division. The time has come for us to be equal… Just as you kill, you are killed. Just as you bombard, you are bombarded. Rejoice at the harm coming to you."
December 26, 2002	Abu Shihab al-Qandahari	Moderator of the Islamist Internet forum al-mojahedoon.net	*Short published article entitled "Nuclear WarIs the Solution for the Destruction of the United States"*: Reuven Paz, "The First Islamic Nuclear Threat Against the United States," International Institute for Counter-Terrorism, January 10, 2003, available at www.ict.org.il.	WMD should be used against the United States to kill a maximum number of Americans. (According to Paz, this article was the first publicly issued threat to use nuclear weapons against the United States from supporters of al-Qa'ida.)	"Indeed, you did read that [the title] correctly. This is the only way to kill the maximum number of Americans." "[Al-Qa'ida] owns 'dirty bombs' and 'bombs with lethal viruses,' which could cover American cities with deadly diseases and turn this nation…into a crowd of contaminated and sick people. The coming days will prove that Qa'idat al-Jihad is capable, with Allah's help, of turning the United States into a lake of lethal radiation, which would seem like the last days of humanity."

Date of Statement	Person Making Statement	Provenance	Source of Statement	Main Points	Selected Quotes
2003	Ayman al-Zawahiri	Senior member of al-Qa'ida's shura council; described as second in command to Usama bin Ladin	*Communication between al-Zawahiri and his operatives*: George Tenet, *At the Center of the Storm*, New York: HarperCollins, 2007.	(Al-Zawahiri canceled plans for a hydrogen cyanide gas attack in New York City, and said this, implying that a more deadly or spectacular attack would replace it.)	"We have something better in mind."
May 2003	Abu Muhammad al-Ablaj	Al-Qa'ida trainer	*E-mail to London-based magazine al-Majalla:* Ben Venzke, "al-Qaeda/al-Ablaj Threat Assessment, v1.0," IntelCenter Report, May 30, 2003, 7, available at http://www.intelcenter.com/ATA- PUB-v1-0.pdf.	We possess sarin gas and nuclear weapons and may use them on infidels.	"As to the use of sarin gas and nuclear [weapons], we will talk about them then and the infidels will know what harms them. They spared no effort in their war on us in Afghanistan and left no weapon unused. They should not therefore rule out the possibility that we will present them with our capabilities."

Date of Statement	Person Making Statement	Provenance	Source of Statement	Main Points	Selected Quotes
May 21, 2003	Shaykh Nasir ibn Hamid al-Fahd	Saudi cleric	*Written fatwa*: Nasir ibn Hamid al-Fahd, "A Treatise on the Legal Status of Using Weapons of Mass Destruction against Infidels," available at http://www.carnegieendowment.org/static/npp/fatwa.pdf.	Only God (not humans) has the power to proscribe the use of weapons of mass destruction. Muslims are not bound by international agreements regarding WMD because such agreements have no standing in Islamic law. The principle of reciprocity, as seen in the *Qur'an*, permits Muslims to attack America in massively destructive ways because of the massive harm America has done to Muslims and their lands. Civilians may be targeted because of the principle of reciprocity, and large numbers of civilian casualties are acceptable as long as they occur during the course of an attack meant to defeat an enemy, not just an attack targeting the innocent.	"This matter is so obvious to Muslims that it needs no demonstration.... Anyone who considers America's aggression against Muslims and their lands during the past decades... will conclude that striking her is permissible merely on the rule of treating as one has been treated. No other arguments need be mentioned. Some brothers have totaled the number of Muslims killed directly or indirectly by their weapons and come up with a figure of nearly 10 million." "Thus the situation in this regard is that if those engaged in jihad establish that the evil of the infidels can be repelled only by attacking them at night with weapons of mass destruction, they may be used even they annihilate all the infidels."

Date of Statement	Person Making Statement	Provenance	Source of Statement	Main Points	Selected Quotes
September 21, 2003	Abu Muhammad al-Ablaj	Al-Qa'ida trainer	*Interview in al-Majalla*: Mahmud Khalil, "Al-Qa'ida's Abu Muhammad al-Ablaj on Bin Ladin, Weapons, U.S. Targets," *al-Majalla*, September 21, 2003, translation at http://www.why-war.com/news/2003/09/21alqaidas.html.	A chemical, biological, or nuclear weapon must be used at a strategic moment.	"Is there a sane person who discloses his [WMD] secrets? Brother, the strategic weapons are not just [a matter of] remov[ing] the pin and strik[ing]. If such was the case, then [they] would have been available and [an attack] would have been carried out before the 'blessed strike' [9/11]. The matter needs time. Such a massive strategic weapon is bound to have reactions commensurate with its size. It must therefore be used at a time that makes the Crusader enemy beg on his knee that he does not want more strikes..."

Date of Statement	Person Making Statement	Provenance	Source of Statement	Main Points	Selected Quotes
November 22, 2003	Shaykh Nasir ibn Hamid al-Fahd	Saudi cleric	*Interview on Saudi national television:* Kelly Uphoff, "Osama bin Laden's Mandate for Nuclear Terror," JINSA Online, December 10, 2004, available at http://www.jinsa.org/articles /articles.html/function/view/categoryid/1701/documentid/2762/history/3,2360,655, 1701,2762.	(In response to criticism from Dr. Ayyid ibn 'Abdallah al Qarni, respected cleric and preacher, and regarding the May 12, 2003 terrorist bombing in Riyadh, Saudi Arabia, al-Fahd ostensibly backtracked on some of the statements made in earlier *fatwas*, including the WMD *fatwa*. His statements were suspected of being coerced by the Saudi government, however.)	Al-Fahd "demanded that this interview be conducted to acquit myself of such actions and so that people will know that we do not approve of such acts, which are prohibited."

Date of Statement	Person Making Statement	Provenance	Source of Statement	Main Points	Selected Quotes
December 25, 2003	Unknown	Unknown website participant	*Website posting*: strike-free.net/dead_list/list.htm, as cited in Walter Laqueur, ed., *Voices of Terror*, New York: Reed Press, 2004.	Unclear	"Rawalpindi 25/12/2003: Pakistan's U.S. led Dictator Musharraf has narrowly survived a second assassination bid this month. 'The Cretin and all his companions are safe and sound' said Major General Shaukat Sultan. An aide said Musharraf, who had been heading home, was in good spirits. The Pakistani nukes will soon get a new erratically and lethal owner and the American apes down with Mad Cow disease don't catch on nothing, awaiting a dirty bomb on nice homeland in a mass hysteria after orange fake alert."
December 2004	Abu Walid al-Masri	Al-Qa'ida insider	*Book manuscript*: Abu Walid al Masri, "The History of the Arab Afghans from the Time of their Arrival in Afghanistan until their Departure with the Taliban," serialized in *Al-Sharq al-Awsat*, December 8–14, 2004.	In inner al-Qa'ida discussions, the conclusion was reached that the group did need to acquire WMD to use in response to WMD attacks on Muslims.	"The conclusion reached was that al-Qa'ida must possess weapons for defense, based on what can be obtained or supplied in the nuclear, biological, or chemical fields, so that in a crisis, if the other side used weapons of mass destruction, it will not escape a deadly punishment…"

Date of Statement	Person Making Statement	Provenance	Source of Statement	Main Points	Selected Quotes
				Usama bin Ladin, though initially unsure about a dramatic increase in weaponry, gave in to pressure from members of al-Qa'ida's leadership to seek radioactive material from contacts in Chechnya.	
December 22, 2004	Abu Mus'ab al-Suri	Prominent al-Qa'ida-linked strategist	*Open letter to U.S. State Department posted on al-Suri's Web site*: "Communique from the Office of Abu Mus'ab al-Suri," December 22, 2004. See translated passages at www.globalterror alert.com/pdf/0705/abumusabalsuri.pdf.	Weapons of mass destruction should be used against the United States because the United States has used them against Islam. Usama bin Ladin should have employed WMD in the 9/11 attacks.	"If I were consulted in the case of that operation [9/11] I would advise the use of planes in flights from outside the U.S. that would carry WMD. Hitting the U.S. with WMD was and is still very complicated. Yet, it is possible after all, with Allah's help, and more important than being possible—it is vital."

Date of Statement	Person Making Statement	Provenance	Source of Statement	Main Points	Selected Quotes
				Using WMD against the United States is complicated, but possible, and should be done.	"The mujahidin may be able to obtain these weapons [nuclear, chemical, biological] by cooperating with whomever already possesses them, by buying them, or by building and using primitive radioactive weapons known as 'dirty bombs'...it is not a far cry from justice to adopt the slogan, 'Dirty Bombs for a Dirty Nation.' This is practically equal treatment. Let the American people—those who voted for killing, destruction, the looting of other nations' wealth, megalomania, and the desire to control others—be contaminated with radiation! We apologize for the radioactive fallout."
July 12, 2005	'Abd al-Qadir Fall Mamur	Fundamentalist imam with ties to al-Qa'ida	*Statement on Contracorrente television program called in via telephone from Senegal*: "Former Imam Threatens Chemical Attack in Italy 'Within 6 Months,'" *Libero* (Milan), 13 July 2005.	The Abu Hafs al-Masri Brigades are planning a nerve gas attack on one of Italy's symbolic cities within six months' time.	"Within six months Italy will be subjected to a chemical attack. This is the time to strike [Prime Minister Silvio] Berlusconi, and it will happen in a short space of time."

Date of Statement	Person Making Statement	Provenance	Source of Statement	Main Points	Selected Quotes
					"The cities which are candidates for being struck are symbolic cities such as Rome, Milan, Bologna, and Venice." The weapons to be used are "non-conventional weapons such as nerve gas, which Italy's current prevention measures are unable to detect."
August 2005	Abu Bakar Ba'asyir	Jemaah Islamiyah Leader	*Interview at Cipinang Prison in Jakarta*: Scott Atran, "The Emir: An Interview with Abu Bakar Ba'asyir, Alleged Leader of the Southeast Asian Jemaah Islamiyah Organization," Spotlight on Terror, 3:9, available at http://jamestown.org/terrorism/news/article.php?articleid=2369782.	The use of nuclear weapons by Muslims is justified where it is necessary, but in general, the goal of Muslims should be to scare enemies rather than kill them.	"Yes, [the use of nuclear weapons by Muslims is justified] if [it is] necessary. But the Islamic Ummah should seek to minimalize [the intensity of the fighting]. Allah has said in verse 8 chapter 60 that we should equip ourself with weapon power—that is an order—but preferably to scare and not to kill our enemy. The main goal is to scare them. If they are scared they won't bother us, and then we won't bother them as well. But if they persist, we have to kill them. In this way, Prophet Muhammad sought to minimalize the fighting."

Date of Statement	Person Making Statement	Provenance	Source of Statement	Main Points	Selected Quotes
October 2005	Abu al-Usud al-Faqir	Author of one al-Qa'ida's WMD manual	*Al-Qa'ida training manual*: Abu al-Usood al-Faqir, "Instances of Radiation Pollution from 1945–1987," al-Faruq website, October 2005. As cited in Sammy Salama and David Wheeler, "From the Horse's Mouth: Unraveling Al-Qa'ida's Target Selection Calculus," CNS Research Story, April 17, 2007, available at cns.miis.edu/pubs/week/070417.htm#fnB5.	Radiological attacks could be very effective and cause the United States and its allies significant economic damage. Jihadists should attempt such attacks.	"The important thing is to disperse radioactive material in a large commercial area so the government is forced to shut down this area which will cause this country massive economic disruption due to the following reasons: 1. The high costs of decontamination of radioactive areas. 2. The high economic losses in this large commercial area due to closure. 3. Subsequent unemployment and loss of jobs. 4. Stoppage of general life in that area. 5. Large compounded problems are to follow due to these losses. Suggested cities: Las Vegas (the city of fornication and gambling that does not sleep)—New York—London—Sydney—Tokyo—Moscow—Other large tourist cities—and commercial capitals of all infidel nations."

Date of Statement	Person Making Statement	Provenance	Source of Statement	Main Points	Selected Quotes
October 2006	Abu Hamza al-Muhajir (Abu 'Ayyub al-Masri)	Leader of al-Qa'ida in Iraq	*Audio recording posted on Web site*: "Islamist Websites Monitor No. 2 Abu Hamza Al-Muhajir: American Military Bases are an Ideal Environment for Trying Out Biological and Dirty Bombs," MEMRI Special Dispatch Series No. 1309, October 6, 2006, available at http://www.memri.org/bin/articles.cgi?Page=archives&Area=sd&ID=SP130906.	Nuclear scientists should join by his [Abu Hamza al-Muhajir's] mujahidin group. American military bases are ideal targets for the testing of WMD weapons.	"[T]he battlefield will accommodate your scientific aspirations." "My final message is [addressed] to those who have special skills and qualifications amongst the experts in [the fields of] chemistry, physics, management, electronics, communications and all the advanced specialties, particularly nuclear scientists and [experts] on explosives. I say [to them]: we have urgent need of you. The front of jihad will suit your aspirations. The American military bases, with their large areas, are an ideal environment for trying out your non-conventional bombs: the biological [bombs] and the so-called 'dirty' bombs..."

Date of Statement	Person Making Statement	Provenance	Source of Statement	Main Points	Selected Quotes
April 2007	Shayk Husayn ibn Mahmud	According to *Al-Sharq al-Awsat,* Shaykh Husayn ibn Mahmud is the pseudonym of an al-Qa'ida leader who frequently writes on Islamist forums.	*Article in* Sada Al-Jihad, *a jihadist e-magazine*: MEMRI Special Dispatch Series No. 1635, June 27, 2007, at www.memri.org/bin/articles.cgi?Page=archives&Area=sd&ID=SP163507.	The enemies of al-Qa'ida have used nuclear and chemical bombs on Muslims, and Allah commands us [al-Qa'ida] to respond in kind.	"Allah commands [us] to fight the enemy the same way he fights us, to kill him in the same way he kills us, and to deliberately kill those who set out to kill us. Today, our enemies hit us with nuclear bombs, cluster [bombs] and chemical [bombs] which have killed many of our men, women and children, destroyed homes and crops, spread disease and burned [people's] bodies. We have the right to fight back by the same means, by the command of Allah who [instructs us] to be ruthless and fierce [with the enemy] and to smite him, in order to teach others a lesson..."

Date of Statement	Person Making Statement	Provenance	Source of Statement	Main Points	Selected Quotes
April 2007	Abu Zabadi	Contributor to Islamist Web site	*Article posted on Islamist Web site Al-Firdaws*: "Is it Legitimate to Use Nuclear Weapons against the West? A Debate on an Islamist Forum," Special Dispatch Series, No. 1538, April 12, 2007.	A first strike nuclear attack would result in indiscriminate killing, which would violate Allah's commandment to preserve the lives of the innocent. The United States has not used nuclear weapons against Muslims, so it would be illegitimate for Muslims to use nuclear weapons to attack the United States. The matter of wiping the United Stats off the face of the earth for its immorality is up to God to decide—some Muslim nations are equally immoral. If Bin Ladin's followers want to respond to U.S. attacks, they should attack the United States on the battlefield, and not attack U.S. civilians.	"Since America and its allies are stronger than the Islamic nation,…" "circumstances forbid us to provoke America and its allies... even if Al-Qaeda succeeds in obtaining a nuclear bomb." "If God wishes to wipe America off the face of the earth because of its great corruption, the matter is in His hands [and not in the hands of the mujahideen]." "If Bin Laden and his followers wish to respond [to U.S. attacks] in kind, they should [confront] the evil troops on the battlefield."

Date of Statement	Person Making Statement	Provenance	Source of Statement	Main Points	Selected Quotes
April 2007	'Abd al-Sham	Contributor to Islamist Web site	*Article posted on Islamic Web site Al-Firdaws (responding to article by Abu Zabadi):* "Is it Legitimate to Use Nuclear Weapons against the West? A Debate on an Islamist Forum," MEMRI Special Dispatch Series, No. 1538, April 12, 2007.	Destruction caused by U.S. conventional weapons is much greater than that caused by a nuclear bomb, which legitimizes Muslim use of a nuclear bomb against the United States. Even things that are normally forbidden to Muslims are permitted when the attack is one of retribution in kind.	"The destructive power of the one-ton bombs dropped on Afghanistan alone is greater than that of the atomic bomb dropped on Hiroshima…" "The principle of retribution in kind applies, for example, when the infidels do something that is completely forbidden to Muslims, such as mutilating corpses. It is prohibited for Muslims [to do such a thing] unless the infidels commit [this crime] against Muslims!!!"

Date of Statement	Person Making Statement	Provenance	Source of Statement	Main Points	Selected Quotes
November 2007	Numan ibn 'Uthman	Former leader of the Libyan Islamic Fighting Group	*Open letter to Ayman al-Zawahiri*: "Terrorism: Jihad Has Failed, Former Libyan Islamist Tells al-Qaeda," *Adnkronos International*, November 7, 2007, available at http://www.adnkronos.com/AKI/English/Security/?id=1.0.1524980329.	At the Kandahar summit in 2000, Usama bin Ladin defined the acquisition of WMD as a "Shari'a Obligation." Al-Qa'ida does not have a strategic vision and would use any acquired WMD for indiscriminate killing, not for deterrence. Provoking the United States with WMD would only bring Western occupation of the entire Middle East, to the detriment of Arab countries.	"During this occasion [an al-Qa'ida summit in Kandahar, Afghanistan in 2000], I had a strong dispute with the martyr Abu Hafs al-Kumandan, because he was heavily involved in acquiring weapons of mass destruction. He wanted to use these weapons to dissuade the United State from attacking Afghanistan. And yet I knew that al-Qaeda did not have any strategic vision and would have used the weapons to kill indistriminately [sic] and not to dissuade....After seven years since that meeting, my convictions on these issues have only grown stronger."
Unknown	Abu Mus'ab al-Zarqawi	Former leader of al-Qa'ida in Iraq	"Al-Qa'ida Denies Jordan WMD Plot," BBC, April 30, 2004.	We [al-Qa'ida] would not hesitate to use a nuclear weapon to strike Israeli towns. We [al-Qa'ida] hope to have a nuclear weapon soon.	"If we had such a bomb—and we ask God that we have such a bomb soon—we would not hesitate for a moment to strike Israeli towns, such as Eilat, Tel Aviv and others."

Date of Statement	Person Making Statement	Provenance	Source of Statement	Main Points	Selected Quotes
Unknown	Abu 'Abdullah al-Kuwayti	Al-Qa'ida member	From http://www.ctc.usma.edu/aq/AFGP- 2002-001120Trans.pdf, as cited in Jerry Mark Long, *Strategic Culture, Al-Qaida, and Weapons of Mass Destruction*, November 20, 2006, 21, available at http://www.dtra.mil/documents/asco/publications/comparitive_strategic_cultures_curriculum/case%20studies/Al%20Qaeda%20(Long)%20rev%20final%020%20Nov.pdf.	We [al-Qa'ida] possess nuclear and biological weapons and may use them to kill hundreds of thousands of Americans that we don't wish to fight.	"If the American people are ready to die as we are ready to die, then our combat groups along with our military, nuclear, and biological equipment will kill hundreds of thousands of people we don't wish to fight."
Unknown	Ayman al-Zawahiri	Senior member of al-Qa'ida's shura council; described as second in command to Usama bin Ladin	*Interview with Pakistani journalist Hamid Mir*: Max Delany, "Under Attack al-Qaeda Makes Nuclear Claim," *The Moscow News*, 3 March 2004.	We [al-Qa'ida] acquired nuclear weapons in Central Asia—our affiliates traveled to several cities, including Moscow and Tashkent.	
Unknown	'Abd al-Aziz al-Muqrin and other unnamed contributors to an online al-Qa'ida manual	Al-Qa'ida members	*Al-Qa'ida manual posted online, entitled "The Base of the Vanguard"*: Jason Burke, "Al-Qaeda Launches Online Terrorist Manual," *The Guardian*, 18 January 2004.	The use of WMD, biological, and nuclear arms in particular, are one potential tactic in global jihad.	

Date of Statement	Person Making Statement	Provenance	Source of Statement	Main Points	Selected Quotes
Unknown	Fath Allah Fathi	A purported former deputy of al-Zarqawi and a leader of Ansar al-Islam	*Interrogation by CIA*: "Europe Target of Chemical Terror Plot, CIA Told," *El Tiempo* (Madrid), 25 January 2005.	A spectacular chemical attack is being planned against an unknown location in Europe.	A chemical attack is being planned against Europe that would be "more spectacular than 11 September." "The decision has been taken to use the chemical bomb, not so much because of its destructive potential, which is spectacular when compared with bombs manufactured with simple explosives, but rather above all because of the chaos effect it would produce among the population."
Unknown	Grand Ayatullah Ahmad Husayni al-Baghdadi	Shi'i cleric	*Remarks made on Al-Jazira*: Translated excerpts at "Iraqi Ayatollah Ahmad al-Baghdadi Talks of America's Annihilation and the Muslim Conquest of the World; Declares Support for Nuclear Bombs for Muslim and Arab Countries," MEMRI #1166, May 18, 2006, available at http://www.memri.org/bin/articles.cgi?Page=archives&Area=sd&ID= SP116606.	If biological and chemical weapons are needed, they will be used by the followers of Allah to conquer the world.	"If the objective and subjective conditions materialize, and there are soldiers, weapons, and money—even if this means using biological, chemical, and bacterial [sic] weapons—we will conquer the world, so that 'There is no God but Allah, and Muhammad is His Prophet' will be triumphant over the domes of Moscow, Washington, and Paris."

NOTE

1. This research was supported by an appointmnet to the U.S. Department of Homeland Security Research Opportunity Progrma administered by the Oak Ridge Institute for Science and Education through a cooperative agreement between the U.S. Department of Energy and the U.S. Department of Homeland Security. ORISE is managed by Oak Ridge Associated Universities (ORAU) under DOE contract number DE-AC05-06OR23100. All opinions expressed in this paper are the author's and do not necessarily reflect the policies and views of DHS, DOE, or ORAU/ORISE.

Index

E

I

T